Fifth Joint Conference on Lexical and Computational Semantics (*SEM 2016)

Berlin, Germany
11 – 12 August 2016

ISBN: 978-1-5108-2757-8

*SEM 2016: The Fifth Joint Conference on Lexical and Computational Semantics

Proceedings of the Conference

August 11-12 2016
Berlin, Germany

*SEM 2016 is sponsored by:

Introduction

*SEM, the Joint Conference on Lexical and Computational Semantics, has been organized yearly since 2012 under the auspices of ACL SIGLEX and SIGSEM. Its long term goal is to become a stable forum for the growing number of NLP researchers working on all aspects of semantics. To this end, each year it brings together researchers interested in the semantics of natural languages and its computational modeling. The conference embraces symbolic and probabilistic approaches, and everything in between. Theoretical contributions as well as practical applications are welcome.

The 2016 edition of *SEM takes place in Berlin on August 11 and 12 and is collocated with ACL. We accepted 27 papers (16 long and 11 short papers) for publication at the conference, out of 66 paper submissions (resulting in an overall acceptance rate of 40

The *SEM 2016 program consists of oral presentations for long papers, a poster session for short papers and three keynote talks by Yoav Artzi, Alexander Koller and Bonnie Webber.

Following the tradition initiated at *SEM 2015, *SEM 2016 will award two Adam Kilgarriff *SEM Best Paper Awards for Lexical Semantics.

We thank EACL and SIGLEX for sponsoring the three keynotes and Google and Lexical Computing for sponsoring the Adam Kilgarriff *SEM Best Paper Award. We would also like to thank Phong Le, *SEM 2016 Publication Chair, for his valuable work in editing these proceedings and the area chairs for their efforts in recruiting reviewers, stimulating discussion among them and for their dedication to carefully select the papers that make *SEM 2016 the high quality event we will all enjoy in Berlin. Last but not least, we thank the reviewers without whom *SEM could not be.

Claire Gardent, General Chair (CNRS and Université de Lorraine, Nancy, France)
Raffaella Bernardi, Program Co-Chair (University of Trento, Italy)
Ivan Titov, Program Co-Chair (University of Amsterdam, the Netherlands)

*SEM 2016 Chairs and Reviewers

General Chair:

Claire Gardent, CNRS and Université de Lorraine, Nancy, France

Program Co-Chairs:

Raffaella Bernardi, University of Trento, Italy
Ivan Titov, University of Amsterdam, the Netherlands

Area Chairs:

Distributional semantics
Kevin Duh, Johns Hopkins University, USA

Lexical semantics, lexical acquisition, WSD
Diana McCarthy, University of Cambridge, UK

Lexical resources, linked data, ontologies
Roberto Navigli, Sapienza University of Rome, Italy

Formal and linguistic semantics
Jonathan Ginzburg, Université Paris-Diderot, France

Semantic parsing and semantic role labeling
Yoav Artzi, Cornell, USA
Yonatan Bisk, ISI, USA

Multi-level Semantics (lexical, sentential, discourse and dialogue)
Annie Louis, University of Essex, UK
Michael Roth, University of Edinburgh, UK

Semantics for applications (textual entailment, IE, QA, summarization, social media)
Elena Cabrio, University of Nice Sophia Antipolis, France

Publication Chair:

Phong Le, University of Amsterdam, the Netherlands

Reviewers:

Omri Abend, Apoorv Agarwal, Eneko Agirre, Nikolaos Aletras, Pascal Amsili, Jacob Andreas, Timothy Baldwin, Mohit Bansal, Pierpaolo Basile, Valerio Basile, Roberto Basili, Beata Beigman Klebanov, I. Beltagy, Chris Biemann, Gemma Boleda, Francis Bond, Georgeta Bordea, Ellen Breitholz, Paul Buitelaar, Heather Burnett, José Camacho-Collados, Danqi Chen, Tao Chen, Martin Chodorow, Christos Christodoulopoulos, Grzegorz Chrupała, Philipp Cimiano, Paul Cook, Robin Cooper, Bonaventura Coppola, Anna Corazza, Inés Crespo, Danilo Croce, Georgiana Dinu, Jacob Eisenstein, Stefan Evert, James Fan, Tim Fernando, Nicholas FitzGerald, Jeffrey Flanigan, Chris Fox, Anette Frank, Daniel Fried, Alona Fyshe, Aldo Gangemi, Spandana Gella, Daniel Gildea, Dan Goldwasser, Jorge Gracia, Eleni Gregoromichelaki, Weiwei Guo, Iryna Gurevych, Daniel Hardt, Felix Hill, Graeme Hirst, Julian Hough, Julie Hunter, Ignacio Iacobacci, Katja Jasinskaja, Sujay Kumar Jauhar, Richard Johansson, Laura Kallmeyer, Stefan Kaufmann, Ruth Kempson, Douwe Kiela, Ioannis Konstas, Valia Kordoni, Andras Kornai, Zornitsa Kozareva, Sebastian

Krause, Shalom Lappin, Dan Lassiter, Jey Han Lau, Kenton Lee, Wang Ling, Ken Litkowski, Zhiyuan Liu, Oier Lopez de Lacalle, Zhengdong Lu, Bernardo Magnini, Emar Maier, Alda Mari, Sebastian Martschat, John Philip McCrae, Yashar Mehdad, Rada Mihalcea, Tristan Miller, Shachar Mirkin, Makoto Miwa, Alessandro Moschitti, Philippe Muller, Smaranda Muresan, Ndapandula Nakashole, Hwee Tou Ng, Vincent Ng, Hiroki Ouchi, Rebecca J. Passonneau, Siddharth Patwardhan, Ted Pedersen, Maciej Piasecki, Mohammad Taher Pilehvar, Christopher Pinon, Massimo Poesio, Christopher Potts, John Prager, Judita Preiss, Valentina Presutti, Laurette Pretorius, Laurent Prévot, Matthew Purver, Roi Reichart, Drew Reisinger, German Rigau, Tim Rocktäschel, Horacio Rodriguez, Michael Rosner, Sascha Rothe, Rachel Rudinger, Kjell Johan Saeboe, Sabine Schulte im Walde, Vivek Srikumar, Christian Stab, Peter Sutton, Stan Szpakowicz, Stefan Thater, Sara Tonelli, Kentaro Torisawa, Yuta Tsuboi, Kateryna Tymoshenko, Christina Unger, Olga Uryupina, Enric Vallduvi, Eva Maria Vecchi, Laure Vieu, Andreas Vlachos, Grégoire Winterstein, Travis Wolfe, Adam Wyner, Feiyu Xu, Mark Yatskar, Heike Zinsmeister, Pierre Zweigenbaum, Diarmuid Ó Séaghdha, Jan Šnajder

Invited Talk: Context and Non-compositional Phenomena in Language Understanding

Yoav Artzi

Cornell University

Abstract

Sentence meaning can be recovered by composing the meaning of words following the syntactic structure. However, robust understanding requires considering non-compositional and contextual cues as well. For example, a robot following instructions must consider its observations to accurately complete its task. Similarly, to correctly map temporal expressions within a document to standard time values, a system must consider previously mentioned events. In this talk, I will address such phenomena within compositional approaches, and focus on the non-compositional parts of the reasoning process.

Joint work with Kenton Lee and Luke Zettlemoyer.

Invited Talk: Top-down and bottom-up views on success in semantics

Alexander Koller

University of Potsdam

Abstract

As participants of *SEM, all of us are excited about the resurgence of research in computational semantics over the past few years. There is a general feeling that modern data-driven approaches to semantics, especially distributional ones, are great success stories. This is in contrast to classical knowledge-based approaches, which are widely accepted as respectable and pretty, but not useful in practice.

In my talk, I will challenge this perception by asking what the measure of success of research in semantics should be. I will distinguish between bottom-up and top-down views on linguistic theories, and argue that we count (computational) truth-conditional semantics as failed for top-down reasons, but data-driven semantics as a success for bottom-up reasons. I will argue that identifying top-down goals for modern computational semantics would help us understand the relationship between classical and modern approaches to semantics, and distinguish research directions in modern semantics that are useful from those that are merely fun.

In the second part of the talk, I will focus on one candidate for a top-down goal that is mentioned frequently, namely similarity of arbitrary phrases based on distributional methods. I will ask whether our evaluation methods for similarity are appropriate, and whether similarity is even a meaningful concept if the task and context are left unspecified. I will conclude with some thoughts on how we might obtain top-down goals by taking a more task-based perspective.

Invited Talk: Exploring for Concurrent Discourse Relations

Bonnie Webber

University of Edinburgh

Abstract

Discourse relations are an element of discourse coherence, indicating how the meaning and/or function of clauses in a text make sense together. Evidence for discourse relations can come from a range of sources, including explicit discourse connectives such as coordinating and subordinating conjunctions and discourse adverbials. While some clauses may require an explicit connective to provide evidence for a discourse relation, other clauses don't.

This talk starts from the observation that there may be more than one piece of explicit evidence for how a clause relates to the rest of the discourse. I first consider why this may be so, before considering the related questions of why there may only be one piece of explicit evidence or none at all. The amount of explicit evidence, however, does not constrain the possibility that a clause bears more than one relation to the previous discourse, what we have called "Concurrent Discourse Relations".

Since we don't fully understand concurrent discourse relations, I present work we have been doing on exploring for evidence from corpora and on getting evidence from crowdsourcing experiments. The goal is to be able to use such evidence to help automatically annotate concurrent relations in corpora and improve the ability of systems to extract information from text by recognizing more of the relations underlying text coherence.

Table of Contents

Conference Program

Thursday, August 11, 2016

9:00–9:10   *Welcome*

9:10–10:00   *Invited Talk: Context and Non-compositional Phenomena in Language Understanding*
Yoav Artzi

10:00–10:30   *Quantificational features in distributional word representations*
Tal Linzen, Emmanuel Dupoux and Benjamin Spector

10:30–11:00   Break

11:00–12:30   Lexical semantics

11:00–11:30   *Automatic Identification of Aspectual Classes across Verbal Readings*
Ingrid Falk and Fabienne Martin

11:30–12:00   *Metaphor as a Medium for Emotion: An Empirical Study*
Saif Mohammad, Ekaterina Shutova and Peter Turney

12:00–12:30   *High-Fidelity Lexical Axiom Construction from Verb Glosses*
Gene Kim and Lenhart Schubert

10:30–11:00	**Break**

11:00–12:30   **Semantics for applications and distributional semantics**

11:00–11:30   *Detecting Stance in Tweets And Analyzing its Interaction with Sentiment*
Parinaz Sobhani, Saif Mohammad and Svetlana Kiritchenko

11:30–12:00   *A Study of Suggestions in Opinionated Texts and their Automatic Detection*
Sapna Negi, Kartik Asooja, Shubham Mehrotra and Paul Buitelaar

12:00–12:30   *You and me... in a vector space: modelling individual speakers with distributional semantics*
Aurélie Herbelot and Behrang QasemiZadeh

12:30–14:10   **Lunch break**

14:10–15:00   *Invited talk: Exploring for Concurrent Discourse Relations*
Bonnie Webber

15:00–15:30   *Random Positive-Only Projections: PPMI-Enabled Incremental Semantic Space Construction*
Behrang QasemiZadeh and Laura Kallmeyer

15:30–16:00   **Break**

Quantificational features in distributional word representations

Tal Linzen[1,2]   **Emmanuel Dupoux**[1]   **Benjamin Spector**[2]
[1]Laboratoire de Sciences Cognitives et Psycholinguistique   [2]Institut Jean Nicod
École Normale Supérieure
PSL Research University
{tal.linzen, benjamin.spector}@ens.fr
emmanuel.dupoux@gmail.com

Abstract

Do distributional word representations encode the linguistic regularities that theories of meaning argue they should encode? We address this question in the case of the logical properties (monotonicity, force) of quantificational words such as *everything* (in the object domain) and *always* (in the time domain). Using the vector offset approach to solving word analogies, we find that the skip-gram model of distributional semantics behaves in a way that is remarkably consistent with encoding these features in some domains, with accuracy approaching 100%, especially with medium-sized context windows. Accuracy in others domains was less impressive. We compare the performance of the model to the behavior of human participants, and find that humans performed well even where the models struggled.

1   Introduction

Vector-space models of lexical semantics (VSMs) represent words as points in a high-dimensional space. Similar words are represented by points that are close together in the space. VSMs are typically trained on a corpus in an unsupervised way; the goal is for words that occur in similar contexts to be assigned similar representations. The context of a word in a corpus is often defined as the set of words that occur in a small window around the word of interest (Lund and Burgess, 1996; Turney and Pantel, 2010). VSM representations have been shown to be useful in improving the performance of NLP systems (Turian et al., 2010; Bansal et al., 2014) as well as in predicting cognitive measures such as similarity judgments and semantic priming (Jones et al., 2006; Hill et al., 2015).

While there is evidence that VSM representations encode useful information about the meaning of open-class words such as *dog* or *table*, less is known about the extent to which they capture abstract linguistic properties, in particular the aspects of word meaning that are crucial in logical reasoning. Some have conjectured that those properties are unlikely to be encoded in VSMs (Lewis and Steedman, 2013), but evidence that VSMs encode features such as syntactic category or verb tense suggests that this pessimism is premature (Mikolov et al., 2013c; Levy and Goldberg, 2014).

The goal of this paper is to evaluate to what extent logical features are encoded in VSMs. We undertake a detailed analysis of words with quantificational features, such as *everybody* or *nowhere*. To assess whether a particular linguistic feature is encoded in a vector space, we adopt the vector offset approach to the analogy task (Turney, 2006; Mikolov et al., 2013c; Dunbar et al., 2015). In the analogy task, a system is requested to fill in the blank in a sentence:

(1)   *man* is to *woman* as *king* is to ___.

The system is expected to infer the relation between the first two words—*man* and *woman*—and find a word that stands in the same relation to *king*. When this task is solved using the offset method, there is no explicit set of relations that the system is trained to identify. We simply subtract the vector for *man* from the vector for *woman* and add it to *king*. If the offset *woman* − *man* represents an abstract gender feature, adding that offset to *king* should lead us to *queen* (Figure 1).

In the rest of this paper, we describe the set of analogy problems that we used to evaluate the VSMs' representation of quantificational features, and explore how accuracy is affected by the con-

1

*Proceedings of the Fifth Joint Conference on Lexical and Computational Semantics (*SEM 2016)*, pages 1–11,
Berlin, Germany, August 11-12, 2016.

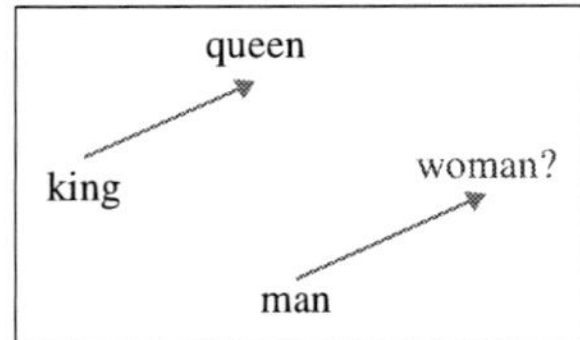

Figure 1: Using the vector offset method to solve the analogy task (Mikolov et al., 2013c).

| | INC. | | DEC. |
	Universal	Existential	Universal
PERSON	*everybody*	*somebody*	*nobody*
OBJECT	*everything*	*something*	*nothing*
PLACE	*everywhere*	*somewhere*	*nowhere*
TIME	*always*	*sometimes*	*never*
MODAL	*must*	*can*	*cannot*
MODAL V.	*require*	*allow*	*forbid*

Table 1: All of the words tested in the experiments (INC = Increasing, DEC = Decreasing).

text windows used to construct the VSM. We then report two experiments that examine the robustness of the results. First, we determine whether the level of performance that we expect from the VSMs is reasonable, by testing how well humans solve the same analogy problems. Second, we investigate how the quality of the representations is affected by the size of the training corpus.

A large and constantly expanding range of VSM architectures have been proposed in the literature (Mikolov et al., 2013a; Pennington et al., 2014; Turney and Pantel, 2010). Instead of exploring the full range of architectures, the present study will focus on the skip-gram model, implemented in word2vec (Mikolov et al., 2013b). This model has been argued to perform either better than or on a par with competing architectures, depending on the task and on hyperparameter settings (Baroni et al., 2014; Levy et al., 2015). Particularly pertinent to our purposes, Levy et al. (2015) find that the skip-gram model tends to recover formal linguistic features more accurately than traditional distributional models.

2 Quantificational words

We focus on words that quantify over the elements of a domain, such as *everyone* or *nowhere*. We restrict our attention to single words that include the domain of quantification as part of their meaning – that is, we exclude determiners (*every*) and phrases (*every person*). The meaning of a quantifier is determined by three factors: quantificational force, polarity and domain of quantification. We describe these factors in turn.

2.1 Quantificational force

We focus on universal and existential quantificational words, which can be translated into first-order logic using a universal ($\forall$) or existential ($\exists$) quantifier. For example, *everybody* and *nobody* are both universal:

(2)   Everybody smiles:
$\forall x.person(x) \rightarrow smiles(x)$

(3)   Nobody smiles:
$\forall x.person(x) \rightarrow \neg smiles(x)$

Somebody is existential:

(4)   Somebody smiles:
$\exists x.person(x) \wedge smiles(x)$

English has quantificational expressions that don't fall into either category (*three people*, *most things*). Those are usually not encoded as a single English word, and are therefore not considered in this paper.

2.2 Polarity

Quantifiers that can be expressed as a single word are in general either increasing or decreasing. A quantifier is increasing if any predicate that is true of the quantifier can be broadened without affecting the truth value of the sentence (Barwise and Cooper, 1981). For example, since *everyone* is increasing, (5-a) entails (5-b):

(5)   a.   Everybody went out to a death metal concert last night.
        b.   Everybody went out last night.

By contrast, in decreasing quantifiers such as *nobody* the truth of broader predicates entails the truth of narrower ones:

(6)   a.   Nobody went out last night.
        b.   Nobody went out to a death metal concert last night.

2.3 Domain

We studied six domains. The first three domains are intuitively straightforward: PERSON (e.g., *everybody*); OBJECT (e.g., *everything*); and PLACE (e.g., *everywhere*). The three additional domains are described below.

TIME: Temporal adverbs such as *always* and *seldom* are naturally analyzed as quantifying over situations or events (Lewis, 1975; de Swart, 1993). The sentence *Caesar always awoke before dawn*, for example, can be seen as quantifying over waking events and stating that each of those events occurred before dawn.

MODAL: Modal auxiliaries such as *must* or *can* quantify over relevant possible worlds (Kripke, 1959). Consider, for example, the following sentences:

(7)   a.   Anne must go to bed early.
         b.   Anne can go to bed early.

Assuming deontic modality, such as the statement of a rule, (7-a) means that in all worlds in which the rule is obeyed, Anne goes to bed early, whereas (7-b) means that there exists at least one world consistent with the speaker's orders in which she goes to bed early.

MODAL VERB: Verbs such as *request* and *forbid* can be paraphrased using modal auxiliaries: *he allowed me to stay up late* is similar in meaning to *he said I can stay up late*. It is plausible to argue that *allow* is existential and increasing, just like *can*.

3   Evaluation

In what follows, we use the following notation (Levy and Goldberg, 2014):

(8) $a : a^* :: b : \underline{\quad}$

The offset model is typically understood as in Figure 1: the analogy task is solved by finding $x = a^* - a + b$. In practice, since the space is continuous, x is unlikely to precisely identify a word in the vocabulary. The guess is then taken to be the word x^* that is nearest to x:

$$x^* = \arg\max_{x'} \cos(x', a^* - a + b) \qquad (1)$$

where cos denotes the cosine similarity between the vectors. This point has a significant effect on the results of the offset method, as we will see below. Following Mikolov et al. (2013c) and Levy and Goldberg (2014), we normalize a, a^* and b prior to entering them into Equation 1.

Trivial responses: x^* as defined above is almost always trivial: in our experiments the nearest neighbor of x was either a^* (11% of the time) or b (88.9% of the time). Only in a single analogy out of the 2160 we tested was it not one of those two options. Following Mikolov et al. (2013c), then, our guess x^* will be the nearest neighbor of x that is not a, a^* or b.

Baseline: The fact that the nearest neighbor of $a^* - a + b$ tends to be b itself suggests that $a^* - a$ is typically small in comparison to the distance between b and any of its neighbors. Even if b is excluded as a guess, then, one might be concerned that the analogy target b^* is closer to b than any of its neighbors. If that is the case, our success on the analogy task would not be informative: our results would stay largely the same if $a^* - a$ were replaced by a random vector of the same magnitude (Linzen, 2016). To address this concern, we add a baseline that solves the analogy task by simply returning the nearest neighbor of b, ignoring a and a^* altogether.

Multiplication: Levy and Goldberg (2014) point out that the word x^* that is closest to $a^* - a + b$ in terms of cosine similarity is the one that maximizes the following expression:

$$\arg\max_{x'}(\cos(x', a^*) - \cos(x', a) + \cos(x', b)) \qquad (2)$$

They report that replacing addition with multiplication improves accuracy on the analogy task:

$$\arg\max_{x'} \frac{\cos(x', a^*) \cos(x', b)}{\cos(x', a)} \qquad (3)$$

We experiment with both methods.

Synonyms: Previous studies required an exact match between the guess and the analogy target selected by the experimenter. This requirement may underestimate the extent to which the space encodes linguistic features, since the bundle of semantic features expressed by the intended target can often be expressed by one or more other words. This is the case for *everyone* and *everybody*, *prohibit* and *forbid* or *can't* and *cannot*. As such, we considered synonyms of b^* to be exact matches. Likewise, we considered synonyms of a, a^* and b to be trivial responses and excluded them from consideration as guesses.

This treatment of synonyms is reasonable when the goal is to probe the VSM's semantic representations (as it often is), but may be inappropriate for other purposes. If, for example, the analogy task is used as a method for generating inflected forms, *prohibiting* would not be an appropriate guess for *like : liking :: forbid :* ___.

Partial success metrics: We did not restrict the guesses to words with quantificational features: all of the words in the vocabulary, including words like *penguin* and *melancholy*, were potential guesses. In addition to counting exact matches ($x^* = b^*$), then, we keep track of the proportion of cases in which x^* was a quantificational word in one of the six relevant domains.

Within the cases in which x^* was a quantificational word, we separately counted how often x^* had the expected domain, the expected polarity and the expected force. To be able to detect such partial matches, we manually added some words to our vocabulary that were not included in the set in Table 1. These included items starting with *any*, such as *anywhere* or *anybody*, as well as additional temporal adverbs (*seldom*, *often*).

Finally, we record the rank of b^* among the 100 nearest neighbors of x, where a rank of 1 indicates an exact match. It was often the case that b^* was not among the 100 nearest neighbors of x; we therefore record how often b^* was ranked at all.

4 Experimental setup

4.1 Analogies

For each ordered pair of domains ($6 \times 5 = 30$ pairs in total), we constructed all possible analogies where a and a^* were drawn from one domain (the source domain) and b and b^* from the other (the target domain). Since there are three words per domain, we had six possible analogies per domain pair, for a total of 180 analogies.

Each set of four words was used to construct multiple analogies. Those analogies are in general not equivalent. For example, the words *everybody*, *nobody*, *everywhere* and *nowhere* make up the following analogies:

(9)   *everybody : nobody :: everywhere :* ___

(10)   *nobody : everybody :: nowhere :* ___

(11)   *everywhere : nowhere :: everybody :* ___

(12)   *nowhere : everywhere :: nobody :* ___

The neighborhoods of *everywhere* and *nobody* may well differ in density. Since the density of the neighborhood of b affects the results of the offset

method, the result is not invariant to a permutation of the words in an analogy. It is, however, invariant to replacing a within-domain analogy with an across-domain one. The following analogy is equivalent to (9):

(13)   *everybody : everywhere :: nobody :* ___

This analogy would be solved by finding the nearest neighbor of *everywhere* − *everybody* + *nobody*, which is, of course, the same as the nearest neighbor of *nobody* − *everybody* + *everywhere* used to solve (9). We do not include such analogies.

4.2 VSMs

We trained our VSMs using the skip-gram with negative sampling algorithm implemented in `hyperwords`,[1] which extends `word2vec` to allow finer control over hyperparameters. The vectors were trained on a concatenation of ukWaC (Baroni et al., 2009) and a 2013 dump of the English Wikipedia, 3.4 billion words in total.

The skip-gram model has a large number of parameters. We set most of those parameters to values that have been previously shown to be effective (Levy et al., 2015); we list those values below. We only vary three parameters that control the context window. Syntactic category information has been shown to be best captured by narrow context windows that encode the position of the context word relative to the focus word (Redington et al., 1998; Sahlgren, 2006). Our goal in varying these parameters is to identity the contexts that are most conducive to recovering logical information.

Window size: We experimented with context windows of 2, 5 or 10 words on either side of the focus word (i.e., a window of size 2 around the focus word consists of four context words).

Window type: When constructing the vector space, the skip-gram model performs frequency-based pruning: rare words are discarded in all cases and very frequent words are discarded probabilisitically. We experimented with static and dynamic windows. The size of static windows is determined prior to frequency-based word deletion. By contrast, the size of dynamic windows is determined after frequent and infrequent words are deleted. This means that dynamic windows often include words that are farther away from the focus words than the nominal window size, and

---

[1] https://bitbucket.org/omerlevy/hyperwords

Size	Context	Window	B	O	M	O - B
2	Nonpos	Dynamic	.08	.32	.34	.24
2	Nonpos	Static	.06	.23	.24	.17
2	Pos	Dynamic	.06	.29	.32	.24
2	Pos	Static	.06	.24	.27	.19
5	Nonpos	Dynamic	.07	.28	.29	.22
5	Nonpos	Static	.11	.35	.36	.24
5	Pos	Dynamic	.03	.29	.31	.27
5	Pos	Static	.06	.28	.29	.23
10	Nonpos	Dynamic	.08	.28	.29	.19
10	Nonpos	Static	.17	.31	.31	.14
10	Pos	Dynamic	.17	.32	.31	.16
10	Pos	Static	.11	.26	.26	.15

Table 2: Results on all hyperparameter settings, evaluated using three methods: B(aseline), O(ffset) and M(ultiplication).

that words that tend to have very frequent function words around them will systematically have a larger effective context window.

Context type: We experimented with bag-of-words (nonpositional) contexts and positional contexts. In nonpositional contexts, a context word cat is treated in the same way regardless of its distance from the focus word and of whether it follows or precedes it. In positional contexts, on the other hand, context words are annotated with their position relative to the focus words; the context word cat^{-2} is considered to be distinct from cat^{+1}.

Fixed hyperparameters: We used the following values for the rest of the hyperparameters: 500-dimensional words vectors; 15 negative samples per focus word; words with a frequency of less than 100 were discarded; words with unigram probability above 10^{-5} were probabilistically discarded (preliminary experiments showed that a 10^{-3} threshold reduced performance across the board); negative samples were drawn from the unigram frequency distribution, after that distribution was smoothed with exponent $\alpha = 0.75$; we performed one iteration through the data.

5 Results

We first report results averaged across all domains. We then show that there was large variability across domains: the VSMs showed excellent performance on some domains but struggled with others.

Offset method: Overall accuracy was fairly low (mean: 0.29, range: $0.23 - 0.35$), somewhat lower than the 0.4 accuracy that Mikolov et al. (2013c) report for their syntactic features.[2] Strikingly, b^* was among the 100 nearest neighbors of x only in 70% of the cases. When the guess was a quantificational word (61% of the time), it was generally in the right domain (93%). Its polarity was correct 72% of the time, and its force 54% of the time.

The static nonpositional 5-word VSM achieved the best accuracy (35%), best average rank (5.5) and was able to recover the most quantificational features (polarity: 82% correct; force: 63% correct; both proportions are conditioned on the guess being a quantificational word).

Alternatives to the offset method: In line with the results reported by Levy and Goldberg (2014), we found that substituting multiplication for addition resulted in slightly improved performance in 10 out of 12 VSMs, though the improvement in each individual VSM was never significant according to Fisher's exact test (Table 2). If we take each VSM to be an independent observation, the difference across all VSMs is statistically significant in a t-test ($t = 2.45$, $p = 0.03$).

The baseline that ignores a and a^* altogether reached an accuracy of up to 0.17, sometimes accounting for more than half the accuracy of the offset method. The success of the baseline is significant, given that chance level is very low (recall that all but the rarest words in the corpus were possible guesses). Still, the offset method was significantly more accurate than the baseline in all VSMs ($10^{-12} < p < 0.003$, Fisher's exact test).

Differences across domains: We examine the performance of the offset method in the best-performing VSM in greater detail. There were dramatic differences in accuracy across target domains. When b^* was a PERSON, guesses were correct 73% of the time; the correct guess was one of the top 100 neighbors 87% of the time, and its average rank was 1.31. Conversely, when b^* was a MODAL VERB, the guess was never correct; in fact, in this target tomain, b^* was one of the 100 nearest neighbors of x only 7% of the time, and the average rank in these cases was 59 (see Table

---

[2]Note that the figure reported by Mikolov et al. (2013c) collapses across several different types of syntactic features, some of which are encoded with accuracy higher than 0.4 and some with lower accuracy (Levy and Goldberg, 2014; Linzen, 2016).

a	a^*	b	b^*	x_1^*	x_2^*	x_3^*	Rank
sometimes	always	somebody	everybody	nobody	anybody	everybody	3
forbid	require	nobody	everybody	need	needed	any-one	n/a
can	must	somebody	everybody	nobody	whoever	no-one	4
always	sometimes	everybody	somebody	often	or	occasionally	n/a
require	permit	everything	something	anything	everybody	sneakily	13
forbid	require	nothing	everything	need	needed	turn-round	n/a
must	can	everything	something	anything	things	you"ll	5
never	always	nothing	everything	something	anything	everything	3
cannot	must	never	always	once	always	hadn't	2
everybody	somebody	always	sometimes	some-one	if	whoever's	n/a
everything	nothing	always	never	certainly	indeed	certaintly	37
nobody	somebody	never	sometimes	you've	"if	myslef	n/a
somebody	everybody	can	must	cannot	could	will	4
forbid	require	cannot	must	can	need	must	3
everything	something	must	can	should	might	ought	9
sometimes	always	can	must	could	must	cannot	2
cannot	must	forbid	require	prohibit	enjoin	forswear	n/a
sometimes	always	permit	require	anyads.co.uk	re-confirm	withold	n/a
somebody	nobody	permit	forbid	npdes	restrictions	eu/eea	n/a
something	everything	permit	require	npdes	h-1b	authorizations	n/a

Table 3: A sample of errors made by the [5, Nonpositional, Static] VSM (an error is an analogy problem where the correct answer was not the nearest neighbor of $x = a^* - a + b$). Four analogies are shown per target domain; x_1^*, x_2^* and x_3^* are the nearest, second nearest and third nearest neighbors of x, respectively. The rank is marked as *n/a* the correct answer was not one of the 100 nearest neigbors of x.

3 for examples of the errors of the offset method). Variability across source domains was somewhat less pronounced; Figure 2a shows the interaction between source and target domain.

In light of the differences across domains, we repeated our investigation of the influence of context parameters, this time restricting the source and target domains to PERSON, PLACE and OBJECT. Exact match accuracy ranged from 0.5 for the static nonpositional 2-word window to 0.83 for the static nonpositional 5-word window. The latter VSM achieved almost perfect accuracy in cases where the guess was a quantificational word (domain: 1.0, polarity: 0.97, force: 1.0). We conclude that in some domains logical features can be robustly recovered from distributional information; note, however, that even the baseline method occasionally succeeds on these domains (Figure 2c).

Effect of context parameters: Overall, the influence of context parameters on accuracy was not dramatic. When the VSMs are compared based on the extent that the offset method improves over the baseline (O − B in Table 2), a somewhat clearer picture emerges: the improvement is greatest in intermediate window sizes, either 5-word windows or dynamic 2-word windows. This contrasts with findings on the acquisition of syntactic categories, where narrower contexts performed best (Redington et al., 1998), suggesting that the cues to quantificational features are further from the focus word than cues to syntactic category.

One candidate for such a cue is the word's compatibility with negative polarity items (NPI) such as *any*. NPIs are often licensed by decreasing quantifiers (Fauconnier, 1975): *nobody ate any cheese* is grammatical, but **everybody ate any cheese* isn't. Whereas contextual cues to syntactic category—e.g., *the* before nouns—are often directly adjacent to the focus word, *any* will typically be part of a different constituent from the focus word, and is therefore quite likely to fall outside a narrow context window.

We did not find a systematic effect of the type of context (positional vs. nonpositional). However, as Section 7 below shows, this parameter does affect performance when the VSMs are trained on smaller corpora.

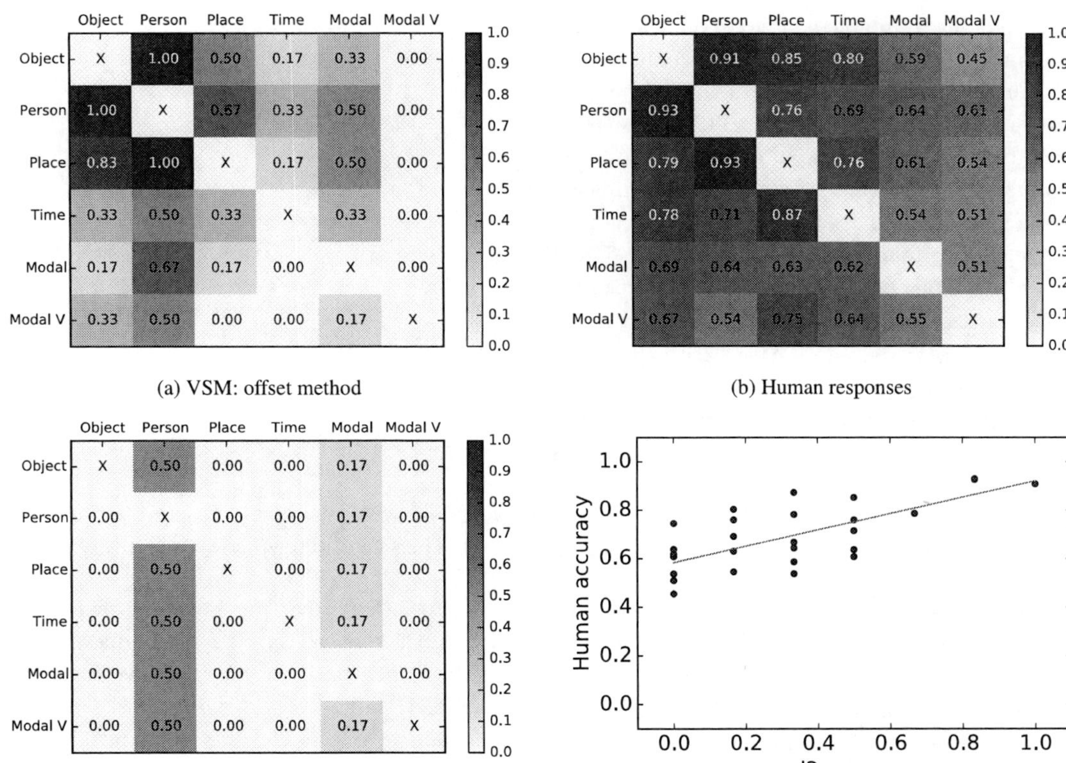

(a) VSM: offset method

(b) Human responses

(c) VSM: baseline (accuracy depends only on the target domain)

(d) Correlation between human responses and the accuracy of the offset method (each point represents a source + domain pair)

Figure 2: On the left: accuracy of the best model (static nonpositional 5-word context), broken down by source (in the y-axis) and target (in the x-axis) domain. On the right: human responses.

6 How well do humans do the task?

Some of the analogies are intuitively fairly difficult: quantification over possible deontic worlds (*require* vs. *forbid*) is quite different from quantification over individuals (*everybody* vs. *nobody*). Those are precisely the domains in which the VSMs performed poorly. Are we asking too much of our VSM representations? Can humans perform this task?[3]

To answer this question, we gave the same analogies to human participants recruited through Amazon Mechanical Turk. We divided our 180 quantificational analogies into five lists of 36 analogies each. Each list additionally contained four practice trials presented in the beginning of the list and ten catch trials interspersed throughout the list. These additional trials contained simple analogies, such as *big : bigger :: strong : ___* or *brother : sister :: son : ___*. Each of the lists was presented to ten participants (50 participants in total). They were asked to type in a word that had the same relationship to the third word as the first two words had to each other.

We excluded participants that made more than three mistakes on the catch trials (three participants) as well as one participant who did not provide any answer to some of the questions. While mean accuracy varied greatly among subjects (range: $0.22 - 1$; mean: 0.68; median: 0.69; standard deviation: 0.17), it was in general much higher than the accuracy of the VSMs.

Figure 2b presents the human participants' aver-

---

[3]These two questions are highly related from a cognitive modeling perspective, but in general it is far from clear that human performance on a logical task is an appropriate yardstick for a computational reasoning system. In the domain of quantifier monotonicity, in particular, there are documented discrepancies between normative logic and human reasoning (Chemla et al., 2011; Geurts and van Der Slik, 2005). In many cases it may be preferable for a reasoning system to conform to normative logic rather than mimic human behavior precisely.

age accuracy by source and target domain. Mean accuracy was 0.45 or higher for all combinations of source and target domains. Logistic regression confirmed that having MODAL VERB and MODAL as either the source or target domain led to lower accuracy. There were no statistically significant differences between those two domains or among the remaining four domains, with the exception of TIME as a target domain, which was less accurate than PLACE, OBJECT and PERSON.

The VSMs did not have access to the morphological structure of the words. This makes the comparison with humans difficult: it is hard to see how human participants could be stopped from accessing that knowledge when performing an analogy such as *nowhere : somewhere :: nobody : ___*. Notably, however, the difference in performance between the morphologically marked domains and the other domains is if anything *more* marked in the VSMs than in humans. Moreover, there is a fairly small difference in the accuracy of our human participants between PLACE and TIME as target domains, even though the former is morphologically marked and the latter isn't.

7 Effect of training corpus size

The VSMs trained on our 3.4 billion token corpus achieved very good performance on the analogy task, at least in some of the domains. How dependent is the performance of the models on the size of the training corpus? To address this question, we sampled four subcorpora from our Wikipedia corpus, with 100K, 1M, 3M and 10M sentences. As the average sentence length in the corpus is 18 words, the corpora contained 1.8M, 18M, 54M and 180M tokens, respectively.

Given that VSM accuracy was low in some of the domains even when the spaces were trained on 3.4G tokens, we limit our experiments in this section to the OBJECT and PERSON domains. We made two changes to the hyperparameters settings that were not modulated in the VSMs trained on the full corpus. First, we lowered the threshold for rare word deletion (100K / 1M sentences: 10; 3M sentences: 50; 10M sentences: 100). Second, we experimented with smaller vectors (100, 300 and 500), under the assumption that it may be more difficult to train large vectors on a small data set. As before, we experimented with window sizes of 2, 5 and 10 words on either side of the focus

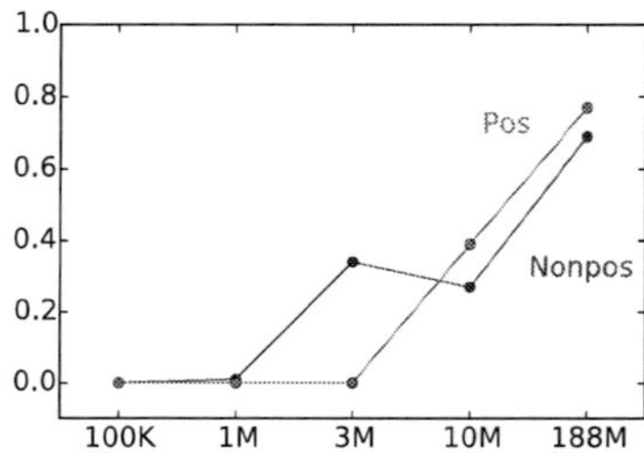

Figure 3: Effect of training corpus size (in sentences) on the accuracy of the analogy task, averaged across vector and window size settings.

word and with positional and nonpositional contexts. The size of the windows was always static.

Figure 3 shows the accuracy of the analogy task averaged across vector sizes and window sizes. VSMs trained on the 100K and 1M subcorpora completely failed to perform the task: with the exception of one model that performed one out the 12 analogies correctly, accuracy was always 0. The VSMs trained on the 3M and 10M sentences subcorpora perform better (between 0.27 and 0.39 on average), though still much worse than the VSMs trained on the full corpus. The type of context had a large effect on the success of the model: VSMs with positional contexts trained on the 3M subcorpus had extremely low accuracy, whereas on the 10M subcorpus positional contexts performed better than nonpositional ones. The performance advantage of positional contexts was larger on the 10M corpus than on the full corpus.

Hart and Risley (1995) estimate that American children are exposed to between 3 and 11 million words every year, depending on the socioeconomic status of their family. The 1M and 3M sentence corpora therefore represent plausible amounts of exposure for a child; the adults tested in Section 6 may have seen the equivalent of 10M sentences. The degraded performance of the VSMs on these smaller training corpora suggests that distributional information alone is unlikely to be sufficient for humans' acquisition of quantification, and that an adequate cognitive model would need to consider richer types of context, such as syntactic context and discourse structure, or to make explicit reference to the way these words are used in logical reasoning.

8 Related work

There is a large body of work on the evaluation of VSMs (Turney and Pantel, 2010; Hill et al., 2015). A handful of recent papers have looked at distributional representations of logical words. Baroni et al. (2012) extracted corpus-based distributional representations for quantifier phrases such as *all cats* and *no dogs*, and trained a classifier to detect entailment relations between those phrases; for example, the classifier might learn that *all cats* entails *some cats*. Bernardi et al. (2013) introduce a phrase similarity challenge that relies on the correct interpretation of determiners (e.g., *orchestra* is expected to be similar to *many musicians*), and use it to evaluate VSMs and composition methods. Hermann et al. (2013) discuss the difficulty of accounting for negation in a distributional semantics framework.

Another line of work seeks to combine the graded representations of content words such as *mammal* or *book* with a symbolic representation of logical words (Garrette et al., 2014; Lewis and Steedman, 2013; Herbelot and Vecchi, 2015). Our work, which focuses on the quality of graded representation of logical words, can be seen as largely orthogonal to this line of work.

Finally, our study is related to recent neural network architectures designed to recognize entailment and other logical relationships between sentences (Bowman et al., 2015; Rocktäschel et al., 2016). Those systems learn word vector representations that are optimized to perform an explicit entailment task (when trained in conjunction with a compositional component). In future work, it may be fruitful to investigate whether those representations encode logical features more faithfully than the unsupervised representations we experimented with.

9 Conclusion

The skip-gram model, like earlier models of distributional semantics, represents words in a vector space using only their bag-of-words contexts in a corpus. We tested whether the representations that this model acquires for words with quantificational content encode the logical features that theories of meaning predict they should encode. We addressed this question using the offset method for solving the analogy task, $a : a^* :: b : \_\_\_$ (e.g., *everyone* : *someone* :: *everywhere* : *___*).

Distributional methods successfully recovered quantificational features in many cases. Accuracy was higher when the context window was of an intermediate size, sometimes approaching 100% on simpler domains. Performance on other domains was poorer, however. Humans given the same task also showed variability across domains, but achieved better accuracy overall, suggesting that there is room for improving the VSMs. Finally, we showed that the VSMs require large amounts of training data to perform the task well, suggesting that the simplest form of distributional learning is not sufficient for acquiring logical features given the amount of language input that humans are exposed to.

Acknowledgements

We thank Marco Baroni, Emmanuel Chemla, Anne Christophe and Omer Levy for comments and technical assistance. This research was supported by the European Research Council (grant ERC-2011-AdG 295810 BOOTPHON) and the Agence Nationale pour la Recherche (grants ANR-10-IDEX-0001-02 PSL and ANR-10-LABX-0087 IEC).

References

Mohit Bansal, Kevin Gimpel, and Karen Livescu. 2014. Tailoring continuous word representations for dependency parsing. In *Proceedings of the 52nd Annual Meeting of the Association for Computational Linguistics (Volume 2: Short Papers)*, pages 809–815, Baltimore, Maryland, June. Association for Computational Linguistics.

Marco Baroni, Silvia Bernardini, Adriano Ferraresi, and Eros Zanchetta. 2009. The WaCky wide web: a collection of very large linguistically processed web-crawled corpora. *Language Resources and Evaluation*, 43(3):209–226.

Marco Baroni, Raffaella Bernardi, Ngoc-Quynh Do, and Chung-chieh Shan. 2012. Entailment above the word level in distributional semantics. In *Proceedings of the 13th Conference of the European Chapter of the Association for Computational Linguistics*, pages 23–32. Association for Computational Linguistics.

Marco Baroni, Georgiana Dinu, and Germán Kruszewski. 2014. Don't count, predict! A systematic comparison of context-counting vs. context-predicting semantic vectors. In *Proceedings of the 52nd Annual Meeting of the Association for Computational Linguistics*, pages 238–247.

Jon Barwise and Robin Cooper. 1981. Generalized quantifiers and natural language. *Linguistics and Philosophy*, 4(2):159–219.

Raffaella Bernardi, Georgiana Dinu, Marco Marelli, and Marco Baroni. 2013. A relatedness benchmark to test the role of determiners in compositional distributional semantics. In *Proceedings of the 51st Annual Meeting of the Association for Computational Linguistics (Volume 2: Short Papers)*, pages 53–57. Association for Computational Linguistics.

Samuel R. Bowman, Christopher Potts, and Christopher D. Manning. 2015. Recursive neural networks can learn logical semantics. In *Proceedings of the 3rd Workshop on Continuous Vector Space Models and their Compositionality (CVSC)*.

Emmanuel Chemla, Vincent Homer, and Daniel Rothschild. 2011. Modularity and intuitions in formal semantics: the case of polarity items. *Linguistics and Philosophy*, 34(6):537–570.

Henriëtte de Swart. 1993. *Adverbs of quantification: A generalized quantifier approach*. New York: Garland.

Ewan Dunbar, Gabriel Synnaeve, and Emmanuel Dupoux. 2015. Quantitative methods for comparing featural representations. In *Proceedings of the 18th International Congress of Phonetic Sciences*.

Gilles Fauconnier. 1975. Pragmatic scales and logical structure. *Linguistic Inquiry*, 6(3):353–375.

Dan Garrette, Katrin Erk, and Raymond Mooney. 2014. A formal approach to linking logical form and vector-space lexical semantics. In Harry C. Bunt, Johannes Bos, and Stephen Pulman, editors, *Computing meaning*, pages 27–48. Dordrecht: Springer.

Bart Geurts and Frans van Der Slik. 2005. Monotonicity and processing load. *Journal of Semantics*, 22(1):97–117.

Betty Hart and Todd R. Risley. 1995. *Meaningful differences in the everyday experience of young American children*. Baltimore: P. H. Brookes.

Aurélie Herbelot and Eva Maria Vecchi. 2015. Building a shared world: mapping distributional to model-theoretic semantic spaces. In *Proceedings of the 2015 Conference on Empirical Methods in Natural Language Processing*, pages 22–32, Lisbon, Portugal, September. Association for Computational Linguistics.

Karl Moritz Hermann, Edward Grefenstette, and Phil Blunsom. 2013. "not not bad" is not "bad": A distributional account of negation. *Proceedings of the ACL Workshop on Continuous Vector Space Models and their Compositionality*.

Felix Hill, Roi Reichart, and Anna Korhonen. 2015. Simlex-999: Evaluating semantic models with (genuine) similarity estimation. *Computational Linguistics*.

Michael N. Jones, Walter Kintsch, and Douglas J.K. Mewhort. 2006. High-dimensional semantic space accounts of priming. *Journal of Memory and Language*, 55(4):534–552.

Saul A. Kripke. 1959. A completeness theorem in modal logic. *The Journal of Symbolic Logic*, 24(1):1–14.

Omer Levy and Yoav Goldberg. 2014. Linguistic regularities in sparse and explicit word representations. In *Proceedings of the Eighteenth Conference on Computational Language Learning*, pages 171–180.

Omer Levy, Yoav Goldberg, and Ido Dagan. 2015. Improving distributional similarity with lessons learned from word embeddings. *Transactions of the Association for Computational Linguistics*, 3:211–225.

Mike Lewis and Mark Steedman. 2013. Combining distributional and logical semantics. *Transactions of the Association for Computational Linguistics*, 1:179–192.

David Lewis. 1975. Adverbs of quantification. In Edward L. Keenan, editor, *Formal semantics of natural language*, pages 178–188. Cambridge University Press.

Tal Linzen. 2016. How (not) to compare semantic spaces using word analogies. In *Proceedings of the First ACL Workshop on Evaluating Vector Space Representations for NLP*.

Kevin Lund and Curtis Burgess. 1996. Producing high-dimensional semantic spaces from lexical co-occurrence. *Behavior Research Methods*, 28(2):203–208.

Tomas Mikolov, Kai Chen, Greg Corrado, and Jeffrey Dean. 2013a. Efficient estimation of word representations in vector space. *Proceedings of ICLR*.

Tomas Mikolov, Ilya Sutskever, Kai Chen, Greg Corrado, and Jeff Dean. 2013b. Distributed representations of words and phrases and their compositionality. In *Advances in Neural Information Processing Systems*, pages 3111–3119.

Tomas Mikolov, Wen-tau Yih, and Geoffrey Zweig. 2013c. Linguistic regularities in continuous space word representations. In *Proceedings of NAACL-HLT*, pages 746–751.

Jeffrey Pennington, Richard Socher, and Christopher D. Manning. 2014. Glove: Global vectors for word representation. *Proceedings of the 2014 Conference on Empirical Methods in Natural Language Processing (EMNLP)*, 12:1532–1543.

Martin Redington, Nick Chater, and Steven Finch. 1998. Distributional information: A powerful cue for acquiring syntactic categories. *Cognitive Science*, 22(4):425–469.

Tim Rocktäschel, Edward Grefenstette, Karl Moritz Hermann, Tomáš Kočiský, and Phil Blunsom. 2016. Reasoning about entailment with neural attention. In *International Conference for Learning Representations*.

Magnus Sahlgren. 2006. *The Word-Space Model: Using distributional analysis to represent syntagmatic and paradigmatic relations between words in high-dimensional vector spaces*. Ph.D. thesis, Stockholm University.

Joseph Turian, Lev-Arie Ratinov, and Yoshua Bengio. 2010. Word representations: A simple and general method for semi-supervised learning. In *Proceedings of the 48th Annual Meeting of the Association for Computational Linguistics*, pages 384–394, Uppsala, Sweden, July. Association for Computational Linguistics.

Peter D. Turney and Patrick Pantel. 2010. From frequency to meaning: Vector space models of semantics. *Journal of Artificial Intelligence Research*, 37(1):141–188.

Peter D. Turney. 2006. Similarity of semantic relations. *Computational Linguistics*, 32(3):379–416.

Automatic Identification of Aspectual Classes across Verbal Readings

Ingrid Falk and Fabienne Martin
University of Stuttgart
`firstname.lastname@ling.uni-stuttgart.de`

Abstract

The automatic prediction of aspectual classes is very challenging for verbs whose aspectual value varies across readings, which are the rule rather than the exception. This paper sheds a new perspective on this problem by using a machine learning approach and a rich morpho-syntactic and semantic valency lexicon. In contrast to previous work, where the aspectual value of corpus clauses is determined on the basis of features retrieved from the corpus, we use features extracted from the lexicon, and aim to predict the aspectual value of verbal *readings* rather than verbs. Studying the performance of the classifiers on a set of manually annotated verbal readings, we found that our lexicon provided enough information to reliably predict the aspectual value of verbs across their readings. We additionally tested our predictions for unseen predicates through a task based evaluation, by using them in the automatic detection of temporal relation types in TempEval 2007 tasks for French. These experiments also confirmed the reliability of our aspectual predictions, even for unseen verbs.

1 Introduction

It is well known that the aspectual value of a sentence plays an important role in various NLP tasks, like for instance the assessment of event factuality (Saurí and Pustejovsky, 2012), automatic summarisation (Kazantseva and Szpakowicz, 2010), the detection of temporal relations (Costa and Branco, 2012) or machine translation (Meyer et al., 2013). Since, however, the aspectual value of a sentence results from a complex interplay between lexical features of the predicate and its linguistic context, the automatic detection of this aspectual value is quite challenging.

Studies on the computational modelling of aspectual classes emerged about two decades ago with the work of Passonneau (1988) and Klavans and Chodorow (1992), among others. In probably the most extensive study on the field, Siegel and McKeown (2000) extract clauses from a corpus and classify them into states and events, sorting the latter into culminated and non-culminated events in a subsequent step. The classification is based on features inspired by classic Vendlerian aspectual diagnostics, themselves collected from the corpus. Since, however, these features are collected on a type level, this method does not give satisfying results for verbs whose aspectual value varies across readings (henceforth 'aspectually polysemous verbs'), which are far from exceptional (see section 3)[1].

This problem is directly addressed by Zarcone and Lenci (2008). These authors classify corpus clauses into the four Vendlerian aspectual categories (states, activities, accomplishments and achievements), and like Siegel and McKeown, base their classification on (classic aspectual) features collected from the corpus. However, they additionally employ some syntactic properties of the predicate, a move that enables them to better account for the influence of the linguistic context on the aspectual value of the verb across readings.

Friedrich and Palmer (2014), who extend Siegel and McKeown's (2000) model to distributional features, also address the problem of aspectually polysemous verbs, by making use of instance-based syntactic and semantic features, obtained from an automatic syntactic analysis of the clause.

---

[1]Type-based classification selects a dominant sense for any given verb and then always assigns it for each reading of this verb.

*Proceedings of the Fifth Joint Conference on Lexical and Computational Semantics (*SEM 2016)*, pages 12–22,
Berlin, Germany, August 11-12, 2016.

The approach we present here is designed to tackle the issue of aspectual variability and is complementary to the methods just described. As we know from detailed work on verbal syntax and semantics in the tradition of Dowty (1979), Levin (1993), Rappaport and Levin (1998) and subsequent work, many morpho-syntactic and semantic properties of the verb exert a strong influence on its aspectual value in context. As far as we know, no study on the computational modelling of aspectual classes has tried to systematically take advantage of these correlations between lexical properties and lexical aspect. We aim to capitalise on these correlations with the help of a rich French lexical resource, "Les Verbes Français" (Dubois and Dubois-Charlier (1997; François et al. (2007), henceforth LVF). The LVF is a valency lexicon of French verbs providing a detailed morpho-syntactic and semantic description for each reading (use) of a verb.

Differently from previous work, the instances we classify aspectually are verbal readings as delineated in the LVF (rather than corpus phrases). We therefore study lexical aspect on an intermediate level between the coarse-grained type (verb) level and the fine-grained corpus utterance level. Also, while in previous approaches, the features are collected from corpora, those we make use of are retrieved from the lexicon entries. The substantial advantage of this approach, that heavily makes use of the colossal amount of information manually coded in the LVF, is that it enables us to fully investigate the aspectual flexibility of verbs across readings and the factors that determine it.

For our automatic aspectual classification, we firstly extracted verbal readings from the LVF for a set of 167 frequent verbs chosen in such a way that each of the four Vendlerian aspectual classes are roughly equally represented. A semanticist manually annotated each of the corresponding 1199 readings based on a refinement of the classic Vendlerian 4-way aspectual categorisation. This refinement is motivated by recent studies in theoretical linguistics converging in the view that the traditional quadripartite aspectual typology has to be further refined (see (Hay et al., 1999; Piñón, 2006; Mittwoch, 2013) among many others). Such a refinement enables one to better account for the variable degree of aspectual flexibility among predicates, so as to *e.g.* delineate between 'strictly stative' predicates (e.g. *know*), and

those stative predicates that also naturally display an activity reading (e.g. *think*). This annotation provides the gold standard for our classification experiments. For each annotated reading, we then collected morpho-syntactic and semantic features from the LVF, chosen for their relevance for the aspectual value of the verb in context. Based on these features, we trained classifiers to automatically predict the aspectual class of the LVF readings.

We assessed the accuracy of our automatic aspectual classification in a task based evaluation as follows. Costa and Branco (2012) showed that (type-based/verb-level) aspectual indicators improve temporal relation classification in TempEval challenges (Verhagen et al., 2007), which emerged in conjunction with TimeML and Time-Banks (Pustejovsky and Mani, 2003). The tasks involved in these challenges require temporal reasoning. Following Branco and Costa's example, we performed TempEval tasks on the French TempEval data, using aspectual indicators derived from the predictions generated by our classifier. This way, we could show that our aspectual classification based on lexical features is reliable.

The paper is structured as follows. Section 2 presents the resource used. Section 3 explains on which criteria verbal readings were manually annotated. Section 4 describes the features collected from the LVF. Section 5 presents the automatic aspectual classification based on these features. Section 6 presents the aspectual indicators derived from the classification. Section 7 describes how our automatic classification was evaluated through TempEval tasks.

2 The Resource – LVF

The LVF, which roughly covers 12 300 verbs (lemmas) for a total of 25 610 readings, is a detailed and extensive lexical resource providing a systematic description of the morpho-syntactic and syntactico-semantic properties of French verbs[2]. The basic lexical units are readings of the verbs, determined by their defining syntactic environment (argument structure, adjuncts) and a semiformal semantic decomposition (with a finite repertoire of '*opérateurs*'). Once the idiosyn-

---

[2] The paper version is available online at `http://talep.lif.univ-mrs.fr/FondamenTAL/`. Online access and electronic versions in XML are available at `http://rali.iro.umontreal.ca/rali/?q=fr/lvf`.

crasies are put aside, this decomposition very roughly uses the same inventory of labels and features as in the lexical templates found in e.g. Pinker (1989) or Jackendoff (1983). In Table 1, we give the sample entries for the verb *élargir* 'widen' to illustrate LVF's basic layout.

Syntactic description (Table 1a). Each reading of a verb is coupled with a representation of its syntactic frames. In principle, a verbal reading can be coupled with a transitive frame (labelled 'T'), a reflexively marked frame ('P') and an intransitive frame ('A', 'N') unmarked by the reflexive. The syntactic description additionally specifies some semantic features of the main arguments (e.g. whether the subject and direct object are animate and/or inanimate, whether the indirect object refers to a location, etc). This information is often crucial for the aspectual value of the reading (e.g. a 'human-only' intransitive frame strongly indicates unergativity and henceforth atelicity).

Semantic description (Table 1b). Each entry in the LVF is also characterised by a semi-formal semantic decomposition providing a rough approximation of the meaning of each verbal reading. Each entry is therefore paired with a finite set of primitive semantic features and labels on the basis of which verbal readings are sorted into 14 semantic classes (*eg. psych-verbs, verbs of physical state and behaviour*, etc.). The semantic features and labels used in the semantic decomposition provide other cues about the type of verbs (unergative/ unaccusative verbs, manner/ result verbs, etc.) which is instantiated by each reading. For instance, for the reading 01 of *élargir* 'widen' ('*élargir01*' for short) in Table 1b, 'r/d +qt [p]' roughly corresponds to BECOME(more(p)) ('r/d' stands for '(make) become'; '+qt' stands for an increase along a scale). From this, one can safely infer that *élargir01* is a 'degree achievement' verb.

Derivational properties. The LVF also indicates when a verb is formed through a derivational process, and in the positive case, provides information about the category of the verbal root, thus enabling one to identify deadjectival or denominal verbs. Finally, for each entry is specified which suffix is used for the available reading-preserving deverbal nominalisations and adjectives (*-ment, -age, -ion, -eur, -oir, -ure* or zero-derived nominalisations, and *-able, -ant, -é* adjectives).

3   The annotation

We retrieved 1199 entries (verbal readings) for the selected 167 frequent verbs mentioned earlier. On average, each verb has roughly 15 readings, while 50% have more than 13[3]. These readings were manually annotated according to a fine-grained aspectual classification on a 'telicity scale' of eight values.

At the bottom of the scale are readings that are unambiguously ('strictly') stative (i.e. for which any other aspectual value is excluded), rated with 1 (S-STA). For instance, *élargir02* (see Table 1a) is rated with 1, given (a.o.) its incompatibility with the progressive. Those are distinguished from stative verbs that also display a dynamic reading (e.g. *penser* 'think'), rated with 2 (STA-ACT). Readings that are unambiguously dynamic and atelic ('strict activity' readings) are rated with 3 (S-ACT).

At the top are found achievement readings for which any other aspectual value is excluded, rated with 8 (S-ACH). At the middle of the scale are found 'variable telicity' readings, that have no preference for the telic use in a neutral context and are compatible both with *for-* and *in-* adverbials, rated with 4 (ACT-ACC). For instance, *élargir01* is rated with 4, because (a.o.) it is compatible both with *for-* and *in-* adverbials and has no preference for the telic reading in a neutral context. These variable telicity readings are distinguished from 'weak accomplishment' readings, rated with 5 (W-ACC). Out of context, weak accomplishment readings trigger an inference of completion and have a preference for the telic use; however, they are nevertheless acceptable with a *for*-adverbial (on the relevant interpretation of this adverbial). For instance, *remplir01* 'fill' (*Pierre a rempli le seau d'eau* 'Peter filled the bucket with water') is rated with 5, because it by default triggers an inference of completion, but is nevertheless still acceptable with a *for*-adverbial under the 'partitive' reinterpretation of this adverbial. Under this reinterpretation, described e.g. by Smollett (2005) or Champollion (2013), the sentence triggers an inference of non-completion (Bott (2010), see e.g. *Peter filled the bucket with water for 10 minutes*). 'Strong' accomplishment readings — like *remplir09* (*Cette nouvelle a rempli Pierre de*

---

[3]Interestingly, the average number of 15 readings per verb very closely matches the number of event categories per verb obtained in the experiment reported by Marvel and Koenig (2015), who propose a new method of automatically categorising event descriptions.

id	frame	encoded information
01	T1308	transitive, human subject, inanimate direct object, instrumental adjunct
	P3008	reflexive, inanimate subject, instrumental adjunct
	A30	intransitive with adjunct, inanimate subject
02	N1i	intransitive, animate subject, prep. phrase headed by *de* (*of*)
	A90	intransitive with adjunct, subject human or thing
	T3900	transitive, inanimate subject, object human or thing

(a) Syntactic descriptions

id	example[a]	semantic decomposition	sem. primitive	sem. class
01	On *élargit* une route/ La route *(s')élargit*.	`r/d+qt large`	become	Transformation
02	Cette veste *élargit* Paul aux épaules/ La robe *élargit* la taille.	`d large a.som`	become	Transformation
03	On *élargit* ses connaissances.	`r/d large abs`	become	Transformation
04	On *élargit* le débat à la politique étrangère.	`f.ire abs VRS`	directed move	Enter/Exit

(b) The four readings illustrated by sample sentences and their semantic description

[a]Literal translations – 01: One widens a road/the road is REFL widened/the road widens. 02: This jacket widens Paul 'at the' shoulders/ The dress widens the waist. 03: One widens one's knowledge. 04: One extends the debate to foreign policy.

Table 1: LVF entries for *élargir*

joie 'This news filled Peter with joy') — are incompatible with the partitive reinterpretation of *for*-adverbials.[4] Those are rated with 6 (S-ACC). Finally, accomplishments that share a proper subset of properties with achievements are rated with 7 (ACC-ACH).

The annotator evaluated each entry with a definite or singular indefinite internal argument, in order to abstract away from the role of the determiner in the aspectual value of the VP (see e.g. Verkuyl (1993)).

We also used a coarser grained aspectual scale and group the verbal readings into the following classes: ATElic (rating 1–3), with VARiable telicity (rating 4), and TELic (5 or more). Table 2 gives an overview of the distribution of the aspectual ratings.

The first finding is that verbs display a considerable aspectual variability across readings, which confirms the need to go beyond the type level for the computational modelling of aspectual classes. The aspectual value of 2/3 of the 151 verbs with more than one reading varies with the instantiated reading (on the 8 value scale). With respect to the coarser grained scale, roughly half of the verbs (82, for a total of 793 readings) have readings in more than one of the three overarching aspectual classes.

4 The features

The LVF connects each verbal reading with specific morphological, syntactic and semantic features. Among such features, those that influence the lexical aspect of the verb in context are known to be pervasive: Verbs encoding the BECOME operator in their event structure generally have a telic use; intransitive manner verbs are mostly activity verbs (see e.g. Rappaport Hovav and Levin (1998) and subsequent work); ditransitive verbs like *give* are mostly result verbs (see e.g. Pylkkänen (2008)) and thus accomplishments.[5]. We took advantage of many of these features for our classification. Also, some semantic classes give very clear hints to the lexical aspect of its members. For instance, readings instantiating the class of 'enter/exit verbs' are telic, those instantiating the 'transformation' class are never atelic only, etc.[6] We also made use of features conveyed by the semantic decomposition, in particular its main component (BECOME, DO, ITER, STATE, etc.).

We also took advantage of the encoded information on the suffixes used in reading-preserving nominalisations. For instance, readings with an intransitive but no transitive frame can in prin-

---

[4]The *for*-adverbial is nevertheless compatible with *remplir09*, but only under its (non-partitive) 'result state-related interpretation', under which it scopes on the result state, cf. Piñón (1999); see e.g. *This news filled Peter with joy for ten minutes*.

[5]Relevant features are sometimes coded in an indirect way. For instance, the difference between verbs like *donner x à y* 'give x to y', that subcategorise the indirect object, and verbs like *dire x à y* 'say x to y', that do not, is retrievable through the difference in the associated syntactic frames.

[6]On this respect, note that the semantic decomposition of *élargir02*, which involves BECOME, shows the limits of the analysis provided by the LVF: Under the 'spatial' use of which *élargir02* is an instance, degree achievements do not describe events in which an individual undergoes change over time (see Deo et al. (2013)).

1	2	3	4	5	6	7	8	1-3	4	5-8
S-STA	ACT-STA	S-ACT	ACT-ACC	W-ACC	S-ACC	ACC-ACH	S-ACH	ATE	VAR	TEL
182	67	175	195	172	227	29	152	424	195	580

(a) 8 value scale   (b) 3 value scale

Table 2: Aspectual distribution of the 1199 manually annotated verbal readings

Features collected from corpus *Example Clause*	Related features in LVF
frequency	–
not or never *She can **not** explain why.*	–
temporal adverb *I saw to it **then**.*	durative adverbial in semantic decomposition
implicit or no external argument *He was admitted to the hospital.*	canonical passive, refl. constr. w. instrumental adj.
past/pres participle *… blood pressure going up.*	–
in adverbial *She built it **in an hour**.*	–
4 tense related features	–
manner adverb *She studied **diligently**.*	manner argument or adjunct
evaluative adverb *They performed **horribly**.*	+ql in semantic decomposition
for adverbial *I sang **for** ten minutes.*	durative adverbial in semantic decomposition
continuous adverb *She will live **indefinitely**.*	+re (iterative operator) in semantic decomposition

Table 3: Siegel and McKeown's (2000) and LVF features.

Features collected from corpus	Related features in LVF
temporal adverbs	temporal arg. or adj.
intentional adverbs	–
frequency adverbs	+qt in sem. decomp.
iterative adverbs	+re in sem. decomp.
tense	–
only subject	A* or N* frame
presence of direct obj	T* frame
presence of indirect obj	N* frame
presence of locative arg	encoded in frame sem class = L
presence of sent. compl. canonical passive	encoded in frame T* and A* schema
subj & dobj, number, animacy, definiteness	plural subj or obj human/animal subj or obj thing subj or obj

Table 4: Zarcone and Lenci's (2008) and LVF features.

ciple characterise unaccusative (telic) or unergative (atelic) verbs. But only the latter undergo *-eur* nominalisation, as in English (see Keyser and Roeper (1984)). The availability of the *-eur* nominalisation is therefore a reliable aspectual feature too.

Tables 3 and 4 compare features used in some previous aspectual classifications and their equivalents in the LVF. As one can check, the LVF features cover most of the features used in Siegel and McKeown (2000) and Zarcone and Lenci (2008)[7]. For obvious reasons, features related to grammatical aspect conveyed by tenses are not covered in our valency lexicon. But overall, our set of features roughly corresponds to those used in previous work, for a total of 38 features.

5 Classifying LVF entries

The items we classified are the 1199 readings for the 167 verbs selected. Our classification task consisted in predicting the right (coarse-grained) aspectual class for these readings (ATE, VAR or TEL). In this supervised learning setting, we applied the classifiers shown in Table 5 with the implementation provided by Weka (Hall et al., 2009), mostly with their default settings[8]. We measured the performance of the classifiers by assessing the accuracy in 10-fold cross-validation, and compared it to the accuracy of a baseline classifier which always assigns the majority class (TEL, rules.ZeroR). We also performed a linear forward feature selection using the Naïve Bayes algorithm[9]. This way, nine features were selected, coding, among others:

- the presence of a temporal or manner argument/adjunct in the semantic decomposition;

- the main primitive in the semantic decomposition;

- the use of the suffixes *-ment* and *-ure* in the reading-preserving nominalisation;

- the relative polysemy of the lemma (indicated by the number of its readings);

- a subject that must be inanimate;

- the presence of a reflexive reading.

---

[7]The features used by Friedrich and Palmer (2014) are mainly derived from those of Siegel and McKeown (2000).

[8]For libsvm (the SVM implementation), we used a linear kernel and normalisation. We selected roughly one classifier from each class.

[9]An exhaustive search with the 38 features in this group was computationally too time-consuming.

Algorithm	*complete*	*selected*
`trees.j48`	61.80	63.00
`rules.jrip`	63.89	61.56
`lazy.kstar`	62.89	**67.47**
`functions.libsvm`	62.72	61.13
`bayes.naivebayes`	60.22	65.80
`baseline`	48.37	48.37

Table 5: Classification accuracy for LVF readings, with *complete* feature set and *selected* in feature selection process.

The results in Table 5 show that the features retrieved from the LVF enable one to predict the aspectual class considerably better than the baseline: The accuracy ranges from 12 points to almost 20 above the baseline accuracy of 48.37. The best configuration, achieving an accuracy of 67.48%, is the `lazy.kstar` classifier based on the feature set reduced by feature selection. A comparison with the results reported in previous work is difficult, due to the great discrepancies in the experimental settings (see the introduction). However, our results clearly show that the aspectual class characterising verbal readings can be predicted with a reasonable precision on the basis of lexical-related information only. They once again empirically confirm the well-documented correlations between lexical aspect and the morpho-syntactic/semantic properties of the verb.

6 Aspectual indicators

In this section, we take a more qualitative look at the results obtained in section 5. We assessed the quality of the predictions of our model (henceforth LVF-model) in two ways. Firstly, we derived *aspectual indicators for the type level*, describing the general 'aspectual profile' of a verb across all its readings. These are later used in the task based evaluation described in section 7[10]. Secondly, we looked at the aspectual values assigned to the readings of particular verbs (see *indicators for the verbal readings* below).

Indicators for the type-level. The aspectual indicators for the type-level are computed on the basis of the aspectual values predicted for each reading of the verb. As shown in Table 6, they are designed to reflect how aspectual values vary across the readings of the verb. For example, the indica-

v.	var	> 1 telicity value for same lemma?
m.	maj	Telicity value of majority
t.	tel	Any telic reading?
a.	ate	Any atelic reading?

(a) Nominal and binary aspectual indicators

1.	%tel	Proportion of telic readings
2.	%ate	Proportion of atelic readings
3.	%var	Proportion of flexible readings
4.	probest.max	Max of probability estimates
5.	probest.min	Min of probability estimates
6.	probest.avg	Average of probability estimates

(b) Numeric aspectual indicators.

Table 6: Aspectual indicators

tor 'v' in Table 6a shows whether there is any variation at all, 't' assesses the presence of at least one telic reading, etc. Whereas the indicators in Table 6a provide qualitative cues, those in Table 6b convey quantitative information. The first three give the proportion of readings of a particular aspectual class. The last three are computed from the probability estimates generated by the `libsvm` classifier.

In order to get an idea of the quality of our predictions, we computed from automatic predictions the aspectual indicators for all annotated verbs. We provide some of them in Table 7 for verbs judged aspectually polysemous by the annotator. These 'automatic' aspectual indicators are given in normal font. For the same verbs, we also computed the 'manual' aspectual indicators, i.e. those computed on the basis of the manual annotations (when possible)[11]. These are set in bold face. The verbs in Table 7a are dominantly telic, those in 7b dominantly atelic and those in 7c dominantly variable. As one can check, the dominant aspectual value is correctly assigned in most cases. Also, in most cases, the proportion of uses of the non-preferred readings closely matches the proportion obtained manually. Unsurprisingly, the sample of verbs predicted to be 'mostly telic' are mostly (quasi-)achievement verbs or strong accomplishments describing 'non-gradual' changes (verbs lexicalising changes involving a two-point scale, e.g. *dead* or *not dead* for *kill*, see e.g. Beavers (2008)). Unsurprisingly again, many verbs predicted to be 'mostly variable' are degree achievement verbs. More remarkably, *remplir* 'fill' is

---

[10]Assigning a value to the type level was necessary to test our predictions on the TempEval corpus, since aligning each utterance of this corpus with a specific LVF-reading is not feasible.

[11]Indicators derived from the probability estimates are not computable from the manual annotations.

rightly predicted to be 'mostly telic', although it is a verb of gradual change. The model therefore preserves here the crucial distinction between degree achievements associated with a close scale like *remplir*, tolerating atelic readings under some uses although they conventionally encode a maximal point (see Kennedy and Levin (2008)), and achievement verbs associated with an open scale like *élargir* 'widen', that also accept both *for-* and *in-* adverbials, but do not show a preference for the telic reading in absence of any adverbial. These observations suggest that even if predictions for some readings are wrong, the aspectual indicators might still rightly capture the general 'aspectual profile' of verbs at the type level.

Indicators for the verbal readings. We also inspected the predicted values for some predicates and compared them to the values assigned manually. For predicates showing a high degree of aspectual variability like *élargir* 'widen' (see Table 7c), the results are very good: *élargir01* ('They are widening the road') is correctly analysed as VAR and *élargir04* ('They are extending the majority') as TEL. Interestingly, *élargir02* ('This jacket widens Pierre's shoulders') is correctly analysed as ATE, despite of the fact that it is wrongly analysed by the LVF as instantiating the class of change of state verbs (see footnote 6). This suggests that the computational model could leverage the information provided by the syntactic frames associated to *élargir02* (see Table 1b) to outweigh the wrongly assigned semantic class and produce the correct aspectual prediction.

7 Task based evaluation

Reliable automatic aspectual classifications are expected to enhance existing solutions to temporal relation classification. Thus, if our LVF-model improves such a solution, we can conclude that our learned aspectual values are reliable. We therefore evaluated the predictive power of the LVF-model on unseen verbs through such tasks, following the method proposed in Costa and Branco (2012). While Costa and Branco (2012) collected their aspectual indicators from the web and improved the temporal relation detection in the Portuguese TimeBank (PTiB), we derive ours from the predictions generated using the LVF-model, as described in section 6 and use them in TempEval tasks for the French TimeBank.

The data used in these experiments are the French

lemma	m	t	a	%tel	%ate	%var
casser	**TEL**	**1**	**0**	**95.00**	**0**	**0.05**
'break'	TEL	1	1	95.65	4.35	0
mourir	**TEL**	**1**	**1**	**75.00**	**25.00**	**0**
'die'	TEL	1	1	75.00	25.00	0
remplir	**TEL**	**1**	**1**	**70.00**	**30.00**	**0**
'fill'	TEL	1	1	80.00	20.00	0

(a) Mostly telic

lemma	m	t	a	%tel	%ate	%var
regarder	**ATE**	**0**	**1**	**0**	**91.67**	**8.33**
'look at'	ATE	1	1	16.67	83.33	0
chanter	**ATE**	**0**	**1**	**0**	**66.67**	**33.33**
'sing'	ATE	0	1	0	66.67	33.33
étudier	**ATE**	**1**	**1**	**30.00**	**60.00**	**10.00**
'study'	ATE	1	1	20.00	80.00	0

(b) Mostly atelic

lemma	m	t	a	%tel	%ate	%var
vieillir	**VAR**	**0**	**1**	**0**	**11.11**	**88.89**
'get older'	VAR	0	1	0	22.22	77.78
embellir	**VAR**	**0**	**1**	**0**	**33.33**	**66.67**
'beautify'	VAR	1	0	33.33	0	66.67
élargir	**VAR**	**1**	**1**	**25.00**	**25.00**	**50.00**
'widen'	VAR	1	1	25.00	25.00	50.00

(c) Mostly variable

Table 7: Aspectual indicators computed from predictions and from manual annotations. Indicators in **bold face** are computed based on manual annotations. The names of the indicators refer to the labels used in Table 6.

TempEval data, a corpus for French annotated in ISO-TimeML (FTiB in the following) described in Bittar et al. (2011). This data contains about 15 000 tokens[12] annotated with temporal relations. Of these, roughly 2/3 are marked between 2 event arguments and 1/3 between an event and a temporal expression. The classification tasks we are concerned with deal with the automatic detection of the type of these temporal relations, namely the tasks A, B and C in the TempEval 2007 challenge[13]. Table 8 gives an overview of the data for each of the three classification tasks. We build our experiments on top of a base system addressing these challenges and show that the performance of this base system can be improved using our aspec-

---

[12]This corresponds to 1/4 of the English TimeBank.

[13]Task A is about temporal relations between an event and a time, task B focuses on relations between events and the document's creation time, and task C is concerned with relations between two events.

	FTiB		PTiB	LVF	
	tlinks	rel. types	tlinks	lemmas(seen)	readings
A	302	10	1659	164(16)	1597
B	264	5	2887	149(14)	1329
C	1172	15	1993	427(40)	3827

Table 8: Event instances for TempEval tasks A, B and C for French and Portuguese (left) and corresponding verbs and readings in LVF (right).

Attribute	A	B	C
event-aspect	×	✓	✓
event-polarity	×	✓	✓
event-pos	×	✓	✓
event-class	✓	✓	✓
event-tense	×	×	×
event-mood*	×	✓	✓
event-vform*	×	✓	✓
order-adjacent	×	N/A	N/A
order-event-first	×	N/A	N/A
order-event-between	✓	N/A	N/A
order-timex-between	×	N/A	N/A
timex-mod	×	×	N/A
timex-type	✓	×	N/A
tlink-relType	class		

Table 9: Features used in the base system for TempEval tasks A, B and C. Features checked (✓) were selected in the feature selection process.

tual indicators.

Like Costa and Branco (2012), we implemented as base system the classifiers proposed for English by Hepple et al. (2007), which only rely on relatively simple annotation attributes. Table 9 lists the features used in the context of our FTiB data, basically the same as in Hepple et al. (2007) and Costa and Branco (2012). As in their work, we also determined the final set of features by performing an exhaustive search on all possible feature combinations for each task, using again the Naïve Bayes algorithm. The features marked '✓' are those finally selected this way. Using this set of features, we trained the same classifiers and under the same conditions described in section 5 on the FTiB data. The accuracy of the resulting models in 10-fold cross-validation on the three TempEval tasks are shown in italics in Table 10.

Following again Costa and Branco (2012), we then enhanced this basic set of features with each of the aspectual indicators computed from the predictions generated by the LVF-model. The aspectual indicators are listed in Table 6; we described their computation in section 6. This way, we obtained 10 enhanced feature sets, one for each as-

pectual indicator. Using these feature sets and the same classifiers as before, we learned models on the FTiB data and computed their accuracy in 10 fold cross-validation.

The improvements achieved this way are shown in Table 10. Whenever an aspectual indicator improves the results of the base system, we give its accuracy (in bold face) below the accuracy of the base system. The superscripts refer to the lines in Table 6 and show which of the aspectual indicators was used to enhance the base feature set to obtain the reported improved accuracy[14].

The results given in Table 10 show that the accuracy of 8 out of the 15 tested classifiers could be improved by 1-3 points by adding the aspectual indicators. The indicator which produced the most and largest improvements was the average over the probability estimates, suggesting that this value best reflects the dominant aspectual value of the verb. Overall, the improvement obtained through our classification is quantitatively comparable to the enhancement realised by Costa and Branco (2012): Their results show an improvement similar in size to ours for 9 out of the same 15 classifiers. They evaluate on a test set, whereas we compare accuracy in 10-fold cross-validation. This was necessary since the French TimeBank is considerably smaller (roughly 1/4 of Costa and Branco's data set for Portuguese, see PTiB column in Table 8). As mentioned earlier, a qualitative comparison is nevertheless difficult, given the substantial differences between the data and the methodology used here and there.

The results clearly show however that the LVF-model trained on our annotated lexical entries performs well on unseen predicates.

8 Conclusion and future work

This paper focuses on the issue of aspectual variability for the computational modelling of aspectual classes, by using a machine learning approach and a rich morpho-syntactic and semantic valency lexicon. In contrast to previous work, where the aspectual value of corpus clauses is determined at the type (verb) level on the basis of features retrieved from the corpus, we make use of features retrieved from the lexicon in order to predict an aspectual value for each *reading* of a same verb (as they are delineated in this lexicon). We firstly

---

[14]We only show improvements of at least 1%, and only show the largest gains in performance.

Classifier	A	B	C
`trees.j48`	*0.71*	*0.81*	*0.40*
	0.73[1]	**0.82**[3]	**0.41**[a]
`rules.jrip`	*0.71*	*0.83*	*0.36*
	0.73[6]	**0.84**[6]	**0.37**[m]
`lazy.kstar`	*0.72*	*0.82*	*0.42*
		0.85[5]	
`functions.libsvm`	*0.74*	*0.83*	*0.40*
		0.85[6]	
`bayes.naivebayes`	*0.73*	*0.84*	*0.40*
`baseline`	*0.72*	*0.62*	*0.29*

Table 10: Accuracy of classifiers obtained on FTiB with base and enhanced feature sets. Values for the base classifiers are in italics. In bold face improvements of an enhanced classifier, no values represent no improvement. Superscripts give the aspectual indicator used to enhance the base feature set and obtain the improved result. They refer to rows in Table 6.

studied the performance of the classifier on a set of manually annotated verb readings. Our results experimentally confirm the theoretical assumption that a sufficiently detailed lexicon provides enough information to reliably predict the aspectual value of verbs across their readings. Secondly, we tested the predictions for unseen predicates through a task based evaluation: We used the aspectual values predicted by the LVF-model to improve the detection of temporal relation classes in TempEval 2007 tasks for French. Our predictions resulted in improvements quantitatively similar to those achieved by Costa and Branco (2012) for Portuguese and thus confirm the reliability of our aspectual predictions for unseen verbs.

The investigation reported here can be further pursued in many interesting ways. One possible line of work consists in exploring the aspectual realisation and distribution of the LVF readings in corpus data. This would also provide means to relate our findings for verbal readings to corpus instances.

Our study strongly relies on the LVF lexical database, a very extensive source of morpho-syntactic and semantic information. For other languages, this kind of information, when it is available, is generally not contained in a single lexicon. Therefore, a further interesting research direction would be to evaluate the applicability of our technique to suitable information from distributed resources. On this respect, recent efforts made for linking linguistic and lexical data and making these data accessible and interoperable would certainly be very helpful. For English in particular, available suitable resources are already abundant.

One of these is the *Pattern Dictionary of English Verbs*, see (Hanks, 2008). Other interesting data bases are FrameNet (Baker et al., 1998), VerbNet (Levin, 1993; Kipper Schuler, 2006) and PropBank (Palmer et al., 2005), especially since these different resources have been mapped together by (Loper et al., 2007), thus giving access to both the lexical and distributional properties defining each entry.

Increasing the reliability of automatic identification of aspectual classes also represents interesting opportunities for several NLP applications. A finer-grained and more reliable automatic assessment of aspectual classes can among others be quite useful for increasing the accuracy of textual entailment recognition, and, particularly, the sensitivity of systems to event factuality (Saurí and Pustejovsky, 2009). For instance, for telic perfective sentences, while the inference of event completion amounts to an entailment with strong accomplishments and (quasi-)achievements (at least in absence of an adverb signalling incompletion like *partly*), the same inference is to some extent defeasible with weak accomplishments. Integrating finer-grained distinctions among predicates could also enable one to better disambiguate verbal modifiers like durative adverbials. A *for*-adverbial typically signals that the event is incomplete when it modifies a weak accomplishment; e.g., *Peter filled the truck for one hour* suggests that the filling event is not finished, see (Bott, 2010) a.o. However, the same adverbial does not trigger this inference when it applies to a strong accomplishment or a (quasi)-achievement. For instance, *They broke the law for five days* does not suggest that the breaking event is not finished. A system that performs better in the identification of fine grained aspectual classes would therefore evaluate with more precision the probability that the reported event is completed in the actual world.

Acknowledgments

This research was funded by the German Science Foundation, SFB 732 *Incremental specification in context*, Project B5 *Polysemy in a Conceptual System*. For feedback and discussions, we thank Achim Stein and the reviewers of *Sem 2016.

References

Collin F. Baker, Charles J. Fillmore, and John B. Lowe. 1998. The Berkeley FrameNet project. In *Pro-

ceedings of the 17th International Conference on Computational Linguistics, volume 1, pages 86–90, Montreal, Quebec, Canada. Association for Computational Linguistics.

John Beavers. 2008. Scalar complexity and the structure of events. In John Dölling and Tatjana Heyde-Zybatow, editors, *Event Structures in Linguistic Form and Interpretation*. De Gruyter, Berlin.

André Bittar, Pascal Amsili, Pascal Denis, and Laurence Danlos. 2011. French TimeBank: An ISO-TimeML annotated reference corpus. pages 130–134. Association for Computational Linguistics.

Oliver Bott. 2010. *The Processing of Events*. John Benjamins, Amsterdam/Philadelphia.

Lucas Champollion. 2013. The scope and processing of *for*-adverbials: A reply to Deo and Piñango. In Todd Snider, editor, *Proceedings of Semantics and Linguistic Theory (SALT) 23*, pages 432–452. CLC publications, Cornell University, Ithaca:NY.

Francisco Costa and António Branco. 2012. Aspectual type and temporal relation classification. pages 266–275. Association for Computational Linguistics.

Ashwini Deo, Itamar Francez, and Andrew Koontz-Garboden. 2013. From change to value difference. In Todd Snider, editor, *Semantics and Linguistic Theory (SALT) 23*, pages 97–115. CLC publications, Cornell University, Ithaca:NY.

David Dowty. 1979. *Word Meaning and Montague Grammar : The semantics of Verbs and Times in Generative Semantics and in Montague's PTQ*. D. Reidel Pub. Co., Dordrecht; Boston.

Jean Dubois and Françoise Dubois-Charlier. 1997. *Les Verbes français*. Larousse.

Jacques François, Denis Le Pesant, and Danielle Leeman. 2007. Présentation de la classification des Verbes Français de Jean Dubois et Françoise Dubois-Charlier. *Langue française*, 153(1):3–19.

Annemarie Friedrich and Alexis Palmer. 2014. Automatic prediction of aspectual class of verbs in context. volume 2, pages 517–523. Association for Computational Linguistics.

Mark Hall, Eibe Frank, Geoffrey Holmes, Bernhard Pfahringer, Peter Reutemann, and Ian H. Witten. 2009. The WEKA data mining Software: An update. *SIGKDD Explor. Newsl.*, 11(1):10–18.

Patrick Hanks. 2008. Mapping Meaning onto Use: A Pattern Dictionary of English Verbs. Utah. AACL.

Jennifer Hay, Christopher Kennedy, and Beth Levin. 1999. Scalar structure underlies telicity in 'degree achievements'. In Devon Strolovitch Tanya Matthews, editor, *Semantics and Linguistic Theory (SALT) 9*, pages 127–144.

Mark Hepple, Andrea Setzer, and Robert Gaizauskas. 2007. USFD: Preliminary exploration of features and classifiers for the TempEval-2007 Task. pages 438–441. Association for Computational Linguistics.

Ray Jackendoff. 1983. *Semantics and Cognition*. MIT Press, Cambridge, Mass.

Anna Kazantseva and Stan Szpakowicz. 2010. Summarizing short stories. *Computational Linguistics*, 36(1):71–106.

Christopher Kennedy and Beth Levin. 2008. Measure of change: The adjectival core of verbs of variable telicity. In Louise McNally and Christopher Kennedy, editors, *Adjectives and Adverbs: Syntax, Semantics, and Discourse*, pages 156–182. Oxford University Press, Oxford.

Samuel Keyser and Thomas Roeper. 1984. On the middle and ergative construction in English. *Linguistic Inquiry*, 15:381–416.

Karin Kipper Schuler. 2006. *VerbNet: A Broad-Coverage, Comprehensive Verb Lexicon*. Ph.D. thesis, University of Pennsylvania.

Judith L. Klavans and Martin Chodorow. 1992. Degrees of stativity: The lexical representation of verb aspect. In *COLING 1992 Volume 4: The 15th International Conference on Computational Linguistics*.

Beth Levin. 1993. *English Verb Classes and Alternations: A Preliminary Investigation*. University of Chicago Press, Chicago.

Edward Loper, Szu ting Yi, and Martha Palmer. 2007. Combining lexical resources: Mapping between propbank and verbnet. In *Proceedings of the 7th International Workshop on Computational Linguistics*.

Aron Marvel and Jean-Pierre Koenig. 2015. Event categorization beyond verb senses. In *Proceedings of the 11th Workshop on Multiword Expressions, NAACL 2015*, pages 569–574.

Thomas Meyer, Cristina Grisot, and Andrei Popescu-Belis. 2013. Detecting narrativity to improve English to French translation of simple past verbs. In *Proceedings of the Workshop on Discourse in Machine Translation*, pages 33–42, Sofia, Bulgaria, August. Association for Computational Linguistics.

Anita Mittwoch. 2013. On the criteria for distinguishing accomplishments from activities, and two types of aspectual misfits. In Boban Arsenijevic, Berit Gehrke, and Rafael Marín, editors, *Studies in the Composition and Decomposition of Event Predicates*, pages 27–48. Springer, Berlin.

Martha Palmer, Paul Kingsbury, and Daniel Gildea. 2005. The proposition bank: An annotated corpus of semantic roles. *Computational Linguistics*, 31(1):71–106.

Rebecca J. Passonneau. 1988. A computational model of the semantics of tense and aspect. *Computational Linguistics*, 14(2):44–60.

Christopher Piñón. 1999. Durative adverbials for result states. In *Proceedings of the 18th West Coast Conference in Formal Linguistics*, pages 420–433. Cascadilla Press, Somerville, MA.

Christopher Piñón. 2006. Weak and strong accomplishments. In Katalin Kiss, editor, *Event Structure and the Left Periphery. Studies on Hungarian*, pages 91–106. Springer, Dordrecht.

Steven Pinker. 1989. *Learnability and Cognition: The Acquisition of Argument Structure*. MIT Press, Cambridge, Mass.

James Pustejovsky and Inderjeet Mani. 2003. Annotation of temporal and event expressions. In *Companion Volume of the Proceedings of HLT-NAACL 2003 - Tutorial Abstracts*.

Liina Pylkkänen. 2008. *Introducing Arguments*. MIT Press, Cambridge, MA.

Malka Rappaport Hovav and Beth Levin. 1998. Building verb meanings. In Miriam Butt and Wilhelm Geuder, editors, *The Projection of Arguments: Lexical and Compositional Factors*, pages 97–134. CSLI Publications, Chicago.

Roser Saurí and James Pustejovsky. 2009. FactBank: A corpus annotated with event factuality. 43(3):227–268.

Roser Saurí and James Pustejovsky. 2012. Are you sure that this happened? Assessing the factuality degree of events in text. *Computational Linguistics*, 38(2):261–299.

Eric V. Siegel and Kathleen R. McKeown. 2000. Learning methods to combine linguistic indicators: Improving aspectual classification and revealing linguistic insights. *Computational Linguistics*, 26(4):595–628.

Rebecca Smollett. 2005. Quantized direct object don't delimit after all. In Henk Verkuyl, Henriëtte de Swart, and Angeliek van Hout, editors, *Perspectives on Aspect*, pages 41–59. Kluwer Academic Publishers, Amsterdam.

Marc Verhagen, Robert Gaizauskas, Frank Schilder, Mark Hepple, Graham Katz, and James Pustejovsky. 2007. Semeval-2007 task 15: Tempeval temporal relation identification. In *Proceedings of the Fourth International Workshop on Semantic Evaluations (SemEval-2007)*, pages 75–80, Prague, Czech Republic. Association for Computational Linguistics.

Henk Verkuyl. 1993. *A Theory of Aspectuality : The Interaction between Temporal and Atemporal Structure*. Cambridge University Press, Cambridge; New York.

Alessandra Zarcone and Alessandro Lenci. 2008. Computational models for event type classification in context. In *Proceedings of the Sixth International Conference on Language Resources and Evaluation (LREC'08)*, Marrakech, Morocco. European Language Resources Association (ELRA).

Metaphor as a Medium for Emotion: An Empirical Study

Saif M. Mohammad
National Research Council Canada
saif.mohammad@nrc-cnrc.gc.ca

Ekaterina Shutova
University of Cambridge, UK
es407@cam.ac.uk

Peter D. Turney
Allen Institute for Artificial Intelligence
petert@allenai.org

Abstract

It is generally believed that a metaphor tends to have a stronger emotional impact than a literal statement; however, there is no quantitative study establishing the extent to which this is true. Further, the mechanisms through which metaphors convey emotions are not well understood. We present the first data-driven study comparing the emotionality of metaphorical expressions with that of their literal counterparts. Our results indicate that metaphorical usages are, on average, significantly more emotional than literal usages. We also show that this emotional content is not simply transferred from the source domain into the target, but rather is a result of meaning composition and interaction of the two domains in the metaphor.

1 Introduction

Metaphor gives our expression color, shape and character. Metaphorical language is a result of complex knowledge projection from one domain, typically a physical, closely experienced one, to another, typically more abstract and vague one (Lakoff and Johnson, 1980). For instance, when we say "He *shot down* all of my arguments", we project knowledge and inferences from the domain of *battle* (the *source* domain) onto our reasoning about arguments and debates (the *target* domain). While preserving the core meaning of the sentence, the use of metaphor allows us to introduce additional connotations and emphasize certain aspects of the target domain, while downplaying others. Consider the following examples:

(1) a. The new measures *are strangling* business.

  b. The new measures tightly regulate business.

When we talk about "*strangling* business" in (1a) we express a distinct viewpoint on governmental regulation of business, as opposed to a more neutral factual statement expressed in (1b).

The interplay of metaphor and emotion has been an object of interest in fields such as linguistics (Blanchette et al., 2001; Kovecses, 2003), political science (Lakoff and Wehling, 2012), cognitive psychology (Crawford, 2009; Thibodeau and Boroditsky, 2011) and neuroscience (Aziz-Zadeh and Damasio, 2008; Jabbi et al., 2008). A number of computational approaches for sentiment polarity classification of metaphorical language have also been proposed (Veale and Li, 2012; Kozareva, 2013; Strzalkowski et al., 2014). However, there is no quantitative study establishing the extent to which metaphorical language is used to express emotion nor a data-supported account of the mechanisms by which this happens.

Our study addresses two questions: (i) whether a metaphorical statement is likely to convey a stronger emotional content than its literal counterpart; and (ii) how this emotional content arises in the metaphor, i.e. whether it comes from the source domain, or from the target domain, or rather arises compositionally through interaction of the source and the target. To answer these questions, we conduct a series of experiments, in which human subjects are asked to judge metaphoricity and emotionality of a sentence in a range of settings. We test two experimental hypotheses.

Hypothesis 1: metaphorical uses of words tend to convey more emotion than their literal paraphrases in the same context.

Hypothesis 2: the metaphorical sense of a word tends to carry more emotion than the literal sense of the same word.

To test Hypothesis 1, we compare the emotional content of a metaphorically used word to that of

*Proceedings of the Fifth Joint Conference on Lexical and Computational Semantics (*SEM 2016)*, pages 23–33,
Berlin, Germany, August 11-12, 2016.

its literal paraphrase in a fixed context, as in the following example.

(2) a. Hillary *brushed off* the accusations.

b. Hillary dismissed the accusations.

To test Hypothesis 2, we compare the emotional content of the metaphorical sense of a word to a literal sense of that same word in its literal context, as follows.

(3) a. Hillary *brushed off* the accusations.

b. He brushed off the snow.

Here, *brushed off* is metaphorical in the context of "accusations" but literal in the context of "snow".

Our experiments focus on metaphors expressed by a verb, since this is the most frequent type of metaphor, according to corpus studies (Cameron, 2003; Shutova and Teufel, 2010). In order to obtain a sufficient coverage across metaphorical and literal verb senses we extract our data from Word-Net. For 1639 senses of 440 verbs, we annotate their usage as metaphorical or literal using the crowdsourcing platform, CrowdFlower[1]. We then create datasets of pairs of these usages to test Hypotheses 1 and 2.

Our results support both hypotheses, providing evidence that metaphor is an important mechanism for expressing emotions. Further, the fact that metaphorical uses of words tend to carry more emotion than their literal uses indicates that the emotional content is not simply transferred from the source domain into the target, but rather is a result of meaning composition and interaction of the two domains in the metaphor. For this project, we created a dataset in which verb senses are annotated for both metaphoricity and emotionality. In addition, the metaphorical uses are paired with their human-validated interpretations in the form of literal paraphrases. We have made this dataset freely available online.[2] We expect that this dataset, the first of its kind, will find many applications in NLP, including the development and testing of metaphor identification and interpretation systems, modeling regular polysemy in word sense disambiguation, distinguishing between near-synonyms in natural language generation, and, not least, the development of sentiment analysis systems that can operate on real-world, metaphor-rich texts.

---

[1] www.crowdflower.com

[2] http://saifmohammad.com/WebPages/metaphor.html

2 Related Work

Word sense, metaphor and emotion: The standard approach to word sense disambiguation (WSD) is to develop a model for each polysemous word (Navigli, 2009). The model for a word predicts the intended sense, based on context. A problem with this approach to WSD is that good coverage of common polysemous English words would require about 3,200 distinct models. Kilgarriff (1997) has argued there are systematic relations among word senses across different words, focusing in particular on metaphor as a ubiquitous source of polysemy. This area of research is known as regular polysemy. Thus, there is a systematic relation between metaphor and word sense (Kilgarriff, 1997; Turney et al., 2011) and the emotion associated with a word depends on the sense of the word (Strapparava and Valitutti, 2004; Mohammad and Turney, 2013).[3] This raises the question of whether there is a systematic relation between presence of metaphor and the emotional content of words. As far as we know, this is the first paper to quantitatively explore this question.

Gibbs et al. (2002) conducted a study that looked at how listeners respond to metaphor and irony when they are played audio tapes describing emotional experiences. They found that on average metaphors were rated as being more emotional than non-metaphoric expressions. However, that work did not compare paraphrase pairs that differed in just one word (metaphorically or literally used) and thus did not control for context. Citron and Goldberg (2014) compared metaphorical and literal sentences differing only in one word, and found that metaphorical sentences led to more activity in the the amygdala and the anterior portion of the hippocampus. They hypothesized that this is because metaphorical sentences are more emotionally engaging than literal sentences.

Metaphor annotation: Metaphor annotation studies have typically been corpus-based and involved either continuous annotation of metaphorical language (i.e., distinguishing between literal and metaphorical uses of words in a given text), or search for instances of a specific metaphor in a corpus and an analysis thereof. The majority of corpus-linguistic studies were concerned with metaphorical expressions and mappings within a limited domain, e.g., WAR, BUSINESS, FOOD or

---

[3] Words used in different senses convey different affect.

PLANT metaphors (Santa Ana, 1999; Izwaini, 2003; Koller, 2004; Skorczynska Sznajder and Pique-Angordans, 2004; Lu and Ahrens, 2008; Low et al., 2010; Hardie et al., 2007), in a particular genre or type of discourse (Charteris-Black, 2000; Cameron, 2003; Lu and Ahrens, 2008; Martin, 2006; Beigman Klebanov and Flor, 2013).

Two recent studies (Steen et al., 2010; Shutova and Teufel, 2010) moved away from investigating particular domains to a more general study of how metaphor behaves in unrestricted continuous text. Steen and colleagues (Pragglejaz Group, 2007; Steen et al., 2010) proposed a metaphor identification procedure (MIP), in which every word is tagged as literal or metaphorical, based on whether it has a "more basic meaning" in other contexts than the current one. The basic meaning was defined as "more concrete; related to bodily action; more precise (as opposed to vague); historically older" and its identification was guided by dictionary definitions. Shutova and Teufel (2010) extended MIP to the identification of conceptual metaphors along with the linguistic ones. Lönneker (2004) investigated metaphor annotation in lexical resources. Their Hamburg Metaphor Database contains examples of metaphorical expressions in German and French, which are mapped to senses from EuroWordNet[4] and annotated with source–target domain mappings taken from the Master Metaphor List (Lakoff et al., 1991).

Emotion annotation: Sentiment analysis is defined as detecting the evaluative or affective attitude in text. A vast majority of work in sentiment analysis has focused on developing classifiers for valence prediction (Kiritchenko et al., 2014; Dong et al., 2014; Socher et al., 2013; Mohammad et al., 2013), i.e., determining whether a piece of text expresses positive, negative, or neutral attitude. However, there is a growing interest in detecting a wider range of emotions such as joy, sadness, optimism, etc. (Holzman and Pottenger, 2003; Alm et al., 2005; Brooks et al., 2013; Mohammad, 2012). Much of the this work has been influenced by the idea that some emotions are more basic than others (Ekman, 1992; Ekman and Friesen, 2003; Plutchik, 1980; Plutchik, 1991). Mohammad (2012) polled the Twitter API for tweets that have hashtag words such as *#anger* and *#sadness* corresponding to the eight Plutchik basic emo-

tions. He showed that these hashtag words act as good labels for the rest of the tweets. Suttles and Ide (2013) used a similar distant supervision technique and collected tweets with emoticons, emoji, and hashtag words corresponding to the Plutchik emotions. Emotions have also been annotated in lexical resources such as the Affective Norms for English Words, the NRC Emotion Lexicon (Mohammad and Turney, 2013), and WordNet Affect (Strapparava and Valitutti, 2004). The annotated corpora mentioned above have largely been used as training and test sets, and the lexicons have been used to provide features for emotion classification. (See Mohammad (2016) for a survey on affect datasets.) None of this work explicitly studied the interaction between metaphor and emotions.

3 Experimental Setup

To test Hypotheses 1 and 2, we extracted pairs of metaphorical and literal instances from WordNet. In WordNet, each verb sense corresponds to a *synset*, which consists of a set of near-synonyms, a *gloss* (a brief definition), and one or more *example sentences* that show the usage of one or more of the near-synonyms. We will refer to each of these sentences as the *verb-sense sentence*, or just *sentence*. The portion of the sentence excluding the target verb will be called the *context*. We will refer to each pair of target verb and verb-sense sentence as an *instance*. We extracted the following types of instances from WordNet:

Instance 1
Target verb: *erase*
Sentence: *The Turks erased the Armenians.*

Here, *erase* is used metaphorically. We will refer to such instances as *metaphorical instances*.

Now consider an instance similar to the one above, but where the target verb is replaced by its near-synonym or hypernym. For example:

Instance 2
Target verb: *kill*
Sentence: *The Turks killed the Armenians.*

The sentence in Instance 2 has a different target verb (although with a very similar meaning to the first) and an identical context w.r.t. Instance 1. However, in this instance, the target verb is used literally. We will refer to such instances as *literal instances*. To test Hypothesis 1, we will compare pairs such as Instance 1–Instance 2. We will then ask human annotators to examine these instances

---

[4]http://www.illc.uva.nl/EuroWordNet/

both individually and in pairs to determine how much emotion the target verbs convey in the sentences.

Another instance of the verb *erase*, corresponding to a different sense, is shown below:

Instance 3

Target verb: *erase*

Sentence: *Erase the formula on the blackboard.*

This instance contains a literal use of *erase*. To test Hypothesis 2, we will compare pairs such as Instance 1–Instance 3 that have the same target verb, but different contexts such that one instance is metaphorical and another is literal. We will ask human annotators to examine these instances both individually and in pairs to determine how much emotion the target verbs convey in the sentences.

In the sub-sections below, we describe: (3.1) How we compiled instance pairs to test Hypotheses 1 and 2. This involved annotating instances as metaphorical or literal. (3.2) How we annotated pairs of instances to determine which is more metaphorical. (3.3) How we annotated instances for emotionality. And finally, (3.4) how we annotated pairs of instances to determine which is more emotional.

3.1 Compiling pairs of instances

In order to create datasets of pairs such as Instance 1–Instance 2 and Instance 1–Instance 3, we first determine whether WordNet verb instances are metaphorical or literal. Specifically, we chose verbs with at least three senses (so that there is a higher chance of at least one sense being metaphorical) and less than ten senses (to avoid highly ambiguous verbs). In total, 440 verbs satisfied this criterion, yielding 1639 instances. We took example sentences directly from WordNet and automatically checked to make sure that the verb appeared in the gloss and the example sentence. In cases where the example sentence did not contain the focus word, we ignored the synset. We used the Questionnaire 1 to annotate these instances for metaphoricity:

Questionnaire 1: Literal or Metaphorical?

Instructions

You will be given a focus word and a sentence that contains the focus word (highlighted in bold). You will be asked to rate whether the focus word is used in a literal sense or a metaphorical sense in that sentence. Below are some typical properties of metaphorical and literal senses:

Literal usages tend to be:
- more basic, straightforward meaning; more physical, closely tied to our senses: vision, hearing, touching, tasting

Metaphorical usages tend to be:
- more complex; more distant from our senses; more abstract; more vague; often surprising; tend to bring in imagery from a different domain

Example 1

Focus Word: *shoot down*
Sentence: *The enemy **shot down** several of our aircraft.*

Question: In the above sentence, is the focus word used in a literal sense or a metaphorical sense?

- the focus word's usage is metaphorical
- the focus word's usage is literal

Solution: the focus word's usage is literal

Example 2

Focus Word: *shoot down*
Sentence: *He **shot down** the student's proposal.*

Question: In the above sentence, is the focus word used in a literal sense or a metaphorical sense?

- the focus word's usage is metaphorical
- the focus word's usage is literal

Solution: the focus word's usage is metaphorical

Your Task

Focus Word: *answer*
Sentence: *This steering wheel **answers** to the slightest touch.*

In the above sentence, is the focus word used in a literal sense or a metaphorical sense?
- the focus word's usage is metaphorical
- the focus word's usage is literal

This questionnaire, and all of the others described ahead in this paper, were annotated through the crowdsourcing platform Crowd-Flower. The instances in all of these questionnaires were presented in random order. Each instance was annotated by at least ten annotators. CrowdFlower chooses the majority response as the answer to each question. For our experiments, we chose a stronger criterion for an instance to be considered metaphorical or literal – 70% or more of the annotators had to agree on the choice of the category. The instances for which this level of agreement was not reached were discarded from further analysis. This strict criterion was chosen so that greater confidence can be placed on the results obtained from the annotations. Nonetheless, we release the full set of 1,639 annotated instances for other uses and further research. Additionally, we selected only those instances whose focus verbs had at least one metaphorical sense (or instance) and at least one literal sense (or instance). This resulted in a *Master Set* of 176 metaphorical instances and 284 literal instances.

3.1.1 Instances to test Hypothesis 1

For each of the 176 metaphorical instances in the Master Set, the three authors of this paper independently chose a synonym of the target verb that would make the instance literal. For example, for Instance 1 shown earlier, *kill* was chosen as synonym of *erase* (forming Instance 2). The synonym was chosen either from the list of near-synonyms in the same synset as the target word or from WordNet hypernyms of the target word. The three authors discussed amongst themselves to resolve disagreements. Five instances were discarded because of lack of agreement. Thus corresponding to each of the remaining 171 metaphorical instances, 171 literal instances were generated that had non-identical, similar meaning target verbs, but identical contexts. This set of 171 pairs of instances forms the dataset used to test Hypothesis 1, and we will refer to these instance pairs as the *Hypothesis 1 Pairs* and to the set of 342 (171×2) instances as the *Hypothesis 1 Instances*.

3.1.2 Instances to test Hypothesis 2

In order to test Hypothesis 2, we compare instances with the same target verb, but corresponding to its different senses. We use all of the 460 (176+284) instances in the Master Set, and refer to them as *Hypothesis 2 Instances*. As for Hypothesis 1, we also group these instances into pairs. For each of the verbs in the Master Set, all possible pairs of metaphorical and literal instances were generated. For example, if a verb had two metaphorical instances and three literal instances, then $2 \times 3 = 6$ pairs of instances were generated. In total, 355 pairs of instances were generated. We will refer to his set of instance pairs as *Hypothesis 2 Cross Pairs* (pairs in which one instance is labeled metaphoric and the other is literal).

Rather than viewing instances as either metaphorical or literal, one may also consider a graded notion of metaphoricity. That is, on a scale from most literal to most metaphorical, instances may have different degrees of metaphoricity (or literalness). Therefore, we also evaluate pairs where the individual instances have not been explicitly labeled as metaphorical or literal; instead, they have been marked according to whether one instance is more metaphorical than the other. For each of the verbs in the Master Set, all possible pairs of instances were generated. For example, if a verb had five instances in the Master Set, then ten pairs of instances were generated. This

resulted in 629 pairs in total. We will refer to them as *Hypothesis 2 All Pairs* (all possible pairs of instances, without regard to their labels).

3.2 Relative metaphoricity annotation

For each of the pairs in both *Hypothesis 2 Cross Pairs* and in *Hypothesis 2 All Pairs*, we ask annotators which instance is more metaphorical, as shown in Questionnaire 2 below:

Questionnaire 2: Which is more metaphorical?

Instructions

You will be given two sentences with similar meanings. Each sentence contains a focus word. You will be asked to compare how the focus words are used in the two sentences. You will be asked to decide whether the focus word's usage in one sentence is more metaphorical than the focus word's usage in the other sentence.

– Description of metaphorical and literal usages same as in Questionnaire 1 (not repeated here due to space constraints)–

Your Task

Focus Word 1: *attack*
Sentence 1: *I **attacked** the problem as soon as I was up.*
Focus word 2: *attack*
Sentence 2: *The Serbs **attacked** the village at night.*

Which is more metaphorical?
- focus word's usage in the sentence 1 is more metaphorical
- the focus word's usage in sentence 2 is more metaphorical
- the usages in the two sentences are equally metaphorical or equally literal

---

The instance pairs within a question were presented in random order. The questions themselves were also in random order.

3.3 Absolute emotion annotation

For each of the Hypothesis 1 and Hypothesis 2 instances, we used responses to Questionnaire 3 shown below to determine if the target verb conveys an emotion in the sentence.

Questionnaire 3: Does the focus word convey emotion?

Instructions

You will be given a focus word and a sentence that includes the focus word. You will be asked to rate whether the focus word conveys some emotion in the sentence.

Your Task

Focus Word: *answer*
Sentence: *This steering wheel **answers** to the slightest touch.*

How much emotion is conveyed?
- the focus word conveys some emotion
- the focus word conveys no emotion

3.4 Relative emotion annotation

Just as instances can have degrees of metaphoricity, they can have degrees of emotion. Thus, for
each of the Hypothesis 1 Pairs we asked annotators to mark which instance is more emotional, as
shown in Questionnaire 4 below:

**Questionnaire 4: Which of the two given sentences
conveys more emotion?**

Instructions

You will be given two sentences with similar meanings.
Each sentence contains a focus word. You will be asked to
compare how the focus words are used in the two sentences
and whether the focus word conveys more emotion in one
sentence than in the other sentence.

Your Task

Focus Word 1: *attack*
Sentence 1: *I **attacked** the problem as soon as I was up.*

Focus word 2: *start*
Sentence 2: *I **started** on the problem as soon as I was up.*

Which conveys more emotion?
- focus word in first sentence conveys more emotion
- focus word in second sentence conveys more emotion
- focus words in the two sentences convey a similar degree
of emotion

The order in which the instance pairs were presented for annotation was determined by random
selection. Whether the metaphorical or the literal
instance of a pair was chosen as the first instance
shown in the question was also determined by random selection. The same questionnaire was used
for Hypothesis 2 pairs as well.

4 Results and data analysis

4.1 Hypothesis 1 results

An analysis of the responses to Questionnaire 3
for the Hypothesis 1 instances is shown in Table 1. Recall that the annotators were given 342 instances where half were metaphoric and half were
literal. Additionally each literal instance was created by replacing the target verb in a metaphorical
instance with a synonym of the target verb. Recall
also that the 342 instances were presented in random order. Table 1 shows that a markedly higher
number of metaphorical instances (39.8%) are
considered emotional than literal ones (16.1%).
Fisher's exact test shows that this difference is significant with greater than 95% confidence[5].

---

[5]In the following experiments, we use Fisher's exact test
for two-by-two tables of event counts and we use the binomial exact test (i.e., the Clopper-Pearson interval) for binary
(heads/tails) event counts (Agresti, 1996).

Table 1: Summary of responses to Q3 (emotional
or not emotional) for Hypothesis 1 Instances (342
instances – 171 metaphorical and 171 literal).

# instances that are:	
emotional	191 (55.8%)
not emotional	151 (44.2%)
Total	**342 (100%)**
# instances that are:	
metaphorical and emotional	136 (39.8%)
metaphorical and not emotional	35 (10.2%)
literal and emotional	55 (16.1%)
literal and not emotional	116 (33.9%)
Total	**342 (100%)**

Table 2: Summary of responses to Q4 (which is
more emotional) for Hypothesis 1 Pairs (171 pairs
of metaphorical and literal instances).

# instances that are:	
metaphorical and more emotional	143 (83.6%)
literal and more emotional	17 (09.9%)
similarly emotional	11 (06.4%)
Total	**171 (100%)**

An analysis of the responses to Questionnaire
4 for the Hypothesis 1 pairs is shown in Table 2.
Here, the annotators were given pairs of instances
where one is metaphorical and one is literal (and
the two instances differ only in the target verb),
and the annotators were asked to determine which
instance is more emotional. Metaphorical instances were again predominantly marked as more
emotional (83.6%) than their literal counterparts
(9.9%). This difference is significant with greater
than 95% confidence, using the binomial exact
test. Thus, results from both experiments support
Hypothesis 1.

4.2 Hypothesis 2 results

Table 3 shows an analysis of the responses to
Questionnaire 3 for the Hypothesis 2 instances.
Recall that the annotators were given 460 instances where 176 were metaphoric and 284 were
literal. The data corresponds to verbs that have
both metaphorical and literal senses. The various
instances generated for each verb have the same
focus verb but different context (verb-sense sentence). The 460 instances were again presented
in random order. Table 3 shows that a markedly
higher number of metaphorical instances are considered emotional (14.1%), whereas much fewer
of the literal instances are considered emotional
(3.7%). This difference is significant with greater
than 95% confidence, using Fisher's exact test.

Table 3: Summary of responses to Q3 (emotional or not emotional) for Hypothesis 2 Instances (460 instances – 176 metaphorical and 284 literal).

# instances that are:	
emotional	82 (17.8%)
not emotional	378 (82.2%)
Total	**460 (100%)**
# instances that are:	
metaphorical and emotional	65 (14.1%)
metaphorical and not emotional	111 (24.1%)
literal and emotional	17 (03.7%)
literal and not emotional	267 (58.0%)
Total	**460 (100%)**

Table 4: Summary of responses to Q4 (which is more emotional) for Hypothesis 2 Cross Pairs (355 pairs of metaphorical and literal instances).

# instances that are:	
metaphorical and more emotional	211 (59.4%)
literal and more emotional	31 (08.7%)
similarly emotional	113 (31.8%)
Total	**355 (100%)**

Hypothesis 2 All Pairs received lower overall emotionality scores than Hypothesis 1 Pairs. Some variation is expected because the two datasets are not identical. Additionally, when an annotator finds the same word in many literal (non-emotional contexts) as in the Hypothesis 2 setup (but not in Hypothesis 1 setup), then they are less likely to tell us that the same word, even though now used in a metaphorical context, is conveying emotion. Despite the lower overall emotionality of Hypothesis 2 All Pairs, our hypothesis that metaphorical instances are more emotional than the literal ones still holds. Further, experiments with pairs of emotions (described below) avoid the kind of bias mentioned above, and also demonstrate the higher relative emotionality of metaphorical instances.

Table 4 shows the analysis for Hypothesis 2 Cross Pairs in the relative emotion annotation setting. The annotators were given pairs of instances where one is metaphorical and one is literal (and the two instances have the same focus verb in different context). The annotators were asked to determine which instance is more emotional. Metaphorical instances were marked as being more emotional than their literal counterparts in 59.4% of cases. Literal instances were marked as more emotional only in 8.7% of cases. This difference is significant with greater than 95% confidence, using the binomial exact test.

An analysis of the responses to Questionnaire 4 for the Hypothesis 2 All Pairs is shown in Table 5. This dataset included all possible pairs of instances associated with each verb in the Master Set. Thus in addition to pairs where one is highly metaphorical and one highly literal, this set also includes pairs where both instances may be highly metaphorical or both highly literal. Observe that

---

Q1: drain-v-1 The rain water *drains* into this big vat. LIT 0.9
drain-v-2 The [..] class *drains* me of energy. MET 0.8
drain-v-3 We *drained* the oil tank. LIT 0.9
drain-v-4 Life in the camp *drained* him. MET 0.91

Q1 and Q3, Hypothesis 1 (Table 1):
Life in the camp *drained* him. MET some emotion
Life in the camp *weakened* him. LIT some emotion
The [..] class *drains* me of energy. MET some emotion
The [..] class *depletes* me of energy. LIT some emotion

Q1 and Q4, Hypothesis 1 (Table 2):
Life in the camp *drained* him. MET
Life in the camp *weakened* him. LIT
– the first sentence conveys more emotion
The exercise class *drains* me of energy. MET
The exercise class *depletes* me of energy. LIT
– the first sentence conveys more emotion

Q1 and Q3, Hypothesis 2 (Table 3):
Life in the camp *drained* him. MET some emotion
The rain water *drains* into this big vat. LIT no emotion
The [..] class *drains* me of energy. MET some emotion
We *drained* the oil tank. LIT no emotion

Q1 and Q4, Hypothesis 2 (Table 4):
Life in the camp *drained* him. MET
The rain water *drains* into this big vat. LIT
– the first sentence conveys more emotion
We *drained* the oil tank. LIT
The exercise class *drains* me of energy. MET
– the second sentence conveys more emotion

Figure 1: Complete annotation cycle for the verb *drain* (some sense pairs are omitted for brevity). LIT stands for literal and MET for metaphoric. The annotations in Q1 are accompanied by their confidence scores.

once again a higher number of instances that were marked as more metaphorical were also marked as being more emotional (than less or similarly emotional). This difference is significant with greater than 95% confidence (binomial exact test).

Overall, these results support Hypothesis 2, that metaphorical senses of the same word tend to carry more emotion than its literal senses. Figure 1 demonstrates the complete annotation cycle (Q1 to Q4) for the verb *drain*.

Table 5: Summary of responses to Q4 (which is more emotional) for Hypothesis 2 All Pairs (629 pairs of instances). Note that in addition to pairs where one is highly metaphorical and one highly literal, the All Pairs set also includes pairs where both instances may be highly metaphorical or both highly literal.

# instances that are more metaphorical and more emotional	227 (36.1%)
# instances that are more metaphorical but less emotional	28 (04.4%)
# instances that are more metaphorical but similarly emotional	119 (18.9%)
# instances that are similarly metaphorical and similarly emotional	196 (31.2%)
# instances that are similarly metaphorical but differ in emotionality	59 (09.4%)
Total	**629 (100%)**

5 Discussion

It is generally believed that the senses of a word can be divided into a metaphorical subset and a literal subset (Kilgarriff, 1997). It is easy to find examples of this particular pattern of polysemy, but a few examples do not justify the claim that this pattern is a widespread regularity. The annotations of our dataset confirm the hypothesis that the metaphorical/literal distinction is a common pattern for polysemous verbs (as many as 38% of all verb senses we annotated were metaphorical). As far as we know, this is the first study that gives a solid empirical foundation to the belief that the metaphorical/literal distinction is a central form of regular polysemy.

Furthermore, the annotated dataset can be used for research into the nature of metaphorical/literal regular polysemy. Previous research on metaphor annotation identified metaphorical uses of words in text, thus analysing data for only one sense at a time. In contrast, our dataset allows one to analyse a range of metaphorical and literal uses of the same word, potentially shedding light on the origins of regular polysemy and metaphor. Such a structure of the dataset also provides a new framework for computational modelling of metaphor. A system able to systematically capture metaphorical sense extensions will be in a better position to generalise to unseen metaphors rather than a system trained on individual examples of metaphorical word uses in their specific contexts. The large size and coverage across many senses makes this dataset particularly attractive for computational modeling of metaphor. Our analysis also suggests that the work on emotion detection in text may be useful to support algorithms for handling metaphorical sense extension. Perhaps emotion analysis may yield insights into other forms of regular polysemy (Boleda et al., 2012).

We hypothesized that literal paraphrases tend to express less emotion than their metaphorical counterparts. This conjecture is related to Hypothesis 1. All of the sentence pairs that we used to test Hypothesis 1 are essentially a special type of paraphrase, in which only one word is varied. The results in Section 4.1 support Hypothesis 1, and thus they lend some degree of support to our hypothesis about paraphrases. It might be argued that we have only tested a special case of paraphrase, and we agree that further experiments are needed, with more general types of paraphrase (including, for instance, multi-word paraphrases). We leave this as a topic for future work. However, our results confirm the validity of our hypothesis with respect to metaphorical and literal lexical substitutes.

The results of our experiments are also relevant to many other NLP tasks modelling lexical meaning, for instance, natural language generation (NLG). It can be difficult to make the correct choice among several near-synonyms in NLG (Inkpen and Hirst, 2006); for example, the near-synonyms *error*, *mistake*, *slip*, and *blunder* convey the same core meaning but have different connotations. The degree to which two words are near-synonyms is proportional to the degree to which one can substitute for another in a given context (Inkpen and Hirst, 2006). Substituting a metaphoric term with a literal one tends to change the meaning of the sentence in an important respect—its emotional content. The degree of metaphor in the generated sentences would thus become an important factor in selecting the most appropriate candidate in NLG. It follows from Hypothesis 1 that terms with the same degree of metaphor will be more substitutable than terms with different degrees of metaphor. Therefore NLG systems can benefit from taking the degree of metaphor into account.

Our experiments and data also provide new insights into the nature of metaphorical emotions. Our results confirm both hypotheses, supporting the claim that metaphorical uses of words carry stronger emotions than their literal uses, as well

Table 6: Summary of data annotated for metaphoricity and emotionality.

File	Data	Annotations
1. Data-metaphoric-or-literal.txt	WordNet Verb-Sense Instances (1639)	metaphorical or Literal (Questionnaire 1)
2. Data-Table1-emotional-or-not.txt	Hypothesis 1 Instances (342)	metaphorical or Literal (Questionnaire 1) and Emotional or Not Emotional (Questionnaire 3)
3. Data-Table2-which-is-more-emotional.txt	Hypothesis 1 Instance Pairs (171)	metaphorical or Literal (Questionnaire 1) and Which Instance is More Emotional (Questionnaire 4)
4. Data-Table3-emotional-or-not.txt	Hypothesis 2 Instances (460)	metaphorical or Literal (Questionnaire 1) and Emotional or Not Emotional (Questionnaire 3)
5. Data-Table4-which-is-more-emotional.txt	Hypothesis 2 Instance Pairs (355)	metaphorical or Literal (Questionnaire 1) and Which Instance is More Emotional (Questionnaire 4)
6. Data-Table5-which-is-more-emotional.txt	Hypothesis 2 Unmarked Pairs (629)	Which Instance is more metaphorical (Questionnaire 2) and Which Instance is More Emotional (Questionnaire 4)

The judge *clapped* him in jail. MET some emotion
The judge *put* him in jail. LIT no emotion
The wings of the birds *clapped* loudly. LIT no emotion

This writer *fractures* the language. MET some emotion
This writer *misuses* the language. LIT no emotion
The pothole *fractured* a bolt on the axle. LIT no emot.

The spaceship *blazed* out into space. MET some emot.
The spaceship *departed* out into space. LIT no emotion
The summer sun can cause a pine to *blaze*. LIT no emot.

Figure 2: Hypothesis 1 and 2 pairs merged into triples, demonstrating higher emotionality arising through metaphorical composition.

as their literal paraphrases. This suggests that emotional content is not merely a property of the source or the target domain (and the respective word senses), but rather it arises through metaphorical composition. Figure 2 shows some examples of this phenomenon in our dataset. This is the first such finding, and it highlights the importance of metaphor as a mechanism for expressing emotion. This, in turn, suggests that joint models of metaphor and emotion are needed in order to create real-world systems for metaphor interpretation, as well as for sentiment analysis. All of the data created as part of this project, as summarized in Table 6, is made freely available.[6]

6 Conclusions

This paper confirms the general belief that metaphorical language tends to have a stronger emotional impact than literal language. As far as we know, our study is the first attempt to clearly formulate and test this belief. We formulated two hypotheses regarding emotionality of metaphors. Hypothesis 1: metaphorical uses of words tend to convey more emotion than their literal paraphrases in the same context. Hypothesis 2: the metaphorical sense of a word tends to carry more emotion than the literal sense of the same word. We conducted systematic experiments to show that both hypotheses are true for verb metaphors. A further contribution of this work is to the areas of sentiment analysis and metaphor detection. At training time, sentiment classifiers could, for example, use the information that a particular word or expression is metaphorical as a feature, and similarly, metaphor detection systems could use the information that a particular word or expression conveys sentiment as a feature.

The results are significant for the study of regular polysemy as the senses of many verbs readily divide into literal and metaphorical groups. We hope that research in regular polysemy will be able to build on the datasets that we have released. Our results also support the idea that a metaphor conveys emotion that goes beyond the source and target domains taken separately. The act of bridging the two domains creates something new, beyond the component domains. This remains a rich topic for further research. Finally, we hope that the results in this paper will encourage greater collaboration between the Natural Language Processing research communities in sentiment analysis and metaphor analysis. All of the data annotated for metaphoricity and emotionality is made freely available.

Acknowledgments

We are grateful to the *SEM reviewers for their insightful comments. Ekaterina Shutova's research is supported by the Leverhulme Trust Early Career Fellowship.

---

[6]http://saifmohammad.com/WebPages/metaphor.html

References

Alan Agresti. 1996. *Categorical data analysis*, volume 996. New York: John Wiley & Sons.

Cecilia Ovesdotter Alm, Dan Roth, and Richard Sproat. 2005. Emotions from text: Machine learning for text-based emotion prediction. In *Proceedings of the Joint Conference on HLT–EMNLP*, Vancouver, Canada.

Lisa Aziz-Zadeh and Antonio Damasio. 2008. Embodied semantics for actions: findings from functional brain imaging. *Journal of Physiology - Paris*, 102(1-3).

Beata Beigman Klebanov and Michael Flor. 2013. Argumentation-relevant metaphors in test-taker essays. In *Proceedings of the First Workshop on Metaphor in NLP*, pages 11–20, Atlanta, Georgia.

Isabelle Blanchette, Kevin Dunbar, John Hummel, and Richard Marsh. 2001. Analogy use in naturalistic settings: The influence of audience, emotion and goals. *Memory and Cognition*, 29(5).

Gemma Boleda, Sebastian Padó, and Jason Utt. 2012. Regular polysemy: A distributional model. In *Proceedings of the First Joint Conference on Lexical and Computational Semantics-Volume 1: Proceedings of the main conference and the shared task, and Volume 2: Proceedings of the Sixth International Workshop on Semantic Evaluation*, pages 151–160. Association for Computational Linguistics.

Michael Brooks, Katie Kuksenok, Megan K Torkildson, Daniel Perry, John J Robinson, Taylor J Scott, Ona Anicello, Ariana Zukowski, Paul Harris, and Cecilia R Aragon. 2013. Statistical affect detection in collaborative chat. In *Proceedings of the 2013 conference on Computer supported cooperative work*, pages 317–328. ACM.

Lynne Cameron. 2003. *Metaphor in Educational Discourse*. Continuum, London.

Jonathan Charteris-Black. 2000. Metaphor and vocabulary teaching in esp economics. *English for Specific Purposes*, 19(2):149–165.

Francesca MM Citron and Adele E Goldberg. 2014. Metaphorical sentences are more emotionally engaging than their literal counterparts. *Journal of cognitive neuroscience*.

Elizabeth Crawford. 2009. Conceptual Metaphors of Affect. *Emotion Review*, 1(2).

Li Dong, Furu Wei, Chuanqi Tan, Duyu Tang, Ming Zhou, and Ke Xu. 2014. Adaptive recursive neural network for target-dependent twitter sentiment classification. In *Proceedings of the 52nd Annual Meeting of the Association for Computational Linguistics*, pages 49–54.

Paul Ekman and Wallace V Friesen. 2003. *Unmasking the face: A guide to recognizing emotions from facial clues*. Ishk.

Paul Ekman. 1992. An Argument for Basic Emotions. *Cognition and Emotion*, 6(3):169–200.

Raymond W Gibbs, John S Leggitt, and Elizabeth A Turner. 2002. Whats special about figurative language in emotional communication. *The verbal communication of emotions. Interdisciplinary perspectives*, pages 125–149.

Andrew Hardie, Veronika Koller, Paul Rayson, and Elena Semino. 2007. Exploiting a semantic annotation tool for metaphor analysis. In *Proceedings of the Corpus Linguistics Conference*, Birmingham, UK.

Lars E. Holzman and William M. Pottenger. 2003. Classification of emotions in internet chat: An application of machine learning using speech phonemes. Technical report, Leigh University.

Sattar Izwaini. 2003. Corpus-based study of metaphor in information technology. In *Proceedings of the Workshop on Corpus-based Approaches to Figurative Language, Corpus Linguistics 2003*, Lancaster.

Mbemba Jabbi, Jojanneke Bastiaansen, and Christian Keysers. 2008. A common anterior insula representation of disgust observation, experience and imagination shows divergent functional connectivity pathways. *PLoS ONE*, 3(8):e2939.

Adam Kilgarriff. 1997. I don't believe in word senses. *Computers and the Humanities*, 31(2):91–113.

Svetlana Kiritchenko, Xiaodan Zhu, and Saif M. Mohammad. 2014. Sentiment analysis of short informal texts. *Journal of Artificial Intelligence Research*, 50:723–762.

Veronika Koller. 2004. *Metaphor and Gender in Business Media Discourse: A Critical Cognitive Study*. Palgrave Macmillan, Basingstoke: New York.

Z. Kovecses. 2003. *Metaphor and Emotion Language, Culture, and Body in Human Feeling*. Cambridge University Press, Cambridge.

Zornitsa Kozareva. 2013. Multilingual affect polarity and valence prediction in metaphor-rich texts. In *Proceedings of the 51st Annual Meeting of the Association for Computational Linguistics (Volume 1: Long Papers)*, pages 682–691, Sofia, Bulgaria, August. Association for Computational Linguistics.

George Lakoff and Mark Johnson. 1980. *Metaphors We Live By*. University of Chicago Press, Chicago.

George Lakoff and Elisabeth Wehling. 2012. *The Little Blue Book: The Essential Guide to Thinking and Talking Democratic*. Free Press, New York.

George Lakoff, Jane Espenson, and Alan Schwartz. 1991. The master metaphor list. Technical report, University of California at Berkeley.

Birte Lönneker. 2004. Lexical databases as resources for linguistic creativity: Focus on metaphor. In *Proceedings of the LREC 2004 Workshop on Language Resources for Linguistic Creativity*, pages 9–16, Lisbon, Portugal.

Graham Low, Zazie Todd, Alice Deignan, and Lynne Cameron. 2010. *Researching and Applying Metaphor in the Real World*. John Benjamins, Amsterdam/Philadelphia.

Louis Lu and Kathleen Ahrens. 2008. Ideological influences on building metaphors in taiwanese presidential speeches. *Discourse and Society*, 19(3):383–408.

James Martin. 2006. A corpus-based analysis of context effects on metaphor comprehension. In A. Stefanowitsch and S. T. Gries, editors, *Corpus-Based Approaches to Metaphor and Metonymy*, Berlin. Mouton de Gruyter.

Saif M. Mohammad and Peter D. Turney. 2013. Crowdsourcing a word–emotion association lexicon. *Computational Intelligence*, 29(3):436–465.

Saif M. Mohammad, Svetlana Kiritchenko, and Xiaodan Zhu. 2013. NRC-Canada: Building the state-of-the-art in sentiment analysis of tweets. In *Proceedings of the International Workshop on Semantic Evaluation*, SemEval '13, Atlanta, Georgia, USA, June.

Saif M. Mohammad. 2012. #emotional tweets. In *Proceedings of the First Joint Conference on Lexical and Computational Semantics*, *SEM '12, pages 246–255, Montréal, Canada. Association for Computational Linguistics.

Saif M. Mohammad. 2016. Sentiment analysis: Detecting valence, emotions, and other affectual states from text. In Herb Meiselman, editor, *Emotion Measurement*. Elsevier.

Roberto Navigli. 2009. Word sense disambiguation: A survey. *ACM Computing Surveys (CSUR)*, 41(2):10.

Robert Plutchik. 1980. A General Psychoevolutionary Theory of Emotion. *Emotion: Theory, research, and experience*, 1(3):3–33.

Robert Plutchik. 1991. *The emotions*. University Press of America.

Pragglejaz Group. 2007. MIP: A method for identifying metaphorically used words in discourse. *Metaphor and Symbol*, 22:1–39.

Otto Santa Ana. 1999. Like an animal I was treated?: anti-immigrant metaphor in US public discourse. *Discourse Society*, 10(2):191–224.

Ekaterina Shutova and Simone Teufel. 2010. Metaphor corpus annotated for source - target domain mappings. In *Proceedings of LREC 2010*, pages 3255–3261, Malta.

Hanna Skorczynska Sznajder and Jordi Pique-Angordans. 2004. A corpus-based description of metaphorical marking patterns in scientific and popular business discourse. In *Proceedings of European Research Conference on Mind, Language and Metaphor (Euresco Conference)*, Granada, Spain.

Richard Socher, Alex Perelygin, Jean Y. Wu, Jason Chuang, Christopher D. Manning, Andrew Y. Ng, and Christopher Potts. 2013. Recursive deep models for semantic compositionality over a sentiment treebank. In *Proceedings of the Conference on Empirical Methods in Natural Language Processing*, EMNLP '13. Association for Computational Linguistics.

Gerard J. Steen, Aletta G. Dorst, J. Berenike Herrmann, Anna A. Kaal, Tina Krennmayr, and Trijntje Pasma. 2010. *A method for linguistic metaphor identification: From MIP to MIPVU*. John Benjamins, Amsterdam/Philadelphia.

Carlo Strapparava and Alessandro Valitutti. 2004. Wordnet affect: an affective extension of wordnet. In *LREC*, volume 4, pages 1083–1086.

Tomek Strzalkowski, Samira Shaikh, Kit Cho, George Aaron Broadwell, Laurie Feldman, Sarah Taylor, Boris Yamrom, Ting Liu, Ignacio Cases, Yuliya Peshkova, and Kyle Elliot. 2014. Computing affect in metaphors. In *Proceedings of the Second Workshop on Metaphor in NLP*, pages 42–51, Baltimore, MD, June. Association for Computational Linguistics.

Jared Suttles and Nancy Ide. 2013. Distant supervision for emotion classification with discrete binary values. In *Computational Linguistics and Intelligent Text Processing*, pages 121–136. Springer.

Paul H. Thibodeau and Lera Boroditsky. 2011. Metaphors we think with: The role of metaphor in reasoning. *PLoS ONE*, 6(2):e16782, 02.

Peter D. Turney, Yair Neuman, Dan Assaf, and Yohai Cohen. 2011. Literal and metaphorical sense identification through concrete and abstract context. In *Proceedings of the 2011 Conference on the Empirical Methods in Natural Language Processing*, pages 680–690.

Tony Veale and Guofu Li. 2012. Specifying viewpoint and information need with affective metaphors: A system demonstration of the metaphor magnet web app/service. In *Proceedings of the ACL 2012 System Demonstrations*, ACL '12, pages 7–12.

High-Fidelity Lexical Axiom Construction from Verb Glosses

Gene Kim
University of Rochester
Department of Computer Science
gkim21@cs.rochester.edu

Lenhart Schubert
University of Rochester
Department of Computer Science
schubert@cs.rochester.edu

Abstract

This paper presents a rule-based approach to constructing lexical axioms from Word-Net verb entries in an expressive semantic representation, Episodic Logic (EL). EL differs from other representations in being syntactically close to natural language and covering phenomena such as generalized quantification, modification, and intensionality while still allowing highly effective inference. The presented approach uses a novel preprocessing technique to improve parsing precision of coordinators and incorporates frames, hand-tagged word senses, and examples from WordNet to achieve highly consistent semantic interpretations. EL allows the full content of glosses to be incorporated into the formal lexical axioms, without sacrificing interpretive accuracy, or verb-to-verb inference accuracy on a standard test set.

Evaluation of semantic parser performance is based on *EL-match*, introduced here as a generalization of the *smatch* metric for semantic structure accuracy. On gloss parses, the approach achieves an *EL-match* F1 score of 0.83, and a whole-axiom F1 score of 0.45; verb entailment identification based on extracted axioms is competitive with the state-of-the-art.

1 Introduction

Words encapsulate a great deal of knowledge, and in conjunction with language syntax, allow human beings to construct sentences that convey novel ideas to one another. Any system intended for broad natural language understanding will need to be able to perform inferences on the words that are the building blocks of language. For this reason,

> **Gloss** – *slam2.v* : "strike violently"
> **Axiom** – ((x slam2.v y) ** e)
>   → ((x (violently.adv (strike.v y))) ** e)

Figure 1: Example of rule extraction from machine readable dictionaries for WordNet entry of *slam2.v*.

there have been many attempts to transduce informal lexical knowledge from machine readable dictionaries into a formally structured form (Calzolari, 1984; Chodorow et al., 1985; Harabagiu et al., 1999; Moldovan and Rus, 2001; Hobbs, 2008; Allen et al., 2013).

Consider an example of the types of knowledge these approaches seek to extract in Figure 1. WordNet defines *slam2.v*, i.e., sense 2 of the verb *slam*, as "strike violently". This gloss states an implication that if "x slams y" characterizes an event e, then "x strikes y violently" also characterizes event e. All language phenomena must be able to be represented and reasoned about for such axioms to be useful in a language understanding system. This is where previous approaches share a common shortcoming: the logical representations that the lexical knowledge is mapped into are insufficient for representing many common natural language devices or for performing inference.

The contributions of this paper are the following:

- We demonstrate limitations in previous approaches to extracting lexical knowledge from machine readable dictionaries, particularly in their choices of logical representation.

- We present an approach to extracting lexical axioms in EL, which is a logical representation that overcomes these limitations. Our approach includes novel preprocessing and

*Proceedings of the Fifth Joint Conference on Lexical and Computational Semantics (*SEM 2016)*, pages 34–44,
Berlin, Germany, August 11-12, 2016.

information synthesis strategies for making precise axioms.

- We present *EL-smatch*, a generalized *smatch* scoring metric for partial scoring of semantic parses with complex operators and predicates.

The remainder of the paper presents related work in Section 2, background in Section 3, then a description of our semantic parsing approach in Section 4. A description of *EL-smatch* is presented in Section 5, followed by experimental results in Section 6, and future work and conclusions in Section 7.

2 Related Work

There have been many approaches in the past to extracting lexical information from machine-readable dictionaries. Early approaches to this problem focused on surface-level techniques, including hypernym extraction (Calzolari, 1984; Chodorow et al., 1985), pattern matching (Alshawi, 1989; Vossen et al., 1989; Wilks et al., 1989), and co-occurrence data extraction (Wilks et al., 1989).

In an evaluation of such methods, Ide & Veronis (1993) identified key challenges that thwart progress on this problem—challenges that persist to this day. Among these are the fact that dictionary glosses are often abstract, sometimes miss important information (such as arguments), and may be inconsistent with one another. Evidently there is a need for sophisticated extraction techniques to acquire accurate and consistent knowledge from dictionaries.

Most modern approaches to this problem use WordNet (Miller, 1995) as the lexical resource because of the linguistic and semantic annotations that accompany the glosses. Some work encodes WordNet glosses into variants of first-order logic (FOL) (Harabagiu et al., 1999; Moldovan and Rus, 2001; Hobbs, 2008), such as Hobbs Logical Form (HLF) (Hobbs, 1985), while other work encodes them into OWL-DL (OWL Working Group, 2004; Allen et al., 2011; Allen et al., 2013; Orfan and Allen, 2015; Mostafazadeh and Allen, 2015). A particularly noteworthy line of work is that by Allen et al. (2013), which integrates information from a high-level ontology with glosses of semantically related clusters of words to construct inference-supporting micro-theories of concepts corresponding to these words. While these advances are significant, they are limited by the expressivity of the representations used, in comparison with the richness of natural language.

2.1 Limitations of Logical Representations Used by Previous Approaches

As discussed by Schubert (2015), the choice of semantic representation is an important component of the natural language understanding problem. Because of space constraints, we will discuss only a few of the relevant issues and point the reader to (Schubert, 2015) for a more in-depth analysis of the issues at hand. The logical representation used for robust language understanding must satisfy the following requirements:

- Express the semantic content of most, if not all, possible natural language constructions;

- Have associated methods of inference;

- Have a formal interpretation.

The semantic representations used by previous approaches fall short on at least one of the above requirements. FOL struggles to express predicate modification (especially nonintersective modification), nonstandard quantifiers such as *most* or *at least 50*, and modality. Approaches that rely on functionalizing predication and connectives as a means of allowing for arbitrary propositional attitudes ultimately fail because quantifiers cannot be functionalized; thus they cannot capture the meaning of sentences with a modally embedded quantifier such as the following (with *believes* taking scope over *every*):

Kim believes that every galaxy harbors life.

HLF (Hobbs, 1985) is another common choice of semantic representation. It strives to capture sentential meaning within a subset of FOL by treating all words as predicates, including negation, disjunction, quantifiers, and modifiers. But it is unable to distinguish between events and propositions and between predicate and sentence modifiers, and the formal interpretation of quantification in HLF can lead to contradiction (Schubert, 2015).

OWL-DL (OWL Working Group, 2004) was designed for knowledge engineering on specific domains and thus cannot handle many common natural language phenomena, such as predicate and sentence reification, predicate modification, self-reference, and uncertainty. There have been many efforts to allow for such phenomena, with varying degrees of success. As just one example, consider the common practice in OWL-DL of treating predicate modification as predicate intersection. For example, "whisper loudly" is represented as whisper $\sqcap \forall_{of}$-1.(loudly). *whisper* is the set of individual whispering events and $\forall_{of}$-1.(loudly) is the set of individual events that are modified by the adverb *loudly*. But according to WordNet, to whisper is to speak softly, so under an intersective interpretation of the modifiers, a loud whisper is both soft and loud. Similarly, WordNet glosses the verb *spin* as *revolve quickly*, so that under an intersective interpretation, a slow spin is both quick and slow. Analogously for nouns, a large pond or large brochure would be both large and small (*brochure* is glossed as *a small book*, and *pond* as *a small lake*). Even more difficult issues, from an OWL-DL perspective, are generalized quantifiers, uncertainty, attitudes, and reification, such as exemplified in the sentence

When self-driving cars are properly adopted, vehicles that need humans to drive them will probably be banned, according to Tesla CEO Elon Musk.

For a fuller discussion of issues in representations based on FOL, HLF, OWL-DL, etc., again see (Schubert, 2015).

3 Background

This section describes background material underlying our semantic parsing approach. First, we describe WordNet (Miller, 1995), our input lexical resource. Then, we describe Episodic Logic (EL), our choice of semantic representation for lexical axioms.

3.1 WordNet

WordNet is a lexical knowledge base that contains glosses for words, enumerates the word senses of each word, groups synonyms into *synsets*, encodes generality/specificity relations as *hypernym/hyponyms*, and provides schematic sentence structures for each word in the form of simple *frames*. The semantic annotations accompanying the glosses help in building a robust parser by reducing the amount of inference necessary for building axioms and assisting in handling mistakes

in the glosses. Also, a significant proportion of the words in WordNet glosses have been tagged with their word senses and part-of-speech in the Princeton Annotated Gloss Corpus.[1] This helps with the important but often neglected word sense disambiguation (WSD) aspect of the interpretation problem; certainly ambiguous or faulty WSD can lead to misunderstandings and faulty inferences (is *Mary had a little lamb* about ownership or dining?). We use WordNet 3.0, which at the time of writing is the most recent version that is fully available for the UNIX environment, and focus on the verbs in this paper.

3.2 Episodic Logic

EL (Schubert and Hwang, 2000) was designed to be close to natural language, with the intuition that a logical representation that retains much of the expressivity of natural language will be able to more fully represent the complex constructs in natural language. EL provides constructs that are not common in most FOL-based languages, such as predicate modifiers, generalized quantifiers, reification, and ways of associating episodes (events or situations) with arbitrarily complex sentences. Importantly, EL is backed by a comprehensive inference system, EPILOG, which has been shown to be competitive with FOL theorem provers despite its substantially greater expressivity (Morbini and Schubert, 2009).

EL uses infix notation for readability, with the "subject" argument preceding the predicate and any additional arguments following the predicate. For associating episodes with logical sentences, EL introduces two modal operators '**' and '*'. $[\Phi$ ** $e]$ means that Φ *characterizes* (i.e. describes as a whole) episode e and $[\Phi$ * $e]$ means that Φ is true in (i.e. describes a piece or aspect of) episode e.

We show that EL overcomes some of the limitations of previous work that have been discussed using an example. Below is the EL representation for the sentence *Kim believes that every galaxy harbors life.*

```
(Kim.name believe.v
  (That (∀x (x galaxy.n)
           (x harbor.v (K life.n)))))
```

That and K are sentence and predicate reifica-

36

---

[1]http://wordnet.princeton.edu/glosstag.shtml

tion operators, respectively and $(\forall x\ \Phi(x)\ \Psi(x))$ is equivalent to $(\forall x\ (\Phi(x)\ \rightarrow\ \Psi(x)))$.[2] For discussion of the semantic types of the operators alluded to in this section and the connection to Davidsonian event semantics and other variants of event/situation semantics, see the papers describing EL (Schubert and Hwang, 2000; Schubert, 2000).

4 Gloss Axiomatization

In this section, we describe our approach to semantic parsing and axiomatization of WordNet entries. Our approach consists of three major steps:

1. Argument structure inference (Section 4.1)

2. Semantic parsing of the gloss (Section 4.2)

3. Axiom construction (Section 4.3)

Figure 2 shows the entire process for the previously introduced example, *slam2.v*. The argument inference step refines the WordNet sentence frames using the provided examples. Specific pronouns associated with argument position are inserted as dummy arguments into the corresponding argument positions in the gloss, and the modified gloss is semantically parsed into EL. Axiom construction replaces the dummy arguments with variables and constructs a scoped axiom relating the entry word and the semantic parse of the gloss using the characterization operator '**'. In the simple example *slam2.v*, most of the subroutines used in each step have no effect. All transformations outside the scope of the BLLIP parser are performed with hand-written rules, which were fine-tuned using a development set of 550 verb synset entries.

4.1 Argument Structure Inference

We initially use the frames in WordNet to hypothesize the argument structures. For example, the frames for *quarrel1.v* are [Somebody quarrel1.v] and [Somebody quarrel1.v PP]. From this we hypothesize that *quarrel1.v* has a subject argument that is a person, no object argument, and may include a prepositional phrase adjunct.

Then we refine the frames by looking at the examples and gloss(es) available for the *synset*.

The examples for *quarrel1.v*: *"We quarreled over the question as to who discovered America"* and *"These two fellows are always scrapping[3] over something"* suggest that the subject argument can be plural and the PP can be specialized to PP-OVER. We identify the arguments and semantic types of the examples through a semantic parse, which is obtained using the method described in Section 4.2. Then we either update existing frames or introduce additional frames based on the agreement among examples and the number of available examples. We similarly obtain semantic types for arguments from glosses. For example, *paint1.v* has the gloss *"make a painting"* and the frame [Somebody -s Something]. Based on the gloss, we infer that the semantic type for the object argument is *painting*. Gloss-based argument structure inference can be done during the gloss parsing step, to avoid redundant computation.

Finally, we merge redundant frames. For example, frames that differ only in that one has *somebody* in a certain argument position where the other has *something* are merged into one frame where we simply use *something* (as a category allowing for both things and persons). Also there are rules for merging predicate complement types (Adjective/Noun & PP → Adjective/Noun/PP) and adding dative alternations to ditransitive frames [Somebody -s Somebody Something] → [Somebody -s Something to Somebody].

4.2 Semantic Parsing of Glosses

Sentence-level semantic parsers for EL have been developed previously, which we can use for semantic parsing of the glosses (Schubert, 2002; Schubert and Tong, 2003; Gordon and Schubert, 2010; Schubert, 2014). For the parser to be effective, some preprocessing of the glosses is necessary because glosses often omit arguments, resulting in an incomplete sentence. There are also some serious shortcomings to general semantic parsers, particularly in handling coordinators *and/or*. In this section, we describe the complete semantic parsing process of glosses and the details of each step. Throughout our semantic parsing implementation, we use the tree-to-tree transduction tool (TTT) (Purtee and Schubert, 2012) for trans-

---

[2]However, EL's quantifier syntax also allows, e.g., $(\mathtt{most.det}\ x\ \Phi(x)\ \Psi(x))$, which is not reducible to FOL.

[3]*quarrel1.v* and *scrap2.v* are in the same synset, so they share example sentences and are interchangeable in this context.

WordNet entry

slam2.v

Tagged gloss: `(VB strike1) (RB violently1)`

Frames: `[Somebody slam2.v Something]`
`[Somebody slam2.v Somebody]`

Examples: ("slam the ball")

4.3 Axiom Construction

Axiom: `(∀x1 (∀y1 (∀e [[x1 slam2.v y1] ** e]`
`[[[x1 (violently1.adv (strike1.v y1))] ** e]`
`and [x1 person1.n] [y1 thing12.n]`

4.1 Argument Structure Inference

Refined Frames:

`[Somebody slam2.v Something]`

4.2 Semantic Parsing

Parse: `(Me.pro (violently1.adv`
`(strike1.v It.pro)))`

Figure 2: Example gloss axiomatization process for WordNet entry *slam2.v*. The numbering corresponds to the subsections where these stages are discussed in detail.

parent and modular tree transformations[4] and the BLLIP parser (Charniak, 2000) to get Treebank parses.

The general outline of the gloss processing steps is described below:

1. Create separate POS-tagged word sequences for distinct glosses:

   a. Label gloss g with POS tags using the Princeton Annotated Gloss Corpus, backing off to the synset type in the sense key.[5]

   b. Split multigloss trees along semicolons for individual POS tagged glosses $p_1, p_2, ..., p_n$.

2. Create an easy-to-parse sentence for each gloss:

   a. Factor out coordinators, leaving the first conjunct in the gloss. Save the coordinated phrases c_{p_i} for later insertion.

   b. Insert dummy arguments (*I*, *it*, *them*).

   c. Drop POS tags to create new gloss g_i'.

3. Syntactically parse each gloss sentence into initial LFs:

   a. Parse g_i' into tree t_i using the BLLIP parser.

   b. Refine POS tags in t_i using the Princeton Annotated Gloss Corpus.

   c. Run t_i through the sentence-level semantic parser to get logical form s_i.

4. Refine the initial LFs:

   a. Reinsert coordinated phrases c_{p_i} into s_i.

b. Introduce word senses into the logical form.

We now describe the sentence-level semantic parser, coordinator factorization, argument insertion/inference, and word sense introduction in more detail.

4.2.1 Sentence Level Semantic Parser

The sentence-level semantic (EL) parser we use is modeled after the partial interpreter used by the KNEXT system (Van Durme et al., 2009; Gordon and Schubert, 2010). First, the parser applies corrective and disambiguating transformations to raw Treebank trees. For example, these correct certain systematic prepositional phrase (PP) attachment errors, distinguish copular *be* from other forms, assimilate verb particles into the verb, particularize SBAR constituents to relative clauses, adverbials, or clausal nominals, insert traces for dislocated constituents, etc. Second, the parser uses about 100 rules to compositionally interpret Treebank parses into initial interpretations. Finally, coreference resolution, quantifier, coordinator, and tense scoping, temporal deindexing, (non-embedded) Skolemization, equality reduction, conjunction splitting and other canonicalization operations are applied to refine the logical form.

4.2.2 Argument Insertion and Inference

WordNet glosses (and glosses in general) only include arguments when necessary to specify some semantic type for the argument. Figure 3 displays example glosses from WordNet that demonstrate this treatment of arguments. Both the subject and object arguments in the gloss of *slam2.v* are omitted, and the subject is omitted from the gloss of *paint1.v*, while the object in the gloss is included.

---

[4]We do not explicitly state where TTT is used in the algorithm since it is a general tree transformation tool, which is used throughout the algorithm whenever a tree transformation is necessary.

[5]Every word in the glosses of the Princeton Annotated Gloss Corpus is labeled with the POS tag or the sense key. The synset type distinguishes between nouns, verbs, adjectives, and adverbs.

Argument position	English text	EL atom
subject	I/my/myself	Me.pro
direct object	it	It.pro
indirect object	them	They.pro

Table 1: Mappings between dummy argument position, text, and EL atoms.

---

slam2.v – subject strike *object* violently
paint1.v – subject make a painting

Figure 3: Example glosses demonstrating the treatment of arguments in glosses. Underlined words are arguments and italicized arguments indicate where an argument should exist, but does not in the gloss.

We make arguments explicit and unify their treatment in order to improve Treebank and semantic parses and simplify the axiom construction step, described in Section 4.3. Figure 4 shows unified versions of the glosses that appear in Figure 3, *slam2.v* and *paint1.v*. In this unified treatment, all arguments are represented by argument position-specific dummy arguments. Table 1 lists the dummy arguments and their relation to the argument position and EL. Dummy arguments are inserted into the POS tagged gloss p_i based on the inferred argument structure from Section 4.1 and the insertions are achieved through pattern matching of the POS tags.

Finally, some glosses contain references to the subject using the terms *one, one's,* or *oneself* (e.g. *sprawl1.v : sit or lie with one's limbs spread out*). These are mapped to *I, my,* and *myself,* respectively to correctly corefer with the dummy subject argument *I*.

4.2.3 Coordinator Factorization

Treebank and semantic parsers are prone to errors for coordinated phrases, often mistaking them for appositives, or vice-versa. To minimize such errors, we developed a method of factorizing coordinated phrases. The conjuncts can usually be identified by syntactic and semantic relatedness. This

---

slam2.v – I'll strike *it* violently
paint1.v – I'll make *it*; (*it* : a painting)

Figure 4: Unified versions of WordNet glosses from Figure 3.

can be seen in the WordNet gloss for *edit1.v*: *prepare for publication or presentation by correcting, revising, or adapting.* We use linguistic phrase types as a proxy for syntactic and semantic relatedness. That is, we identify coordinated groups of verb phrases, noun phrases, adjectival phrases, and prepositional phrases. These phrase groups are pulled out of the sentence, and only the first phrase in the group is left in the sentence.

The phrase groups are identified using a set of rules that were fine-tuned with reference to the development set of verb synsets. The rules tend to handle common modifications, such as adjectives in noun phrases. For ambiguous cases, such as prepositional modification, factorization is not performed.

The phrase groups are passed through a modified sentence-level semantic parser (stopping short of the coordinator scoping step), and embedded back into the gloss logical form before the coordinator scoping step in the semantic parsing of the gloss. The place of insertion is identified by matching the first phrase in the phrase group with a phrase in the logical form.

4.2.4 Word Sense Introduction

Word sense introduction is assisted by the hand-tagged word senses in WordNet. All words that are not hand-tagged with a word sense are given the lowest numbered word sense with a frame matching the context of its use in the gloss. Generally, the lower numbered word senses in WordNet are the most relevant senses of the word.

4.3 Axiom Construction

Finally, we take the results from Sections 4.1 and 4.2 and construct the axiom. Dummy arguments in the parsed gloss are correlated with the arguments in the frame using the mapping in Table 1. We replace the arguments with variables, introduce logical formulas asserting the semantic types (from the argument structure in Section 4.1), and construct an axiom asserting that the truth of the entry word with the proper argument structure (without semantic types) implies the truth of the semantic parse of the gloss and semantic types of the arguments. Before axiom construction, the example from Figure 2, *slam2.v*, has the following refined frame and semantic parse of the gloss from Sections 4.1 and 4.2, respectively:

```
[Somebody slam2.v Something]
[Me.pro
    (violently1.adv (strike1.v It.pro))]
```

After we replace the arguments and create formulas asserting the semantic types, we have:

```
[x1 slam2.v y1]
[x1 (violently1.adv (strike1.v y1))]
[x1 person1.n], [y1 thing12.n]
```

Finally, we construct an axiom of form $(\forall x\ \Phi(x)\ \Psi(x))$ (equivalent to $(\forall x\ (\Phi(x) \rightarrow \Psi(x)))$) and using the modal *characterization* operator **:

```
(∀x1,y1,e
  [[x1 slam2.v y1] ** e]
  [[[x1 (violently1.adv
        (strike1.v y1))] ** e]
   and [x1 person1.n] [y1 thing12.n]
```

We can easily generate converse axioms as well, such as that if a person strikes something violently, then it is probably the case that he or she slams it (in the *slam2.v* sense). EL allows us to express a degree of uncertainty in the formulation of the converse, and this is appropriate to the extent that lexical glosses cannot be expected to provide complete, "airtight" definitions, but rather just the most important semantic content. However, in this paper we limit ourselves to discussion of the "forward" version of gloss-derived axioms.

5   *EL-smatch*

In this section we introduce *EL-smatch*, a generalized formulation of *smatch* (Cai and Knight, 2013), the standard evaluation metric for AMR parsing (Banarescu et al., 2013). *Smatch* represents each logical form as a conjunction of triples of three types:

1. *instance(variable, type)*

2. *relation(variable, variable)*

3. *attribute(variable, value)*

Every node instance of the logical form is associated with a variable, and the nodes are described and related to each other using the above triples. Thus, *type* and *value* can both only be atomic constants. The *smatch* score is then defined as the *maximum f-score (of triples) obtainable via a one-to-one matching of variables between the two formulas* (Cai and Knight, 2013).

In order to capture complex types of EL, we introduce an additional triple:

instance(variable, variable).

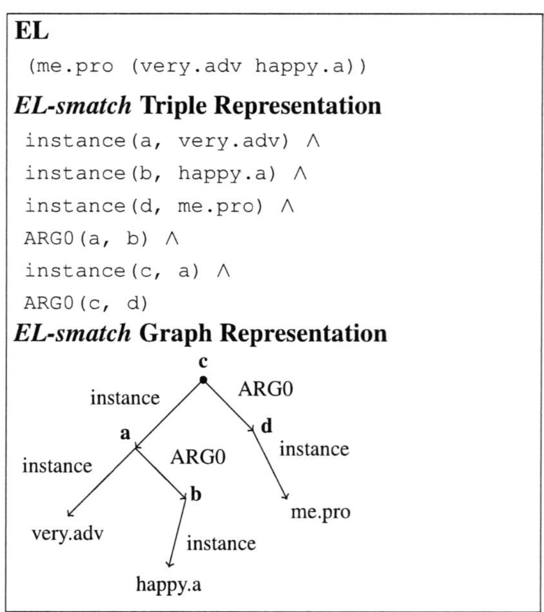

Figure 5: Example of syntactic mapping from EL to *EL-smatch* triple and graph representations for sentence "I am very happy".

The first variable argument is associated with the instance, and the second variable argument, with the type.

With this addition to the representation, we can syntactically map EL formulas into a conjunction of triples by introducing a node variable for every component of the formula and then describing and relating the components using the triples. Since the representation used by *smatch* is the same as that of AMR, we can map the triple representation into a graph representation in the same manner as AMR formulas. Figure 5 shows an example of the use of the new instance triple in mapping the EL formula for "I am very happy" into these representations. However, this mapping does not relate the semantics of EL to AMR since the interpretation of the triples differ for AMR and EL formulas.

6   Experiments

We conducted two experiments to demonstrate the efficacy of our approach for semantic parsing and the usefulness of the resulting axioms for inference.[6]

---

[6]One reviewer suggested comparing our axioms with ontologies linked to WordNet, such as SUMO (Niles and Pease, 2001) and DOLCE (Gangemi et al., 2002), or with the hypernym hierarchy of WordNet. Such an experiment was performed by Allen et al. (2013), which showed that WordNet glosses contain information that is not found in the structural

Measure	Precision	Recall	F1
EL-smatch	0.85	0.82	0.83
Full Axiom	0.29	1.00	0.45

Table 2: Performance against gold standard parses of 50 synsets.

6.1 Semantic Parsing Evaluation

We constructed a gold standard set of axioms by selecting 50 random WordNet synsets that were not used during development. Gold standard axioms for these synsets were written by the first author, then refined in collaboration between the two authors.[7] The 50 synsets resulted in 52 axioms and 2,764 triples in the gold standard. The results in Table 2 show the system performance using both *EL-smatch* and full axiom metrics. In the full axiom metric, the precision measures the number of axioms that are completely correct, and the recall measures the number of axioms generated (which can vary due to merged glosses and multiple frames). The *EL-smatch* score of 0.83 shows that the axioms are generally good, even when not completely correct. Generating completely correct axioms is difficult because there are multiple non-trivial subproblems, such as prepositional attachment and word sense disambiguation. *EL-smatch* displays a more fine-grained measure of our system performance than the full axiom metric.

6.2 Inference Evaluation

To our knowledge, no earlier work evaluates inference in a manner that captures the details of semantically rich lexical axioms. Therefore, in order to compare our results to previous work, we evaluate a stripped-down version of our inference mechanism on a manually created verb entailment dataset (Weisman et al., 2012). This dataset contains 812 directed verb pairs, $v1 \rightarrow v2$, which are annotated 'yes' if the annotator could think of plausible contexts under which the entailment from $v1$ to $v2$ holds. For example, *identify* entails *recognize* in some contexts, does not entail *describe* is any context. Though the dataset is not rich, many previous systems (Mostafazadeh and Allen, 2015; Weisman et al., 2012; Chklovski and

Method	Precision	Recall	F1
Our Approach	0.43	0.53	0.48
TRIPS	0.50	0.45	0.47
Supervised	0.40	0.71	0.51
VerbOcean	0.33	0.15	0.20
Random	0.28	0.29	0.28

Table 3: Performance against gold standard parses of 50 synsets.

Pantel, 2004) have evaluated on this dataset, establishing it as a basic standard of comparison. In order to fit our axioms to this dataset, we remove semantic roles (verb arguments and adjuncts) from our axioms. Also, since the dataset has no word senses, the inferences begin with every synset that contains a sense of the starting word, and the final predicted entailments suppress sense distinctions. When generating inferences, we find verbs in the consequent of the axiom that are not modified by a negation or negating adverb (e.g., *nearly, almost,* etc.). Such inferences are chained up to three times, or until an abstract word is reached (e.g., *be, go,* etc.), which glosses do not sufficiently describe. This blacklist contains 24 abstract words.

Table 3 shows the results on this dataset. *TRIPS* is an approach by Mostafazadeh & Allen (2015), which constructs axioms from WordNet using the TRIPS parser and represents its axioms in OWL-DL, *Supervised* is a supervised learning approach by Weisman et al. (2012), *VerbOcean* classifies entailments according to the strength relation of the VerbOcean knowledege-base (Chklovski and Pantel, 2004), and *Random* is a method that randomly classifies the pair with probability equal to the distribution in the testset (27.7%). The performance of our system is competitive with state-of-the-art systems *TRIPS* and *Supervised* on this task. Our system performance splits the performance of *TRIPS* and *Supervised* in all three measures.

The inference capabilities of our axioms exceed what is evaluated by this testset. Because of space constraints, an example of a more expressive inference using extracted axioms is included in supplementary material[8].

6.3 Error Analysis

In the semantic parsing evaluation, most of the parsing errors arose from a failure in the sentence

---

relations of WordNet. A similar experiment by us is unlikely to shed additional light on the topic.

[7]Due to time constraints, this evaluation was performed on a gold standard developed primarily by only one annotator. We hope to remedy this in future work including an analysis of interannotator agreement.

[8]http://www.cs.rochester.edu/u/gkim21/papers/high-fidelity-lex-supplementary.pdf

parser or preprocessing directly preceding the sentence parser. That is, 17 out of the 52 axioms had errors arising from the sentence parser. These errors arose from either linguistic patterns that we did not encounter in our development set or in complex sentences (e.g. *take a walk for one's health or to aid digestion, as after a meal*). Many of these can be avoided in the future by increasing the development set. Fortunately, the semantic parser uses keywords to mark ambiguous attachments or phrases, so that in many cases, axioms that are not fully parsed can be identified and ignored, rather than using an incorrectly parsed axiom.

WSD and incorrect scoping of semantic types are also major sources of errors. The challenge of WSD was minimized by the subset of hand-tagged word senses in WordNet. We may be able to reduce such errors in the future by merging together redundant or overly specific word senses. Incorrect scoping of semantic types is particularly problematic when the semantic type is specified in the gloss itself, as the type constraint needed to move across scopes. Our system performed well on coordinator scoping. We correctly scoped 23 of the 27 instances of coordinators in the dataset. Coordinators are generally a great source of error in parsers and this result is evidence of the effectiveness of our coordinator handling mechanism. In all four instances, the disjunctions were extracted from the gloss correctly, but were not reintroduced into the axiom. As such, this error did not make these axioms incorrect, rather incomplete.

7 Future Work and Conclusions

There are many attractive directions for future work. The scope of this project can be broadened to include nouns, adjectives, and adverbs, as required for any system that actually tackles the natural language understanding problem. There are also many ways to refine and deepen the gloss interpretation process. The parses may be improved by looking through the *hypernym* graph and borrowing results from parses of parents (generalizations) of words. We can also incorporate techniques from Allen et al. (2011; 2013) and Mostafazadeh & Allen (2015) to integrate results from related sets of glosses. The high-level TRIPS ontology could be used to improve robustness in the face of inconsistencies in WordNet and interpretation errors. Also, more sophisticated WSD techniques, such as those from the SENSEVAL-3 task on WSD (Litkowski, 2004), could be used to improve semantic precision, and argument coherence could be improved using techniques from Mostafazadeh & Allen (Mostafazadeh and Allen, 2015). Another possible avenue is concurrent use of information from multiple dictionaries, such as Wiktionary, VerbNet, and WordNet, to construct more complete and reliable axioms, in particular with respect to argument structure and types.

We argued that the semantic representations used in previous approaches to extracting lexical axioms from dictionaries are insufficient for achieving a natural language understanding system. We presented an approach to extracting lexical axioms of verbs from WordNet into EL, an expressive semantic representation that overcomes the shortcomings of the representations used in the past. We also presented a generalized *smatch* scoring metric, *EL-smatch*, which we used to evaluate our system. The evaluation shows that our approach constructs precise verb axioms from Word-Net. Furthermore, we demonstrate that the generated axioms perform competitively against the state of the art in a verb entailment task. We aim to apply these axioms to more comprehensive language understanding tasks and commonsense reasoning tests when we have sufficient coverage of the lexicon.

Acknowledgments

The work was supported by a Sproull Graduate Fellowship from the University of Rochester and NSF grant IIS-1543758. We are also grateful to Nasrin Mostafazadeh, Omid Bakhshandeh, and the anonymous reviewers for their helpful comments.

References

James Allen, William de Beaumont, Nate Blaylock, George Ferguson, Jansen Orfan, and Mary Swift. 2011. Acquiring commonsense knowledge for a cognitive agent. In *Proceedings of the AAAI Fall Symposium Series: Advances in Cognitive Systems (ACS 2011)*, Arlington, VA, USA.

James Allen, Will de Beaumont, Lucian Galescu, Jansen Orfan, Mary Swift, and Choh Man Teng. 2013. Automatically deriving event ontologies for a commonsense knowledge base. In *Proceedings of the 10th International Conference on Computational Semantics (IWCS 2013) – Long Papers*, pages

23–34, Potsdam, Germany, March. Association for Computational Linguistics.

Hiyan Alshawi. 1989. Analysing the dictionary definitions. In Bran Boguraev and Ted Briscoe, editors, *Computational Lexicography for Natural Language Processing*, pages 153–169. Longman Publishing Group, White Plains, NY, USA.

Laura Banarescu, Claire Bonial, Shu Cai, Madalina Georgescu, Kira Griffitt, Ulf Hermjakob, Kevin Knight, Philipp Koehn, Martha Palmer, and Nathan Schneider. 2013. Abstract Meaning Representation for sembanking. In *Proceedings of the 7th Linguistic Annotation Workshop and Interoperability with Discourse*, pages 178–186, Sofia, Bulgaria, August. Association for Computational Linguistics.

Shu Cai and Kevin Knight. 2013. Smatch: an evaluation metric for semantic feature structures. In *Proceedings of the 51st Annual Meeting of the Association for Computational Linguistics (Volume 2: Short Papers)*, pages 748–752, Sofia, Bulgaria, August. Association for Computational Linguistics.

Nicoletta Calzolari. 1984. Detecting patterns in a lexical data base. In *Proceedings of the 10th International Conference on Computational Linguistics and 22nd Annual Meeting of the Association for Computational Linguistics*, pages 170–173, Stanford, California, USA, July. Association for Computational Linguistics.

Eugene Charniak. 2000. A maximum-entropy-inspired parser. In *Proceedings of the 1st North American Chapter of the Association for Computational Linguistics Conference*, NAACL 2000, pages 132–139, Stroudsburg, PA, USA. Association for Computational Linguistics.

Timothy Chklovski and Patrick Pantel. 2004. VerbOcean: Mining the web for fine-grained semantic verb relations. In Dekang Lin and Dekai Wu, editors, *Proceedings of EMNLP 2004*, pages 33–40, Barcelona, Spain, July. Association for Computational Linguistics.

Martin S. Chodorow, Roy J. Byrd, and George E. Heidorn. 1985. Extracting semantic hierarchies from a large on-line dictionary. In *Proceedings of the 23rd Annual Meeting on Association for Computational Linguistics*, ACL '85, pages 299–304, Stroudsburg, PA, USA. Association for Computational Linguistics.

Aldo Gangemi, Nicola Guarino, Claudio Masolo, Alessandro Oltramari, and Luc Schneider. 2002. Sweetening ontologies with DOLCE. In *Proceedings of the 13th International Conference on Knowledge Engineering and Knowledge Management. Ontologies and the Semantic Web*, EKAW '02, pages 166–181, London, UK. Springer-Verlag.

Jonathan Gordon and Lenhart Schubert. 2010. Quantificational sharpening of commonsense knowledge. In *Proceedings of the AAAI 2010 Fall Symposium on Commonsense Knowledge*.

Sanda Harabagiu, George Miller, and Dan Moldovan. 1999. WordNet 2 - A morphologically and semantically enhanced resource. In *SIGLEX99: Standardizing Lexical Resources*, pages 1–8, College Park, MD, USA, June. Association for Computational Linguistics.

Jerry R. Hobbs. 1985. Ontological promiscuity. In *Proceedings of the 23rd Annual Meeting of the Association for Computational Linguistics*, pages 60–69, Chicago, Illinois, USA, July. Association for Computational Linguistics.

Jerry R. Hobbs. 2008. Deep lexical semantics. In *Computational Linguistics and Intelligent Text Processing, 9th International Conference, CICLing Proceedings*, volume 4919 of *Lecture Notes in Computer Science*, pages 183–193, Haifa, Israel, February. Springer.

Nancy Ide and Jean Véronis. 1993. Knowledge extraction from machine-readable dictionaries: An evaluation. In *EAMT Workshop*, volume 898 of *Lecture Notes in Computer Science*, pages 19–34. Springer.

Ken Litkowski. 2004. Senseval-3 task: Word sense disambiguation of WordNet glosses. In Rada Mihalcea and Phil Edmonds, editors, *Senseval-3: Third International Workshop on the Evaluation of Systems for the Semantic Analysis of Text*, pages 13–16, Barcelona, Spain, July. Association for Computational Linguistics.

George A. Miller. 1995. WordNet: A lexical database for english. *Communications of the ACM*, 38(11):39–41, November.

Dan Moldovan and Vasile Rus. 2001. Logic form transformation of WordNet and its applicability to question answering. In *Proceedings of 39th Annual Meeting of the Association for Computational Linguistics*, pages 402–409, Toulouse, France, July. Association for Computational Linguistics.

Fabrizio Morbini and Lenhart K. Schubert. 2009. Evaluation of EPILOG: a reasoner for Episodic Logic. In *Proceedings of the Ninth International Symposium on Logical Formalizations of Commonsense Reasoning*.

Nasrin Mostafazadeh and James F. Allen. 2015. Learning semantically rich event inference rules using definition of verbs. In *Computational Linguistics and Intelligent Text Processing - 16th International Conference, CICLing Proceedings, Part I*, volume 9041 of *Lecture Notes in Computer Science*, pages 402–416, Cairo, Egypt, April. Springer.

Ian Niles and Adam Pease. 2001. Towards a standard upper ontology. In *Proceedings of the International Conference on Formal Ontology in Information Systems - Volume 2001*, FOIS '01, pages 2–9, New York, NY, USA. ACM.

Jansen Orfan and James Allen. 2015. Learning new relations from concept ontologies derived from definitions. In *Proceedings of the AAAI 2015 Spring Symposium Series on Logical Formalizations of Commonsense Reasoning*.

W3C OWL Working Group. 2004. *OWL Web Ontology Language Guide*. W3C Recommendation. Available at https://www.w3.org/TR/2004/REC-owl-guide-20040210.

Adam Purtee and Lenhart Schubert. 2012. TTT: A tree transduction language for syntactic and semantic processing. In *Proceedings of the Workshop on Applications of Tree Automata Techniques in Natural Language Processing*, ATANLP '12, pages 21–30, Stroudsburg, PA, USA. Association for Computational Linguistics.

Lenhart K. Schubert and Chung Hee Hwang. 2000. Episodic Logic meets Little Red Riding Hood: A comprehensive natural representation for language understanding. In Lucja M. Iwańska and Stuart C. Shapiro, editors, *Natural Language Processing and Knowledge Representation*, pages 111–174. MIT Press, Cambridge, MA, USA.

Lenhart Schubert and Matthew Tong. 2003. Extracting and evaluating general world knowledge from the Brown corpus. In *Proceedings of the HLT-NAACL 2003 Workshop on Text Meaning*, pages 7–13, Stroudsburg, PA, USA. Association for Computational Linguistics.

Lenhart K. Schubert. 2000. The situations we talk about. In Jack Minker, editor, *Logic-based Artificial Intelligence*, pages 407–439. Kluwer Academic Publishers, Norwell, MA, USA.

Lenhart Schubert. 2002. Can we derive general world knowledge from texts? In *Proceedings of the Second International Conference on Human Language Technology Research*, HLT '02, pages 94–97, San Francisco, CA, USA. Morgan Kaufmann Publishers Inc.

Lenhart Schubert. 2014. From treebank parses to episodic logic and commonsense inference. In *Proceedings of the ACL 2014 Workshop on Semantic Parsing*, pages 55–60, Baltimore, MD, June. Association for Computational Linguistics.

Lenhart Schubert. 2015. Semantic representation. In *Proceedings of the Twenty-Ninth AAAI Conference on Artificial Intelligence*.

Benjamin Van Durme, Phillip Michalak, and Lenhart K. Schubert. 2009. Deriving generalized knowledge from corpora using WordNet abstraction. In *Proceedings of the 12th Conference of the European Chapter of the Association for Computational Linguistics*, EACL '09, pages 808–816, Stroudsburg, PA, USA. Association for Computational Linguistics.

Piek Vossen, Willem Meijs, and M. den Broeder. 1989. Meaning and structure in dictionary definitions. In *Computational Lexicography for Natural Language Processing*, pages 171–192. Longman Publishing Group, White Plains, NY, USA.

Hila Weisman, Jonathan Berant, Idan Szpektor, and Ido Dagan. 2012. Learning verb inference rules from linguistically-motivated evidence. In *Proceedings of the 2012 Joint Conference on Empirical Methods in Natural Language Processing and Computational Natural Language Learning*, EMNLP-CoNLL '12, pages 194–204, Stroudsburg, PA, USA. Association for Computational Linguistics.

Yorick Wilks, Dan Fass, Cheng-ming Guo, James E. McDonald, Tony Plate, and Brian M. Slator. 1989. A tractable machine dictionary as a resource for computational semantics. In *Computational Lexicography for Natural Language Processing*, pages 193–228. Longman Publishing Group, White Plains, NY, USA.

Implicit Semantic Roles in a Multilingual Setting

Jennifer Sikos   **Yannick Versley**   **Anette Frank**
Department of Computational Linguistics
Heidelberg University, Germany
Leibniz Science Campus "Empirical Linguistics and Computational Language Modeling"
{sikos, versley, frank}@cl.uni-heidelberg.de

Abstract

Extending semantic role labeling (SRL) to detect and recover non-local arguments continues to be a challenge. Our work is the first to address the detection of implicit roles from a multilingual perspective. We map predicate-argument structures across English and German sentences, and we develop a classifier that distinguishes implicit arguments from other translation shifts. Using a combination of alignment statistics and linguistic features, we achieve a precision of 0.68 despite a limited training set, which is a significant gain over the majority baseline. Our approach does not rely on pre-existing knowledge bases and is extendible to any language pair with parallel data and dependency parses.

1 Introduction

Understanding events and their participants is a core NLP task, and SRL is the standard approach for identification and labeling of these events in text. SRL systems (Täckström et al., 2015; Roth and Woodsend, 2014) have benefited NLP applications, and many approaches have been proposed to transfer semantic roles from English to other languages without further reliance on manual annotation (Kozhevnikov and Titov, 2013; Padó and Lapata, 2009). However, event structures – both predicates and their arguments – are known to shift in the translation process, and this poor correspondence presents a bottleneck for the transference of semantic roles across languages. In some cases, the semantic content of an entire argument can be missing from the scope of its translated predicate.

Arguments that are omitted are often treated as noise in state-of-the-art projection models; however, our work views them as a valuable source of data - such arguments serve as naturally occurring training data for *implicit* role detection. We target arguments that have been dislocated from their predicates, or are dropped entirely, in translated sentences. These non-isomorphic event structures can not only be leveraged as new training data for implicit role detection, but analyzing the shifts that trigger these implicit roles can guide improvements to systems that perform cross-lingual semantic role projection.

Implicit Roles If a predicate is known to have multiple semantic arguments, only a subset might be expressed within the local boundary of its clause or sentence. SRL models typically restrict their search for semantic arguments to this local domain and are not designed to recover arguments situated in the broader discourse context. Non-local role linking extends the SRL task by recovering the semantic arguments not instantiated in the local scope of the predicate. One complicating factor is that these implicit arguments can either be found in the context, and thereby are recoverable, or they could be existentially interpreted and might not correspond to any referent in the text at all. In the examples below, the argument for the predicate <u>withdrawn</u> in (1) is resolvable while the implicit argument for <u>reading</u> in (2) is not:

(1)   El Salvador is now the only Latin American country which still has troops in [Iraq][1]. Nicaragua, Honduras, and the Dominican Republic have <u>withdrawn</u> their troops ∅.
Implicit role: Location

(2)   I was sitting <u>reading</u> ∅ in the chair.
Implicit role: Theme

Implicit role labeling systems consistently report low performance due to lack of training data. Combining the few existing resources improves

---

[1] In this and other examples throughout the paper, the brackets [] indicate the antecedent of the implicit argument.

*Proceedings of the Fifth Joint Conference on Lexical and Computational Semantics (*SEM 2016)*, pages 45–54,
Berlin, Germany, August 11-12, 2016.

performance (Feizabadi and Padó, 2015) when they contribute diversity in predicate and argument types. Since much of the multilingual parallel corpora vary in domain and genre, mining these corpora for implicit roles should provide new training data that is sufficiently diverse to benefit the implicit role labeling task.

Predicate-Argument Structures across Languages Translational correspondences have been used in previous work to acquire resources for supervised monolingual tasks, such as word sense disambiguation (Diab and Resnik, 2002). Similarly, semantic role annotations can be transferred to new languages when predicate-argument structures are stable across language pairs (Padó and Lapata, 2009). In this work, we target predicate-argument structures that do not express such stability and have shifted in the translation process. In example (3), the role *farmers* is dropped entirely in the aligned German sentence:

(3) The only change is that [farmers] are not required to produce.

Die einzige Neuerung ist, dass nicht gefordert
The only change is, that not required
wird zu produzieren.
are to produce.

The challenge in detecting implicit roles across languages is that these omissions represent only a fraction of the kinds of poor alignments that can occur. In fact, different types of translational shifts may occur that do not constitute cases of implicit role omission. Such factors include: change in part-of-speech from a verbal predicate to a noun or adjective, light verb constructions, single predicates that are expressed as both a verb and complement in the target language, and expressions with no direct translations (Samardžic et al., 2010).

Aims and Contributions To find implicit (non-local) semantic roles in translation, we distinguish role omissions from other types of translation shifts. We test linguistic features to automatically detect such role omissions in parallel corpora. We divide our work into alignment (Section 3.1) and classification (Section 3.2), with an annotation task for data construction (Section 4).

Our contributions are (i) a novel method for automatically identifying implicit roles in discourse, (ii) a classifier that is able to distinguish general translational divergences from true cases of implicit roles, (iii) an annotated, multilingual dataset of manually tagged implicit arguments, and (iv) a classifier that achieves precision of 0.68 despite a small training set size, which is a significant improvement over a majority class baseline. Finally, we perform detailed analysis of our annotation and automatic classification results.

2 Related Work

2.1 Implicit Semantic Role Labeling

Previous resources for implicit SRL were developed over diverging schemas, texts, and predicate types. An initial dataset was constructed in the SemEval-2010 Shared Task "Linking Events and Their Participants in Discourse", under the FrameNet paradigm; authors annotated short stories with implicit arguments and their antecedents, resulting in approx. 500 resolvable and 700 nonresolvable implicit roles out of roughly 3,000 frame instances (Ruppenhofer et al., 2010). Gerber and Chai (2010) focused on the implicit arguments of a constrained set of 10 nominal predicates in the NomBank scheme, annotating 966 implicit role instances for these specific predicates.

Numerous studies on the recovery of implicit roles have concluded that a lack of training data has been the stopping point towards improvements on the implicit role labeling task (Gorinski et al., 2013; Laparra and Rigau, 2013). To address this problem, Silberer and Frank (2012) generated artificial training data by removing arguments from coreference chains and showed that adding such instances yields performance gains. However, their quality was low and later work (Roth and Frank, 2015) has shown that smaller numbers of naturally occurring training data performed better. Roth and Frank (2015) applied a graph-based method for automatically acquiring high-quality data for non-local SRL using comparable monolingual corpora. They detect implicit semantic roles across documents and their antecedents from the prior context, again following cross-document links. In contrast, our work does not rely on semantic resources (SRL and lexical ontologies), but builds on parallel corpora enriched with dependencies and word alignments. Finally, Stern and Dagan (2014) generate training data for implicit SRL from textual entailment data sets. However, this type of resource needs to be manually curated.

2.2 Cross-lingual Annotation Projection

Aside from English, resources for SRL only exist for a select number of languages. For the languages that have such resources, annotated data still tends to vastly underrepresent the variability and breadth of coverage that exists for English. To extend SRL to new languages without reliance on manual annotation, models for role transference have been developed under both the supervised (Padó and Lapata, 2009; Akbik et al., 2015) and unsupervised (Kozhevnikov and Titov, 2013) setting. Most relevant to our work are previous studies that address the problem of projecting semantic role annotations across parallel corpora.

To transfer semantic annotations across languages, Padó and Lapata (2009) score the constituents of word-aligned parallel sentences and project role labels for the arguments that achieve highest constituent alignment scores. Akbik et al (2015) use filtered projection by constraining alignments through lexical and syntactic filters to ensure accuracy in predicate and argument role projection. Complete predicate-argument mappings are then used to bootstrap a classifier to recover further unaligned predicates and arguments.

3 Detecting Implicit Roles across Languages

We hypothesize that implicit semantic roles can be found in translated sentences, even in corpora where sentences are typically close translations. Our goal is to distinguish implicit roles from other translation shifts that cause poor alignment in SRL projection. A model is constructed based on lexical, syntactic, and alignment properties of parallel predicate-argument structures, and this classifier is, to the best of our knowledge, the first to detect a wide range of omitted roles in multilingual, parallel corpora. Our implicit role detection applies to both core and non-core arguments and is not dependent on large-scale SRL resources.

3.1 Identifying Poorly Aligned Arguments

Our first goal is to find candidates for implicit arguments by aligning predicate-argument structures across parallel English and German sentences.

Predicate and Argument Identification We target all non-auxiliary verbs as predicates, and detect their dependents through grammatical relations in dependency parses. We extract subjects, direct objects, indirect objects, prepositional objects, adverbial or nominal modifiers as well as embedded clauses. These recover both the core and non-core arguments (adjuncts) of the predicate.[2] Arguments are attached to their nearest predicate and cannot be attached to more than one, as might occur in cases of embedded clauses.

Aligning Arguments for Detection of Unaligned Roles We use word alignments between parallel source (sl) and target (tl) language sentences as input. A predicate in the source language p^{sl} is mapped to a predicate in the target language p^{tl} if there exists a word alignment link between them, and their arguments are then aligned using the scoring function $ArgAL_p$ (Eq 3). $ArgAL_p$ uses word alignment links between the source and target arguments a^{sl}, a^{tl} of the aligned predicate pair to produce an optimal mapping between corresponding predicate-argument structures.

For scoring, we adapt Padó and Lapata (2009)'s constituent alignment-based overlap measure (Eq 1) to dependencies, where $yield(a)$ denotes the set of words in the yield (headword and dependents) of an argument a, and $align(a)$ the set of words in the target language that are aligned to the yield of a. Because the automatic word alignment tool gives predictions for links in both directions, we apply this asymmetric measure from the English-German and German-English links and average their results (Eq 2). The *ascore* is computed for the Cartesian product $A^{sl} \times A^{tl}$ over all source and target arguments of the aligned predicates p^{sl} and p^{tl}. We select the argument alignments $A'^{sl} \times A'^{tl} \subseteq A^{sl} \times A^{tl}$ that return the maximal sum of scores for all arguments across the aligned argument structure (Eq 3).

Anticipating noise in the word alignments, we set a threshold to enforce accurate mappings between arguments. From the obtained mappings, we consider any argument whose alignment score does not exceed a threshold Θ as *unaligned* and thus as a candidate for an implicit role. The selection of threshold Θ is discussed in Section 5.

$$ovlp(a^{sl}, a^{tl}) = \frac{|\ align(a^{sl}) \cap yield(a^{tl})\ |}{|\ align(a^{sl}) \cup yield(a^{tl})\ |} \quad (1)$$

$$ascore(a^{sl}, a^{tl}) = \frac{ovlp(a^{sl}, a^{tl}) + ovlp(a^{tl}, a^{sl})}{2} \quad (2)$$

---

[2]Since we are treating arguments and adjuncts alike, in the following we loosely refer to both types of dependents as 'arguments'.

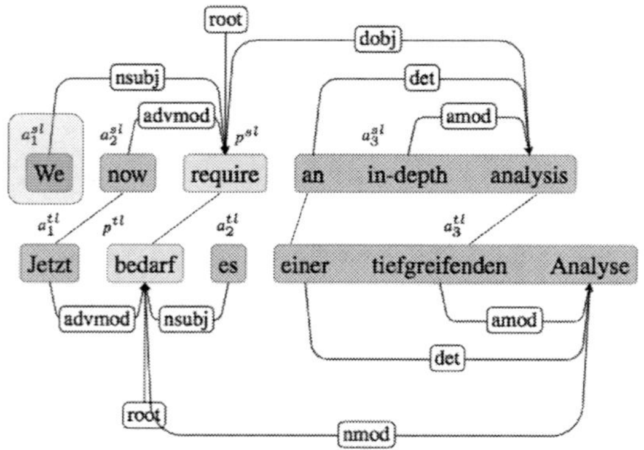

Alignment Type	Aligned Arguments	Alignment Score
headword	$a_1^{sl},-$	0
	a_2^{sl},a_1^{tl}	1
	$a_3^{sl},-$	0
ascore	$a_1^{sl},-^{tl}$	0
	a_2^{sl},a_1^{tl}	$(1+1)/2 = 1.0$
	a_3^{sl},a_3^{tl}	$(2/3 + 2/3)/2 = 0.67$

Figure 1: Predicate-argument structures with noisy word alignments (left), and alignment scores for the arguments (right). *Headword* scoring aligns only headwords of the source (a^{sl}) and target (a^{tl}) arguments, while *ascore* uses headwords and dependents of an entire argument span for alignment.

$$ArgAL_p = \underset{A'^{sl} \times A'^{tl} \subseteq A^{sl} \times A^{tl}}{\arg\max} \sum_{A^{sl} \times A^{tl}} ascore(a^{sl}, a^{tl})$$

where

$$A^{sl} \times A^{tl} = \{\langle a^{sl}, a^{tl}\rangle \mid a^{sl} \in \langle p^{sl}, a^{sl}\rangle, a^{tl} \in \langle p^{tl}, a^{tl}\rangle\} \tag{3}$$

An example of the alignment scoring is given in Figure 1, where predicates and arguments are detected over parallel English-German sentences, and word alignments are automatically generated. The argument 'an in-depth analysis' consists of a headword and two dependents, with two noisy word alignments that link the arguments across languages. Given these word alignment links, the *ascore* (Eq 2) is computed by taking the number of alignments and the yield of the arguments for both English and German, and these scores are then averaged for a final alignment score of 0.67. In this case, the scoring function still produces correct mappings across the predicate-argument structures despite imperfect word alignments, and an implicit role, *We*, is correctly unaligned to the German sentence.

3.2 Classification of Poor Alignments as Implicit Roles

Our objective is to build a classifier that automatically detects implicit roles across parallel corpora. To achieve this goal, we construct a classifier that takes as input an unaligned argument in English and, based on linguistic features in the aligned English and German sentences, determines whether this unaligned argument is an implicit role in German. Our dataset, described in Section 4.2, consists of instances of poorly aligned roles that have been annotated as either *implicit, not implicit,*

or *not a role of the predicate*. In classification, we reduce the annotation classes (*implicit/not implicit/not a role of the predicate*) to a binary decision where the positive class represents the implicit roles, and the negative class is any unaligned argument that annotators determined as either *not implicit* or *not a semantic role*. We reduced the task to a binary decision to avoid sparsity in the classification.

Features We hypothesize that we can predict the existence of an implicit role through features of the predicate-argument structures in the source and target languages. These features include monolingual predicate-argument structures, as well as cross-lingual features that represent the quality of the alignments across the parallel sentences. Monolingual features encode the syntactic properties of the arguments and predicates for source and target sentences, as well as sentential-level features that include the presence of modal and auxiliary verbs and conjunctions. To incorporate cross-lingual information, the alignment scores described in Section 3.1 are kept as features to the classifier, based on our assumption that the overall alignment between source and target predicate-argument structures should impact the classification of an implicit role. Both monolingual and cross-lingual features apply to surrounding predicate/arguments, where arguments can either be aligned or unaligned, and predicates that have fully aligned structures are considered *complete*. A complete list of features is shown in Table 1.

Classifiers We experimented with three classifiers, a Support Vector Machine (SVM) with a lin-

TYPE	FEATURE	XLING
Argument	Lemma	
	POS	
	Grammatical relation to predicate	
	Distance to predicate	
	Number of dependents	
	Syntactic path to predicate	
	Alignment type of neighboring argument (*aligned, unaligned*)	+
Predicate	Lemma	
	POS	
	Total number of arguments	
	Number of aligned arguments	+
	Number of unaligned arguments	+
	$ArgAL_p$ score	+
	Alignment type of neighboring predicate (*complete, incomplete*)	+
Sentential	Presence of a modal or auxiliary	
	Sentence-final punctuation marks before end	
	Conjunction between $p^{sl}, p^{sl}\text{-}1$	
	Sum of $ArgAL_p$ scores	
	Total number of arguments	
	Total number of predicates	
	Sum of $ArgAL_p$ scores over all predicates	+

Table 1: Features investigated for classification, where Xling are cross-lingual features.

ear kernel, Decision Tree, and Gradient Boosting, under the framework of the Scikit-learn library (Pedregosa et al., 2011).

4 Constructing a Dataset for Classifying Implicit Arguments

This section presents the construction of our experimental dataset for implicit role detection.

4.1 Corpora and Tools

We conduct our experiments over the Europarl corpus (Koehn, 2005), which contains over 1.9 million aligned sentences in our target languages. Anticipating noise in the automatic word alignments, we first take sentences from manually word-aligned German-English Europarl data (Padó and Lapata, 2005) to conduct our initial experiments. These sentences give us an upper bound for the number of implicit roles we should expect to obtain. Automatic word alignments are generated with GIZA++ (Och and Ney, 2003).

Predicates and their arguments are first detected through dependency parses on English and German parallel corpora. Parses are generated for English with ClearNLP (Choi and McCallum, 2013). German sentences are run through the MarMot morphological analyzer (Mueller et al., 2013), and dependency parses for German are then generated using the RBG Parser (Lei et al., 2014). The Universal Dependencies project facilitates cross-lingual consistency in parsing and provides better compatibility amongst multiple languages. We trained the RBG Parser with the Universal Dependencies tagset (Rosa et al., 2014), and thus our argument detection can be applied to other languages in the Universal Dependencies project.

4.2 Annotation of Poorly Aligned Arguments

Annotation Instances Our goal is to find any argument that is either missing or dislocated from its predicate in translation. With this objective in mind, we focused our annotation on incomplete predicate structures whose argument(s) remained unaligned. Any argument with scores below the alignment threshold (see Section 3.1) was a candidate for annotation.

Annotation Task and Guidelines Three annotators worked on this task. Each annotator was a native German speaker with high fluency in English, and had taken at least one undergraduate course in linguistics. Annotators were given guidelines that define predicates as *events* or *scenarios*, and semantic roles as an element that has a semantic dependence on the predicate, including the *who, what, where, when,* and *why* type of information. Implicit roles were defined as "any role that is missing from the scope, or clausal boundary, of the predicate". Each annotator was trained on a test set of 10 example sentences.

Annotators were given pairs of sentences with aligned predicates in English and German, where the English predicate had a poorly aligned argument. Annotation instances were presented as: two preceding English sentences, the English sentence with both the argument and predicate highlighted, the German sentence with the aligned predicate highlighted, and two preceding German sentences. An example of the annotation task is shown in Figure 2.

The annotation task was broken into two subtasks. First, annotators were asked to judge whether the marked argument is a correct semantic role for the English predicate. The second sub-

```
Context - 2 preceding English sentences

    ————

The only change is that [farmers] are not –required– to
produce .
Die einzige Neuerung ist , dass nicht –gefordert– wird
zu produzieren .

    ————

Context - 2 preceding German sentences

  ——————————————

[farmers]
Can 'farmers' be considered a role of the English
predicate 'required'?

If 'no': please choose:
not a role of English predicate

Can 'farmers' be considered an implicit role for
the German predicate 'gefordert'?

If 'no': please choose:
not an implicit role of German predicate
If 'yes': please indicate the location of the German
translation of 'farmers' by marking it in (**)
```

Figure 2: Example annotation task. Aligned predicates are marked in dashes (–) and implicit role candidates are surrounded by squared brackets [].

task asked annotators to judge whether a translation for the argument was available in the scope of the highlighted German predicate. If it was not available in the scope, they were asked to annotate the example as *implicit*.

Difficult Annotation Cases The annotations were adjudicated by one of the authors, and the annotator with the highest agreement with the adjudicator was asked to complete the entire dataset.

Cases that resulted in higher annotator disagreement included arguments of nominal predicates that were themselves the argument of the aligned predicate. In Example 4 below, *30 August* is a role for the nominal predicate *participation* but not continue:

(4)   The massive participation [from 30 August]
      must <u>continue</u>.

Other difficult annotation cases included roles that were partially, or entirely, encoded in the translated predicate. These included temporal adjuncts that could either be interpreted as present tense or implicit in the translated sentence:

(5)   I will [now] <u>give</u> the floor to the President

      Ich <u>gebe</u> dem Präsidenten das Wort
      I   give the   President   the floor

After a review of these difficult cases, annotation guidelines were modified and annotators were re-trained.

Annotation Quality Inter-annotator agreement was measured by Cohen's Kappa scores over 114 instances, and the entire 700 candidates were then completed by Annotator 1. One of the authors adjudicated for agreement. Results are given in Table 2 where "Role + Implicit" reports Kappa scores over all three categories - *not a role, implicit, and not implicit,* while "Implicit" reports agreement over binary *implicit* vs *non-implicit* decisions.

ANNOTATOR vs ADJUDICATOR	ROLE + IMPLICIT	IMPLICIT
ANNOTATOR 1	0.76	0.96
ANNOTATOR 2	0.48	0.92
ANNOTATOR 3	0.29	0.69

Table 2: Kappa agreements

Annotation Results In total, we took 700 poorly aligned arguments whose scores were below the alignment threshold (Section 3.1), where 500 were selected from manual word alignments and 200 from GIZA++ alignments. The 500 candidate arguments were sampled from 987 gold-aligned Europarl sentences, in which over 3,000 arguments fell below the threshold. The 200 candidates were sampled from 500 automatically aligned Europarl sentence pairs (excluding the sentences from the manually aligned dataset), with nearly 3,000 arguments below the threshold, to estimate the difference in implicit roles between manual and automatic word alignments.

Over the completed dataset, results for the annotation types are given in Table 3. Out of the manually aligned Europarl sentences, annotations produced 45 positive implicit role instances (9% of the annotated candidates). The automatic alignments, with 200 examples, contained 6 instances (3% of the annotated candidates) of implicit roles. Over the total 700 instances, 24.5% were classified as 'not a predicate role', 68.3% as 'not implicit', and 7.2% as 'implicit'.

	INSTANCES	NOT A ROLE	NOT IMPLICIT	IMPLICIT
Manual	500	154	301	45
GIZA++	200	18	176	6

Table 3: Final annotation dataset.

Classifier	P	R	F1
Majority Baseline	0	0	0
SVM-ablated	**0.6805**	**0.4444**	**0.5128**
SVM-all	0.1555	0.2238	0.18333
Decision Tree-ablated	0.6682	0.4155	0.4934
Decision Tree-all	0.4134	0.2222	0.2748
Gradient Boosting-ablated	0.6688	0.3777	0.4631
Gradient Boosting-all	0.6466	0.2222	0.3268

Table 4: Precision, Recall and F_1 for the positive class (*implicit role*), with stratified 5-fold CV.

5 Classification Experiments and Results

5.1 Argument Alignment and Scoring

With the scoring function described in Section 3.1, perfectly aligned arguments should produce a score of 1.0. We experimentally set the threshold Θ for the minimum alignment score at 0.2 for arguments such that arguments with imperfect word alignments will still be aligned.

5.2 Classification of Implicit Arguments

The data set constructed in Section 4 resulted in 51 manually validated implicit roles and 649 negative instances that were input for classification.

We measure precision, recall, and F_1 scores, and for the SVM and Gradient Boosting classifiers we experimented with parameters to optimize precision. The SVM classifier with a linear kernel produced the highest scores, but results were closely followed by Decision Tree and Gradient Boosting classifiers. For the SVM classifier, we experimented with different regularization {0.5, 1, 10, 20} and class weight increments {None, 1:2, 1:10} and found the highest precision scores were achieved with C=0.5 and class weight 1:2. In Gradient Boosting, we experimented with max depth {1, 2, 3} and found the highest precision scores were obtained with a max depth of 2. Since the data set is heavily biased towards the negative class, we divided training and test sets with a stratified 5-fold cross-validation (CV). We later experimented with upsampling for the positive class but found no significant improvement.

Feature Ablation To determine the optimal feature set, we performed ablation tests by incrementally removing a feature and performing training/testing over the reduced feature set. Ablation was performed individually for each classifier. After these tests, we eliminated features that caused

Type	Feature
a^{sl}	lemma, POS, path to predicate
$a^{sl}+1$	POS, path to predicate
$a^{sl}-1$	alignment type, number of dependents
p^{tl}	POS
$p^{tl}-1$	sum of $ArgAL_p$ scores
$p^{tl}+1$	POS, number of arguments, number of unaligned arguments, sum of $ArgAL_p$ scores, alignment type

Table 5: Final feature set used in classification. Notation is defined in Section 3.1, where $\pm$ 1 are the arguments/predicates preceding (–1) and following (+1) the candidate.

a drop in performance and used only the best performing features in the final classification. The final feature set is shown in Table 5.

The SVM model obtains the best results of 0.68 precision and F_1-score of 0.51 with the ablated feature set, closely followed by the other classifier models and outperforming the majority baseline, which always predicts the negative class (see Table 4 for both ablated and full feature results).

Feature Analysis The final feature set used in the classification experiment included both cross-lingual features of the predicate and arguments on source/target sentences, as well as monolingual predicate and argument features. The ablation results support our initial hypothesis that the surrounding predicate/argument structures and alignment scores are relevant to the detection of an omitted role.

5.3 Analysis of Results

Translation Shifts that Trigger Implicit Roles Through observation of the positive instances, we determined a number of syntactic environments that trigger omission of semantic roles from English to German. Shift in voice, finite to infinite verb forms, and coordination could all motivate the deletion of a role across translated sentences. While these syntactically licensed implicit roles composed 57% of our positive instances, a large number (43%) were not found to have an explanation on syntactic grounds alone. In these cases, the arguments seem to have been omitted by pragmatic or semantic factors. The distribution of these shift types over our dataset is given in Table 6.

Voice A change from active (source) to passive (target). Subjects are dropped in translation:

(6) The more [we] <u>refuse</u> to democratize the institutions ....

> Je mehr die Demokratisierung der
> The more the democratization of the
> Institutionen <u>verweigert</u> wird ...
> institution <u>refused</u> are

Coordination An argument might be the repeated subject of two conjoined clauses, but expressed as a shared argument in the parallel sentence:

(7) I was faced with this system *and* [I] do not <u>know</u> any parliament

> Ich fand dieses System vor *und* <u>kenne</u> kein
> I faced this system before and know no
> Parlament
> parliament

Extraposition Complex clausal embeddings can cause roles to be extraposed from their predicates in the target language text:

(8) ...but would also want to <u>encourage</u> both parties [to observe the spirit of this new agreement].

> ...er kann die beiden Parteien nur <u>veranlassen</u>
> ...it can that both parties only encourage
> wollen, [den Geist dieses neuen Abkommens
> want, the spirit of-this new agreement
> zu achten].
> to observe

Coordination and extraposition are borderline cases with regard to the non-locality of roles. PropBank does annotate coordinated arguments, and in these cases the syntactic parse tree can be leveraged for recovery of the non-local role. However, we still consider these implicit arguments since they are expressed outside of the local scope of the predicates.

Nonfinite Similar to change in voice, the subject of a finite verb can be dropped when the translated verb is nonfinite:

(9) I would ask that [they] <u>reconsider</u> these decisions

> Ich bitte, diese Entscheidung <u>zu überdenken</u>
> I ask, these decisions to reconsider

Semantic/Pragmatic A role can be dropped in translation without a structural shift that licenses the omission. In these instances, the role could have been incorporated into the aligned sentence without a change to the syntactic environment.

(10) ... I am <u>asking</u> you to do this directly, [in this House].

> ...<u>wende</u> ich mich hiermit direkt an Sie .
> ...turn I myself hereby directly to you

Since the directionality of our implicit role search focused on English to German, we do not account for syntactic shifts that could cause omissions in the opposite direction, i.e. German to English. There are imperative constructions in German that overtly encode the addressee of the command ("go outside" in English can be translated as "go *you* outside" in German) which can trigger implicit roles in translation from German to English.

Shift Type	Count	%
Voice	7	14%
Coordination	8	16%
Extraposition	8	16%
Nonfinite	6	11%
Semantic/Pragmatic	22	43%

Table 6: Shift types that trigger implicit roles.

Semantic Role Types of Omitted Arguments We adopt the VerbNet roleset (Kipper et al., 2000) to manually label semantic role across all our implicit argument instances. A full analysis of the role types, shown in Table 7, found that a majority of implicit roles are *Agent* and *Theme*. This reflects the general distributions for role frequency (Merlo and Van Der Plas, 2009), but could also be due to the syntactic shifts that produce a higher omission of the subject, such as passivization and coordination, which are commonly filled by the *Agent* and *Theme* roles.

Core Role	Count	Non-Core Role	Count
Agent	15	Time	6
Theme	14	Topic	5
Recipient	3	Location	3
Experiencer	2	Manner	1
Cause	2		

Table 7: Thematic roles, both core and non-core, of the implicit cases.

Antecedents to the Implicit Role The analyses above described the shift types that trigger argument omission, but only two of these types, coordination and extraposition, would guarantee the missing argument to be recoverable from the non-local context. Cases where the annotators were able to recover the antecedent roles, either from the previous clause or sentences, were less than the majority (21 out of the 51 cases), while many instances were not instantiated in the non-local context. Table 8 gives the proportion of recovered antecedents according to shift types. The fact that extraposition and coordination cases yield higher number of resolvable roles can be exploited in future work for antecedent linking.

Shift Type	Resolvable	Not resolvable
Voice	1	6
Coordination	8	0
Extraposition	8	0
Nonfinite	1	5
Semantic/Pragmatic	3	19

Table 8: Availability of the antecedent in the surrounding context.

6 Conclusion and Future Work

In this work, we investigated the hypothesis that implicit semantic roles can be identified in translation. Our method is knowledge-lean and achieves respectable performance despite a small training set. While the present work has focused on missing arguments of verbal predicates, implicit role detection in this multilingual framework can be easily extended to nominal predicates. Combining both predicate types is expected to improve the overall results, as some of the noise we are currently observing pertains to implicit roles occurring with nouns. Additional noise is produced by the automatic word alignments, which can be addressed by employing triangulation techniques using multiple language pairs. Further, with our current classifier we can predict role omissions across parallel sentences with better accuracy than reliance on noisy word alignments alone, and with these predictions we can generate better candidates for annotation and reduce the time and cost of future annotation effort.

A next step from the current work would be to automatically recover the antecedent of the implicit role in the target language when it is available. By doing so, we can construct new training data for monolingual implicit role labeling, improve transference of semantic roles across parallel corpora, and generate novel training data for implicit role labeling for new languages.

7 Acknowledgments

This research has been conducted within the Leibniz Science Campus "Empirical Linguistics and Computational Modeling", funded by the Leibniz Association under grant no. SAS-2015-IDS-LWC and by the Ministry of Science, Research, and Art (MWK) of the state of Baden-Württemberg. We thank our annotators Leo Born, Max Müller-Eberstein and Julius Steen for their contribution.

References

Alan Akbik, Laura Chiticariu, Marina Danilevsky, Yunyao Li, Shivakumar Vaithyanathan, and Huaiyu Zhu. 2015. Generating High Quality Proposition Banks for Multilingual Semantic Role Labeling. In *Proceedings of the 53rd Annual Meeting of the Association for Computational Linguistics and the 7th International Joint Conference on Natural Language Processing*, pages 397–407, Beijing, China.

Jinho D. Choi and Andrew McCallum. 2013. Transition-based Dependency Parsing with Selectional Branching. In *Proceedings of the 51st Annual Meeting of the Association for Computational Linguistics*, pages 1052–1062, Sofia, Bulgaria.

Mona Diab and Philip Resnik. 2002. An unsupervised method for word sense tagging using parallel corpora. In *Proceedings of the 40th Annual Meeting on Association for Computational Linguistics*, pages 255–262. Association for Computational Linguistics.

Parvin Sadat Feizabadi and Sebastian Padó. 2015. Combining Seemingly Incompatible Corpora for Implicit Semantic Role Labeling. In *Proceedings of the Fourth Joint Conference on Lexical and Computational Semantics*, pages 40–50, Denver, Colorado, June.

Matthew Gerber and Joyce Y Chai. 2010. Beyond NomBank: A study of implicit arguments for nominal predicates. In *Proceedings of the 48th Annual Meeting of the Association for Computational Linguistics*, pages 1583–1592.

Philip Gorinski, Josef Ruppenhofer, and Caroline Sporleder. 2013. Towards weakly supervised resolution of null instantiations. In *Proceedings of the 10th International Conference on Computational Semantics (IWCS 2013)*, pages 119–130.

Karin Kipper, Hoa Trang Dang, Martha Palmer, et al. 2000. Class-based construction of a verb lexicon. In *AAAI/IAAI*, pages 691–696.

Philipp Koehn. 2005. Europarl: A parallel corpus for statistical machine translation. In *MT summit*, volume 5, pages 79–86.

Mikhail Kozhevnikov and Ivan Titov. 2013. Cross-lingual Transfer of Semantic Role Labeling Models. In *Proceedings of the 51st Annual Meeting of the Association for Computational Linguistics*, pages 1190–1200, Sofia, Bulgaria, August.

Egoitz Laparra and German Rigau. 2013. ImpAr: A Deterministic Algorithm for Implicit Semantic Role Labelling. In *ACL (1)*, pages 1180–1189.

Tao Lei, Yu Xin, Yuan Zhang, Regina Barzilay, and Tommi Jaakkola. 2014. Low-Rank Tensors for Scoring Dependency Structures. In *Proceedings of the 52nd Annual Meeting of the Association for Computational Linguistics*, pages 1381–1391, Baltimore, Maryland.

Paola Merlo and Lonneke Van Der Plas. 2009. Abstraction and generalisation in semantic role labels: PropBank, VerbNet or both? In *Proceedings of the Joint Conference of the 47th Annual Meeting of the ACL and the 4th International Joint Conference on Natural Language Processing of the AFNLP: Volume 1-Volume 1*, pages 288–296. Association for Computational Linguistics.

Thomas Mueller, Helmut Schmid, and Hinrich Schütze. 2013. Efficient Higher-Order CRFs for Morphological Tagging. In *Proceedings of the 2013 Conference on Empirical Methods in Natural Language Processing*, pages 322–332, Seattle, Washington, USA.

Franz Josef Och and Hermann Ney. 2003. A Systematic Comparison of Various Statistical Alignment Models. *Computational Linguistics*, 29(1):19–51.

Sebastian Padó and Mirella Lapata. 2005. Cross-lingual projection of role-semantic information. In *Proceedings of HLT/EMNLP 2005*, Vancouver, BC.

Sebastian Padó and Mirella Lapata. 2009. Cross-lingual Annotation Projection for Semantic Roles. *Journal of Artificial Intelligence Research*, 36(1):307–340.

F. Pedregosa, G. Varoquaux, A. Gramfort, V. Michel, B. Thirion, O. Grisel, M. Blondel, P. Prettenhofer, R. Weiss, V. Dubourg, J. Vanderplas, A. Passos, D. Cournapeau, M. Brucher, M. Perrot, and E. Duchesnay. 2011. Scikit-learn: Machine learning in Python. *Journal of Machine Learning Research*, 12:2825–2830.

Rudolf Rosa, Jan Masek, David Marecek, Martin Popel, Daniel Zeman, and Zdenek Zabokrtský. 2014. HamleDT 2.0: Thirty Dependency Treebanks Stanfordized. In *LREC*, pages 2334–2341.

Michael Roth and Anette Frank. 2015. Inducing Implicit Arguments from Comparable Texts: A Framework and its Applications. *Computational Linguistics*, 41(4):625–664.

Michael Roth and Kristian Woodsend. 2014. Composition of Word Representations Improves Semantic Role Labelling. In *EMNLP*, pages 407–413.

Josef Ruppenhofer, Caroline Sporleder, Roser Morante, Collin Baker, and Martha Palmer. 2010. Semeval-2010 task 10: Linking events and their participants in discourse. In *Proceedings of the 5th International Workshop on Semantic Evaluation*, pages 45–50.

Tanja Samardžic, Lonneke Van Der Plas, Goljihan Kashaeva, and Paola Merlo. 2010. The Scope and the Sources of Variation in Verbal Predicates in English and French. In *Proceedings of the Ninth International Workshop on Treebanks and Linguistic Theories*, pages 199–211.

Carina Silberer and Anette Frank. 2012. Casting Implicit Role Linking as an Anaphora Resolution Task. In *Proceedings of the First Joint Conference on Lexical and Computational Semantics-Volume 1: Proceedings of the main conference and the shared task, and Volume 2: Proceedings of the Sixth International Workshop on Semantic Evaluation*, pages 1–10.

Asher Stern and Ido Dagan. 2014. Recognizing implied predicate-argument relationships in textual inference. In *Proceedings of the 52nd Annual Meeting of the Association for Computational Linguistics (Volume 2: Short Papers)*, pages 739–744, Baltimore, Maryland.

Oscar Täckström, Kuzman Ganchev, and Dipanjan Das. 2015. Efficient inference and structured learning for semantic role labeling. *Transactions of the Association for Computational Linguistics*, 3:29–41.

Driving inversion transduction grammar induction
with semantic evaluation

Meriem Beloucif and **Dekai Wu**
Human Language Technology Center
Hong Kong University of Science and Technology
Clear Water Bay, Hong Kong
`mbeloucif|dekai@cs.ust.hk`

Abstract

We describe a new technique for improving statistical machine translation training by adopting scores from a recent crosslingual semantic frame based evaluation metric, XMEANT, as outside probabilities in expectation-maximization based ITG (inversion transduction grammars) alignment. Our new approach strongly biases early-stage SMT learning towards semantically valid alignments. Unlike previous attempts that have proposed using semantic frame based evaluation metrics as the objective function for late-stage tuning of less than a dozen loglinear mixture weights, our approach instead applies the semantic metric at one of the earliest stages of SMT training, where it may impact millions of model parameters. The choice of XMEANT is motivated by empirical studies that have shown ITG constraints to cover almost all crosslingual semantic frame alternations, which resemble the crosslingual semantic frame matching measured by XMEANT. Our experiments purposely restrict training data to small amounts to show the technique's utility in the absence of a huge corpus, to study the effects of semantic generalizations while avoiding overreliance on memorization. Results show that directly driving ITG training with the crosslingual semantic frame based objective function not only helps to further sharpen the ITG constraints, but still avoids excising relevant portions of the search space, and leads to better performance than either conventional ITG or GIZA++ based approaches.

1 Introduction

We propose a new technique that biases early stage statistical machine translation (SMT) learning towards semantics. Our algorithm adopts the crosslingual evaluation metric XMEANT (Lo *et al.*, 2014) to initialize expectation-maximization (EM) outside probabilities during inversion transduction grammar or ITG (Wu, 1997) induction. We show that injecting a crosslingual semantic frame based objective function in the actual learning of the translation model helps to bias the training of the SMT model towards semantically more relevant structures. Our approach is highly motivated by recent research which showed that including a semantic frame based objective function during the formal feature weights tuning stage increases the translation quality. More precisely, Lo *et al.* (2013a); Lo and Wu (2013); Lo *et al.* (2013b); Beloucif *et al.* (2014) showed that tuning against a semantic frame based evaluation metric like MEANT (Lo *et al.*, 2012), improves the translation adequacy.

Our choice to improve ITG alignments is motivated by the fact that they have already previously been empirically shown to cover essentially 100% of crosslingual semantic frame alternations, even though they rule out the majority of incorrect alignments (Addanki *et al.*, 2012). Our technique uses XMEANT for rewarding good translations while learning bilingual correlations of the translation model. We also show that integrating a semantic frame based objective function much earlier in the training pipeline not only produces more semantically correct alignments but also helps to learn bilingual correlations without memorizing from a huge amounts of parallel corpora. We report results and examples showing that this way for inducing ITGs gives a better translation quality compared to the conventional ITGs and GIZA++ (Och

*Proceedings of the Fifth Joint Conference on Lexical and Computational Semantics (*SEM 2016)*, pages 55–63,
Berlin, Germany, August 11-12, 2016.

and Ney, 2000) alignments.

2 Related work

The choice of XMEANT, a crosslingual version of MEANT (Lo and Wu, 2011, 2012; Lo *et al.*, 2012), is motivated by the work of Lo *et al.* (2014) who showed that XMEANT can correlate better with human adequacy judgement than most other metrics under some conditions. Furthermore, previous empirical studies have shown that the crosslingual semantic frame matching measured by XMEANT is fully covered within ITG constraints (Addanki *et al.*, 2012).

2.1 Inversion transduction grammars

Inversion transduction grammars (ITGs, Wu (1997)) are a subset of syntax-directed transduction grammar (Lewis and Stearns, 1968; Aho and Ullman, 1972). A transduction is a set of bisentences that define the relation between an input language L_0 and an output language L_1. Accordingly, a transduction grammar is able to generate, translate or accept a transduction or a set of bisentences. Inversion transductions are a subset of transduction which are synchronously generated and parsed by inversion transduction grammars (ITGs, (Wu, 1997)).

An ITG can always be written in a 2-normal form and it is represented by a tuple $\langle N, V_0, V_1, R, S \rangle$ where N is a set of nonterminals, V_0 and V_1 are the bitokens of L_0 and L_1 respectively, R is a set of transduction rules and $S \in N$ is the start symbol.

We can write each transduction rule as follows:

$$S \rightarrow A$$
$$A \rightarrow [BC]$$
$$A \rightarrow \langle BC \rangle$$
$$A \rightarrow e/\epsilon$$
$$A \rightarrow \epsilon/f$$
$$A \rightarrow e/f$$

ITGs allow both straight and inverted rules, straight transduction rules use square brackets and take the form $A \rightarrow [BC]$ and inverted rules use inverted brackets and take the form $A \rightarrow \langle BC \rangle$. Straight transduction rules generate transductions with the same order in L_0 and L_1 which means that, in the parse tree, the children instantiated by straight rules are read in the same order.

The rule probability function p is defined using fixed probabilities for the structural rules, and a translation table t that is trained using IBM model 1 (Brown *et al.*, 1993) in both directions.

There are different classes of inversion transduction grammars. LTGs or linear transduction grammars (Saers *et al.*, 2010) impose harsher constraints than ITGs but still cover almost 100% of verb frame alternations (Addanki *et al.*, 2012). There are also many ways to formulate the model over ITGs: Wu (1995); Zhang and Gildea (2005); Chiang (2007); Cherry and Lin (2007); Blunsom *et al.* (2009); Haghighi *et al.* (2009); Saers *et al.* (2010); Neubig *et al.* (2011).

In this work, we use BITGs or bracketing transduction grammars (Saers *et al.*, 2009) which only use one single nonterminal category and surprisingly achieve a good result.

2.2 Semantic frame based evaluation metrics

2.2.1 MEANT's algorithm

Unlike *n*-gram or edit-distance based metrics, the MEANT family of metrics (Lo and Wu, 2011, 2012; Lo *et al.*, 2012) adopt the principle that a good translation is one in which humans can successfully understand the general meaning of the input sentence as captured by the basic event structure: *who did what to whom, for whom, when, where, how and why* (Pradhan *et al.*, 2004). Recent work have shown that the semantic frame based metric, MEANT, correlates better with human adequacy judgment than most common evaluation metrics (Lo and Wu, 2011, 2012; Lo *et al.*, 2012) such as BLEU (Papineni *et al.*, 2002), NIST (Doddington, 2002), METEOR (Banerjee and Lavie, 2005), CDER (Leusch *et al.*, 2006), WER (Nießen *et al.*, 2000), and TER (Snover *et al.*, 2006).

Algorithm one in figure 2 shows how a MEANT score is computed (Lo and Wu, 2011, 2012; Lo *et al.*, 2012).

2.2.2 XMEANT: crosslingual MEANT

XMEANT (Lo *et al.*, 2014) is the crosslingual version of the semantic evaluation metric MEANT. It has been shown that the crosslingual evaluation metric, XMEANT, correlates even better with human adequacy judgment than MEANT, and also better than most evaluation metrics like BLEU (Papineni *et al.*, 2002), NIST (Doddington, 2002), METEOR (Banerjee and Lavie, 2005), CDER (Leusch *et al.*, 2006), WER (Nießen *et al.*, 2000), and TER (Snover *et al.*, 2006).

Unlike MEANT which needs expensive manmade references, XMEANT uses the foreign in-

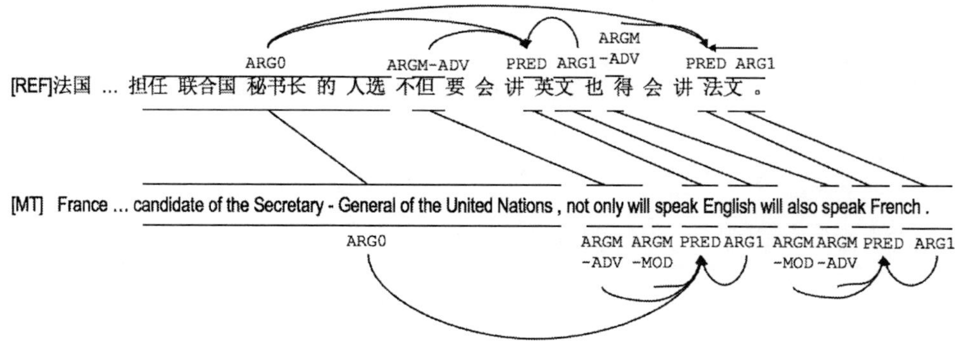

Figure 1: Example of how XMEANT aligns words and phrases

put to evaluate the MT translation output. Figure 1 shows an example of shallow semantic parsing in a Chinese input sentence and an English MT output. It also shows how XMEANT aligns the role fillers between two parallel sentences from different languages based on their semantic frames matching.

Figure 2 underlines the differences between MEANT and XMEANT algorithms. XMEANT uses MEANT's f-score based method for aggregating lexical translation probabilities within semantic role filler phrases. Each token of the role fillers in the output/input string is aligned to the token of the role fillers in the input/output string that has the maximum lexical translation probability. In contrast to MEANT which measures lexical similarity using a monolingual context vector model, XMEANT instead substitutes simple crosslingual lexical translation probabilities. The crosslingual phrasal similarities are computed as follows:

$$
\begin{aligned}
\mathbf{e}_{i,\mathrm{pred}} &\equiv \text{the output side of the pred of aligned frame } i \\
\mathbf{f}_{i,\mathrm{pred}} &\equiv \text{the input side of the pred of aligned frame } i \\
\mathbf{e}_{i,j} &\equiv \text{the output side of the ARG } j \text{ of aligned frame } i \\
\mathbf{f}_{i,j} &\equiv \text{the input side of the ARG } j \text{ of aligned frame } i \\
p(e,f) &= \sqrt{t(e|f)\,t(f|e)} \\
\mathrm{prec}_{\mathbf{e},\mathbf{f}} &= \frac{\sum_{e\in\mathbf{e}} \max_{f\in\mathbf{f}} p(e,f)}{|\mathbf{e}|} \\
\mathrm{rec}_{\mathbf{e},\mathbf{f}} &= \frac{\sum_{f\in\mathbf{f}} \max_{e\in\mathbf{e}} p(e,f)}{|\mathbf{f}|} \\
s_{i,\mathrm{pred}} &= \frac{2\cdot \mathrm{prec}_{\mathbf{e}_{i,\mathrm{pred}},\mathbf{f}_{i,\mathrm{pred}}} \cdot \mathrm{rec}_{\mathbf{e}_{i,\mathrm{pred}},\mathbf{f}_{i,\mathrm{pred}}}}{\mathrm{prec}_{\mathbf{e}_{i,\mathrm{pred}},\mathbf{f}_{i,\mathrm{pred}}} + \mathrm{rec}_{\mathbf{e}_{i,\mathrm{pred}},\mathbf{f}_{i,\mathrm{pred}}}} \\
s_{i,j} &= \frac{2\cdot \mathrm{prec}_{\mathbf{e}_{i,j},\mathbf{f}_{i,j}} \cdot \mathrm{rec}_{\mathbf{e}_{i,j},\mathbf{f}_{i,j}}}{\mathrm{prec}_{\mathbf{e}_{i,j},\mathbf{f}_{i,j}} + \mathrm{rec}_{\mathbf{e}_{i,j},\mathbf{f}_{i,j}}}
\end{aligned}
$$

where the joint probability p is defined as the har-

monic mean of the two directions of the translation table t trained using IBM model 1 (Brown *et al.*, 1993). $\mathrm{prec}_{\mathbf{e},\mathbf{f}}$ is the precision and $\mathrm{rec}_{\mathbf{e},\mathbf{f}}$ is the recall of the phrasal similarities of the role fillers. $s_{i,\mathrm{pred}}$ and $s_{i,j}$ are the f-scores of the phrasal similarities of the predicates and role fillers of the arguments of type j between the input and the MT output.

Our approach uses the XMEANT score of every bisentence in the training data and uses it to initialize the outside probability of the expectation-maximization algorithm, then uses this crucial information for weighting meaningful sentences to inducing bracketing inversion transduction grammars. We show in this paper that using this semantic objective function at an early stage of training SMT system, we are not only able to learn more semantic bilingual correlations between the two languages, but we are also able get rid of the heavy memorization that most of the conventional alignment systems rely heavily on.

2.3 Alignment

Word alignment is considered to be a necessary step in training SMT systems, it helps to learn bilingual correlations between the input and the output languages. In this work, we compare the alignment produced by our system to the traditional GIZA++ alignment and the conventional ITG alignment. Most of the conventional alignment algorithms: IBM models (Brown *et al.*, 1990) and hidden Markov models or HMM (Vogel *et al.*, 1996) are flat and directed. In fact, (a) they allow the unstructured movement of words leading to a weak word alignment, (b) consider translations in one direction in isolation, and (c)

Figure 2: MEANT vs XMEANT algorithms

Algorithm 1 MEANT algorithm

1. Apply *an output language* automatic shallow semantic parsing to *the reference translation* and to *the machine translation*.

2. Apply maximum weighted bipartite matching to align the semantic frames between *the reference translation* and *the machine translation*, according to **the lexical similarity** of the semantic predicates.

3. For each pair of aligned semantic frames, apply maximum weighted bipartite matching to align arguments between *the reference translation* and *the machine translation*, according to **the lexical similarity** of the semantic role fillers.

4. Compute the weighted f-score over the matching role labels of these aligned predicates and role fillers.

Algorithm 2 XMEANT algorithm

1. Apply *an input language* automatic shallow semantic parser *to the foreign input* and *an output language* automatic shallow semantic parser *to the MT output*.

2. Apply the maximum weighted bipartite matching algorithm to align the semantic frames between *the foreign input* and *the MT output* according to **the lexical translation probabilities** of the predicates.

3. For each pair of the aligned frames, apply the maximum weighted bipartite matching algorithm to align the arguments between *the foreign input* and *the MT output* according to the **aggregated phrasal translation probabilities** of the role fillers.

4. Compute the weighted f-score over the matching role labels of these aligned predicates and role fillers according to the definitions similar to MEANT.

Figure 2: MEANT vs XMEANT algorithms

need two separate alignments to form a single *bidirectional alignment*. The harmonization of two directed alignments is typically done heuristically. This means that there is no model that considers the final bidirectional alignment that the translation system is trained on to be optimal. Inversion transduction grammars (Wu, 1997), on the other hand, have proven that learning word alignments using a system that is compositionally-structured, can provide *optimal bidirectional alignments*. Although this structured optimality comes at a higher cost in terms of time complexity, it allows preexisting structured information to be incorporated into the model. It also allows models to be compared in a meaningful way. Saers and Wu (2009) proposed a better method of producing word alignment by training inversion transduction grammars (Wu, 1997). One problem encountered with such model was that the exhaustive biparsing that runs in $O(n^6)$. Saers *et al.* (2009) proposed a more efficient algorithm that runs in $O(n^3)$.

Zens and Ney (2003) showed that ITG constraints allow a higher flexibility in word-ordering for longer sentences than the conventional IBM model. Furthermore, they demonstrate that applying ITG constraints for word alignment leads to learning a significantly better alignment than the constraints used in conventional IBM models for both German-English and French-English language pairs. Zhang and Gildea (2005) on the other hand showed that the tree learned while training using ITG constraints gives much more accurate word alignments than those trained on manually annotated treebanks like in Yamada

and Knight (2001) in both Chinese-English and German-English. Haghighi *et al.* (2009) show that using ITG constraints for supervised word alignment methods not only produce alignments without lower alignment error rates but also produces a better translation quality.

Some of the previous work on word alignment used morphological and syntactic features (De Gispert *et al.*, 2006). Log linear models have been proposed to incorporate those features (Chris *et al.*, 2011). The problem with those approaches is that they require language specific knowledge and they always work better on more morphological rich languages.

A few studies that try to integrate some semantic knowledge in computing word alignment are proposed by Jeff *et al.* (2011) and Theerawat and David (2014). However, the former needs to have a prior word alignment learned on lexical items. The latter proposes a semantically oriented word alignment, but requires extracting word similarities from the monolingual data first, before producing alignment using word similarities.

3   Adopting XMEANT scores as EM outside probabilities

We implemented a token based BITG system as our ITG baseline, our choice of BITG is motivated by previous work that showed that BITG alignments outperformed alignments from GIZA++ (Saers *et al.*, 2009).

Figure 3 shows the BITG induction algorithm that we used in this paper. We initialize it with

---

Algorithm Token based ITG-indcution and alignment.

C ▷ The parallel corpus
c ▷ The rule counts
$G = \langle N, W_0, W_1, R, S \rangle$ ▷ The empty ITG
$A \in N$ ▷ The bracketing symbol
p ▷ The rule probability function to estimate
a ▷ The alignments
$sum \leftarrow 0$ ▷ The sum of all counts
$R \leftarrow R \cup \{S \to A, A \to [AA], A \to \langle AA \rangle\}$
$p(S \to A) = 1$
$p(A \to [AA]) = \frac{1}{4}$
$p(A \to \langle AA \rangle) = \frac{1}{4}$
for parallel sentences $e_{0..T}/f_{0..V} \in C$ **do**
    for $0 \leq s < T$ **do**
        $W_0 \leftarrow W_0 \cup \{e_{s..s+1}\}$
        $R \leftarrow R \cup \{A \to e_{s..s+1}/\epsilon\}$
        $c_{A \to e_{s..s+1}/\epsilon} \leftarrow c_{A \to e_{s..s+1}/\epsilon} + 1$
        $sum \leftarrow sum + 1$
    for $0 \leq u < V$ **do**
        $W_1 \leftarrow W_1 \cup \{f_{u..u+1}\}$
        $R \leftarrow R \cup \{A \to \epsilon/f_{u..u+1}\}$
        $c_{A \to \epsilon/f_{u..u+1}} \leftarrow c_{A \to \epsilon/f_{u..u+1}} + 1$
        $sum \leftarrow sum + 1$
    for $0 \leq s < T$ **do**
        for $0 \leq u < V$ **do**
            $R \leftarrow R \cup \{A \to e_{s..s+1}/f_{u..u+1}\}$
            $c_{A \to e_{s..s+1}/f_{u..u+1}} \leftarrow c_{A \to e_{s..s+1}/f_{u..u+1}} + 1$
            $sum \leftarrow sum + 1$
for rule $A \to e/f \in R$ **do**
    $p(A \to e/f) \leftarrow \frac{1}{2} \frac{c_{A \to e/f}}{sum}$
repeat
    $p \leftarrow reestimate\_with\_em(G, p, C)$
until convergence
for parallel sentences $e_{0..T}/f_{0..V} \in C$ **do**
    $a_{e_{0..T}/f_{0..V}} \leftarrow viterbi\_parse(G, p, e_{0..T}/f_{0..V})$
return a

Figure 3: Token based BITG induction algorithm

Table 1: Comparison of translation quality for three methods used to train Moses for Chinese-English MT under small corpus IWSLT 2007 conditions

	cased		uncased	
System	BLEU	TER	BLEU	TER
Giza++ based induction	19.23	63.94	19.83	63.40
ITG based induction	20.05	63.19	20.42	62.61
XMEANT outside probabilities based	**27.59**	**59.48**	**28.54**	**58.81**

uniform structural probabilities, setting aside half of the probability mass for lexical rules. This probability mass is distributed among the lexical rules according to co-occurrence counts from the training data, assuming each sentence to contain one empty token to account for singletons. The novelty in our model consists of adopting the XMEANT score of each bisentence as the initial value for the outside probabilities as follows:

$$\beta_{(0,|\mathbf{e}_i|,0,|\mathbf{f}_i|)} = XMEANT(\mathbf{e}_i, \mathbf{f}_i) \qquad (1)$$

where i represents the bisentences number i in the corpus.

These initial probabilities are refined with 10 iterations of expectation maximization where the expectation step is calculated using beam pruned parsing (Saers *et al.*, 2009) with a beam width of 100. On the last iteration, we extract the alignments imposed by the Viterbi parses as the word alignments outputted by the system.

In our experiments, we tried to show that including semantic earlier in learning SMT systems can help us get rid of the expensive huge corpora used in the traditional SMT training. Although Chinese is not a low resource language, we tried purposely to simulate low resource conditions, we used a relatively small corpus (IWSLT07). The training set contained 39,953 sentences. The dev set and test set were the same for all systems in order to keep

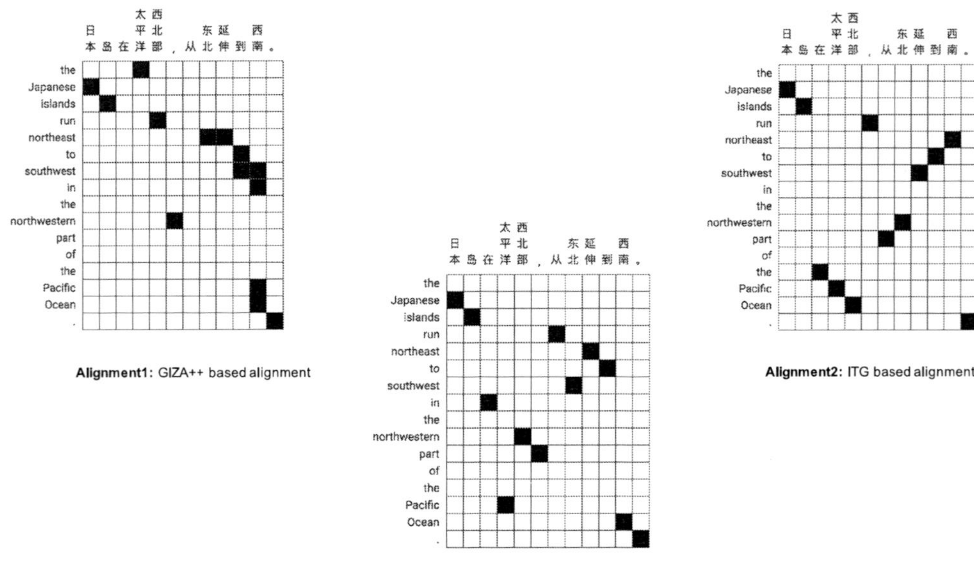

Alignment1: GIZA++ based alignment

Alignment3: XMEANT as outside probability based alignment

Alignment2: ITG based alignment

Figure 4: Alignments of bisentences produced by the three discussed alignment systems

the experiments comparable.

We compare the performance of our proposed semantic frame based alignment to the conventional ITG alignment and to the traditional GIZA++ baseline with grow-diag-final-and to harmonize both alignment directions. We tested the different alignments described above by using the standard Moses toolkit (Koehn *et al.*, 2007), and a 6-gram language model learned with the SRI language model toolkit (Stolcke, 2002) to train our model.

4 Results

We compared the performance of the semantic frame based ITG alignment against both the conventional ITG alignment and the traditional GIZA++ alignment. We evaluated our MT output using the surface based evaluation metric BLEU (Papineni *et al.*, 2002) and the edit distance evaluation metric TER (Snover *et al.*, 2006). Table 1 shows that the alignment based on our proposed algorithm helps achieving much higher scores in term of BLEU and TER in comparison to both conventional ITG and GIZA++ alignment.

Figure 4 illustrates the alignments generated by the three systems described in this paper for a given example. The traditional GIZA++ alignment (top left) and the conventional ITG alignment (top right) fail to align all the crucial parts

of the given bisentence. The English sentence can be divided into three major parts: "the Japanese islands", "run northeast to southwest" and "in the northwest part of the pacific ocean.". The conventional ITG based alignment only succeeds to align the first part of the sentence. GIZA++ based system correctly aligns part one and parts of part two. We note from the sentence's gloss (figure 5) that our proposed alignment outperforms the two other alignments by capturing the relevant information in both part one and part three, and also successfully aligns the token "in" to "在".

Figure 6 shows four interesting examples extracted from our translated data and compared to the translations obtained by other systems. We see from the examples that ITG based models can produce a slightly better outputs compared to GIZA++ based alignment, but our semantic frame based alignment highly outperform both alignments. We clearly see how the outputs from our new submitted system capture more strong bilingual correlations although we are using the same small corpus for every system. In example 2 and 4, our system produces a translation that is as good as the human reference. For example number one, our system produces a more precise translation than the human reference since the Chinese character "偷" is normally translated to "stolen" and not "pickpocketed". Example 3, our proposed system

English: the Japanese islands run northeast to southwest in the northwestern part of the Pacific Ocean.
Chinese: 日本　　　島 在 太平洋　　　西北部 ， 　　从 东北 延伸到 西南 　　。
Gloss: Japanese islands in pacific ocean northwestern   part from northeast run to southwest .

Figure 5: The gloss of the bisentence used in figure 4

Example 1

Input	在 地铁 里 钱包 被 偷 了 。
Gloss	in subway in wallet steal
Reference	I had my wallet pickpocketed in the subway .
GIZA++	the subway in my wallet was stolen .
ITG	the subway in my wallet was stolen .
XMEANT based	my wallet was stolen in the subway .

Example 2

Input	我 想 往 日本 寄 航空 邮件 。
Gloss	I want to Japan send air mail
Reference	I 'd like to send it to Japan by airmail .
GIZA++	I 'd like to Japan by air mail .
ITG	I 'd like to call to Japan by air mail .
XMEANT based	I 'd like to send it to Japan by air mail .

Example 3

Input	在 这儿 能 买到 歌剧 的 票吗 ?
Gloss	at here can buy opera ticket?
Reference	can I get an opera ticket here ?
GIZA++	here you can buy tickets
ITG	where can I buy tickets for " The here ?
XMEANT based	where can I buy a ticket for the opera here ?

Example 4

Input	我 的 座位 在 哪里 ?
Gloss	I 's seat at where
Reference	where is my seat ?
GIZA++	my seat is?
ITG	my seat is where ?
XMEANT based	where 's my seat ?

Figure 6: Four interesting examples comparing the output from the three discussed alignment systems

give the most accurate and understandable translation among all systems. The only small problem with this output is the fact that the Chinese character "在" which represents "at" but sometimes gets translated to "where".

The results and examples we see above show that we should be more focused on incorporating semantic information during the actual early-stage learning of the translation model's structure, rather than merely tuning a handful of late-stage loglinear mixture weights against a semantic objective function.

5 Conclusion

We presented a semantic frame based alignment method that adopts the crosslingual semantic evaluation metric, XMEANT, as expectation maximization (EM) outside probabilities for inversion transduction grammar (ITG) induction. We show that our new approach biases early stage SMT training towards semantics by injecting a semantic frame objective function in the initial steps of learning the translation model. Incorporating the semantic frame based objective function at the early stage of induction biases ITG alignments at a point where it still has the potential to influence millions of model parameters. Finally, we show that directly driving ITG induction with a crosslingual semantic frame objective function not only helps to further sharpen the ITG constraints, but still avoids excising relevant portions of the search space, and leads to better performance than either conventional ITG or GIZA++ based approaches.

6 Acknowledgment

This material is based upon work supported in part by the Defense Advanced Research Projects Agency (DARPA) under LORELEI contract HR0011-15-C-0114, BOLT contracts HR0011-12-C-0014 and HR0011-12-C-0016, and GALE contracts HR0011-06-C-0022 and HR0011-06-C-0023; by the European Union under the Horizon 2020 grant agreement 645452 (QT21) and FP7 grant agreement 287658; and by the Hong Kong

Research Grants Council (RGC) research grants GRF16210714, GRF16214315, GRF620811 and GRF621008. Any opinions, findings and conclusions or recommendations expressed in this material are those of the authors and do not necessarily reflect the views of DARPA, the EU, or RGC.

References

Karteek Addanki, Chi-kiu Lo, Markus Saers, and Dekai Wu. LTG vs. ITG coverage of cross-lingual verb frame alternations. In *16th Annual Conference of the European Association for Machine Translation (EAMT-2012)*, Trento, Italy, May 2012.

Alfred V. Aho and Jeffrey D. Ullman. *The Theory of Parsing, Translation, and Compiling*. Prentice-Halll, Englewood Cliffs, New Jersey, 1972.

Satanjeev Banerjee and Alon Lavie. METEOR: An automatic metric for MT evaluation with improved correlation with human judgments. In *Workshop on Intrinsic and Extrinsic Evaluation Measures for Machine Translation and/or Summarization*, Ann Arbor, Michigan, June 2005.

Meriem Beloucif, Chi kiu Lo, and Dekai Wu. Improving meant based semantically tuned smt. In *11 th International Workshop on spoken Language Translation (IWSLT 2014), 34-41 Lake Tahoe, California*, 2014.

Phil Blunsom, Trevor Cohn, Chris Dyer, and Miles Osborne. A Gibbs sampler for phrasal synchronous grammar induction. In *Joint Conference of the 47th Annual Meeting of the Association for Computational Linguistics and 4th International Joint Conference on Natural Language Processing of the AFNLP (ACL-IJCNLP 2009)*, pages 782–790, Suntec, Singapore, August 2009.

Peter F. Brown, John Cocke, Stephen A. Della Pietra, Vincent J. Della Pietra, Frederik Jelinek, John D. Lafferty, Robert L. Mercer, and Paul S. Roossin. A statistical approach to machine translation. *Computational Linguistics*, 16(2):79–85, 1990.

Peter F. Brown, Stephen A. Della Pietra, Vincent J. Della Pietra, and Robert L. Mercer. The mathematics of machine translation: Parameter estimation. *Computational Linguistics*, 19(2):263–311, 1993.

Colin Cherry and Dekang Lin. Inversion transduction grammar for joint phrasal translation modeling. In *Syntax and Structure in Statistical Translation (SSST)*, pages 17–24, Rochester, New York, April 2007.

David Chiang. Hierarchical phrase-based translation. *Computational Linguistics*, 33(2):201–228, 2007.

Dyer Chris, Clark Jonathan, Lavie Alon, and A.Smith Noah. Unsupervised word alignment with arbitrary features. In *49th Annual Meeting of the Association for Computational Linguistics*, 2011.

Adrià De Gispert, Deepa Gupta, Maja Popovic, Patrik Lambert, Jose B.Marino, Marcello Federico, Hermann Ney, and Rafael Banchs. Improving statistical word alignment with morpho-syntactic transformations. In *Advances in Natural Language Processing*, pages 368–379, 2006.

George Doddington. Automatic evaluation of machine translation quality using n-gram co-occurrence statistics. In *The second international conference on Human Language Technology Research (HLT '02)*, San Diego, California, 2002.

Aria Haghighi, John Blitzer, John DeNero, and Dan Klein. Better word alignments with supervised ITG models. In *Joint Conference of the 47th Annual Meeting of the Association for Computational Linguistics and 4th International Joint Conference on Natural Language Processing of the AFNLP (ACL-IJCNLP 2009)*, pages 923–931, Suntec, Singapore, August 2009.

Ma Jeff, Matsoukas Spyros, and Schwartz Richard. Improving low-resource statistical machine translation with a novel semantic word clustering algorithm. In *Proceedings of the MT Summit XIII*, 2011.

Philipp Koehn, Hieu Hoang, Alexandra Birch, Chris Callison-Burch, Marcello Federico, Nicola Bertoldi, Brooke Cowan, Wade Shen, Christine Moran, Richard Zens, Chris Dyer, Ondrej Bojar, Alexandra Constantin, and Evan Herbst. Moses: Open source toolkit for statistical machine translation. In *Interactive Poster and Demonstration Sessions of the 45th Annual Meeting of the Association for Computational Linguistics (ACL 2007)*, pages 177–180, Prague, Czech Republic, June 2007.

Gregor Leusch, Nicola Ueffing, and Hermann Ney. CDer: Efficient MT evaluation using block movements. In *11th Conference of the European Chapter of the Association for Computational Linguistics (EACL-2006)*, 2006.

Philip M. Lewis and Richard E. Stearns. Syntax-directed transduction. *Journal of the Association for Computing Machinery*, 15(3):465–488, 1968.

Chi-kiu Lo and Dekai Wu. MEANT: An inexpensive, high-accuracy, semi-automatic metric for evaluating translation utility based on semantic roles. In *49th Annual Meeting of the Association for Computational Linguistics: Human Language Technologies (ACL HLT 2011)*, 2011.

Chi-kiu Lo and Dekai Wu. Unsupervised vs. supervised weight estimation for semantic MT evaluation metrics. In *Sixth Workshop on Syntax, Semantics and Structure in Statistical Translation (SSST-6)*, 2012.

Chi-kiu Lo and Dekai Wu. Can informal genres be better translated by tuning on automatic semantic metrics? In *14th Machine Translation Summit (MT Summit XIV)*, 2013.

Chi-kiu Lo, Anand Karthik Tumuluru, and Dekai Wu. Fully automatic semantic MT evaluation. In *7th Workshop on Statistical Machine Translation (WMT 2012)*, 2012.

Chi-kiu Lo, Karteek Addanki, Markus Saers, and Dekai Wu. Improving machine translation by training against an automatic semantic frame based evaluation metric. In *51st Annual Meeting of the Association for Computational Linguistics (ACL 2013)*, 2013.

Chi-kiu Lo, Meriem Beloucif, and Dekai Wu. Improving machine translation into Chinese by tuning against Chinese MEANT. In *International Workshop on Spoken Language Translation (IWSLT 2013)*, 2013.

Chi-kiu Lo, Meriem Beloucif, Markus Saers, and Dekai Wu. XMEANT: Better semantic MT evaluation without reference translations. In *52nd Annual Meeting of the Association for Computational Linguistics (ACL 2014)*, 2014.

Graham Neubig, Taro Watanabe, Eiichiro Sumita, Shinsuke Mori, and Tatsuya Kawahara. An unsupervised model for joint phrase alignment and extraction. In *49th Annual Meeting of the Association for Computational Linguistics: Human Language Technologies (ACL HLT 2011)*, pages 632–641, Portland, Oregon, June 2011.

Sonja Nießen, Franz Josef Och, Gregor Leusch, and Hermann Ney. A evaluation tool for machine translation: Fast evaluation for MT research. In *The Second International Con-*

ference on Language Resources and Evaluation (LREC 2000), 2000.

Franz Josef Och and Hermann Ney. Improved statistical alignment models. In *The 38th Annual Meeting of the Association for Computational Linguistics (ACL 2000)*, pages 440–447, Hong Kong, October 2000.

Kishore Papineni, Salim Roukos, Todd Ward, and Wei-Jing Zhu. BLEU: a method for automatic evaluation of machine translation. In *40th Annual Meeting of the Association for Computational Linguistics (ACL-02)*, pages 311–318, Philadelphia, Pennsylvania, July 2002.

Sameer Pradhan, Wayne Ward, Kadri Hacioglu, James H. Martin, and Dan Jurafsky. Shallow semantic parsing using support vector machines. In *Human Language Technology Conference of the North American Chapter of the Association for Computational Linguistics (HLT-NAACL 2004)*, 2004.

Markus Saers and Dekai Wu. Improving phrase-based translation via word alignments from stochastic inversion transduction grammars. In *Third Workshop on Syntax and Structure in Statistical Translation (SSST-3)*, pages 28–36, Boulder, Colorado, June 2009.

Markus Saers, Joakim Nivre, and Dekai Wu. Learning stochastic bracketing inversion transduction grammars with a cubic time biparsing algorithm. In *11th International Conference on Parsing Technologies (IWPT'09)*, pages 29–32, Paris, France, October 2009.

Markus Saers, Joakim Nivre, and Dekai Wu. Word alignment with stochastic bracketing linear inversion transduction grammar. In *Human Language Technologies: The 2010 Annual Conference of the North American Chapter of the Association for Computational Linguistics (NAACL HLT 2010)*, pages 341–344, Los Angeles, California, June 2010.

Matthew Snover, Bonnie Dorr, Richard Schwartz, Linnea Micciulla, and John Makhoul. A study of translation edit rate with targeted human annotation. In *7th Biennial Conference Association for Machine Translation in the Americas (AMTA 2006)*, pages 223–231, Cambridge, Massachusetts, August 2006.

Andreas Stolcke. SRILM – an extensible language modeling toolkit. In *7th International Conference on Spoken Language Processing (ICSLP2002 - INTERSPEECH 2002)*, pages 901–904, Denver, Colorado, September 2002.

Songyot Theerawat and Chiang David. Improving word alignment using word similarity. In *52nd Annual Meeting of the Association for Computational Linguistics*, 2014.

Stephan Vogel, Hermann Ney, and Christoph Tillmann. HMM-based word alignment in statistical translation. In *The 16th International Conference on Computational linguistics (COLING-96)*, volume 2, pages 836–841, 1996.

Dekai Wu. Trainable coarse bilingual grammars for parallel text bracketing. In *Third Annual Workshop on Very Large Corpora (WVLC-3)*, pages 69–81, Cambridge, Massachusetts, June 1995.

Dekai Wu. Stochastic inversion transduction grammars and bilingual parsing of parallel corpora. *Computational Linguistics*, 23(3):377–403, 1997.

Kenji Yamada and Kevin Knight. A syntax-based statistical translation model. In *39th Annual Meeting of the Association for Computational Linguistics and 10th Conference of the European Chapter of the Association for Computational Linguistics*, pages 523–530, Toulouse, France, July 2001.

Richard Zens and Hermann Ney. A comparative study on reordering constraints in statistical machine translation. In *41st Annual Meeting of the Association for Computational Linguistics (ACL-2003)*, pages 144–151, Stroudsburg, Pennsylvania, 2003.

Hao Zhang and Daniel Gildea. Stochastic lexicalized inversion transduction grammar for alignment. In *43rd Annual Meeting of the Association for Computational Linguistics (ACL-05)*, pages 475–482, Ann Arbor, Michigan, June 2005.

Natural Solution to FraCaS Entailment Problems

Lasha Abzianidze
TiLPS, Tilburg University, the Netherlands
L.Abzianidze@uvt.nl

Abstract

Reasoning over several premises is not a common feature of RTE systems as it usually requires deep semantic analysis. On the other hand, FraCaS is a collection of entailment problems consisting of multiple premises and covering semantically challenging phenomena. We employ the tableau theorem prover for natural language to solve the FraCaS problems in a *natural* way. The expressiveness of a type theory, the transparency of natural logic and the schematic nature of tableau inference rules make it easy to model challenging semantic phenomena. The efficiency of theorem proving also becomes challenging when reasoning over several premises. After adapting to the dataset, the prover demonstrates state-of-the-art competence over certain sections of FraCaS.

1 Introduction

Understanding and automatically processing the natural language semantics is a central task for computational linguistics and its related fields. At the same time, inference tasks are regarded as the best way of testing an NLP systems's semantic capacity (Cooper et al., 1996, p. 63). Following this view, recognizing textual entailment (RTE) challenges (Dagan et al., 2005) were regularly held which evaluate the RTE systems based on the RTE dataset. The RTE data represents a set of text-hypotheses pairs that are human annotated on the inference relations: *entailment*, *contradiction* and *neutral*. Hence it attempts to evaluate the systems on human reasoning. In general, the RTE datasets are created semi-automatically and are often motivated by the scenarios found in the applications like question answering, relation extraction, infor-

mation retrieval and summarization (Dagan et al., 2005; Dagan et al., 2013). On the other hand, the semanticists are busy designing theories that account for the valid logical relations over natural language sentences. These theories usually model reasoning that depends on certain semantic phenomena, e.g., Booleans, quantifiers, events, attitudes, intensionality, monotonicity, etc. These types of reasoning are weak points of RTE systems as the above mentioned semantic phenomena are underrepresented in the RTE datasets.

In order to test and train the weak points of an RTE system, we choose the FraCaS dataset (Cooper et al., 1996). The set contains complex entailment problems covering various challenging semantic phenomena which are still not fully mastered by RTE systems. Moreover, unlike the standard RTE datasets, FraCaS also allows multi-premised problems. To account for these complex entailment problems, we employ the theorem prover for higher-order logic (Abzianidze, 2015a), which represents the version of formal logic motivated by *natural logic* (Lakoff, 1970; Van Benthem, 1986). Though such expressive logics usually come with the inefficient decision procedures, the prover maintains efficiency by using the inference rules that are specially tailored for the reasoning in natural language. We introduce new rules for the prover in light of the FraCaS problems and test the rules against the relevant portion of the set. The test results are compared to the current state-of-the-art on the dataset.

The rest of the paper is structured as follows. We start with introducing a tableau system for natural logic (Muskens, 2010). Section 3 explores the FraCaS dataset in more details. In Section 4, we describe the process of adapting the theorem prover to FraCaS, i.e. how specific semantic phenomena are modeled with the help of tableau rules. Several premises with monotone quantifiers in-

*Proceedings of the Fifth Joint Conference on Lexical and Computational Semantics (*SEM 2016)*, pages 64–74,
Berlin, Germany, August 11-12, 2016.

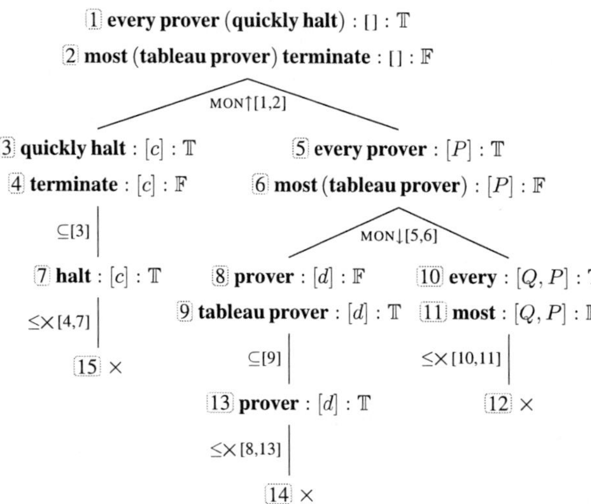

Figure 1: A closed tableau proves that *every prover halts quickly* entails *most tableau provers terminate*. Each branch growth is marked with the corresponding rule application.

crease the search space for proofs. In Section 5, we present several rules that contribute to shorter proofs. In the evaluation part (Section 6), we analyze the results of the prover on the relevant FraCaS sections and compare them with the related RTE systems. We end with possible directions of future work.

2 Tableau theorem prover for natural language

Reasoning in formal logics (i.e., a formal language with well-defined semantics) is carried out by automated theorem provers, where the provers come in different forms based on their underlying proof system. In order to mirror this scenario for reasoning in natural language, Muskens (2010) proposed to approximate natural language with a version of natural logic (Lakoff, 1970; Van Benthem, 1986; Sánchez-Valencia, 1991) while a version of analytic tableau method (Beth, 1955; Hintikka, 1955; Smullyan, 1968), hereafter referred to as *natural tableau*, is introduced as a proof system for the logic. The version of natural logic employed by Muskens (2010) is higher-order logic formulated in terms of the typed lambda calculus (Church, 1940).[1] As a result, the logic is

much more expressive (in the sence of modeling certian phenomena in an intuitive way) than first-order logic, e.g., it can naturally account for generalized quantifiers (Montague, 1973; Barwise and Cooper, 1981), monotonicity calculus (Van Benthem, 1986; Sánchez-Valencia, 1991; Icard and Moss, 2014) and subsective adjectives.

What makes the logic *natural* are its terms, called Lambda Logical Forms (LLFs), which are built up only from variables and lexical constants via the functional application and λ-abstraction. In this way the LLFs have a more natural appearance than, for instance, the formulas of first-order logic. The examples of LLFs are given in the nodes of the tableau proof tree in Figure 1, where the type information for terms is omitted. A tableau node can be seen as a statement of truth type which is structured as a triplet of a main LLF, an argument list of terms and a truth sign. The semantics associated with a tableau node is that the application of the main LLF to the terms of an argument list is evaluated according to the truth sign. For instance, the node 9 is interpreted as the term **tableau prover** d being true, i.e. d is in the extension of **tableau prover**. Notice that LLFs not only resemble surface forms in terms of lexical elements but most of their constituents are in correspondence too. This facilitates the automatized generation of LLFs from surface forms.

The natural tableau system of (Muskens, 2010), like any other tableau systems (D'Agostino et al., 1999), tries to prove statements by refuting them. For instance, in case of an entailment proof, a tableau starts with the counterexample where the premises are true and the conclusion is false. The proof is further developed with the help of schematic inference rules, called tableau rules (see Figure 2). A tableau is closed if all its branches are closed, i.e. are marked with a closure ($\times$) sign. A tableau branch intuitively corresponds to a situation while a closed branch represents an inconsistent situation. Refutation of a statement fails if a closed tableau is obtained. Hence the closed tableau serves as a proof for the statement. The proof of an entailment in terms of the closed tableau is demonstrated in Figure 1. The tableau starts with the counterexample (1,2) of the entailment. It is further developed by applying the rule (MON↑) to 1 and 2, taking into account that

<hr>

[1]More specifically, the logic is two-sorted variant of Russell's type theory, which according to Gallin (1975) represents a more general and neat formulation of Montague (1970)'s intensional logic. For theorem proving, we employ one-sorted type theory, i.e. with the entity e and truth t types, and hence omit a type s for world-time pairs.

$$
\frac{G\,A : [\vec{C}] : \mathbb{T} \qquad H\,B : [\vec{C}] : \mathbb{F}}{A : [\vec{d}] : \mathbb{T} \quad G : [P, \vec{C}] : \mathbb{T} \qquad B : [\vec{d}] : \mathbb{F} \quad H : [P, \vec{C}] : \mathbb{F}} \; \mathrm{MON}{\uparrow}
$$

G or H is mon$\uparrow$ and $\vec{d}$ and P are fresh

$$
\frac{G\,A : [\vec{C}] : \mathbb{T} \qquad H\,B : [\vec{C}] : \mathbb{F}}{A : [\vec{d}] : \mathbb{F} \quad G : [P, \vec{C}] : \mathbb{T} \qquad B : [\vec{d}] : \mathbb{T} \quad H : [P, \vec{C}] : \mathbb{F}} \; \mathrm{MON}{\downarrow}
$$

G or H is mon$\downarrow$ and $\vec{d}$ and P are fresh

$$
\frac{A\,N : [\vec{C}] : \mathbb{T}}{N : [\vec{C}] : \mathbb{T}} \subseteq \text{ where } A \text{ is subsective}
$$

$$
\frac{A : [\vec{C}] : \mathbb{T} \qquad B : [\vec{C}] : \mathbb{F}}{\times} \leq\!\times \; \begin{array}{l}\text{where } A \text{ entails } B \\ \text{written as } A \leq B\end{array}
$$

Figure 2: The tableau rules employed by the tableau proof in Figure 1

every is upward monotone in the second argument position. The rule application is carried out until all branches are closed or no new rule application is possible. In the running example, all the branches close as ($\leq\!\times$) identifies inconsistencies there; for instance, ⟨4⟩ and ⟨7⟩ are inconsistent according to ($\leq\!\times$) assuming that a knowledge base (KB) provides that *halting* entails *termination*, i.e. **halt $\leq$ terminate**.

The natural tableau system was succesfully applied to the SICK textual entailment problems (Marelli et al., 2014) by Abzianidze (2015a). In particular, the theorem prover for natural language, called LangPro, was implemented that integrates three modules: the parsers for Combinatory Categorial Grammar (CCG) (Steedman, 2000), LLFgen that generates LLFs from the CCG derivation trees, and the natural logic tableau prover (NLogPro) which builds tableau proofs. The pipeline architecture of the prover is depicted in Figure 3: the sentences of an input problem are first parsed, then converted into LLFs, which are further processed by NLogPro. For a CCG parser, there are at least two options, C&C (Clark and Curran, 2007; Honnibal et al., 2010) and Easy-CCG (Lewis and Steedman, 2014). The inventory of rules (IR) of NLogPro is a crucial component for the prover; it contains most of the rules found

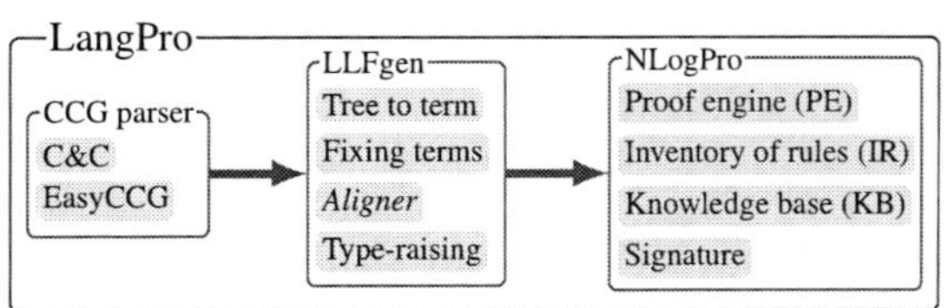

Figure 3: The architecture of LangPro

in (Muskens, 2010) and also additional rules that were collected from SICK. In order to make theorem proving robust, LangPro employs a conservative extension of the type theory for accessing the syntactic information of terms (Abzianidze, 2015b): in addition to the basic semantic types e and t, the extended type theory incorporates basic syntactic types n, np, s and pp corresponding to the primitive categories of CCG.

Abzianidze (2015a) shows that on the unseen portion of SICK LangPro obtains the results comparable to the state-of-the-art scores while achieving an almost perfect precision. Based on this inspiring result, we decide to adapt and test LangPro on the FraCaS problems, from the semantics point of view much more harder than the SICK ones.[2]

3 FraCaS dataset

The FraCaS test suite (Cooper et al., 1996) is a set of 346 test problems. It was prepared by the FraCaS consortium as an initial benchmark for semantic competence of NLP systems. Each FraCaS problem is a pair of premises and a yes-no-unknown question that is annotated with a gold judgment: *yes* (entailment), *no* (contradiction), or *unknown* (neutral). The problems mainly consist of short sentences and resemble the problems found in introductory logic books. To convert the test suite into the style of RTE dataset, MacCartney and Manning (2007) translated the questions into declarative sentences. The judgments were copied from the original test suite with slight modifications.[3] Several problems drawn from the obtained FraCaS dataset are presented in Table 1.

Unlike other RTE datasets, the FraCaS problems contain multiple premises (45% of the total

---

[2] An online version of LangPro is available at: `http://lanthanum.uvt.nl/labziani/tableau/`

[3] More details about the conversion, including information about several *noisy* problems (e.g., a problem missing a premise or hypothesis, or having a non-standard gold answer) can be found in MacCartney (2009). The FraCaS RTE dataset is available at: `http://www-nlp.stanford.edu/~wcmac/downloads/fracas.xml`

problems) and are structured in sections according to the semantic phenomena they concern. The sections cover generalized quantifiers (GQs), plurals, anaphora, ellipsis, adjectives, comparatives, temporal reference, verbs and attitudes. Due to the challenging problems it contains, the FraCaS dataset can be seen as one of the most complex RTE data from the semantics perspective. Unfortunately, due to its small size the dataset is not representative enough for system evaluation purposes. The above mentioned facts perhaps are the main reasons why the FraCaS data is less favored for developing and assessing the semantic competence of RTE systems. Nevertheless, several RTE systems (MacCartney and Manning, 2008; Angeli and Manning, 2014; Lewis and Steedman, 2013; Tian et al., 2014; Mineshima et al., 2015) were trained and evaluated on (the parts of) the dataset. Usually the goal of these evaluations is to show that specific theories/frameworks and the corresponding RTE systems are able to model deep semantic reasoning over the phenomena found in FraCaS. Our aim is also the same in the rest of the sections.

4 Modeling semantic phenomena

Modeling a new semantic phenomenon in the natural tableau requires introduction of special rules. The section presents the new rules that account for certain semantic phenomena found in FraCaS.

FraCaS Section 1, in short FrSec-1, focuses on GQs and their monotonicity properties. Since the rules for monotonicity are already implemented in LangPro, in order to model monotonicity behavior of a new GQ, it is sufficient to define its monotonicity features in the signature. For instance, *few* is defined as $\mathbf{few}_{n\downarrow,vp\downarrow,s}$ while *many* and *most* are modeled as $\mathbf{many}_{n,vp\uparrow,s}$ and $\mathbf{most}_{n,vp\uparrow,s}$ respectively.[4] The contrast between monotonicity properties of the first arguments of **few** and **many** is conditioned solely by the intuition behind the FraCaS problems: *few* is understood as an absolute amount while *many* as proportional (see Fr-56 and 76 in Table 1). Accounting for the monotonicity properties of *most*, i.e. $\mathbf{most}_{n,vp\uparrow,s}$, is not sufficient for fully capturing its semantics. For instance, solving Fr-26 requires more than just up-

ID	FraCaS entailment problem
6 no	**P**: No really great tenors are modest. **C**: There are really great tenors who are modest.
26 yes	**P1**: Most Europeans are resident in Europe. **P2**: All Europeans are people. **P3**: All people who are resident in Europe can travel freely within Europe. **C**: Most Europeans can travel freely within Europe.
44 yes	**P1**: Few committee members are from southern Europe. **P2**: All committee members are people. **P3**: All people who are from Portugal are from southern Europe. **C**: There are few committee members from Portugal.
56 unk	**P1**: Many British delegates obtained interesting results from the survey. **C**: Many delegates obtained interesting results from the survey.
76 yes	**P1**: Few committee members are from southern Europe. **C**: Few female committee members are from southern Europe.
85 no	**P1**: Exactly two lawyers and three accountants signed the contract. **C**: Six lawyers signed the contract.
99 yes	**P1**: Clients at the demonstration were all impressed by the system's performance. **P2**: Smith was a client at the demonstration. **C**: Smith was impressed by the system's performance.
100 yes	**P**: Clients at the demonstration were impressed by the system's performance. **C**: Most clients at the demonstration were impressed by the system's performance.
211 no	**P1**: All elephants are large animals. **P2**: Dumbo is a small elephant. **C**: Dumbo is a small animal.

Table 1: Samples of the FraCaS problems

ward monotonicity of *most* in its second argument. We capture the semantics, concerning *more than a half*, of *most* by the following new rule:

$$\cfrac{\mathbf{most}_q \ N \ A : [\,] : \mathbb{T} \\ \mathbf{most}_q \ N \ B : [\,] : \mathbb{X}}{\begin{array}{l} A : [c_e] : \mathbb{T} \\ B : [c_e] : \mathbb{X} \\ N : [c_e] : \mathbb{T} \end{array}} \text{MOST}, \quad \begin{array}{l} \text{where } q \equiv (n, vp, s) \\ \text{and } \mathbb{X} \text{ is either } \mathbb{T} \text{ or } \mathbb{F} \end{array}$$

With (MOST), now it is possible to prove Fr-26 (see Figure 4). The rule efficiently but partially captures the semantics of *most*. Modeling its complete semantics would introduce unnecessary inefficiency in the theorem proving.[5]

FrSec-1 involves problems dedicated to the conservativity phenomenon (1). Although we have

---

[4] Following the conventions in (Sánchez-Valencia, 1991), we mark the argument types with monotonicity properties associated with the argument positions. In this way, $\mathbf{few}_{n\downarrow,vp\downarrow,s}$ is downward monotone in its noun and VP arguments, where vp abbreviates (np, s).

[5] For complete proof-theoretic semantics of *most* wrt *same* and *all* in syllogistic logic see Endrullis and Moss (2015). Similar rules that account for additional semantics of *few* and *many* are presented in Section 5 as they coincide with efficient rules for other quantifiers.

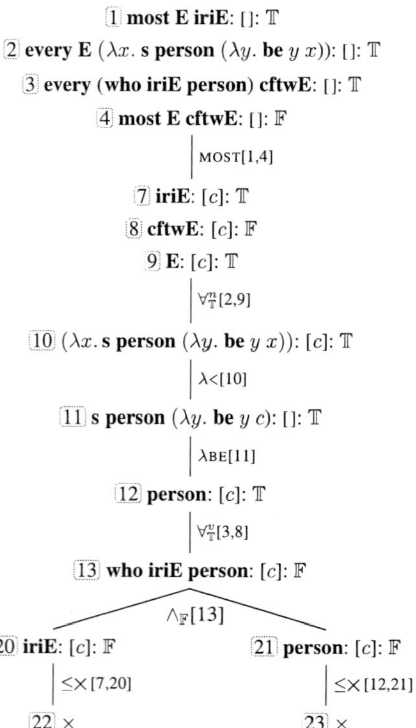

Figure 4: The tableau proof, generated by Lang-Pro, classifies Fr-26 as entailment. The abbreviations **cftwE**, **iriE** and **E** stand for the LLFs of *can freely travel within Europe*, *is resident in Europe* and *European*, respectively. The nodes that do not contribute to the closure of the tableau are omitted. The proof also employs the admissible rules $(\forall_{\mathbb{T}}^{n})$ and $(\forall_{\mathbb{T}}^{v})$ from Section 5.

not specially modeled the conservativity property of GQs in LangPro, it is able to solve all 16 poblems about conservativity except one. The reason is that conservativity is underrepresented in FraCaS. Namely, the problems cover conservativity in the form of (2) instead of (1) (see Fr-6).

$$Q\ A\ \text{are}\ B \leftrightarrow Q\ A\ \text{are}\ A\ \text{who are}\ B \qquad (1)$$

$$Q\ A\ \text{are}\ B \leftrightarrow \text{There are}\ Q\ A\ \text{who are}\ B \qquad (2)$$

We capture (2) with the help of the existing rules for GQs and (THR✕), from (Abzianidze, 2015b), which treats the expletive constructions, like *there is*, as a universal predicate, i.e., any entity not satisfying it leads to inconsistency (✕).

$$\frac{\textbf{be}\ c\ \textbf{there}\ :\ []\ :\ \mathbb{F}}{\times}\text{THR}\times$$

But these rules are not enough for solving Fr-44 because the monotonicity rules cannot lead to the solution when applied to the following nodes representing P1 and C of Fr-44, respectively.

$$\textbf{few}\ M\ (\textbf{be from}\ S)\ :\ []\ :\ \mathbb{T} \qquad (3)$$

$$\textbf{few}\ (\textbf{from}\ P\ M)\ (\lambda x.\ \textbf{be}\ x\ \textbf{there})\ :\ []\ :\ \mathbb{F} \qquad (4)$$

To solve Fr-44, we introduce a new tableau rule (THR_PP) which acts as a paraphrase rule. After the rule is applied to (4), (MON↓) can be applied to the resulted node and (3) which contrasts *being from southern Europe* to *being from Portugal*.

$$\frac{Q\ (p_{\text{np,n,n}}A\ N)(\lambda x.\ \textbf{be}\ x\ \textbf{there})\ :\ []\ :\ \mathbb{X}}{Q\ N\ (\textbf{be}\ (p\ A))\ :\ []\ :\ \mathbb{X}}\text{THR\_PP}$$

FrSec-2 covers the problems concerning plurals. Usually the phrases like bare plurals, definite plurals and definite descriptions (e.g., *the dog*) do not get special treatment in wide-coverage semantic processing and by default are treated as indefinites. Since we want to take advantage of the expressive power of the logic and its proof system, we decide to separately model these phrases. We treat bare plurals and definite plurals as GQs of the form $\mathbf{s}_{\text{n,vp,s}}\ N_{\text{n}}$, where **s** stands for the plural morpheme. The quantifier **s** can be ambiguous in LLFs due to the ambiguity related to the plurals: they can be understood as *more than one*, *universal* or *quasi-universal* (i.e. *almost every*). Since most of the problems in FraCaS favor the latter reading, we model **s** as a quasi-universal quantifier. We introduce the following lexical knowledge, $\mathbf{s} \leq \mathbf{a}$ and $\mathbf{s} \leq \mathbf{most}$, in the KB and allow the existential quantification rules (e.g., $\exists_{\mathbb{T}}$) to apply the plural terms $\mathbf{s}\ N$. With this treatment, for instance, the prover is able to prove the entailment in Fr-100.

We model the definite descriptions as generalized quantifiers of the form $\mathbf{the}\ N$, where the rules make **the** act as the universal and existential quantifiers when marked with $\mathbb{T}$ and as the existential quantifier in case of $\mathbb{F}$. Put differently, $(\forall_{\mathbb{T}})$, $(\exists_{\mathbb{T}})$ and $(\exists_{\mathbb{F}})$ allow the quantifier in their antecedent nodes to match **the**.

$$\frac{g_{\mathsf{q}}\ N\ V\ :\ []\ :\ \mathbb{T}}{N\ :\ [c_e]\ :\ \mathbb{F}\quad V\ :\ [c_e]\ :\ \mathbb{T}}\forall_{\mathbb{T}}$$
$$g \in \{\textbf{every}, \textbf{the}\}\ \text{and}\ c_e\ \text{is old}$$

$$\frac{g_{\mathsf{q}}\ N\ V\ :\ []\ :\ \mathbb{F}}{N\ :\ [c_e]\ :\ \mathbb{F}\quad V\ :\ [c_e]\ :\ \mathbb{F}}\exists_{\mathbb{F}}$$
$$g \in \{\textbf{a}, \textbf{the}\}\ \text{and}\ c_e\ \text{is old}$$

$$\frac{g_{\mathsf{q}}\ N\ V\ :\ []\ :\ \mathbb{T}}{\begin{array}{c}N\ :\ [c_e]\ :\ \mathbb{T}\\ V\ :\ [c_e]\ :\ \mathbb{T}\end{array}}\exists_{\mathbb{T}}$$
$$g \in \{\textbf{a}, \textbf{s}, \textbf{the}\}\ \text{and}\ c_e\ \text{is fresh}$$

This choice guarantees that, for example, *the demonstration* in the premises of Fr-99 co-refer and allow the proof for entailment. This approach also maintains the link if there are different surface forms co-referring, e.g., *the demonstration* and *the presentation*, in contrast to the approach in Abzianidze (2015a).

FrSec-2 also involves several problems with contrasting cardinal phrases like **exactly** n and m, where $n < m$ (see Fr-85). We account for these problems with the closure rule ($\times$EXCT), where the type q, the predicate $\texttt{greater}/2$ and the domain for E act as constraints.

$$\frac{\begin{array}{c} E_{\mathrm{q,q}} N_{\mathrm{q}} : [\vec{C}] : \mathbb{T} \\ M_{\mathrm{q}} : [\vec{C}] : \mathbb{T} \end{array}}{\times}\times\text{EXCT} \quad \begin{array}{l} \text{such that} \\ E \in \{\textbf{just}, \textbf{exactly}\} \\ \text{and } \texttt{greater}(M, N) \end{array}$$

FrSec-5 contains RTE problems pertaining to various types of adjective. First-order logic has problems with modeling *subsective* or *privative* adjectives (Kamp and Partee, 1995), but they are naturally modeled with higher-order terms. A subsective term, e.g., $\textbf{small}_{\mathrm{n,n}}$, is a relation over a *comparison class* and an entity, e.g., $\textbf{small}_{\mathrm{n,n}}\ \textbf{animal}_{\mathrm{n}}\ c_e$ is of type t as n is a subtype of et according to the extended type theory (Abzianidze, 2015b). The rule ($\subseteq$) in Figure 2 accounts for the subsective property. With the help of it, the prover correctly identifies Fr-211 as contradiction (see Figure 5). In case of the standard first-order *intersective* analysis, the premises of Fr-211 would be translated as:

$\texttt{small(dumbo)} \wedge \texttt{elephant(dumbo)} \wedge$
$\forall \texttt{x}\big(\texttt{elephant(x)} \rightarrow (\texttt{large(x)} \wedge \texttt{animal(x)})\big)$

which is a contradiction given that $\texttt{small}$ and $\texttt{large}$ are contradictory predicates. Therefore, due to the *principle of explosion* everything, including the conclusion and its negation, would be entailed from the premises.

FrSec-9, about attitudes, is the last section we explore. Though the tableau system of (Muskens, 2010) employs intensional types, LangPro only uses extensional types due to simplicity of the system and the paucity of intensionality in RTE problems. Despite the fact, with the proof-theoretic approach and extensional types, we can still account for a certain type of reasoning on attitude verbs by modeling entailment properties of the verbs in the style of Nairn et al. (2006) and Karttunen (2012). For example, *know* has (+/+) property meaning that when it occurs in a positive embedding context, it entails its sentential complement with a positive polarity. Similarly, *manage to* is (+/+)

1. **every elephant** $(\lambda x.\, \textbf{s}\ (\textbf{large animal})\ (\lambda y\ \textbf{be}\ y\ x)) : [\,] : \mathbb{T}$

  2. **a** (**small elephant**) $(\lambda x.\, \textbf{be}\ x\ \textbf{dumbo}) : [\,] : \mathbb{T}$

  3. **a** (**small animal**) $(\lambda x.\, \textbf{be}\ x\ \textbf{dumbo}) : [\,] : \mathbb{T}$

$$\lambda\text{BE}[3]$$

  4. **small animal** : [**dumbo**] : $\mathbb{T}$

$$\lambda\text{BE}[2]$$

  5. **small elephant** : [**dumbo**] : $\mathbb{T}$

$$\subseteq[5]$$

  6. **elephant** : [**dumbo**] : $\mathbb{T}$

$$\forall_{\mathbb{T}}^{n}[1,6]$$

  7. $\lambda x.\, \textbf{s}\ (\textbf{large animal})\ (\lambda y.\, \textbf{be}\ y\ x) : [\textbf{dumbo}] : \mathbb{T}$

$$\lambda_{<}[7]$$

  8. **s** (**large animal**) $(\lambda y.\, \textbf{be}\ y\ \textbf{dumbo}) : [\,] : \mathbb{T}$

$$\lambda\text{BE}[8]$$

  9. **large animal** : [**dumbo**] : $\mathbb{T}$

$$>[4,9]$$

  10. **small** : [**animal**, **dumbo**] : $\mathbb{T}$

  11. **large** : [**animal**, **dumbo**] : $\mathbb{T}$

$$\times\,|\,[10,11]$$

  12. $\times$

Figure 5: The closed tableau by LangPro proves Fr-211 as contradiction.

and (-/-) because *John managed to run* entails *John run* and *John did not manage to run* entails *John did not run*. We accommodate the entailment properties in the tableau system in a straightforward way, e.g., terms with (+/+) property, like **know** and **manage**, are modeled via the rule (+/+) where $?p$ is an optional prepositional or particle term. The rest of the three entailment properties for attitude verbs are captured in the similar way.

$$\frac{h_{\alpha,\mathrm{vp}}^{++}(?p_{\alpha,\alpha}\ V_{\alpha}) : [d] : \mathbb{T}}{V_{\alpha} : [\vec{E}] : \mathbb{T}}+/+$$
$$\text{such that if } \alpha = \mathrm{vp}, \text{ then } \vec{E} = d;$$
$$\text{otherwise } \alpha = \mathrm{s} \text{ and } \vec{E} \text{ is empty}$$

We also associate the entailment properties with the phrases *it is true that* and *it is false that* and model them via the corresponding tableau rules.

Our account for intensionality with the extensional types represents a syntactic approach rather than semantic. From the semantics perspective, the extensional types license John knowing all true statement if he knows at least one of them. But using the proof system, a syntactic machinery, we avoid such unwanted entailments with the absence of rules. In future, we could incorporate intensional types in LangPro if there is representative RTE data for the intensionality phenomenon.

The rest of the FraCaS sections were skipped during the adaptation phase for several reasons. FrSec-3 and FrSec-4 are about anaphora and ellipsis respectively. We omitted these sections as recently pronoun resolution is not modeled in the natural tableau and almost all sentences involving ellipsis are wrongly analyzed by the CCG parsers. In the current settings of the natural tableau, we treat auxiliaries as vacuous, due to this reason LangPro cannot properly account for the problems in FrSec-8 as most of them concern the aspect of verbs. FrSec-6 and FrSec-7 consists of problems with comparatives and temporal reference respectively. To account the latter phenomena, the LLFs of certain constructions needs to be specified further (e.g., for comparative phrases) and additional tableau rules must be introduced that model *calculations* on time and degrees.

5 Efficient theorem proving

Efficiency in theorem proving is crucial as we do not have infinite time to wait for provers to terminate and return an answer. Smaller tableau proofs are also easy for verifying and debugging. The section discusses the challenges for efficient theorem proving induced by the FraCaS problems and introduces new rules that bring efficiency to some extent.

The inventory of rules is a main component of a tableau method. Usually tableau rules are such inference rules that their consequent expressions are not larger than the antecedent expressions and are built up from sub-parts of the antecedent expressions. The natural tableau rules also satisfy these properties which contribute to the termination of tableau development. But there is still a big chance that a tableau does not terminate or gets unnecessarily large. The reasons for this is a combination of branching rules, δ-rules (introducing fresh entity terms), γ-rules (triggered for each entity term), and non-equivalent rules (the antecedents of which must be accessible by other rules too).[6]

Efficeint theorem proving with LangPro becomes more challenging with multi-premised problems and monotonic GQs. More nodes in a tableau give rise to more choice points in rule applications and monotonic GQs are usually available for both monotonic and standard semantic rules.

To encourage short tableau proofs, we introduce eight *admissible* rules — the rules that are redundant from completeness point of view but represent *smart* shortcuts of several rule applications.[7] Half of the rules for the existential (e.g., *a* and *the*) and universal (e.g., *every*, *no* and *the*) quantifiers are γ-rules.[8] To make application of these rules more efficient, we introduce two admissible rules for each of the γ-rules. For instance, $(\forall_{\mathbb{T}}^{n})$ and $(\forall_{\mathbb{T}}^{v})$ are admissible rules which represent the efficient but incomplete versions of $(\forall_{\mathbb{T}})$:

$$\frac{q\,N\,V : [\,] : \mathbb{T} \quad N : [c] : \mathbb{T}}{V : [c] : \mathbb{T}}\forall_{\mathbb{T}}^{n} \qquad \frac{q\,N\,V : [\,] : \mathbb{T} \quad V : [c] : \mathbb{F}}{N : [c] : \mathbb{F}}\forall_{\mathbb{T}}^{v}$$
$$\text{where } q \in \{\mathbf{every}, \mathbf{the}\}$$

Their efficiency is due to choosing a relevant entity c_e, rather than any entity like $(\forall_{\mathbb{T}})$ does: $(\forall_{\mathbb{T}}^{n})$ chooses the entity that satisfies the noun term while $(\forall_{\mathbb{T}}^{v})$ picks the one not satisfying the verb term. Moreover, the admissible rules are not branching unlike their γ counterparts. Other four admissible rules account for *a* and *the* in a false context and *no* in a true context in the similar way.

The monotonicity rules, (MON↑) and (MON↓), are inefficient as they are branching δ-rules. On the other hand, the rules for GQs are also inefficient for being a γ or δ-rule. Both types of rules are often applicable to the same GQs, e.g., *every* and *a*, as most of GQs have monotonicity properties. Instead of triggering these two types of rules separately, we introduce two admissible rules, (∃FUN↑) and (ØFUN↓), which trigger them in tandem:

$$\frac{g_{\mathsf{q}}\,N\,A : [\,] : \mathbb{T}\;\boxed{1} \quad g_{\mathsf{q}}\,N\,B : [\,] : \mathbb{F}\;\boxed{2}}{A : [c_e] : \mathbb{T}\;\boxed{3} \quad B : [c_e] : \mathbb{F}\;\boxed{4} \quad N : [c_e] : \mathbb{T}\;\boxed{5}}∃\mathrm{FUN}{\uparrow}$$
$$g \in \{\mathbf{a}, \mathbf{s}, \mathbf{many}, \mathbf{every}\}$$

$$\frac{h_{\mathsf{q}}\,N\,A : [\,] : \mathbb{F} \quad h_{\mathsf{q}}\,N\,B : [\,] : \mathbb{T}}{A : [c_e] : \mathbb{T} \quad B : [c_e] : \mathbb{F} \quad N : [c_e] : \mathbb{T}}Ø\mathrm{FUN}{\downarrow}$$
$$h \in \{\mathbf{no}, \mathbf{few}\}$$

---

[6]For instance, (MON↑) and (MON↓) in Figure 2 are both branching and δ. They are also non-equivalent since their consequents are semantically weaker than their antecedents; this requires that after their application, the antecedent nodes are still reusable for further rule applications. On the other hand, $(\forall_{\mathbb{T}})$ is non-equivalent and γ; for instance, for any en-

tity term c_e, it is applicable to **every dog bark** : [ ] : $\mathbb{T}$ and asserts that either c is not **dog** or c does **bark**.

[7]In other words, if a closed tableau makes use of an admissible rule, the tableau can still be closed with a different rule application strategy that ignores the admissible rule.

[8]Remember from Section 4 that *the* is treated like the universal and existential quantifiers in certain cases.

ID	FraCaS entailment problem
64 unk	**P**: At most ten female commissioners spend time at home.
	C: At most ten commissioners spend time at home.
88 unk	**P**: Every representative and client was at the meeting.
	C: Every representative was at the meeting.
109 no	**P**: Just one accountant attended the meeting.
	C: Some accountants attended the meeting.
215 unk	**P1**: All legal authorities are law lecturers.
	P2: All law lecturers are legal authorities.
	C: All competent legal authorities are competent law lecturers.

Table 2: Problems with false proofs

For instance, if $g = $ **every**, a single application of ($\exists$FUN$\uparrow$) already yields the fine-grained semantics: there is c_e that is A and N but not B. If the nodes were processed by the rules for **every**, ($\forall_\mathbb{F}$) would first entail ④ and ⑤ from ② and then ($\forall_\mathbb{T}$) or ($\forall_\mathbb{T}^n$) would introduce ③ from ①. ($\exists$FUN$\uparrow$) also represents a more specific version of the admissible rule (FUN$\uparrow$) of Abzianidze (2015a), which itself is an efficient and partial version of (MON$\uparrow$).

($\exists$FUN$\uparrow$) and ($\emptyset$FUN$\downarrow$) not only represent admissible rules but they also model semantics of *few* and *many* not captured by the monotonicity rules. For instance, if **few dog bark** : [] : $\mathbb{F}$ and **few dog bite** : [] : $\mathbb{T}$, then a set of entities that are **dog** and **bark**, denoted by $[\![\mathbf{dog}]\!] \cap [\![\mathbf{bark}]\!]$, is strictly larger than $[\![\mathbf{dog}]\!] \cap [\![\mathbf{bite}]\!]$ (despite the absolute or relative readings of *few*). Due to this set relation, there is an entity in $[\![\mathbf{dog}]\!] \cap [\![\mathbf{bark}]\!]$ and not in $[\![\mathbf{bite}]\!]$. Therefore, we get the inference encoded in ($\emptyset$FUN$\downarrow$). Similarly, it can be shown that *many* satisfies the inference in ($\exists$FUN$\uparrow$).

6 Evaluation

After adapting the prover to the FraCaS sections for GQs, plurals, adjectives and attitudes, we evaluate it on the relevant sections and analyze the performance. Obtained results are compared to related RTE systems.

We run two version of the prover, ccLangPro and easyLangPro, that employ CCG derivations produced by C&C and EasyCCG respectively. In order to abstract from the parser errors to some extent, the answers from both provers are aggregated in LangPro: a proof is found iff one of the parser-specific provers finds a proof. The evaluation results of the three versions of LangPro on the relevant FraCaS sections are presented in Table 3 along with the confusion matrix for LangPro.

Meas%	ccLP	eLP	**LP**
Prec	**94**	93	**94**
Rec	73	71	**81**
Acc	80	79	**85**

Gold**LP**	YES	NO	UNK
YES	**60**	0	14
NO	1	**14**	2
UNK	4	0	**47**

Table 3: Measures of ccLangPro (ccLP), easy-LangPro (eLP) and LangPro (LP) on FraCaS sections 1, 2, 5, 9 and the confusion matrix for LP.

The results show that LangPro performs slightly better with C&C compared to EasyCCG. This is due to LLFgen which is mostly tuned on the C&C derivations. Despite this bias, easyLangPro proves 8 problems that were not proved by ccLangPro. In case of half of these problems, C&C failed to return derivations for some of the sentences while in another half of the problems the errors in C&C derivations were crucial, e.g., in the conclusion of Fr-44 *committee members* was not analyzed as a constituent. On the other hand, ccLangPro proves 10 problems unsolved by easyLangPro, e.g., Fr-6 was not proved because EasyCCG analyzes *really* as a modifier of *are* in the conclusion, or even more unfortunate, the morphological analyzer of EasyCCG cannot get the lemma of *clients* correctly in Fr-99 and as a result the prover cannot relate **clients** to **client**.

The precision of LangPro is high due to its sound inference rules. Fr-109 in Table 2 was the only case when entailment and contradiction were confused: plurals are not modeled as strictly more than one.[9] The false proves are mostly due to a lack of knowledge about adjectives. Lang-Pro does not know a default comparison class for *clever*, e.g., *clever person→clever* but *clever politician↛clever*). Fr-215 was proved as entailment because we have not modeled intensionality of adjectives. Since EasyCCG was barely used during adaptation (except changing most of NP modifiers into noun modifiers), it analyzed *at most* in Fr-64 as a sentential modifier which was not modeled as downward monotone in the signature. Hence, by default, it was considered as upward monotone leading to the proof for entailment.

There are several reasons behind the problems that were not proved by the prover. Several problems for adjectives were not proved as they con-

---

[9]Moreover, Fr-109 is identical to Fr-107 which has *yes* as a gold answer. Another inconsistency in gold answers of Fr-87 and Fr-88 (due to the ambiguous premise) is a reason for a false proof. While Fr-87 was correctly proved by the prover, obviously Fr-88 was misclassified automatically.

Sec (Sing/All)	Single-premised (Acc %)							Multi-premised (Acc %)					Overall (Acc %)				
	BL	NL07,08	LS P/G	NLI	T14a,b	M15	**LP**	BL	LS P/G	T14a,b	M15	**LP**	BL	LS P/G	T14a,b	M15	**LP**
1 GQs (44/74)	45	84 **98**	70 89	95	80 93	82	93	57	50 80	80 **97**	73	93	50	62 85	80 **95**	78	93
2 Plur (24/33)	58	~~42~~ **75**	-	~~38~~	-	67	**75**	67	-	-	67	67	61	-	-	67	**73**
5 Adj (15/22)	40	60 80	-	**87**	-	**87**	**87**	43	-	-	29	43	41	-	-	68	**73**
9 Att (9/13)	67	~~56~~ 89	-	~~22~~	-	78	**100**	50	-	-	**75**	**75**	62	-	-	77	**92**
1,2,5,9 (92/142)	50	- **88**	-	-	-	78	**88**	56	-	-	66	**80**	52	-	-	74	**85**

Table 4: Comparison of RTE systems tested on FraCaS: NL07 (MacCartney and Manning, 2007), NL08 (MacCartney and Manning, 2008), LS (Lewis and Steedman, 2013) with Parser and Gold syntax, NLI (Angeli and Manning, 2014), T14a (Tian et al., 2014), T14b (Dong et al., 2014) and M15 (Mineshima et al., 2015). BL is a majority (*yes*) baseline. Results for non-applicable sections are strikeout.

tained comparative constructions, not covered by the rules. Some problems assume the universal reading of plurals. A couple of problems involving *at most* were not solved as the parsers often analyze the phrase in a wrong way.[10]

We also check the FraCaS sections how representative they are for higher-order GQs (HOGQs). After replacing all occurrences of **most**, **several**, **many**, **s** and **the** with the indefinite **a** in LLFs, LangPro$^{-\text{HOGQ}}$ (without the HOGQs) achieves an overall accuracy of 81% over FrSec-1,2,5,9. Compared to LangPro only 6 problems, including Fr-56, 99, were misclassified while Fr-26, 100 were solved. This shows that the dataset is not representative enough for HOGQs.

In Table 4, the current results are compared to the RTE systems that have been tested on the single or multi-premised FraCaS problems.[11] According to the table, the current work shows that the natural tableau system and LangPro are successful in deep reasoning over multiple premises.

The natural logic approach in MacCartney and Manning (2008) and Angeli and Manning (2014) models monotonicity reasoning with the exclusion relation in terms of the string edit operations over phrases. Since the approach heavily hinges on a sequence of edits that relates a premise to a conclusion, it cannot process multi-premised problems properly. Lewis and Steedman (2013) and Mineshima et al. (2015) both base on first-order logic representations. While Lewis and Steedman (2013) employs distributional relation clustering to model the semantics of content words, Mineshima et al. (2015) extends first-order logic

with several higher-order terms (e.g., for *most*, *believe*, *manage*) and augments first-order inference of Coq with additional inference rules for the higher-order terms. Tian et al. (2014) and Dong et al. (2014) build an inference engine that reasons over abstract denotations, formulas of relational algebra or a sort of description logic, obtained from Dependency-based Compositional Semantic trees (Liang et al., 2011). Our system and approach differ from the above mentioned ones in its unique combination of expressiveness of high-order logic, *naturalness* of logical forms (making them easily obtainable) and flexibility of a semantic tableau method. All these allow to model surface and deep semantic reasoning successfully in a single system.

7 Future work

We have modeled several semantic phenomena in the natural tableau theorem prover and obtained high results on the relevant FraCaS sections. Concerning the FraCaS dataset, in future work we plan to account for the comparatives and temporal reference in the natural tableau. After showing that the natural tableau can successfully model deep reasoning (e.g., the FraCaS problems) and (relatively) wide-coverage and surface reasoning (e.g., the SICK dataset), we see the RTE datasets, like RTE-1 (Dagan et al., 2005) and SNLI (Bowman et al., 2015), involving texts obtained from newswire or crowd-scouring as a next step for developing the theory and the theorem prover.

Acknowledgments

The author thanks the anonymous reviewers for their valuable comments and feedback. The research is a part of the project "Towards Logics that Model Natural Reasoning" supported by the NWO grant (project number 360-80-050).

---

[10]Tableau proofs of the FraCaS problems are available at: `http://lanthanum.uvt.nl/langpro/fracas`

[11]Since the FraCaS data is small and usually the problems are seen during the system development, the comparison should be understood in terms of an expressive power of a system and the underlying theory.

References

Lasha Abzianidze. 2015a. A tableau prover for natural logic and language. In *Proceedings of the 2015 Conference on Empirical Methods in Natural Language Processing*, pages 2492–2502, Lisbon, Portugal, September. Association for Computational Linguistics.

Lasha Abzianidze. 2015b. Towards a wide-coverage tableau method for natural logic. In Tsuyoshi Murata, Koji Mineshima, and Daisuke Bekki, editors, *New Frontiers in Artificial Intelligence: JSAI-isAI 2014 Workshops, LENLS, JURISIN, and GABA, Kanagawa, Japan, October 27-28, 2014, Revised Selected Papers*, pages 66–82. Springer Berlin Heidelberg, Berlin, Heidelberg, June.

Gabor Angeli and Christopher D. Manning. 2014. Naturalli: Natural logic inference for common sense reasoning. In *Proceedings of the 2014 Conference on Empirical Methods in Natural Language Processing (EMNLP)*.

Jon Barwise and Robin Cooper. 1981. Generalized quantifiers and natural language. *Linguistics and Philosophy*, 4(2):159–219.

Evert W. Beth. 1955. Semantic Entailment and Formal Derivability. *Koninklijke Nederlandse Akademie van Wentenschappen, Proceedings of the Section of Sciences*, 18:309–342.

Samuel R. Bowman, Gabor Angeli, Christopher Potts, and Christopher D. Manning. 2015. A large annotated corpus for learning natural language inference. In *Proceedings of the 2015 Conference on Empirical Methods in Natural Language Processing*, pages 632–642, Lisbon, Portugal, September. Association for Computational Linguistics.

Alonzo Church. 1940. A formulation of the simple theory of types. *Jurnal of Symbolic Logic*, 5(2):56–68, June.

Stephen Clark and James R. Curran. 2007. Wide-coverage efficient statistical parsing with ccg and log-linear models. *Computational Linguistics*, 33.

Robin Cooper, Dick Crouch, Jan Van Eijck, Chris Fox, Josef Van Genabith, Jan Jaspars, Hans Kamp, David Milward, Manfred Pinkal, Massimo Poesio, Steve Pulman, Ted Briscoe, Holger Maier, and Karsten Konrad. 1996. *FraCaS: A Framework for Computational Semantics*. Deliverable D16.

Ido Dagan, Oren Glickman, and Bernardo Magnini. 2005. The pascal recognising textual entailment challenge. In *Proceedings of the PASCAL Challenges Workshop on Recognising Textual Entailment*.

Ido Dagan, Dan Roth, Mark Sammons, and Fabio Massimo Zanzotto. 2013. *Recognizing Textual Entailment: Models and Applications*. Synthesis Lectures on Human Language Technologies. Morgan & Claypool Publishers.

Marcello D'Agostino, Dov M. Gabbay, Reiner Hhnle, and Joachim Posegga, editors. 1999. *Handbook of Tableau Methods*. Springer.

Yubing Dong, Ran Tian, and Yusuke Miyao. 2014. Encoding generalized quantifiers in dependency-based compositional semantics. In *Proceedings of the 28th Pacific Asia Conference on Language, Information, and Computation*, pages 585–594, Phuket,Thailand, December. Department of Linguistics, Chulalongkorn University.

Jörg Endrullis and Lawrence S. Moss. 2015. Syllogistic logic with "most". In Valeria de Paiva, Ruy de Queiroz, S. Lawrence Moss, Daniel Leivant, and G. Anjolina de Oliveira, editors, *Logic, Language, Information, and Computation: 22nd International Workshop, WoLLIC 2015, Bloomington, IN, USA, July 20-23, 2015, Proceedings*, pages 124–139. Springer Berlin Heidelberg, Berlin, Heidelberg.

Daniel Gallin. 1975. *Intensional and Higher-Order Modal Logic: With Applications to Montague Semantics*. American Elsevier Pub. Co.

Jaakko Hintikka. 1955. *Two Papers on Symbolic Logic: Form and Content in Quantification Theory and Reductions in the Theory of Types*. Number 8 in Acta philosophica Fennica. Societas Philosophica.

Matthew Honnibal, James R. Curran, and Johan Bos. 2010. Rebanking ccgbank for improved np interpretation. In *Proceedings of the 48th Meeting of the Association for Computational Linguistics (ACL 2010)*, pages 207–215, Uppsala, Sweden.

Thomas F. Icard and Lawrence S. Moss. 2014. Recent progress on monotonicity. *Linguistic Issues in Language Technology*, 9.

Hans Kamp and Barbara Partee. 1995. Prototype theory and compositionality. *Cognition*, 57(2):129–191.

Lauri Karttunen. 2012. Simple and phrasal implicatives. In **SEM 2012: The First Joint Conference on Lexical and Computational Semantics – Volume 1: Proceedings of the main conference and the shared task, and Volume 2: Proceedings of the Sixth International Workshop on Semantic Evaluation (SemEval 2012)*, pages 124–131, Montréal, Canada, 7-8 June. Association for Computational Linguistics.

George Lakoff. 1970. Linguistics and natural logic. In Donald Davidson and Gilbert Harman, editors, *Semantics of Natural Language*, volume 40 of *Synthese Library*, pages 545–665. Springer Netherlands.

Mike Lewis and Mark Steedman. 2013. Combined distributional and logical semantics. *Transactions of the Association for Computational Linguistics (TACL)*, 1:179–192.

Mike Lewis and Mark Steedman. 2014. A* CCG parsing with a supertag-factored model. In *Proceedings of the 2014 Conference on Empirical Methods in Natural Language Processing (EMNLP)*, pages 990–1000, Doha, Qatar, October. Association for Computational Linguistics.

P. Liang, M. I. Jordan, and D. Klein. 2011. Learning dependency-based compositional semantics. In *Association for Computational Linguistics (ACL)*, pages 590–599.

Bill MacCartney and Christopher D. Manning. 2007. Natural logic for textual inference. In *Proceedings of the ACL-PASCAL Workshop on Textual Entailment and Paraphrasing*, RTE '07, pages 193–200, Stroudsburg, PA, USA. Association for Computational Linguistics.

Bill MacCartney and Christopher D. Manning. 2008. Modeling semantic containment and exclusion in natural language inference. In Donia Scott and Hans Uszkoreit, editors, *COLING*, pages 521–528.

Bill MacCartney. 2009. *Natural language inference*. Phd thesis, Stanford University.

Marco Marelli, Stefano Menini, Marco Baroni, Luisa Bentivogli, Raffaella Bernardi, and Roberto Zamparelli. 2014. A sick cure for the evaluation of compositional distributional semantic models. In Nicoletta Calzolari, Khalid Choukri, Thierry Declerck, Hrafn Loftsson, Bente Maegaard, Joseph Mariani, Asuncion Moreno, Jan Odijk, and Stelios Piperidis, editors, *Proceedings of the Ninth International Conference on Language Resources and Evaluation (LREC'14)*, Reykjavik, Iceland. European Language Resources Association (ELRA).

Koji Mineshima, Pascual Martínez-Gómez, Yusuke Miyao, and Daisuke Bekki. 2015. Higher-order logical inference with compositional semantics. In *Proceedings of the 2015 Conference on Empirical Methods in Natural Language Processing*, pages 2055–2061, Lisbon, Portugal, September. Association for Computational Linguistics.

R. Montague. 1970. English as a formal language. In Bruno et al. (eds.) In Visentini, editor, *Linguaggi nella società e nella tecnica. Milan: Edizioni di Comunità.*, pages 188–221.

Richard Montague. 1973. The proper treatment of quantification in ordinary English. In K. J. J. Hintikka, J. Moravcsic, and P. Suppes, editors, *Approaches to Natural Language*, pages 221–242. Reidel, Dordrecht.

Reinhard Muskens. 2010. An analytic tableau system for natural logic. In Maria Aloni, Harald Bastiaanse, Tikitu de Jager, and Katrin Schulz, editors, *Logic, Language and Meaning*, volume 6042 of *Lecture Notes in Computer Science*, pages 104–113. Springer Berlin Heidelberg.

Rowan Nairn, Cleo Condoravdi, and Lauri Karttunen. 2006. Computing relative polarity for textual inference. In *Proceedings of the Fifth International Workshop on Inference in Computational Semantics (ICoS-5)*.

Víctor Sánchez-Valencia. 1991. Categorial grammar and natural reasoning. ILTI Publication Series for Logic, Semantics, and Philosophy of Language LP-91-08, University of Amsterdam.

Raymond M. Smullyan. 1968. *First-order Logic*. Springer-Verlag.

Mark Steedman. 2000. *The Syntactic Process*. MIT Press, Cambridge, MA, USA.

Ran Tian, Yusuke Miyao, and Takuya Matsuzaki. 2014. Logical inference on dependency-based compositional semantics. In *Proceedings of the 52nd Annual Meeting of the Association for Computational Linguistics (Volume 1: Long Papers)*, pages 79–89, Baltimore, Maryland, June. Association for Computational Linguistics.

Johan Van Benthem. 1986. *Essays in Logical Semantics*, volume 29 of *Studies in Linguistics and Philosophy*. Springer Netherlands.

How Factuality Determines Sentiment Inferences

Manfred Klenner and Simon Clematide
Computational Linguistics
University of Zurich, Switzerland
{klenner|siclemat}@cl.uzh.ch

Abstract

In a complex sentence comprised of one or more subclauses, the overt or hidden attitudes between the various entities depend on the factuality projection of the verbs, their polar effects, and the modality and affirmative status (negated or not) of the clauses. If factuality is given, some referents might even be considered to benefit or to suffer from the (effects of the) described situation, independently of their relations to the other referents. An interesting question is, how the reader evaluates all this from his/her perspective. We introduce an approach based on Description Logics that integrates these various perspectives into a joint model.

1 Introduction

Sentences can express a positive or negative relationship between people, organizations, and nations etc. For instance, in the sentence "the EU supports Greece", a positive attitude of the EU towards Greece is expressed. At the same time, a positive effect that is meant to be true, is asserted. That is, Greece benefits from the situation described. If the reader has a negative attitude towards the beneficiary (Greece), he might regard the apparent benefactor (EU) as his opponent. However, if the sentence is embedded into a non-factive verb like "to pretend" ("The EU pretends to support Greece"), neither the positive relationship between the referents nor the positive effect on Greece hold any longer. Instead, the matrix verb "to pretend" casts a negative effect on the EU. If the reader adheres to this common sense verb connotation, he will adopt the negative attitude towards the EU. Furthermore, if some actor criticizes that the EU supports Greece, factuality of the embedded clause is given (compared

to "pretend"). Thus, the positive effect on Greece still takes place, but now there is a negative attitude of this actor of the matrix clause towards both referents of the complement clause. Finally, if an actor criticizes that the EU does *not* support Greece, his attitude towards Greece is positive (but negative towards the EU).

Given a text, we would like to be able to answer the following questions: What is good or bad *for* the entities mentioned in the text? What is good or bad *of* these entities? What are the attitudes of the entities towards each other? And last but not least, what follows from the reader's stance, i.e. his prior attitudes towards some entities?

A user of our system then could mine texts for proponents and opponents of his, in the sense that entities that do things (or like others that) he likes are proponents, and entities that act in the opposite way (or like others he dislikes) are opponents.

In contrast to existing work (e.g. Deng and Wiebe (2015)), we stress the point that verb signatures in the sense of Karttunen (2012) that capture (non-)factuality information regarding complement clauses need to be taken into account in order to properly draw such inferences. We focus on complex sentences where a matrix verb restricts its subclauses with respect to factuality depending on its affirmative status (i.e. whether the matrix clause is affirmative or negated). The interplay of (non-)factuality with negation, the various polar restrictions projected by the verbs, and the aforementioned relational layer give rise to a complex model.

We have implemented a joint model with Description Logics (DL), namely OWL (Horrocks and Patel-Schneider, 2011) and SWRL (Horrocks and Patel-Schneider, 2004). The model is language-independent. However, the mapping from a sentence to input structures is mediated by a dependency parser, a predicate-argument extractor and a verb lexicon covering the polar restric-

*Proceedings of the Fifth Joint Conference on Lexical and Computational Semantics (*SEM 2016)*, pages 75–84,
Berlin, Germany, August 11-12, 2016.

tions – these components are language-dependent. We give English examples in this paper, although our pipeline (and the empirical evaluation) is for German. Our English example sentences were manually converted to OWL representations.

2 Related Work

The topic of event factuality in natural language applications is thoroughly discussed in Saurí and Pustejovsky (2009). For their FactBank annotations, they differentiate between *factual* (it is the case) and *counterfactual* (it is not the case).

The *certainty* (epistemic modality) to which factuality holds is a continuum, but according to Saurí and Pustejovsky (2009) it has often been divided into the following three-fold distinction that they also adhere to: *certain*, *probable*, and *possible*. Saurí and Pustejovsky (2009) additionally provide annotation labels for cases where the factuality is underspecified. An important trait of their approach lies in the fact that these annotations are always relative to sources mentioned in the text, typically subjects or objects of source-introducing predicates, for instance, "*said the minister*". In our work, we focus on the identification and extraction of *certain facts* that convey polar effects, opposition or support.

A rule-based approach to sentiment inference is Neviarouskaya et al. (2009). Each verb instantiation is described from an *internal* and an *external* perspective. For example, "to admire a mafia leader" is classified as affective positive (the subject's attitude towards the direct object) given the internal perspective while it is (as a whole) a negative judgment, externally (here the concepts introduced by the Appraisal theory are used, cf. Martin and White (2005)). However, the authors do not give any details about how they carry out rule application, and factuality does not play any role in their work.

The same is true for Reschke and Anand (2011). They capture the polarity of a verb frame instantiation as a function of the polarity of the verb's roles. In our approach, we do not assume to know the polarity of the roles in advance, but intend to infer them contextually. In their approach, if a murderer looses something positive, then this is positive as a whole. It is hard to see how less drastic cases are to be treated. For instance, "the thief looses all his friends" – is this positive? We would say: it is negative for the thief and that the friends have a negative attitude towards the thief.

How Description Logics can be used to identify so-called polarity conflicts was described in Klenner (2015). However, attitudes and the factuality of situations were not part of that model.

3 The Verb Model: Polarity Frames

The basis of our approach is a verb resource that we call polarity frames (Klenner et al., 2014; Klenner and Amsler, 2016). The current lexicon is comprised of 330 German verbs that instantiate 690 polarity frames. A verb can have more than one polarity frame due to polysemy. We are particularly interested in those verbs that subcategorize complement clauses (78 verbs), since they are crucial for complex inferences.

For each argument of a polarity frame (agent, patient, theme, etc.), we specify whether it casts a polar effect on its argument filler. For instance, the patient argument of "to help" receives a positive effect. We distinguish between polar roles that indicate that something is good/bad *of* or *for* someone. The agent role is an *of-role* – it is good *of* A to help B. The patient role (depending on the verb also theme or recipient) is a *for-role*, i.e. it is good *for* B if A helps her.

Given the verb "to help", there are at least two polarity frames, the transitive one ("A helps B") and the one with an embedded (infinitival) subclause ("A helps to XCOMP"). In the first frame, both argument fillers receive a positive effect. The agent is a positive *of-role*, which we call the *posof* role. Accordingly, the patient is a *posfor* role. Both roles are generalizations of the traditional semantic roles.

In the second frame ("A helps to XCOMP"), the agent again is the bearer of the *posof* role. But now it is XCOMP that receives a positive effect, i.e. it is good for the situation denoted by XCOMP to receive help. Thus, not only entities but also situations are affected by the polarity that a verb casts on its arguments. In order to distinguish roles for situations from roles for entities, we call the roles for positively and negatively affected subclauses *poscl* and *negcl*, respectively. This nomenclature (*posof, posfor, poscl*) eases the development of general inference rules over entities and situations.

3.1 Verb Signatures

Verbs that subcategorize a clausal complement are further specified for factuality of the clausal com-

Label	Explanation	Matrix Verb
F	factual in any case	to regret
NF	non-factual in any case	to hope
AF	factual if affirmative	to force
ANF	non-factual if affirmative	to forget
NaF	factual if non-affirmative	to forget
NaNF	non-factual if non-affirmative	to manage
NaO	true or false if non-affirmative	to help

Table 1: (Non-)Factuality of subclauses

Verb	of-role	for-role	cl-role	aff	neg
criticize	of	n/a	negcl	AF	NaF
approve	of	n/a	poscl	AF	NaF
help	posof	n/a	poscl	AF	NaO
help	posof	posfor	n/a	n/a	n/a
survive	n/a	posfor	n/a	n/a	n/a

Table 2: Polarity frames

plement. Factuality means that the situation described in the subclause is meant (by the author) to be true (to hold). We follow the work of Karttunen (2012), who distinguishes factive, non-factive and implicative verbs. Factuality of the subclause depends on the matrix verb's signature and the presence or absence of negation in the matrix clause.

Table 1 summarizes the signatures of example matrix verbs and introduces our short labels (e.g. AF). Factive verbs, such as "to regret", cast factuality on their subclause, whether the main clause is negated or not. If A regrets that COMP, then COMP is true in the sense that the speaker believes (or a least asserts) COMP to be true. The same holds for "A does NOT regret that COMP" (factuality here is constant under negation, thus factuality is a presupposition of factive verbs). Subclauses of non-factive verbs, on the other hand, are never meant to be factual (e.g. "to pretend", "to hope").

Then, there are verbs called implicatives that cast a mixture of factuality and non-factuality. Two-way implicatives, like "to forget to", have non-factual subclauses in an affirmative use, but factual subclauses if negated. One-way implicatives only give rise to factuality in either the affirmative (like "to force") or negated matrix verb contexts (like "to refuse"). For instance, if A forces B to lie, B lies. If A does not force B to lie, then B might lie as well, we just cannot tell.

Non-factuality blocks some, but not all inferences. In "A hopes that B wins", the subclause is non-factual, so B does not receive a positive effect (he is not a beneficiary): this inference is blocked. However, the attitude of the *of-role* of the (factual) matrix sentence (A) towards the *for-role* of the (non-factual) embedded verb holds (a positive relationship): it is not blocked. Relationship inference *within* a non-factual clause, however, is blocked, e.g. if A hopes that B loves C, the inference that B has a positive attitude towards C is blocked.

Table 2 shows the polarity frames of some verbs. The polar roles *poscl* and *negcl* stand for positive and negative effects of the verb on its subclause (*cl-role*), respectively, while *of* indicates a neutral effect. The last two columns relate to the verb signatures as introduced in Table 1, the second last column reports the restriction whether the matrix verb is aff(irmative) and the last column whether it is neg(ated). For example, the subclause of "help" (row 3) is factual if the "help" sentence is affirmative (AF), but its truth value is unspecified (NaO) if negated.

4 Preprocessing Pipeline

Our polarity frames provide a mapping from grammatical roles to our generalized set of semantic roles, which we call the *polar semantic roles* of a verb. For instance, the subject of "to survive" is mapped to a *posfor* role while the subject of "to cheat" realizes a *negof* role. In order to provide a proper mapping, we have to identify these grammatical roles given a dependency parse. Among others, passive voice, but also implicit arguments given control or raising verbs raise the need to reconstruct the real fillers of the grammatical roles of the verbs from the surface structure of the dependency parse. Also coreference needs to be coped with.

We have implemented a rule-based polar semantic role labeler. Extraction rules were automatically learned from treebank parses and the corresponding, manually annotated verb frame instantiations. Given a parse tree and a gold standard annotation of the underlying verb frames, paths between the verbs and the heads of their grammatical roles can be derived and saved as extraction patterns. Given proper verb frame instances, each filler of a grammatical role is mapped to a polar role according to the polarity frame of the verb.

Clearly, there is a great number of syntactic variations that need to be accounted for. However, 80 to 100 well-chosen correct sentences might already cover the most frequent cases of syntactic variation (cf. Klenner and Amsler (2016)).

Effect	Attitude	Reader
beneficiary	pro	MyOpponent
benefactor	con	MyProponent
victim		SympathyEntity
villain		NonSympathyEntity

Table 3: Projections: Concepts and Properties

5 The Overall Model

We strive to combine three different perspectives in a joint model. Firstly, there is the question of who actually profits (or has a disadvantage) from the described situation. We call this the layer of *effect projection*. Secondly, there is the relational level that determines the attitudes of the participants towards each other, this is called the *attitude projection*. Both are derived from the input text and represent the way the text puts the world (the *text perspective*). Thirdly, there is the perspective of the reader, the *reader projection*: what he or she takes from it. From the *text perspective*, the attitudes of the author (the author projection) sometimes are evident, but in the sentences envisaged by our approach this is normally not the case. We focus on sentences that report the view of the subject of the matrix clause ("A criticizes that . . . ").

Table 3 shows the concepts and properties (relations) of these projection layers: The inference task is to instantiate them given a sentence, only *(Non)SympathyEntity* are specified in advance by the user (reader). The starting point of the inference process are the instantiated polarity frames derived from an input sentence, say, "the EU helps Greece". We know from a dependency parse that "Greece" is the object of "help" and the polarity lexicon tells us that the object of "help" realizes a *posfor* role. This is the core of our lexical resource: grammatical roles are mapped to semantic roles (mainly specializations of for-roles and of-roles). The sentence is affirmative and since no modal verbs or modifiers are present it is factual. In a factual, affirmative sentence, the filler of the *posfor* role is a beneficiary. A *beneficiary* in our setting is someone who actually benefits from the situation described and must not be confused with the thematic role *beneficiary* from the literature: If the sentence would be negated, the beneficiary status of Greece no longer would hold. It would still occupy the *posfor* role, but since negated, it would no longer count as an entity that has received a positive, beneficial effect from the situation. On the contrary, it would now be a *victim*, since it is

denied help.

The properties *pro* and *con* establish the attitude projection. A *pro* relation represents a positive attitude, while *con* means a negative attitude. The filler of any *of-role* of a verb that also has a *posfor* role obviously has a positive attitude (a pro relation) towards the filler of the *posfor* role (here: EU pro Greece), provided again a factual affirmative use. If the filler of the *posfor* role moreover is an instance of *SympathyEntity* of the reader – this is given in advance, the user (modelled reader) has to specify which entities he likes or dislikes – then (among others) the filler of the *of-role* (EU) becomes an instance of the concept *MyProponent* of the reader (since the filler, EU, has, according to the sentence, a positive attitude, a *pro* relation, towards someone the reader likes, here Greece).

The attitude projection is realized with SWRL rules which refer to OWL concepts (e.g. *factual*) and A-Box representations of the sentence. They instantiate OWL properties which in turn are used by other OWL concepts to draw conclusions related to effects and reader projections.

6 Description Logics Model

Description Logics seem to be well suited for such intermingled inference tasks that we envisage. One must not care about the actual order the inferences are drawn, and global consistency checks help to identify and get rid of unwanted side effects. One drawback of pure Description Logics is that relational concepts are a problem. We cannot define a concept *opponent* that relates two individuals A and B, we always have to state a direction[1] namely that B is an opponent of A, i.e., B is an *A-opponent*, so to speak. We have chosen this possibility to define relational concepts w.r.t. the reader. We define the concepts *MyOpponent* and *MyProponent* to capture the reader's perspective. However, we found it much more convenient to use SWRL rules (Horrocks and Patel-Schneider, 2004) instead of pure OWL concepts (Horrocks and Patel-Schneider, 2011) to define the remaining relational inference layer.

Our system was developed in the Protégé editor, which eased the semantical engineering task. HermiT (Glimm et al., 2014) was used for SWRL and OWL reasoning. In the following, we introduce the properties, instance representations, concepts,

---

[1]We could introduce a property *opponent*, but reasoning at the level of properties is limited.

of-role	the agent
posof	the filler gets a positive effects
negof	the filler gets a negative effects
for-role	the patient,recipient, beneficiary or theme
posfor	a positive for-role
negfor	a negative for-role
cl-role	the subclause
poscl	subclause filler receives a positive effect
negcl	subclause filler receives a negative effect

Table 4: Properties for verb argument roles

criticize-1 : (aff AND AF)	help-1 : (aff AND AF)
criticize-1 of-role minister-1	help-1 posof EU
criticize-1 negcl help-1	help-1 posfor Greece
survive-1 : affirmative	help-1 poscl survive-1
survive-1 posfor Greece	criticize: factual

Table 5: A-Box representation

and SWRL rules of our model.

6.1 Properties

OWL properties represent two-placed relations between concepts, they have domain and range restrictions (we do not specify the concrete restrictions here). We have properties that realize the semantic roles of polarity frames. They are used to represent verb instantiations. We have a property *for-role* with subproperties *posfor* and *negfor* and a property *of-role* with *posof*, *negof* as subproperties. These are roles for entities. For situations, a general role *cl-role* denotes a non-polar subclause restriction (e.g. the verb "to remember that" casts it). *negcl* and *poscl* denote positive and negative effects that the matrix verb casts on its complement clause. These roles also have inversed roles, indicated by a preceding initial I (e.g. *I-posof*), to cope with the problem of bidirectional relational properties in Description Logics. Table 4 summarizes our role inventory.

pro and *con* of the attitude layer are also realized as properties. These properties are to be inferred by the system (as specified in section 7), in contrast to the verb argument properties from Table 4 which are instantiated via the dependency tree and the polarity frame lexicon.

6.2 Sentence Representation (A-Box)

We represent sentences and their verb instantiations in a manner that is inspired by Davidson's approach (Davidson, 1966), i.e. verbs are referred to by a constant that represents a verbal event instantiation. Technically, mentions of entities and events are represented by their base form followed by a digit. For example, *survive-1* is an instance of a survive event, and *minister-1* represents a reference to a member of the class of ministers. Our example sentence "The minister has criticized that the EU has helped Greece to survive" is represented by the A-Box assertions from Table 5. The specifications are given in a slightly simpli-

fied Manchester syntax (Horridge et al., 2006).

criticize-1 is an instance of both the classes *aff*(firmative) and *AF* (i.e. factual if affirmative; and, not shown here, *NaF*, i.e. factual if non-affirmative), and it has the role *negcl* with *help-1* as its filler. The concepts *affirmative* and *non-affirmative* are used to represent the affirmative or negated use of a predicate in a sentence.

6.3 Concept Hierarchy (T-Box)

As mentioned, we distinguish between the perspective of the reader, *MyView*, and the perspective of the text, *TextView*, see Fig.1. *TextView* tells us what the author believes to be true. One task of the reader as part of the understanding of a text is to find out what the text entails (class *Implication*) about the described situation (class *Situation*). A situation is either affirmative (class *affirmative*) or negated (class *non-affirmative*), which is known given the sentence (thus, both are primitive concepts). The whole sentence is meant to be true (if no modals are present), so the matrix clause is by definition factual (be it affirmative or non-affirmative). The factuality of an embedded situation (class *Embedded*) depends on the factuality class of the embedding situation denoted by the (embedding) verb (see Fig.1 for the subclasses of *Embedded*, e.g. AF). A factuality class like AF of a situation stems directly from the verb signatures, e.g. in Table 5, where *criticize-1* is an instance of *AF* since the verb "to criticize" bears that signature: whatever affirmative "to criticize" embeds, it is factual[2]. Thus, all subclasses of *Embedded* are primitive concepts (given by the verb signatures). Whether an embedded (individual) situation is factual or non-factual (its *Factuality_Status*) depends on the factuality class of the embedding verb and whether the embedding verb is affirmative or non-affirmative: *factual* and *non-factual* are defined classes. The definition of *factual* in Manchester syntax is:

(I-cl-role some (F or (affirmative and AF) or

---

[2]Clearly, in: "A criticizes that B intends to lie", the intention is factual, not the lying.

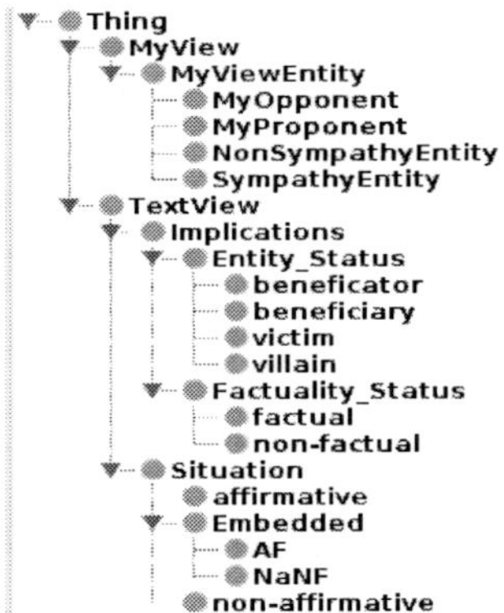

Figure 1: T-Box

(non-affirmative and NaF)))

I-cl-role is the inverse of *cl-role* (describing the embedding of situations). A situation is *factual* if it is embedded (*I-cl-role*) into a situation that is described by a factive verb (class *F* in Table 1), or is *affirmative* and has the signature *AF* or is *non-affirmative* and of type *NaF*. Given this (together with the definition of *non-factual*), we are able to determine the factuality status of an embedded situation of any depth of embedding.

6.3.1 Effect Projection Concepts

We now turn to the *effect layer* represented by the concept *EntityStatus*. We distinguish four classes and call them programmatically *benefactor*, *beneficiary*, *villain*, and *victim*. We just give the definition of *beneficiary*. The idea behind our definition is that the beneficiary of a situation is somebody who benefits from it independently of any attitude that somebody might have towards him. So if A wins, A is the beneficiary, whether A is liked by someone or not. What must be the case is that A occupies the *posfor* role of a situation that is *factual* (not just imagined) and *affirmative* (i.e. not negated). Here is the definition of *beneficiary*:

(I-posfor some (affirmative and factual))

For convenience, we also give the predicate logic equivalent:

$\forall x \exists y \ : \ \text{I-posfor}(x, y) \land \text{affirmative}(y) \land \text{factual}(y) \ \rightarrow \ \text{beneficiary}(x)$

6.3.2 Reader Projection Concepts

The *reader layer* depends on prior information concerning the stance of the reader towards real-world entities (his prior attitudes). The user of our system thus has to specify these kind of preferences in advance. He might state that Greece has his sympathy. This brings us to the concepts of the *MyView* class. We distinguish *SympathyEntity*, *NonSympathyEntity*, all primitive concepts. A *SympathyEntity* is either an entity that especially the reader (and maybe only he) likes (e.g. his dog) or an entity (concrete or abstract) that he, as most people from his culture, believe to be valuable (e.g. freedom). *NonSympathyEntity* is defined correspondingly.

Given the user's prior attitudes, his (non-)sympathies, and given a sentence from which the attitude projections (attitudes among the referents of the sentence) has been derived, the question is what actually makes referents opponents or proponents of the reader.

We exemplify the concept of *MyProponent* here. Trivially, any *SympathyEntity* is also an instance of *MyProponent*. However, there are more sophisticated ways to become someone who is in line with the reader's world view (*MyView*). Namely, if someone has a positive attitude (a *pro* relation) towards a *SympathyEntity* of the reader. Or, if someone is against (a *con* relation) someone the reader does not like (a *NonSympathyEntity*). Here is the definition of *MyProponent*:

(SympathyEntity or (pro some SympathyEntity) or (con some NonSympathyEntity))

The definition relies on the properties *pro* and *con*. We now turn to the part of our model which describes how to infer the referents' attitudes towards each other. The way they behave as indicated by the text determines their relationship and if at least one of the involved participants is a *SympathyEntity* or *NonSympathyEntity* of the reader, the reader projection, i.e., his opponents and proponents can be derived. If A supports B and B is a *NonSympathyEntity* of the reader, then A is an opponent of the reader (since A *con* B holds, but see the next section for the definition of these inferred properties).

7 Attitude Projection Rules

We use SWRL rules to specify the attitude inference layer. SWRL rules are neatly coupled with OWL concepts (T-Box) and instances (A-Box). For instance, we can refer to an instance of class *factual* by a predicate of the form *fac-*

#	Input Predicates	
1	posfor(help,GR)	negcl(criticize,help)
2	posof(help,EU)	of-role(criticize,min.)
3	poscl(help,survive)	posfor(survive,GR)
4	aff(criticize)	aff(help)
5	aff(survive)	factual(criticize)

Table 6: Input representation

#	Inference	Rule
i1	beneficiary(Greece)	OWL def.
i2	pro(EU,Greece)	r1
i3	con(minister,EU)	r2
i4	disapprove(minister,survive)	r3
i5	con(minister,Greece)	r4
i6	con(EU,minister)	r5

Table 7: Inferences

tual(?x)[3]. Properties are referred to accordingly, e.g. *negcl(?s,?s2)* binds *?s* and *?s2* to any A-Box expression (in Manchester Syntax) of the form: *someInstance1 negcl someInstance2*, e.g. *criticize-1 negcl help-1* from Table 5. This might be somewhat intransparent to readers unfamiliar with OWL and SWRL. For convenience, we have translated Table 5 into Table 6, where A-Box expressions are mapped to a notation closer to SWRL. We also have stripped indices, e.g. *criticize-1* is now just *criticize*.

In order to introduce our scheme, we go through the example sentence S (repeated):

S: *The minister has criticized that the EU has helped Greece to survive.*

The instantiations from Table 6 are based on the polarity frames of the verbs and the dependency parse of the sentence. Since no negation is present, it holds that *aff(criticize)*, *aff(help)*, *aff(survive)* (line 4 and 5), where *aff* means affirmative use. The matrix clause (since no modal is present) is factual (line 5), i.e., *factual(criticize)*. Note that *posfor(help,Greece)* just means that Greece occupies a particular polar role. Whether Greece actually gets a positive effect depends on the factuality as determined by the matrix verb and its affirmative status (and also the affirmative status of the complement verb itself).

Before reading the further outline of our rule component, the reader is invited to verify that the following inferences drawn from the example sentence S are in line with his/her intuition (i4 and i6 needs further explanation, though):

Greece as a beneficiary (i1 from Table 7) follows from the OWL definition (Greece takes the *posfor* role in a factual affirmative sentence).

In general, the goal is to find out whether A is for (*pro*) B or whether A is against (*con*) B. A verb might (directly) reveal the relation between

the participants within the same clause: if A helps B, then A is *pro* B. If A criticizes B, then A is *con* B (at least in a certain – the given – context, not necessarily in a fundamental, irreconcilable way). Provided, of course, the situation is factual and affirmative.

```
r1 aff(?s),posof(?s,?x),factual(?s),
    posfor(?s,?y) -> pro(?x,?y)
```

Rule r1 states: An actor *?x* (the *posof* role, in general, any of-role) is *pro ?y* if in a single factual, affirmative sentence *?s*, *?y* is the filler of the *posfor* role (i2 from Table 7): *pro(EU,Greece)*.

If a sentence *?s* embeds a sentence *?s2*, then rules like the following are in charge:

```
r2 factual(?s),aff(?s),negcl(?s,?s2),
    of_role(?s,?x),of_role(?s2,?y)
        -> con(?x,?y)
```

According to r2, an affirmative and factual matrix clause *?s* that embeds an affirmative subclause *?s2* (the factuality of *?s2* is irrelevant) bearing a negative effect (*negcl*) gives rise to a *con* relation between the *of-role* of the matrix clause and the *of-role* of the subclause (see i3 from Table 7): *con(minister, EU)*.

More complicated scenarios arise in the case of multiple embeddings. According to Table 2, "to criticize" has a *negcl* role while "to help" has a *poscl* role. If A criticizes that B helps C to D (D=survive), then, obviously, A disapproves D. That is, a *negcl* on a *poscl* gives *disapprove*, see rule r3.

```
r3 aff(?s),factual(?s),negcl(?s,?s2),
    aff(?s2),of_role(?s,?x),poscl(?s2,?s3)
        -> disapprove(?x,?s3)
```

The matrix clause must be factual: if A (just) *might* criticize that COMP, nothing can be inferred about A's (dis-)approval regarding COMP (and COMP of COMP). Rule r3 triggers and produces i4 from Table 7: *disapprove(minister,survive)*.

The next rule describes how disapprove propagates to a *con* relation (factuality is irrelevant).

---

[3]We follow the SWRL notation to indicate variables by a leading question mark.

```
r4 aff(?s),posfor(?s,?y),disapproves(?x,?s)
     -> con(?x,?y)
```

If someone disapproves an affirmative situation that is positive (*posfor*) for someone, then he is against this person. Rule r4 produces i5 from Table 7: *con(minister,Greece)*.

One could also think of rules like the following:

```
r5 pro(?x,?z),con(?y,?z) -> con(?x,?y)
```

If A is *pro* B and C is *con* B then we might be allowed to guess that A is *con* C. In our example it follows that EU is *con* minister, see i6 from Table 7. Note that these transitively given *pro* and *con* relations are only safe if they stem from the same sentence. It is not true *in general* that I am against someone who dislikes a person I like. If (rule r5) A admires B while C finds B boring, A and C are opponents, but only conditional on B, so to speak. In general, pros and cons can only deliver situation-specific attitudes.

Now that we have seen examples of the effect projection (*beneficiary(Greece)*), the attitude projection (e.g. *con(minister,EU)*) let us end with an example of the reader projection. If the reader is skeptical about the EU (these days), i.e., the EU is a *NonSympathyEntity* of his, then *minister* becomes a instance of *MyProponent* (via the definition of *MyProponent* and the derived attitude *con(minister,EU)*).

The author projection also can be plugged in easily. Take the sentence "The minister criticizes the ridiculous initiative". We only have to derive *con(author,initiative)* from the use of "ridiculous" and we can exploit the full capacity of our reasoning scheme, e.g. we could derive *pro(author,minister)*.

8 Empirical Evaluation

Our inference rules were tuned on the basis of 80 constructed development sentences (Dev80) that concisely capture our modelled phenomena. They combine verbs from our lexicon in sentences that are comprised of subclause embeddings up to three levels. Affirmative and negated use of these verbs are combined with (non-)factuality at each level of embedding. This was meant to base our model on an increased generative complexity of natural language – even if such sentences are rare in real texts. Our goal was to model competence and at same time make it applicable. The sample sentence S from the last section is an example of such a constructed sentence. For each sentence,

Relations	A	B	Gold	System
benefactor	2	2	4	5
beneficiary	10	5	7	16
victim	35	40	42	52
villain	4	5	6	11
con	68	50	68	67
pro	35	23	29	37
total	154	125	156	188

Table 8: Statistics for Test80: Annotators A and B, the adjudicated gold standard G, and the system output (setting I)

we manually instantiated the polarity frames, i.e., we identified the polarity frame and the fillers of the grammatical roles. It was the tuning of the rule component we were after, not the impact of the preprocessing pipeline (extraction from the dependency trees) on the overall performance. The final performance of our system on Dev80 was: precision 83.89% and recall 93.72%.

The final test corpus (Test80) contains 80 unseen sentences drawn from the German newspaper treebank TüBa-D/Z (Telljohann et al., 2009). About 10% of its 95,000 sentences contain a verb that is modelled in our lexicon. In about 5,000 sentences our extraction component triggers. 540 cases show subclause embedding. In 46 sentences the verb of the matrix clause and the verb of the subclause are in our lexicon, and 6 of them involve negation. We included these cases into our test set and added 34 randomly chosen affirmative and negated sentences containing a single verb from the lexicon. For these sentences, we evaluated two different settings. In setting I, the treebank parses were used, in setting II the output of the ParZu dependency parser (Sennrich et al., 2013).

Table 8 shows the descriptive statistics for Test80 (column system showing the results for setting I)[4]. Two raters A and B independently annotated all test sentences according to simple guidelines that treat the prediction of the inferred effects and attitudes as a textual entailment task (Dagan et al., 2013).[5] After a reconciliation session only two cases had to be adjudicated by a third rater

---

[4]We cannot evaluate *MyProponent* and *MyOpponent* since these concepts depend on the individual preferences of the annotators.

[5]The annotators have to formulate factual entailment candidates that they then accept or reject. Given our running example sentence, they would typically create and check entailment sentences such as "Therefore, it is the case that the EU has a positive attitude towards Greece" for *pro*, or "Therefore, it is the case that the EU acts in a positive manner" for *benefactor*.

in order to establish a gold standard G. The pairwise agreement between A and B is 43% (Cohen's $\kappa = 0.19$), between A and G 69% ($\kappa = 0.56$), B and G 61% ($\kappa = 0.44$). κ between A and B is low, but this is mostly due to the difficulty of spotting candidate entities and relations in complex nested sentences, and not due to different annotation categories assigned to the same candidate. Humans are selective annotators and focus on the most striking attitudes more than on the more hidden ones. During reconciliation, missing annotations of one annotator could be easily spotted and adopted in view of the annotations of the other.

The overall performance of the system is 59.04% precision and 71.15% recall (setting I). If we replace perfect parse trees with parser output (setting II), precision is almost unaffected (58.84%), while recall drops to 50.64%.

We have identified some systematic errors of our system. Among others, it instantiates concepts from the effect layer (beneficiary etc.) too often, especially entities that are non-actors (e.g. "A criticizes the proposal" gives *victim(proposal)*). The gold standard only allows actors (person, company etc.) to occupy these roles. A better classification for actors would help in these cases.

A central claim of this paper is that factuality is important for sentiment inferences since it licences or suppresses reasoning. Given our test set comprised of 80 sentences, 41 verb mentions were classified as non-factual and thus were blocked for certain inferences. If we switch off factuality detection (i.e., every verb is factual), a precision drop of 12.9% results (while recall increases only slightly by 1.2%).

9 Comparison with Deng & Wiebe

Recently, Deng and Wiebe (2014) and Deng and Wiebe (2015) have introduced an advanced conceptual framework for inferring sentiment implicatures. Their work is most similar to our approach. Various model versions exist, the latest one (Deng and Wiebe, 2015) also copes with event-level sentiment inference, which brings it even closer to our model. Probabilistic Soft Logic is used for the specification of the rules and for drawing inferences. The goal of the systems is to detect entity pairs that are in a PosPair or NegPair relation. This is similar to our pro/con relations.

First of all, factuality is not taken into account in their framework, while we have shown that it is crucial for certain inference steps. Although their model is based on the idea of good/bad-for verbs, they do not envisage to propagate (as we do) such effects, i.e. determine whether these effects have occurred or not (clearly, factuality is crucial here). In contrast to our approach, their model is a probabilistic one. However, it is obviously not the layer of inference rules (the attitude projection in our terms) which establishes the source of uncertainty, it is the preprocessing where three existing sentiment systems and two SVM classifiers are used for polarity detection (i.e. identifying targets, polarity spans etc.). This obscures the fact that some inference rules might contribute to false predictions as well. For instance there is a rule (3.10 from Table 1, (Deng and Wiebe, 2015)) that more or less states that I am against any action of someone I do not like. Clearly, we hardly would be against a good deed of an opponent of us. We believe, though, that such over-generalized rules also exist in our model and that we should find a means to focus on that kind of failure (not so much on propagated errors from the preprocessing stages).

10 Conclusions

Our model strives to answer the following questions, given a text and the personal profile of a single user: who benefits (or suffers) from the situations described, what does the text (implicitly) tell us about the relationship of the actors involved, which topics does an actor like or dislike and – given all this – what does this imply for the user: who are proponents or opponents of his or hers.

The basis or our model is a language-specific verb polarity lexicon with polar effects on the bearers of what we call the *for-roles* and the *of-roles* of the verb. This and the predicate argument structures of a sentence lead to an A-Box representation of the sentence. OWL concepts and a set of SWRL rules then derive what the text implies about (the author's view of) reality and what the reader might make of it.

Acknowledgments

We would like to thank Noëmi Aepli and Don Tuggener for their support and the reviewers for their helpful comments. This work was conducted using the Protégé resource, which is supported by grant GM10331601 from the National Institute of General Medical Sciences of the United States National Institutes of Health.

References

Ido Dagan, Dan Roth, Mark Sammons, and Fabio Zanzotto. 2013. *Recognizing Textual Entailment: Models and Applications*, volume 6 of *Synthesis Lectures on Human Language Technologies*. Morgan & Claypool.

Donald Davidson. 1966. The logical form of action sentences. In Nicholas Rescher and Alan Ross Anderson, editors, *The Logic of Decision and Action*, pages 81–95. University of Pittsburgh Press.

Lingjia Deng and Janyce Wiebe. 2014. Sentiment propagation via implicature constraints. *Meeting of the European Chapter of the Association for Computational Linguistics (EACL-2014)*.

Lingjia Deng and Janyce Wiebe. 2015. Joint prediction for entity/event-level sentiment analysis using probabilistic soft logic models. In *Proceedings of the 2015 Conference on Empirical Methods in Natural Language Processing, EMNLP 2015, Lisbon, Portugal, September 17-21, 2015*, pages 179–189.

Birte Glimm, Ian Horrocks, Boris Motik, Giorgos Stoilos, and Zhe Wang. 2014. HermiT: An OWL 2 reasoner. *Journal of Automated Reasoning*, 53(3):245–269.

Matthew Horridge, Nick Drummond, John Goodwin, Alan Rector, Robert Stevens, and Hai H Wang. 2006. The Manchester OWL syntax. In *OWL: Experiences and Directions (OWLED)*.

Ian Horrocks and Peter F. Patel-Schneider. 2004. A proposal for an OWL rules language. In *Proc. of the Thirteenth International World Wide Web Conference (WWW 2004)*, pages 723–731. ACM.

Ian Horrocks and Peter F. Patel-Schneider. 2011. KR and reasoning on the Semantic Web: OWL. In John Domingue, Dieter Fensel, and James A. Hendler, editors, *Handbook of Semantic Web Technologies*, chapter 9, pages 365–398. Springer.

Lauri Karttunen. 2012. Simple and phrasal implicatives. In *Proceedings of the First Joint Conference on Lexical and Computational Semantics - Volume 1: Proceedings of the Main Conference and the Shared Task, and Volume 2: Proceedings of the Sixth International Workshop on Semantic Evaluation*, SemEval '12, pages 124–131, Stroudsburg, PA, USA. Association for Computational Linguistics.

Manfred Klenner and Michael Amsler. 2016. Sentiframes: A resource for verb-centered german sentiment inference. In *Proceedings of the Tenth International Conference on Language Resources and Evaluation (LREC 2016)*, Paris, France, may. European Language Resources Association (ELRA).

Manfred Klenner, Michael Amsler, and Nora Hollenstein. 2014. Verb polarity frames: a new resource and its application in target-specific polarity classification. In *Proceedings of KONVENS 2014*, pages 106–115.

Manfred Klenner. 2015. Verb-centered sentiment inference with description logics. In *6th Workshop on Computational Approaches to Subjectivity, Sentiment & Social Media Analysis*, pages 134–140, September.

J. R. Martin and P. R. R. White. 2005. *Appraisal in English*. Palgrave, London.

Alena Neviarouskaya, Helmut Prendinger, and Mitsuru Ishizuka. 2009. Semantically distinct verb classes involved in sentiment analysis. In Hans Weghorn and Pedro T. Isaías, editors, *IADIS AC (1)*, pages 27–35. IADIS Press.

Kevin Reschke and Pranav Anand. 2011. Extracting contextual evaluativity. In *Proceedings of the Ninth International Conference on Computational Semantics*, pages 370–374.

Roser Saurí and James Pustejovsky. 2009. FactBank: a corpus annotated with event factuality. *Language Resources and Evaluation*, 43(3):227–268.

Rico Sennrich, Martin Volk, and Gerold Schneider. 2013. Exploiting synergies between open resources for german dependency parsing, pos-tagging, and morphological analysis. In *Recent Advances in Natural Language Processing (RANLP 2013)*, pages 601–609, September.

Heike Telljohann, Erhard W. Hinrichs, Sandra Kübler, Heike Zinsmeister, and Kathrin Beck. 2009. Stylebook for the Tübingen treebank of written German (TüBa-D/Z). Technical report, Universität Tübingen, Seminar für Sprachwissenschaft.

Sense Embedding Learning for Word Sense Induction

Linfeng Song[1], **Zhiguo Wang**[2], **Haitao Mi**[2] and **Daniel Gildea**[1]
[1]Department of Computer Science, University of Rochester, Rochester, NY 14627
[2]IBM T.J. Watson Research Center, Yorktown Heights, NY 10598

Abstract

Conventional word sense induction (WSI) methods usually represent each instance with discrete linguistic features or co-occurrence features, and train a model for each polysemous word individually. In this work, we propose to learn sense embeddings for the WSI task. In the training stage, our method induces several sense centroids (embedding) for each polysemous word. In the testing stage, our method represents each instance as a contextual vector, and induces its sense by finding the nearest sense centroid in the embedding space. The advantages of our method are (1) distributed sense vectors are taken as the knowledge representations which are trained discriminatively, and usually have better performance than traditional count-based distributional models, and (2) a general model for the whole vocabulary is jointly trained to induce sense centroids under the mutli-task learning framework. Evaluated on SemEval-2010 WSI dataset, our method outperforms all participants and most of the recent state-of-the-art methods. We further verify the two advantages by comparing with carefully designed baselines.

1 Introduction

Word sense induction (WSI) is the task of automatically finding sense clusters for polysemous words. In contrast, word sense disambiguation (WSD) assumes there exists an already-known sense inventory, and the sense of a word type is disambiguated according to the sense inventory. Therefore, clustering methods are generally applied in WSI tasks, while classification methods are utilized in WSD tasks. WSI has been successfully applied to many NLP tasks such as machine translation (Xiong and Zhang, 2014), information retrieval (Navigli and Crisafulli, 2010) and novel sense detection (Lau et al., 2012).

However, existing methods usually represent each instance with discrete hand-crafted features (Bordag, 2006; Chen et al., 2009; Van de Cruys and Apidianaki, 2011; Purandare and Pedersen, 2004), which are designed manually and require linguistic knowledge. Most previous methods require learning a specific model for each polysemous word, which limits their usability for downstream applications and loses the chance to jointly learn senses for multiple words.

There is a great advance in recent distributed semantics, such as word embedding (Mikolov et al., 2013; Pennington et al., 2014) and sense embedding (Reisinger and Mooney, 2010; Huang et al., 2012; Jauhar et al., 2015; Rothe and Schütze, 2015; Chen et al., 2014; Tian et al., 2014). Comparing with word embedding, sense embedding methods learn distributed representations for senses of a polysemous word, which is similar to the sense centroid of WSI tasks.

In this work, we point out that the WSI task and the sense embedding task are highly interrelated, and propose to jointly learn sense centroids (embeddings) of all polysemous words for the WSI task. Concretely, our method induces several sense centroids (embedding) for each polysemous word in training stage. In testing stage, our method represents each instance as a contextual vector, and induces its sense by finding the nearest sense centroid in the embedding space. Comparing with existing methods, our method has two advantages: (1) distributed sense embeddings are taken as the knowledge representations which are trained discriminatively, and usually have better performance than traditional count-based dis-

85

*Proceedings of the Fifth Joint Conference on Lexical and Computational Semantics (*SEM 2016)*, pages 85–90,
Berlin, Germany, August 11-12, 2016.

tributional models (Baroni et al., 2014), and (2) a general model for the whole vocabulary is jointly trained to induce sense centroids under the mutli-task learning framework (Caruana, 1997). Evaluated on SemEval-2010 WSI dataset, our method outperforms all participants and most of the recent state-of-the-art methods.

2 Methodology

2.1 Word Sense Induction

WSI is generally considered as an unsupervised clustering task under the distributional hypothesis (Harris, 1954) that the word meaning is reflected by the set of contexts in which it appears. Existing WSI methods can be roughly divided into feature-based or Bayesian. Feature-based methods first represent each instance as a context vector, then utilize a clustering algorithm on the context vectors to induce all the senses. Bayesian methods (Brody and Lapata, 2009; Yao and Van Durme, 2011; Lau et al., 2012; Goyal and Hovy, 2014; Wang et al., 2015), on the other hand, discover senses based on topic models. They adopt either the LDA (Blei et al., 2003) or HDP (Teh et al., 2006) model by viewing each target word as a corpus and the contexts as pseudo-documents, where a context includes all words within a window centred by the target word. For sense induction, they first extract pseudo-documents for the target word, then train topic model, finally pick the most probable topic for each test pseudo-document as the sense.

All of the existing WSI methods have two important factors: 1) how to group similar instances (clustering algorithm) and 2) how to represent context (knowledge representation). For clustering algorithms, feature-based methods use k-means or graph-based clustering algorithms to assign each instance to its nearest sense, whereas Bayesian methods sample the sense from the probability distribution among all the senses for each instance, which can be seen as soft clustering algorithms. As for knowledge representation, existing WSI methods use the vector space model (VSM) to represent each context. In feature-based models, each instance is represented as a vector of values, where a value can be the count of a feature or the co-occurrence between two words. In Bayesian methods, the vectors are represented as co-occurrences between documents and senses or between senses and words. Overall existing meth-

ods separately train a specific VSM for each word. No methods have shown distributional vectors can keep knowledge for multiple words while showing competitive performance.

2.2 Sense Embedding for WSI

As mentioned in Section 1, sense embedding methods learn a distributed representation for each sense of a polysemous word. There are two key factors for sense embedding learning: (1) how to decide the number of senses for each polysemous word and (2) how to learn an embedding representation for each sense. To decide the number of senses in factor (1), one group of methods (Huang et al., 2012; Neelakantan et al., 2014) set a fixed number K of senses for each word, and each instance is assigned to the most probable sense according to Equation 1, where $\mu(w_t, k)$ is the vector for the k-th sense centroid of word w, and v_c is the representation vector of the instance.

$$s_t = \arg\max_{k=1,..,K} sim(\mu(w_t, k), v_c) \qquad (1)$$

Another group of methods (Li and Jurafsky, 2015) employs non-parametric algorithms to dynamically decide the number of senses for each word, and each instance is assigned to a sense following a probability distribution in Equation 2, where S_t is the set of already generated senses for w_t, and γ is a constant probability for generating a new sense for w_t.

$$s_t \sim \begin{cases} p(k|\mu(w_t, k), v_c) \; \forall \, k \in S_t \\ \gamma \; \text{for new sense} \end{cases} \qquad (2)$$

From the above discussions, we can obviously notice that WSI task and sense embedding task are inter-related. The two factors in sense embedding learning can be aligned to the two factors of WSI task. Concretely, deciding the number of senses is the same problem as the clustering problem in WSI task, and sense embedding is a potential knowledge representation for WSI task. Therefore, sense embedding methods are naturally applicable to WSI.

In this work, we apply the sense embedding learning methods for WSI tasks. Algorithm 1 lists the flow of our method. The algorithm iterates several times over a Corpus (Line 2-3). For each token w_t, it calculates the context vector v_c (Line 4) for an instance, and then gets the most possible

Algorithm 1 Sense Embedding Learning for WSI

1: **procedure** TRAINING(Corpus C)
2:      **for** $iter$ in [$1..I$] **do**
3:         **for** w_t in C **do**
4:             $v_c \leftarrow$ context_vec(w_t)
5:             $s_t \leftarrow$ sense_label(w_t, v_c)
6:             update(w_t, s_t)
7:         **end for**
8:      **end for**
9: **end procedure**

---

sense label s_t for w_t (Line 5). Finally, both the sense embeddings for s_t and global word embeddings for all context words of w_t are updated (Line 6). We introduce our strategy for *context_vec* in the next section. For *sense_label* function, a sense label is obtained by either Equation 1 or Equation 2. For the *update* function, vectors are updated by the Skip-gram method (same as Neelakantan et al. (2014)) which tries to predict context words with the current sense. In this algorithm, the senses of all polysemous words are learned jointly on the whole corpus, instead of training a single model for each individual word as in the traditional WSI methods. This is actually an instance of multi-task learning, where WSI models for each target word are trained together, and all of these models share the same global word embeddings.

Comparing to the traditional methods for WSI tasks, the advantages of our method include: 1) WSI models for all the polysemous words are trained jointly under the multi-task learning framework; 2) distributed sense embeddings are taken as the knowledge representations which are trained discriminatively, and usually have better performance than traditional count-based distributional models (Baroni et al., 2014). To verify the two statements, we carefully designed comparative experiments described in the next section.

3 Experiment

3.1 Experimental Setup and baselines

We evaluate our methods on the test set of the SemEval-2010 WSI task (Manandhar et al., 2010). It contains 8,915 instances for 100 target words (50 nouns and 50 verbs) which mostly come from news domain. We choose the April 2010 snapshot of Wikipedia (Shaoul and Westbury, 2010) as our training set, as it is freely available and domain general. It contains around 2 million documents

and 990 million tokens. We train and test our models and the baselines according to the above data setting, and compare with reported performance on the same test set from previous papers.

For our sense embedding method, we build two systems: *SE-WSI-fix* which adopts Multi-Sense Skip-gram (MSSG) model (Neelakantan et al., 2014) and assigns 3 senses for each word type, and *SE-WSI-CRP* (Li and Jurafsky, 2015) which dynamically decides the number of senses using a Chinese restaurant process. For *SE-WSI-fix*, we learn sense embeddings for the top 6K frequent words in the training set. For *SE-WSI-CRP*, we first learn word embeddings with word2vec[1], then use them as pre-trained vectors to learn sense embeddings. All training is under default parameter settings, and all word and sense embeddings are fixed at 300 dimensions. For fair comparison, we create *SE-WSI-fix-cmp* by training the MSSG model on the training data of the SemEval-2010 WSI task with the same setting of *SE-WSI-fix*.

We also design baselines to verify the two advantages of our sense embedding methods. One (*CRP-PPMI*) uses the same CRP algorithm as *SE-WSI-CRP*, but with Positive PMI vectors as pre-trained vectors. The other (*WE-Kmeans*) uses the vectors learned by *SE-WSI-fix*, but separately clusters all the context vectors into 3 groups for each target word with kmeans. We compute a context vector by averaging the vectors of all selected words in the context[2].

3.2 Comparing on SemEval-2010

We compare our methods with the following systems: (1) *UoY* (Korkontzelos and Manandhar, 2010) which is the best system in the SemEval-2010 WSI competition; (2) *NMF$_{lib}$* (Van de Cruys and Apidianaki, 2011) which adopts non-negative matrix factorization to factor a matrix and then conducts word sense clustering on the test set; (3) *NB* (Choe and Charniak, 2013) which adopts naive Bayes with the generative story that a context is generated by picking a sense and then all context words given the sense; and (4) *Spectral* (Goyal and Hovy, 2014) which applies spectral clustering on a set of distributional context vectors.

Experimental results are shown in Table 1. Let us see the results on supervised recall (80-20 SR)

---

[1] https://code.google.com/p/word2vec/
[2] A word is selected only if its length is greater than 3, not the target word, or not in a self-constructed stoplist.

System	V-Measure(%)			Paired F-score(%)			80-20 SR(%)			FS	#CI
	All	Noun	Verb	All	Noun	Verb	All	Noun	Verb	All	
UoY (2010)	15.7	20.6	8.5	49.8	38.2	66.6	62.4	59.4	66.8	-	11.5
NMF$_{lib}$ (2011)	11.8	13.5	9.4	45.3	42.2	49.8	62.6	57.3	70.2	-	4.80
NB (2013)	**18.0**	**23.7**	**9.9**	52.9	52.5	53.5	65.4	62.6	69.5	-	3.42
Spectral (2014)	4.5	4.6	4.2	**61.5**	**54.5**	**71.6**	-	-	-	60.7	1.87
SE-WSI-fix-cmp	16.3	20.8	9.7	54.3	54.2	54.3	**66.3**	**63.6**	**70.2**	**66.4**	2.61
SE-WSI-fix	9.8	13.5	4.3	55.1	50.7	61.6	62.9	58.5	69.2	63.0	2.50
SE-WSI-CRP	5.7	7.4	3.2	55.3	49.4	63.8	61.2	56.3	67.9	61.3	2.09
CRP-PPMI	2.9	3.5	2.0	57.7	53.3	64.0	59.2	53.6	67.4	59.2	1.76
WE-Kmeans	4.6	5.0	4.1	51.2	46.5	57.6	58.6	53.3	66.4	58.6	2.54

Table 1: Result on SemEval-2010 WSI task. *80-20 SR* is the supervised recall of 80-20 split supervised evaluation. *FS* is the F-Score of 80-20 split supervised evaluation. *#CI* is the average number of clusters (senses)

first, as it is the main indicator for the task. Overall, *SE-WSI-fix-cmp*, which jointly learns sense embedding for 6K words, outperforms every comparing systems which learns for each single word. This shows that sense embedding is suitable and promising for the task of word sense induction. Trained on out-of-domain data, *SE-WSI-fix* outperforms most of the systems, including the best system in the shared task (*UoY*), and *SE-WSI-CRP* works better than *Spectral* and all the baselines. This also shows the effectiveness of the sense embedding methods. Besides, *SE-WSI-CRP* is 1.7 points lower than *SE-WSI-fix*. We think the reason is that *SE-WSI-CRP* induces fewer senses than *SE-WSI-fix* (see the last column of Table 1). Since both systems induce fewer senses than the golden standard which is 3.85, inducing fewer senses harms the performance. Finally, simple as it is, *NB* shows a very good performance. However *NB* can not benefit from large-scale data as its number of parameters is small, and it uses EM algorithm which is generally slow. Sense embedding methods have other advantages that they train a general model while *NB* learns specific model for each target word.

As for the unsupervised evaluations, *SE-WSI-fix* achieves a good V-Measure score (VM) with a few induced senses. Pedersen (2010) points out that bad models can increase VM by increasing the number of clusters, but doing this will harm performance on both Paired F-score (PF) and SR. Even though *UoY*, *NMF$_{lib}$* and *NB* show better VM, they (especially *UoY*) induced more senses than *SE-WSI-fix*. *SE-WSI-fix* has higher PF than all others, and higher SR than *UoY* and *NMF$_{lib}$*.

Trained on the official training data of SemEval-2010 WSI task, *SE-WSI-fix-cmp* achieves the top performance on both VM and PF, while it induces a reasonable number of averaged senses. Comparatively *SE-WSI-CRP* has lower VM and induces fewer senses than *SE-WSI-fix*. One possible reason is that the "rich gets richer" nature of CRP makes it conservative for making new senses. But its PF and SR show that it is still a highly competitive system.

To verify the advantages of our method, we first compare *SE-WSI-CRP* with *CRP-PPMI* as their only difference is the vectors for representing contexts. We can see that *SE-WSI-CRP* performs significantly better than *CRP-PPMI* on both SR and VM. *CRP-PPMI* has higher PF mainly because it induces fewer number of senses. The above results prove that using sense embeddings have better performance than using count-based distributional models. Besides, *SE-WSI-fix* is significantly better than *WE-Kmeans* on every metric. As *WE-Kmeans* and *SE-WSI-fix* learn sense centroids in the same vectors space, while the latter performs joint learning. Therefore, the joint learning is better than learning separately.

4 Related Work

Kågebäck et al. (2015) proposed two methods to utilize distributed representations for the WSI task. The first method learned centroid vectors by clustering all pre-computed context vectors of each target word. The other method simply adopted *MSSG* (Neelakantan et al., 2014) and changed context vector calculation from the average of all context word vectors to weighted average. Our work has further contributions. First, we clearly point out the two advantages of sense embedding methods: 1) joint learning under the mutli-task learning framework, 2) better knowledge representation by discriminative training, and verify them by experiments. In addition, we adopt various sense embedding methods to show that sense embedding methods are generally promising for WSI, not just one method is better than other methods. Finally, we compare our methods with recent state-of-the-art WSI methods on both supervised and unsupervised metrics.

5   Conclusion

In this paper, we show that sense embedding is a promising approach for WSI by adopting two different sense embedding based systems on the SemEval-2010 WSI task. Both systems show highly competitive performance while they learn a general model for thousands of words (not just the tested polysemous words). we believe that the two advantages of our method are: 1) joint learning under the mutli-task learning framework, 2) better knowledge representation by discriminative training, and verify them by experiments.

Acknowledgments

Funded by NSF IIS-1446996. We would like to thank Yue Zhang for his insightful comments on the first version of the paper, and the anonymous reviewers for the insightful comments.

References

Marco Baroni, Georgiana Dinu, and Germán Kruszewski. 2014. Don't count, predict! a systematic comparison of context-counting vs. context-predicting semantic vectors. In *Proceedings of the 52nd Annual Meeting of the Association for Computational Linguistics (Volume 1: Long Papers)*, pages 238–247, Baltimore, Maryland, June. Association for Computational Linguistics.

D. Blei, A. Ng, and M. Jordan. 2003. Latent Dirichlet allocation. *Journal of Machine Learning Research*, 3:993–1022, Jan.

Stefan Bordag. 2006. Word sense induction: Triplet-based clustering and automatic evaluation. In *EACL*. Citeseer.

Samuel Brody and Mirella Lapata. 2009. Bayesian word sense induction. In *Proceedings of the 12th Conference of the European Chapter of the ACL (EACL 2009)*, pages 103–111, Athens, Greece, March. Association for Computational Linguistics.

Rich Caruana. 1997. Multitask learning. *Machine learning*, 28(1):41–75.

Ping Chen, Wei Ding, Chris Bowes, and David Brown. 2009. A fully unsupervised word sense disambiguation method using dependency knowledge. In *Proceedings of Human Language Technologies: The 2009 Annual Conference of the North American Chapter of the Association for Computational Linguistics*, pages 28–36, Boulder, Colorado, June. Association for Computational Linguistics.

Xinxiong Chen, Zhiyuan Liu, and Maosong Sun. 2014. A unified model for word sense representation and disambiguation. In *Proceedings of the 2014 Conference on Empirical Methods in Natural Language Processing (EMNLP)*, pages 1025–1035, Doha, Qatar, October. Association for Computational Linguistics.

Do Kook Choe and Eugene Charniak. 2013. Naive Bayes word sense induction. In *Proceedings of the 2013 Conference on Empirical Methods in Natural Language Processing*, pages 1433–1437, Seattle, Washington, USA, October. Association for Computational Linguistics.

Kartik Goyal and Eduard H Hovy. 2014. Unsupervised word sense induction using distributional statistics. In *COLING*, pages 1302–1310.

Zellig S Harris. 1954. Distributional structure. *Word*, 10(2-3):146–162.

Eric Huang, Richard Socher, Christopher Manning, and Andrew Ng. 2012. Improving word representations via global context and multiple word prototypes. In *Proceedings of the 50th Annual Meeting of the Association for Computational Linguistics (Volume 1: Long Papers)*, pages 873–882, Jeju Island, Korea, July. Association for Computational Linguistics.

Sujay Kumar Jauhar, Chris Dyer, and Eduard Hovy. 2015. Ontologically grounded multi-sense representation learning for semantic vector space models. In *Proceedings of the 2015 Conference of the North American Chapter of the Association for Computational Linguistics: Human Language Technologies*, pages 683–693, Denver, Colorado, May–June. Association for Computational Linguistics.

Ioannis Korkontzelos and Suresh Manandhar. 2010. Uoy: Graphs of unambiguous vertices for word sense induction and disambiguation. In *Proceedings of the 5th International Workshop on Semantic Evaluation*, pages 355–358, Uppsala, Sweden, July. Association for Computational Linguistics.

Mikael Kågebäck, Fredrik Johansson, Richard Johansson, and Devdatt Dubhashi. 2015. Neural context embeddings for automatic discovery of word senses. In *Proceedings of the 1st Workshop on Vector Space Modeling for Natural Language Processing*, pages 25–32, Denver, Colorado, June. Association for Computational Linguistics.

Jey Han Lau, Paul Cook, Diana McCarthy, David Newman, and Timothy Baldwin. 2012. Word sense induction for novel sense detection. In *Proceedings of the 13th Conference of the European Chapter of the Association for Computational Linguistics*, pages 591–601, Avignon, France, April. Association for Computational Linguistics.

Jiwei Li and Dan Jurafsky. 2015. Do multi-sense embeddings improve natural language understanding? In *Proceedings of the 2015 Conference on Empirical Methods in Natural Language Processing*, pages 1722–1732, Lisbon, Portugal, September. Association for Computational Linguistics.

Suresh Manandhar, Ioannis P Klapaftis, Dmitriy Dligach, and Sameer S Pradhan. 2010. Semeval-2010 task 14: Word sense induction & disambiguation. In *Proceedings of the 5th international workshop on semantic evaluation*, pages 63–68. Association for Computational Linguistics.

Tomas Mikolov, Ilya Sutskever, Kai Chen, Greg S Corrado, and Jeff Dean. 2013. Distributed representations of words and phrases and their compositionality. In *Advances in Neural Information Processing Systems*, pages 3111–3119.

Roberto Navigli and Giuseppe Crisafulli. 2010. Inducing word senses to improve web search result clustering. In *Proceedings of the 2010 Conference on Empirical Methods in Natural Language Processing*, pages 116–126, Cambridge, MA, October. Association for Computational Linguistics.

Arvind Neelakantan, Jeevan Shankar, Alexandre Passos, and Andrew McCallum. 2014. Efficient non-parametric estimation of multiple embeddings per word in vector space. In *Proceedings of the 2014 Conference on Empirical Methods in Natural Language Processing (EMNLP)*, pages 1059–1069, Doha, Qatar, October. Association for Computational Linguistics.

Ted Pedersen. 2010. Duluth-wsi: Senseclusters applied to the sense induction task of semeval-2. In *Proceedings of the 5th International Workshop on Semantic Evaluation*, pages 363–366, Uppsala, Sweden, July. Association for Computational Linguistics.

Jeffrey Pennington, Richard Socher, and Christopher Manning. 2014. Glove: Global vectors for word representation. In *Proceedings of the 2014 Conference on Empirical Methods in Natural Language Processing (EMNLP)*, pages 1532–1543, Doha, Qatar, October. Association for Computational Linguistics.

Amruta Purandare and Ted Pedersen. 2004. Word sense discrimination by clustering contexts in vector and similarity spaces. In Hwee Tou Ng and Ellen Riloff, editors, *HLT-NAACL 2004 Workshop: Eighth Conference on Computational Natural Language Learning (CoNLL-2004)*, pages 41–48, Boston, Massachusetts, USA, May 6 - May 7. Association for Computational Linguistics.

Joseph Reisinger and Raymond J. Mooney. 2010. Multi-prototype vector-space models of word meaning. In *Human Language Technologies: The 2010 Annual Conference of the North American Chapter of the Association for Computational Linguistics*, pages 109–117, Los Angeles, California, June. Association for Computational Linguistics.

Sascha Rothe and Hinrich Schütze. 2015. Autoextend: Extending word embeddings to embeddings for synsets and lexemes. In *Proceedings of the 53rd Annual Meeting of the Association for Computational Linguistics and the 7th International Joint Conference on Natural Language Processing (Volume 1: Long Papers)*, pages 1793–1803, Beijing, China, July. Association for Computational Linguistics.

Cyrus Shaoul and Chris Westbury. 2010. The westbury lab wikipedia corpus.

Y. W. Teh, M. I. Jordan, M. J. Beal, and D. M. Blei. 2006. Hierarchical Dirichlet processes. *Journal of the American Statistical Association*, 101(476):1566–1581.

Fei Tian, Hanjun Dai, Jiang Bian, Bin Gao, Rui Zhang, Enhong Chen, and Tie-Yan Liu. 2014. A probabilistic model for learning multi-prototype word embeddings. In *Proceedings of COLING 2014, the 25th International Conference on Computational Linguistics: Technical Papers*, pages 151–160, Dublin, Ireland, August. Dublin City University and Association for Computational Linguistics.

Tim Van de Cruys and Marianna Apidianaki. 2011. Latent semantic word sense induction and disambiguation. In *Proceedings of the 49th Annual Meeting of the Association for Computational Linguistics: Human Language Technologies*, pages 1476–1485, Portland, Oregon, USA, June. Association for Computational Linguistics.

Jing Wang, Mohit Bansal, Kevin Gimpel, Brian Ziebart, and Clement Yu. 2015. A sense-topic model for word sense induction with unsupervised data enrichment. *Transactions of the Association for Computational Linguistics*, 3:59–71.

Deyi Xiong and Min Zhang. 2014. A sense-based translation model for statistical machine translation. In *Proceedings of the 52nd Annual Meeting of the Association for Computational Linguistics (Volume 1: Long Papers)*, pages 1459–1469, Baltimore, Maryland, June. Association for Computational Linguistics.

Xuchen Yao and Benjamin Van Durme. 2011. Nonparametric bayesian word sense induction. In *Proceedings of TextGraphs-6: Graph-based Methods for Natural Language Processing*, pages 10–14. Association for Computational Linguistics.

Improving Zero-Shot-Learning for German Particle Verbs by using Training-Space Restrictions and Local Scaling

Maximilian Köper and **Sabine Schulte im Walde** and **Max Kisselew** and **Sebastian Padó**
Institut für Maschinelle Sprachverarbeitung, Universität Stuttgart
Pfaffenwaldring 5B, 70569 Stuttgart, Germany
{koepermn,schulte,kisselmx,pado}@ims.uni-stuttgart.de

Abstract

Recent models in distributional semantics consider derivational patterns (e.g., $use \rightarrow use + ful$) as the result of a compositional process, where base term and affix are combined. We exploit such models for German particle verbs (PVs), and focus on the task of learning a mapping function between base verbs and particle verbs. Our models apply particle-verb motivated training-space restrictions relying on nearest neighbors, as well as recent advances from zero-shot-learning. The models improve the mapping between base terms and derived terms for a new PV derivation dataset, and also across existing derivation datasets for German and English.

1 Introduction

Lazaridou et al. (2013) were the first to apply distributional semantic models (DSMs) to the task of deriving the meaning of morphologically complex words from their parts. They relied on high-dimensional vector representations to model the derived term (e.g., *useful*) as a result of a compositional process that combines the meanings of the base term (e.g., *to use*) and the affix (e.g., *ful*). For evaluation, they compared the predicted vector of the complex word with the original, corpus-based vector.

More recently, Kisselew et al. (2015) put the task of modeling derivation into the perspective of zero-shot-learning: instead of using cosine similarities they predicted the derived term by learning a mapping function between the base term and the derived term. Once the predicted

vector was computed, a nearest neighbor search was applied to validate if the prediction corresponded to the derived term. In zero-shot-learning the task is to predict novel values, i.e., values that were never seen in training. More formally, zero-shot-learning trains a classifier $f : X \rightarrow Y$ that predicts novel values for Y (Palatucci et al., 2009). It is often applied across vector spaces, such as different domains (Mikolov et al., 2013; Lazaridou et al., 2015).

The experiments by Kisselew et al. (2015) were performed over six derivational patterns for German (cf. Table 1), including particle verbs (PVs) with two different particle prefixes (*an* and *durch*), which were particularly difficult to predict. PVs such as *anfangen* (to start) are compositions of a base verb (BV) such as *fangen* (to catch) and a verb particle such as *an*. Predicting PV meaning is challenging because German PVs are highly productive (Springorum et al., 2013b; Springorum et al., 2013a), and the particles are notoriously ambiguous (Lechler and Roßdeutscher, 2009; Haselbach, 2011; Kliche, 2011; Springorum, 2011). Furthermore, the particles often trigger meaning shifts when they combine with base verbs (Springorum et al., 2013b), so the resulting PVs represent frequent cases of non-literal meaning.

In this paper, we focus on predicting the meanings of German PV derivations. Our models provide two contributions to the research field of predicting derivations: (i) We suggest a novel idea of restricting the available training data, which has a positive impact on the mapping quality. (ii) We integrate a correction method for popular nearest neighbors into our models, so-called *hubs* (Radovanović et al., 2010), to improve the prediction quality.

*Proceedings of the Fifth Joint Conference on Lexical and Computational Semantics (*SEM 2016)*, pages 91–96,
Berlin, Germany, August 11-12, 2016.

POS	Affix	Example	Inst.
adj/adj	un-	sagbar - unsagbar	80
adj/adj	anti-	religiös - antireligiös	80
noun/noun	-in	Bäcker - Bäckerin	80
noun/noun	-chen	Schiff - Schiffchen	80
verb/verb	an-	backen - anbacken	80
verb/verb	durch-	sehen - durchsehen	80

Table 1: German dataset (Kisselew et al., 2015).

POS	Affix	Example	Inst.
verb/verb	auf-	nehmen - aufnehmen	171
verb/verb	ab-	setzen - absetzen	287
verb/verb	mit-	streiken - mitstreiken	216
verb/verb	ein-	laufen - einlaufen	185
verb/verb	zu-	drücken - zudrücken	50
verb/verb	an-	legen - anlegen	221
verb/verb	aus-	malen - ausmalen	280

Table 2: New German PV derivation dataset.

2 Prediction Experiments

As in Kisselew et al. (2015), we treat every derivation type as a specific learning problem: we take a set of word pairs with a particular derivation pattern (e.g., "-in", Bäcker::Bäcker**in**), and divide this set into training and test pairs by performing 10-fold cross-validation. For the test pairs, we predict the vectors of the derived terms (e.g., $\overrightarrow{Bäckerin}$). The search space includes all corpus words across parts-of-speech, except for the base term. The performance is measured in terms of recall-out-of-5 (McCarthy and Navigli, 2009), counting how often the correct derived term is found among the five nearest neighbors of the predicted vector.

2.1 Derivation Datasets

We created a new collection of German particle verb derivations[1] relying on the same resource as Kisselew et al. (2015), the semi-automatic derivational lexicon for German *DErivBase* (Zeller et al., 2013). From DErivBase, we induced all pairs of base verbs and particle verbs across seven different particles. Non-existing verbs were manually filtered out. In total, our collection contains 1 410 BV–PV combinations across seven particles, cf. Table 2.

In addition, we apply our models to two existing collections for derivational patterns, the German dataset from Kisselew et al. (2015), comprising six derivational patterns with 80 in-

stances each (cf. Table 1), and the English dataset from Lazaridou et al. (2013), comprising 18 derivational patterns (3 prefixes and 15 suffixes) and 7 449 instances (cf. Table 3).

POS	Affix	Example	Inst.
verb/adj	-able	believe - believable	227
noun/adj	-al	doctor - doctoral	295
verb/noun	-er	repeat - repeater	874
noun/adj	-ful	use - useful	103
noun/adj	-ic	algorithm - algorithmic	330
verb/noun	-ion	erupt - eruption	687
noun/noun	-ist	drama - dramatist	294
adj/noun	-ity	accessible - accessibility	422
noun/verb	-ize	cannibal - cannibalize	155
noun/adj	-less	word - wordless	172
adj/adv	-ly	diagonal - diagonally	1,897
verb/noun	-ment	equip - equipment	215
adj/noun	-ness	empty - emptiness	652
noun/adj	-ous	religion - religious	207
noun/adj	-y	sport - sporty	454
adj/adj	in-	dispensable - indispensable	151
verb/verb	re-	write - rewrite	136
adj/adj	un-	familiar - unfamiliar	178

Table 3: English dataset (Lazaridou et al., 2013).

2.2 Word Embedding Vectors

We relied on the German and English *COW* web corpora[2] (Schäfer and Bildhauer, 2012) to obtain vector representations. The corpora contain 20 billion words and 9 billion words, respectively. We parsed the corpora using state-of-the-art pipelines integrating the MarMoT tagger and the MATE parser (Müller et al., 2013; Bohnet, 2010), and induced window co-occurrences for all corpus lemma–POS pairs and co-occurring nouns, verbs and adjectives in a 5-lemma window. We then created 400-dimensional word representations using the *hyperwords* toolkit (Levy et al., 2015), with context distribution smoothing of 0.75 and positive point-wise mutual information weighting together with singular value decomposition. The resulting vector space models contain approximately 460 000 lemmas for German and 240 000 lemmas for English.

2.3 Prediction Methods

2.3.1 Baseline

A baseline method that simply guesses the derived term has a chance of approx. $\frac{1}{460\,000}$ for German and $\frac{1}{240\,000}$ for English to predict the correct term. We thus apply a more informed baseline, the same as in Kisselew et al. (2015), and

---

[1] The dataset is available from `http://www.ims.uni-stuttgart.de/data/pv-deriv-dataset/`.

[2] `http://corporafromtheweb.org`

predict the derived term at exactly the same position as the base term.

2.3.2 Additive Method (AvgAdd)

AvgAdd is a re-implementation of the best method in Kisselew et al. (2015):[3] For each affix, the method learns a difference vector by computing the dimension-wise differences between the vector representations of base term A and derived term B. The method thus learns a centroid $\vec{c}$ for all relevant training pairs (N) with the same affix:

$$\vec{c} = \frac{1}{N} \sum_{i=0}^{n} (B_i - A_i) \tag{1}$$

For each PV test instance with this affix, the learned centroid vector is added dimension-wise to the vector representation of the base term to predict a position for the derived term.

2.3.3 Restricting the Training Space (BestAdd)

Avg-Add learns a vector representation based on the full available training data for each derivational pattern. In this paper, we suggest a method $BestAdd_k$ that restricts the training items of a given base term to those BV–PV training instances that include the k nearest base verbs (using $k = 1, 3, 5$) according to their *cosine*. The motivation for our adjusted method relies on the observation that particles are very ambiguous and thus differ in their meanings across particle verbs. For example, the meanings of 'an' include a directed contact as in *sprechen::ansprechen* (to speak/to speak to s.o.) and in *schreiben::anschreiben* (to write/to write to s.o.), and also a start of an action as in *spielen::anspielen* (to play/to start playing) and in *stimmen::anstimmen* (to pitch/to start singing). We assume that base verbs that are distributionally similar also behave in a similar way when combined with a specific particle, and that a more restricted training set that is however specified for BV semantics outperforms a larger training set across wider BV meanings.

2.3.4 3CosMul

We also re-implemented *3CosMul* (Levy and Goldberg, 2014), a method that has been proven successful in solving analogy tasks, such as *man*

---

[3]We also conducted experiments with the least-squares error objective method *LexFun* but the results were clearly inferior to the *AvgAdd* method.

(A) is to *king* (B) as *woman* (C) is to *queen* (D). *3CosMul* does not explicitly predict a position in space but selects a target D in space that is close to B and C but not close to A. We applied *3CosMul* by always using the most similar training instance (as for *BestAdd* with $k = 1$).

2.4 Local Scaling

All methods introduced in the previous section perform a nearest neighbor search at the predicted position. We suggest to improve the prediction quality at this stage by mitigating the hubness problem (Dinu et al., 2015). *Hubs* are objects in vector space that are likely to appear disproportionately often among nearest neighbors, without necessarily being semantically related. Hubness has been shown an intrinsic problem of high-dimensional spaces (Tomasev, 2014). In order to reduce hubness, three unsupervised methods to re-scale the high-dimensional distances have been proposed (Schnitzer et al., 2014): local scaling, global scaling, and shared nearest neighbors. We focus on a local scaling (LS) type of hubness-correcting distance measure, namely the non-iterative contextual measure NI (Jégou et al., 2007):

$$NI(x, y) = \frac{d_{xy}}{\sqrt{\mu_x \cdot \mu_y}} \tag{2}$$

NI relies on the average distance μ of x and y to their k nearest neighbors. It increases the similarity between x and y in cases where we observe low average similarities between x, y and its k nearest neighbors. Intuitively, if a word x is not even close to its nearest neighbors but comparably close to y then we increase the similarity between x and y.

For *3CosMul*, we adapt local scaling by scaling over the neighborhood information for all four parts (A, B, C and D) in the analogy:

$$3CosMul{+}LS\ (D) = \frac{3CosMul(D)}{\sqrt[4]{\mu_A \cdot \mu_B \cdot \mu_C \cdot \mu_D}}$$

3 Results

3.1 *BestAdd* and Local Scaling

Table 4 presents macro-averaged recall-out-of-5 scores, giving equal weight to each derivation regardless of the number of instances. Across the three datasets, the default results (i.e., without local scaling) obtained with our novel method

	Particle Verbs (DE)		**Kisselew (DE)**		**Lazaridou (EN)**	
Method	Default	+ NI_{15}	Default	+ NI_{15}	Default	+ NI_{15}
Baseline	10.79%		16.08%		15.36%	
AvgAdd	11.82%	+1.28%	24.26%	+3.14%	24.19%	+2.95%
$BestAdd_1$	10.22%	+1.19%	33.91%	+3.97%	27.32%	+1.87%
$BestAdd_3$	**14.26%**	**+2.24%**	**38.50%**	**+4.17%**	37.06%	+1.40%
$BestAdd_5$	14.44%	+1.97%	38.07%	+4.61%	**38.49%**	**+2.12%**
3CosMul	10.06%	-0.73%	33.91%	+ 1.04%	27.88%	+0.90%

Table 4: Macro-averaged recall-out-of-5 across methods, with and without local scaling NI_{15}.

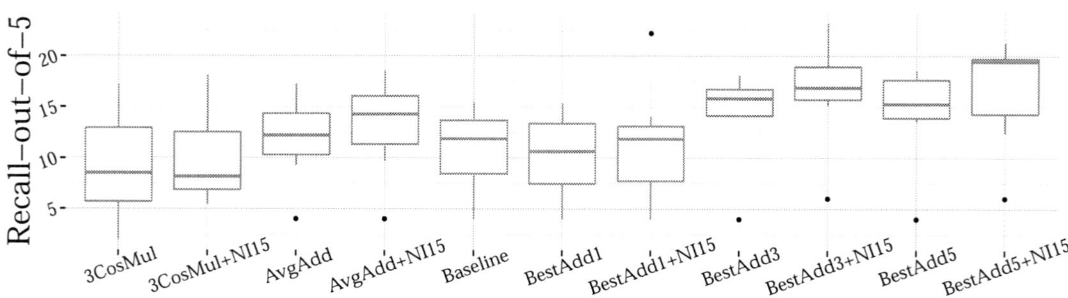

Figure 1: Recall-out-of-5 results across methods, for the German PV derivation dataset.

BestAdd (with $k = \{3,5\}$) are significantly[4] above *AvgAdd* ($p < 0.01$), the previously best method for the existing German and English datasets. *BestAdd* with $k = 1$ and *3CosMul* perform at a similar level than *AvgAdd*, but for our new PV derivation dataset do not even outperform the baseline. Restricting the training process to a small selection of nearest neighbors therefore has a positive impact on the prediction quality.

Furthermore, local scaling relying on $k = 15$ nearest neighbors (NI_{15}) improves the prediction results in all but one cases. These improvements are however not significant.

The results in Table 4 also demonstrate that predicting particle verbs is the most challenging derivation task, as the results are significantly lower than for the other two datasets. Figure 1 once more illustrates the recall-out-of-5 results for our new PV dataset. In the following, we zoom into dataset derivation types.

3.2 Improvement across Derivation Types and Languages

Figures 2 to 4 break down the results from Table 4 across the German and English derivation types.

The blue bars show the *BestAdd_3* results, and the green stacked bars represent the additional gain using local scaling (NI_{15}). The yellow points correspond to baseline performance, and the dotted black lines to the *AvgAdd* results.

We can see that *BestAdd_3* not only outperforms the previously best method *AvgAdd* on average but also for each derivation type. Also, local scaling provides an additional positive impact for all but one particle type in German, *ab-*, and for all but three derivation types in English, *-able, -al, -less*.

At the same time, we can see that the impact of local scaling is different across derivation types. For example, looking into the data we observe that *mit* PVs are often wrongly mapped to nouns, and *BestAdd* and local scaling correct this behavior: The nearest neighbors of the verb *erledigen* (to manage sth.) with *BestAdd_3* are *Botengang* (errand), *Haushaltsarbeit* (domestic work), *Hausmeisterarbeit* (janitor work), and further six compounds with the nominal head *Arbeit* (work). Additional local scaling predicts the correct PV *miterledigen* (to manage sth. in addition) as second nearest neighbor.

---

[4]Significance relies on χ^2.

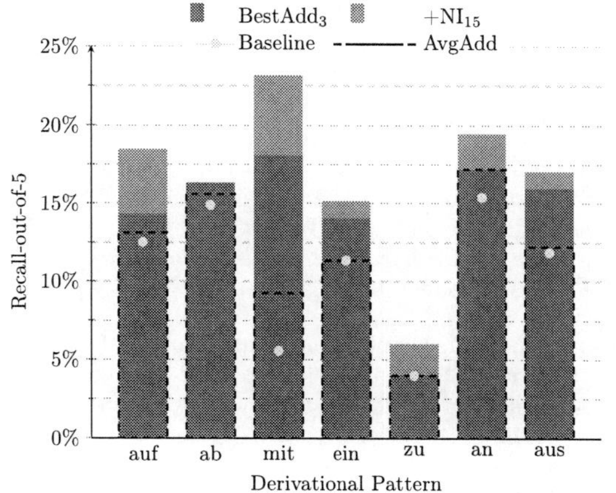

Figure 2: Performance gain across particle types.

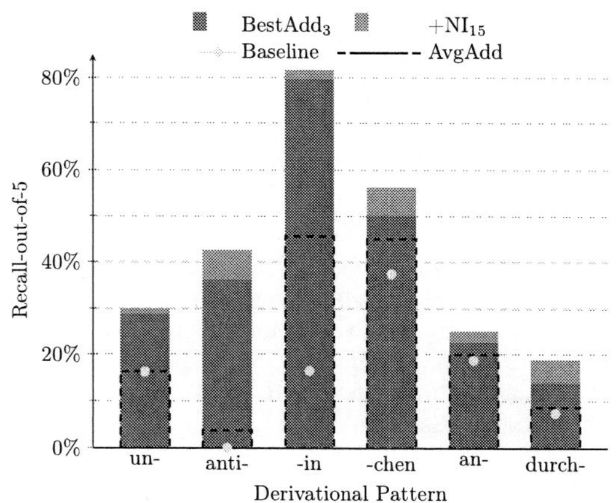

Figure 3: Performance gain for derivation types in Kisselew et al. (2015).

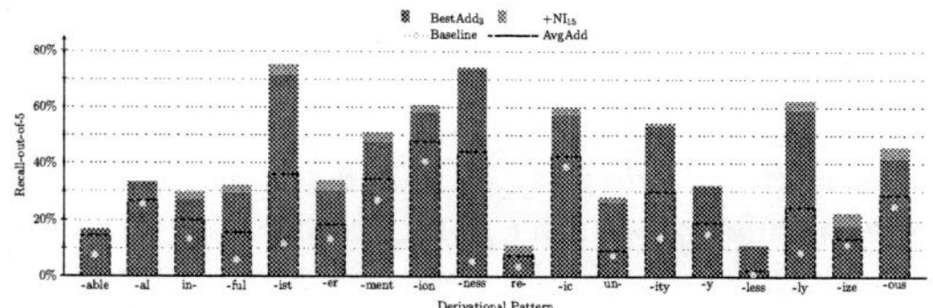

Figure 4: Performance gain for derivation types in Lazaridou et al. (2013).

3.3 Recall-out-of-x across Particle Types

Figure 5 focuses on the particle types, but varies the strength of the evaluation measure. Relying on *BestAdd*$_3$ with local scaling NI$_{15}$, we apply recall-out-of-x with $x \in [1, 10]$. With one exception (*zu*), all particle types achieve a performance of 15-23% for recall-out-of-5, so *zu* had a negative impact on the average score in Table 4. Looking at recall-out-of-10, the performances go up to 20-30%. While PVs with the rather non-ambiguous *mit* are again modeled best, also PVs with strongly ambiguous particles (such as *an* and *auf*) are modeled well.

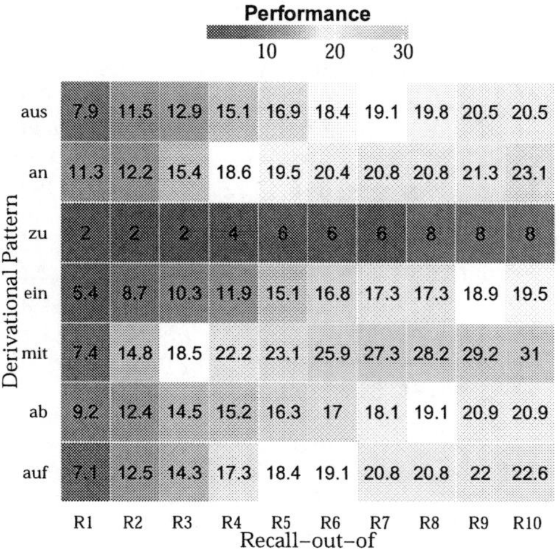

Figure 5: Recall-out-of-[1,10] across particles.

4 Conclusion

We suggested two ways to improve the prediction of derived terms for English and German. Both (i) particle-verb motivated training-space restrictions and (ii) local scaling to address hubness in high-dimensional spaces had a positive impact on the prediction quality of derived terms across datasets. Particle-specific explorations demonstrated the difficulty of this derivation, and differences across particle types.

Acknowledgments

The research was supported by the DFG Collaborative Research Centre SFB 732 (Max Kisselew, Maximilian Köper, Sebastian Padó) and the DFG Heisenberg Fellowship SCHU-2580/1 (Sabine Schulte im Walde).

References

Bernd Bohnet. 2010. Top accuracy and fast dependency parsing is not a contradiction. In *Proceedings of the 23rd International Conference on Computational Linguistics*, pages 89–97, Beijing, China.

Georgiana Dinu, Angeliki Lazaridou, and Marco Baroni. 2015. Improving zero-shot learning by mitigating the hubness problem. In *Proceedings of the International Conference on Learning Representations, Workshop Track*, San Diego, CA, USA.

Boris Haselbach. 2011. Deconstructing the meaning of the German temporal verb particle *"nach"* at the syntax-semantics interface. In *Proceedings of Generative Grammar in Geneva*, pages 71–92, Geneva, Switzerland.

Hervé Jégou, Hedi Harzallah, and Cordelia Schmid. 2007. A contextual dissimilarity measure for accurate and efficient image search. In *Proceedings of the Conference on Computer Vision & Pattern Recognition*, pages 1–8, Minneapolis, MN, USA.

Max Kisselew, Sebastian Padó, Alexis Palmer, and Jan Šnajder. 2015. Obtaining a better understanding of distributional models of German derivational morphology. In *Proceedings of the 11th International Conference on Computational Semantics*, pages 58–63, London, UK.

Fritz Kliche. 2011. Semantic Variants of German Particle Verbs with *"ab"*. *Leuvense Bijdragen*, 97:3–27.

Angeliki Lazaridou, Marco Marelli, Roberto Zamparelli, and Marco Baroni. 2013. Compositional-ly derived representations of morphologically complex words in distributional semantics. In *Proceedings of the 51st Annual Meeting of the Association for Computational Linguistics*, pages 1517–1526, Sofia, Bulgaria.

Angeliki Lazaridou, Georgiana Dinu, and Marco Baroni. 2015. Hubness and pollution: Delving into cross-space mapping for zero-shot learning. In *Proceedings of the 53rd Annual Meeting of the Association for Computational Linguistics*, pages 270–280, Beijing, China.

Andrea Lechler and Antje Roßdeutscher. 2009. German particle verbs with *"auf"*. Reconstructing their composition in a DRT-based framework. *Linguistische Berichte*, 220:439–478.

Omer Levy and Yoav Goldberg. 2014. Linguistic regularities in sparse and explicit word representations. In *Proceedings of the 18th Conference on Computational Natural Language Learning*, pages 171–180, Baltimore, MD, USA.

Omer Levy, Yoav Goldberg, and Ido Dagan. 2015. Improving distributional similarity with lessons learned from word embeddings. *Transactions of the Association for Computational Linguistics*, 3:211–225.

Diana McCarthy and Roberto Navigli. 2009. The English lexical substitution task. *Language Resources and Evaluation*, 43(2):139–159.

Tomas Mikolov, Quoc V. Le, and Ilya Sutskever. 2013. Exploiting similarities among languages for machine translation. *CoRR*, abs/1309.4168.

Thomas Müller, Helmut Schmid, and Hinrich Schütze. 2013. Efficient higher-order CRFs for morphological tagging. In *Proceedings of the Conference on Empirical Methods in Natural Language Processing*, pages 322–332, Seattle, WA, USA.

Mark Palatucci, Dean Pomerleau, Geoffrey Hinton, and Tom Mitchell. 2009. Zero-shot learning with semantic output codes. In *Advances in Neural Information Processing Systems 22*, pages 1410–1418.

Miloš Radovanović, Alexandros Nanopoulos, and Mirjana Ivanović. 2010. Hubs in space: Popular nearest neighbors in high-dimensional data. *Journal of Machine Learning Research*, 11:2487–2531.

Roland Schäfer and Felix Bildhauer. 2012. Building large corpora from the web using a new efficient tool chain. In *Proceedings of the 8th International Conference on Language Resources and Evaluation*, pages 486–493, Istanbul, Turkey.

Dominik Schnitzer, Arthur Flexer, and Nenad Tomasev. 2014. A case for hubness removal in high-dimensional multimedia retrieval. In *Advances in Information Retrieval - 36th European Conference on IR Research*, pages 687–692.

Sylvia Springorum, Sabine Schulte im Walde, and Antje Roßdeutscher. 2013a. Sentence generation and compositionality of systematic neologisms of German particle verbs. Talk at the Conference on Quantitative Investigations in Theoretical Linguistics, Leuven, Belgium.

Sylvia Springorum, Jason Utt, and Sabine Schulte im Walde. 2013b. Regular meaning shifts in German particle verbs: A case study. In *Proceedings of the 10th International Conference on Computational Semantics*, pages 228–239, Potsdam, Germany.

Sylvia Springorum. 2011. DRT-based analysis of the German verb particle *"an"*. *Leuvense Bijdragen*, 97:80–105.

Nenad Tomasev. 2014. *The Role Of Hubness in High-dimensional Data Analysis*. Ph.D. thesis.

Britta Zeller, Jan Šnajder, and Sebastian Padó. 2013. DErivBase: Inducing and evaluating a derivational morphology resource for German. In *Proceedings of the 51st Annual Meeting of the Association for Computational Linguistics*, pages 1201–1211, Sofia, Bulgaria.

When Hyperparameters Help:
Beneficial Parameter Combinations in Distributional Semantic Models

Alicia Krebs
a.m.krebs@student.rug.nl

Denis Paperno
denis.paperno@unitn.it

Center for Mind and Brain Sciences (CIMeC), University of Trento, Rovereto, Italy

Abstract

Distributional semantic models can predict many linguistic phenomena, including word similarity, lexical ambiguity, and semantic priming, or even to pass TOEFL synonymy and analogy tests (Landauer and Dumais, 1997; Griffiths et al., 2007; Turney and Pantel, 2010). But what does it take to create a competitive distributional model? Levy et al. (2015) argue that the key to success lies in hyperparameter tuning rather than in the model's architecture. More hyperparameters trivially lead to potential performance gains, but what do they actually do to improve the models? Are individual hyperparameters' contributions independent of each other? Or are only specific parameter combinations beneficial? To answer these questions, we perform a quantitative and qualitative evaluation of major hyperparameters as identified in previous research.

1 Introduction

In a rigorous evaluation, (Baroni et al., 2014) showed that neural word embeddings such as skip-gram have an edge over traditional count-based models. However, as argued by Levy and Goldberg (2014), the difference is not as big as it appears, since skip-gram is implicitly factorizing a word-context matrix whose cells are the pointwise mutual information (PMI) of word context pairs shifted by a global constant. Levy et al. (2015) further suggest that the performance advantage of neural network based models is largely due to hyperparameter optimization, and that the optimization of count based models can result in similar performance gains. In this paper we take this claim as the starting point. We experiment with

three hyperparameters that have the greatest effect on model performance according to Levy et al. (2015): subsampling, shifted PMI and context distribution smoothing. To get a more detailed picture, we use a greater range of hyperparameter values than in previous work, comparing all hyperparameter value combinations, and perform a qualitative analysis of their effect.

2 Hyperparameters Explored

2.1 Context Distribution Smoothing (CDS)

Mikolov et al. (2013b) smoothed the original contexts distribution raising unigram frequencies to the power of alpha. Levy and Goldberg (2015) used this technique in conjunction with PMI.

$$PMI(w, c) = \log \frac{\hat{P}(w, c)}{\hat{P}(w) \cdot \hat{P}_\alpha(c)}$$

$$\hat{P}_\alpha(c) = \frac{\#(c)^\alpha}{\sum_c \#(c)^\alpha}$$

After CDS, either PPMI or Shifted PPMI may be applied. We implemented CDS by raising every count to the power of α, exploring several values for α, from .25 to .95 to 1 (no smoothing).

2.2 Shifted PPMI

Levy and Goldberg introduced Shifted Positive Pointwise Mutual Information (SPPMI) as an association measure more efficient than PPMI. For every word w and every context c, the SPPMI of w is the higher value between 0 and its PMI value minus the log of a constant k.

$$PPMI(w, c) = \max(\log \frac{P(w, c)}{P(w)P(c)}, 0)$$

$$SPPMI_k(w, c) = \max(PMI(w, c) - \log k, 0)$$

*Proceedings of the Fifth Joint Conference on Lexical and Computational Semantics (*SEM 2016)*, pages 97–101,
Berlin, Germany, August 11-12, 2016.

2.3 Subsampling

Subsampling was used by Mikolov et al. as a means to remove frequent words that provide less information than rare words (Mikolov et al., 2013a). Each word in the corpus with frequency above treshold t can be ignored with probability p, computed for each word using its frequency f:

$$p = 1 - \sqrt{\frac{t}{f}}$$

Following Mikolov et al., we used $t = 10^{-5}$. In word2vec, subsampling is applied before the corpus is processed. Levy and Goldberg explored the possibility of applying subsampling afterwards, which does not affect the context window's size, but found no significant difference between the two methods. In our experiments, we applied subsampling before processing.

3 Evaluation Setup

3.1 Corpus

For maximum consistency with previous research, we used the cooccurrence counts of the best count-based configuration in Baroni et al. (2014), extracted from the concatenation of the web-crawled ukWack corpus (Baroni et al., 2009), Wikipedia, and the BNC, for a total of 2.8 billion tokens, using a 2-word window and the 300K most frequent tokens as contexts. This corpus will be referred to as WUB. For comparison with a smaller corpus, similar to the one in Levy and Goldberg's setup, we also extracted cooccurrence data from Wikipedia alone, leaving the rest of the configuration identical. This corpus will be referred to as Wiki.

3.2 Evaluation Materials

Three data sets were used to evaluate the models. The MEN data set contains 3000 word pairs rated by human similarity judgements. Bruni et al. (2014) report an accuracy of 78% on this data-set using an approach that combines visual and textual features. The WordSim data set is a collection of word pairs associated with human judgements of similarity or relatedness. The similarity set contains 203 items (WS sim) and the relatedness set contains 252 items (WS rel). Agirre et al. achieved an accuracy of 77% on this data set using a context window approach (Agirre et al., 2009). The TOEFL data set includes 80 multiple-choice synonym questions (Landauer and Dumais,

1997). For this data set, corpus-based approaches have reached an accuracy of 92.50% (Rapp, 2003).

4 Results

4.1 Context Distribution Smoothing

Our results show that smoothing is largely ineffective when used in conjunction with PPMI. It also becomes apparent that .95 is a better parameter than .75 for smoothing purposes.

		MEN	WS rel	WS sim	toefl
WUB	.25	.6128	.3740	.5814	.62
	.50	.6592	.4419	.6283	.68
	.70	.6938	.5113	.6708	.72
	.75	.7008	.5249	.6788	.75
	.80	.7069	.5393	.6866	.76
	.85	.7119	.5517	.6950	**.77**
	.90	.7162	.5625	.6998	**.77**
	.95	.7197	**.5730**	**.7043**	**.77**
	1.0	**.7208**	.5708	.7001	.76
Wiki	.75	.7194	.4410	.6906	.76
	.85	.7251	.4488	.7001	.76
	.95	**.7277**	**.4534**	.7083	**.77**
	1.0	.7224	.4489	**.7158**	.76

Table 1: Context Distribution Smoothing

4.2 Shifted PPMI

When using SPPMI, Levy and Goldberg (2014) tested three values for k: 1, 5 and 15. On the MEN data set, they report that the best k value was 5 (.721), while on the WordSim data set the best k value was 15 (.687). In our experiments, where (in contrast to Levy and Goldberg) all other hyperparameters are set to 'vanilla' values, the best k value was 3 for all data sets.

4.3 Smoothing and Shifting Combined

The results in Table 3 show that Context Distribution Smoothing is effective when used in conjunction with Shifted PPMI. With CDS, 5 turns out to be a better value than 3 for k. These results are also consistent with the previous experiment: a smoothing of .95 is in most cases better than .75.

4.4 Subsampling

Under the best shifting and smoothing configuration, subsampling can improve the model's performance score by up to 9.2% (see Table 4). But in

		MEN	WS rel	WS sim	toefl
WUB	1	.7208	.5708	.7001	**.76**
	2	.7298	.5880	.7083	.75
	3	**.7314**	**.5891**	**.7113**	**.76**
	4	.7308	.5771	.7071	**.76**
	5	.7291	.5651	.7034	.75
	10	.7145	.5138	.6731	.72
	15	.6961	.4707	.6464	.71
Wiki	1	.7224	.4489	.7158	.76
	3	**.7281**	**.4575**	**.7380**	**.77**
	4	.7269	.4553	.7376	.75
	5	.7250	.4504	.7334	.76

Table 2: Shifted PPMI

	MEN	WS rel	WS sim	toefl
WUB				
log(1) cds(1.0)	.7208	.5708	.7001	.76
log(3) cds(.75)	.7319	.5969	.7146	.73
log(3) cds(.90)	.7371	.6170	.7285	.76
log(3) cds(.95)	.7379	.6201	.7315	.76
log(4) cds(.75)	.7363	.6071	.7212	.75
log(4) cds(.90)	.7398	.6222	.7351	.76
log(4) cds(.95)	.7403	**.6265**	.7392	**.77**
log(5) cds(.75)	.7387	.6115	.7281	.76
log(5) cds(.90)	.7412	.6223	.7404	**.77**
log(5) cds(.95)	**.7414**	.6257	**.7434**	**.77**
Wiki				
log(1) cds(1.0)	.7224	.4489	.7158	**.76**
log(5) cds(.75)	**.7424**	.4787	.7378	.75
log(5) cds(.85)	.7399	.4795	.7418	.75
log(5) cds(.95)	.7362	**.4806**	.7443	.75

Table 3: CDS and Shifted PPMI

	MEN	WS rel	WS sim	toefl
WUB				
log(1) cds(1.0)	.7284	.5043	.6750	**.75**
log(5) cds(.95)	**.7577**	**.5539**	**.7505**	.73
Wiki				
log(1) cds(1.0)	.7260	.5186	.6965	.72
log(5) cds(.95)	**.7661**	**.5729**	**.7446**	**.76**

Table 4: CDS and SPPMI with subsampling

the absence of shifting and smoothing, subsampling does not produce a consistent performance change, which ranges from -6.7% to $+7\%$.

The nature of the task is also important here: on WS rel, subsampling improves the model's performance by 9.2%. We assume that diversifying contextual cues is more beneficial in a relatedness task than in others, especially on a smaller corpus.

5 Qualitative Analysis

CDS and SPPMI increase model performance because they reduce statistical noise, which is illustrated in Table 5. It shows the top ten neighbours of the word *doughnut* in the vanilla PPMI configuration vs. SPPMI with CDS, in which there are more semantically related neighbours (in bold).

To visualize which dimensions of the vectors are discarded when shifting and smoothing, we randomly selected a thousand word vectors and compared the number of dimensions with a positive value for each vector in the vanilla configuration vs. log(5)cds(.95). For instance, the word *segmentation* has 1105 positive dimensions in the vanilla configuration, but only 577 in the latter.

For visual clarity, only vectors with 500 or less contexts are shown in Figure 1.

This figure indicates that the process of shifting and smoothing appears to be largely independent from the number of contexts of a vector: a word with a high number of positive contexts in the vanilla configuration may very well end up with zero positive contexts under SPPMI with CDS.

The independence of the number of positive contexts under the vanilla configuration from the probability of having at least one positive context under SPPMI with CDS is confirmed by the Chi-Square test ($\chi = 344.26$, p = .9058).

We further analysed a sample of 1504 vectors that lose all positive dimensions under SPPMI with CDS. We annotated a portion of those vectors, and found that the vast majority were numerical expressions, such as dates, prices or measurements, e.g. *1745*, which may appear in many different contexts, but is unlikely to have a high number of occurrences with any of them. This explains why its number of positive contexts drops to zero when SPPMI and CDS are applied.

6 Count vs Predict and Corpus Size

We conducted the same experimentations on two corpora: the WUB corpus (Wikipedia+ukWack+BNC) used by Baroni et al., and the smaller Wiki corpus comparable

log(1) cds(1.0)		log(5) cds(.95)	
doughnut	1.0	doughnut	1.0
lukeylad	.467	**donut**	.242
ricardo308	.388	**doughnuts**	.213
katie8731	.376	**donuts**	.203
holliejm	.288	**kreme**	.179
donut	.200	lukeylad	.167
lumic	.187	**krispy**	.149
notveryfast	.183	:dance	.115
adricsghost	.178	bradys	.105
doughnuts	.178	holliejm	.102

Table 5: Top 10 neighbours of *doughnut*. Semantically related neighbors are given in bold.

>0	>300	>750	>1000	>1500
8:23	1900s	e4	1024	51
01-06-2005	7.45pm	8.4	1928.	1981.
ec3n	41.	331	1924.	17
5935	1646	1745	45,000	2500
$1.00	$25	1/3	630	1960s

Table 6: Sample of words with zero positive dimensions after SPPMI with CDS

predict	MEN	WS rel	WS sim	toefl
WUB	.80	.70	.80	.91
Wiki	.7370	.4951	.7714	.83

best count	MEN	WS rel	WS sim	toefl
WUB	.7577	.6265	.7505	.77
Wiki	.7661	.5729	.7446	.77

Table 7: Performance of count vs. predict models as a function of corpus size

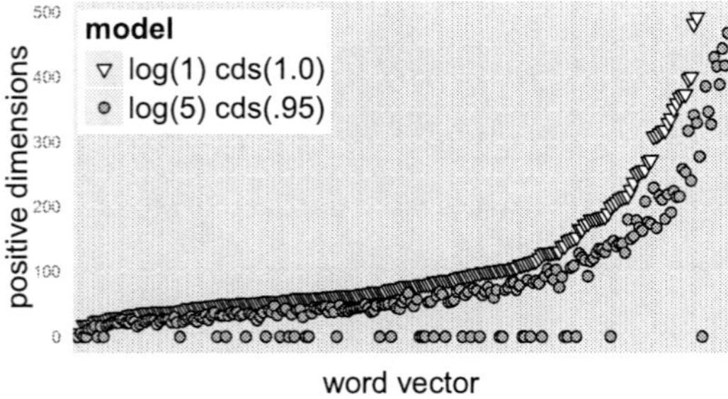

Figure 1: Along the X axis, vectors are ordered by the ascending number of positive dimensions in the vanilla model. The Y axis represents the number of positive dimensions in two models.

to the one that Levy et al. employed. With these two corpora, we found the same general pattern of results, with the exception of the WordSim relatedness task benefitting greatly from a larger corpus and MEN favoring steeper smoothing (.75) under the smaller corpus. This suggests that the smoothing hyperparameter should be adjusted to the corpus size and the task at hand.

For comparison, we give the results for a word2vec model trained on the two corpora using the best configuration reported by Baroni et al. (2014): CBOW, 10 negative samples, CDS, window 5, and 400 dimensions. We find that PPMI is more efficient when using the Wikipedia corpus alone, but when using the larger corpus the predict model still outperforms all count models.

7 Conclusion

Our investigation showed that the interaction of different hyperparameters matters more than the implementation of any single one. Smoothing only shows its potential when used in combination with shifting. Similarly, subsampling only becomes interesting when shifting and smoothing are applied. When it comes to parameter values, we recommend using .95 as a smoothing hyperparameter and log(5) as a shifting hyperparameter.

Qualitatively speaking, the hyperparameters help largely by reducing statistical noise in cooccurrence data. SPPMI works by removing low PMI values, which are likely to be noisy. CDS effectively lowers PMI values for rare contexts, which tend to be more noisy, allowing for a higher threshold for SPPMI ($\log 5$ vs. $\log 3$) to be effective. Subsampling gives a greater weight to underexploited data from rare words at the expense of frequent ones, but it amplifies the noise as well as the signal, and should be combined with the other noise-reducing hyperparameters to be useful.

In terms of corpus size, we've seen that similar performance can be achieved with a smaller corpus if the right hyperparameters are used. One exception is the WordSim relatedness task, in which models require more data to achieve the same level of performance, and benefit from subsampling much more than in the similarity task.

While the best predictive model from Baroni et al. trained on the WUB corpus still outperforms our best count model on the same corpus, hyperparameter tuning does significantly improve the performance of count models and should be used when a corpus is too small to build a predictive model.

References

Eneko Agirre, Enrique Alfonseca, Keith Hall, Jana Kravalova, Marius Paşca, and Aitor Soroa. 2009. A study on similarity and relatedness using distributional and wordnet-based approaches. In *Proceedings of Human Language Technologies: The 2009 Annual Conference of the North American Chapter of the Association for Computational Linguistics*, pages 19–27. Association for Computational Linguistics.

Marco Baroni, Silvia Bernardini, Adriano Ferraresi, and Eros Zanchetta. 2009. The wacky wide web: A collection of very large linguistically processed web-crawled corpora. *Language Resources and Evaluation*, 43(3):209–226.

Marco Baroni, Georgiana Dinu, and Germán Kruszewski. 2014. Dont count, predict! a systematic comparison of context-counting vs. context-predicting semantic vectors. In *Proceedings of the 52nd Annual Meeting of the Association for Computational Linguistics*, volume 1, pages 238–247.

Elia Bruni, Nam-Khanh Tran, and Marco Baroni. 2014. Multimodal distributional semantics. *J. Artif. Intell. Res.(JAIR)*, 49(1–47).

Thomas L. Griffiths, Mark Steyvers, and Joshua B. Tenenbaum. 2007. Topics in semantic representation. *Psychological Review*, 114(2):211–244.

Thomas K. Landauer and Susan T. Dumais. 1997. A solution to plato's problem: The latent semantic analysis theory of acquisition, induction, and representation of knowledge. *Psychological Review*, 104(2):211–240.

Omer Levy and Yoav Goldberg. 2014. Neural word embedding as implicit matrix factorization. In *Advances in Neural Information Processing Systems*, pages 2177–2185.

Omer Levy, Yoav Goldberg, and Ido Dagan. 2015. Improving distributional similarity with lessons learned from word embeddings. *Transactions of the Association for Computational Linguistics*, 3:211–225.

Tomas Mikolov, Kai Chen, Greg Corrado, and Jeffrey Dean. 2013a. Efficient estimation of word representations in vector space. *arXiv preprint arXiv:1301.3781*.

Tomas Mikolov, Ilya Sutskever, Kai Chen, Greg S Corrado, and Jeff Dean. 2013b. Distributed representations of words and phrases and their compositionality. In *Advances in Neural Information Processing Systems*, pages 3111–3119.

Reinhard Rapp. 2003. Word sense discovery based on sense descriptor dissimilarity. In *Proceedings of the Ninth Machine Translation Summit*, pages 315–322.

Peter D. Turney and Patrick Pantel. 2010. From frequency to meaning: Vector space models of semantics. *Journal of Artificial Intelligence Research*, 37(1):141–188.

Leveraging VerbNet to build Corpus-Specific Verb Clusters

Daniel W Peterson and **Jordan Boyd-Graber** and **Martha Palmer**
University of Colorado
{daniel.w.peterson, jordan.boyd.graber, martha.palmer}@colorado.edu

Daisuke Kawhara
Kyoto University, JP
dk@i.kyoto-u.ac.jp

Abstract

In this paper, we aim to close the gap from extensive, human-built semantic resources and corpus-driven unsupervised models. The particular resource explored here is VerbNet, whose organizing principle is that semantics and syntax are linked. To capture patterns of usage that can augment knowledge resources like VerbNet, we expand a Dirichlet process mixture model to predict a VerbNet class for each sense of each verb, allowing us to incorporate annotated VerbNet data to guide the clustering process. The resulting clusters align more closely to hand-curated syntactic/semantic groupings than any previous models, and can be adapted to new domains since they require only corpus counts.

1   Introduction

In this paper, we aim to close the gap from extensive, human-built semantic resources and corpus-driven unsupervised models. The work done by linguists over years of effort has been validated by the scientific community, and promises real traction on the fuzzy problem of deriving meaning from words. However, lack of coverage and adaptability currently limit the usefulness of this work.

The particular resource explored here is VerbNet (Kipper-Schuler, 2005), a semantic resource built upon the foundation of verb classes by Levin (1993). Levin's verb classes are built on the hypothesis that syntax and semantics are fundamentally linked. The semantics of a verb affect the allowable syntactic constructions involving that verb, creating regularities in language to which speakers are extremely sensitive. It follows that grouping verbs by allowable syntactic realizations leads from syntax to meaningful semantic groupings. This seed grew into VerbNet, a process which involved dozens of linguists and a decade of work, making careful decisions about the allowable syntactic frames for various verb senses, informed by text examples.

VerbNet is useful for semantic role labeling and related tasks (Giuglea and Moschitti, 2006; Yi, 2007; Yi et al., 2007; Merlo and van der Plas, 2009; Kshirsagar et al., 2014), but its widespread use is limited by coverage. Not all verbs have a VerbNet class, and some polysemous verbs have important senses unaccounted for. In addition, VerbNet is not easily adaptable to domain-specific corpora, so these omissions may be more prominent outside of the general-purpose corpora and linguistic intuition used in its construction. Its great strength is also its downfall: adding new verbs, new senses, and new classes requires trained linguists - at least, to preserve the integrity of the resource.

According to Levin's hypothesis, knowing the set of allowable syntactic patterns for a verb sense is sufficient to make meaningful semantic classifications. Large-scale corpora provide an extremely comprehensive picture of the possible syntactic realizations for any particular verb. With enough data in the training set, even infrequent verbs have sufficient data to support learning. Kawahara et al. (2014) showed that, using a Dirichlet Process Mixture Model (DPMM), a VerbNet-like clustering of verb senses can be built from counts of syntactic features.

We develop a model to extend VerbNet, using a large corpus with machine-annotated dependencies. We build on prior work by adding partial supervision from VerbNet, treating VerbNet classes as additional latent variables. The resulting clusters are more similar to the evaluation set, and each cluster in the DPMM predicts its VerbNet class distribution naturally. Because the technique is data-driven, it is easily adaptable to domain-specific corpora.

*Proceedings of the Fifth Joint Conference on Lexical and Computational Semantics (*SEM 2016)*, pages 102–107,
Berlin, Germany, August 11-12, 2016.

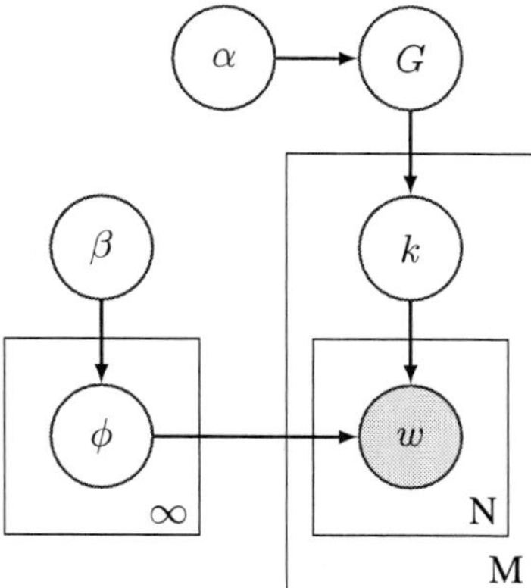

Figure 1: The DPMM used in Kawahara et al. (2014) for clustering verb senses. M is the number of verb senses, and N is the sum total of slot counts for that verb sense.

2 Prior Work

Parisien and Stevenson (2011) and Kawahara et al. (2014) showed distinct ways of applying the Hierarchical Dirichlet Process (Teh et al., 2006) to uncover the latent clusters from cluster examples. The latter used significantly larger corpora, and explicitly separated verb sense induction from the syntactic/semantic clustering, which allowed more fine-grained control of each step.

In Kawahara et al. (2014), two identical DPMM's were used. The first clustered verb instances into senses, and one such model was trained for each verb. These verb-sense clusters are available publicly, and are used unmodified in this paper. The second DPMM clusters verb senses into VerbNet-like clusters of verbs. The result is a resource that, like Verbnet, inherently captures the inherent polysemy of verbs. We focus our improvements on this second step, and try to derive verb clusters that more closely align to VerbNet.

2.1 Dirichlet Process Mixture Models

The DPMM used in Kawahara et al. (2014) is shown in Figure 1. The clusters are drawn from a Dirichlet Process with hyperparameter α and base distribution G. The Dirichlet process prior creates a clustering effect described by the Chinese Restaurant Process. Each cluster is chosen proportionally to the number of elements it already contains, i.e.

$$P(k|\alpha, C_k(*)) \propto \begin{cases} C_k(*), & \text{if } C_k(*) > 0 \\ \alpha, & \text{if } k = k_{new}, \end{cases} \quad (1)$$

where $C_k(*)$ is the count of clustered items already in cluster k.

Each cluster k has an associated multinomial distribution over vocabulary items (e.g. slot:token pairs), ϕ_k, which is drawn from G, a Dirichlet distribution of the same size as the vocabulary, parameterized by a constant β. Because the Dirichlet is the multinomial's conjugate prior, we can actually integrate out ϕ_k analytically, given counts of vocabulary items drawn from ϕ_k. For a particular vocabulary item w, we compute

$$P(w|\phi_k, \beta) = \frac{C_k(w) + \beta}{C_k(*) + |V|\beta}, \quad (2)$$

where $C_k(w)$ is the number of times w has been drawn from ϕ_k, $C_k(*) = \sum_i C_k(i)$, and $|V|$ is the size of the vocabulary.

When assigning a verb instance to a sense, a single instance may have multiple syntactic arguments w. Using Bayes's law, we update each assignment iteratively using Gibbs sampling, using equations (1) and (2), according to

$$P(k|\alpha, C_k(*), \phi_k, \beta) \propto$$
$$P(k|\alpha, C_k(*)) \prod_w P(w|\phi_k, \beta). \quad (3)$$

$\beta < 1$ encourages the clusters to have a sparse representation in the vocabulary space. $\alpha = 1$ is a typical choice, and encourages a small number of clusters to be used.

2.2 Step-wise Verb Cluster Creation

By separating the verb sense induction and the clustering of verb senses, the features can be optimized for the distinct tasks. According to (Kawahara et al., 2014), the best features for inducing verb classes are joint slot:token pairs. For the verb clustering task, slot features which ignore the lexical items were the most effective. This aligns with Levin's hypothesis of diathesis alternations - the syntactic contexts are sufficient for the clustering.

In this paper, we re-create the second stage clustering with the same features, but add supervision. Supervised Topic Modeling (Mimno and McCallum, 2008; Ramage et al., 2009) builds on the Bayesian framework by adding, for each item, a prediction about a variable of interest, which is observed at least some of the time. This encourages the topics to be useful at predicting a supervised signal, as well as coherent as topics. We do not have explicit knowledge of VerbNet class for any of the first-level DPMM's verb senses, so our supervision is informed only at the level of the verb.

3 Supervised DPMM

Adding supervision to the DPMM is fairly straightforward: at each step, we sample both a mixture component k and a VerbNet class y. For this, we assign each cluster (mixture component) a unique distribution ρ over VerbNet classes, drawn from a fixed-size Dirichlet prior with parameter γ. As before, this allows us to estimate the likelihood of a VerbNet class y knowing only the counts of assigned senses, $C_k(y)$, for each y, as

$$P(y|\rho_k,\gamma) = \frac{C_k(y) + \gamma}{C_k(*) + |S|\gamma}, \quad (4)$$

where $|S|$ is the number of classes in the supervision.

The likelihood of choosing a class for a particular verb requires us to form an estimate of that verb's probability of joining a particular VerbNet class. We initialize η from SemLink, as $\eta(y) = \omega * C_v^{SL}(y) + \delta$, for fixed constants ω and δ, and with $C_v^{SL}(y)$ as the count, in SemLink, of times verb v was assigned to VerbNet class y. We then draw a verb-specific distribution θ over VerbNet classes, from a Dirichlet with parameters η, so that η acts as pseudo-counts, steering θ to give high weight to VerbNet classes aligned with SemLink for each verb. We compute

$$P(y|\theta,\eta) = \frac{C_v(y) + \eta(y)}{C_v(*) + \sum \eta}, \quad (5)$$

where $C_v(y)$ is the number of times verb v is assigned to VerbNet class y by our model.

We sample the VerbNet class for a verb sense as a product of experts (Hinton, 2002), the θ_v for the verb v, and ρ_k for the assigned cluster k. This encourages alignment between the VerbNet classes observed in SemLink and the VerbNet classes predicted by the clusters, and is computationally straightforward. We simply compute

$$P(y|\rho_k,\gamma,\theta_v,\eta) \propto P(y|\rho_k,\gamma)P(y|\theta_v,\eta). \quad (6)$$

Sampling a cluster for a verb sense now depends on the VerbNet class y,

$$P(k|y,\alpha,\phi_k,\beta,\rho_k,\gamma,\theta_v,\eta) \propto$$
$$\left(P(k|\alpha, C_k(*)) \times \right.$$
$$P(y|\rho_k,\gamma,\theta_v,\eta) \times \quad (7)$$
$$\left. \prod_w P(w|\phi_k,\beta) \right).$$

We then update y based on Equation 6, and then resample for the next batch.

The supervised process is depicted in Figure 2. In brief, we know for each verb an η, a given by counts from SemLink, which we use as a prior for θ. We sample, in addition to the cluster label k, a VerbNet class y, which depends on θ and ρ, where ρ is the distribution over VerbNet classes in cluster k. ρ is drawn from a Dirichlet distribution paramaterized by $\gamma < 1$, encouraging each cluster to have a sparse distribution over VerbNet classes. Because y depends on both θ and ρ, the clusters are encouraged to align with VerbNet classes.

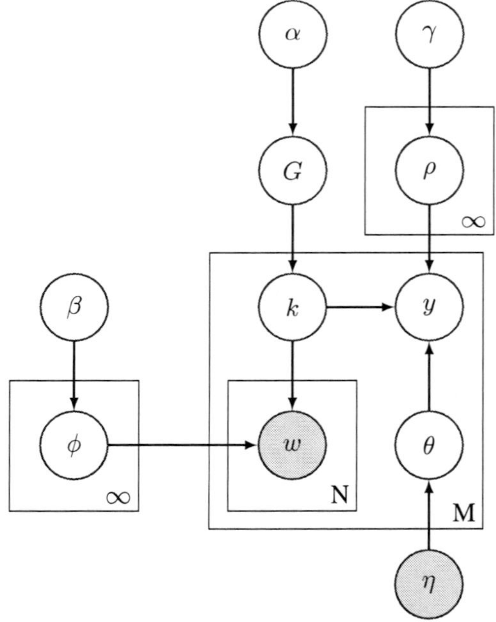

Figure 2: The Supervised DPMM used in this work for clustering verb senses. M is the number of verb senses, and N is the sum total of slot counts for that verb sense. θ is initialized to reflect the VerbNet class preferences for each verb, when they are known.

3.1 Modeling Choices

When incorporating supervision, the more direct method of downstream sampling of the VerbNet class may be preferred to using a prior. However, the verb senses are generated through a DPMM, and we do not have a gold-label assignment of VerbNet classes to each sense. Instead, we estimate, for each verb in VerbNet, a distribution θ describing the likelihood a verb will participate in a particular class, using counts from SemLink.

When sampling a cluster for a verb sense with a verb in VerbNet, we sample y from a product of experts. We cannot incorporate θ as a prior when sampling y, because we have multiple verbs, with distinct distributions $\theta_{v_1}, \theta_{v_2}, \ldots$.

Because the product-of-experts is a discrete probability distribution, it is easy to marginalize out this variable when sampling k, using

$$P(k|\alpha, \phi_k, \beta, \rho_k, \gamma, \theta) \propto$$
$$\sum_y P(k|y, \alpha, \phi_k, \beta, \rho_k, \gamma, \theta_v, \eta). \quad (8)$$

Either way, once a cluster is selected, we should update the ρ and θ. So, once a cluster is selected, we still sample a discrete y. We compare performance for sampling k with assigned y and with marginalized y.

When incorporating supervision, we flatten VerbNet, using only the top-level categories, simplifying the selection process for y. In Kawahara et al. (2014), slot features were most effective features at producing a VerbNet-like structure; we follow suit.

4 Results

For evaluation, we compare using the same dataset and metrics as Kawahara et al. (2014). There, the authors use the polysemous verb classes of Korhonen et al. (2003), a subset of frequent polysemous verbs. This makes the test set a sort of mini-VerbNet, suitable for evaluation. They also define a normalized modified purity and normalized inverse purity for evaluation, explained below.

The standard purity of a hard clustering averages, for each cluster's majority gold standard class, the percentage of clustered items of that class. Because the clustering is polysemous, a typical automatically-induced cluster K will contain only some senses of the verbs. We take this partial membership into account when deciding the

cluster's majority class. We define $c_{iv} \in [0,1]$ as the proportion of instances of verb v grouped into cluster K_i. We also treat induced clusters containing only one verb sense as errors, rather than treating them as clusters of perfect purity. Therefore, the normalized modified purity (nmPU), with respect to the gold standard clusters G, is,

$$\text{nmPU} = \frac{1}{N} \sum_{i \text{ s.t. } |K_i| > 1} \max_j \delta_{K_i}(K_i \cap G_j), \quad (9)$$

where

$$\delta_{K_i}(K_i \cap G_j) = \sum_{v \in K_i \cap G_j} c_{iv}. \quad (10)$$

This nmPU is analagous to clustering precision: it measures, on average, how well the clustering avoids matching items that should not be clustered. We also define a recall analogue, the normalized inverse purity (niPU), as,

$$\text{niPU} = \frac{1}{N} \sum_j \max_i \delta_{G_j}(K_i \cap G_j). \quad (11)$$

This measures how well each gold standard cluster is recovered. We report each metric, and the F1 score combining them, to compare the clustering accuracy with respect to the gold standard G.

We use the clustering from Kawahara et al. (2014) as a baseline for comparison. However, for evaluation, the authors only clustered senses of verbs in the evaluation set. Since we would like to test the effectiveness of adding supervision, we treat all verbs in the evaluation set as unsupervised, with no initialization of θ. Therefore, to compare apples-to-apples, we calculate the nPU, niPU, and F1 of the Kawahara et al. (2014) full clustering against the evaluation set. Our model also computes the full clustering, but with supervision for known verbs (other than the evaluation set).

Parameters were selected using a grid search, and cross-validation. The results are summarized in Table 1, comparing the unsupervised DPMM baseline (**DPMM**) to the supervised DPMM (**SDPMM**), and the supervised DPMM sampling k with y marginalized out (**mSDPMM**).

5 Comparison of Produced Clusters

The supervised sampling scheme produces fewer clusters than the unsupervised baseline. This is in

Model	Example Clusters	
Gold	**push** (0.20), **pull** (0.17)	**give** (1.0), **lend** (1.0), **generate** (0.33), **allow** (0.25), **pull** (0.17), **pour** (0.17)
DPMM	**push** (0.40), **drag** (0.27), **pull** (0.08)	**lend** (0.30), **give** (0.13),
SDPMM	**drag** (0.87), **push** (0.43), **pull** (0.42), **pour** (0.39), **drop** (0.31), **force** (0.09)	**give** (0.82), **pour** (0.02), **ship** (0.002)

Table 2: Example clusters from the evaluation dataset (**Gold**), and along with the most-aligned clusters from the unsupervised baseline (**DPMM**) and our semi-supervised clustering scheme (**SDPMM**). Weights given in parentheses describe the total proportion of verb instances assigned to each cluster.

Model	nmPU	niPU	F1	N
DPMM	**55.72**	60.33	57.93	522
SDPMM	51.00	**75.71**	**60.95**	122
mSDPMM	51.04	75.00	60.74	129

Table 1: Clustering accuracy on verbs in the Korhonen et al. (2003) dataset. N is the number of clusters spanned by the evaluation set.

part because it produces fewer "singleton" clusters, containing only one verb sense from the evaluation set. The SDPMM produces only 16% singleton clusters, compared with 34% of singleton clusters from the unsupervised DPMM.

The supervised clusters also tend to cluster more of the senses of each verb into the same cluster. The predominant SDPMM cluster for a verb, which has the highest percentage of a verb's total instances, tends to have 224% the number of instances as the predominant unsupervised DPMM cluster. This tendency does not prevent verbs being assigned multiple clusters, however. On average, the supervised clustering uses 30% fewer clusters for each verb, a smaller reduction than the 70% overall drop in the number of clusters.

A few example clusters are presented in Table 2.

6 Conclusions and Future Directions

The supervision tends to encourage a smaller number of clusters, so the precision-like metric, nmPU, is lower, but the recall-like metric, niPU, is much higher. Marginalizing out the variable y when sampling k does not make an appreciable difference to the F1 score. Swapping out the Dirichlet process for a Pitman-Yor process may bring finer control over the number of clusters.

We have expanded the work in Kawahara et al. (2014) by explicitly modeling a VerbNet class for each verb sense, drawn from a product of experts

based on the cluster and verb. This allowed us to leverage data from SemLink with VerbNet annotation, to produce a higher-quality clustering. It also allows us to describe each cluster in terms of alignment to VerbNet classes. Both of these improvements bring us closer to extending VerbNet's usefulness, using only automated dependency parses of corpora. We may speculate, and should test, whether the improved verb clusters will prove useful in end-to-end semantic tasks.

References

Ana-Maria Giuglea and Alessandro Moschitti. 2006. Semantic role labeling via framenet, verbnet and propbank. In *Proceedings of the Joint 21st International Conference on Computational Linguistics and 44th Annual Meeting of the Association for Computational Linguistics (COLING-ACL 2006)*.

Geoffrey E Hinton. 2002. Training products of experts by minimizing contrastive divergence. *Neural computation*, 14(8):1771–1800.

Daisuke Kawahara, Daniel W. Peterson, and Martha Palmer. 2014. A step-wise usage-based method for inducing polysemy-aware verb classes. In *Proceedings of the 52nd Annual Meeting of the Association for Computational Linguistics (ACL2014)*.

Karin Kipper-Schuler. 2005. *VerbNet: A Broad-Coverage, Comprehensive Verb Lexicon*. Ph.D. thesis, University of Pennsylvania.

Anna Korhonen, Yuval Krymolowski, and Zvika Marx. 2003. Clustering polysemic subcategorization frame distributions semantically. In *Proceedings of the 41st Annual Meeting of the Association for Computational Linguistics (ACL2003)*, pages 64–71.

Meghana Kshirsagar, Nathan Schneider, and Chris Dyer. 2014. Leveraging heterogeneous data sources for relational semantic parsing. In *Proceedings of ACL 2014 Workshop on Semantic Parsing*.

Beth Levin. 1993. *English verb classes and alternations: A preliminary investigation*. The University of Chicago Press.

Paola Merlo and Lonneke van der Plas. 2009. Abstraction and generalisation in semantic role labels: Propbank, verbnet or both? In *Proceedings of IJC-NLP/ACL 2009*.

David Mimno and Andrew McCallum. 2008. Topic models conditioned on arbitrary features with dirichlet-multinomial regression. In *UAI*.

Christopher Parisien and Suzanne Stevenson. 2011. Generalizing between form and meaning using learned verb classes. In *Proceedings of the 33rd Annual Meeting of the Cognitive Science Society (CogSci2011)*.

Daniel Ramage, David Hall, Ramesh Nallapati, and Christopher D Manning. 2009. Labeled lda: A supervised topic model for credit attribution in multi-labeled corpora. In *Proceedings of the 2009 Conference on Empirical Methods in Natural Language Processing: Volume 1-Volume 1*, pages 248–256. Association for Computational Linguistics.

Yee Whye Teh, Michael I. Jordan, Matthew J. Beal, and David M. Blei. 2006. Hierarchical Dirichlet processes. *Journal of the American Statistical Association*, 101(476).

Szu-ting Yi, Edward Loper, and Martha Palmer. 2007. Can semantic roles generalize across genres? In *Proceedings of NAACL HLT 2007*.

Szu-ting Yi. 2007. *Automatic Semantic Role Labeling*. Ph.D. thesis, University of Pennsylvania.

Adding Context to Semantic Data-Driven Paraphrasing

Vered Shwartz   **Ido Dagan**
Computer Science Department
Bar-Ilan University
Ramat-Gan, Israel
`vered1986@gmail.com dagan@cs.biu.ac.il`

Abstract

Recognizing lexical inferences between pairs of terms is a common task in NLP applications, which should typically be performed within a given context. Such context-sensitive inferences have to consider both term meaning in context as well as the fine-grained relation holding between the terms. Hence, to develop suitable lexical inference methods, we need datasets that are annotated with fine-grained semantic relations in-context. Since existing datasets either provide out-of-context annotations or refer to coarse-grained relations, we propose a methodology for adding context-sensitive annotations. We demonstrate our methodology by applying it to phrase pairs from PPDB 2.0, creating a novel dataset of *fine-grained* lexical inferences *in-context* and showing its utility in developing context-sensitive methods.

1 Introduction

Recognizing lexical inference is an essential component in semantic tasks. In question answering, for instance, identifying that *broadcast* and *air* are synonymous enables answering the question "When was 'Friends' first aired?" given the text "'Friends' was first broadcast in 1994". Semantic relations such as synonymy *(tall, high)* and hypernymy *(cat, pet)* are used to infer the meaning of one term from another, in order to overcome lexical variability.

In semantic tasks, such terms appear within corresponding contexts, thus making two aspects necessary in order to correctly apply inferences: First, the meaning of each term should be considered within its context (Szpektor et al., 2007; Pantel et al., 2007), e.g., *play* entails *compete* in certain contexts, but not in the context of playing the national anthem at a sports competition. Second, the soundness of inferences within context is conditioned on the fine-grained semantic relation that holds between the terms, as studied within natural logic (MacCartney and Manning, 2007). For instance, in upward-monotone sentences a term entails its hypernym ("my *iPhone*'s battery is low" $\Rightarrow$ "my *phone*'s battery is low"), while in downward monotone ones it entails its hyponym ("talking on the *phone* is prohibited" $\Rightarrow$ "talking on the *iPhone* is prohibited").

Accordingly, developing algorithms that properly apply lexical inferences in context requires datasets in which inferences are annotated *in-context* by *fine-grained* semantic relations. Yet, such a dataset is not available (see 2.1). Most existing datasets provide *out-of-context* annotations, while the few available *in-context* annotations refer to coarse-grained relations, such as relatedness or similarity.

In recent years, the PPDB paraphrase database (Ganitkevitch et al., 2013) became a popular resource among semantic tasks, such as monolingual alignment (Sultan et al., 2014) and recognizing textual entailment (Noh et al., 2015). Recently, Pavlick et al. (2015) classified each paraphrase pair to the fine-grained semantic relation that holds between the phrases, following natural logic (MacCartney and Manning, 2007). To that end, a subset of PPDB paraphrase-pairs were manually annotated, forming a fine-grained lexical inference dataset. Yet, annotations are given *out-of-context*, limiting its utility.

In this paper, we aim to fill the current gap in the inventory of lexical inference datasets, and present a methodology for adding context to out-of-context datasets. We apply our methodology on a subset of phrase pairs from Pavlick et al. (2015),

*Proceedings of the Fifth Joint Conference on Lexical and Computational Semantics (*SEM 2016)*, pages 108–113,
Berlin, Germany, August 11-12, 2016.

	x	y	contexts	out-of-context relation	in-context relation
1	piece	strip	Roughly 1,500 gold and silver **pieces** were found and the hoard contains roughly 5kgs of gold and 2.5kgs of silver. A huge political storm has erupted around Australia after labor leader Kevin Rudd was found to have gone to a **strip** club during a taxpayer funded trip.	Equivalence	Independent
2	competition	race	Three countries withdrew from the **competition**: Germany, Spain and Switzerland. Morgan Tsvangirai, the leader of the Movement for Democratic Change (MDC), Zimbabwe's main opposition party, has said that he will pull out of the **race** to become the president of Zimbabwe.	Reverse Entailment	Equivalence
3	boy	family	The birth of the **boy**, whose birth name is disputed among different sources, is considered very important in the entertainment world. Bill will likely disrupt the Obama **family**'s vacation to Martha's Vineyard.	Forward Entailment	Other-related
4	jump	walk	Amid wild scenes of joy on the pitch he **jumped** onto the podium and lifted the trophy, the fourth of Italy's history. In a game about rescuing hostages a hero might **walk** past Coca-Cola machine's one week and Pepsi the next.	Other-related	Alternation

Table 1: Illustration of annotation shifts when context is given. [1] the sense of *strip* in the given context is different from the one which is equivalent to *piece*. [2] the term *race* is judged out-of-context as more specific than *competition*, but is considered equivalent to it in a particular context. [3] a meronymy relation is (often) considered out-of-context as entailment, while in a given context this judgment doesn't hold. [4] general relations may become more concrete when the context is given.

creating a novel dataset for fine-grained lexical inference in-context. For each term-pair, we add a pair of context sentences, and re-annotate these term-pairs with respect to their contexts.[1] We show that almost half of the semantically-related term-pairs become unrelated when the context is specified. Furthermore, a generic out-of-context relation may change within a given context (see table 1). We further report baseline results that demonstrate the utility of our dataset in developing fine-grained context-sensitive lexical inference methods.

2 Background

2.1 Lexical Inference Datasets

Figure 1 lists prominent human-annotated datasets used for developing lexical inference methods. In these datasets, each entry consists of an (x, y) term-pair, annotated to whether a certain semantic relation holds between x and y. Each dataset either specifies fine-grained semantic relations (see 2.2), or groups several semantic relations under a single coarse-grained relation (e.g. lexical substitution, similarity).

In some datasets, term-pairs are annotated to whether the relation holds between them in some (unspecified) contexts (*out-of-context*), while in others, the annotation is given with respect to a given context (*in-context*). In these datasets, each entry consists of a term-pair, x and y, and context, where some of the datasets provide a single context in which x occurs while others provide a separate context for each of x and y (corresponding to the *1 context* and *2 contexts* columns in Figure 1). The latter simulates a frequent need in NLP applications, for example, a question answering system recognizes that *broadcast* entails *air* given the context of the question ("When was 'Friends' first aired?") and that of the candidate passage ("'Friends' was first broadcast in 1994").

We observe that most lexical inference datasets provide *out-of-context* annotations. The existing *in-context* datasets are annotated for coarse-grained semantic relations, such as similarity or relatedness, which may not be sufficiently informative.

---

[1] The dataset and annotation guidelines are available at:
`http://u.cs.biu.ac.il/`
`~nlp/resources/downloads/`
`context-sensitive-fine-grained-dataset.`

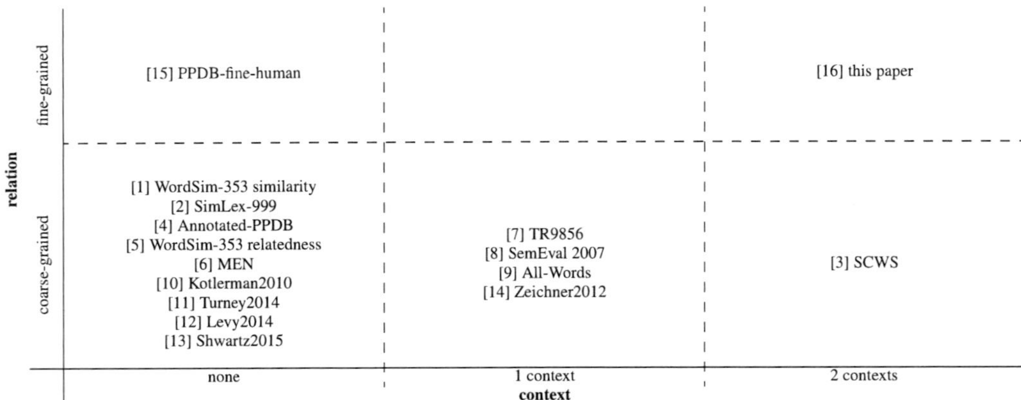

Figure 1: A map of prominent lexical inference datasets. **Word similarity**: [1] Zesch et al. (2008), [2] Hill et al. (2014), [3] Huang et al. (2012), [4] Wieting et al. (2015). **Term relatedness**: [5] Zesch et al. (2008), [6] Bruni et al. (2014), [7] Levy et al. (2015). **Lexical substitution**: [8] McCarthy and Navigli (2007), [9] Kremer et al. (2014), **Lexical inference**: [10] Kotlerman et al. (2010), [11] Turney and Mohammad (2014), [12] Levy et al. (2014), [13] Shwartz et al. (2015), [14] Zeichner et al. (2012), [15] Pavlick et al. (2015) (see 2.2), [16].

$\equiv$	Equivalence	is the same as
$\sqsubset$	Forward Entailment	is more specific than
$\sqsupset$	Reverse Entailment	is more general than
$\char`\^$	Negation	is the exact opposite of
|	Alternation	is mutually exclusive with
$\sim$	Other-Related	is related in some other way to
#	Independence	is not related to

Table 2: Semantic relations in PPDB 2.0. Like Pavlick et al., we conflate *negation* and *alternation* into one relation.

2.2   PPDB with Semantic Relations

The PPDB paraphrase database (Ganitkevitch et al., 2013) is a huge resource of automatically derived paraphrases. In recent years, it has been used for quite many semantic tasks, such as semantic parsing (Wang et al., 2015), recognizing textual entailment (Noh et al., 2015), and monolingual alignment (Sultan et al., 2014).

Recently, as part of the PPDB 2.0 release, Pavlick et al. (2015) re-annotated PPDB with fine-grained semantic relations, following natural logic (MacCartney and Manning, 2007) (see table 2). This was done by first annotating a subset of PPDB pharaphase-pairs that appeared in the SICK dataset of textual entailment (Marelli et al., 2014). Annotators were instructed to select the appropriate semantic relation that holds for each paraphrase pair. These human annotations were later used to train a classifier and predict the semantic relation for all paraphrase pairs in PPDB. Considering the widespread usage of PPDB in applications, this extension may likely lead to applying lexical inferences based on such fine-grained semantic relations.

In this paper, we focus on human-annotated datasets, and therefore find the above mentioned subset of human-annotated paraphrases particularly relevant; we refer to this dataset as PPDB-fine-human. This dataset, as well as the PPDB 2.0 automatically created resource, are still missing a key feature in lexical inference, since the semantic relation for each paraphrase pair is specified out of context.

3   Dataset Construction Methodology

In this section, we present a methodology of adding context to lexical inference datasets, that we apply on PPDB-fine-human.

3.1   Selecting Phrase-Pairs

PPDB-fine-human is a quite large dataset (14k pairs), albeit with some phrase-pairs that are less useful for our purpose. We therefore applied the following filtering and editing on the phrase pairs:

Relation Types   We expected that phrase pairs that were annotated out-of-context as *independent* will remain independent in almost every context; indeed, out of a sample of 100 such pairs that we annotated within context, only 8% were annotated with another semantic relation. As this was too sparse to justify the cost of human annotations, we chose to omit such phrase pairs.

Grammaticality-based   Filtering   Many phrases in PPDB-fine-human are ungrammatical, e.g. *boy is*. We consider such phrases less useful for our purpose, as semantic applications usually apply lexical inferences on syntactically coherent constituents. We therefore parse the original SICK (Marelli et al., 2014) sentences containing these phrases, and omit pairs in which one of the phrases is not a constituent.

Filtering Trivial Pairs In order to avoid trivial paraphrase pairs, we filter out inflections *(Iraq, Iraqi)* and alternate spellings *(center, centre)*, by omitting pairs that share the same lemma, or those that have Levenshtein distance $\leq$ 3. In addition, we omit pairs that have lexical overlaps *(a young lady, lady)* and filter out pairs in which one of the two phrases is just a stop word.

Removing Determiners The annotation seems to be indifferent to the presence of a determiner, e.g., the labelers annotated all of *(kid, the boy)*, *(the boy, the kid)*, and *(a kid, the boy)* as *reverse entailment*. To avoid repetitive pairs, and to get a single "normalized" phrase, we remove preceding determiners, e.g., yielding *(kid, boy)*.

Finally, it is interesting to note that `PPDB-fine-human` includes term-pairs in which terms are of different grammatical categories. Our view is that such cross-category term-pairs are often relevant for semantic inference (e.g. *(bicycle, riding)*) and therefore we decided to stick to the PPDB setting, and kept such pairs.

At the end of this filtering process we remained with 1385 phrase pairs from which we sampled 375 phrase pairs for our dataset, preserving the relative frequency across relation types in PPDB.

3.2 Adding Context Sentences

We used Wikinews[2] to extract context sentences. We used the Wikinews dump from November 2015, converted the Wiki Markup to clean text using WikiExtractor[3], and parsed the corpus using spaCy.[4]

For each (x, y) phrase-pair, we randomly sampled 10 sentence-pairs of the form (s_x, s_y), such that s_x contains x and s_y contains y. In the sampling process we require, for each of the two terms, that its 10 sentences are taken from different Wikinews articles, to obtain a broader range of the term's senses. This yields 10 tuples of the form (x, y, s_x, s_y) for each phrase pair and 3750 tuples in total.[5]

We split the dataset to 70% train, 25% test, and 5% validation sets. Each of the sets contains different term-pairs, to avoid overfitting for the most common relation of a term-pair in the training set.

3.3 Annotation Task

Our annotation task, carried out on Amazon Mechanical Turk, followed that of Pavlick et al. (2015). We used their guidelines, and altered them only to consider the contexts. We instructed annotators to select the relation that holds between the terms (x and y) while interpreting each term's meaning *within* its given context (s_x and s_y). To ensure the quality of workers, we applied a qualification test and required a US location, and a 99% approval rate for at least 1,000 prior HITS. We assigned each annotation to 5 workers, and, following Pavlick et al. (2015), selected the gold label using the majority rule, breaking ties at random. We note that for 91% of the examples, at least 3 of the annotators agreed.[6]

The annotations yielded moderate levels of agreement, with Fleiss' Kappa $\kappa = 0.51$ (Landis and Koch, 1977). For a fair comparison, we replicated the original out-of-context annotation on a sample of 100 pairs from our dataset, yielding agreement of $\kappa = 0.46$, while the in-context agreement for these pairs was $\kappa = 0.51$. As expected, adding context improves the agreement, by directing workers toward the same term senses while revealing rare senses that some workers may miss without context.[7]

4 Analysis

Figure 2 displays the confusion matrix of relation annotations in context compared to the out-of-context annotations. Most prominently, while the original relation holds in many of the contexts, it is also common for term-pairs to become independent. In some cases, the semantic relation is changed (as in table 1).

---

[5]Our dataset is comparable in size to most of the datasets in Figure 1. In particular, the SCWS dataset (Huang et al., 2012), which is the most similar to ours, contains 2003 term-pairs with context sentences.

[6]We also released an additional version of the dataset, including only the agreeable 91%.

[7]The gap between the reported agreement in Pavlick et al. (2015) ($\kappa = 0.56$) and our agreement for out-of-context annotations ($\kappa = 0.46$) may be explained by our filtering process, removing obvious and hence easily consensual pairs.

	in-context					
out-of-context	≡	⊏	⊐	|	∼	#
≡	60.54	6.9	0.38	0.38	9.58	22.22
⊏	2.96	41.13	1.41	0	11.69	42.82
⊐	5.97	1.67	37.92	2.08	13.19	39.17
|	1.25	1.88	5.42	41.46	2.92	47.08
∼	1.52	0.7	2.03	4.56	31.46	59.75

Figure 2: percentages of each relation annotation in-context, for annotations out-of-context. The diagonal shows out-of-context relations that hold in-context, and the last column shows term-pairs that become independent, usually due to sense-shifts. In all other cells, semantic relations are changed. Recall that we didn't annotate out-of-context independent pairs.

4.1 Baseline Results

To demonstrate our dataset's utility, we report several baseline performances on our test set (table 3). The first two are context-insensitive, assigning the same label to a term-pair in all its contexts; the first assigns manual labels from `PPDB-fine-human`, and the second assigns PPDB 2.0 classifier predictions. We also trained a context-sensitive logistic regression classifier on our train set, using the available PPDB 2.0 features, plus additional context-sensitive features. To represent words as vectors, we used pretrained GloVe embeddings of 300 dimensions, trained on Wikipedia (Pennington et al., 2014), and added the following features:

$$max_{w \in s_y} \vec{x} \cdot \vec{w} \qquad (1)$$

$$max_{w \in s_x} \vec{y} \cdot \vec{w} \qquad (2)$$

$$max_{w_x \in s_x, w_y \in s_y} \vec{w_x} \cdot \vec{w_y} \qquad (3)$$

(1) and (2) measure similarities between a term and its most similar term in the other term's context, and (3) measures the maximal word similarity across the contexts.

This context-sensitive method, trained on our dataset, notably outperforms context insensitive baselines, thus illustrating the potential utility of our dataset for developing fine-grained context-sensitive lexical inference methods. Yet, the absolute performance is still mediocre, emphasizing the need to develop better such methods, using our dataset or similar ones created by our methodology.

5 Conclusion

In this paper, we presented a methodology for adding context to context-insensitive lexical inference datasets, and demonstrated it by creating such dataset over PPDB 2.0 fine-grained

	precision	recall	F_1
PPDB-fine-human	**0.722**	0.380	0.288
PPDB2 classifier	0.611	0.565	0.556
in-context classifier	0.677	**0.685**	**0.670**

Table 3: Baseline performance on the test set (mean over all classes). (1) `PPDB-fine-human` manual annotations (out-of-context). (2) PPDB 2.0 classifier predictions (out-of-context). (3) our context-sensitive logistic regression classifier. Like Pavlick et al., we conflate the *forward entailment* and *reverse entailment* relations in all baselines.

paraphrase-pair annotations. We then demonstrated that our dataset can indeed be used for developing fine-grained context-sensitive lexical inference methods, which outperform the corresponding context-insensitive baselines.

Acknowledgments

We would like to thank Ellie Pavlick and Chris Callison-Burch for their assistance and insightful comments.

This work was partially supported by an Intel ICRI-CI grant, the Israel Science Foundation grant 880/12, and the German Research Foundation through the German-Israeli Project Cooperation (DIP, grant DA 1600/1-1).

References

Elia Bruni, Nam-Khanh Tran, and Marco Baroni. 2014. Multimodal distributional semantics. *JAIR*, 49:1–47.

Juri Ganitkevitch, Benjamin Van Durme, and Chris Callison-Burch. 2013. PPDB: The paraphrase database. In *HLT-NAACL*, pages 758–764.

Felix Hill, Roi Reichart, and Anna Korhonen. 2014. Simlex-999: Evaluating semantic models with (genuine) similarity estimation. *arXiv preprint arXiv:1408.3456*.

Eric H Huang, Richard Socher, Christopher D Manning, and Andrew Y Ng. 2012. Improving word representations via global context and multiple word prototypes. In *ACL 2012*, pages 873–882. Association for Computational Linguistics.

Lili Kotlerman, Ido Dagan, Idan Szpektor, and Maayan Zhitomirsky-Geffet. 2010. Directional distributional similarity for lexical inference. *Natural Language Engineering*, 16(04):359–389.

Gerhard Kremer, Katrin Erk, Sebastian Padó, and Stefan Thater. 2014. What substitutes tell us-analysis of an all-words lexical substitution corpus. In *EACL 2014*.

J Richard Landis and Gary G Koch. 1977. The measurement of observer agreement for categorical data. *biometrics*, pages 159–174.

Omer Levy, Ido Dagan, and Jacob Goldberger. 2014. Focused entailment graphs for open ie propositions. In *CoNLL 2014*, pages 87–97, Ann Arbor, Michigan, June. Association for Computational Linguistics.

Ran Levy, Liat Ein-Dor, Shay Hummel, Ruty Rinott, and Noam Slonim. 2015. Tr9856: A multi-word term relatedness benchmark. In *ACL 2015*, page 419.

Bill MacCartney and Christopher D Manning. 2007. Natural logic for textual inference. In *Proceedings of the ACL-PASCAL Workshop on Textual Entailment and Paraphrasing*, pages 193–200. Association for Computational Linguistics.

Marco Marelli, Luisa Bentivogli, Marco Baroni, Raffaella Bernardi, Stefano Menini, and Roberto Zamparelli. 2014. Semeval-2014 task 1: Evaluation of compositional distributional semantic models on full sentences through semantic relatedness and textual entailment. *SemEval-2014*.

Diana McCarthy and Roberto Navigli. 2007. Semeval-2007 task 10: English lexical substitution task. In *Proceedings of the 4th International Workshop on Semantic Evaluations*, pages 48–53. Association for Computational Linguistics.

Tae-Gil Noh, Sebastian Padó, Vered Shwartz, Ido Dagan, Vivi Nastase, Kathrin Eichler, Lili Kotlerman, and Meni Adler. 2015. Multi-level alignments as an extensible representation basis for textual entailment algorithms. **SEM 2015*, page 193.

Patrick Pantel, Rahul Bhagat, Bonaventura Coppola, Timothy Chklovski, and Eduard H Hovy. 2007. Isp: Learning inferential selectional preferences. In *HLT-NAACL*, pages 564–571.

Ellie Pavlick, Johan Bos, Malvina Nissim, Charley Beller, Benjamin Van Durme, and Chris Callison-Burch. 2015. Adding semantics to data-driven paraphrasing. In *ACL 2015*, Beijing, China, July. Association for Computational Linguistics.

Jeffrey Pennington, Richard Socher, and Christopher D. Manning. 2014. Glove: Global vectors for word representation. In *EMNLP 2014*, pages 1532–1543.

Vered Shwartz, Omer Levy, Ido Dagan, and Jacob Goldberger. 2015. Learning to exploit structured resources for lexical inference. *CoNLL 2015*, page 175.

Md Arafat Sultan, Steven Bethard, and Tamara Sumner. 2014. Back to basics for monolingual alignment: Exploiting word similarity and contextual evidence. *TACL 2014*, 2:219–230.

Idan Szpektor, Eyal Shnarch, and Ido Dagan. 2007. Instance-based evaluation of entailment rule acquisition. In *ACL 2007*, page 456.

Peter D Turney and Saif M Mohammad. 2014. Experiments with three approaches to recognizing lexical entailment. *Natural Language Engineering*, 21(03):437–476.

Yushi Wang, Jonathan Berant, and Percy Liang. 2015. Building a semantic parser overnight. In *ACL 2015*.

John Wieting, Mohit Bansal, Kevin Gimpel, and Karen Livescu. 2015. From paraphrase database to compositional paraphrase model and back. *TACL 2015*, 3:345–358.

Naomi Zeichner, Jonathan Berant, and Ido Dagan. 2012. Crowdsourcing inference-rule evaluation. In *ACL 2012*, pages 156–160. Association for Computational Linguistics.

Torsten Zesch, Christof Müller, and Iryna Gurevych. 2008. Using wiktionary for computing semantic relatedness. In *AAAI*, volume 8, pages 861–866.

So-Called Non-Subsective Adjectives

Ellie Pavlick
University of Pennsylvania
epavlick@seas.upenn.edu

Chris Callison-Burch
University of Pennsylvania
ccb@cis.upenn.edu

Abstract

The interpretation of adjective-noun pairs plays a crucial role in tasks such as recognizing textual entailment. Formal semantics often places adjectives into a taxonomy which should dictate adjectives' entailment behavior when placed in adjective-noun compounds. However, we show experimentally that the behavior of *subsective* adjectives (e.g. *red*) versus *non-subsective* adjectives (e.g. *fake*) is not as cut and dry as often assumed. For example, inferences are not always symmetric: while *ID* is generally considered to be mutually exclusive with *fake ID*, *fake ID* is considered to entail *ID*. We discuss the implications of these findings for automated natural language understanding.

Privative Non-Subsective ($AN \cap N = \emptyset$)			
anti-	artificial	counterfeit	deputy
erstwhile	ex-	fabricated	fake
false	fictional	fictitious	former
hypothetical	imaginary	mock	mythical
onetime	past	phony	pseudo-
simulated	spurious	virtual	would-be
Plain Non-Subsective ($AN \not\subset N$ and $AN \cap N \neq \emptyset$)			
alleged	apparent	arguable	assumed
believed	debatable	disputed	doubtful
dubious	erroneous	expected	faulty
future	historic	impossible	improbable
likely	mistaken	ostensible	plausible
possible	potential	predicted	presumed
probable	proposed	putative	questionable
seeming	so-called	supposed	suspicious
theoretical	uncertain	unlikely	unsuccessful

Table 1: 60 non-subsective adjectives from Nayak et al. (2014). Noun phrases involving non-subsective adjectives are assumed not to entail the head noun. E.g. *would-be hijacker* $\not\Rightarrow$ *hijacker*. (See Section 2 for definition of privative vs. plain).

1 Introduction

Most adjectives are *subsective*, meaning that an instance of an adjective-noun phrase is an instance of the noun: a *red car* is a *car* and a *successful senator* is a *senator*. In contrast, adjective-noun phrases involving *non-subsective* adjectives, such as *imaginary* and *former* (Table 1), denote a set that is disjoint from the denotation of the nouns they modify: an *imaginary car* is not a *car* and a *former senator* is not a *senator*. Understanding whether or not adjectives are subsective is critical in any task involving natural language inference. For example, consider the below sentence pair from the Recognizing Textual Entailment (RTE) task (Giampiccolo et al., 2007):

1. (a) U.S. District Judge Leonie Brinkema accepted would-be hijacker Zacarias Moussaoui's guilty pleas ...

   (b) Moussaoui participated in the Sept. 11 attacks.

In this example, recognizing that 1(a) does not entail 1(b) hinges on understanding that a *would-be hijacker* is not a *hijacker*.

The observation that adjective-nouns (ANs) involving non-subsective adjectives do not entail the underlying nouns (Ns) has led to the generalization that the deletion of non-subsective adjectives tends to result in contradictory utterances: *Moussaoui is a would-be hijacker* entails that it is not the case that *Moussaoui is a hijacker*. This generalization has prompted normative rules for the treatment of such adjectives in various NLP tasks. In information extraction, it is assumed that systems cannot extract useful rules from sentences containing non-subsective modifiers (Angeli et al., 2015), and in RTE, it is assumed that systems should uniformly penalize insertions and deletions of non-subsective adjectives (Amoia and Gardent, 2006).

*Proceedings of the Fifth Joint Conference on Lexical and Computational Semantics (*SEM 2016)*, pages 114–119,
Berlin, Germany, August 11-12, 2016.

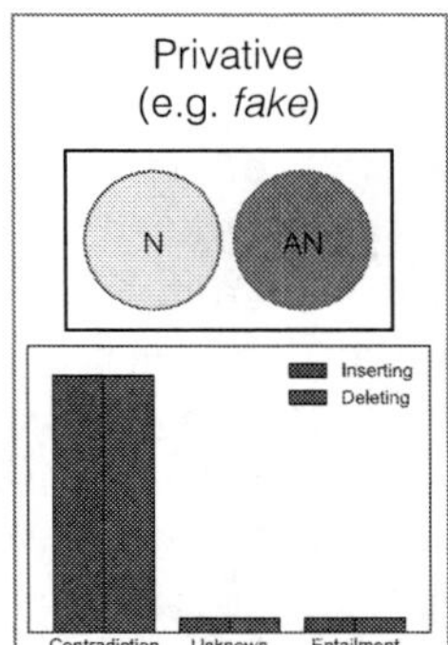

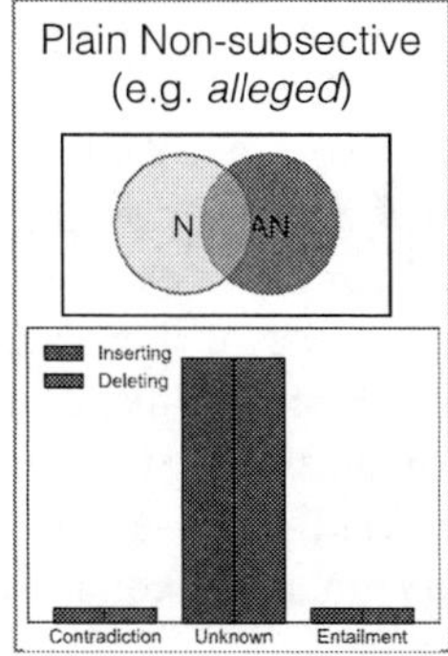

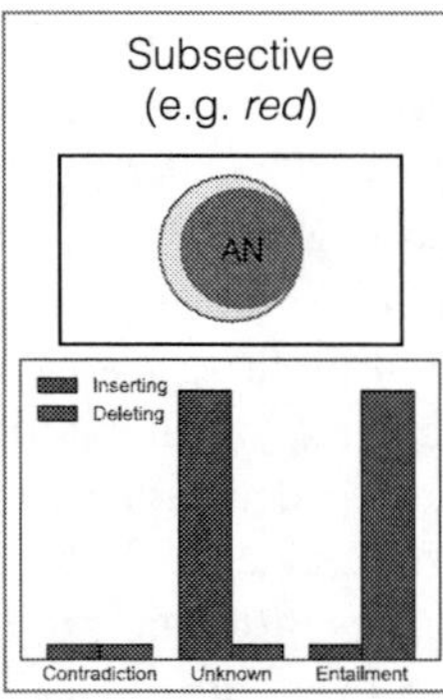

Figure 1: Three main classes of adjectives. If their entailment behavior is consistent with their theoretical definitions, we would expect our annotations (Section 3) to produce the insertion (blue) and deletion (red) patterns shown by the bar graphs. Bars (left to right) represent CONTRADICTION, UNKNOWN, and ENTAILMENT

While these generalizations are intuitive, there is little experimental evidence to support them. In this paper, we collect human judgements of the validity of inferences following from the insertion and deletion of various classes of adjectives and analyze the results. Our findings suggest that, in practice, most sentences involving non-subsective ANs can be safely generalized to statements about the N. That is, non-subsective adjectives often behave like normal, subsective adjectives. On further analysis, we reveal that, when adjectives do behave non-subsectively, they often exhibit asymmetric entailment behavior in which insertion leads to contradictions ($ID \Rightarrow \neg\ fake\ ID$) but deletion leads to entailments ($fake\ ID \Rightarrow ID$). We present anecdotal evidence for how the entailment associated with inserting/deleting a non-subsective adjective depends on the salient properties of the noun phrase under discussion, rather than on the adjective itself.

2 Background and Related Work

Classes of Adjectives. Adjectives are commonly classified taxonomically as either subsective or non-subsective (Kamp and Partee, 1995). Subsective adjectives are adjectives which pick out a subset of the set denoted by the unmodified noun; that is, $AN \subset N$[1]. For non-subsective adjectives, in contrast, the AN cannot be guaranteed to be a subset of N. For example, *clever* is subsective, and so a *clever thief* is always a *thief*. However,

alleged is non-subsective, so there are many possible worlds in which an *alleged thief* is not in fact a *thief*. Of course, there may also be many possible worlds in which the *alleged thief* is a *thief*, but the word *alleged*, being non-subsective, does not guarantee this to hold.

Non-subsective adjectives can be further divided into two classes: *privative* and *plain*. Sets denoted by privative ANs are completely disjoint from the set denoted by the head N ($AN \cap N = \emptyset$), and this mutual exclusivity is encoded in the meaning of the A itself. For example, *fake* is considered to be a quintessential privative adjective since, given the usual definition of *fake*, a *fake ID* can not actually be an *ID*. For plain non-subsective adjectives, there may be worlds in which the AN is and N, and worlds in which the AN is not an N: neither inference is guaranteed by the meaning of the A. As mentioned above, *alleged* is quintessentially plain non-subsective since, for example, an *alleged thief* may or may not be an actual *thief*. In short, we can summarize the classes of adjectives in the following way: subsective adjectives entail the nouns they modify, privative adjectives contradict the nouns they modify, and plain non-subsective adjectives are compatible with (but do not entail) the nouns they modify. Figure 1 depicts these distinctions.

While the hierarchical classification of adjectives described above is widely accepted and often applied in NLP tasks (Amoia and Gardent, 2006; Amoia and Gardent, 2007; Boleda et al., 2012; McCrae et al., 2014), it is not undisputed. Some linguists take the position that in fact privative ad-

---

[1] We use the notation N and AN to refer both the the natural language expression itself (e.g. *red car*) as well as its denotation, e.g. $\{x|x\ is\ a\ red\ car\}$.

jectives are simply another type of subsective adjective (Partee, 2003; McNally and Boleda, 2004; Abdullah and Frost, 2005; Partee, 2007). Advocates of this theory argue that the denotation of the noun should be expanded to include both the properties captured by the privative adjectives as well as those captured by the subsective adjectives. This expanded denotation can explain the acceptability of the sentence *Is that gun real or fake?*, which is difficult to analyze if *gun* entails $\neg$*fake gun*. More recent theoretical work argues that common nouns have a "dual semantic structure" and that non-subsective adjectives modify part of this meaning (e.g. the functional features of the noun) without modifying the extension of the noun (Del Pinal, 2015). Such an analysis can explain how we can understand a *fake gun* as having many, but not all, of the properties of a *gun*.

Several other studies abandon the attempt to organize adjectives taxonomically, and instead focus on the properties of the modified noun. Nayak et al. (2014) categorize non-subsective adjectives in terms of the proportion of properties that are shared between the N and the AN and Pustejovsky (2013) focus on syntactic cues about exactly which properties are shared. Bakhshandh and Allen (2015) analyze adjectives by observing that, e.g., *red* modifies `color` while *tall* modifies `size`. In Section 5, we discuss the potential benefits of pursuing these property-based analyses in relation to our experimental findings.

Recognizing Textual Entailment. We analyze adjectives within the context of the task of Recognizing Textual Entailment (RTE) (Dagan et al., 2006). The RTE task is defined as: given two natural language utterances, a premise p and a hypothesis h, would a typical human reading p likely conclude that h is true? We consider the RTE task as a three-way classification: ENTAILMENT, CONTRADICTION, or UNKNOWN (meaning p neither entails nor contradicts h).

3 Experimental Design

Our goal is to analyze how non-subsective adjectives effect the inferences that can be made about natural language. We begin with the set of 60 non-subsective adjectives identified by Nayak et al. (2014), which we split into plain non-subsective and privative adjectives (Table 1).[2] We search

---

[2]The division of these 60 adjectives into privative/plain is based on our own understanding of the literature, not on

through the Annotated Gigaword corpus (Napoles et al., 2012) for occurrences of each adjective in the list, restricting to cases in which the adjective appears as an adjective modifier of (is in an *amod* dependency relation with) a common noun (NN). For each adjective, we choose 10 sentences such that the adjective modifies a different noun in each. As a control, we take a small sample 100 ANs chosen randomly from our corpus. We expect these to contain almost entirely subsective adjectives.

For each selected sentence s, we generate s' by deleting the non-subsective adjective from s. We then construct two RTE problems, one in which $p = s$ and $h = s'$ (the *deletion* direction), and one in which $p = s'$ and $h = s$ (the *insertion* direction). For each RTE problem, we ask annotators to indicate on a 5-point scale how likely it is that p entails h, where a score of -2 indicates definite contradiction and a score of 2 indicates definite entailment. We use Amazon Mechanical Turk, requiring annotators to pass a qualification test of simple RTE problems before participating. We solicit 5 annotators per p/h pair, taking the majority answer as truth. Workers show moderate agreement on the 5-way classification ($\kappa = 0.44$).

Disclaimer. This design does not directly test the taxonomic properties of non-subsective ANs. Rather than asking "Is this instance of AN an instance of N?" we ask "Is this statement that is true of AN also true of N?" While these are not the same question, theories based on the former question often lead to overly-cautious approaches to answering the latter question. For example, in information extraction, the assumption is often made that sentences with non-subsective modifiers cannot be used to extract facts about the head N (Angeli et al., 2015). We focus on the latter question, which is arguably more practically relevant for NLP, and accept that this prevents us from commenting on the underlying taxonomic relations between AN and N.

4 Results

Expectations. Based on the theoretical adjective classes described in Section 2, we expect that both the insertion and the deletion of privative adjectives from a sentence should result in judgments of CONTRADICTION: i.e. it should be the case that *fake ID* $\Rightarrow \neg$ *ID* and *ID* $\Rightarrow \neg$ *fake ID*. Similarly, we expect plain non-subsective adjectives

---

Nayak et al. (2014).

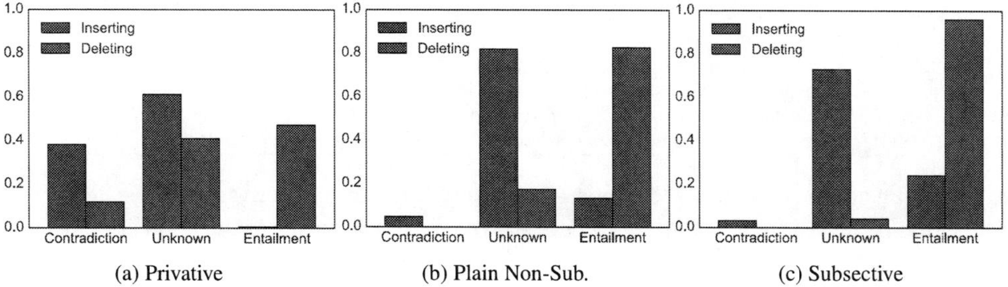

(a) Privative   (b) Plain Non-Sub.   (c) Subsective

Figure 2: Observed entailment judgements for insertion (blue) and deletion (red) of adjectives. Compare to expected distributions in Figure 1.

to receive labels of UNKNOWN in both directions. We expect the subsective adjectives to receive labels of ENTAILMENT in the deletion direction (*red car* $\Rightarrow$ *car*) and labels of UNKNOWN in the insertion direction (*car* $\not\Rightarrow$ *red car*). Figure 1 depicts these expected distributions.

Observations. The observed entailment patterns for insertion and deletion of non-subsective adjectives are shown in Figure 2. Our control sample of subsective adjectives (Figure 2c) largely produced the expected results, with 96% of deletions producing ENTAILMENTs and 73% of insertions producing UNKNOWNs.[3] The entailment patterns produced by the non-subsective adjectives, however, did not match our predictions. The plain non-subsective adjectives (e.g. *alleged*) behave nearly identically to how we expect regular, subsective adjectives to behave (Figure 2b). That is, in 80% of cases, deleting the plain non-subsective adjective was judged to produce ENTAILMENT, rather than the expected UNKNOWN. The examples in Table 2 shed some light onto why this is the case. Often, the differences between N and AN are not relevant to the main point of the utterance. For example, while an *expected surge in unemployment* is not a *surge in unemployment*, a policy that deals with an *expected surge* deals with a *surge*.

The privative adjectives (e.g. *fake*) also fail to match the predicted distribution. While insertions often produce the expected CONTRADICTIONs, deletions produce a surprising number of ENTAILMENTs (Figure 2a). Such a pattern does not fit into any of the adjective classes from Figure 1. While some ANs (e.g. *counterfeit money*) behave in the prototypically privative way, others

---

(1)	Swiss officials on Friday said they've launched an investigation into Urs Tinner's **alleged role**.
(2)	To deal with an **expected surge** in unemployment, the plan includes a huge temporary jobs program.
(3)	They kept it close for a half and had a **theoretical chance** come the third quarter.

Table 2: Contrary to expectations, the deletion of plain non-subsective adjectives often preserves the (plausible) truth in a model. E.g. *alleged role* $\not\Rightarrow$ *role*, but *investigation into alleged role* $\Rightarrow$ *investigation into role*.

(e.g. *mythical beast*) have the property in which N$\Rightarrow\neg$AN, but AN$\Rightarrow$N (Figure 3). Table 3 provides some telling examples of how this AN$\Rightarrow$N inference, in the case of privative adjectives, often depends less on the adjective itself, and more on properties of the modified noun that are at issue in the given context. For example, in Table 3 Example 2(a), a *mock debate* probably contains enough of the relevant properties (namely, arguments) that it can entail *debate*, while in Example 2(b), a *mock execution* lacks the single most important property (the death of the executee) and so cannot entail *execution*. (Note that, from Example 3(b), it appears the jury is still out on whether *leaps in artificial intelligence* entail *leaps in intelligence...*)

5 Discussion

The results presented suggest a few important patterns for NLP systems. First, that while a non-subsective AN might not be an instance of the N (taxonomically speaking), statements that are true of an AN are often true of the N as well. This is relevant for IE and QA systems, and is likely to become more important as NLP systems focus more on "micro reading" tasks (Nakashole and Mitchell, 2014), where facts must be inferred from single documents or sentences, rather than by exploiting

---

[3] A full discussion of the 27% of insertions that deviated from the expected behavior is given in Pavlick and Callison-Burch (2016).

(1a)	ENTAIL.	Flawed **counterfeit software** can corrupt the information entrusted to it.
(1b)	CONTRA.	Pharmacists in Algodones denied selling **counterfeit medicine** in their stores.
(2a)	ENTAIL.	He also took part in a **mock debate** Sunday.
(2b)	CONTRA.	Investigation leader said the prisoner had been subjected to a **mock execution**.
(3a)	ENTAIL.	The plants were grown under **artificial light** and the whole operation was computerised.
(3b)	UNKNOWN	Thrun predicted that leaps in **artificial intelligence** would lead to driverless cars on the roads by 2030.

Table 3: Entailment judgements for the *deletion* of various privative adjectives from a sentence. Whether or not deletion results in CONTRADICTION depends on which properties of the noun are most relevant.

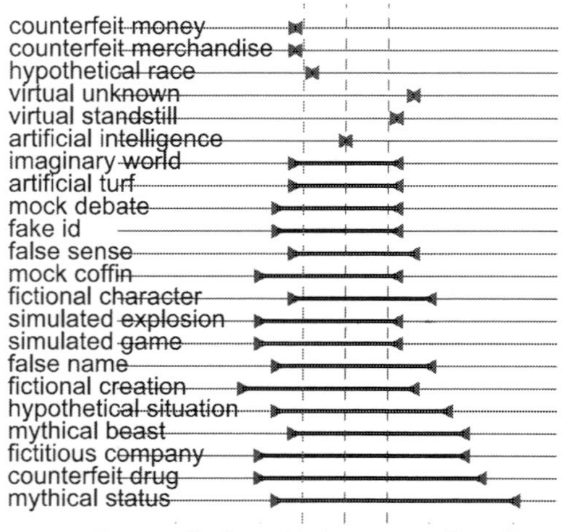

Figure 3: Entailments scores for insertion (blue) and deletion (red) for various ANs. E.g. the bottom line says that *status* $\Rightarrow\neg$ *mythical status* (insertion produces CONTRADICTION), but *mythical status* $\Rightarrow$ *status* (deletion produces ENTAILMENT).

the massive redundancy of the web. Second, the asymmetric entailments associated with privative adjectives suggests that the contradictions generated by privative adjectives may not be due to a strict denotational contradiction, but rather based on implicature: i.e. if an *ID* is in fact *fake*, the speaker is obligated to say so, and thus, when *ID* appears unmodified, it is fair to assume it is not a *fake ID*. Testing this hypothesis is left for future research. Finally, the examples in Tables 2 and 3 seem to favor a properties-oriented analysis of adjective semantics, rather than the taxonomic analysis often used. Nayak et al. (2014)'s attempt to characterize adjectives in terms of the number of properties the AN shares with N is a step in the right direction, but it seems that what is relevant is not *how many* properties are shared, but rather *which* properties are shared, and which properties are at issue in the given context.

6   Conclusion

We present experimental results on textual inferences involving non-subsective adjectives. We show that, contrary to expectations, the deletion of non-subsective adjectives from a sentence does not necessarily result in non-entailment. Thus, in applications such as information extraction, it is often possible to extract true facts about the N from sentences involving a non-subsective AN. Our data suggests that inferences involving non-subsective adjectives require more than strict reasoning about denotations, and that a treatment of non-subsective adjectives based on the properties of the AN, rather than its taxonomic relation to the N, is likely to yield useful insights.

Acknowledgments

This research was supported by a Facebook Fellowship, and by gifts from the Alfred P. Sloan Foundation, Google, and Facebook. This material is based in part on research sponsored by the NSF grant under IIS-1249516 and DARPA under number FA8750-13-2-0017 (the DEFT program). The U.S. Government is authorized to reproduce and distribute reprints for Governmental purposes. The views and conclusions contained in this publication are those of the authors and should not be interpreted as representing official policies or endorsements of DARPA and the U.S. Government.

We would like to thank the anonymous reviewers for their very thoughtful comments. We would also like to thank the Mechanical Turk annotators for their contributions.

References

Nabil Abdullah and Richard A Frost. 2005. Adjectives: A uniform semantic approach. In *Advances in Artificial Intelligence*, pages 330–341. Springer.

Marilisa Amoia and Claire Gardent. 2006. Adjective based inference. In *Proceedings of the Workshop KRAQ'06 on Knowledge and Reasoning for*

Language Processing, pages 20–27. Association for Computational Linguistics.

Marilisa Amoia and Claire Gardent. 2007. A first order semantic approach to adjectival inference. In *Proceedings of the ACL-PASCAL Workshop on Textual Entailment and Paraphrasing*, pages 185–192, Prague, June. Association for Computational Linguistics.

Gabor Angeli, Melvin Jose Johnson Premkumar, and Christopher D. Manning. 2015. Leveraging linguistic structure for open domain information extraction. In *Proceedings of the 53rd Annual Meeting of the Association for Computational Linguistics and the 7th International Joint Conference on Natural Language Processing (Volume 1: Long Papers)*, pages 344–354, Beijing, China, July. Association for Computational Linguistics.

Omid Bakhshandh and James Allen. 2015. From adjective glosses to attribute concepts: Learning different aspects that an adjective can describe. In *Proceedings of the 11th International Conference on Computational Semantics*, pages 23–33, London, UK, April. Association for Computational Linguistics.

Gemma Boleda, Eva Maria Vecchi, Miquel Cornudella, and Louise McNally. 2012. First order vs. higher order modification in distributional semantics. In *Proceedings of the 2012 Joint Conference on Empirical Methods in Natural Language Processing and Computational Natural Language Learning*, pages 1223–1233, Jeju Island, Korea, July. Association for Computational Linguistics.

Ido Dagan, Oren Glickman, and Bernardo Magnini. 2006. The PASCAL recognizing textual entailment challenge. In *Machine Learning Challenges. Evaluating Predictive Uncertainty, Visual Object Classification, and Recognising Tectual Entailment*, pages 177–190. Springer.

Guillermo Del Pinal. 2015. Dual content semantics, privative adjectives and dynamic compositionality. *Semantics and Pragmatics*, 5.

Danilo Giampiccolo, Bernardo Magnini, Ido Dagan, and Bill Dolan. 2007. The third PASCAL recognizing textual entailment challenge. In *Proceedings of the ACL-PASCAL Workshop on Textual Entailment and Paraphrasing*, pages 1–9, Prague, June. Association for Computational Linguistics.

Hans Kamp and Barbara Partee. 1995. Prototype theory and compositionality. *Cognition*, 57(2):129–191.

John P. McCrae, Francesca Quattri, Christina Unger, and Philipp Cimiano. 2014. Modelling the semantics of adjectives in the ontology-lexicon interface. In *Proceedings of the 4th Workshop on Cognitive Aspects of the Lexicon (CogALex)*, pages 198–209, Dublin, Ireland, August. Association for Computational Linguistics and Dublin City University.

Louise McNally and Gemma Boleda. 2004. Relational adjectives as properties of kinds. *Empirical issues in formal syntax and semantics*, 8:179–196.

Ndapandula Nakashole and Tom M Mitchell. 2014. Micro reading with priors: Towards second generation machine readers. In *Proceedings of the 4th Workshop on Automated Knowledge Base Construction (AKBC), at NIPS. Montreal, Canada*.

Courtney Napoles, Matthew Gormley, and Benjamin Van Durme. 2012. Annotated gigaword. In *Proceedings of the Joint Workshop on Automatic Knowledge Base Construction and Web-scale Knowledge Extraction*, pages 95–100.

Neha Nayak, Mark Kowarsky, Gabor Angeli, and Christopher D. Manning. 2014. A dictionary of nonsubsective adjectives. Technical Report CSTR 2014-04, Department of Computer Science, Stanford University, October.

Barbara H Partee. 2003. Are there privative adjectives. In *Conference on the Philosophy of Terry Parsons, University of Massachusetts, Amherst*.

Barbara Partee. 2007. Compositionality and coercion in semantics: The dynamics of adjective meaning. *Cognitive foundations of interpretation*, pages 145–161.

Ellie Pavlick and Chris Callison-Burch. 2016. Most baies are little and most problems are huge: Compositional entailment in adjective nouns. In *Proceedings of the 54th Annual Meeting of the Association for Computational Linguistics (ACL 2016)*, Berlin, Germany. Association for Computational Linguistics.

James Pustejovsky. 2013. Inference patterns with intensional adjectives. In *Proceedings of the 9th Joint ISO - ACL SIGSEM Workshop on Interoperable Semantic Annotation*, pages 85–89, Potsdam, Germany, March. Association for Computational Linguistics.

Linguistic Style Accommodation in Disagreements

Elise van der Pol, **Sharon Gieske** and **Raquel Fernández**
Institute for Logic, Language and Computation
University of Amsterdam
{elisevanderpol|sharongieske}@gmail.com, raquel.fernandez@uva.nl

Abstract

We investigate style accommodation in online discussions, in particular its interplay with content agreement and disagreement. Using a new model for measuring style accommodation, we find that speakers coordinate on style more noticeably if they disagree than if they agree, especially if they want to establish rapport and possibly persuade their interlocutors.

1 Introduction

In interactive communication, speakers tend to adapt their linguistic behaviour to one another at several levels, including pitch, speech rate, and the words and constructions they use. This phenomenon has been studied from different perspectives, most notably cognitive psychology and sociology. For instance, the Interactive Alignment Model (Pickering and Garrod, 2004) claims that priming mechanisms, which are an inherent feature of humans' cognitive architecture, lead to interpersonal coordination during dialogue. In contrast, Communication Accommodation Theory (Shepard et al., 2001) focuses on the external factors influencing linguistic accommodation (e.g., the wish to build rapport) and argues that converging on linguistic patterns reduces the social distance between interlocutors, which results in speakers being viewed more favourably.

Within the latter sociolinguistic view, a common methodology used to study linguistic accommodation is to focus on stylistic accommodation, as reflected in the use of function words, such as pronouns, quantifiers, and articles (Chung and Pennebaker, 2007). Previous research has shown that matching of function words signals relative social status between speakers (Niederhoffer and Pennebaker, 2002) and can be used to predict re-

lationship initiation and stability in speed dating conversations (Ireland et al., 2011). Furthermore, Danescu-Niculescu-Mizil et al. (2012) found that speakers adapt their linguistic style more when they talk to interlocutors who have higher social status and Noble and Fernández (2015) showed that this is also the case for interlocutors with a more central position in a social network.

In this paper, we investigate style accommodation in online discussions. Rather than looking into status- or network-based notions of power differences, we capitalise on the argumentative character of such discussions to study how argumentative aspects such as agreement and disagreement relate to style accommodation. In particular, we focus on the interplay between alignment of beliefs—interlocutors' (dis)agreement on *what* is said—and alignment of linguistic style—interlocutors' coordination or lack thereof on *how* content is expressed. Our aim is to investigate the following hypotheses:

H1: Speakers accommodate their linguistic style more to that of their addressees' if they agree with them on content than if they disagree.

H2: Speakers who disagree on content coordinate their linguistic style more towards addressees they want to persuade than towards those they want to distance themselves from.

Given evidence for the relationship between affiliation and mimicry (Lakin and Chartrand, 2003; Scissors et al., 2008), H1 seems a sensible conjecture. Hypothesis H2 is grounded on the assumption that individuals who disagree with their interlocutors may want to persuade them to change their mind. This creates a certain power difference, with the persuader being in a more dependent position. As shown by Danescu-Niculescu-Mizil et al. (2012), such dependence can lead to increased style matching.

*Proceedings of the Fifth Joint Conference on Lexical and Computational Semantics (*SEM 2016)*, pages 120–124,
Berlin, Germany, August 11-12, 2016.

2 Data

For our investigation we use the Internet Argument Corpus (IAC) (Walker et al., 2012), which contains a collection of online discussions scraped from internet fora. About 10,000 Quote-Response (Q-R) pairs have been annotated with scalar judgments over a multitude of dimensions, including level of agreement/disagreement (scale 5 to –5). Although the corpus does not include an annotation that directly indicates level of persuasiveness, we approximate persuasion by making use of two additional annotated dimensions: nice/nastiness (scale 5 to –5) and sarcasm (scale 1 to –1). We assume that responses that are perceived as nicer are more likely to be persuasive than those perceived as nasty. Similarly, we take sarcastic responses as being more likely to signal a distancing attitude than a persuasion goal.

Each Q-R pair has been judged by 5 to 7 annotators on Amazon Mechanical Turk and their scores have been averaged for each dimension. Walker et al. (2012) report relatively low inter-annotator agreement (measured with Krippendorf's α): 0.62 for agreement/disagreement, 0.46 for nice/nastiness, and only 0.22 for sarcasm.[1] We therefore chose to leverage only a subset of the corpus for which there is substantial agreement on either side of the scales. For the nice/nasty and agreement/disagreement judgments, we only consider Q-R pairs with strong majorities, i.e., Q-R pairs where all judgments except at most one are either ≥ 0 or ≤ 0. For sarcasm, we only consider Q-R pairs where there is at most one neutral judgment (value 0) and at most one judgment opposite to the majority.

In addition, to be able to assess the style of individual authors, we restrict our analysis to Q-R pairs with response authors who contribute responding posts in at least 10 different Q-R pairs. The resulting dataset after applying all these constraints contains a total of 5,004 Q-R pairs, 14% of which correspond to agreeing responses, 65% to disagreeing responses, and 21% to neutral responses. This mirrors the distribution in the full, unfiltered corpus: 13% agreeing, 67% disagreeing, and 20% neutral responses.

3 Measuring Linguistic Accommodation

We measure linguistic style accommodation with respect to 8 different functional markers (personal pronouns, impersonal pronouns, articles, prepositions, quantifiers, adverbs, conjunctions, and auxiliary verbs) using the lists made available by Noble and Fernández (2015).[2] Our starting point is the linguistic coordination measure proposed by Danescu-Niculescu-Mizil et al. (2012), which uses a subtractive conditional probability to capture the increase in the probability of using a marker given that it has been used by the previous conversation participant. In our notation:

$$C^m = p(R_i^m | Q_j^m) - p(R_i^m) \qquad [1]$$

Here $p(R_i^m | Q_j^m)$ refers to the probability that a response R by author i contains marker m given that the quoted post by j also contains m. How much coordination C there is in i's responses to j corresponds to the difference between this conditional probability and the prior probability $p(R_i^m)$ for author i, i.e., the probability that any response by i contains a linguistic marker of category m.

Given the sparsity of data in online discussion fora with regards to repeated interactions between the same individuals i and j, we compute a score for each Q-R pair (rather than for the set of Q-R pairs between specific authors i and j). Therefore, the conditional probability in Equation [1] corresponds to a variable that takes value 1 if both Q and R contain m and 0 if only Q does (and is undefined if Q does not contain m). The prior again corresponds to the proportion of responses by the author of R that exhibit m in the entire dataset.

A problem with this measure (both in the original formulation by Danescu-Niculescu-Mizil et al. and our own with a boolean term) is that it does not account for utterance length: clearly, a longer response has more chances to contain a marker m than a shorter response. Indeed length has been observed to be an important confounding factor in the computation of stylistic coordination (Gao et al., 2015). We therefore proposed an extension of the original measure to account for both aspects independently: the *presence* of a marker in a post (1 vs. 0) and its *frequency* given the post length.

In our model, alignment between Q and R and the prior for the author of R with respect to

---

[1] According to Walker et al. (2012), these α scores were computed using an ordinal scale (except for sarcasm) on a dataset comprising both the set of Q-R pairs we take as starting point here and data from an additional experiment referred to as P123 by the authors. See their paper for details.

[2] These lists of markers are based on Linguistic Inquiry and Word Count (LIWC) by Pennebaker et al. (2007).

marker class m correspond to feature vectors $\vec{a}$ and $\vec{b}$, respectively, with a first feature indicating marker presence and a second feature accounting for marker frequency. Thus, for a given Q-R pair:

a_1: presence of m in R given that Q contains m
a_2: proportion of words in R that are m

Similarly, for a given author i, the prior includes the following features:

b_1: proportion of responses R by i containing m
b_2: proportion of words by i that are m

After rescaling all features to range $[0, 1]$, $\vec{a}$ and $\vec{b}$ are scalarized by taking the dot product with a so-called weight vector $\vec{w}$, which determines the importance of each feature (*presence* vs. *frequency*). This *linear scalarization* is a standard technique in multi-objective optimization (Roijers et al., 2013). To determine the SA_m score of a given Q-R pair for a marker class m, as in the original measure we finally take the difference between the alignment observed in the Q-R pair and the prior encoding the linguistic style of the responding author:

$$SA_m = (\vec{a} \cdot \vec{w}) - (\vec{b} \cdot \vec{w}) \qquad [2]$$

An advantage of this measure is that it allows us to explore the effects of using different weights for different features, in our case *presence* vs. *frequency*, but potentially other features (such as syntactic alignment) as well. In the current setting, if $w_2 = 0$, we obtain the original measure where only the presence of a marker is recorded, without taking into account frequency and hence post length. In contrast, if $w_1 = 0$, only relative marker frequency is considered and no importance is given to the mere presence of a marker in a post. If the two weights are above zero, both features are taken into account.

4 Analysis and Results

For each Q-R pair in our dataset, we compute SA_m for each marker m, as well as the average style accommodation over all markers, which we refer to simply as SA. To test the hypotheses put forward in the Introduction, we retrieve clearly agreeing Q-R pairs (agreement annotation > 1, $N = 468$) and clearly disagreeing Q-R pairs (agreement annotation < -1, $N = 2519$). All our analyses are performed on these subsets.

According to hypothesis H1, more style accommodation is expected to be present in agreeing responses. We find a significant difference in SA_m

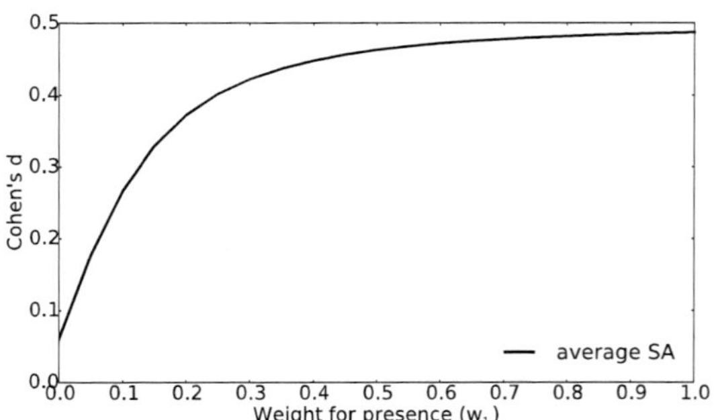

Figure 1: Effect size (Cohen's d) when comparing SA in agreeing and disagreeing Q-R pairs with different feature weights; w_1 (*presence*) in the x-axis.

for all markers between agreeing and disagreeing Q-R pairs (Welch two sample t-test, $p < 0.001$; effect size Cohen's d between .22 and .37 for all markers). Contrary to hypothesis H1, however, in all cases the level of style accommodation is higher in *disagreeing* responses than in agreeing ones. Example (1) in Table 1 shows a typical Q-R pair with high content agreement but low SA. As illustrated by this example, strongly agreeing responses often consist of short explicit expressions of agreement, with less potential for stylistic alignment. In contrast, disagreeing responses tend to be longer (as already observed by conversational analysts such as Pomerantz (1984)) and have therefore more chances to include stylistic markers matching the quoted post.

Indeed, although across the board disagreeing responses exhibit more SA, the statistical significance of this difference decreases as we lower the weight of the *presence* features (and thus give more importance to frequency and post lenght). Figure 1 shows the evolution of the effect size (Cohen's d) with different values for w_1. When only frequency is taken into account ($w_1 = 0$), the effect size is very low. However, as soon as w_1 receives some weight (from $w_1 = 0.1$ onwards), a more significant difference can be observed for disagreeing Q-R pairs (Welch two sample t-test, $p < 0.001, d > 0.2$).[3]

We now concentrate on disagreeing Q-R pairs to investigate our second hypothesis. According to H2, disagreeing responses with a persuasive

---

[3] As suggested by one anonymous reviewer, we also performed our analysis on a balanced dataset constructed by under-sampling the category of disagreeing Q-R pairs. Our findings also hold in this balanced setting.

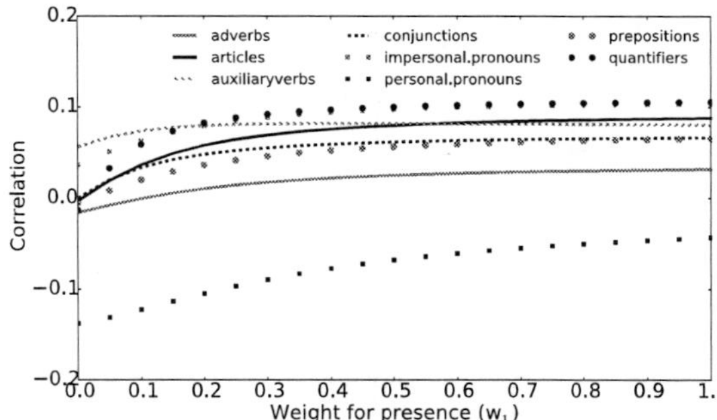

Figure 2: Correlation between SA and nice/nastiness annotations in disagreeing Q-R pairs.

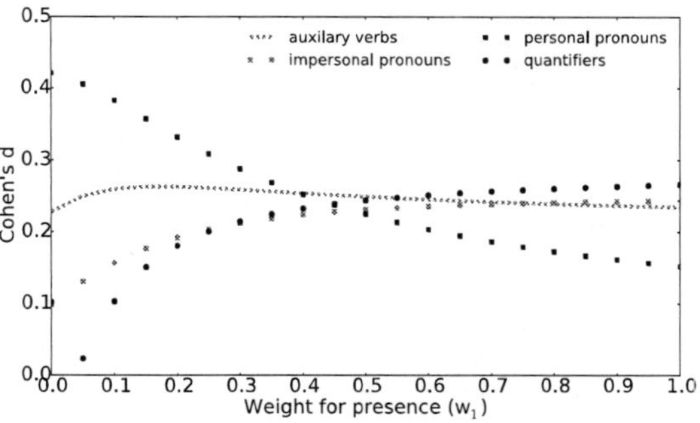

Figure 3: Effect size (Cohen's d) when comparing SA in disagreeing nice vs. nasty Q-R pairs with different feature weights; w_1 in the x-axis.

aim will show higher style accommodation. As mentioned earlier, we use the nice/nastiness and sarcasm annotations as a proxy for persuasion or lack thereof. We observe a tendency towards positive correlation between style accommodation and niceness: i.e., responses with higher SA tend to be perceived as nicer. Nevertheless, the correlations observed, although often significant ($p < 0.05$), are extremely weak (Pearson's $r < 0.1$). Interestingly, however, in this case there is one type of marker that stands out: accommodation on personal pronouns is *negatively* correlated with level of niceness. This can be observed in Figure 2, which plots SA for all markers separately for different feature weighting schemes. As can be seen, the negative correlation for personal pronouns is stronger the more weight we give to marker frequency (lower values of w_1 in the plot). This correlation is significant ($p < 0.05$) for all values of w_2 higher than 0.1.

We next discard neutral values on the nice/nastiness dimension and focus on Q-R pairs that have clearly been annotated as nice (score > 1) or nasty (score < -1). We find significant differences for four marker types: auxiliary verbs, quantifiers, impersonal and personal pronouns. Not surprisingly, given the correlations observed above, the three former markers show more SA in nice disagreeing responses, while SA with respect to personal pronouns is higher in nasty responses. Examples (2) and (3) in Table 1 illustrate this. Figure 3 shows the effect size of these differences (Cohen's d) for these four marker types, for different feature weight values. As clearly seen in the plot, personal pronouns also contrast with the other markers on their behaviour with different weighting schemes. The

(1) **Q:** Micheal Moore tends to manipulate people, just in a different way than the President or the media does… not with fear, with knowledge and anger.   **R:** Well said. I agree 100%.   *agreement*= 5, *nice/nasty*= 5, $SA_{avg}=-.39$ ($\vec{w}=[0.5, 0.5]$)

(2) **Q:** And the problem is, if one of these assumption is proven incorrect, then the whole theory collapses.   **R:** And one of these assumption has not been proven incorrect.   *agreement*= −2, *nice/nasty*= 5 , $SA_{quant} = .31$ ($\vec{w}=[0.5, 0.5]$)

(3) **Q:** But he does have a point…   **R:** I see. Then you have none?   *agreement*= −1, *nice/nasty*= −2, $SA_{pers.pro}=.24$ ($\vec{w}=[0.5, 0.5]$)

Table 1: Example Q-R pairs.

higher accommodation on personal pronouns (in nasty responses) is much more pronounced when marker frequency receives a high weight.

Finally, regarding sarcasm, we observe a tendency for all markers to exhibit lower levels of style accommodation in sarcastic disagreeing responses. This tendency is statistically significant for three marker types: auxiliary verbs, quantifiers, and impersonal pronouns (Welch two sample t-test, $p < 0.05$ for $w_1 > 0.25$). Accommodation on personal pronouns does not appear to be related to sarcasm. We remark, however, that these results need to be taken with care since only 3% of all Q-R pairs in the dataset (5% in disagreeing pairs) are reliably annotated as sarcastic.

5 Conclusions

We have investigated style accommodation in online discussions by means of a new model that takes into account the *presence* of a marker in both quoted text and response and the relative *frequency* of that marker given the length of a post.

Contrary to our first hypothesis, we found more accommodation in disagreeing responses than in agreeing ones. Thus, if speakers fully align on content, there seems to be less need to also align on style; in contrast, when there is a content disagreement, speakers may want to maintain rapport by exhibiting style accommodation. In support of our second hypothesis, we observed more accommodation in disagreeing responses that were perceived as nice by annotators. In a discussion, such responses are presumably more persuasive than those perceived as nasty or sarcastic, where style accommodation was lower.

We found pronounced differences for personal pronouns: in the current dataset, accommodation on personal pronouns signals distancing (nasty perception). The fact that personal pronouns stand out confirms previous findings showing that this marker class can be a particularly powerful indicator of social dynamics (Pennebaker, 2011).

Our analysis has shown that the relative weight given to *presence* and *frequency* features can have a substantial impact on the results obtained. We hope that the model put forward will help to further understand confounding factors in the computation of style accommodation. We leave a thorough investigation of these issues to future work.

Acknowledgements

We are grateful to the *SEM anonymous reviewers for their useful comments and suggestions. This research has received funding from the Netherlands Organisation for Scientific Research (NWO) under the VIDI grant n. 276-89-008, *Asymmetry in Conversation*.

References

Cindy Chung and James W. Pennebaker. 2007. The psychological functions of function words. *Social Communication*, pages 343–359.

Cristian Danescu-Niculescu-Mizil, Lillian Lee, Bo Pang, and Jon Kleinberg. 2012. Echoes of power: Language effects and power differences in social interaction. In *Proceedings of the 21st international conference on World Wide Web*, pages 699–708. ACM.

Shuyang Gao, Greg Ver Steeg, and Aram Galstyan. 2015. Understanding confounding effects in linguistic coordination: an information-theoretic approach. *PloS One*, 10(6):e0130167.

Molly E. Ireland, Richard B. Slatcher, Paul W. Eastwick, Lauren E. Scissors, Eli J. Finkel, and James W. Pennebaker. 2011. Language style matching predicts relationship initiation and stability. *Psychological Science*, 22(1):39–44.

Jessica L. Lakin and Tanya L. Chartrand. 2003. Using nonconscious behavioral mimicry to create affiliation and rapport. *Psychological Science*, 14(4):334–339.

Kate G Niederhoffer and James W Pennebaker. 2002. Linguistic style matching in social interaction. *Journal of Language and Social Psychology*, 21(4):337–360.

Bill Noble and Raquel Fernández. 2015. Centre stage: How social network position shapes linguistic coordination. In *Proceedings of the 6th Workshop on Cognitive Modeling and Computational Linguistics*, pages 29–38, Denver, Colorado, June. Association for Computational Linguistics.

James W. Pennebaker, Martha E. Francis, and Roger J. Booth. 2007. Linguistic Inquiry and Word Count (LIWC): A computerized text analysis program. Technical report, LIWC.net, Austin, Texas.

James W. Pennebaker. 2011. *The Secret Life of Pronouns: What*. Bloomsbury Press.

Martin J. Pickering and Simon Garrod. 2004. Toward a mechanistic psychology of dialogue. *Behavioral and Brain Sciences*, 27(02):169–190.

Anita Pomerantz. 1984. Agreeing and disagreeing with assessments: Some features of preferred/dispreferred turn shaped. In *Structures of Social Action*. Cambridge University Press.

Diederik Marijn Roijers, Peter Vamplew, Shimon Whiteson, and Richard Dazeley. 2013. A survey of multi-objective sequential decision-making. *Journal of Artificial Intelligence Research*.

Lauren E. Scissors, Alastair J. Gill, and Darren Gergle. 2008. Linguistic mimicry and trust in text-based CMC. In *Proceedings of the 2008 ACM conference on Computer supported cooperative work*, pages 277–280. ACM.

Carolyn A. Shepard, Howard Giles, and Beth A. Le Poire. 2001. Communication accommodation theory. In W. P. Robinson and H. Giles, editors, *The new Handbook of Language and Social Psychology*, pages 33–56. John Wiley & Sons Ltd.

Marilyn A Walker, Jean E Fox Tree, Pranav Anand, Rob Abbott, and Joseph King. 2012. A corpus for research on deliberation and debate. In *Proceedings of the Eighth International Conference on Language Resources and Evaluation (LREC)*, pages 812–817.

Unsupervised Text Segmentation Using
Semantic Relatedness Graphs

Goran Glavaš, Federico Nanni, Simone Paolo Ponzetto
Data and Web Science Group
University of Mannheim
B6 26, DE-68161 Mannheim, Germany
`{goran,federico,simone}@.informatik.uni-mannheim.de`

Abstract

Segmenting text into semantically coherent fragments improves readability of text and facilitates tasks like text summarization and passage retrieval. In this paper, we present a novel unsupervised algorithm for linear text segmentation (TS) that exploits word embeddings and a measure of semantic relatedness of short texts to construct a *semantic relatedness graph* of the document. Semantically coherent segments are then derived from maximal cliques of the relatedness graph. The algorithm performs competitively on a standard synthetic dataset and outperforms the best-performing method on a real-world (i.e., non-artificial) dataset of political manifestos.

1 Introduction

Despite the fact that in mainstream natural language processing (NLP) and information retrieval (IR) texts are modeled as bags of unordered words, texts are sequences of semantically coherent segments, designed (often very thoughtfully) to ease readability and understanding of the ideas conveyed by the authors. Although authors may explicitly define coherent segments (e.g., as paragraphs), many texts, especially on the web, lack any explicit segmentation.

Linear text segmentation aims to represent texts as sequences of semantically coherent segments. Besides improving readability and understandability of texts for readers, automated text segmentation is beneficial for NLP and IR tasks such as text summarization (Angheluta et al., 2002; Dias et al., 2007) and passage retrieval (Huang et al., 2003; Dias et al., 2007). Whereas early approaches to unsupervised text segmentation measured the co-herence of segments via raw term overlaps between sentences (Hearst, 1997; Choi, 2000), more recent methods (Misra et al., 2009; Riedl and Biemann, 2012) addressed the issue of sparsity of term-based representations by replacing term-vectors with vectors of latent topics.

A topical representation of text is, however, merely a vague approximation of its meaning. Considering that the goal of TS is to identify *semantically* coherent segments, we propose a TS algorithm aiming to directly capture the semantic relatedness between segments, instead of approximating it via topical similarity. We employ word embeddings (Mikolov et al., 2013) and a measure of semantic relatedness of short texts (Šarić et al., 2012) to construct a relatedness graph of the text in which nodes denote sentences and edges are added between semantically related sentences. We then derive segments using the maximal cliques of such similarity graphs.

The proposed algorithm displays competitive performance on the artifically-generated benchmark TS dataset (Choi, 2000) and, more importantly, outperforms the best-performing topic modeling-based TS method on a real-world dataset of political manifestos.

2 Related Work

Automated text segmentation received a lot of attention in NLP and IR communities due to its usefulness for text summarization and text indexing. Text segmentation can be performed in two different ways, namely (1) with the goal of obtaining linear segmentations (i.e. detecting the sequence of different segments in a text) , or (2) in order to obtain hierarchical segmentations (i.e. defining a structure of subtopics between the detected segments). Like the majority of TS methods (Hearst, 1994; Brants et al., 2002; Misra et al., 2009; Riedl

*Proceedings of the Fifth Joint Conference on Lexical and Computational Semantics (*SEM 2016)*, pages 125–130,
Berlin, Germany, August 11-12, 2016.

and Biemann, 2012), in this work we focus on linear segmentation of text, but there is also a solid body of work on hierarchical TS, where each top-level segment is further broken down (Yaari, 1997; Eisenstein, 2009).

Hearst (1994) introduced TextTiling, one of the first unsupervised algorithms for linear text segmentation. She exploits the fact that words tend to be repeated in coherent segments and measures the similarity between paragraphs by comparing their sparse term-vectors. Choi (2000) introduced the probabilistic algorithm using matrix-based ranking and clustering to determine similarities between segments. Galley et al. (2003) combined content-based information with acoustic cues in order to detect discourse shifts whereas Utiyama and Isahara (2001) and Fragkou et al. (2004) minimized different segmentation cost functions with dynamic programming.

The first segmentation approach based on topic modeling (Brants et al., 2002) employed the probabilistic latent semantic analysis (pLSA) to derive latent representations of segments and determined the segmentation based on similarities of segments' latent vectors. More recent models (Misra et al., 2009; Riedl and Biemann, 2012) employed the latent Dirichlet allocation (LDA) (Blei et al., 2003) to compute the latent topics and displayed superior performance to previous models on standard synthetic datasets (Choi, 2000; Galley et al., 2003). Misra et al. (2009) used dynamic programming to find globally optimal segmentation over the set of LDA-based segment representations, whereas Riedl and Biemann (2012) introduced TopicTiling, an LDA-driven extension of Hearst's TextTiling algorithm where segments are, represented as dense vectors of dominant topics of terms they contain (instead of as sparse term vectors). Riedl and Biemann (2012) show that TopicTiling outperforms at-that-time state-of-the-art methods for unsupervised linear segmentation (Choi, 2000; Utiyama and Isahara, 2001; Galley et al., 2003; Fragkou et al., 2004; Misra et al., 2009) and that it is also faster than other LDA-based methods (Misra et al., 2009).

In the most closely related work to ours, Malioutov and Barzilay (2006) proposed a graph-based TS approach in which they first construct the fully connected graph of sentences, with edges weighted via the cosine similarity between bag-of-words sentence vectors, and then run the minimum normalized multiway cut algorithm to obtain the segments. Similarly, Ferret (2007) builds the similarity graph, only between words instead of between sentences, using sparse co-occurrence vectors as semantic representations for words. He then identifies topics by clustering the word similarity graph via the Shared Nearest Neighbor algorithm (Ertöz et al., 2004). Unlike these works, we use the dense semantic representations of words and sentences (i.e., embeddings), which have been shown to outperform sparse semantic vectors on a range of NLP tasks. Also, instead of looking for minimal cuts in the relatedness graph, we exploit the maximal cliques of the relatedness graph between sentences to obtain the topic segments.

3 Text Segmentation Algorithm

Our TS algorithm, dubbed GRAPHSEG, builds a *semantic relatedness graph* in which nodes denote sentences and edges are created for pairs of semantically related sentences. We then determine the coherent segments by finding maximal cliques of the relatedness graph. The novelty of GRAPHSEG is in the fact that it directly exploits the semantics of text instead of approximating the meaning with topicality.

3.1 Semantic Relatedness of Sentences

The measure of semantic relatedness between sentences we use is an extension of a salient *greedy lemma alignment* feature proposed in a supervised model by Šarić et al. (2012). They greedily align content words between sentences by the similarity of their distributional vectors and then sum the similarity scores of aligned word pairs. However, such greedily obtained alignment is not necessarily optimal. In contrast, we compute the optimal alignment by (1) creating a weighted complete bipartite graph between the sets of content words of the two sentences (i.e., each word from one sentence is connected with a relatedness edge to all of the words in the other sentence) and (2) running a bipartite graph matching algorithm known as the Hungarian method (Kuhn, 1955) that has the polynomial complexity. The similarities of content words between sentences (i.e., the weights of the bipartite graph) are computed as the cosine of the angle between their corresponding embedding vectors (Mikolov et al., 2013).

Let A be the set of word pairs in the optimal alignment between the content-word sets of the two sentences S_1 and S_2, i.e., $A = \{(w_1, w_2) \mid w_1 \in S_1 \wedge w_2 \in S_2\}$. We then compute the semantic relatedness for two given sentences S_1 and S_2 as follows:

$$sr(S_1, S_2) = \sum_{(w_1, w_2) \in A} \cos(v_1, v_2) \cdot \min(ic(w_1), ic(w_2))$$

where v_i is the embedding vector of the word w_i and $ic(w)$ is the information content (IC) of the word w, computed based on the relative frequency of w in some large corpus C:

$$ic(w) = -\log \frac{freq(w) + 1}{|C| + \sum_{w' \in C} freq(w')}.$$

We utilize the IC weighting of embedding similarity because we assume that matches between less frequent words (e.g., *guitar* and *ukulele*) contribute more to sentence relatedness than pairs of similar but frequent words (e.g., *do* and *make*). We used Google Books Ngrams (Michel et al., 2011) as a large corpus C for estimating relative frequencies of words in a language.

Because there will be more aligned pairs between longer sentences, the relatedness score will be larger for longer sentences merely because of their length (regardless of their actual similarity). Thus, we normalize the $sr(S_1, S_2)$ score first with the length of S_1 and then with the length S_2 and we finally average these two normalized scores:

$$rel(S_1, S_2) = \frac{1}{2} \cdot \left(\frac{sr(S_1, S_2)}{|S_1|} + \frac{sr(S_1, S_2)}{|S_2|} \right).$$

3.2 Graph-Based Segmentation

All sentences in a text become nodes of the relatedness graph G. We then compute the semantic similarity, as described in the previous subsection, between all pairs of sentences in a given document. For each pair of sentences for which the semantic relatedness is above some treshold value τ we add an edge between the corresponding nodes of G. Next, we employ the Bron-Kerbosch algorithm (Bron and Kerbosch, 1973) to compute the set $\mathcal{Q}$ of all maximal cliques of G. We then create the initial set of segments SG by merging adjacent sentences found in at least one maximal clique $Q \in \mathcal{Q}$ of graph G. Next, we merge the adjacent segments sg_i and sg_{i+1} for which there is at least one clique $Q \in \mathcal{Q}$ containing at least one sentence from sg_i and one sentence from sg_{i+1}. Finally, given the

Step	Sets
Cliques $\mathcal{Q}$	$\{1, 2, 6\}, \{2, 4, 7\}, \{3, 4, 5\}, \{1, 8, 9\}$
Init. seg.	$\{1, 2\}, \{3, 4, 5\}, \{6\}, \{7\} \{8, 9\}$
Merge seg.	$\{1, 2, 3, 4, 5\}, \{6\}, \{7\}, \{8, 9\}$
Merge small	$\{1, 2, 3, 4, 5\}, \{6, 7\}, \{8, 9\}$

Table 1: Creating segments from graph cliques ($n = 2$). In the third step we merge segments $\{1, 2, 3\}$ and $\{4, 5\}$ because the second clique contains sentences 2 (from the left segment) and 4 (from the right segment). In the final step we merge single sentence segments (assuming $segs(\{1, 2, 3, 4, 5\}, \{6\}) < segs(\{6\}, \{7\})$ and $segs(\{7\}, \{8, 9\}) < segs(\{6\}, \{7\}))$.

minimal segment size n, we merge segments sg_i with less than n sentences with the semantically more related of the two adjacent segments – sg_{i-1} or sg_{i+1}. The relatedness between two adjacent segments ($sgr(sg_i, sg_{i+1})$) is computed as the average relatedness between their respective sentences:

$$sgr(SG_1, SG_2) = \frac{1}{|SG_1||SG_2|} \sum_{\substack{S_1 \in SG_1 \\ S_2 \in SG_2}} rel(S_1, S_2).$$

We exemplify the creation of segments from maximal cliques in Table 1. The complete segmentation algorithm is fleshed out in Algorithm 1.[1]

4 Evaluation

In this section, we first introduce the two evaluation datasets that we use one being the commonly used synthetic dataset and the other a realistic dataset of politi- cal manifestos. Following, we present the experimental setting and finally describe and discuss the results achieved by our GRAPHSEG algorithm and how it compares to other TS models.

4.1 Datasets

Unsupervised methods for text segmentation have most often been evaluated on synthetic datasets with segments from different sources being concatenated in artificial documents (Choi, 2000; Galley et al., 2003). Segmenting such artificial texts is easier than segmenting real-world documents. This is why besides on the artificial Choi dataset we also evaluate GRAPHSEG on a real-world dataset of political texts from the Manifesto Project,[2,3] manually

---

[1] We make the GraphSeg tool freely available at the following address: `https://gg42554@bitbucket.org/gg42554/graphseg.git`

[2] `https://manifestoproject.wzb.eu`

[3] We used the set of six documents manifestos – three Republican and three Democrat manifestos from the 2004,

Algorithm 1: *Segment(text, τ, n)*

$G \leftarrow (V \leftarrow \varnothing, E \leftarrow \varnothing)$
$S \leftarrow sentences(text)$
$SG \leftarrow \varnothing$
// constructing the similarity graph
for each sentence $S_i \in S$ **do**
  $V \leftarrow V \cup \{S_i\}$
for each pair $(S_i, S_j) \mid S_i, S_j \in S$ **do**
  if $rel(S_i, S_j) > \tau$ **do**
    $E \leftarrow E \cup (\{S_i\}, \{S_j\})$
// creating initial segments from cliques
$Q \leftarrow cliques(G)$
for each clique $Q \in \mathcal{Q}$ **do**
  for each $(S_i, S_j), S_i, S_j \in Q$ **do**
    if $j - i = 1$ **do**
      if $sg(S_i) = \varnothing$ **and** $sg(S_j) = \varnothing$ **do**
        $SG \leftarrow SG \cup \{S_i, S_j\}$
      elif $sg(S_i) \neq \varnothing$ **and** $sg(S_j) = \varnothing$ **do**
        $sg(S_i) \leftarrow sg(S_i) \cup \{S_j\}$
      elif $sg(S_i) = \varnothing$ **and** $sg(S_j) \neq \varnothing$ **do**
        $sg(S_j) \leftarrow sg(S_j) \cup \{S_i\}$
// merging adjacent segments
for each segment $sg_i \in SG$ **do**
  if $\exists Q \in \mathcal{Q} \mid (\exists S_j, S_k \in Q \mid$
        $S_j \in sg_i \wedge S_k \in sg_{i+1})$ **do**
    $SG \leftarrow SG \setminus \{sg_i, sg_{i+1}\}$
    $SG \leftarrow SG \cup (sg_i \cup sg_{i+1})$
// merging too small segments
for each segment $sg_i \in SG$ **do**
  if $|sg_i| < n$ **do**
    if $sgr(sg_{i-1}, sg_i) > sgr(sg_i, sg_{i+1})$ **do**
      $SG \leftarrow SG \setminus \{sg_{i-1}, sg_i\}$
      $SG \leftarrow SG \cup (sg_{i-1} \cup sg_i)$
    else do
      $SG \leftarrow SG \setminus \{sg_i, sg_{i+1}\}$
      $SG \leftarrow SG \cup (sg_i \cup sg_{i+1})$
return SG

labeled by domain experts with segments of seven different topics (e.g., economy and welfare, quality of life, foreign affairs). The selected manifestos contain between 1000 and 2500 sentences, with segments ranging in length from 1 to 78 sentences, which is in sharp contrast to the Choi dataset where all segments are of similar size.

4.2 Experimental Setting

To allow for comparison with previous work, we evaluate GRAPHSEG on four subsets of the Choi dataset, differing in number of sentences the seg-

ments contain. For the evaluation on the Choi dataset, the GRAPHSEG algorithm made use of the publicly available word embeddings built from a Google News dataset.[4]

Both LDA-based models (Misra et al., 2009; Riedl and Biemann, 2012) and GRAPHSEG rely on corpus-derived word representations. Thus, we evaluated on the Manifesto dataset both the domain-adapted and domain-unadapted variants of these methods. The domain-adapted variants of the models used the unlabeled domain corpus – a test set of 466 unlabeled political manifestos – to train the domain-specific word representations. This means that we obtain (1) in-domain topics for the LDA-based TopicTiling model of Riedl and Biemann (2012) and (2) domain-specific embeddings for the GRAPHSEG algorithm. On the Manifesto dataset we also evaluate a baseline that randomly (50% chance) starts a new segment at points m sentences apart, with m being set to half of the average length of gold segments.

We evaluate the performance using two standard TS evaluation metrics – P_k (Beeferman et al., 1999) and WindowDiff (WD) (Pevzner and Hearst, 2002). P_k is the probability that two randomly drawn sentences mutually k sentences apart are classified incorrectly – either as belonging to the same segment when they are in different gold segments or as being in different segments when they are in the same gold segment. Following Riedl and Biemann (2012), we set k to half of the document length divided by the number of gold segments. WindowDiff is a stricter version of P_k as, instead of only checking if the randomly chosen sentences are in the same predicted segment or not, it compares the exact number of segments between the sentences in the predicted segmentation with the number of segments in between the same sentences in the gold standard. Lower scores indicate better performance for both these metrics.

The GRAPHSEG algorithm has two parameters: (1) the sentence similarity treshold τ which is used when creating edges of the sentence relatedness graph and (2) the minimal segment size n, which we utilize to merge adjacent segments that are too small. In all experiments we use grid-search in a folded cross-validation setting to jointly optimize both parameters. In view of comparison with other models, the parameter optimization is justified be-

---

2008, and 2012 U.S. elections

[4]`https://drive.google.com/file/d/`
`0B7XkCwpI5KDYNlNUTTlSS21pQmM/edit?usp=`
`sharing`

Method	3-5		6-8		9-11		3-11	
	P_k	WD	P_k	WD	P_k	WD	P_k	WD
Choi (2000)	12.0	–	9.0	–	9.0	–	12.0	–
Brants et al. (2002)	7.4	–	8.0	–	6.8	–	10.7	–
Fragkou et al. (2004)	5.5	–	3.0	–	1.3	–	7.0	–
Misra et al. (2009)	23.0	–	15.8	–	14.4	–	16.1	–
GRAPHSEG	5.6	8.7	7.2	9.4	6.6	9.6	7.2	9.0
Misra et al. (2009)*	2.2	–	2.3	–	4.1	–	2.3	–
Riedl and Biemann (2012)*	1.2	1.3	0.8	0.9	0.6	0.7	1.0	1.1

Table 2: Performance on different portions of the Choi dataset (*with domain-adapted topic model).

Method	P_k	WD
Random baseline	40.60	49.17
Riedl and Biemann (2012)	33.39	38.31
GRAPHSEG	28.09	34.04
Riedl and Biemann (2012)*	32.94	37.59
GRAPHSEG*	28.08	34.00

Table 3: Performance on the Manifesto dataset (*domain-adapted variant).

cause other models, e.g., TopicTiling (Riedl and Biemann, 2012), also have parameters (e.g., number of topics for the topic model) which are optimized using cross-validation.

4.3 Results and Discussion

In Table 2 we report the performance of GRAPH-SEG and prominent TS methods on the synthetic Choi dataset. GRAPHSEG performs competitively, outperforming all methods but (Fragkou et al., 2004) and domain-adapted versions of LDA-based models (Misra et al., 2009; Riedl and Biemann, 2012). However, the approach by (Fragkou et al., 2004) uses the gold standard information – the average gold segment size – as input. On the other hand, the LDA-based models adapt their topic models on parts of the Choi dataset itself. Despite the fact that they use different documents for training the topic models from those used for evaluating segmentation quality, the evaluation is still tainted because snippets from the original documents appear in multiple artificial documents – some of which belong to the the training set and others to the test set, as admitted by Riedl and Biemann (2012) and this is why their reported performance on this dataset is overestimated.

In Table 3 we report the results on the Manifesto dataset. Results of both TopicTiling and GRAPHSEG indicate that the realistic Manifesto dataset is much more difficult to segment than the artificial Choi dataset. The GRAPHSEG algorithm significantly outperforms the TopicTiling method ($p < 0.05$, Student's t-test). In-domain training of word representations, topics for TopicTiling and word embeddings for *GraphSeg*, does not significantly improve the performance for neither of the two models. This result contrasts previous findings (Misra et al., 2009; Riedl and Biemann, 2012) in which the performance boost was credited to the in-domain trained topics and supports our hypothesis that the performance boost of the LDA-based methods' with in-domain trained topics originates from information leakage between different portions of the synthetic Choi dataset.

5 Conclusion

In this work we presented GRAPHSEG, a novel graph-based algorithm for unsupervised text segmentation. GRAPHSEG employs word embeddings and extends a measure of semantic relatedness to construct a relatedness graph with edges established between semantically related sentences. The segmentation is then determined by the maximal cliques of the relatedness graph and improved by semantic comparison of adjacent segments.

GRAPHSEG displays competitive performance compared to best-performing LDA-based methods on a synthetic dataset. However, we identify and discuss evaluation issues pertaining to LDA-based TS on this dataset. We also performed an evaluation on the real-world dataset of political manifestos and showed that in a realistic setting GRAPHSEG significantly outperforms the state-of-the-art LDA-based TS model.

Acknowledgments

We thank the Manifesto Project researchers for making the topically annotated manifestos freely available for research purposes. We thank the anonymous reviewers for their useful comments.

References

Roxana Angheluta, Rik De Busser, and Marie-Francine Moens. 2002. The use of topic segmentation for automatic summarization. In *Proceedings of the ACL-2002 Workshop on Automatic Summarization*, pages 11–12.

Doug Beeferman, Adam Berger, and John Lafferty. 1999. Statistical models for text segmentation. *Machine learning*, 34(1-3):177–210.

David M Blei, Andrew Y Ng, and Michael I Jordan. 2003. Latent dirichlet allocation. *the Journal of machine Learning research*, 3:993–1022.

Thorsten Brants, Francine Chen, and Ioannis Tsochantaridis. 2002. Topic-based document segmentation with probabilistic latent semantic analysis. In *Proceedings of CIKM*, pages 211–218. ACM.

Coen Bron and Joep Kerbosch. 1973. Algorithm 457: Finding all cliques of an undirected graph. *Communications of the ACM*, 16(9):575–577.

Freddy YY Choi. 2000. Advances in domain independent linear text segmentation. In *Proceedings of NAACL*, pages 26–33. Association for Computational Linguistics.

Gaël Dias, Elsa Alves, and José Gabriel Pereira Lopes. 2007. Topic segmentation algorithms for text summarization and passage retrieval: An exhaustive evaluation. In *AAAI*, volume 7, pages 1334–1339.

Jacob Eisenstein. 2009. Hierarchical text segmentation from multi-scale lexical cohesion. In *Proceedings of HLT-NAACL*, pages 353–361. Association for Computational Linguistics.

Levent Ertöz, Michael Steinbach, and Vipin Kumar. 2004. Finding topics in collections of documents: A shared nearest neighbor approach. *Clustering and Information Retrieval*, pages 83–103.

Olivier Ferret. 2007. Finding document topics for improving topic segmentation. In *ACL*, volume 7, pages 480–487. Citeseer.

Pavlina Fragkou, Vassilios Petridis, and Ath Kehagias. 2004. A dynamic programming algorithm for linear text segmentation. *Journal of Intelligent Information Systems*, 23(2):179–197.

Michel Galley, Kathleen McKeown, Eric Fosler-Lussier, and Hongyan Jing. 2003. Discourse segmentation of multi-party conversation. In *Proceedings of ACL*, pages 562–569. Association for Computational Linguistics.

Marti A Hearst. 1994. Multi-paragraph segmentation of expository text. In *Proceedings of the ACL*, pages 9–16. Association for Computational Linguistics.

Marti A Hearst. 1997. TextTiling: Segmenting text into multi-paragraph subtopic passages. *Computational linguistics*, 23(1):33–64.

Xiangji Huang, Fuchun Peng, Dale Schuurmans, Nick Cercone, and Stephen E Robertson. 2003. Applying machine learning to text segmentation for information retrieval. *Information Retrieval*, 6(3-4):333–362.

Harold W Kuhn. 1955. The hungarian method for the assignment problem. *Naval research logistics quarterly*, 2(1-2):83–97.

Igor Malioutov and Regina Barzilay. 2006. Minimum cut model for spoken lecture segmentation. In *Proceedings of COLING-ACL*, pages 25–32. Association for Computational Linguistics.

Jean-Baptiste Michel, Yuan Kui Shen, Aviva Presser Aiden, Adrian Veres, Matthew K Gray, Joseph P Pickett, Dale Hoiberg, Dan Clancy, Peter Norvig, Jon Orwant, Steven Pinker, Martin A. Nowak, and Aiden Erez Lieberman. 2011. Quantitative analysis of culture using millions of digitized books. *Science*, 331(6014):176–182.

Tomas Mikolov, Ilya Sutskever, Kai Chen, Greg S Corrado, and Jeff Dean. 2013. Distributed representations of words and phrases and their compositionality. In *Proceedings of NIPS*, pages 3111–3119.

Hemant Misra, François Yvon, Joemon M Jose, and Olivier Cappe. 2009. Text segmentation via topic modeling: An analytical study. In *Proceedings of CIKM*, pages 1553–1556. ACM.

Lev Pevzner and Marti A Hearst. 2002. A critique and improvement of an evaluation metric for text segmentation. *Computational Linguistics*, 28(1):19–36.

Martin Riedl and Chris Biemann. 2012. TopicTiling: A text segmentation algorithm based on LDA. In *Proceedings of ACL 2012 Student Research Workshop*, pages 37–42. Association for Computational Linguistics.

Frane Šarić, Goran Glavaš, Mladen Karan, Jan Šnajder, and Bojana Dalbelo Bašić. 2012. TakeLab: Systems for measuring semantic text similarity. In *Proceedings of SemEval*, pages 441–448. Association for Computational Linguistics.

Masao Utiyama and Hitoshi Isahara. 2001. A statistical model for domain-independent text segmentation. In *Proceedings of ACL*, pages 499–506. Association for Computational Linguistics.

Yaakov Yaari. 1997. Segmentation of expository texts by hierarchical agglomerative clustering. In *Proceedings of RANLP*.

Improving Text-to-Pictograph Translation Through Word Sense Disambiguation

Leen Sevens[*], **Gilles Jacobs**[**], **Vincent Vandeghinste**[*], **Ineke Schuurman**[*],
Frank Van Eynde[*]
[*]Centre for Computational Linguistics (KU Leuven)
`firstname@ccl.kuleuven.be`
[**]Language and Translation Technology Team (Universiteit Gent)
`gillesm.jacobs@ugent.be`

Abstract

We describe the implementation of a Word Sense Disambiguation (WSD) tool in a Dutch Text-to-Pictograph translation system, which converts textual messages into sequences of pictographic images. The system is used in an online platform for Augmentative and Alternative Communication (AAC). In the original translation process, the appropriate sense of a word was not disambiguated before converting it into a pictograph. This often resulted in incorrect translations. The implementation of a WSD tool provides a better semantic understanding of the input messages.

1 Introduction

In today's digital age, people with Intellectual Disabilities (ID) often have trouble partaking in online activities such as email, chat, and social network websites. Not being able to access or use information technology is a major form of social exclusion. There is a dire need for digital communication interfaces that enable people with ID to contact one another.

Vandeghinste et al. (2015) are developing a Text-to-Pictograph and Pictograph-to-Text translation system for the WAI-NOT[1] communication platform. WAI-NOT is a Flemish non-profit organization that gives people with severe communication disabilities the opportunity to familiarize themselves with the Internet. Their safe website environment offers an email client that makes use of the Dutch pictograph translation solutions. The Text-to-Pictograph translation system (Vandeghinste et al., 2015; Sevens et al., 2015a) au-

tomatically augments written text with Beta[2] or Sclera[3] pictographs and is primarily conceived to improve the *comprehension* of textual content. The Pictograph-to-Text translation system (Sevens et al., 2015b) allows the user to insert a series of Beta or Sclera pictographs, automatically translating this image sequence into natural language text where possible. This facilitates the *construction* of textual content.

The Text-to-Pictograph translation process did not yet perform Word Sense Disambiguation (WSD) to select the appropriate sense of a word before converting it into a pictograph. Instead, the most frequent sense of the word was chosen. This sometimes resulted in incorrect pictograph translations (see Figure 1).

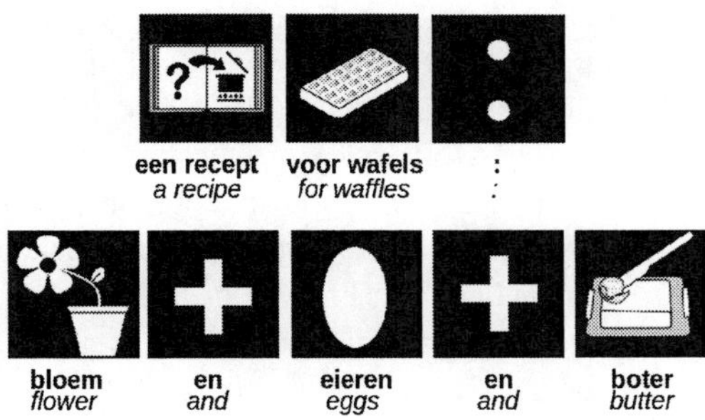

Figure 1: Example of Dutch-to-Sclera translation. The word *bloem* means both *flower* and *flour*. The most common sense is *flower*, which would be the wrong choice within the context of baking. Note that the pictograph language is a simplified language. Function words and number information are not represented.

We describe the implementation of a WSD tool

---

[1]http://www.wai-not.be/

[2]The Beta set consists of more than 3,000 coloured pictographs: https://www.betasymbols.com/

[3]Sclera pictographs are mainly black-and-white pictographs. Over 13,000 pictographs are available and more are added upon user request: http://www.sclera.be/

*Proceedings of the Fifth Joint Conference on Lexical and Computational Semantics (*SEM 2016)*, pages 131–135,
Berlin, Germany, August 11-12, 2016.

in the Dutch Text-to-Pictograph translation system. After a discussion of related work (section 2), we present both the Text-to-Pictograph translation tool and the WSD tool (section 3). We then proceed to describe the implementation procedure (section 4). Our evaluations show that improvements over the baseline in the Text-to-Pictograph translation tool were made (section 5). Finally, we conclude and describe future work (section 6).

2   Related work

There are not many works related to the task of translating text for pictograph-supported communication. Mihalcea and Leong (2008) describe a system for the automatic construction of simple pictographic sentences. They also use Word-Net (Miller, 1995) as a lexical resource, but they do not use the WordNet relations between concepts in the same manner as the Text-to-Pictograph translation system does. Furthermore, their system does not translate the entire message. However, it should be noted that they make use of WSD in a way that is very similar to the approach described below. The WSD tool also relies on WordNet as a lexical database. Their system, though, is focused on English and the effectiveness of WSD within the context of a pictograph translation system was not evaluated.

Quite similar to the Text-to-Pictograph translation system are SymWriter[4] and Blissymbols (Hehner et al., 1983). These systems allow users to insert arbitrary text, which is then semi-automatically converted into pictographs. However, they do not provide automatic translation aids based on linguistic knowledge to properly disambiguate lexical ambiguities, which can lead to erroneous translation (Vandeghinste, 2012).

There is contradictory evidence that Natural Language Processing tools and Information Retrieval tasks benefit from WSD. Within the field of Machine Translation, Dagan and Itai (1994) and Vickrey et al. (2005) show that proper incorporation of WSD leads to an increase in translation performance for automatic translation systems. On the other hand, Carpuat and Wu (2005) argue that it is difficult, at the least, to use standard WSD models to obtain significant improvements to statistical Machine Translation systems, even when supervised WSD models are used. In later research, Carpuat and Wu (2007)

and Chan et al. (2007) demonstrate that WSD can improve machine translation by using probabilistic methods that select the most likely translation phrase. Navigli (2009) underlines the general agreement that WSD needs to show its relevance in vivo. Full-fledged applications should be built including WSD either as an integrated or a pluggable component. As such, we set out to implement WSD and evaluate its effects within the Text-to-Pictograph translation system.

3   Description of the tools

The following sections describe the architecture of the Text-to-Pictograph translation system (section 3.1) and the WSD tool (section 3.2).

3.1   The Text-to-Pictograph translation system

The Text-to-Pictograph translation system translates text into a series of Beta or Sclera pictographs, cf. Vandeghinste et al. (2015) and Sevens et al. (2015a).

The source text first undergoes shallow linguistic processing, consisting of several sub-processes, such as tokenization, part-of-speech tagging, and lemmatization.

For each word in the source text, the system then returns all possible WordNet synsets identifiers (identifiers of sets of synonymous words) that are connected to that word. WordNets are an essential component of the Text-to-Pictograph translation system. For the Dutch system, Cornetto (Vossen et al., 2008; van der Vliet et al., 2010) was used. The synsets are filtered, keeping only those where the part-of-speech tag of the synset matches the part-of-speech tag of the word. Therefore, the semantic ambiguity of words across different grammatical categories (such as the noun *kom* 'bowl' and the verb *kom* 'come') has never formed an obstacle.

The WordNet synsets are used to connect pictographs to natural language text (see Figure 2). This greatly improves the lexical coverage of the system, as pictographs are connected to sets of words that have the same meaning, instead of just individual words. Additionally, if a synset is not covered by a pictograph, the links between synsets can be used to look for alternative pictographs with a similar meaning (such as the *dog* pictograph as a hyperonym for *poodle*). However, using pictographs through synset propagation (making use of the WordNet relations) is controlled by penalties for not using the proper concept.

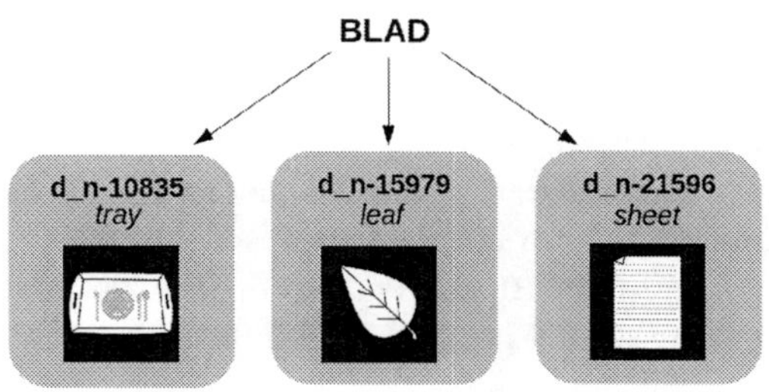

Figure 2: The Dutch word *blad* is linked to three different pictographs through its synsets.

Vandeghinste and Schuurman (2014) manually linked 5710 Sclera pictographs and 2760 Beta pictographs to synsets in Cornetto.

For every word in the sentence, the system checks whether one or more pictographs can be found for it. An A* algorithm[5] calculates the optimal pictograph sequence for the source text.

During the optimal path calculation step, the original system would sometimes be confronted with an equally likely choice between two or more pictographs, corresponding to different meanings of the same word (see Figure 2). In that case, the most commonly occurring sense according to DutchSemCor (Vossen et al., 2010) was chosen.

3.2 The Word Sense Disambiguation tool

We used the Dutch WSD tool that was made available by Ruben Izquiero[6] within the framework of the DutchSemCor project (Vossen et al., 2010).

DutchSemCor delivered a one-million word Dutch corpus that is fully sense-tagged with senses and domain names from the Cornetto database. It was constructed as a balanced-sense lexical sample for the 3000 most frequent and polysemous Dutch words, with about 100 examples for each sense. Part of the corpus was built semi-automatically and other parts manually. In the first phase, 25 examples were collected for each sense and manually tagged by annotators. The remainder of the corpus was tagged by a supervised WSD system, which was built using the manually tagged data from the first phase. The super-

vised system searched for the remaining 75 examples of the different senses to complete the corpus. Low-confidence examples were validated by annotators. In the last phase, even more examples were added to represent the context variety and the sense distribution as reflected in external corpora.

The resulting WSD system was built from the final sense-annotated corpus. The feature set that led to the best performance (81.62% token accuracy) contained words in a 1-token window around the target word, in combination with a bag-of-words representation of the context words. This WSD system takes natural language text as input and returns the confidence values of all senses according to Support Vector Machines.[7] Note that senses correspond to Cornetto synsets in both the Text-to-Pictograph translation tool and the WSD system.

4   Implementation

During the pre-processing phase, we let the Text-to-Pictograph translation system automatically assign a number to every sentence and every word. These numbers correspond to the sentences' position within the broader message and the words' position within the sentences. The WSD tool's output is numbered in a similar way. This way, if a particular input word appears multiple times within a message, the number label allows us to safely match that word with its correct WSD output counterpart.

The WSD tool is implemented after the shallow linguistic analysis and synset retrieval steps. The input to the WSD tool are the original sentences. Instead of only outputting one winning sense per word, we adapted the WSD tool to output the scores of each possible sense of the target word. As mentioned above, in the Text-to-Pictograph translation system, senses correspond to synsets which are attached to the word objects in the message. The WSD scores will now be added as a new feature of these synsets.

Next, we adapt the A* path-finding algorithm to include the WSD score in the penalty calculation as a bonus: A high WSD score biases the selection of the pictograph towards the winning sense. The score is weighted by a trainable parameter to determine the importance of WSD in relation to the

---

[5]A pathfinding algorithm that uses a heuristic to search the most likely paths first. Its input is the pictographically annotated source message, together with the pictographs penalties, depending on the number and kind of synset relations the system had to go through to connect them to the words.

[6]https://github.com/cltl/svm_wsd

[7]For a more detailed explanation on how the WSD system was built and tuned, we refer to Vossen et al. (2010).

Condition	BLEU	NIST	WER	PER
Beta				
No WSD	0.2572	5.0377	53.1435	45.5516
WSD	0.2721**	5.1976**	51.7200	43.7722
Sclera				
No WSD	0.1370	3.8321	72.1379	63.8621
WSD	0.1461*	3.9273	71.1724	62.8966

Table 1: Evaluation. $^*p < 0.05, ^{**}p < 0.01$

other system parameters.[8]

We have tuned these parameters through an automated procedure. The original tuning corpus consists of 50 messages from the WAI-NOT corpus, which were manually translated to Beta and Sclera pictographs by Vandeghinste et al. (2015). To the original tuning corpus, we added five more hand-picked messages from the corpus that included a polysemous word, that had at least two pictographs linked to at least two of its synsets. Biasing the tuning corpus like this was necessary, since the original set had very few ambiguous words.

We used the local hill climber algorithm as described in Vandeghinste et al. (2015), which varies the parameter values when running the Text-to-Pictograph translation script. The BLEU metric (Papineni et al., 2002) was used as an indicator of relative improvement. In order to maximize the BLEU score, we ran five trials of the local hill climbing algorithm, until BLEU converged onto a fixed score. Each trial was run with random initialization values, and varied the values between certain boundaries. From these trials, we took the best scoring parameter values.

5 Extrinsic evaluation

The evaluation set for the full Text-to-Pictograph translation system consists of 50 other messages from the WAI-NOT corpus, which were manually translated to Beta and Sclera pictographs by Vandeghinste et al. (2015).[9] We run the system with and without the WSD module. The system without WSD takes the most frequent sense for each word.[10] The automatic evaluation measures used are BLEU, NIST, Word Error Rate

(WER) and Position-independent word Error Rate (PER).[11] We have added significance levels for the BLEU and NIST scores, by comparing the *no WSD* condition with the *WSD* condition. Significance was calculated using bootstrap resampling (Koehn, 2004).

The results are presented in Table 1.[12] Significant improvements were made for Beta and Sclera (in the BLEU condition). The observation that WSD does not more significantly improve the evaluation results can be explained by the fact that the evaluation set is small and does not contain many polysemous words with multiple senses which are linked to a pictograph in the evaluation set. Only six examples were found.

For that reason, we selected another 20 sentences from the WAI-NOT corpus that contain a word that has at least two pictographs attached to at least two of its synsets (belonging to the same grammatical category) and manually calculated the precision of their pictograph translations, focussing on the ambiguous words, before and after implementing the WSD tool. For Beta, choosing the most frequent sense for each word led to a correct translation for 14 out of 20 ambiguous words, while the addition of the WSD tool gave a correct translation for 18 out of 20 words. For Sclera, we get 11 out of 20 correct translations for the most frequent sense condition, and 17 out of 20 correct translations for the WSD condition. Looking back at Figure 1, the system will now correctly pick the flour pictograph instead of the flower pictograph within the context of baking.

6 Conclusion and future plans

We set out to implement and evaluate the effect of WSD on the Text-to-Pictograph translation system for the Dutch language. Improvements over the baseline system were made. We can affirm that disambiguation works in most cases where senses of ambiguous words are linked to pictographs in the lexical database. The system with WSD is now less likely to pick the wrong pictograph for an ambiguous word, effectively improving picto-

---

[8]See Vandeghinste et al. (2015) for an in-depth description of the other parameters.

[9]Creating a gold standard is difficult, as no parallel corpora are available. Translating the messages into Beta and Sclera pictographs is a meticulous and time-intensive process. This explains why the dataset is small.

[10]It is important to note that these two systems use two different sets of parameters for finding the optimal path as a result of separate parameter tuning.

[11]These metrics are used for measuring a Machine Translation output's closeness to one or more reference translations. We consider pictograph translation as a Machine Translation problem.

[12]The gap between the results for Sclera and the results for Beta is explained by Vandeghinste et al. (2015). The Sclera pictograph set consists of a much larger amount of pictographs than Beta, so several different paraphrasing reference translations are possible.

graphic communication for the end-users. Future work consists of implementing other WSD algorithms and enriching both the tuning corpus and the evaluation corpus with more expert reference translations of Dutch text into Beta and Sclera pictographs.

English and Spanish versions of the Text-to-Pictograph translation system are being developed.

Acknowledgments

We would like to thank IWT and the European Commissions Competitiveness and Innovation Programme for funding Leen Sevens doctoral research and the Able-To-Include project, which allows further development and valorisation of the tools. We also thank the people from WAI-NOT for their valuable feedback.

References

Marine Carpuat and Dekai Wu. 2005. Word Sense Disambiguation vs. Statistical Machine Translation. In *Proceedings of the 43th Annual Meeting on Association for Computational Linguistics*, pages 387–394. Association for Computational Linguistics.

Marine Carpuat and Dekai Wu. 2007. Improving Statistical Machine Translation Using Word Sense Disambiguation. *EMNLP-CoNLL*, 7:61–72.

Yee Seng Chan, Hwee Tou Ng, and David Chiang. 2007. Word Sense Disambiguation Improves Statistical Machine Translation. *Annual Meeting - Association for Computational Linguistics*, 45:33.

Ido Dagan and Alon Itai. 1994. Word Sense Disambiguation Using a Second Language Monolingual Corpus. *Computational Linguistics*, 20(4):563–596.

Barbara Hehner, Peter A. Reich, Shirley McNaughton, and Jinny Storr. 1983. *Blissymbols for Use*. Blissymbolics Communication Institute.

Philipp Koehn. 2004. Statistical significance tests for machine translation evaluation. In *Proceedings of 2004 Conference on Empirical Methods on Natural Language Processing (EMNLP 2004)*, pages 388–395, Barcelona, Spain. Association for Computational Linguistics.

Rada Mihalcea and Chee Wee Leong. 2008. Toward Communicating Simple Sentences Using Pictorial Representations. *Machine Translation*, 22(3):153–173.

George Miller. 1995. WordNet: A Lexical Database fro English. *Communications of the ACM*, 28(11):39–41.

Roberto Navigli. 2009. Word Sense Disambiguation: A Survey. *ACM Computing Surveys*, 41(2):30–35.

Kishore Papineni, Salim Roukos, Todd Ward, and Wei-Jing Zhu. 2002. BLEU: A Method for Automatic Evaluation of Machine Translation. In *Proceedings of the 40th Annual Meeting on Association for Computational Linguistics (ACL 2002)*, pages 311–318, Philadelphia, USA. Association for Computational Linguistics.

Leen Sevens, Vincent Vandeghinste, Ineke Schuurman, and Frank Van Eynde. 2015a. Extending a Dutch Text-to-Pictograph Converter to English and Spanish. In *Proceedings of 6th Workshop on Speech and Language Processing for Assistive Technologies (SLPAT 2015)*, Dresden, Germany.

Leen Sevens, Vincent Vandeghinste, Ineke Schuurman, and Frank Van Eynde. 2015b. Natural Language Generation from Pictographs. In *Proceedings of 15th European Workshop on Natural Language Generation (ENLG 2015)*, pages 71–75, Brighton, UK. Association for Computational Linguistics.

Hennie van der Vliet, Isa Maks, Piek Vossen, and Roxane Segers. 2010. The Cornetto Database: Semantic issues in Linking Lexical Units and Synsets. In *Proceedings of the 14th EURALEX 2010 International Congress*, Leeuwarden, The Netherlands.

Vincent Vandeghinste and Ineke Schuurman. 2014. Linking Pictographs to Synsets: Sclera2Cornetto. In *Proceedings of the 9th International Conference on Language Resources and Evaluation (LREC)*, pages 3404–3410, Reykjavik, Iceland.

Vincent Vandeghinste, Ineke Schuurman, Leen Sevens, and Frank Van Eynde. 2015. Translating Text into Pictographs. *Natural Language Engineering*, pages 1–28.

Vincent Vandeghinste. 2012. Bridging the Gap between Pictographs and Natural Language. In *Proceedings of the RDWG Online Symposium on Easy-to-Read on the Web*.

David Vickrey, Luke Biewald, Marc Teyssier, and Daphne Koller. 2005. Word-Sense Disambiguation for Machine Translation. In *Proceedings of the Conference on Human Language Technology and Empirical Methods in Natural Language Processing*, pages 771–778. Association for Computational Linguistics.

Piek Vossen, Isa Maks, Roxane Segers, and Hennie van der Vliet. 2008. Integrating Lexical Units, Synsets, and Ontology in the Cornetto Database. In *Proceedings of the 6th International Conference on Language Resources and Evaluation (LREC)*, Marrakech, Morocco.

Piek Vossen, Attila Grg, Ruben Izquierdo, and Antal Van den Bosch. 2010. DutchSemCor: Targeting the ideal sense-tagged corpus. In *Proceedings of the 8th International Conference on Language Resources and Evaluation (LREC)*, Istanbul, Turkey.

Taking the best from the Crowd:
Learning Question Passage Classification from Noisy Data

Azad Abad
University of Trento
azad.abad@unitn.it

Alessandro Moschitti
Qatar Computing Research Institute
amoschitti@qf.org.qa

Abstract

In this paper, we propose methods to take into account the disagreement between crowd annotators as well as their skills for weighting instances in learning algorithms. The latter can thus better deal with noise in the annotation and produce higher accuracy. We created two passage reranking datasets: one with crowdsource platform, and the second with an expert who completely revised the crowd annotation. Our experiments show that our weighting approach reduces noise improving passage reranking up to 1.47% and 1.85% on MRR and P@1, respectively.

1 Introduction

One of the most important steps for building accurate QA systems is the selection/reranking of answer passage (AP) candidates typically provided by a search engine. This task requires the automatic learning of a ranking function, which pushes the correct answer passages (i.e., containing the answer to the question) higher in the list.

The accuracy of such function, among other, also depends on the quality of the supervision provided in the training data. Traditionally, the latter is annotated by experts through a rather costly procedure. Thus, sometimes, only noisy annotations obtained via automatic labeling mechanisms are available. For example, the Text REtrieval Conference (TREC[1]) provides open-domain QA datasets, e.g., for factoid QA. This data contains a set of questions, the answer keywords and a set of unannotated candidate APs. The labeling of the latter can be automatically carried out by checking if a given passage contains the correct answer keyword or not. However, this method is prone to

generate passage labels, i.e., containing the answer keyword but not supporting it. For instance, given the following question, Q, from TREC 2002-03 QA, associated with the answer key *Denmark*:

Q: *Where was Hans Christian Anderson born?*

the candidate passage:

AP: *Fairy Tales written by Hans Christian Andersen was published in 1835-1873 in* **Denmark**.

would be wrongly labeled as a correct passage since it contains *Denmark*. Such passages can be both misleading for training and unreliable for evaluating the reranking model, thus requiring manual annotation.

Since the expert work is costly, we can rely on crowdsourcing platforms such as CrowdFlower[2] for labeling data, faster and at lower cost (Snow et al., 2008). This method has shown promising results but it still produces noisy labels. Thus, a solution consists in (i) using redundant annotations from multiple annotators and (ii) resolving their disagreements with a majority voting approach (Sheng et al., 2008; Zhang et al., 2015). However, the consensus mechanism can still produce annotation noise, which (i) depends on crowd workers' skill and the difficulty of the given task; and (ii) can degrade the classifier accuracy.

In this paper, we study methods to take into account the disagreement among the crowd annotators as well as their skills in the learning algorithms. For this purpose, we design several instance weighting strategies, which help the learning algorithm to deal with the noise of the training examples, thus producing higher accuracy.

More in detail: firstly, we define some weight factors that characterize crowd annotators' skill, namely: *Prior Confidence*, which indicates the previous performance of the crowd worker re-

---

[1] http://trec.nist.gov

[2] http://www.crowdflower.com

*Proceedings of the Fifth Joint Conference on Lexical and Computational Semantics (*SEM 2016)*, pages 136–141,
Berlin, Germany, August 11-12, 2016.

ported by the crowdsourcing platform; *Task Confidence*, which is determined by the total number of annotations performed by the crowd worker in the target task; and *Consistency Confidence*, which quantify the agreements between the annotator and the majority voting labels. We used these parameters for building our weighting functions, which aim at reducing the impact of the noisy annotations in learning algorithms.

Secondly, we build a passage reranking dataset based on TREC 2002/2003 QA. We used Crowdflowers for carrying our an intial noisy annotation and we had an expert to manually verify and corrected incorrect labels. This is an important QA resource that we will release to the research community. Additionally, the accuracy of our models, e.g., classifiers and search engines, tested on such gold standard data establish new baselines, useful for future research in the field.

Finally, we conducted comparative experiments on our QA dataset using our weighting strategies. The results show that (i) our rerankers improve on the IR baseline, i.e., BM25, by 17.47% and 19.22% in MRR and P@1, respectively; and (ii) our weighting strategy improves the best reranker (using no-weighting model) up to 1.47% and 1.85% on MRR and P@1, respectively.

2 Related Work

Crowdsourcing has been used in different domains to collect annotations. Kilgarriff (1998) proposed a model for generating golden standard datasets for word-sense disambiguation. The work in (Voorhees, 2000; Volkmer et al., 2007; Alonso and Mizzaro, 2012) considers relevance judgments for building IR systems. Works closer to this paper proposed by Donmez et al. (2009), Qing et al. (2014), Raykar et al. (2010), Whitehill et al. (2009) and Sheng et al. (2008), targeted the quality of crowdsourced annotation and how to deal with noisy labels via probabilistic models. Our approach is different as we do not improve the crowd annotation, but design new weighing methods that can help the learning algorithms to deal with noise. Plank et al. (2014) also propose methods for taking noise into account when training a classifier. However, they modify the loss function of a perceptron algorithms while we assign different weights to the training instances.

Regarding QA and in particular answer sentence/passage reranking there has been a large body of work in the recent years, e.g., see (Radlinski and Joachims, 2006; Jeon et al., 2005; Shen and Lapata, 2007; Moschitti et al., 2007; Surdeanu et al., 2008; Wang et al., 2007; Heilman and Smith, 2010; Wang and Manning, 2010; Yao et al., 2013), but none of them was devoted to exploit annotation properties in their model.

3 Crowdsourced Dataset

Initially, we ran a crowdsourcing task on Crowd-Flower micro-tasking platform and asked the crowd workers to assign a relevant/not relevant annotation label to the given Q/AP pairs. The crowd workers had to decide whether the given AP supports the raised question or not. We consider the TREC corpora described in Section 5.1 and in particular the first 20 APs retrieved by BM25 search engine for every question. We collect 5 judgments for each AP. Additionally, we removed the maximum quota of annotations a crowd worker can perform. We demonstrated that this (i) does not affected the quality of the annotations in Section 5.1; and (ii) allows us to collect reliable statistics about the crowd annotators since they can participate extensively to our annotation project. The intuition behind the idea is: *a crowd worker is more reliable for a given task if (s)he annotates more passages.* Finally, we used control questions discarding the annotation of crowd annotators providing incorrect answers.

Overall, we crowdsourced 527 questions of the TREC 2002/2003 QA task and collected 52,700 judgments. The number of the participant workers was 108 and the minimum and maximum number of answer passages annotated by a single crowd annotator were 21 and 1,050, respectively.

To obtain an accurate gold standard, we asked an expert to revise the passages labeled by crowd annotators when at least one disagreement was present among the annotations. This *super* gold standard is always and only used for testing our models (not for training).

4 Weighting models for learning methods

We define weighing schema for each passage of the training questions. More in detail, each question q is associated with a sorted list of answer passages. In turn, each passage p is associated with a set of annotators $\{a_p^1, a_p^2, ..., a_p^k\}$, where a_p^h is the annotator h, $j_p^h \in \{+1, -1\}$ is her/his judgment, and k is the number of annotators per

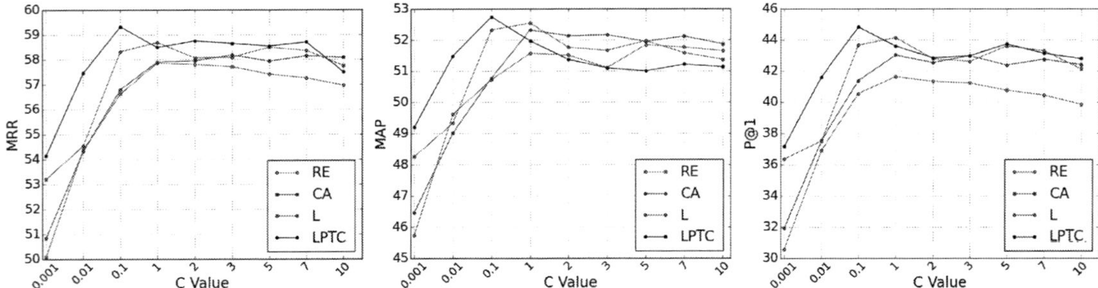

Figure 1: The impact of the C values on different models with (LPTC, L) and without (CA, RE) instance weighting.

passage. We defined a weighting function, $f(\cdot)$, for scoring the passage p as:

$$f(p) = |\sum_{h=1}^{k} j_p^h W(a^h)|. \qquad (1)$$

The weighting function consists of a summation of two factors: (i) j_p^h, which indicates the judgment value the annotators, h, have provided for the passage p; and (ii) $W(u)$, which aims at capturing the reliability of the crowd worker u, using the product of three factors:

$$W(u) = P(u)T(u)C(u), \qquad (2)$$

where *Prior Confidence*, $P(u)$, indicates the prior trust confidence score of the crowd worker, u, provided by the crowdsourcing platform based on the quality of the annotations (s)he has done in the previous tasks. *Task Confidence*, $T(u)$, indicates the total number of annotations performed by the crowd worker u in this task. The score is re-scaled and normalized between (0,1) by considering the maximum and minimum number of annotations the workers have done in this task. *Consistency Confidence*, $C(u)$, indicates the total number of annotation agreements between the annotator u and the majority voting in this task. The score is normalized and re-scaled between (0,1) as well.

We use Eq. 1 in the optimization function of SVMs:

$$\min \quad \frac{||\vec{w}||^2}{2} + c\sum_{i} \xi_i^2 f(p_i), \qquad (3)$$

where $\vec{w}$ is the model, c is the trade-off parameters, ξ_i is the slack variable associated with each training example $\vec{x}_i$, p_i is the passage related to the example x_i (i.e., associated with a constraint), and $f(p_i)$ (Eq. 1) assigns a weight to such constraint.

5 Experiments

5.1 Experimental Setup

QA Corpora. In this paper, we used the questions from TREC 2002 and 2003 from the large newswire corpus, AQUAINT. We created the Q/AP pairs training BM25 on AQUAINT and retrieving candidate passages for each question.

Crowdsourcing Pilot Experiments. Before running the main crowdsourcing task, we evaluated the effect of the initial configurations of the platform on the quality of the collected annotation. We conducted two pilot crowdsourcing experiments, which show that without quota limitation, the collected sets of annotations have both high level of agreement (0.769) calculated with the Kappa statistic (Carletta, 1996).

Classifier Feature. We used the rich set of features described in the state-of-the-art QA system (Tymoshenko and Moschitti, 2015). Such features are based on the similarity between question and the passage text: N-gram overlap (e.g., word lemmas, bi-gram, part-of-speech tags and etc.), tree kernel similarity, relatedness between question category and the related named entity types extracted from the candidate answer, LDA similarity between the topic distributions of question and answer passage.

Reranking Model We used (i) a modified algorithm of SVM-rank [3] using the Eq. 3 to train our rerankers; (ii) the default cost-factor parameter; and (iii) some other specific values to verify if our results would be affected by different C values.

Baselines. We compared our results with three different baselines, namely: **BM25**: we used Terrier search engine[4], which provides BM25 scor-

---

[3]http://svmlight.joachims.org
[4]http://terrier.org

138

Model	MRR	MAP	P@1
	Baselines		
BM25	41.75 ± 6.56	37.25 ± 4.52	25.57 ± 6.17
RE	57.41 ± 7.31	51.75 ± 6.27	41.38 ± 11.12
CA	57.75 ± 6.77	52.09 ± 5.68	42.94 ± 8.55
	Our Weighting Results		
L	58.73 ± 6.88	52.48 ± 6.00	44.12 ± 9.75
P	58.51 ± 5.63	52.07 ± 4.63	43.15 ± 7.32
LP	58.76 ± 6.52	52.60 ± 6.03	44.22 ± 8.72
TC	58.31 ± 5.44	52.09 ± 4.96	42.83 ± 7.69
LTC	58.85 ± 5.85	52.58 ± 5.52	43.74 ± 8.50
LPTC	59.22 ± 6.30	52.63 ± 5.96	44.79 ± 8.82

Table 1: Results over 5 fold cross validation. Our Weighting Results are all better than the Baselines with a statistical significant test of 95%.

ing model to index the answer passages (Robertson and Walker, 1997). The APs are extracted from AQUAINT text corpus and treated as documents. BM25 is used to retrieve 20 candidate answers for each question and rank them by their relevance scores. **RE** (regular expression): we trained a classifier with the noisy annotations produced by labels automatically derived with RE applied to answer keys (no weighting strategy). **CA** (crowd annotations): we train a classier with the same configuration as RE but using majority voting as a source of supervision.

Evaluation Metrics We evaluated the performance of the classifier with the mostly used metrics for QA tasks: the Mean Reciprocal Rank (MRR), which computes the reciprocal of the rank at which the first relevant passage is retrieved, Precision at rank 1 (P@1), which reports the percentage of question with the correct answer at rank 1, and Mean Average Precision (MAP), which measures the average of precision of the correct passages appearing in the ranked AP list. All our results are computed with 5-folds cross validations, thus the above metrics are averaged over 5 folds.

5.2 Weighting Experiments

In these experiments, we used the labels provided by crowd annotators using majority voting for training and testing our models. Most interestingly, we also assign weights to the examples in SVMs with the weighting schemes below:
- **Labels Only (L)**, i.e., we set $P(u) = T(u) = C(u) = 1$ in Eq. 2. This means that the instance weight (Eq. 1) is just the sum of the labels j_p^h.
- **Prior Only (P):** to study the impact of prior annotation skills, we set $C(u) = T(u) = 1$ in Eq. 2, and we only use $P(u)$ (crowdflower trust), i.e., we

do not account for the sign of annotations, j_p^h.
- **Labels & Prior (LP):** the previous model but we also used the sign of the label, j_p^h.
- **Task & Consistency (TC):** we set $P(u) = 1$ such that Eq. 2 takes into account both annotator skill parameters for the specific task, i.e., task and consistency confidence, but only in the current task and no sign of j_p^h.
- **L & TC (LTC):** same as before but we also take into account the sign of the annotator decision.
- **LPTC:** all parameters are used.

Table 1 shows the evaluation of the different baselines and weighting schemes proposed in this paper (using the default c parameter of SVMs). We note that: firstly, the accuracy of BM25 is lower than the one expressed by rerankers trained on noisy labels (-15.66% in MRR, -14.5% in MAP, -15.81 in P@1%).

Secondly, although there is some improvement using crowd annotations for training[5] compared to the noisy training labels (RE), the improvement is not significant (+0.34% in MRR, +0.34% in MAP, +1.56% in P@1). This is due to three reasons: (i) the crowdsourcing annotation suffers from a certain level of noise as well (only 27,350 of the answer passages, i.e., 51.80%, are labeled with "crowd fully in agreement"), (ii) although the RE labels may generate several false positives, these are always a small percentage of the total instances as the dataset is highly unbalanced (9,535 negative vs. 1,005 positive examples); and (iii) RE do not generate many false negatives as they are precise.

Thirdly, the table clearly shows the intuitive fact that it is always better to take into account the sign of the label given by the annotator, i.e., LP vs. L and LTC vs. TC.

Next, when we apply our different weighting schema, we observe that the noise introduced by the crowd annotation can be significantly reduced as the classifier improves by +1.47% in MRR, +0.54% in MAP and +1.85% in P@1, e.g., when using LTC & LPTC compared to CA, which does not provide any weight to the reranker.

Finally, as the trade-off parameter, c, may alone mitigate the noise problem, we compared our models with the baselines according to several value of the parameter. Fig. 1 plots the rank measures averaged over 5-folds: our weighting methods, especially LPTC (black curve), is constantly

---

[5]The test labels are always obtained with majority voting and we removed questions that have no answer in the first 20 passages retrieved by BM25.

better than the baseline, CA, (blue curve) in MRR and P@1.

6 Conclusions

Our study shows that we can effectively exploit the implicit information of crowd workers and apply it to improve the QA task. We demonstrated that (i) the best ranking performance is obtained when the combination of different weighting parameters are used; and (ii) the noise of annotations, present in crowdsourcing data, can be reduced by considering weighting scores extracted from crowd worker performance. In the future, we will explore better weighting criteria to model the noise that is induced by annotations of crowd workers.

Acknowledgement

This work has been partially supported by the EC project CogNet, 671625 (H2020-ICT-2014-2, Researchand Innovation action).

References

Omar Alonso and Stefano Mizzaro. 2012. Using crowdsourcing for trec relevance assessment. 48(6).

Jean Carletta. 1996. Assessing agreement on classification tasks: The kappa statistic. *Comput. Linguist.*

Pinar Donmez, Jaime G. Carbonell, and Jeff Schneider. 2009. Efficiently learning the accuracy of labeling sources for selective sampling. KDD '09, New York, NY, USA.

David A. Ferrucci. 2011. Ibm's watson/deepqa. ISCA '11, New York, NY, USA. ACM.

Michael Heilman and Noah A. Smith. 2010. Good question! statistical ranking for question generation. HLT '10, Stroudsburg, PA, USA. Association for Computational Linguistics.

Jiwoon Jeon, W. Bruce Croft, and Joon Ho Lee. 2005. Finding similar questions in large question and answer archives. CIKM '05, New York, NY, USA. ACM.

Adam Kilgarriff. 1998. Gold standard datasets for evaluating word sense disambiguation programs.

Alessandro Moschitti, Silvia Quarteroni, Roberto Basili, and Suresh Manandhar. 2007. Exploiting syntactic and shallow semantic kernels for question/answer classification. In *In Proceedings of the 45th Conference of the Association for Computational Linguistics.*

Barbara Plank, Dirk Hovy, and Anders Sogaard, 2014. *Learning part-of-speech taggers with inter-annotator agreement loss*, pages 742–751. Association for Computational Linguistics.

Ciyang Qing, Ulle Endriss, Raquel Fernández, and Justin Kruger. 2014. Empirical analysis of aggregation methods for collective annotation. In *Proceedings of the 25th International Conference on Computational Linguistics (COLING-2014).*

Filip Radlinski and Thorsten Joachims. 2006. Query chains: Learning to rank from implicit feedback. *CoRR*, abs/cs/0605035.

Vikas C. Raykar, Shipeng Yu, Linda H. Zhao, Gerardo Hermosillo Valadez, Charles Florin, Luca Bogoni, and Linda Moy. 2010. Learning from crowds. *J. Mach. Learn. Res.*

S. E. Robertson and S. Walker. 1997. On relevance weights with little relevance information. SIGIR '97, pages 16–24, New York, NY, USA. ACM.

Dan Shen and Mirella Lapata. 2007. Using semantic roles to improve question answering. pages 12–21, Prague, Czech Republic, June. Association for Computational Linguistics.

Victor S. Sheng, Foster Provost, and Panagiotis G. Ipeirotis. 2008. Get another label? improving data quality and data mining using multiple, noisy labelers. KDD '08, New York, NY, USA. ACM.

Rion Snow, Brendan O'Connor, Daniel Jurafsky, and Andrew Y. Ng. 2008. Cheap and fast—but is it good?: Evaluating non-expert annotations for natural language tasks. EMNLP '08, Stroudsburg, PA, USA. Association for Computational Linguistics.

Mihai Surdeanu, Massimiliano Ciaramita, and Hugo Zaragoza. 2008. Learning to rank answers on large online qa collections. In *In Proceedings of the 46th Annual Meeting for the Association for Computational Linguistics: Human Language Technologies (ACL-08: HLT*, pages 719–727.

Kateryna Tymoshenko and Alessandro Moschitti. 2015. Assessing the impact of syntactic and semantic structures for answer passages reranking. CIKM '15, pages 1451–1460, New York, NY, USA.

Timo Volkmer, James A Thom, and Seyed MM Tahaghoghi. 2007. Modeling human judgment of digital imagery for multimedia retrieval. *Multimedia, IEEE Transactions on*, 9(5).

Ellen M. Voorhees. 2000. Variations in relevance judgments and the measurement of retrieval effectiveness. *Inf. Process. Manage.*, pages 697–716.

Mengqiu Wang and Christopher D. Manning. 2010. Probabilistic tree-edit models with structured latent variables for textual entailment and question answering. COLING '10, Stroudsburg, PA, USA. Association for Computational Linguistics.

Mengqiu Wang, Noah A Smith, and Teruko Mitamura. 2007. What is the jeopardy model? a quasi-synchronous grammar for qa. *EMNLP-CoNLL*, 7.

Jacob Whitehill, Ting fan Wu, Jacob Bergsma, Javier R. Movellan, and Paul L. Ruvolo. 2009. Whose vote should count more: Optimal integration of labels from labelers of unknown expertise. Curran Associates, Inc.

Xuchen Yao, Benjamin Van Durme, Chris Callison-burch, and Peter Clark. 2013. Answer extraction as sequence tagging with tree edit distance. In *In North American Chapter of the Association for Computational Linguistics (NAACL*.

Jing Zhang, Victor S. Sheng, Jian Wu, Xiaoqin Fu, and Xindong Wu. 2015. Improving label quality in crowdsourcing using noise correction. CIKM '15, New York, NY, USA. ACM.

Orthogonality regularizer for question answering

Chunyang Xiao[1], Guillaume Bouchard[2], Marc Dymetman[1],Claire Gardent[3]

[1]Xerox Research Centre Europe, Grenoble, France
[2]University College London, United Kingdom
[3]CNRS, LORIA, Nancy, France
[1]chunyang.xiao, marc.dymetman@xerox.com
[2]g.bouchard@cs.ucl.ac.uk
[3]claire.gardent@loria.fr

Abstract

Learning embeddings of words and knowledge base elements is a promising approach for open domain question answering. Based on the remark that relations and entities are distinct object types lying in the same embedding space, we analyze the benefit of adding a regularizer favoring the embeddings of entities to be orthogonal to those of relations. The main motivation comes from the observation that modifying the embeddings using prior knowledge often helps performance. The experiments show that incorporating the regularizer yields better results on a challenging question answering benchmark.

1 Introduction

Having a system which is able to answer questions based on a structured knowledge base is a challenging problem. The problem has been addressed recently by researchers working on large knowledge bases such as Reverb (Fader et al., 2011) and Freebase (Bollacker et al., 2008). The creation of question answering (QA) benchmarks for these knowledge bases (KB) has a significant impact on the domain, as shown by the number of QA systems recently proposed in the literature (Berant and Liang, 2014; Berant et al., 2013; Bordes et al., 2014a; Bordes et al., 2014b; Fader et al., 2013; Fader et al., 2014; Yao and Van Durme, 2014; Yih et al., 2014; Dong et al., 2015).

We identify two types of approaches for KB-centric QA systems: parsing-based approaches and information retrieval (IR) based approaches. Parsing-based approaches (Yih et al., 2014; Berant et al., 2013; Berant and Liang, 2014; Reddy et al., 2014) answer factoid questions by learning a structured representation for the sentences, called logical form. This logical form is then used to query the knowledge base and retrieve the answer. IR-based approaches try to identify the best possible match between the knowledge base and the question (Bordes et al., 2014a; Bordes et al., 2014b; Yao and Van Durme, 2014; Dong et al., 2015). In this work, we focus on the second approach, using embedding models, mainly because it is robust to invalid syntax and can exploit information of the answer.

We focus on the Wikianswers (Fader et al., 2013) dataset constructed for Reverb. On Wikianswers, the underlying semantics is very simple (just one single triple). However, the task remains challenging due to the large variety of lexicalizations for the same semantics. We follow the approach of Bordes et .al (2014b) which learns the embeddings of words and KB elements. They model the semantics of natural language sentences and KB triples as the sum of the embeddings of the associated words and KB elements respectively. Despite its simplicity, this model performs surprisingly well in practice. Something even more interesting (Bordes et al., 2014b) is that the system can have a good performance even without using a paraphrase corpus. This makes the system very attractive in practice because in many specific domains, we might have a KB but there may be no paraphrase corpus as in Wikianswers.

In our work, we push the results further when learning a QA system based only on the KB. Our contribution is to introduce a new orthogonality regularizer which distinguishes entities and relations. We also investigate the tradeoff captured by the orthogonality constraints. With a synthetic example, we show that if entities and relations are independent, orthogonal embeddings generate better results. The orthogonality constraint in the context of question answering is new, although it has been successfully used in other contexts (Yao et al., 2014). Like (Bordes et al., 2014b), we use al-

*Proceedings of the Fifth Joint Conference on Lexical and Computational Semantics (*SEM 2016)*, pages 142–147,
Berlin, Germany, August 11-12, 2016.

most no linguistic features such as POS tagging, parsing, etc.

2 The ReVerb Question Answering Task

The ReVerb question answering task was first introduced in (Fader et al., 2013) as follows. Given a large RDF KB and a natural language (NL) question whose answer is given by a triple contained in that KB, the task is to find a correct triple. For example, a correct answer to the NL question "What is the main language in Hong Kong ?" would be the KB triple *(cantonese.e, be-major-language-in.r, hong-kong.e)*. RDF triples are assertions of the form (e_1, r, e_2) where r is a binary relation from some vocabulary R and e_1, e_2 are entities from a vocabulary E.

The KB used is ReVerb[1], a publicly available set of 15 million extractions (Fader et al., 2011) defined over a vocabulary of approximately 600K relations and 3M entities. The test set used for evaluation includes 698 questions extracted from the website Wikianswers, many of which involve paraphrases.

3 Related Work

Fader et al. (2013) present one of the first approaches for dealing with open domain question answering. To map NL questions to KB queries, they first induce a lexicon mapping NL expressions to KB elements using manually defined patterns, alignments and a paraphrase corpus. Using this lexicon, multiple KB queries can be derived from a NL question. These queries are then ranked using a scoring function.

Bordes et al. (2014b) introduce a linguistically leaner IR-based approach which identifies the KB triple most similar to the input NL question. In their approach, KB triples and NL questions are represented as sums of embeddings of KB symbols and words respectively. The similarity between a triple and a question is then simply the dot product of their embeddings. Interestingly, Bordes' (2014b) system performs relatively well (MAP score 0.34) on the Wikianswers dataset even without using the paraphrase corpus. This suggests that the embedding method successfully captures the similarity between NL questions and KB queries. Our work continues this direction by further separating relations with entities.

[1]http://reverb.cs.washington.edu

The idea of distinguishing entities and relations in question answering can also be found in (Yih et al., 2014). However, they base their work by supposing that we can cut the sentence into "entity part" and "relation part" and then calculate the matching score. Our model does not need this cut and simply enforces the entity embeddings and relation embeddings (on the KB side) to be different.

Orthogonality or near orthogonality is a property which is desired in many embedding techniques. In random indexing (Sahlgren, 2005), a near orthogonality is ensured amongst the embeddings of different contexts. In (Zanzotto and Dell'Arciprete, 2012), to approximate tree kernels in a distributed way, different subtree feature embeddings are also constructed to be near orthogonal.

Our work gives yet another motivation for orthogonal embeddings for the special case where the semantics of a sentence is modeled as the sum of its associated word embeddings. In this case, orthogonal word embeddings help to model their independence.

4 Embedding model

Word embeddings are generally learned (Deerwester et al., 1990; Mikolov et al., 2013; Lebret and Collobert, 2015; Faruqui et al., 2014) such that words with similar context will naturally share similar embeddings as measured for instance by cosine similarity. The embeddings learned in (Bordes et al., 2014b) also encode context information. They link the embedding of words with the whole triple-answer in their scoring function. By this means, the word embedding carries the information of the whole triple.

Our model further distinguishes entities and relations. Noting that entities and relations may have some independence (knowing that 'a man eats' doesn't help to tell 'which man'), the distinction is done via orthogonality. We show in the toy example that orthogonality helps to capture this independent structure of the data.

4.1 Scoring function

The model learns the embedding of each word and KB element by trying to score the correct answers highest. Mathematically, let q be the query, and a be the answer-triple to align. Denote the total number of words as N_w and the number of KB elements as N_{kb}. Then denote by $\phi(q) \in \{0, 1\}^{N_w}$

Algorithm 1 Training with orthogonality regularizer

---

1. Sample a positive training pair (q_i, a_i) from D.
2. Create a corrupted triple a_i'
3. If $S(q_i, a_i) - S(q_i, a_i') < 0.1$:
    make a stochastic gradient ascent on $S(q_i, a_i) - S(q_i, a_i') - \lambda|E.R|$
4. Normalize the embedding vector

---

the 1-hot representation indicating the presence or absence of words in the query. Similarly we denote the sparse representation on the KB side as $\psi(a)$. Let $M \in R^{d \times N_w}$ be the embedding matrix for words and $K \in R^{d \times N_{kb}}$ be the embedding matrix for the elements in the KB. d is the low dimension chosen by the user.

The embedding of the sentence is then calculated as $M\,\phi(q)$ and similarly the embedding of the answer-triple as $K\,\psi(a)$. We can score the matching of these embeddings:

$$S(q, a) = (M\,\phi(q))^{\top}(K\,\psi(a))$$

which is the dot product between the embedding of the sentence and the embedding of the triple. The model is introduced in (Bordes et al., 2014b) and we use the same scoring function. Note that the model actually sums up each word embedding to form the embedding of the sentence.

4.2 Inference

The inference procedure is straightforward. Given a question q and a set of possible answer triples noted $A(q)$, the model predicts the answer by returning the triple with the highest score:

$$a' = argmax_{a \in A(q)} S(q, a)$$

4.3 Training

Originally in (Bordes et al., 2014b), given a question to be answered, training is performed by imposing a margin-constraint between the correct answer and negative ones. More precisely, note a' a negative answer to the question q (the correct answer to q being a). Then for each question answer pair, the system tries to maximize the following function by performing a gradient ascent step:

$$min(\epsilon,\ S(q, a) - S(q, a'))$$

with ϵ the margin set to 0.1. In addition, the norms of columns in M and K are constrained to be inferior to 1. The training is done in a stochastic

way by randomly selecting a question answer pair at each step. For each gradient step, the step size is calculated using Adagrad (Duchi et al., 2011). The negative example is created by randomly replacing each element of (e_1, r, e_2) by another one with probability 2/3.

4.4 Enforcing Orthogonal Embeddings

In this work, we are especially interested in the additional assumptions we can make on the model in order to cope with data sparsity. Indeed, when the number of training data supporting the computation of embeddings is small, embedding models are brittle and can lead to disappointing results. We noticed that one important assumption that is not discussed in the basic approach is that the embedding space is the same for relations and entities. That approach has a tendency to learn similar embeddings for entities and relations, even if they have different meanings. Intuitively, we would like to balance that tendency by a "prior knowledge" preference towards choosing embeddings of entities and relations which are orthogonal to each other.

To justify this assumption, consider a simple case where the underlying semantics is (e, r) as in the sentence "John eats". We will use the same letter to indicate an entity or relation and their corresponding embeddings. In (Bordes et al., 2014b), the embedding of the semantics is then calculated as $e + r$ for this very simple case. Now suppose that $\forall e' \neq e,\ ||e - e'||_2 \geq \epsilon$ (i.e John is different from Mary with margin ϵ) and that the same kind of constraints also holds for relations. However, even when these constraints are satisfied, it is not guaranteed that $||e + r - e' - r'||_2 \geq \epsilon$, which means that the model may still get confused on the whole semantics even if each part is clear.

One obvious and linguistically plausible solution is to say that the entities and relations lie in orthogonal spaces. Indeed, if relations and entities are orthogonal $(\forall r, e\ (r \perp e))$, then if two entities e, e' and two relations r, r' are distinct (i.e., $||e - e'||_2 \geq \epsilon$ and $||r - r'||_2 \geq \epsilon$), it follows that $||e + r - e' - r'||_2 = ||e - e'||_2 + |||r - r'||_2 \geq 2\epsilon$ by Pythagorean theorem. That is, two sentences whose semantic representations involve two distinct entities and/or relations will have different values.

In real problems, however, posing a hard orthogonality constraint largely reduces the model's

sentence	Embedding	This work
What is the argument on gun control ?	*(short-gun.e be-type-of.r gun.e)*	**(giuliani.e support.r gun-control.e)**
What year did minnesota become part of US ?	**(minnesota.e become-state-on.r may-11-1858.e)**	*(minnesota.e be-part-of.r united-states.e)*
What is the religious celebration of christians ?	*(christian.e be-all-about.r original-sin.e)*	**(easter.e be-most-important-holiday.r christian.e)**
What do cassava come from ?	*(cassava.e be-source-of.r security.e)*	**(cassava.e be-grow-in.r africa.e)**

Table 1: Some examples for which our system differs from ((Bordes et al., 2014b)). Gold standard answer triples are marked in bold.

expressive power[2], so we decide to add it as a regularizer. More concretely, let the correct triple be (e_1, r, e_2) and the negative one be (e'_1, r', e'_2). Consider that we are in a case not satisfying the margin constraint, then we will try to maximize the following regularized function $S(q, a) - S(q, a') - \lambda |E.R|$ with a gradient step. The regularizer $|E.R| = |e_1.r| + |e_2.r| + |e'_1.r'| + |e'_2.r'|$ is minimized when all the entities and relations live in orthogonal space. The regularization parameter λ is chosen via an automatically constructed development set for which we randomly selected 1/2000 of all the triples in the KB and generate associated questions. We discard these triples from training and choose the λ value based on the score on the development set. The λ value is by this means set to 0.01 with λ in $\{0.5, 0.1, 0.05, 0.01, 0.005, 0.001\}$. Once the λ value is chosen, we retrain the whole system.

5 Experimental results

5.1 Toy example

In this section, we illustrate the benefits of orthogonality via a toy example. We construct a KB containing 50 entities (E) and 50 relations (R) then generate all their cross products obtaining 2500 fact pairs. In consequence the entities and relations are independent.

For every $e_i \in E$, we suppose that there is a single word lexicalizing the entity noted "e_i" . Similarly, we note the lexicalization of r_j "r_j". We separate these 2500 pairs into training (2450) and test (50). Notice that similarly to Wikianswers, this toy dataset involves KB entities and relations whose type is known *a priori*.

The training corpus is built using one simple generation rule : $(e_i, r_j) \rightarrow$ "$e_i\ r_j$" . Negative examples are created by replacing with probability 1/2 both entity and relation with another one. We

Model	Accuracy (1)	Accuracy (2)
Embedding	76%	54%
Ortho_Embedding	90%	68%

Table 2: Results on toy example.

embed all the words and KB symbols in a space of 20 dimensions. We compare the model (Bordes et al., 2014b) with the model where we enforce E and R (and also "E" and "R") to be orthogonal. This means that words or KB symbols in fact live in an embedding space of dimension 10.

At test time, for a given sentence "$e_i\ r_j$", a set of (e, r) pairs is ranked and we compute the proportion of cases where the first ranked pair is correct. Table 2 shows the results for both systems on two configurations: a configuration (Accuracy(1)) where the number of pairs to be ranked is 1250 and another (Accuracy(2)) with 2500 pairs.[3] In both cases, imposing the orthogonality constraint improves performance by a large margin.

5.2 Wikianswers

Wikianswers contains a set of possible triples for each question and we re-rank these triples to report our system's performance. This is the "re-ranking" setting used in (Bordes et al., 2014b). Table 3 compares different systems in this setting. The Embedding scores are taken from (Bordes et al., 2014b) for which we have reimplemented and confirmed the results.

Method	Prec	Recall	F1	MAP
Embedding	0.60	0.60	0.60	0.34
This work	0.63	0.63	0.63	0.36

Table 3: Performance for re-ranking question answer pairs of test set for different systems on Wikianswers

Table 3 shows that our technique improves the performance also on the larger, non-synthetic,

---

[2]Especially, if the embeddings are orthogonal between entities and relations, the knowledge of a given entity can not help to infer the relation and vice versa.

[3]We make sure that the correct answer is included .

dataset provided by Fader (2013) over the Bordes (2014b)'s method. In addition, Table 1 shows some examples where the two systems differ and where the orthogonality regularized embeddings seem to better support the identification of similar relations. For instance, "is the argument on" is mapped to *support.r* rather than *be-type-of.r* and "is the religious celebration of" to *be-most-important-holiday.r* rather then *be-all-about.r*.

6 Conclusion

This paper introduces an embedding model for question answering with orthogonality regularizer. We show that orthogonality helps to capture the differences between entities and relations and that it helps improve performance on an existing dataset.

Acknowledgements

We would like to thank the anonymous reviewers for their constructive feedback.

References

J. Berant and P. Liang. 2014. Semantic parsing via paraphrasing. In *Annual Meeting for the Association for Computational Linguistics (ACL)*.

J. Berant, A. Chou, R. Frostig, and P. Liang. 2013. Semantic parsing on freebase from question-answer pairs. In *Empirical Methods in Natural Language Processing (EMNLP)*.

Kurt Bollacker, Colin Evans, Praveen Paritosh, Tim Sturge, and Jamie Taylor. 2008. Freebase: a collaboratively created graph database for structuring human knowledge. In *SIGMOD Conference*, pages 1247–1250.

Antoine Bordes, Sumit Chopra, and Jason Weston. 2014a. Question answering with subgraph embeddings. In *Empirical Methods in Natural Language Processing (EMNLP)*, pages 615–620.

Antoine Bordes, Jason Weston, and Nicolas Usunier. 2014b. Open question answering with weakly supervised embedding models. *European Conference on Machine Learning and Principles and Practice of Knowledge Discovery (ECML-PKDD)*.

Scott Deerwester, Susan T. Dumais, George W. Furnas, Thomas K. Landauer, and Richard Harshman. 1990. Indexing by latent semantic analysis. *JOURNAL OF THE AMERICAN SOCIETY FOR INFORMATION SCIENCE*, 41(6):391–407.

Li Dong, Furu Wei, Ming Zhou, and Ke Xu. 2015. Question answering over freebase with multi-column convolutional neural networks. In *The 53rd Annual Meeting of the Association for Computational Linguistics and The 7th International Joint Conference of the Asian Federation of Natural Language Processing (ACL-IJCNLP 2015)*. ACL.

John C. Duchi, Elad Hazan, and Yoram Singer. 2011. Adaptive subgradient methods for online learning and stochastic optimization. *Journal of Machine Learning Research*, 12:2121–2159.

Anthony Fader, Stephen Soderland, and Oren Etzioni. 2011. Identifying relations for open information extraction. In *Proceedings of the Conference of Empirical Methods in Natural Language Processing (EMNLP '11)*, Edinburgh, Scotland, UK, July 27-31.

Anthony Fader, Luke Zettlemoyer, and Oren Etzioni. 2013. Paraphrase-driven learning for open question answering. In *Proceedings of the 51st Annual Meeting of the Association for Computational Linguistics (Volume 1: Long Papers)*, pages 1608–1618.

Anthony Fader, Luke Zettlemoyer, and Oren Etzioni. 2014. Open question answering over curated and extracted knowledge bases. *Proceedings of the 20th ACM SIGKDD international conference on Knowledge discovery and data mining - KDD '14*, pages 1156–1165.

Manaal Faruqui, Jesse Dodge, Sujay Kumar Jauhar, Chris Dyer, Eduard H. Hovy, and Noah A. Smith. 2014. Retrofitting word vectors to semantic lexicons. *CoRR*, abs/1411.4166.

Rémi Lebret and Ronan Collobert. 2015. Rehabilitation of count-based models for word vector representations. In *Computational Linguistics and Intelligent Text Processing - 16th International Conference, CICLing 2015, Cairo, Egypt, April 14-20, 2015, Proceedings, Part I*, pages 417–429.

Tomas Mikolov, Ilya Sutskever, Kai Chen, Gregory S. Corrado, and Jeffrey Dean. 2013. Distributed representations of words and phrases and their compositionality. In *Advances in Neural Information Processing Systems 26: 27th Annual Conference on Neural Information Processing Systems 2013. Proceedings of a meeting held December 5-8, 2013, Lake Tahoe, Nevada, United States.*, pages 3111–3119.

Siva Reddy, Mirella Lapata, and Mark Steedman. 2014. Large-scale semantic parsing without question-answer pairs. *Transactions of the Association for Computational Linguistics*, 2:377–392.

Magnus Sahlgren. 2005. An introduction to random indexing. In *In Methods and Applications of Semantic Indexing Workshop at the 7th International Conference on Terminology and Knowledge Engineering*.

Xuchen Yao and Benjamin Van Durme. 2014. Information extraction over structured data: Question answering with freebase. In *Proceedings of ACL*.

Enpeng Yao, Guoqing Zheng, Ou Jin, Shenghua Bao, Kailong Chen, Zhong Su, and Yong Yu. 2014. Probabilistic text modeling with orthogonalized topics. In *The 37th International ACM SIGIR Conference on Research and Development in Information Retrieval, SIGIR '14, Gold Coast , QLD, Australia - July 06 - 11, 2014*, pages 907–910.

Wen-tau Yih, Xiaodong He, and Christopher Meek. 2014. Semantic parsing for single-relation question answering. In *Proceedings of the 52nd Annual Meeting of the Association for Computational Linguistics, ACL 2014, June 22-27, 2014, Baltimore, MD, USA, Volume 2: Short Papers*, pages 643–648.

Fabio Massimo Zanzotto and Lorenzo Dell'Arciprete. 2012. In *International Conference on Machine Learning (ICML)*.

The Role of Modifier and Head Properties in Predicting the Compositionality of English and German Noun-Noun Compounds: A Vector-Space Perspective

Sabine Schulte im Walde and **Anna Hätty** and **Stefan Bott**
Institut für Maschinelle Sprachverarbeitung, Universität Stuttgart
Pfaffenwaldring 5B, 70569 Stuttgart, Germany
{schulte,haettyaa,bottsn}@ims.uni-stuttgart.de

Abstract

In this paper, we explore the role of constituent properties in English and German noun-noun compounds (*corpus frequencies* of the compounds and their constituents; *productivity* and *ambiguity* of the constituents; and *semantic relations* between the constituents), when predicting the degrees of compositionality of the compounds within a vector space model. The results demonstrate that the empirical and semantic properties of the compounds and the head nouns play a significant role.

1 Introduction

The past 20+ years have witnessed an enormous amount of discussions on whether and how the modifiers and the heads of noun-noun compounds such as *butterfly, snowball* and *teaspoon* influence the compositionality of the compounds, i.e., the degree of transparency vs. opaqueness of the compounds. The discussions took place mostly in psycholinguistic research, typically relying on reading time and priming experiments. For example, Sandra (1990) demonstrated in three priming experiments that both modifier and head constituents were accessed in semantically transparent English noun-noun compounds (such as *teaspoon*), but there were no effects for semantically opaque compounds (such as *buttercup*), when primed either on their modifier or head constituent. In contrast, Zwitserlood (1994) provided evidence that the lexical processing system is sensitive to morphological complexity independent of semantic transparency. Libben and his colleagues (Libben et al. (1997), Libben et al. (2003)) were the first who systematically categorised noun-noun compounds with nominal modifiers and heads into four groups representing all possible combinations of

modifier and head transparency (T) vs. opaqueness (O) within a compound. Examples for these categories were *car-wash* (TT), *strawberry* (OT), *jailbird* (TO), and *hogwash* (OO). Libben et al. confirmed Zwitserlood's analyses that both semantically transparent and semantically opaque compounds show morphological constituency; in addition, the semantic transparency of the head constituent was found to play a significant role.

From a computational point of view, addressing the compositionality of noun compounds (and multi-word expressions in more general) is a crucial ingredient for lexicography and NLP applications, to know whether the expression should be treated as a whole, or through its constituents, and what the expression means. For example, studies such as Cholakov and Kordoni (2014), Weller et al. (2014), Cap et al. (2015), and Salehi et al. (2015b) have integrated the prediction of multi-word compositionality into statistical machine translation.

Computational approaches to automatically predict the compositionality of noun compounds have mostly been realised as vector space models, and can be subdivided into two subfields: (i) *approaches that aim to predict the **meaning** of a compound by composite functions*, relying on the vectors of the constituents (e.g., Mitchell and Lapata (2010), Coecke et al. (2011), Baroni et al. (2014), and Hermann (2014)); and (ii) *approaches that aim to predict the **degree of compositionality** of a compound*, typically by comparing the compound vectors with the constituent vectors (e.g., Reddy et al. (2011), Salehi and Cook (2013), Schulte im Walde et al. (2013), Salehi et al. (2014; 2015a)). In line with subfield (ii), this paper aims to distinguish the contributions of modifier and head properties when predicting the compositionality of English and German noun-noun compounds in a vector space model.

*Proceedings of the Fifth Joint Conference on Lexical and Computational Semantics (*SEM 2016)*, pages 148–158,
Berlin, Germany, August 11-12, 2016.

Up to date, computational research on noun compounds has largely ignored the influence of constituent properties on the prediction of compositionality. Individual pieces of research noticed differences in the contributions of modifier and head constituents towards the composite functions predicting compositionality (Reddy et al., 2011; Schulte im Walde et al., 2013), but so far the roles of modifiers and heads have not been distinguished. We use a new gold standard of German noun-noun compounds annotated with *corpus frequencies* of the compounds and their constituents; *productivity* and *ambiguity* of the constituents; and *semantic relations* between the constituents; and we extend three existing gold standards of German and English noun-noun compounds (Ó Séaghdha, 2007; von der Heide and Borgwaldt, 2009; Reddy et al., 2011) to include approximately the same compound and constituent properties. Relying on a standard vector space model of compositionality, we then predict the degrees of compositionality of the English and German noun-noun compounds, and explore the influences of the compound and constituent properties. Our empirical computational analyses reveal that the empirical and semantic properties of the compounds and the head nouns play a significant role in determining the compositionality of noun compounds.

2 Related Work

Regarding relevant psycholinguistic research on the representation and processing of noun compounds, Sandra (1990) hypothesised that an associative prime should facilitate access and recognition of a noun compound, if a compound constituent is accessed during processing. His three priming experiments revealed that in transparent noun-noun compounds, both constituents are accessed, but he did not find priming effects for the constituents in opaque noun-noun compounds.

Zwitserlood (1994) performed an immediate partial repetition experiment and a priming experiment to explore and to distinguish morphological and semantic structures in noun-noun compounds. On the one hand, she confirmed Sandra's results that there is no semantic facilitation of any constituent in opaque compounds. In contrast, she found evidence for morphological complexity, independent of semantic transparency, and that both transparent and also partially opaque compounds (i.e., compounds with one transparent and

one opaque constituent) produce semantic priming of their constituents. For the heads of semantically transparent compounds, a larger amount of facilitation was found than for the modifiers. Differences in the results by Sandra (1990) and Zwitserlood (1994) were supposedly due to different definitions of partial opacity, and different prime–target SOAs.

Libben and his colleagues (Libben et al. (1997), Libben (1998), and Libben et al. (2003)) were the first who systematically categorised noun-noun compounds with nominal modifiers and heads into four groups representing all possible combinations of a constituent's transparency (T) vs. opaqueness (O) within a compound: TT, OT, TO, OO. Libben's examples for these categories were *car-wash* (TT), *strawberry* (OT), *jailbird* (TO), and *hogwash* (OO). They confirmed Zwitserlood's analyses that both semantically transparent and semantically opaque compounds show morphological constituency, and also that the semantic transparency of the head constituent was found to play a significant role. Studies such as Jarema et al. (1999) and Kehayia et al. (1999) to a large extent confirmed the insights by Libben and his colleagues for French, Bulgarian, Greek and Polish.

Regarding related computational work, prominent approaches to model the meaning of a compound or a phrase by a composite function include Mitchell and Lapata (2010), Coecke et al. (2011), Baroni et al. (2014), and Hermann (2014)). In this area, researchers combine the vectors of the compound/phrase constituents by mathematical functions such that the resulting vector optimally represents the meaning of the compound/phrase. This research is only marginally related to ours, since we are interested in the degree of compositionality of a compound, rather than its actual meaning.

Most closely related computational work includes distributional approaches that predict the degree of compositionality of a compound regarding a specific constituent, by comparing the compound vector to the respective constituent vector. Most importantly, Reddy et al. (2011) used a standard distributional model to predict the compositionality of compound-constituent pairs for 90 English compounds. They extended their predictions by applying composite functions (see above). In a similar vein, Schulte im Walde et al. (2013) predicted the compositionality for 244 German compounds. Salehi et al. (2014) defined a crosslingual distributional model that used translations into multiple languages and distributional similarities in the respective languages, to predict the compositionality for the two datasets from Reddy et al. (2011) and Schulte im Walde et al. (2013).

3 Noun-Noun Compounds

Our focus of interest is on noun-noun compounds, such as *butterfly, snowball* and *teaspoon* as well as *car park, zebra crossing* and *couch potato* in English, and *Ahornblatt* 'maple leaf', *Feuerwerk* 'fireworks', and *Löwenzahn* 'dandelion' in German, where both the grammatical head (in English and German, this is typically the rightmost constituent) and the modifier are nouns. We are interested in the degrees of compositionality of noun-noun compounds, i.e., the semantic relatedness between the meaning of a compound (e.g., *snowball*) and the meanings of its constituents (e.g., *snow* and *ball*). More specifically, this paper aims to explore factors that have been found to influence compound processing and representation, such as

- *frequency-based factors*, i.e., the frequencies of the compounds and their constituents (van Jaarsveld and Rattink, 1988; Janssen et al., 2008);

- the *productivity (morphological family size)*, i.e., the number of compounds that share a constituent (de Jong et al., 2002); and

- semantic variables as the *relationship between compound modifier and head*: a teapot is a pot FOR tea; a snowball is a ball MADE OF snow (Gagné and Spalding, 2009; Ji et al., 2011).

In addition, we were interested in the effect of *ambiguity* (of both the modifiers and the heads) regarding the compositionality of the compounds.

Our explorations required gold standards of compounds that were annotated with all these compound and constituent properties. Since most previous work on computational predictions of compositionality has been performed for English and for German, we decided to re-use existing datasets for both languages, which however required extensions to provide all properties we wanted to take into account. We also created a novel gold standard. In the following, we describe the datasets.[1]

---

[1]The datasets are available from `http://www.ims.uni-stuttgart.de/data/ghost-nn/`.

German Noun-Noun Compound Datasets As basis for this work, we created a novel gold standard of German noun-noun compounds: G_hOST-NN (Schulte im Walde et al., 2016). The new gold standard was built such that it includes a representative choice of compounds and constituents from various frequency ranges, various productivity ranges, with various numbers of senses, and with various semantic relations. In the following, we describe the creation process in some detail, because the properties of the gold standard are highly relevant for the distributional models.

Relying on the 11.7 billion words in the web corpus *DECOW14AX*[2] (Schäfer and Bildhauer, 2012; Schäfer, 2015), we extracted all words that were identified as common nouns by the *Tree Tagger* (Schmid, 1994) and analysed as noun compounds with exactly two nominal constituents by the morphological analyser *SMOR* (Faaß et al., 2010). This set of 154,960 two-part noun-noun compound candidates was enriched with empirical properties relevant for the gold standard:

- *corpus frequencies* of the compounds and the constituents (i.e., modifiers and heads), relying on *DECOW14AX*;

- *productivity* of the constituents i.e., how many compound types contained a specific modifier/head constituent;

- *number of senses* of the compounds and the constituents, relying on *GermaNet* (Hamp and Feldweg, 1997; Kunze, 2000).

From the set of compound candidates we extracted a random subset that was balanced[3] for

- the *productivity of the modifiers*: we calculated tertiles to identify modifiers with low/mid/high productivity;

- the *ambiguity of the heads*: we distinguished between heads with 1, 2 and >2 senses.

For each of the resulting nine categories (three productivity ranges × three ambiguity ranges), we randomly selected 20 noun-noun compounds

---

[2]`http://corporafromtheweb.org/decow14/`

[3]We wanted to extract a random subset that at the same time was balanced across frequency, productivity and ambiguity ranges of the compounds and their constituents, but defining and combining several ranges for each of the three criteria and for compounds as well as constituents would have led to an explosion of factors to be taken into account, so we focused on two main criteria instead.

from our candidate set, disregarding compounds with a corpus frequency < 2,000, and disregarding compounds containing modifiers or heads with a corpus-frequency < 100. We refer to this dataset of 180 compounds balanced for modifier productivity and head ambiguity as G_hOST-NN/S.

We also created a subset of 5 noun-noun compounds for each of the 9 criteria combinations, by randomly selecting 5 out of the 20 selected compounds in each mode. This small, balanced subset was then systematically extended by adding all compounds from the original set of compound candidates with either the same modifier or the same head as any of the selected compounds. Taking *Haarpracht* as an example (the modifier is *Haar* 'hair', the head is *Pracht* 'glory'), we added *Haarwäsche, Haarkleid, Haarpflege, etc.* as well as *Blütenpracht, Farbenpracht, etc.*[4] We refer to this dataset of 868 compounds that destroyed the coherent balance of criteria underlying our random extraction, but instead ensured a variety of compounds with either the same modifiers or the same heads, as G_h**OST-NN/XL**.

The two sets of compounds (G_hOST-NN/S and G_hOST-NN/XL) were annotated with the semantic relations between the modifiers and the heads, and compositionality ratings. Regarding *semantic relations*, we applied the relation set suggested by Ó Séaghdha (2007), because (i) he had evaluated his annotation relations and annotation scheme, and (ii) his dataset had a similar size as ours, so we could aim for comparing results across languages. Ó Séaghdha (2007) himself had relied on a set of nine semantic relations suggested by Levi (1978), and designed and evaluated a set of relations that took over four of Levi's relations (BE, HAVE, IN, ABOUT) and added two relations referring to event participants (ACTOR, INST(rument)) that replaced the relations MAKE, CAUSE, FOR, FROM, USE. An additional relation LEX refers to lexicalised compounds where no relation can be assigned. Three native speakers of German annotated the compounds with these seven semantic relations.[5] Regarding *compositionality ratings*, eight native speakers of German annotated all 868 gold-standard compounds with compound–

constituent compositionality ratings on a scale from 1 (definitely semantically opaque) to 6 (definitely semantically transparent). Another five native speakers provided additional annotation for our small core subset of 180 compounds on the same scale. As final compositionality ratings, we use the mean compound–constituent ratings across the 13 annotators.

As alternative gold standard for German noun-noun compounds, we used a dataset based on a selection of noun compounds by von der Heide and Borgwaldt (2009), that was previously used in computational models predicting compositionality (Schulte im Walde et al., 2013; Salehi et al., 2014). The dataset contains a subset of their compounds including 244 two-part noun-noun compounds, annotated by compositionality ratings on a scale between 1 and 7. We enriched the existing dataset with frequencies, and productivity and ambiguity scores, also based on *DECOW14AX* and *GermaNet*, to provide the same empirical information as for the G_hOST-NN datasets. We refer to this alternative German dataset as **VDHB**.

English Noun-Noun Compound Datasets Reddy et al. (2011) created a gold standard for English noun-noun compounds. Assuming that compounds whose constituents appeared either as their hypernyms or in their definitions tend to be compositional, they induced a candidate compound set with various degrees of compound–constituent relatedness from *WordNet* (Miller et al., 1990; Fellbaum, 1998) and *Wiktionary*. A random choice of 90 compounds that appeared with a corpus frequency > 50 in the *ukWaC* corpus (Baroni et al., 2009) constituted their gold-standard dataset and was annotated by compositionality ratings. Bell and Schäfer (2013) annotated the compounds with semantic relations using all of Levi's original nine relation types: CAUSE, HAVE, MAKE, USE, BE, IN, FOR, FROM, ABOUT. We refer to this dataset as **REDDY**.

Ó Séaghdha developed computational models to predict the semantic relations between modifiers and heads in English noun compounds (Ó Séaghdha, 2008; Ó Séaghdha and Copestake, 2013; Ó Séaghdha and Korhonen, 2014). As gold-standard basis for his models, he created a dataset of compounds, and annotated the compounds with semantic relations: He tagged and parsed the written part of the British National Cor-

---

[4]The translations of the example compounds are *hair washing, hair dress, hair care, floral glory*, and *colour glory*.

[5]In fact, the annotation was performed for a superset of 1,208 compounds, but we only took into account 868 compounds with perfect agreement, i.e. IAA=1.

Language	Dataset	#Compounds	Annotation		
			Frequency/Productivity	Ambiguity	Relations
DE	G_hOST-NN/S	180	DECOW	GermaNet	Levi (7)
	G_hOST-NN/XL	868	DECOW	GermaNet	Levi (7)
	VDHB	244	DECOW	GermaNet	–
EN	REDDY	90	ENCOW	WordNet	Levi (9)
	OS	396	ENCOW	WordNet	Levi (6)

Table 1: Noun-noun compound datasets.

pus using *RASP* (Briscoe and Carroll, 2002), and applied a simple heuristics to induce compound candidates: He used all sequences of two or more common nouns that were preceded or followed by sentence boundaries or by words not representing common nouns. Of these compound candidates, a random selection of 2,000 instances was used for relation annotation (Ó Séaghdha, 2007) and classification experiments. The final gold standard is a subset of these compounds, containing 1,443 noun-noun compounds. We refer to this dataset as **OS**.

Both English compound datasets were enriched with frequencies and productivities, based on the *ENCOW14AX*[6] containing 9.6 billion words. We also added the number of senses of the constituents to both datasets, using *WordNet*. And we collected compositionality ratings for a random choice of 396 compounds from the OS dataset relying on eight experts, in the same way as the G_hOST-NN ratings were collected.

Resulting Noun-Noun Compound Datasets
Table 1 summarises the gold-standard datasets. They are of different sizes, but their empirical and semantic annotations have been aligned to a large extent, using similar corpora, relying on WordNets and similar semantic relation inventories based on Levi (1978).

4 VSMs Predicting Compositionality

Vector space models (VSMs) and distributional information have been a steadily increasing, integral part of lexical semantic research over the past 20 years (Turney and Pantel, 2010): They explore the notion of "similarity" between a set of target objects, typically relying on the *distributional hypothesis* (Harris, 1954; Firth, 1957) to determine co-occurrence features that best describe the words, phrases, sentences, etc. of interest.

In this paper, we use VSMs in order to model compounds as well as constituents by distributional vectors, and we determine the semantic relatedness between the compounds and their modifier and head constituents by measuring the distance between the vectors. We assume that the closer a compound vector and a constituent vector are to each other, the more compositional (i.e., the more transparent) the compound is, regarding that constituent. Correspondingly, the more distant a compound vector and a constituent vector are to each other, the less compositional (i.e., the more opaque) the compound is, regarding that constituent.

Our main questions regarding the VSMs are concerned with the influence of constituent properties on the prediction of compositionality. I.e., how do the *corpus frequencies* of the compounds and their constituents, the *productivity* and the *ambiguity* of the constituents, and the *semantic relations* between the constituents influence the quality of the predictions?

4.1 Vector Space Models (VSMs)

We created a standard vector space model for all our compounds and constituents in the various datasets, using co-occurrence frequencies of nouns within a sentence-internal window of 20 words to the left and 20 words to the right of the targets.[7] The frequencies were induced from the German and English *COW* corpora, and transformed to *local mutual information (LMI)* values (Evert, 2005).

Relying on the LMI vector space models, the *cosine* determined the distributional similarity between the compounds and their constituents, which was in turn used to predict the degree

---

[6]http://corporafromtheweb.org/encow14/

[7]In previous work, we systematically compared window-based and syntax-based co-occurrence variants for predicting compositionality (Schulte im Walde et al., 2013). The current work adopted the best choice of co-occurrence dimensions.

of compositionality between the compounds and their constituents, assuming that the stronger the distributional similarity (i.e., the cosine values), the larger the degree of compositionality. The vector space predictions were evaluated against the mean human ratings on the degree of compositionality, using the Spearman Rank-Order Correlation Coefficient ρ (Siegel and Castellan, 1988).

4.2 Overall VSM Prediction Results

Table 2 presents the overall prediction results across languages and datasets. The *mod* column shows the ρ correlations for predicting only the degree of compositionality of compound–modifier pairs; the *head* column shows the ρ correlations for predicting only the degree of compositionality of compound–head pairs; and the *both* column shows the ρ correlations for predicting the degree of compositionality of compound–modifier and compound–head pairs at the same time.

	Dataset	mod	head	both
	G$_h$OST-NN/S	0.48	0.57	0.46
DE	G$_h$OST-NN/XL	0.49	0.59	0.47
	VDHB	0.65	0.60	0.61
EN	REDDY	0.48	0.60	0.56
	OS	0.46	0.39	0.35

Table 2: Overall prediction results (ρ).

The models for VDHB and REDDY represent replications of similar models in Schulte im Walde et al. (2013) and Reddy et al. (2011), respectively, but using the much larger *COW* corpora.

Overall, the *both* prediction results on VDHB are significantly[8] better than all others but REDDY; and the prediction results on OS compounds are significantly worse than all others. We can also compare within-dataset results: Regarding the two G$_h$OST-NN datasets and the REDDY dataset, the VSM predictions for the compound–head pairs are better than for the compound–modifier pairs. Regarding the VDHB and the OS datasets, the VSM predictions for the compound–modifier pairs are better than for the compound–head pairs. These differences do not depend on the language (according to our datasets), and are probably due to properties of the specific gold standards that we did not control. They are, however, also not the main point of this paper.

---

[8]All significance tests in this paper were performed by Fisher r-to-z transformation.

4.3 Influence of Compound Properties on VSM Prediction Results

Figures 1 to 5 present the core results of this paper: They explore the influence of compound and constituent properties on predicting compositionality. Since we wanted to optimise insight into the influence of the properties, we selected the 60 maximum instances and the 60 minimum instances for each property.[9] For example, to explore the influence of head frequency on the prediction quality, we selected the 60 most frequent and the 60 most infrequent compound heads from each gold-standard resource, and calculated Spearman's ρ for each set of 60 compounds with these heads.

Figure 1 shows that the distributional model predicts high-frequency compounds (red bars) better than low-frequency compounds (blue bars), across datasets. The differences are significant for G$_h$OST-NN/XL.

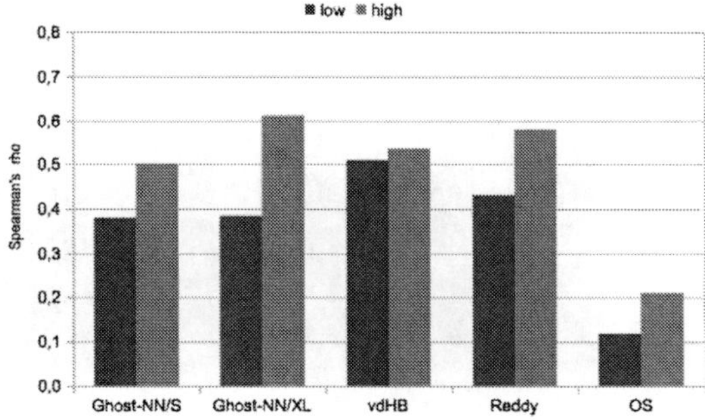

Figure 1: Effect of *compound frequency*.

Figure 2 shows that the distributional model predicts compounds with low-frequency heads better than compounds with high-frequency heads (right panel), while there is no tendency regarding the modifier frequencies (left panel). The differences regarding the head frequencies are significant ($p = 0.1$) for both G$_h$OST-NN datasets.

Figure 3 shows that the distributional model also predicts compounds with low-productivity heads better than compounds with high-productivity heads (right panel), while there is no tendency regarding the productivities of modifiers (left panel). The prediction differences regarding the head productivities are significant for G$_h$OST-NN/S ($p < 0.05$).

---

[9]For REDDY, we could only use 45 maximum/minimum instances, since the dataset only contains 90 compounds.

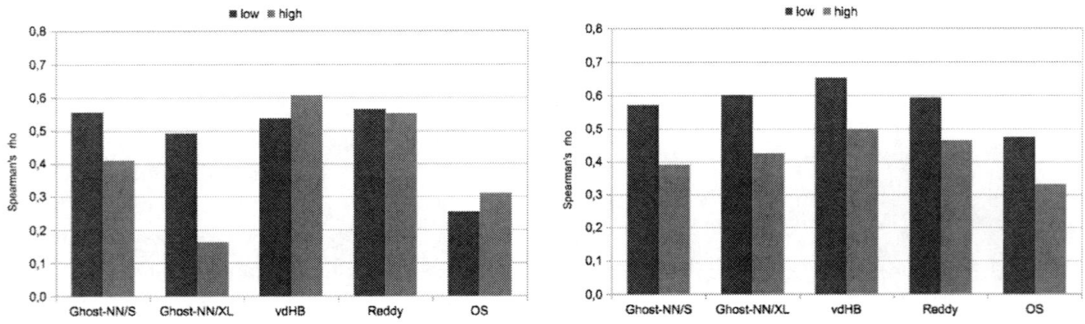

Figure 2: Effect of *modifier/head frequency*.

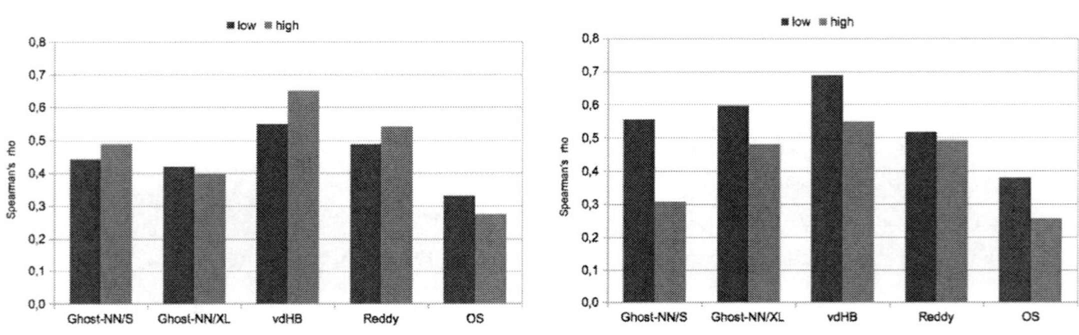

Figure 3: Effect of *modifier/head productivity*.

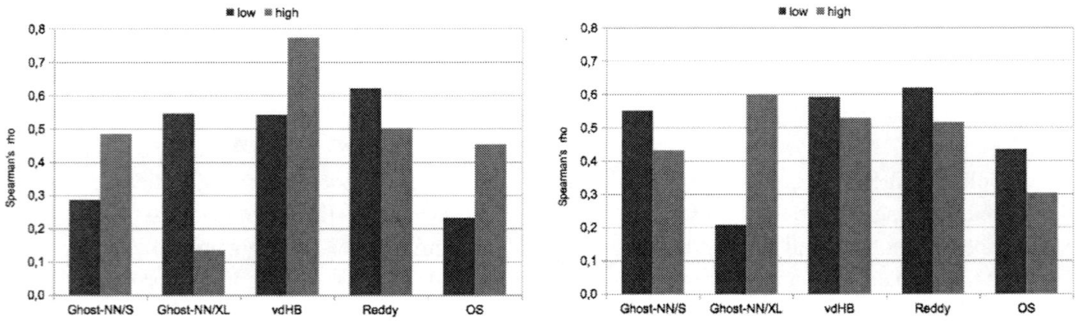

Figure 4: Effect of *modifier/head ambiguity*.

Figure 4 shows that the distributional model also predicts compounds with low-ambiguity heads better than compounds with high-ambiguity heads (right panel) –with one exception (G_hOST-NN/XL)– while there is no tendency regarding the ambiguities of modifiers (left panel). The prediction differences regarding the head ambiguities are significant for G_hOST-NN/XL ($p < 0.01$).

Figure 5 compares the predictions of the distributional model regarding the semantic relations between modifiers and heads, focusing on G_hOST-NN/XL. The numbers in brackets refer to the number of compounds with the respective relation. The plot reveals differences between predictions of compounds with different relations.

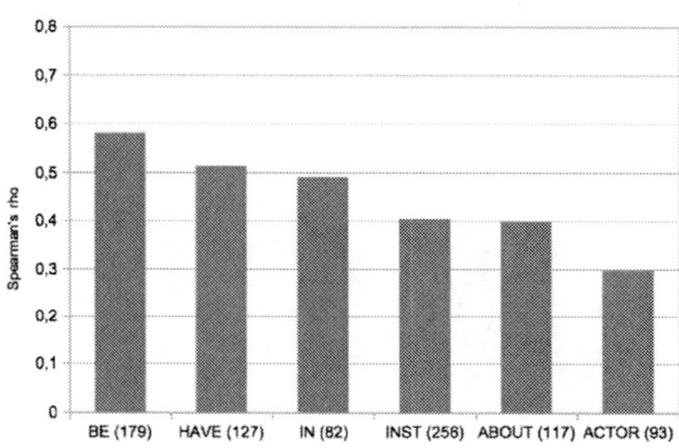

Figure 5: Effect of *semantic relation*.

Table 3 summarises those differences across gold standards that are significant (where filled cells refer to rows significantly outperforming columns). Overall, the compositionality of BE compounds is predicted significantly better than the compositionality of HAVE compounds (in REDDY), INST and ABOUT compounds (in G_hOST-NN) and ACTOR compounds (in G_hOST-NN and OS). The compositionality of ACTOR compounds is predicted significantly worse than the compositionality of BE, HAVE, IN and INST compounds in both G_hOST-NN and OS.

	HAVE	INST	ABOUT	ACTOR
BE	REDDY	G_hOST	G_hOST	G_hOST, OS
HAVE			OS	G_hOST, OS
IN				G_hOST, OS
INST				G_hOST, OS

Table 3: Significant differences: relations.

5   Discussion

While modifier frequency, productivity and ambiguity did not show a consistent effect on the predictions, head frequency, productivity and ambiguity influenced the predictions such that the prediction quality for compounds with low-frequency, low-productivity and low-ambiguity heads was better than for compounds with high-frequency, high-productivity and high-ambiguity heads. The differences were significant only for our new G_hOST-NN datasets. In addition, the compound frequency also had an effect on the predictions, with high-frequency compounds receiving better prediction results than low-frequency compounds. Finally, the quality of predictions also differed for compound relation types, with BE compounds predicted best, and ACTOR compounds predicted worst. These differences were ascertained mostly in the G_hOST-NN and the OS datasets. Our results raise two main questions:

(1) What does it mean if a distributional model predicts a certain subset of compounds (with specific properties) "better" or "worse" than other subsets?

(2) What are the implications for (a) psycholinguistic and (b) computational models regarding the compositionality of noun compounds?

Regarding question (1), there are two options why a distributional model predicts a certain subset of compounds better or worse than other subsets. On the one hand, one of the underlying gold-standard datasets could contain compounds whose compositionality scores are easier to predict than the compositionality scores of compounds in a different dataset. On the other hand, even if there were differences in individual dataset pairs, this would not explain why we consistently find modelling differences for head constituent properties (and compound properties) but not for modifier constituent properties. We therefore conclude that the effects of compound and head properties are due to the compounds' morphological constituency, with specific emphasis on the influences of the heads.

Looking at the individual effects of the compound and head properties that influence the distributional predictions, we hypothesise that high-frequent compounds are easier to predict because they have a better corpus coverage (and less sparse data) than low-frequent compounds, and that they contain many clearly transparent compounds (such as *Zitronensaft* 'lemon juice'), and at the same time many clearly opaque compounds (such as *Eifersucht* 'jealousy', where the literal translations of the constituents are 'eagerness' and 'addiction'). Concerning the decrease in prediction quality for more frequent, more productive and more ambiguous heads, we hypothesise that all of these properties are indicators of ambiguity, and the more ambiguous a word is, the more difficult it is to provide a unique distributional prediction, as distributional co-occurrence in most cases (including our current work) subsumes the contexts of all word senses within one vector. For example, more than half of the compounds with the most frequent and also with the most productive heads have the head *Spiel*, which has six senses in GermaNet and covers six relations (BE, IN, INST, ABOUT, ACTOR, LEX).

Regarding question (2), the results of our distributional predictions confirm psycholinguistic research that identified morphological constituency in noun-noun compounds: Our models clearly distinguish between properties of the whole compounds, properties of the modifier constituents, and properties of the head constituents. Furthermore, our models reveal the need to carefully balance the frequencies and semantic relations of target compounds, and to carefully balance the frequencies, productivities and ambiguities of their head constituents, in order to optimise experiment interpretations, while a careful choice of empirical modifier properties seems to play a minor role.

For computational models, our work provides similar implications. We demonstrated the need to carefully balance gold-standard datasets for multi-word expressions according to the empirical and semantic properties of the multi-word expressions themselves, and also according to those of the constituents. In the case of noun-noun compounds, the properties of the nominal modifiers were of minor importance, but regarding other multi-word expressions, this might differ. If datasets are not balanced for compound and constituent properties, the qualities of model predictions are difficult to interpret, because it is not clear whether biases in empirical properties skewed the results. Our advice is strengthened by the fact that most significant differences in prediction results were demonstrated for our new gold standard, which includes compounds across various frequency, productivity and ambiguity ranges.

6 Conclusion

We explored the role of constituent properties in English and German noun-noun compounds, when predicting compositionality within a vector space model. The results demonstrated that the empirical and semantic properties of the compounds and the head nouns play a significant role. Therefore, psycholinguistic experiments as well as computational models are advised to carefully balance their selections of compound targets according to compound and constituent properties.

Acknowledgments

The research presented in this paper was funded by the DFG Heisenberg Fellowship SCHU 2580/1 (Sabine Schulte im Walde), the DFG Research Grant SCHU 2580/2 *"Distributional Approaches to Semantic Relatedness"* (Stefan Bott), and the DFG Collaborative Research Center SFB 732 (Anna Hätty).

References

Marco Baroni, Silvia Bernardini, Adriano Ferraresi, and Eros Zanchetta. 2009. The WaCky Wide Web: A Collection of Very Large Linguistically Processed Web-Crawled Corpora. *Language Resources and Evaluation*, 43(3):209–226.

Marco Baroni, Raffaella Bernardi, and Roberto Zamparelli. 2014. Frege in Space: A Program for Compositional Distributional Semantics. *Linguistic Issues in Language Technologies*, 9(6):5–110.

Melanie J. Bell and Martin Schäfer. 2013. Semantic Transparency: Challenges for Distributional Semantics. In *Proceedings of the IWCS Workshop on Formal Distributional Semantics*, pages 1–10, Potsdam, Germany.

Ted Briscoe and John Carroll. 2002. Robust Accurate Statistical Annotation of General Text. In *Proceedings of the 3rd Conference on Language Resources and Evaluation*, pages 1499–1504, Las Palmas de Gran Canaria, Spain.

Fabienne Cap, Manju Nirmal, Marion Weller, and Sabine Schulte im Walde. 2015. How to Account for Idiomatic German Support Verb Constructions in Statistical Machine Translation. In *Proceedings of the 11th Workshop on Multiword Expressions*, pages 19–28, Denver, Colorado, USA.

Kostadin Cholakov and Valia Kordoni. 2014. Better Statistical Machine Translation through Linguistic Treatment of Phrasal Verbs. In *Proceedings of the Conference on Empirical Methods in Natural Language Processing*, pages 196–201, Doha, Qatar.

Bob Coecke, Mehrnoosh Sadrzadeh, and Stephen Clark. 2011. Mathematical Foundations for a Compositional Distributional Model of Meaning. *Linguistic Analysis*, 36(1-4):345–384.

Nicole H. de Jong, Laurie B. Feldman, Robert Schreuder, Michael Pastizzo, and Harald R. Baayen. 2002. The Processing and Representation of Dutch and English Compounds: Peripheral Morphological and Central Orthographic Effects. *Brain and Language*, 81:555–567.

Stefan Evert. 2005. *The Statistics of Word Co-Occurrences: Word Pairs and Collocations*. Ph.D. thesis, Institut für Maschinelle Sprachverarbeitung, Universität Stuttgart.

Gertrud Faaß, Ulrich Heid, and Helmut Schmid. 2010. Design and Application of a Gold Standard for Morphological Analysis: SMOR in Validation. In *Proceedings of the 7th International Conference on Language Resources and Evaluation*, pages 803–810, Valletta, Malta.

Christiane Fellbaum, editor. 1998. *WordNet – An Electronic Lexical Database*. Language, Speech, and Communication. MIT Press, Cambridge, MA.

John R. Firth. 1957. *Papers in Linguistics 1934-51*. Longmans, London, UK.

Christina L. Gagné and Thomas L. Spalding. 2009. Constituent Integration during the Processing of Compound Words: Does it involve the Use of Relational Structures? *Journal of Memory and Language*, 60:20–35.

Birgit Hamp and Helmut Feldweg. 1997. GermaNet – A Lexical-Semantic Net for German. In *Proceedings of the ACL Workshop on Automatic Information Extraction and Building Lexical Semantic Resources for NLP Applications*, pages 9–15, Madrid, Spain.

Zellig Harris. 1954. Distributional structure. *Word*, 10(23):146–162.

Karl Moritz Hermann. 2014. *Distributed Representations for Compositional Semantics*. Ph.D. thesis, University of Oxford.

Niels Janssen, Yanchao Bi, and Alfonso Caramazza. 2008. A Tale of Two Frequencies: Determining the Speed of Lexical Access for Mandarin Chinese and English Compounds. *Language and Cognitive Processes*, 23:1191–1223.

Gonia Jarema, Celine Busson, Rossitza Nikolova, Kyrana Tsapkini, and Gary Libben. 1999. Processing Compounds: A Cross-Linguistic Study. *Brain and Language*, 68:362–369.

Hongbo Ji, Christina L. Gagné, and Thomas L. Spalding. 2011. Benefits and Costs of Lexical Decomposition and Semantic Integration during the Processing of Transparent and Opaque English Compounds. *Journal of Memory and Language*, 65:406–430.

Eva Kehayia, Gonia Jarema, Kyrana Tsapkini, Danuta Perlak, Angela Ralli, and Danuta Kadzielawa. 1999. The Role of Morphological Structure in the Processing of Compounds: The Interface between Linguistics and Psycholinguistics. *Brain and Language*, 68:370–377.

Claudia Kunze. 2000. Extension and Use of GermaNet, a Lexical-Semantic Database. In *Proceedings of the 2nd International Conference on Language Resources and Evaluation*, pages 999–1002, Athens, Greece.

Judith N. Levi. 1978. *The Syntax and Semantics of Complex Nominals*. Academic Press, London.

Gary Libben, Martha Gibson, Yeo Bom Yoon, and Dominiek Sandra. 1997. Semantic Transparency and Compound Fracture. Technical Report 9, CLASNET Working Papers.

Gary Libben, Martha Gibson, Yeo Bom Yoon, and Dominiek Sandra. 2003. Compound Fracture: The Role of Semantic Transparency and Morphological Headedness. *Brain and Language*, 84:50–64.

Gary Libben. 1998. Semantic Transparency in the Processing of Compounds: Consequences for Representation, Processing, and Impairment. *Brain and Language*, 61:30–44.

George A. Miller, Richard Beckwith, Christiane Fellbaum, Derek Gross, and Katherine J. Miller. 1990. Introduction to Wordnet: An On-line Lexical Database. *International Journal of Lexicography*, 3(4):235–244.

Jeff Mitchell and Mirella Lapata. 2010. Composition in Distributional Models of Semantics. *Cognitive Science*, 34:1388–1429.

Diarmuid Ó Séaghdha and Ann Copestake. 2013. Interpreting Compound Nouns with Kernel Methods. *Journal of Natural Language Engineering*, 19(3):331–356.

Diarmuid Ó Séaghdha and Anna Korhonen. 2014. Probabilistic Distributional Semantics with Latent Variable Models. *Computational Linguistics*, 40(3):587–631.

Diarmuid Ó Séaghdha. 2007. Designing and Evaluating a Semantic Annotation Scheme for Compound Nouns. In *Proceedings of Corpus Linguistics*, Birmingham, UK.

Diarmuid Ó Séaghdha. 2008. *Learning Compound Noun Semantics*. Ph.D. thesis, University of Cambridge, Computer Laboratory. Technical Report UCAM-CL-TR-735.

Siva Reddy, Diana McCarthy, and Suresh Manandhar. 2011. An Empirical Study on Compositionality in Compound Nouns. In *Proceedings of the 5th International Joint Conference on Natural Language Processing*, pages 210–218, Chiang Mai, Thailand.

Bahar Salehi and Paul Cook. 2013. Predicting the Compositionality of Multiword Expressions Using Translations in Multiple Languages. In *Proceedings of the 2nd Joint Conference on Lexical and Computational Semantics*, pages 266–275, Atlanta, GA.

Bahar Salehi, Paul Cook, and Timothy Baldwin. 2014. Using Distributional Similarity of Multi-way Translations to Predict Multiword Expression Compositionality. In *Proceedings of the 14th Conference of the European Chapter of the Association for Computational Linguistics*, pages 472–481, Gothenburg, Sweden.

Bahar Salehi, Paul Cook, and Timothy Baldwin. 2015a. A Word Embedding Approach to Predicting the Compositionality of Multiword Expressions. In *Proceedings of the Conference of the North American Chapter of the Association for Computational Linguistics/Human Language Technologies*, pages 977–983, Denver, Colorado, USA.

Bahar Salehi, Nitika Mathur, Paul Cook, and Timothy Baldwin. 2015b. The Impact of Multiword Expression Compositionality on Machine Translation Evaluation. In *Proceedings of the 11th Workshop on Multiword Expressions*, pages 54–59, Denver, Colorado, USA.

Dominiek Sandra. 1990. On the Representation and Processing of Compound Words: Automatic Access to Constituent Morphemes does not occur. *The Quarterly Journal of Experimental Psychology*, 42A:529–567.

Roland Schäfer and Felix Bildhauer. 2012. Building Large Corpora from the Web Using a New Efficient Tool Chain. In *Proceedings of the 8th International Conference on Language Resources and Evaluation*, pages 486–493, Istanbul, Turkey.

Roland Schäfer. 2015. Processing and Querying Large Web Corpora with the COW14 Architecture. In *Proceedings of the 3rd Workshop on Challenges in the Management of Large Corpora*, pages 28–34, Mannheim, Germany.

Helmut Schmid. 1994. Probabilistic Part-of-Speech Tagging using Decision Trees. In *Proceedings of the 1st International Conference on New Methods in Language Processing*.

Sabine Schulte im Walde, Stefan Müller, and Stephen Roller. 2013. Exploring Vector Space Models to Predict the Compositionality of German Noun-Noun Compounds. In *Proceedings of the 2nd Joint Conference on Lexical and Computational Semantics*, pages 255–265, Atlanta, GA.

Sabine Schulte im Walde, Anna Hätty, Stefan Bott, and Nana Khvtisavrishvili. 2016. G$_h$oSt-NN: A Representative Gold Standard of German Noun-Noun Compounds. In *Proceedings of the 10th International Conference on Language Resources and Evaluation*, pages 2285–2292, Portoroz, Slovenia.

Sidney Siegel and N. John Castellan. 1988. *Nonparametric Statistics for the Behavioral Sciences*. McGraw-Hill, Boston, MA.

Peter D. Turney and Patrick Pantel. 2010. From Frequency to Meaning: Vector Space Models of Semantics. *Journal of Artificial Intelligence Research*, 37:141–188.

Henk J. van Jaarsveld and Gilbert E. Rattink. 1988. Frequency Effects in the Processing of Lexicalized and Novel Nominal Compounds. *Journal of Psycholinguistic Research*, 17:447–473.

Claudia von der Heide and Susanne Borgwaldt. 2009. Assoziationen zu Unter-, Basis- und Oberbegriffen. Eine explorative Studie. In *Proceedings of the 9th Norddeutsches Linguistisches Kolloquium*, pages 51–74.

Marion Weller, Fabienne Cap, Stefan Müller, Sabine Schulte im Walde, and Alexander Fraser. 2014. Distinguishing Degrees of Compositionality in Compound Splitting for Statistical Machine Translation. In *Proceedings of the 1st Workshop on Computational Approaches to Compound Analysis*, pages 81–90, Dublin, Ireland.

Pienie Zwitserlood. 1994. The Role of Semantic Transparency in the Processing and Representation of Dutch Compounds. *Language and Cognitive Processes*, 9:341–368.

Detecting Stance in Tweets
And Analyzing its Interaction with Sentiment

Parinaz Sobhani
EECS, University of Ottawa
psobh090@uottawa.ca

Saif M. Mohammad and Svetlana Kiritchenko
National Research Council Canada
{saif.mohammad,svetlana.kiritchenko}@nrc-cnrc.gc.ca

Abstract

One may express favor (or disfavor) towards a target by using positive or negative language. Here for the first time we present a dataset of tweets annotated for whether the tweeter is in favor of or against pre-chosen targets, as well as for sentiment. These targets may or may not be referred to in the tweets, and they may or may not be the target of opinion in the tweets. We develop a simple stance detection system that outperforms all 19 teams that participated in a recent shared task competition on the same dataset (SemEval-2016 Task #6). Additionally, access to both stance and sentiment annotations allows us to conduct several experiments to tease out their interactions. We show that while sentiment features are useful for stance classification, they alone are not sufficient. We also show the impacts of various features on detecting stance and sentiment, respectively.

1 Introduction

Stance detection is the task of automatically determining from text whether the author of the text is in favor of, against, or neutral towards a proposition or target. The target may be a person, an organization, a government policy, a movement, a product, etc. For example, one can infer from Barack Obama's speeches that he is in favor of stricter gun laws in the US. Similarly, people often express stance towards various target entities through posts on online forums, blogs, Twitter, Youtube, Instagram, etc.

Automatically detecting stance has widespread applications in information retrieval, text summarization, and textual entailment. Over the last decade, there has been active research in modeling stance. However, most work focuses on congressional debates (Thomas et al., 2006) or debates in online forums (Somasundaran and Wiebe, 2009; Murakami and Raymond, 2010; Anand et al., 2011; Walker et al., 2012; Hasan and Ng, 2013). Here we explore the task of detecting stance in Twitter—a popular microblogging platform where people often express stance implicitly or explicitly.

The task we explore is formulated as follows: given a tweet text and a target entity (person, organization, movement, policy, etc.), automatic natural language systems must determine whether the tweeter is in favor of the given target, against the given target, or whether neither inference is likely. For example, consider the target–tweet pair:

> Target: legalization of abortion   (1)
> Tweet: *The pregnant are more than walking incubators, and have rights!*

Humans can deduce from the tweet that the tweeter is likely in favor of the target.[1]

Note that lack of evidence for 'favor' or 'against', does not imply that the tweeter is neutral towards the target. It may just mean that we cannot deduce stance from the tweet. In fact, this is a common phenomenon. On the other hand, the number of tweets from which we can infer neutral stance is expected to be small. An example is shown below:

> Target: Hillary Clinton   (2)
> Tweet: *Hillary Clinton has some strengths and some weaknesses.*

Stance detection is related to, but different from, sentiment analysis. Sentiment analysis tasks are

---

[1] Note that we use 'tweet' to refer to the text of the tweet and not to its meta-information. In our annotation task, we asked respondents to label for stance towards a given target based on the tweet text alone. However, automatic systems may benefit from exploiting tweet meta-information.

*Proceedings of the Fifth Joint Conference on Lexical and Computational Semantics (*SEM 2016)*, pages 159–169,
Berlin, Germany, August 11-12, 2016.

formulated as determining whether a piece of text is positive, negative, or neutral, or determining from text the speaker's opinion and the target of the opinion (the entity towards which opinion is expressed). However, in stance detection, systems are to determine favorability towards a given (pre-chosen) target of interest. The target of interest may not be explicitly mentioned in the text and it may not be the target of opinion in the text. For example, consider the target–tweet pair below:

> Target: *Donald Trump*   (3)
> Tweet: *Jeb Bush is the only sane candidate in this republican lineup.*

The target of opinion in the tweet is Jeb Bush, but the given target of interest is Donald Trump. Nonetheless, we can infer that the tweeter is likely to be unfavorable towards Donald Trump. Also note that, in stance detection, the target can be expressed in different ways which impacts whether the instance is labeled 'favor' or 'against'. For example, the target in example 1 could have been phrased as 'pro-life movement', in which case the correct label for that instance is 'against'. Also, the same stance (favor or against) towards a given target can be deduced from positive tweets and negative tweets. This interaction between sentiment and stance has not been adequately addressed in past work, and an important reason for this is the lack of a dataset annotated for both stance and sentiment.

Our contributions are as follows:

(1) We create the first tweets dataset labeled for stance, target of opinion, and sentiment. More than 4,000 tweets are annotated for whether one can deduce favorable or unfavorable stance towards one of five targets 'Atheism', 'Climate Change is a Real Concern', 'Feminist Movement', 'Hillary Clinton', and 'Legalization of Abortion'. Each of these tweets is also annotated for whether the target of opinion expressed in the tweet is the same as the given target of interest. Finally, each tweet is annotated for whether it conveys positive, negative, or neutral sentiment.

(2) Partitions of this stance-annotated data were used as training and test sets in the SemEval-2016 shared task competition 'Task #6: Detecting Stance in Tweets' (Mohammad et al., 2016b). Participants were provided with 2,914 training instances labeled for stance for the five targets. The test data included 1,249 instances. The task received submissions from 19 teams. The best performing system obtained an overall average F-score of 67.82. Their approach employed two recurrent neural network (RNN) classifiers: the first was trained to predict task-relevant hashtags on a very large unlabeled Twitter corpus. This network was used to initialize a second RNN classifier, which was trained with the provided training data.

(3) We propose a stance detection system that is much simpler than the SemEval-2016 Task #6 winning system (described above), and yet obtains an even better F-score of 70.32 on the shared task's test set. We use a linear-kernel SVM classifier that relies on features drawn from the training instances—such as word and character n-grams—as well as those obtained using external resources—such as sentiment features from lexicons and word-embedding features from additional unlabeled data.

(4) We conduct experiments to better understand the interaction between stance and sentiment and the factors influencing their interaction. We use the gold labels to determine the extent to which stance can be determined simply from sentiment. We apply the stance detection system (mentioned above in (3)), as a common text classification framework, to determine both stance and sentiment. Results show that while sentiment features are substantially useful for sentiment classification, they are not as effective for stance classification. Word embeddings improve the performance of both stance and sentiment classifiers. Further, even though both stance and sentiment detection are framed as three-way classification tasks on a common dataset where the majority class baselines are similar, automatic systems perform markedly better when detecting sentiment than when detecting stance towards a given target. Finally, we show that stance detection towards the target of interest is particularly challenging when the tweeter expresses opinion about an entity other than the target of interest. In fact, the text classification system performs close to majority baseline for such instances.

All of the stance data, including annotations for target of opinion and sentiment, are made freely available through the shared task website and the homepage for this Stance Project.[2]

---

[2] http://alt.qcri.org/semeval2016/task6/
www.saifmohammad.com/WebPages/StanceDataset.htm

Target	Example Favor Hashtag	Example Against Hashtag	Example Ambiguous Hashtag
Atheism	*#NoMoreReligions*	*#Godswill*	*#atheism*
Climate Change is Concern	-	*#globalwarminghoax*	*#climatechange*
Feminist Movement	*#INeedFeminismBecaus*	*#FeminismIsAwful*	*#Feminism*
Hillary Clinton	*#GOHILLARY*	*#WhyIAmNotVotingForHillary*	*#hillary2016*
Legalization of Abortion	*#proChoice*	*#prayToEndAbortion*	*#PlannedParenthood*

Table 1: Examples of stance-indicative and stance-ambiguous hashtags that were manually identified.

2 A Dataset for Stance from Tweets

The stance annotations we use are described in detail in Mohammad et al. (2016a). We summarize below how we compiled a set of tweets and targets for stance annotation, the questionnaire and crowdsourcing setup used for stance annotation, and an analysis of the stance annotations.

We first identified a list of target entities that were commonly known in the United States and also topics of debate: 'Atheism', 'Climate Change is a Real Concern", 'Feminist Movement', 'Hillary Clinton', and 'Legalization of Abortion'. Next, we compiled a small list of hashtags, which we will call *query hashtags*, that people use when tweeting about the targets. We split these hashtags into three categories: (1) *favor hashtags*: expected to occur in tweets expressing favorable stance towards the target (for example, *#Hillary4President*), (2) *against hashtags:* expected to occur in tweets expressing opposition to the target (for example, *#HillNo*), and (3) *stance-ambiguous hashtags:* expected to occur in tweets about the target, but are not explicitly indicative of stance (for example, *#Hillary2016*). Table 1 lists examples of hashtags used for each of the targets.

Next, we polled the Twitter API to collect close to 2 million tweets containing these hashtags (query hashtags). We discarded retweets and tweets with URLs. We kept only those tweets where the query hashtags appeared at the end. This reduced the number of tweets to about 1.7 million. We removed the query hashtags from the tweets to exclude obvious cues for the classification task. Since we only select tweets that have the query hashtag at the end, removing them from the tweet often still results in text that is understandable and grammatical.

Note that the presence of a stance-indicative hashtag is not a guarantee that the tweet will have the same stance.[3] Further, removal of query hash-

tags may result in a tweet that no longer expresses the same stance as with the query hashtag. Thus we manually annotate the tweet–target pairs after the pre-processing described above. For each target, we sampled an equal number of tweets pertaining to the favor hashtags, the against hashtags, and the stance-ambiguous hashtags. This helps in obtaining a sufficient number of tweets pertaining to each of the stance categories. Note that removing the query hashtag can sometimes result in tweets that do not explicitly mention the target. Consider:

Target: Hillary Clinton   (4)
Tweet: *Benghazi must be answered for #Jeb16*

The query hashtags '#HillNo' was removed from the original tweet, leaving no mention of Hillary Clinton. Yet there is sufficient evidence (through references to Benghazi and #Jeb16) that the tweeter is likely against Hillary Clinton. Further, conceptual targets such as 'legalization of abortion' (much more so than person-name targets) have many instances where the target is not explicitly mentioned.

2.1 Stance Annotation

The core instructions given to annotators for determining stance are shown below.[4] Additional descriptions within each option (not shown here) make clear that stance can be expressed in many different ways, for example by explicitly supporting or opposing the target, by supporting an entity aligned with or opposed to the target, by re-tweeting somebody else's tweet, etc. We also asked a second question pertaining to whether the target of opinion expressed in the tweet is the same as the given target of interest.

---

[3] A tweet that has a seemingly favorable hashtag may in fact oppose the target; and this is not uncommon.

[4] The full set of instructions is made available on the shared task website: http://alt.qcri.org/semeval2016/task6/.

Target of Interest: [target entity]
Tweet: [tweet with query hashtag removed]

Q: From reading the tweet, which of the options below is most likely to be true about the tweeter's stance or outlook towards the target:

1. We can infer from the tweet that the tweeter supports the target

2. We can infer from the tweet that the tweeter is against the target

3. We can infer from the tweet that the tweeter has a neutral stance towards the target

4. There is no clue in the tweet to reveal the stance of the tweeter towards the target (support/against/neutral)

Q2: From reading the tweet, which of the options below is most likely to be true about the focus of opinion/sentiment in the tweet:

1. The tweet explicitly expresses opinion/sentiment about the target

2. The tweet expresses opinion/sentiment about something/someone other than the target

3. The tweet is not expressing opinion/sentiment

For each of the five selected targets, we randomly sampled 1,000 tweets from the 1.7 million tweets initially gathered from Twitter. Each of these tweets was uploaded on CrowdFlower for annotation as per the questionnaire shown above.[5] Each instance was annotated by at least eight annotators. For each target, the data not annotated for stance is used as the *domain corpus*—a set of unlabeled tweets that can be used to obtain information helpful to determine stance, such as relationships between relevant entities.

2.2 Analysis of Stance Annotations

The number of instances that were marked as neutral stance (option 3 in question 1) was less than 1%. Thus, we merged options 3 and 4 into one 'neither in favor nor against' option ('neither' for short). The inter-annotator agreement was 73.1% for question 1 (stance) and 66.2% for Question 2 (target of opinion).[6] These statistics are for the complete annotated dataset, which include instances that were genuinely difficult to annotate for stance (possibly because the tweets were too ungrammatical or vague) and/or instances that received poor annotations from the crowd workers (possibly because the particular annotator did not understand the tweet or its context). We selected instances with agreement equal or greater than 60% (at least 5 out of 8 annotators must agree)

on Question 1 (stance) to create a dataset for machine learning experiments.[7] We will refer to this dataset as the *Stance Dataset*. The inter-annotator agreement on this Stance Dataset is 81.85% for question 1 (stance) and 68.9% for Question 2 (target of opinion). The rest of the instances are kept aside for future investigation. We partitioned the Stance Dataset into training and test sets based on the timestamps of the tweets. All annotated tweets were ordered by their timestamps, and the first 70% of the tweets formed the training set and the last 30% formed the test set. Table 2 shows the distribution of instances in the Stance Dataset.

Table 3 shows the distribution of responses to Question 2 (whether opinion is expressed directly about the given target). Observe that the percentage of 'opinion towards other' varies across different targets from 27% to 46%. Table 4 shows the distribution of instances by target of opinion for the 'favor' and 'against' stance labels. Observe that, as in Example 3, in a number of tweets from which we can infer unfavorable stance towards a target, the target of opinion is someone/something other than the target (about 26.5%). Manual inspection of the data also revealed that in a number of instances, the target is not directly mentioned, and yet stance towards the target was determined by the annotators. About 28% of the 'Hillary Clinton' instances and 67% of the 'Legalization of Abortion' instances were found to be of this kind—they did not mention 'Hillary' or 'Clinton' and did not mention 'abortion', 'pro-life', and 'pro-choice', respectively (case insensitive; with or without hashtag; with or without hyphen). Examples (1) and (4) shown earlier are instances of this, and are taken from our dataset.

3 Labeling the Stance Set for Sentiment

A key research question is the extent to which sentiment is correlated with stance. To that end, we annotated the same Stance Train and Test datasets described above for sentiment in a separate annotation project a few months later. We followed a procedure for annotation on CrowdFlower similar to that described above for stance, but now provided only the tweet (no target). We asked respondents to label the tweets as either positive, negative, or neither. The 'neither' category includes

---

[5] http://www.crowdflower.com

[6] We report absolute agreements here.

[7] The 60% threshold is somewhat arbitrary, but it seemed appropriate in terms of balancing confidence in the majority annotation and having to discard too many instances.

Target	# total	# train	% of instances in Train			# test	% of instances in Test		
			favor	against	neither		favor	against	neither
Atheism	733	513	17.9	59.3	22.8	220	14.5	72.7	12.7
Climate Change is Concern	564	395	53.7	3.8	42.5	169	72.8	6.5	20.7
Feminist Movement	949	664	31.6	49.4	19.0	285	20.4	64.2	15.4
Hillary Clinton	984	689	17.1	57.0	25.8	295	15.3	58.3	26.4
Legalization of Abortion	933	653	18.5	54.4	27.1	280	16.4	67.5	16.1
Total	4163	2914	25.8	47.9	26.3	1249	23.1	51.8	25.1

Table 2: Distribution of instances in the Stance Train and Test sets for Question 1 (Stance).

Target	Opinion towards		
	Target	Other	No one
Atheism	49.3	46.4	4.4
Climate Change is Concern	60.8	30.5	8.7
Feminist Movement	68.3	27.4	4.3
Hillary Clinton	60.3	35.1	4.6
Legalization of Abortion	63.7	31.0	5.4
Total	61.0	33.8	5.2

Table 3: Distribution of instances in the Stance dataset for Question 2 (Target of Opinion).

Stance	Opinion towards		
	Target	Other	No one
favor	94.2	5.1	0.7
against	72.8	26.5	0.7

Table 4: Distribution of target of opinion across stance labels.

mixed and neutral sentiment.

The inter-annotator agreement on the sentiment responses was 85.6%. Table 5 shows the distribution of sentiment labels in the training and test sets. Note that tweets corresponding to all targets, except 'Atheism', are predominantly negative.

4 A Common Text Classification Framework for Stance and Sentiment

Past work has shown that the most useful features for sentiment analysis are word and character n-grams and sentiment lexicons, whereas others such as negation features, part-of-speech features, and punctuation have a smaller impact (Wilson et al., 2013; Mohammad et al., 2013; Kiritchenko et al., 2014b; Rosenthal et al., 2015). More recently, features drawn from word embeddings have been shown to be effective in various text classification tasks such as sentiment analysis (Tang et al., 2014) and named entity recognition (Turian et al., 2010). All of these features are expected to be useful in stance classification as well. However, it is unclear which features will be more useful (and to what extent) for detecting stance as opposed to sentiment. Since we now have a dataset annotated for both stance and sentiment, we create a com-

mon text classification system (machine learning framework and features) and apply it to the Stance Dataset for detecting both stance and sentiment.

There is one exception to the common machine learning framework. The words and concepts used in tweets corresponding to the three stance categories are not expected to generalize across the targets. Thus, the stance system learns a separate model from training data pertaining to each of the targets.[8] Positive and negative language tend to have sufficient amount of commonality regardless of topic of discussion, and hence sentiment analysis systems traditionally learn a single model from all of the training data (Liu, 2015; Kiritchenko et al., 2014b; Rosenthal et al., 2015). Thus our sentiment experiments are also based on a single model trained on all of the Stance Training set.[9]

Tweets are tokenized and part-of-speech tagged with the CMU Twitter NLP tool (Gimpel et al., 2011). We train a linear-kernel Support Vector Machine (SVM) classifier on the Stance training set. SVM is a state-of-the-art learning algorithm proved to be effective on text categorization tasks and robust on large feature spaces. The SVM parameters are tuned using 5-fold cross-validation on Stance Training set. We used the implementation provided in Scikit-learn Machine Learning library (Pedregosa et al., 2011).

The features used in our text classification system are described below:[10]

- *n-grams*: presence or absence of contiguous sequences of 1, 2 and 3 tokens (word n-grams); presence or absence of contiguous sequences of 2, 3, 4, and 5 characters (character n-grams);

- *word embeddings*: the average of the word vectors for words appearing in a given

---

[8]We built a stance system that learns a single model from all training tweets, but its performance was worse.

[9]Training different models for each target did not yield better results.

[10]Use of tweet meta-information is left for future work.

Target	% of instances in Train			% of instances in Test		
	positive	negative	neither	positive	negative	neither
Atheism	60.4	35.1	4.5	59.1	35.5	5.5
Climate Change is Concern	31.7	49.6	18.7	29.6	51.5	18.9
Feminist Movement	17.9	77.3	4.8	19.3	76.1	4.6
Hillary Clinton	32.1	64.0	3.9	25.8	70.2	4.1
Legalization of Abortion	28.8	66.2	5.1	20.4	72.1	7.5
Total	33.1	60.5	6.5	29.5	63.3	7.2

Table 5: Distribution of sentiment in the Stance Train and Test sets.

tweet.[11] We derive 100-dimensional word vectors using Word2Vec Skip-gram model (Mikolov et al., 2013) trained over the Domain Corpus. (Recall that the Domain Corpus is the large set of unlabeled tweets pertaining to the five targets that were not manually labeled for stance).

- *sentiment features*: features drawn from sentiment lexicons as suggested in (Kiritchenko et al., 2014b). The lexicons used include NRC Emotion Lexicon (Mohammad and Turney, 2010), Hu and Liu Lexicon (Hu and Liu, 2004), MPQA Subjectivity Lexicon (Wilson et al., 2005), and NRC Hashtag Sentiment and Emoticon Lexicons (Kiritchenko et al., 2014b).

Some other feature sets that we experimented with, via cross-validation on the training set, included word embeddings trained on a generic Twitter corpus (not the domain corpus), the number of occurrences of each part-of-speech tag, the number of repeated sequences of exclamation or question marks, and the number of words with one character repeated more than two times (for example, *yessss*). However, they did not improve results there, and so we did not include them for the test set experiments.

We evaluate the learned models on the Stance Test set. As the evaluation measure, we use the average of the F1-scores (the harmonic mean of precision and recall) for the two main classes:[12]

For stance classification:

$$F_{avg} = \frac{F_{favor} + F_{against}}{2}$$

For sentiment classification:

$$F_{avg} = \frac{F_{positive} + F_{negative}}{2}$$

Note that F_{avg} can be determined for all of the test instances or for each target data separately. We will refer to the F_{avg} obtained through the former method as *F-micro-across-targets* or *F-microT* (for short). On the other hand, the F_{avg} obtained through the latter method, that is, by averaging the F_{avg} calculated for each target separately, will be called *F-macro-across-targets* or *F-macroT* (for short). F-microT was used as the bottom-line evaluation metric in the SemEval-2016 shared task on stance detection. Note that systems that perform relatively better on the more frequent target classes will obtain higher F-microT scores. On the other hand, to obtain a high F-macroT score a system has to perform well on all target classes.

5 Results of Automatic Systems

In the two subsections below, we present results obtained by the classifiers described above on detecting stance and sentiment, respectively, on the Stance Test set. (Cross-validation experiments on the Stance Training set produced similar results—and are thus not shown.)

5.1 Results for Stance Classification

Table 6 shows the overall results obtained by the automatic stance classifiers. Row i. shows results obtained by a random classifier (a classifier that randomly assigns a stance class to each instance), and row ii. shows results obtained by the majority classifier (a classifier that simply labels every instance with the majority class per target). Observe that F-microT for the majority class baseline is noticeably high. This is mostly due to the differences in the class distributions for the five targets: for most of the targets the majority of the instances are labeled as 'against' whereas for target 'Climate Change is a Real Concern' most of the data are labeled as 'favor'. Therefore, the F-scores for the classes 'favor' and 'against' are more balanced over all targets than for just

---

[11] Averaging is a commonly used vector combination method, although other approaches can also be pursued.

[12] A similar metric was used in the past for sentiment analysis—SemEval 2013 Task 2 (Wilson et al., 2013).

Classifier	F-macroT	F-microT
Benchmarks		
i. random	32.30	34.61
ii. majority	40.09	65.22
iii. first in SemEval'16 Task #6	56.03	67.82
iv. oracle sentiment	53.10	57.20
Our Classifiers		
a. n-grams	58.01	68.98
b. n-grams, embeddings	59.08	**70.32**
c. n-grams, sentiment lexicons	56.40	66.81
d. all three feature sets	**59.21**	69.84

Table 6: Stance Classification: Results obtained by automatic systems.

one target. Row iii. shows results obtained by the winning system (among nineteen participating teams) in the SemEval-2016 shared task on this data.

Results of an Oracle Sentiment Benchmark:
The Stance Dataset with labels for both stance and sentiment allows us, for the first time, to conduct an experiment to determine the extent to which stance detection can be solved with sentiment analysis alone. Specifically, we determine the performance of an oracle system that assigns stance as follows: For each target, select a sentiment-to-stance assignment (mapping all positive instances to 'favor' and all negative instances to 'against' OR mapping all positive instances to 'against' and all negative instances to 'favor') that maximizes the F-macroT score. We call this benchmark the Oracle Sentiment Benchmark. This benchmark is informative because it gives an upper bound of the F-score one can expect when using a traditional sentiment system for stance detection by simply mapping sentiment labels to stance labels.

Row iv. in Table 6 shows the F-scores obtained by the Oracle Sentiment Benchmark on the test set. Observe that the F-macroT score is markedly higher than the corresponding score for the majority baseline, but yet much lower than 100%. This shows that even though sentiment can play a key role in detecting stance, sentiment alone is not sufficient.

Results Obtained by Our Classifier:
Rows a., b., c., and d. show results obtained by our SVM classifier using n-gram features alone, n-grams and word embedding features, n-grams and sentiment lexicon features, and n-grams, word embeddings, and sentiment lexicon features ('all three feature sets'), respectively. The results in row a. show the performance that can be achieved on this test set using only the provided training data and no external resources (such as lexicons and extra labeled or unlabeled data). Observe that the results obtained by our system surpass the results obtained by the winning team in the SemEval shared task (row iii.). Also note that while the n-grams and word embeddings alone provide the highest F-microT score, the sentiment lexicon features are beneficial if one is interested in a higher F-macroT score. Table 7 shows F-scores for tweets pertaining to each of the targets. Observe that the word embedding features are beneficial for four out of five targets. The sentiment lexicon features bring additional improvements for two targets, 'Atheism' and 'Hillary Clinton'.

Recall that the Stance Dataset is also annotated for whether opinion is expressed directly about the target, about somebody/someone other than the target, or no opinion is being expressed. Table 8 shows stance detection F-scores obtained on tweets that express opinion directly towards the target and on tweets that express opinion towards others. (The number of tweets for 'no opinion is being expressed' is small, and thus not covered in this experiment.) Observe that the performance of the classifier is considerably better for tweets where opinion is expressed towards the target, than otherwise. Detecting stance towards a given target from tweets that express opinion about some other entity has not been addressed in our research community, and results in Table 8 show that it is particularly challenging. We hope that this dataset will encourage more work to address this gap in performance.

5.2 Results for Sentiment Classification

Table 9 shows results obtained by various automatic classification systems on the sentiment labels of the Stance Dataset. Observe that the scores obtained by the majority class baseline for the three-way sentiment classification is similar to the majority class baseline for the three-way stance classification. Nonetheless, the text classification system obtains markedly higher scores on sentiment prediction than on predicting stance. Observe also that on this sentiment task (unlike the stance task) the sentiment lexicon features are particularly useful (see row b.). Word embeddings features provide improvements over n-grams (row c.); however, adding them on top of n-grams and

Classifier	Atheism	Climate Concern	Feminist Movement	Hillary Clinton	Legalization of Abortion	F-macroT	F-microT
Majority classifier	42.11	42.12	39.10	36.83	40.30	40.09	65.22
Our classifiers							
a. n-grams	65.19	42.35	57.46	58.63	66.42	58.01	68.98
b. n-grams, embeddings	68.25	**43.80**	**58.72**	57.74	**66.91**	59.08	**70.32**
c. n-grams, sentiment lexicons	65.17	40.08	54.48	60.56	61.70	56.40	66.81
d. all three feature sets	**69.19**	42.35	56.11	**61.74**	66.70	**59.21**	69.84

Table 7: Stance Classification: F-scores obtained for each of the targets (the columns) when one or more of the feature groups are added. Highest scores in each column is shown in bold.

	F-macroT		F-microT	
Classifier	Target	Other	Target	Other
all three features	63.51	38.14	75.31	44.15

Table 8: Stance Classification: F-scores obtained for tweets with opinion towards the target and tweets with opinion towards another entity.

Classifier	F_{Pos}	F_{Neg}	F-microT
Majority classifier	44.22	78.35	61.28
Our classifiers			
a. n-grams	64.78	81.75	73.27
b. n-grams, sentiment lex.	**72.21**	**85.52**	**78.87**
c. n-grams, embeddings	68.85	84.00	76.43
d. all three feature sets	71.90	85.21	78.56

Table 9: Sentiment Classification: Results obtained by automatic systems.

	Opinion towards	
Classifier	Target	Other
all three feature sets	79.64	77.81

Table 10: Sentiment Classification: F-microT on tweets with opinion towards the target and tweets with opinion towards another entity.

sentiment features is not beneficial (row d.).

Table 10 shows the performance of the sentiment classifier on tweets that express opinion towards the given target and those that express opinion about another entity. Observe that the sentiment prediction performance (unlike stance prediction performance) is similar on the two sets of tweets. This shows that the two sets of tweets are not qualitatively different in how they express opinion. However, since one set expresses opinion about an entity other than the target of interest, detecting stance towards the target of interest from them is notably more challenging.

6 Related Work

SemEval-2016 Task #6. The SemEval-2016 Task 'Detecting Stance in Tweets' received submissions from 19 teams, wherein the highest classification F-score obtained was 67.82. The best performing systems used standard text classification features such as those drawn from n-grams, word vectors, and sentiment lexicons. Some teams drew additional gains from noisy stance-labeled data created using distant supervision techniques. A large number of teams used word embeddings and some used deep neural networks such as RNNs and convolutional neural nets. Nonetheless, none of these systems surpassed our results presented here.

Other Stance Detection Work. In work by Somasundaran and Wiebe (2010), a lexicon for detecting argument trigger expressions was created and subsequently leveraged to identify arguments. These extracted arguments, together with sentiment expressions and their targets, were employed in a supervised learner as features for stance classification. Anand et al. (2011) deployed a rule-based classifier with several features such as unigrams, bigrams, punctuation marks, syntactic dependencies and the dialogic structure of the posts. Here, we did not explore dependency features since dependency parsers are not as accurate on tweets. Additionally, Anand et al. (2011) showed that there is no significant difference in performance between systems that use only unigrams and systems that also use other features such as LIWC and opinion or POS generalized dependencies in stance classification. Some of these features were used by the teams participating in the SemEval task over this dataset; however, their systems' performances were lower than the performance showed by our stance detection system. The dialogic relations of agreements and disagreements between posts were exploited by Walker et al. (2012). These relationships are not provided for our Stance dataset.

Sobhani et al. (2015) extracted arguments used in online news comments to leverage them as extra features for detecting stance. Faulkner (2014) investigated the problem of detecting document-level stance in student essays by making use of two sets of features that are supposed to represent stance-taking language. Deng and Wiebe (2014) investigated the relationships and interactions among entities and events explicitly mentioned in the text with the goal of improving sentiment classification. In stance classification, however, the predetermined target of interest may not be mentioned in the text, or may not be the target of opinion in the text. Rajadesingan and Liu (2014) determined stance at user level based on the assumption that if several users retweet one pair of tweets about a controversial topic, it is likely that they support the same side of a debate. In this work, we focus on detecting stance, as well as possible, from a single tweet. Features that help to this end will likely also be useful when there is access to multiple tweets from the same tweeter.

Sentiment Analysis and Related Tasks. There is a vast amount of work in sentiment analysis of tweets, and we refer the reader to surveys (Pang and Lee, 2008; Liu and Zhang, 2012; Mohammad, 2015) and proceedings of recent shared task competitions (Wilson et al., 2013; Rosenthal et al., 2015). Closely-related is the area of aspect based sentiment analysis (ABSA), where the goal is to determine sentiment towards aspects of a product such as speed of processor and screen resolution of a cell phone. We refer the reader to SemEval proceedings for related work on ABSA (Pontiki et al., 2015; Pontiki et al., 2014). Mohammad et al. (2013) and Kiritchenko et al. (2014a) came first in the SemEval-2013 Sentiment in Twitter and SemEval-2014 ABSA shared tasks. We use most of the features they proposed in our classifier. There are other subtasks in opinion mining related to stance classification, such as biased language detection (Recasens et al., 2013; Yano et al., 2010), perspective identification (Lin et al., 2006) and user classification based on their views (Kato et al., 2008). Perspective identification was defined as the subjective evaluation of points of view (Lin et al., 2006). None of the prior work has created a dataset annotated for both stance and sentiment.

7 Conclusions and Future Work

We presented the first dataset of tweets annotated for both stance towards given targets and sentiment. Partitions of the stance-annotated data created as part of this project were used as training and test sets in the SemEval-2016 shared task

'Task #6: Detecting Stance in Tweets' that received submissions from 19 teams. We proposed a simple, but effective stance detection system that obtained an F-score (70.32) higher than the one obtained by the more complex, best-performing system in the competition. We used a linear-kernel SVM classifier that leveraged word and character n-grams as well as sentiment features drawn from available sentiment lexicons and word-embedding features drawn from additional unlabeled data.

Finally, we conducted several experiments to tease out the interactions between the stance and sentiment. Notably, we showed that even though sentiment features are useful for stance detection, they alone are not sufficient. We also showed that even though humans are capable of detecting stance towards a given target from texts that express opinion towards a different target, automatic systems perform poorly on such data.

The features we used are not new to the community and not specifically tailored for stance detection. Nonetheless, they outperform those developed by the 19 teams that participated in the SemEval-2016 shared task on this dataset. This emphasizes the need for more research in exploring novel techniques specifically suited for detecting stance. Some avenues of future work include obtaining more sophisticated features such as those derived from dependency parse trees and automatically generated entity–entity relationship knowledge bases. Knowing that entity X is an adversary of entity Y can be useful in detecting stance towards Y from tweets that express opinion about X. One may also pursue more sophisticated classifiers, for example, deep architectures that jointly model stance, target of opinion, and sentiment. We are also interested in developing stance detection systems that do not require stance-labeled instances for the target of interest, but instead, can learn from existing stance-labeled instances for other targets in the same domain. We also want to model the ways in which stance is conveyed, and how the distribution of stance towards a target changes over time.

Acknowledgments

We thank Colin Cherry and Xiaodan Zhu for helpful discussions. The first author of this paper was supported by the Natural Sciences and Engineering Research Council of Canada under the CREATE program.

References

Pranav Anand, Marilyn Walker, Rob Abbott, Jean E. Fox Tree, Robeson Bowmani, and Michael Minor. 2011. Cats rule and dogs drool!: Classifying stance in online debate. In *Proceedings of the Workshop on Computational Approaches to Subjectivity and Sentiment Analysis*, pages 1–9.

Lingjia Deng and Janyce Wiebe. 2014. Sentiment propagation via implicature constraints. In *Proceedings of the Conference of the European Chapter of the Association for Computational Linguistics*, pages 377–385, Sweden.

Adam Faulkner. 2014. Automated classification of stance in student essays: An approach using stance target information and the Wikipedia link-based measure. In *Proceedings of the Flairs Conference*.

Kevin Gimpel, Nathan Schneider, Brendan O'Connor, Dipanjan Das, Daniel Mills, Jacob Eisenstein, Michael Heilman, Dani Yogatama, Jeffrey Flanigan, and Noah A. Smith. 2011. Part-of-speech tagging for Twitter: Annotation, features, and experiments. In *Proceedings of the Annual Meeting of the Association for Computational Linguistics*.

Kazi Saidul Hasan and Vincent Ng. 2013. Stance classification of ideological debates: Data, models, features, and constraints. In *Proceedings of the International Joint Conference on Natural Language Processing*, pages 1348–1356.

Minqing Hu and Bing Liu. 2004. Mining and summarizing customer reviews. In *Proceedings of the ACM SIGKDD International Conference on Knowledge Discovery and Data Mining*, pages 168–177.

Yoshikiyo Kato, Sadao Kurohashi, Kentaro Inui, Robert Malouf, and Tony Mullen. 2008. Taking sides: User classification for informal online political discourse. *Internet Research*, 18(2):177–190.

Svetlana Kiritchenko, Xiaodan Zhu, Colin Cherry, and Saif M. Mohammad. 2014a. NRC-Canada-2014: Detecting aspects and sentiment in customer reviews. In *Proceedings of the International Workshop on Semantic Evaluation*, Dublin, Ireland, August.

Svetlana Kiritchenko, Xiaodan Zhu, and Saif M. Mohammad. 2014b. Sentiment analysis of short informal texts. *Journal of Artificial Intelligence Research*, 50:723–762.

Wei-Hao Lin, Theresa Wilson, Janyce Wiebe, and Alexander Hauptmann. 2006. Which side are you on? Identifying perspectives at the document and sentence levels. In *Proceedings of the Conference on Computational Natural Language Learning*, pages 109–116.

Bing Liu and Lei Zhang. 2012. A survey of opinion mining and sentiment analysis. In Charu C. Aggarwal and ChengXiang Zhai, editors, *Mining Text Data*, pages 415–463. Springer.

Bing Liu. 2015. *Sentiment Analysis: Mining Opinions, Sentiments, and Emotions*. Cambridge University Press.

Tomas Mikolov, Ilya Sutskever, Kai Chen, Greg S. Corrado, and Jeff Dean. 2013. Distributed representations of words and phrases and their compositionality. In *Advances in Neural Information Processing Systems*, pages 3111–3119.

Saif M. Mohammad and Peter D. Turney. 2010. Emotions evoked by common words and phrases: Using Mechanical Turk to create an emotion lexicon. In *Proceedings of the Workshop on Computational Approaches to Analysis and Generation of Emotion in Text*, pages 26–34.

Saif M. Mohammad, Svetlana Kiritchenko, and Xiaodan Zhu. 2013. NRC-Canada: Building the state-of-the-art in sentiment analysis of tweets. In *Proceedings of the International Workshop on Semantic Evaluation*, Atlanta, Georgia, USA, June.

Saif M. Mohammad, Svetlana Kiritchenko, Parinaz Sobhani, Xiaodan Zhu, and Colin Cherry. 2016a. A dataset for detecting stance in tweets. In *Proceedings of the Language Resources and Evaluation Conference*, Portorož, Slovenia.

Saif M. Mohammad, Svetlana Kiritchenko, Parinaz Sobhani, Xiaodan Zhu, and Colin Cherry. 2016b. SemEval-2016 Task 6: Detecting stance in tweets. In *Proceedings of the International Workshop on Semantic Evaluation*, San Diego, California.

Saif M Mohammad. 2015. Sentiment analysis: Detecting valence, emotions, and other affectual states from text.

Akiko Murakami and Rudy Raymond. 2010. Support or oppose? Classifying positions in online debates from reply activities and opinion expressions. In *Proceedings of the International Conference on Computational Linguistics*, pages 869–875, Beijing, China.

Bo Pang and Lillian Lee. 2008. Opinion mining and sentiment analysis. *Foundations and Trends in Information Retrieval*, 2(1–2):1–135.

Fabian Pedregosa, Gaël Varoquaux, et al. 2011. Scikit-learn: Machine learning in Python. *Journal of Machine Learning Research*, 12:2825–2830.

Maria Pontiki, Dimitrios Galanis, John Pavlopoulos, Harris Papageorgiou, Ion Androutsopoulos, and Suresh Manandhar. 2014. SemEval-2014 Task 4: Aspect based sentiment analysis. In *Proceedings of the International Workshop on Semantic Evaluation*, Dublin, Ireland, August.

Maria Pontiki, Dimitrios Galanis, Haris Papageogiou, Suresh Manandhar, and Ion Androutsopoulos. 2015. SemEval-2015 Task 12: Aspect based sentiment analysis. In *Proceedings of the International Workshop on Semantic Evaluation*, Denver, Colorado.

Ashwin Rajadesingan and Huan Liu. 2014. Identifying users with opposing opinions in Twitter debates. In *Proceedings of the Conference on Social Computing, Behavioral-Cultural Modeling and Prediction*, pages 153–160. Washington, DC, USA.

Marta Recasens, Cristian Danescu-Niculescu-Mizil, and Dan Jurafsky. 2013. Linguistic models for analyzing and detecting biased language. In *Proceedings of the Annual Meeting of the Association for Computational Linguistics*, pages 1650–1659.

Sara Rosenthal, Preslav Nakov, Svetlana Kiritchenko, Saif M. Mohammad, Alan Ritter, and Veselin Stoyanov. 2015. SemEval-2015 Task 10: Sentiment analysis in Twitter. In *Proceedings of the International Workshop on Semantic Evaluations*.

Parinaz Sobhani, Diana Inkpen, and Stan Matwin. 2015. From argumentation mining to stance classification. In *Proceedings of the Workshop on Argumentation Mining*, pages 67–77, Denver, Colorado, USA.

Swapna Somasundaran and Janyce Wiebe. 2009. Recognizing stances in online debates. In *Proceedings of the Annual Meeting of the Association for Computational Linguistics*, pages 226–234, Suntec, Singapore.

Swapna Somasundaran and Janyce Wiebe. 2010. Recognizing stances in ideological on-line debates. In *Proceedings of the NAACL HLT 2010 Workshop CAAGET*, pages 116–124.

Duyu Tang, Furu Wei, Nan Yang, Ming Zhou, Ting Liu, and Bing Qin. 2014. Learning sentiment-specific word embedding for Twitter sentiment classification. In *Proceedings of the Annual Meeting of the Association for Computational Linguistics*, pages 1555–1565.

Matt Thomas, Bo Pang, and Lillian Lee. 2006. Get out the vote: Determining support or opposition from congressional floor-debate transcripts. In *Proceedings of the Conference on Empirical Methods in Natural Language Processing*, pages 327–335.

Joseph Turian, Lev Ratinov, and Yoshua Bengio. 2010. Word representations: a simple and general method for semi-supervised learning. In *Proceedings of the Annual Meeting of the Association for Computational Linguistics*, pages 384–394.

Marilyn A. Walker, Pranav Anand, Robert Abbott, and Ricky Grant. 2012. Stance classification using dialogic properties of persuasion. In *Proceedings of the Conference of the North American Chapter of the Association for Computational Linguistics: Human Language Technologies*, pages 592–596.

Theresa Wilson, Janyce Wiebe, and Paul Hoffmann. 2005. Recognizing contextual polarity in phrase-level sentiment analysis. In *Proceedings of the Conference on Human Language Technology and Empirical Methods in Natural Language Processing*, pages 347–354, Vancouver, British Columbia, Canada.

Theresa Wilson, Zornitsa Kozareva, Preslav Nakov, Sara Rosenthal, Veselin Stoyanov, and Alan Ritter. 2013. SemEval-2013 Task 2: Sentiment analysis in Twitter. In *Proceedings of the International Workshop on Semantic Evaluation*, Atlanta, USA, June.

Tae Yano, Philip Resnik, and Noah A Smith. 2010. Shedding (a thousand points of) light on biased language. In *Proceedings of the NAACL HLT 2010 Workshop on Creating Speech and Language Data with Amazon's Mechanical Turk*, pages 152–158.

A Study of Suggestions in Opinionated Texts and their Automatic Detection

Sapna Negi[1]   **Kartik Asooja**[1]   **Shubham Mehrotra**[1,2]   **Paul Buitelaar**[1]

[1] Insight Centre for Data Analytics, National University of Ireland, Galway
`firstname.lastname@insight-centre.org`

[2] Indian Institute of Information Technology Allahabad, India
`shubhammehrotra94@gmail.com`

Abstract

We study the automatic detection of suggestion expressing text among the opinionated text. The examples of such suggestions in online reviews would be, customer suggestions about improvement in a commercial entity, and advice to the fellow customers. We present a qualitative and quantitative analysis of suggestions present in the text samples obtained from social media platforms. Suggestion mining from social media is an emerging research area, and thus problem definition and datasets are still evolving; this work also contributes towards the same. The problem has been formulated as a sentence classification task, and we compare the results of some popular supervised learning approaches in this direction. We also evaluate different kinds of features with these classifiers. The experiments indicate that deep learning based approaches tend to be promising for this task.

1   Introduction

Online text is becoming an increasingly popular source for acquiring public opinions towards entities like persons, products, services, brands, events, etc. The area of opinion mining focuses on exploiting this abundance of opinions, by mainly performing sentiment based summarisation of text into *positive, negative, and neutral* categories, using sentiment analysis methods. In addition to the online reviews and blogs, people are increasingly resorting to social networks like Twitter, Facebook etc. to instantly express their sentiments and opinions about the products and services they might be experiencing at a given time.

On a closer look, it is noticeable that opinionated text also contains information other than sentiments. This can be validated from the presence of large portions of *neutral* or *objective* or *non-relevant* labelled text in state of the art sentiment analysis datasets. One such information type is suggestions. Table 1 shows the instances of suggestions in sentiment analysis datasets which were built on online reviews. These suggestions may or may not carry positive or negative sentiments towards the reviewed entity. In the recent past, suggestions have gained the attention of the research community, mainly for industrial research, which led to the studies focussing on suggestion detection in reviews (Ramanand et al., 2010; Brun and Hagege, 2013).

The setting up of dedicated suggestion collection forums by brand owners, shows the importance of suggestions for the stakeholders. Therefore, it would be useful if suggestions can be automatically extracted from the large amount of already available opinions. In the cases of certain entities where suggestion collection platforms [1] are already available and active, suggestion mining can be used for summarisation of posts. Often, people tend to provide the context in such posts, which gets repetitive in the case of large number of posts, suggestion mining methods can extract the exact sentence in the post where a suggestion is expressed.

This task has so far been presented as a binary classification of sentences, where the available opinionated text about a certain entity is split into sentences and these sentences are then classified as suggestions or non-suggestions. The previous studies were carried out in a limited scope, mainly for specific domains like reviews, focusing on one use case at a time. The path to the leaf

---

[1] https://feedly.uservoice.com/forums/192636-suggestions/category/64071-mobile

*Proceedings of the Fifth Joint Conference on Lexical and Computational Semantics (*SEM 2016)*, pages 170–178,
Berlin, Germany, August 11-12, 2016.

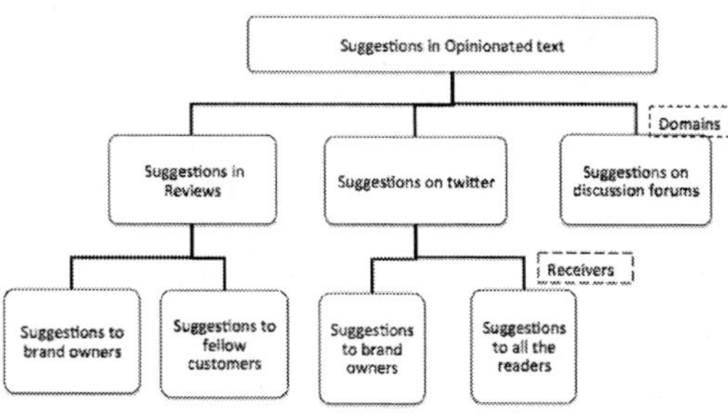

Figure 1: Problem scopes in suggestion detection

nodes in Figure 1 summarises the scope of suggestion mining studies so far. These studies developed datasets for individual tasks and domains, and trained and evaluated classifier models on the same datasets.

We analyse manually labelled datasets from different domains, including the existing datasets, and the datasets prepared by us. The ratio of suggestion and non-suggestion sentences vary across domains, where the datasets from some domains are too sparse for training statistical classifiers. We also introduce two datasets which are relatively richer in suggestions. In Table 1 we report similar linguistic nature of suggestions across these datasets, which presses for domain independent approaches. Therefore, as a deviation from previous studies, this work investigates the generalisation of the problem of suggestion detection i.e. the detection of all suggestions under the root node in Figure 1.

In this work, we compare different methods of suggestion mining using all available datasets. These include manually crafted rules, Support Vector Machines (SVM) with proposed linguistic features, Long Short Term Memory (LSTM) Neural Networks, and Convolutional Neural Networks (CNN). We also compare the results from these approaches with the previous works whose datasets are available. We also perform cross-domain train test experiments. With most of the datasets, Neural Networks (NNs) outperform SVM with the proposed features. However, the overall results for out of domain training remain low. We also compare two different types of word embeddings to be used with the NNs for this task.

2 Problem Definition and Scope

As stated previously, the task of suggestion detection has been framed as binary classification of sentences into *suggestion* (positive class) and *non-suggestion* (negative class).

We previously provided a fine grained problem definition (Negi and Buitelaar, 2015) in order to prepare benchmark datasets and ensure consistency in future task definitions. We identified three parameters which define a suggestion in the context of opinion mining: receiver of suggestion, textual unit of suggestion, and the type of suggestion in terms of its explicit or implicit nature.

While the unit of suggestion still remains as sentence in this work, and the type as explicit expression, we aim for the evaluation of different classifier models for the detection of any suggestion from any opinionated text. The motivation lies in our observation that explicitly expressed suggestions appear in similar linguistic forms irrespective of domain, target entity, and the intended receiver (Table 1). Furthermore, datasets used by the previous studies indicate that aiming the detection of specific suggestions restricts the annotations to suggestions of a specific type, which in turn aggravates class imbalance problem in the datasets (Table 2). It also renders these datasets unsuitable for a generic suggestion detection task, since the negative instances may also comprise of suggestions, but not of the desired type.

3 Related Work

In the recent years, experiments have been performed to automatically detect sentences which contain suggestions. Targeted suggestions were mainly the ones which suggest improvements in a commercial entity. Therefore, online reviews remains the main focus, however, there are a limited number of works focussing on other domains too.

Suggestions for product improvement: Studies like Ramanand et al. (2010) and Brun et al. (2013) employed manually crafted linguistic rules to identify suggestions for product improvement. The evaluation was performed on a small dataset (∼60 reviews). Dong et al. (2013) performed classification of given tweets about Microsoft Windows' phone as suggestions for improvement or not. They compared SVM and Factorisation Machines (FM) based classifiers. For features,

Source, Entity/Topic	Sentence	Sentiment Label	Intended Receiver	Linguistic Properties
Reviews, Electronics	I would recommend doing the upgrade to be sure you have the best chance at trouble free operation.	Neutral	Customer	Subjunctive, Imperative, lexical clue: *recommend*
Reviews, Electronics	My one recommendation to creative is to get some marketing people to work on the names of these things	Neutral	Brand owner	Imperative, lexical clue: *recommendation*
Reviews, Hotels	Be sure to specify a room at the back of the hotel.	Neutral	Customer	Imperative
Reviews, Hotel	The point is, don't advertise the service if there are caveats that go with it.	Negative	Brand Owner	Imperative
Tweets, Windows Phone	Dear Microsoft, release a new zune with your wp7 launch on the 11th. It would be smart	Neutral	Brand owner	Imperative, subjunctive
Discussion thread, Travel	If you do book your own airfare, be sure you don't have problems if Insight has to cancel the tour or reschedule it	Neutral	Thread participants	Conditional, imperative
Tweets, open topics	Again I'm reminded of some of the best advice I've ever received: thank you notes. Always start with the thank you notes.	NA	General public	Imperative, Lexical clue: *advice*
Suggestion forum, Software	Please provide consistency throughout the entire Microsoft development ecosystem!	NA	Brand owner	Imperative, lexical clue: *please*

Table 1: Examples of suggestions from different domains, about different entities and topics, and intended for different receivers. Sentiment labels are the sentiment towards a reviewed entity, if any.

they used certain hash tags and mined frequently appearing word based patterns from a separate dataset of suggestions about Microsoft phones.

Suggestions for fellow customers: In one of our previous works(Negi and Buitelaar, 2015), we focussed on the detection of those suggestions in reviews which are meant for the fellow customers. An example of such suggestion in a hotel review is, *If you do end up here, be sure to specify a room at the back of the hotel.* We used SVM classifier with a set of linguistically motivated features. We also stressed upon the highly subjective nature of suggestion labelling task, and thus performed a study of a formal definition of suggestions in the context of suggestion mining. We also formulated annotation guidelines, and prepared a dataset for the same.

Advice Mining from discussion threads: Wicaksono et al. (2013) detected advice containing sentences from travel related discussion threads. They compared sequential classifiers based on Hidden Markov Model (HMM) and Conditional Random Fields (CRF), considering each thread as a sequence of sentences labelled as advice and non-advice. They also some features which were dependent on the position of a sentence in its thread. This approach was therefore specific to the domain of discussion threads. Their annotations seem to consider implicit expressions of advice as *advice.*

Text Classification using deep learning: Recently NNs are being effectively used for text classification tasks, like sentiment classification and semantic categorisation. LSTM (Graves, 2012), and CNN (Kim, 2014a) are the two most popular neural network architectures in this regard.

Tweet classification using deep learning: To the best of our knowledge, deep learning has only been employed for sentiment based classification of tweets. CNN (Severyn and Moschitti, 2015) and LSTM (Wang et al., 2015) have demonstrated good performance in this regard.

4 Datasets

The required datasets for this task are a set of sentences obtained from opinionated texts, which are labelled as *suggestion* and *non-suggestion*, where suggestions are explicitly expressed.

Existing Datasets: Datasets from most of the previous studies on suggestions for product improvement are unavailable due to their industrial ownership. The currently available datasets are:

1) Twitter dataset about Windows phone: This dataset comprises of tweets which are addressed to Microsoft. The tweets which expressed suggestions for product improvement are labelled as suggestions (Dong et al., 2013). Due to the

short nature of tweets, suggestion detection is performed on the tweet level, rather than the sentence level. The authors indicated that they have labeled the explicit expressions of suggestions in the dataset.

2) Electronics and hotel reviews: A review dataset, where only those sentences which convey suggestions to the fellow customers are considered as suggestions (Negi and Buitelaar, 2015).

3) Travel advice dataset: Obtained from travel related discussion forums. All the advice containing sentences are tagged as *advice* (Wicaksono and Myaeng, 2013). One problem with this dataset is that the statements of facts (*implicit suggestions*) are also tagged as advice, for example, *The temperature may reach upto 40 degrees in summer.*

Introduced Datasets: In this work, we identify additional sources for suggestion datasets, and prepare labelled datasets with larger number of explicitly expressed suggestions.

1) Suggestion forum: Posts from a customer support platform[2] which also hosts dedicated suggestion forums for products. Though most of the forums for commercial products are closed access, we discovered two forums which are openly accessible: Feedly mobile app[3], and Windows app studio[4]. We collected samples of posts for these two products. Posts were then split into sentences using the sentence splitter from Stanford CoreNLP toolkit (Manning et al., 2014). Two annotators were asked to label 1000 sentences, on which the inter-annotator agreement (kappa) of 0.81 was obtained. Rest of the dataset was annotated by only one annotator. Due to the annotation costs, we limited the size of data sample, however this dataset is easily extendible due to the availability of much larger number of posts on these forums.

2) We also prepared a tweet dataset where tweets are a mixture of random topics, and not specific to any given entity or topic. These tweets were collected using the hashtags *suggestion, advice, recommendation, warning*, which increased the chance of appearance of suggestions in this dataset. Due to the noisy nature of tweets, two annotators performed annotation on all the tweets.

The inter-annotator agreement was calculated as 0.72. Only those tweets were retained for which the annotators agreed on the label.

3) We also re-tagged the travel advice dataset from Wicaksono et al. (2013) where only those suggestions which were explicitly expressed were retained as suggestions.

Table 2 details all the available datasets including the ones we are introducing in this work. The introduced datasets contain higher percentage of suggestions. We therefore train models on the introduced datasets, and evaluate them on the existing datasets.

Dataset	Suggestion Type	Suggestions/ Total Instances
Existing Datasets		
Electronics Reviews, (Negi and Buitelaar, 2015)	Only for customers, explicitly expressed	324/3782
Hotel Reviews, (Negi and Buitelaar, 2015)	Only for customers, explicitly expressed	448/7534
Tweets Microsoft phone, (Dong et al., 2013)	Only for brand owners, explicitly expressed	238/3000
Travel advice 1, (Wicaksono and Myaeng, 2013)	Any suggestion, explicitly or implicitly expressed	2192/5199
Introduced Datasets		
Travel advice 2 (Re-labeled Travel advice 1)	Any suggestion, explicitly expressed	1314/5183
Suggestion forum[5]	Any suggestion, explicitly expressed	1428/5724
Tweets with hashtags: *suggestion, advice, recommendation, warning*	Any suggestion, explicitly expressed	1126/4099

Table 2: Available suggestion detection datasets

5 Automatic Detection of Suggestions

Some of the conventional text classification approaches have been previously studied for this task, primarily, rules and SVM classifiers. Each approach was only evaluated on the datasets prepared within the individual works. We employ these two approaches on all the available datasets for all kinds of suggestion detection task. We then perform a study of the employability of LSTM and CNN for this kind of text classification task. We evaluate all the statistical classifiers in both domain dependent and independent training. The results demonstrate that deep learning methods have an advantage over the conventional approaches for this task.

5.1 Rule based classification

This approach uses a set of manually formulated rules aggregated from the previous rule based experiments (Ramanand et al., 2010; Goldberg et al., 2009). These rules exclude the rules provided by Brun et al. (2013), because of their dependency on in-house (publicly unavailable) components from Brun et al. (2013). Only those rules have been used which do not depend on any domain specific vocabulary. A given text is labeled as a suggestion, if at least one of the rules is true.

1. Modal verbs (MD) followed by a base form of verb (VB), followed by an adjective.
2. At-least one clause starts with a present tense of verb (VB, VBZ, VBP). This is a naive method for detecting imperative sentences. Clauses are identified using the parse trees; the sub-trees under S and SBAR are considered as clauses.
3. Presence of any of the suggestion keywords/phrases *suggest, recommend, hopefully, go for, request, it would be nice, adding, should come with, should be able, could come with, i need, we need, needs, would like to, would love to.*
4. Presence of templates for suggestions expressed in the form of wishes [*would like *(if), I wish, I hope, I want, hopefully, if only, would be better if, *(should)*, would that, can't believe .*(didn't).*, (don't believe).*(didn't), (do want), I can has*].

The part of speech tagging and parsing is performed using Stanford parser (Manning et al., 2014). Table 3 shows the results of rule based classification for the positive class i.e. suggestion class. With the available datasets, detection of negative instances is always significantly better than the positive ones, due to class imbalance.

5.2 Statistical classifiers

SVM was used in almost all the related work either as a proposed classifier with some feature engineering, or for comparison with other classifiers.

Support Vector Machines: SVM classifiers are popularly used for text classification in the research community. We perform the evaluation of a classifier using SVM with the standard n-gram

Dataset	Prec.	Rec.	F1
Electronics Reviews	0.229	0.660	0.340
Hotel Reviews	0.196	0.517	0.285
Travel discussion 2	0.312	0.378	0.342
Microsoft Tweets	0.207	0.756	0.325
New Tweets	0.200	0.398	0.266
Suggestion Forum	0.461	0.879	0.605

Table 3: Results of Suggestion Detection using rule based classifier. Reported metrics are only for the suggestion class.

features (uni, bi-grams) and the features proposed in our previous work (Negi and Buitelaar, 2015). These features are sequential POS patterns for imperative mood, sentence sentiment score obtained using SentiWordNet, and information about *nsubj* dependency present in the sentence. We use LibSVM[6] implementation with the parameters specified previously in Negi and Buitelaar (2015). No oversampling is used, instead class weighting is applied by using class weight ratio depending upon the class distribution of the negative and positive class respectively in the training dataset.

Deep Learning based classifiers: Recent findings about the impressive performance of deep learning based models for some of the natural language processing tasks calls for similar experiments in suggestion mining. We therefore present the first set of deep learning based experiments for the same. We experiment with two kinds of neural network architectures: LSTM and CNN. LSTM effectively captures sequential information in text, while retaining the long term dependencies. In a standard LSTM model for text classification, text can be fed to the input layer as a sequence of words, one word at a time. Figure 2 shows the architecture of LSTM neural networks for binary text classification.

On the other hand, CNN is known to effectively capture local co-relations of spatial or temporal structures, therefore a general intuition is that CNN might capture well the good n-gram features at different positions in a sentence.

5.3 Features

Features for SVM: The feature evaluation of (Negi and Buitelaar, 2015) indicated that POS tags, certain keywords (lexical clues), POS

---

[6]https://www.csie.ntu.edu.tw/ cjlin/libsvm/

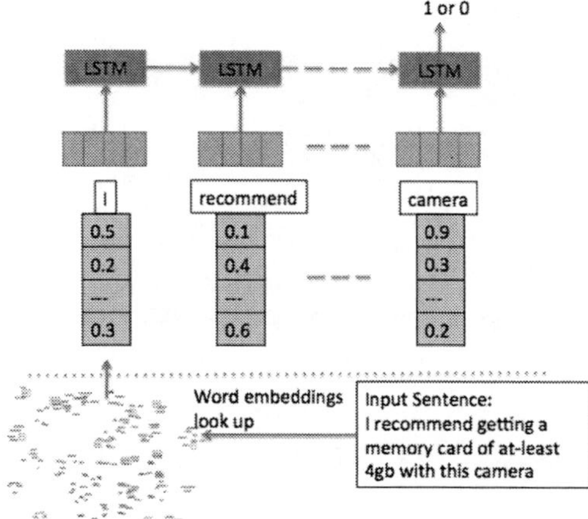

Figure 2: Architecture for using LSTM as a binary text classifier

patterns for imperative mood, and certain dependency information about the subject, can be useful features for the detection of suggestions. In the previous works, the feature types were manually determined. We now aim to eliminate the need of manual determination of feature types. A recently popular approach of doing this is to use neural networks with *word embeddings* (Bengio et al., 2003) based feature vectors, instead of using classic count-based feature vectors.

Word embeddings for Neural Networks: In simpler terms, word embeddings are automatically learnt vector representations for lexical units. Baroni et al. (2014) compared the word embeddings obtained through different methods, by using them for different semantic tasks. Based on those comparisons, we use a pre-trained COMPOSES[7] embeddings, which were developed by Baroni et al. (2014). These embeddings/word vectors are of size 400. For experiments on twitter datasets, we used Glove (Pennington et al., 2014) based word embeddings learnt on Twitter data[8], which comprises of 200 dimensions.

We additionally experiment with dependency based word embeddings (Deps)[9] (Levy and Goldberg, 2014). These embeddings determine

---

[7]Best predict vectors on http://clic.cimec.unitn.it/composes/semantic-vectors.html

[8]http://nlp.stanford.edu/projects/glove/

[9]Dependency-Based on https://levyomer.wordpress.com/2014/04/25/dependency-based-word-embeddings/

the context of a word on the basis of linguistic dependencies, instead of window based context used by COMPOSES. Therefore, Deps tends to perform better in determining the functional similarity between words, as compared to COMPOSES.

Additional feature for NNs: For neural network based classifiers, we also experimented with POS tags as an additional feature with the pre-trained word embeddings. This tends to decrease the precision and increase the recall, but results in an overall decrease of F-1 score in most of the runs. Therefore, we do not report the results of these experiments.

5.4 Configurations

NN Configuration: Considering the class imbalance in the datasets, we employ oversampling of the minority class (positive) to adjust the class distribution of training data. While performing cross validation, we perform oversampling on training data for each fold separately after cross-validating.

LSTM: For LSTM based classification, we use 2 hidden layers of 100 and 50 neurons respectively, and 1 softmax output layer. We also utilize L2 regularization to counter overfitting. For LSTMs, we use the softsign activation function.

CNN: We used a filter window of 2 with 40 feature maps in CNN, thus giving 40 bigram based filters (Kim, 2014b). A subsampling layer with max pooling is used.

In-Domain and Cross-Domain Evaluation: In the case of statistical classifiers, we perform the experiments in two sets. The first set of experiments (Table 4, 6) evaluate a classifier (and feature types) for the cases where labeled data is available for a specific domain, entity, or receiver specific suggestions. In this case, evaluation is performed using a 10 fold cross validation with SVM and 5 fold with NN classifiers. The second set of experiments evaluate the classifiers (and feature types) for a generic suggestion detection task, where the model can be trained on any of the available datasets. These experiments evaluate the classifier algorithms, as well as the training datasets. In the case of twitter, training is performed on twitter dataset, while evaluation for this cross-domain setting is performed on the Microsoft tweet dataset.

Data	Precision			Recall			F1 score		
	SVM	LSTM	CNN	SVM	LSTM	CNN	SVM	LSTM	CNN
Hotel	**0.580**	0.576	0.505	0.512	**0.717**	0.703	0.543	**0.639**	0.578
Electronics	0.645	**0.663**	0.561	0.621	**0.681**	0.671	0.640	**0.672**	0.612
Travel advice 2	0.458	**0.609**	0.555	**0.732**	0.630	0.621	0.566	**0.617**	0.586
Microsoft Tweets	0.468	**0.591**	0.309	**0.903**	0.514	0.766	**0.616**	0.550	0.441
New tweets	**0.693**	0.619	0.590	0.580	0.674	**0.752**	0.632	0.645	**0.661**
Suggestion forum	0.661	**0.738**	0.665	0.760	0.716	**0.772**	0.712	**0.727**	0.713

Table 4: In-domain training: Performance of SVM (10 fold), LSTM, and CNN (5 fold) using cross validation on the available datasets. The listed results are for the suggestion class only. SVM uses features from Negi and Buitelaar (2015), and neural networks use pre-trained word embeddings (COMPOSES for normal text and Twitter Glove for tweets).

Dataset	Related work	F1 type	F1 (Related Work)	SVM	LSTM	CNN
Travel Advice 1	(Wicaksono and Myaeng, 2013)	Weighted F-1 score for both classes	0.756	0.680	**0.762**	0.692
Microsoft tweets	(Dong et al., 2013)	F-1 score for suggestions only	**0.694**	0.616	0.550	0.441

Table 5: Comparison of the performance of SVM (Negi and Buitelaar, 2015), LSTM and CNN with the best results reported in two of the related works whose datasets are available. 5 fold cross validation was used. The related works used different kinds of F1 scores.

Dataset	LSTM		CNN	
	COMP.	Deps	COMP.	Deps
Hotel	**0.638**	0.607	**0.578**	0.550
Electronics	**0.672**	0.608	**0.611**	0.556
Travel advice 2	0.617	**0.625**	**0.586**	0.564
Sugg Forum	**0.752**	0.732	**0.714**	0.695

Table 6: F-1 score for the suggestion class, using *COMPOSES* and *Deps* embeddings with LSTM and CNN. 5 fold cross validation.

Pre-processing: We also compared experiments on tweets with pre-processing, and without pre-processing the tweets. The pre-processing involved removing URLs and hashtags, and normalisation of punctuation repetition. Pre-processing tends to decrease the performance in all the experiments. Therefore, none of the experiments reported by us use pre-processing on tweets.

6 Results and Discussions

Tables 4, 7 show the Precision, Recall and F-1 score for the suggestion class (positive class). In general, rule based classifier shows a higher recall, but very low precision, leading to very low F-1 scores as compared to statistical classifiers, where LSTM emerges as a winner in majority of the runs. Below we summarise different observations from the results.

Embeddings: COMPOSES embeddings prove to be a clear winner in our experiments. Deps outperform COMPOSES in only 3 cases out of all the experiments reported in Tables 6, 8. It was observed that using Deps always resulted in higher recall, however F-1 scores dropped due to a simultaneous drop in precision. Also, Deps embeddings tend to perform better with LSTM, as compared to CNN.

Comparison with Related Work: Table 5 compares the results from those works whose datasets are available. It shows that LSTM outperforms the best results from Wicaksono et al. by a small margin, provided that they used features which are only valid for dicussion threads, while the LSTM uses generic features (embeddings). The table also shows a comparison of other approaches with the factorization machine based approach adopted by Dong et al. (2013) for classifying Microsoft tweets, which provides a much higher F-1 score. This can be attributed to the use of fine tuning (oversampling, thresholding) for the class imbalance problem. Dong et al. also report results using FM and SVM which do not use fine tuning; those results are in line with our SVM and LSTM results. Additionally, they also use hashtags and suggestion templates extracted from an unavailable dataset of suggestions for Microsoft phones.

Train/Test	Precision			Recall			F-1 score		
	SVM	LSTM	CNN	SVM	LSTM	CNN	SVM	LSTM	CNN
Sugg-Forum/Hotel	0.327	**0.425**	0.348	0.156	**0.482**	0.379	0.211	**0.452**	0.363
Sugg-Forum/Electronics	0.109	**0.500**	0.376	0.519	0.532	0.411	0.180	**0.516**	0.393
Sugg-Forum/Travel advice	0.386	**0.52**	0.395	0.212	0.235	**0.531**	0.273	0.323	**0.453**
Travel advice/Hotel	0.147	**0.244**	0.206	0.616	0.616	0.582	0.238	**0.349**	0.304
New Tweets/Microsoft Tweets	0.112	**0.189**	0.164	0.122	0.351	**0.458**	0.117	**0.246**	0.241

Table 7: Cross-domain evaluation: Performance of SVM, LSTM, CNN when trained on new suggestion rich datasets and tested on the existing suggestion datasets. The listed results are for the positive (suggestion) class only.

Train/Test	LSTM		CNN	
	COMP	Deps	COMP	Deps
Sugg-Forum/Hotel	**0.450**	0.38	0.363	**0.367**
Sugg-Forum/Electronics	**0.510**	0.470	**0.393**	0.384
Sugg-Forum/Travel Advice	0.323	**0.340**	**0.453**	0.330
Travel advice/Hotel	0.316	**0.349**	**0.304**	0.292

Table 8: Evaluation of *COMPOSES* and *Dependency* embeddings with LSTM and CNN in a cross domain train-test setting.

SVM versus NNs: In most cases, the neural network based classifiers outperformed SVM, see tables 4, 7. Although SVM in combination with feature engineering and parameter tuning, proves to be a competent alternative, specially with the more balanced new datasets. The newly introduced datasets (suggestions about Feedly app and Windows platform) produce better results than the existing sparse datasets for the in-domain evaluation, see table 4. This can be again attributed to the better class representation in this dataset.

Text type: The results of tweet datasets in general show much lower classification accuracy than the datasets of standard texts for cross domain training, see table 7. In the case of in-domain evaluation for the Microsoft tweet dataset, SVM performs better than neural networks, and vice versa in the case of the new tweet dataset, see table 4.

7 Conclusion and Future Work

In this work, we presented an insight into the problem of suggestion detection, which extracts different kinds of suggestions from opinionated text. We point to new sources of suggestion rich datasets, and provide two additional datasets which contain larger number of suggestions as compared to the previous datasets. We compare various approaches for suggestion detection, including the ones used in the previous works, as well as the deep learning approaches for sentence classification which have not yet been applied to this problem.

Since suggestions tend to exhibit similar linguistic nature, irrespective of topics and intended receiver of the suggestions, there is a scope of learning domain independent models for this task. Therefore, we apply the discussed approaches both in a domain dependent, and domain independent setting, in order to evaluate the domain independence of the proposed models.

Neural networks in general performed better, in both in-domain and cross-domain evaluation. The initial results for domain independent training are poor. In light of the findings from this work, domain transfer approaches would be an interesting direction for future works in this problem.

The results also point out the challenges and complexity of the task. Preparing datasets where suggestions are labeled at a phrase or clause level might reduce the complexities arising due to long sentences.

Acknowledgement

This work has been funded by the European Unions Horizon 2020 programme under grant agreement No 644632 MixedEmotions, and the Science Foundation Ireland under Grant Number SFI/12/RC/2289 (Insight Center).

References

[Baroni et al.2014] Marco Baroni, Georgiana Dinu, and Germán Kruszewski. 2014. Don't count, predict! a systematic comparison of context-counting vs. context-predicting semantic vectors. In *Proceedings of the 52nd Annual Meeting of the Association for Computational Linguistics (Volume 1: Long Papers)*, pages 238–247, Baltimore, Maryland, June. Association for Computational Linguistics.

[Bengio et al.2003] Yoshua Bengio, Réjean Ducharme, Pascal Vincent, and Christian Janvin. 2003. A neural probabilistic language model. *J. Mach. Learn. Res.*, 3:1137–1155, March.

[Brun and Hagege2013] C. Brun and C. Hagege. 2013. Suggestion mining: Detecting suggestions for improvements in users comments. In *Proceedings of 14th International Conference on Intelligent Text Processing and Computational Linguistics*.

[Dong et al.2013] Li Dong, Furu Wei, Yajuan Duan, Xiaohua Liu, Ming Zhou, and Ke Xu. 2013. The automated acquisition of suggestions from tweets. In Marie desJardins and Michael L. Littman, editors, *AAAI*. AAAI Press.

[Goldberg et al.2009] Andrew B. Goldberg, Nathanael Fillmore, David Andrzejewski, Zhiting Xu, Bryan Gibson, and Xiaojin Zhu. 2009. May all your wishes come true: A study of wishes and how to recognize them. In *Proceedings of Human Language Technologies: The 2009 Annual Conference of the North American Chapter of the Association for Computational Linguistics*, NAACL '09, pages 263–271, Stroudsburg, PA, USA. Association for Computational Linguistics.

[Graves2012] Alex Graves. 2012. Supervised sequence labelling. In *Supervised Sequence Labelling with Recurrent Neural Networks*, pages 5–13. Springer Berlin Heidelberg.

[Kim2014a] Yoon Kim. 2014a. Convolutional neural networks for sentence classification. *arXiv preprint arXiv:1408.5882*.

[Kim2014b] Yoon Kim. 2014b. Convolutional neural networks for sentence classification. In *Proceedings of the 2014 Conference on Empirical Methods in Natural Language Processing (EMNLP)*, pages 1746–1751, Doha, Qatar, October. Association for Computational Linguistics.

[Levy and Goldberg2014] Omer Levy and Yoav Goldberg. 2014. Dependency-based word embeddings. In *ACL*.

[Manning et al.2014] Christopher D. Manning, Mihai Surdeanu, John Bauer, Jenny Finkel, Steven J. Bethard, and David McClosky. 2014. The Stanford CoreNLP natural language processing toolkit. In *Association for Computational Linguistics (ACL) System Demonstrations*, pages 55–60.

[Negi and Buitelaar2015] Sapna Negi and Paul Buitelaar. 2015. Towards the extraction of customer-to-customer suggestions from reviews. In *Proceedings of the 2015 Conference on Empirical Methods in Natural Language Processing*, pages 2159–2167, Lisbon, Portugal, September. Association for Computational Linguistics.

[Pennington et al.2014] Jeffrey Pennington, Richard Socher, and Christopher D. Manning. 2014. Glove: Global vectors for word representation. In *Empirical Methods in Natural Language Processing (EMNLP)*, pages 1532–1543.

[Ramanand et al.2010] J Ramanand, Krishna Bhavsar, and Niranjan Pedanekar. 2010. Wishful thinking - finding suggestions and 'buy' wishes from product reviews. In *Proceedings of the NAACL HLT 2010 Workshop on Computational Approaches to Analysis and Generation of Emotion in Text*, pages 54–61, Los Angeles, CA, June. Association for Computational Linguistics.

[Severyn and Moschitti2015] Aliaksei Severyn and Alessandro Moschitti. 2015. Unitn: Training deep convolutional neural network for twitter sentiment classification. In *Proceedings of the 9th International Workshop on Semantic Evaluation (SemEval 2015)*, pages 464–469, Denver, Colorado, June. Association for Computational Linguistics.

[Wang et al.2015] Xin Wang, Yuanchao Liu, Chengjie SUN, Baoxun Wang, and Xiaolong Wang. 2015. Predicting polarities of tweets by composing word embeddings with long short-term memory. In *Proceedings of the 53rd Annual Meeting of the Association for Computational Linguistics and the 7th International Joint Conference on Natural Language Processing (Volume 1: Long Papers)*, pages 1343–1353, Beijing, China, July. Association for Computational Linguistics.

[Wicaksono and Myaeng2013] Alfan Farizki Wicaksono and Sung-Hyon Myaeng. 2013. Automatic extraction of advice-revealing sentences foradvice mining from online forums. In *K-CAP*, pages 97–104. ACM.

You and me... in a vector space:
modelling individual speakers with distributional semantics

Aurélie Herbelot
Centre for Mind/Brain Sciences
University of Trento
`aurelie.herbelot@unitn.it`

Behrang QasemiZadeh
DFG Collaborative Research Centre 991
Heinrich-Heine-Universität Düsseldorf
`zadeh@phil.hhu.de`

Abstract

The linguistic experiences of a person are an important part of their individuality. In this paper, we show that people can be modelled as vectors in a semantic space, using their personal interaction with specific language data. We also demonstrate that these vectors can be taken as representative of 'the kind of person' they are. We build over 4000 speaker-dependent subcorpora using logs of Wikipedia edits, which are then used to build distributional vectors that represent individual speakers. We show that such 'person vectors' are informative to others, and they influence basic patterns of communication like the choice of one's interlocutor in conversation. Tested on an information-seeking scenario, where natural language questions must be answered by addressing the most relevant individuals in a community, our system outperforms a standard information retrieval algorithm by a considerable margin.

1 Introduction

Distributional Semantics (DS) (Turney and Pantel, 2010; Clark, 2012; Erk, 2012) is an approach to computational semantics which has historical roots in the philosophical work of Wittgenstein, and in particular in the claim that 'meaning is use', i.e. words acquire a semantics which is a function of the contexts in which they are used (Wittgenstein, 1953). The technique has been used in psycholinguistics to model various phenomena, from priming to similarity judgements (Lund and Burgess, 1996), and even aspects of language acquisition (Landauer and Dumais, 1997; Kwiatkowski et al., 2012). The general idea is that an individual speaker develops the verbal side of his or her conceptual apparatus from the linguistic experiences he or she is exposed to, together with the perceptual situations surrounding those experiences.

One natural consequence of the distributional claim is that meaning is both speaker-dependent and community-bound. On the one hand, depending on *who* they are, speakers will be exposed to different linguistic and perceptual experiences, and by extension develop separate vocabularies and conceptual representations. For instance, a chef and a fisherman may have different representations of the word *fish* (Wierzbicka, 1984). On the other hand, the vocabularies and conceptual representations of individual people should be close enough that they can successfully communicate: this is ensured by the fact that many linguistic utterances are shared amongst a community.

There is a counterpart to the claim that 'language is speaker-dependent': speakers are language-dependent. That is, the type of person someone is can be correlated with their linguistic experience. For instance, the fact that *fish* and *boil* are often seen in the linguistic environment of an individual may indicate that this individual has much to do with cooking (contrast with high co-occurrences of *fish* and *net*). In some contexts, linguistic data might even be the only source of information we have about a person: in an academic context, we often infer from the papers a person has written and cited which kind of expertise they might have.

This paper offers a model of individuals based on (a subset of) their linguistic experience. That is, we model how, by being associated with particular types of language data, people develop a uniqueness representable as a vector in a semantic space. Further, we evaluate those 'person vectors' along one particular dimension: the type of knowledge

*Proceedings of the Fifth Joint Conference on Lexical and Computational Semantics (*SEM 2016)*, pages 179–188,
Berlin, Germany, August 11-12, 2016.

we expect them to hold.

The rest of this paper is structured as follows. We first give a short introduction to the topic of modelling linguistic individuality (§2) and we discuss how DS is a suitable tool to represent the associated characteristics for a given person (§3). We describe a model of individuals in a community using 'person vectors' (§4). We then highlight the challenges associated with evaluating such vectors, and propose a prediction task which has for goal to identify someone with a particular expertise, given a certain information need (§5, §6). Concretely, we model a community of over 4000 individuals from their linguistic interaction with Wikipedia (§7). We finally evaluate our model on the suggested task and compare results against a standard information retrieval algorithm.

2   Individuality and how it is seen

A speaker's linguistic experience—what they read, write, say and hear—is individual in all the ways language can be described, from syntax to pragmatics, including stylistics and register. One area of work where linguistic individuality has been extensively studied is author profiling and identification (Zheng et al., 2006; Stamatatos, 2009). It has been shown, in particular, how subtle syntactic and stylistic features (including metalinguistic features such as sentence length) can be a unique signature of a person. This research, often conducted from the point of view of forensic linguistics, has person identification as its main goal and does not delve much into semantics, for the simple reason that the previously mentioned syntactic and structural clues often perform better in evaluation (Baayen et al., 1996).

This paper questions in which way the semantic aspects of someone's linguistic experience contributes to their individuality. One aspect that comes to mind is variations in word usage (as mentioned in the introduction). Unfortunately, this aspect of the problem is also the most difficult to approach computationally, for sheer lack of data: we highlight in §5 some of the reasons why obtaining (enough) speaker-specific language data remains a technical and privacy minefield. Another aspect, which is perhaps more straightforwardly modellable, is the extent to which the type of linguistic material someone is exposed to broadly correlates with *who they are*. It is likely, for instance, that the authors of this paper write and read a lot about linguistics, and this correlates with broad features of theirs, e.g. they are computational linguists and are interested in language. So, as particular stylistic features can predict *who* a person is, a specific semantic experience might give an insight into *what kind* of person they are.

In what follows, we describe how, by selecting a *public subset* of a person's linguistic environment, we can build a representation of that person which encapsulates and summarises a part of their individuality. The term 'public subset' is important here, as the entire linguistic experience of an individual is (at this point in time!) only accessible to them, and the nature of the subset dictates which aspect of the person we can model. For instance, knowing what a particular academic colleague has written, read and cited may let us model their work expertise, while chatting with them at a barbecue party might give us insight into their personal life.

We further contend that what we know about a person conditions the type of interaction we have with them: we are more likely to start a conversation about linguistics with someone we see as a linguist, and to talk about the bad behaviour of our dog with a person we have primarily modelled as a dog trainer. In other words, the model we have of people helps us successfully communicate with them.

3   Some fundamentals of DS

The basis of any DS system is a set of word meaning representations ('distributions') built from large corpora. In their simplest form,[1] distributions are vectors in a so-called *semantic space* where each dimension represents a term from the overall system's vocabulary. The value of a vector along a particular dimension expresses how characteristic the dimension is for the word modelled by the vector (as calculated using, e.g., Pointwise Mutual Information). It will be found, typically, that the vector *cat* has high weight along the dimension *meow* but low weight along *politics*. More complex architectures result in compact representations with reduced dimensionality, which can integrate a range of non-verbal information such as visual and sound features (Feng and Lapata, 2010; Kiela and Clark, 2015).

Word vectors have been linked to conceptual

---

[1]There are various possible ways to construct distributions, including predictive language models based on neural networks (Mikolov et al., 2013).

representations both theoretically (Erk, 2013) and experimentally, for instance in psycholinguistic and neurolinguistic work (Anderson et al., 2013; Mitchell et al., 2008). The general idea is that a distribution encapsulates information about *what kind of thing* a particular concept might be. Retrieving such information in ways that can be verbalised is often done by looking at the 'nearest neighbours' of a vector. Indeed, a natural consequence of the DS architecture is that similar words cluster in the same area of the semantic space: it has been shown that the distance between DS vectors correlates well with human similarity judgements (Baroni et al., 2014b; Kiela and Clark, 2014). So we can find out what a cat is by inspecting the subspace in which the vector *cat* lives, and finding items such as *animal, dog, pet, scratch* etc.

In what follows, we use this feature of vector spaces to give an interpretable model of an individual, i.e., we can predict that a person might be a linguist by knowing that their vector is the close neighbour of, say, *semantics, reference, model*.

4 A DS model of a community

4.1 People in semantic spaces

Summing up what we have said so far, we follow the claim that we can theoretically talk about the linguistic experience of a speaker in distributional terms. The words that a person has read, written, spoken or heard, are a very individual signature for that person. The sum of those words carries important information about the type of concepts someone may be familiar with, about their social environment (indicated by the registers observed in their linguistic experience) and, broadly speaking, their interests.

We further posit that people's individuality can be modelled as vectors in a semantic space, in a way that the concepts surrounding a person's vector reflect their experience. For instance, a cook might 'live' in a subspace inhabited by other cooks and concepts related to cooking. In that sense, the person can be seen as any other concept inhabiting that space.

In order to compute such person vectors, we expand on a well-known result of compositional distributional semantics (CDS). CDS studies how words combine to form phrases and sentences. While various, more or less complex frameworks have been proposed (Clark et al., 2008; Mitchell and Lapata, 2010; Baroni et al., 2014a), it has re-

peatedly been found that simple addition of vectors performs well in modelling the meaning of larger constituents (i.e., we express the meaning of *black cat* by simply summing the vectors for *black* and *cat*). To some extent, it is also possible to get the 'gist' of simple sentences by summing their constituent words. The fundamental idea behind simple addition is that, given a coherent set of words (i.e. words which 'belong together and are close in the semantic space), their sum will express the general topic of those words by creating a centroid vector sitting in their midst. This notion of coherence is important: summing two vectors that are far away from each other in the space will result in a vector which is far from both the base terms (this is one of the intuitions used in (Vecchi et al., 2011) to capture semantically anomalous phrases).

We take this idea further by assuming that people are on the whole coherent (see (Herbelot, 2015) for a similar argument about proper names): their experiences reflect who they are. For instance, by virtue of being a chef, or someone interested in cooking, someone will have many interconnected experiences related to food. In particular, a good part of their *linguistic* experiences will involve talking, reading and writing about food. It follows that we can represent a person by summing the vectors corresponding to the words they have been exposed to. When aggregating the vocabulary most salient for a chef, we would hopefully create a vector inhabiting the 'food' section of the space. As we will see in §6, the model we propose is slightly more complex, but the intuition remains the same.

Note that, in spite of being 'coherent', people are not one-sided, and a cook can also be a bungee-jumper in their spare time. So depending on the spread of data we have about a person, our method is not completely immune to creating vectors which sit a little too far away from the topics they encapsulate. This is a limit of our approach which could be solved by attributing a set of vectors, rather than a single representation, to each person. In this work, however, we do not consider this option and assume that the model is still discriminative enough to distinguish people.

4.2 From person vectors to interacting agents

In what sense are person vectors useful representations? We have said that, as any distribution in a semantic space, they give information about *the type of thing/person* modelled by the vector. We also mentioned in §2 that knowing who someone is (just like knowing *what* something is) influences our interaction with them. So we would like to model in which ways our people representations help us successfully communicate with them.

For the purpose of this paper, we choose an information retrieval task as our testbed, described in §5. The task, which involves identifying a relevant knowledge holder for a particular question, requires us to embed our person vectors into simple agent-like entities, with a number of linguistic, knowledge-processing and communicative capabilities. A general illustration of the structure of each agent is shown in Fig. 1. An agent stores (and dynamically updates) a) a person vector; b) a memory which, for the purpose of our evaluation (§5), is a store of linguistic experiences (some data the person has read or written, e.g. information on Venezuelan cocoa beans). The memory acts as a knowledge base which can be queried, i.e. relevant parts can be 'remembered' (e.g. the person remember reading about some Valrhona cocoa, with a spicy flavour). Further, the agent has some awareness of others: it holds a model of its community consisting of other people's vectors (e.g., the agent knows Bob, who is a chef, and Alice, who is a linguist). When acted by a particular communication need, the agent can direct its attention to the appropriate people in its community and engage with them.

5 Evaluating person vectors

5.1 The task

To evaluate our person vectors, we choose a task which relies on having a correct representation of the expertise of an individual.

Let's imagine a person with a particular *information* need, for instance, getting sightseeing tips for a holiday destination. Let's also say that we are in a pre-Internet era, where information is typically sought from other actors in one's real-world community. The communication process associated with satisfying this information need takes two steps: a) identifying the actors most likely to hold relevant knowledge (perhaps a friend who has done the trip before, or a local travel agent); b) asking them to share relevant knowledge.

In the following, we replicate this situation using a set of agents, created as described in §4.

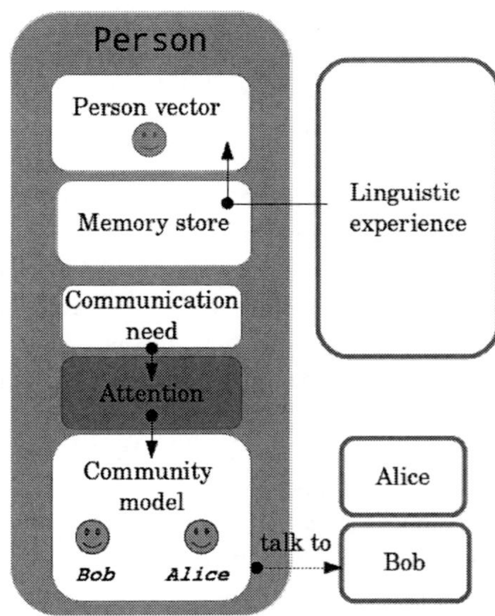

Figure 1: A person is exposed to a set of linguistic experiences. Computationally, each experience is represented as a vector in a memory store. The sum of those experiences make up the individual's 'person vector'. The person also has a model of their community in the form of other individuals' person vectors. In response to a particular communication need, the person can direct their attention to the relevant actors in that community.

We assume that those agents are fully connected and aware of each other, in a way that they can direct specific questions to the individuals most likely to answer them. Our evaluation procedure tests whether, for a given information need, expressed in natural language by one agent (e.g. *What is Venezuelan chocolate like?*), the community is modelled in a way that an answer can be successfully obtained (i.e. an agent with relevant expertise has been found, and 'remembers' some information that satisfies the querier's need). Note that we are not simulating any real communication between agents, which would require that the information holder generates a natural language answer to the question. Rather, the contacted agent simply returns the information in its memory store which seems most relevant to the query at hand. We believe this is enough to confirm that the person vector was useful in acquiring the information: if the querying agent contacts the 'wrong' person, the system has failed in successfully fulfulling the information need.

5.2 Comparative evaluation

We note that the task we propose can be seen as an information retrieval (IR) problem over a distributed network: a query is matched to some relevant knowledge unit, with all available knowledge being split across a number of 'peers' (the individuals in our community). So in order to know how well the system does at retrieving relevant information, we can use as benchmark standard IR software.

We compare the performance of our system with a classic, centralised IR algorithm, as implemented in the *Apache Lucene* search engine. Lucene is an open source library for implementing (unstructured) document retrieval systems, which has been employed in many full-text search engine systems (for an overview of the library, see (Bialecki et al., 2012)). We use the out-of-the-box 'standard' indexing solution provided by Lucene,[2] which roughly implements a term-by-document Vector Space Model, in which terms are lemmatised and associated to documents using their *tf-idf* scores (Spärck-Jones, 1972) computed from the input Wikipedia corpus of our evaluation. Similarly, queries are parsed using Lucene's standard query parser and then searched and ranked by the computed 'default' similarities.[3]

Our hypothesis is that, if our system can match the performance of a well-known IR system, we can also conclude that the person vectors were a good summary of the information held by a particular agent.

5.3 Data challenges

Finding data to set up the evaluation of our system is an extremely challenging task. It involves finding a) personalised linguistic data which can be split into coherent 'linguistic experiences'; b) realistic natural language queries; c) a gold standard matching queries and relevant experiences. There is very little openly available data on people's personal linguistic experience. What is available comes mostly from the Web science and user personalisation communities and such data is either not annotated for IR evaluation purposes (e.g. (von der Weth and Hauswirth, 2013)), or proprietary and not easily accessible or re-distributable (e.g. (Collins-Thompson et al., 2011)). Conversely, standard IR datasets do not give any information about users' personal experiences. We attempt to solve this conundrum by using information freely available on Wikipedia. We combine a Wikipedia-based Question Answering (QA) dataset with contributor logs from the online encyclopedia.

We use the freely available 'WikiQA' dataset of (Yang et al., 2015).[4] This dataset contains 3047 questions sampled from the Bing search engine's data. Each question is associated with a Wikipedia page which received user clicks at query time. The dataset is further annotated with the particular sentence in the Wikipedia article which answers the query – if it exists. Many pages that were chosen by the Bing users do not actually hold the answer to their questions, reducing the data to 1242 queries and the 1194 corresponding pages which can be considered relevant for those queries (41% of all questions). We use this subset for our experiments, regarding each document in the dataset as a 'linguistic experience', which can be stored in the memory of the agent exposed to it.

To model individuals, we download a log of Wikipedia contributions (March 2015). This log is described as a 'log events to all pages and users'. We found that it does not, in fact, contain all possible edits (presumably because of storage issues). Of the 1194 pages in our WikiQA subset, only 625 are logged. We record the usernames of all contributors to those 625 documents, weeding out contributors whose usernames contain the string *bot* and have more than 10,000 edits (under the assumption that those are, indeed, bots). Finally, for each user, we download and clean all articles they have contributed to.

In summary, we have a dataset which consists of a) 662 WikiQA queries linked to 625 documents relevant for those queries; b) a community of 4379 individuals/agents, with just over 1M documents spread across the memories of all agents.

6 Implementation

Our community is modelled as a distributed network of 4379 agents $\{a_1, \ldots, a_{4379}\}$. Each agent a_k has two components: a) a personal profile component, which fills the agent's memory with information from the person's linguistic experience (i.e., documents she/he reads or edits) and calculates the corresponding person vector; b) an 'attention' component which gets activated when

---

[2]Ver. 5.4.1, obtained from `http://apache.lauf-forum.at/lucene/java/5.4.1`.

[3]For an explanation of query matching and similarity computation see `http://lucene.apache.org/core/5_4_1/core/org/apache/lucene/search/similarities/Similarity.html`.

[4]`http://aka.ms/WikiQA`

a communication need is felt. All agents share a common semantic space $\mathcal{S}$ which gives background vectorial representations for words in the system's vocabulary. In our current implementation, $\mathcal{S}$ is given by the CBOW semantic space of (Baroni et al., 2014b), a 400-dimension vector space of 300,000 items built using the neural network language model of (Mikolov et al., 2013). This space shows high correlation with human similarity judgements (i.e., $\rho = 0.80$) over the 3000 pairs of the *MEN dataset* (Bruni et al., 2012). Note that using a standard space means the we assume shared meaning presentations across the community (i.e., at this stage, we don't model inter-speaker differences at the lexical item level).

Person vectors: A person vector is the normalised sum of that person's linguistic experiences:

$$\vec{p} = \sum_{1..k..n} \vec{e_k}. \tag{1}$$

As mentioned previously, in our current setup, linguistic experiences correspond to documents.

Document/experience vectors: we posit that the (rough) meaning of a document can be expressed as an additive function acting over (some of) the words of that document. Specifically, we sum the 10 words that are most characteristic for the document. While this may seem to miss out on much of the document's content, it is important to remember that the background DS representations used in the summation are already rich in content: the vector for *Italy*, for instance, will typically sit next to *Rome*, *country* and *pasta* in the semantic space. The summation roughly captures the document's content in a way equivalent to a human describing a text as being *about so and so*.

We need to individually build document vectors for potentially sparse individual profiles, without necessitating access to the overall document collection of the system (because a_k is not necessarily aware of a_m's experiences). Thus, standard measures such as *tf-idf* are not suitable to calculate the importance of a word for a document. We alleviate this issue by using a static list of word entropies (calculated over the ukWaC 2 billion words corpus, (Baroni et al., 2009)) and the following weighting measure:

$$w_t = \frac{freq(t)}{log(H(t) + 1)}, \tag{2}$$

where $freq(t)$ is the frequency of term t in the document and $H(t)$ is its entropy, as calculated over a larger corpus. The representation of the document is then the weighted sum of the 10 terms[5] with highest importance for that text:

$$\vec{e} = \sum_{t \in t_1...t_{10}} w_t * \vec{t}. \tag{3}$$

Note that both vectors $\vec{t}$ and $\vec{e}$ are normalised to unit length.

For efficiency reasons, we compute weights only over the first 20 lines of documents, also following the observation that the beginning of a document is often more informative as to its topic than the rest (Manning et al., 2008).

Attention: The 'attention' module directs the agent to the person most relevant for its current information need. In this paper, it is operationalised as cosine similarity between vectors. The module takes a query q and translates it into a vector $\vec{q}$ by summing the words in the query, as in Eq. 3. It then goes through a 2-stage process: 1) find potentially helpful people by calculating the cosine distance between $\vec{q}$ and all person vectors $\vec{p_1}...\vec{p_n}$; 2) query the m most relevant people, who will calculate the distance between $\vec{q}$ and all documents in their memory, $D_k = \{d_1...d_t\}$. Receive the documents corresponding to the highest scores, ranked in descending order.

7 Describing the community

7.1 Qualitative checks

As a sanity check, it is possible to inspect where each experience/document vector sits in the semantic space, by looking at its 'nearest neighbours' (i.e., the m words closest to it in the space). We show below two documents with their nearest neighbours, as output by our system:

```
Artificial_intelligence:
ai artificial intelligence intelligent
computational research researchers
computing cognitive computer

Anatoly_Karpov:
chess ussr moscow tournament ukraine
russia soviet russian champion opponent
```

We also consider whether each user inhabits a seemingly coherent area of the semantic space. The following shows a user profile, as output by our system, which corresponds to a person with an interest in American history:

---

[5] We experimented with a range of values, not reported here for space reasons.

184

# agents	# docs
2939	1-100
944	100-500
226	500-1000
145	1000-2000
82	2000-5000
15	10000-200000

Table 1: Distribution of documents across people. For example, 2939 agents contain 1–100 documents.

```
name = [...]
topics = confederate indians american
americans mexican mexico states army
soldiers navy
coherence = 0.452686176513
p_vector:0.004526 0.021659 [...] 0.029680
```

The profile includes a username and the 10 nearest neighbours to the user's p_k vector (which give a human-readable representation of the broad expertise of the user), the corresponding coherence figure (see next section for information about coherence) and the actual person vector for that agent.

7.2 Quantitative description

Distribution of documents across agents: An investigation of the resulting community indicates that the distribution of documents across people is highly skewed: 12% of all agents only contain one document, 31% contain less than 10 documents. Table 1 shows the overall distribution.

Topic coherence: We compute the 'topic coherence' of each person vector, that is, the extent to which it focuses on related topics. We expect that it will be easier to identify a document answering a query on e.g. baking if it is held by an agent which contains a large proportion of other cooking-related information. Following the intuition of (Newman et al., 2010), we define the coherence of a set of documents $d_1, \cdots, d_n$ as the mean of their pairwise similarities:

$$Coherence(d_{1...n}) = mean\{Sim(d_i, d_j), \\ ij \in 1 \ldots n, i < j\} \tag{4}$$

where Sim is the cosine similarity between two documents.

The mean coherence over the 4379 person vectors is 0.40 with a variance of 0.06. The high variance is due to the number of agents containing one document only (which have coherence 1.0). When only considering the agents with at least two documents, the mean coherence is 0.32, with variance

# relevant docs	# agents containing doc
176	1
169	2-4
100	5-9
64	10-19
45	20-49
49	50-99
19	100-199
3	200-399

Table 2: Redundancy of relevant documents across people. For example, 176 documents are found in one agent; 169 documents are found in 2–4 agents, etc.

0.01. So despite a high disparity in memory sizes, the coherence is roughly stable. For reference, a cosine similarity of 0.32 in our semantic space corresponds to a fair level of relatedness: for instance, some words related to *school* at the 0.30 level are *studied, lessons, attend, district, church.*

Information redundancy: we investigate the redundancy of the created network with respect to our documents of interest: given a document D which answers one or more query in the dataset, we ask how many memory stores contain D. This information is given in Table 2. We observe that 176 documents are contained in only one agent out of 4379. Overall, around 70% of the documents that answer a query in the dataset are to be found in less than 10 agents. So as far as our pages of interest are concerned, the knowledge base of our community is minimally redundant, making the task all the more challenging.

8 Evaluation

The WikiQA dataset gives us information about the document d_{gold} that was clicked on by users after issuing a particular query q. This indicates that d_{gold} was relevant for q, but does not give us information about which other documents might have also be deemed relevant by the user. In this respect, the dataset differs from fully annotated IR collections like the TREC data (Harman, 1993). In what follows, we report *Mean Reciprocal Rank (MRR)*, which takes into account that only one document per query is considered relevant in our dataset:

$$MRR = \sum_{q \in Q} P(q), \tag{5}$$

where Q is the set of all queries, and $P(q)$ is the precision of the system for query q. $P(q)$ itself is

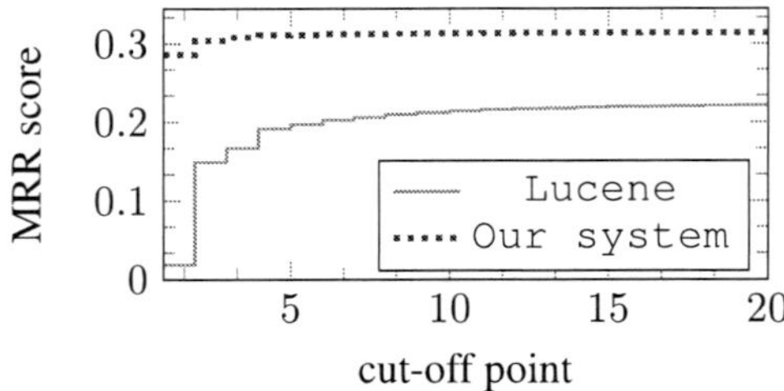

Figure 2: MRR for Lucene and our system (best 5 person vectors).

given by:

$$P(q) = \begin{cases} \frac{1}{r_q} & \text{if } r_q < \text{cutoff} \\ 0 & \text{otherwise} \end{cases},$$

where r_q is the rank at which the correct document is returned for query q, and the cutoff is a predefined number of considered results (e.g., top 20 documents).

The MRR scores for Lucene and our system are shown in Fig. 2. The x-axis shows different cut-off points (e.g., cut-off point 10 means that we are only considering the top 10 documents returned by the system). The graph gives results for the case where the agent contacts the $p = 5$ people potentially most relevant for the query. We also tried $m = \{10, 20, 50\}$ and found that end results are fairly stable, despite the fact that the chance of retrieving at least one 'useful' agent increases. This is due to the fact that, as people are added to the first phase of querying, confusion increases (more documents are inspected) and the system is more likely to return the correct page at a slightly lower rank (e.g., as witnessed by the performance of Lucene's centralised indexing mechanism).

Our hypothesis was that matching the performance of an IR algorithm would validate our model as a useful representation of a community. We find, in fact, that our method considerably outperforms Lucene, reaching $MRR = 0.31$ for $m = 5$ against $MRR = 0.22$. This is a very interesting result, as it suggests that retaining the natural relationship between information and knowledge holders increases the ability of the system to retrieve it, and this, despite the intrinsic difficulty of searching in a distributed setting. This is especially promising, as the implementation presented here is given in its purest form, without heavy pre-processing or parameter setting. Aside from a short list of common stopwords, the agent only uses simple linear algebra operations over raw, non-lemmatised data.

MRR figures are not necessarily very intuitive, so we inspect how many times an agent is found who *can* answer the query (i.e. its memory store contains the document that was marked as holding the answer to the query in WikiQA). We find that the system finds a helpful hand 39% of the time for $m = 5$ and 52% at $m = 50$. These relatively modest figures demonstrate the difficulty of our task and dataset. We must however also acknowledge that finding appropriate helpers amongst a community of 4000 individuals is highly non-trivial.

Overall, the system is very precise once a good agent has been identified (i.e., it is likely to return the correct document in the first few results). This is shown by the fact that the MRR only increases slightly between cut-off point 1 and 20, from 0.29 to 0.31 (compare with Lucene, which achieves $MRR = 0.02$ at rank 1). This behaviour can be explained by the fact that the agent overwhelmingly prefers 'small' memory sizes: 78% of the agents selected in the first phase of the querying process contain less than 100 documents. This is an important aspect which should guide further modelling. We hypothesise that people with larger memory stores are perhaps less attractive to the querying agent because their profiles are less topically defined (i.e., as the number of documents browsed by a user increases, it is more likely that they cover a wider range of topics). As pointed out in §4, we suggest that our person representations may need more structure, perhaps in the form of several coherent 'topic vectors'. It makes intuitive sense to assume that a) the interests of a person are not necessarily close to each other (e.g. someone may be a linguist and a hobby gardener); b) when a person with an information need selects 'who can help' amongst their acquaintances, they only consider the relevant aspects of an individual (e.g., the hobby gardener is a good match for a query on gardening, irrespectively of their other persona as a linguist).

Finally, we note that all figures reported here are below their true value (including those pertaining to *Lucene*). This is because we attempt to retrieve the page labelled as containing the answer to the query in the WikiQA dataset. Pages which are relevant but not contained in WikiQA are incorrectly given a score of 0. For instance, the query *what classes are considered humanities* returns *Outline of the humanities* as the first answer, but the chosen document in WikiQA is *Humanities*.

9 Conclusion

We have investigated the notion of 'person vector', built from a set of linguistic experiences associated with a real individual. These 'person vectors' live in the same semantic space as concepts and, as any semantic vector, give information about the kind of entity they describe, i.e. what kind of person someone is. We modelled a community of speakers from 1M 'experiences' (documents read or edited by Wikipedians), shared across over 4000 individuals. We tested the representations obtained for each individual by engaging them into an information-seeking task necessitating some understanding of the community for successful communication. We showed that our system outperforms a standard IR algorithm, as implemented by the Lucene engine. We hope to improve our modelling by constructing structured sets of person vectors that explicitly distinguish the various areas of expertise of an individual.

One limit of our approach is that we assumed person vectors to be unique across the community, i.e. that there is some kind of ground truth about the representation of a person. This is of course unrealistic, and the picture that Bob has of Alice should be different from the picture that Kim has of her, and again different from the picture that Alice has of herself. Modelling these fine distinctions, and finding an evaluation strategy for such modelling, is reserved for future work.

A more in-depth analysis of our model would also need to consider more sophisticated composition methods. We chose addition in this paper for its ease of implementation and efficiency, but other techniques are known to perform better for representing sentences and documents (Le and Mikolov, 2014)).

We believe that person vectors, aside from being interesting theoretical objects, are also useful constructs for a range of application, especially in the social media area. As a demonstration of this, we have made our system available at `https://github.com/PeARSearch` in the form of a distributed information retrieval engine. The code for the specific experiments presented in this paper is at `https://github.com/PeARSearch/PeARS-evaluation`.

Acknowledgements

We thank Germán Kruszewski, Angeliki Lazaridou and Ann Copestake for interesting discussions about this work. The first author is funded through ERC Starting Grant COMPOSES (283554).

References

Andrew J Anderson, Elia Bruni, Ulisse Bordignon, Massimo Poesio, and Marco Baroni. 2013. Of words, eyes and brains: Correlating image-based distributional semantic models with neural representations of concepts. In *EMNLP*, pages 1960–1970.

Harald Baayen, Hans Van Halteren, and Fiona Tweedie. 1996. Outside the cave of shadows: Using syntactic annotation to enhance authorship attribution. *Literary and Linguistic Computing*, 11(3):121–132.

Marco Baroni, Silvia Bernardini, Adriano Ferraresi, and Eros Zanchetta. 2009. The WaCky wide web: a collection of very large linguistically processed web-crawled corpora. *Language resources and evaluation*, 43(3):209–226.

Marco Baroni, Raffaela Bernardi, and Roberto Zamparelli. 2014a. Frege in space: A program of compositional distributional semantics. *Linguistic Issues in Language Technology*, 9.

Marco Baroni, Georgiana Dinu, and Germán Kruszewski. 2014b. Don't count, predict! a systematic comparison of context-counting vs. context-predicting semantic vectors. In *Proceedings of ACL*, pages 238–247.

A. Bialecki, R. Muir, and G. Ingersoll. 2012. Apache Lucene 4. pages 17–24.

Elia Bruni, Gemma Boleda, Marco Baroni, and Nam-Khanh Tran. 2012. Distributional semantics in technicolor. In *Proceedings of ACL*, pages 136–145.

Stephen Clark, Bob Coecke, and Mehrnoosh Sadrzadeh. 2008. A compositional distributional model of meaning. In *Proceedings of the Second Quantum Interaction Symposium (QI-2008)*, pages 133–140.

Stephen Clark. 2012. Vector space models of lexical meaning. In Shalom Lappin and Chris Fox, editors, *Handbook of Contemporary Semantics – second edition*. Wiley-Blackwell.

Kevyn Collins-Thompson, Paul N Bennett, Ryen W White, Sebastian de la Chica, and David Sontag. 2011. Personalizing web search results by reading level. In *Proceedings of the 20th ACM international conference on Information and knowledge management*, pages 403–412. ACM.

Katrin Erk. 2012. Vector space models of word meaning and phrase meaning: A survey. *Language and Linguistics Compass*, 6(10):635–653.

Katrin Erk. 2013. Towards a semantics for distributional representations. In *Proceedings of the Tenth International Conference on Computational Semantics (IWCS2013)*.

Yansong Feng and Mirella Lapata. 2010. Visual information in semantic representation. In *NAACL-HLT2010*, pages 91–99, Los Angeles, California, June.

Donna K. Harman. 1993. The first text retrieval conference (TREC-1). *Information Processing & Management*, 29(4):411–414.

Aurélie Herbelot. 2015. Mr Darcy and Mr Toad, gentlemen: distributional names and their kinds. In *Proceedings of the 11th International Conference on Computational Semantics*, pages 151–161.

Douwe Kiela and Stephen Clark. 2014. A systematic study of semantic vector space model parameters. In *Proceedings of the 2nd Workshop on Continuous Vector Space Models and their Compositionality (CVSC) at EACL*, pages 21–30.

Douwe Kiela and Stephen Clark. 2015. Multi-and cross-modal semantics beyond vision: Grounding in auditory perception. In *EMNLP*.

Tom Kwiatkowski, Sharon Goldwater, Luke Zettlemoyer, and Mark Steedman. 2012. A probabilistic model of syntactic and semantic acquisition from child-directed utterances and their meanings. In *EACL*, pages 234–244, Avignon, France.

Thomas K Landauer and Susan T Dumais. 1997. A solution to Plato's problem: The latent semantic analysis theory of acquisition, induction, and representation of knowledge. *Psychological review*, pages 211–240.

Quoc V Le and Tomas Mikolov. 2014. Distributed representations of sentences and documents. *arXiv preprint arXiv:1405.4053*.

Kevin Lund and Curt Burgess. 1996. Producing high-dimensional semantic spaces from lexical co-occurrence. *Behavior Research Methods, Instruments, & Computers*, 28:203–208, June.

Christopher D Manning, Prabhakar Raghavan, and Hinrich Schütze. 2008. *Introduction to information retrieval*, volume 1. Cambridge University Press, Cambridge, UK.

Tomas Mikolov, Kai Chen, Greg Corrado, and Jeffrey Dean. 2013. Efficient estimation of word representations in vector space. *arXiv preprint arXiv:1301.3781*.

Jeff Mitchell and Mirella Lapata. 2010. Composition in Distributional Models of Semantics. *Cognitive Science*, 34(8):1388–1429, November.

Tom M. Mitchell, Svetlana V. Shinkareva, Andrew Carlson, Kai-Min Chang, Vicente L. Malave, Robert A. Mason, and Marcel Adam Just. 2008. Predicting human brain activity associated with the meanings of nouns. *Science*, 320(5880):1191–1195.

David Newman, Jey Han Lau, Karl Grieser, and Timothy Baldwin. 2010. Automatic evaluation of topic coherence. In *NAACL*, pages 100–108.

Karen Spärck-Jones. 1972. A statistical interpretation of term specificity and its application in retrieval. *Journal of documentation*, 28(1):11–21.

Efstathios Stamatatos. 2009. A survey of modern authorship attribution methods. *Journal of the American Society for information Science and Technology*, 60(3):538–556.

Peter D. Turney and Patrick Pantel. 2010. From frequency to meaning: Vector space models of semantics. *Journal of Artificial Intelligence Research*, 37:141–188.

Eva Maria Vecchi, Marco Baroni, and Roberto Zamparelli. 2011. (Linear) maps of the impossible: capturing semantic anomalies in distributional space. In *Proceedings of the Workshop on Distributional Semantics and Compositionality*, pages 1–9. Association for Computational Linguistics.

Christian von der Weth and Manfred Hauswirth. 2013. Dobbs: Towards a comprehensive dataset to study the browsing behavior of online users. In *Web Intelligence (WI) and Intelligent Agent Technologies (IAT), 2013*, volume 1, pages 51–56. IEEE.

Anna Wierzbicka. 1984. Cups and mugs: Lexicography and conceptual analysis. *Australian Journal of Linguistics*, 4(2):205–255.

Ludwig Wittgenstein. 1953. *Philosophical investigations*. Wiley-Blackwell (reprint 2010).

Yi Yang, Wen-tau Yih, and Christopher Meek. 2015. WIKIQA: A Challenge Dataset for Open-Domain Question Answering. In *EMNLP*.

Rong Zheng, Jiexun Li, Hsinchun Chen, and Zan Huang. 2006. A framework for authorship identification of online messages: Writing-style features and classification techniques. *Journal of the American Society for Information Science and Technology*, 57(3):378–393.

Random Positive-Only Projections:
PPMI-Enabled Incremental Semantic Space Construction

Behrang QasemiZadeh
DFG SFB 991
Heinrich-Heine-Universität Düsseldorf
Düsseldorf, Germany
zadeh@phil.hhu.de

Laura Kallmeyer
DFG SFB 991
Heinrich-Heine-Universität Düsseldorf
Düsseldorf, Germany
kallmeyer@phil.hhu.de

Abstract

We introduce *positive-only projection* (PoP), a new algorithm for constructing semantic spaces and word embeddings. The PoP method employs random projections. Hence, it is highly scalable and computationally efficient. In contrast to previous methods that use random projection matrices $\mathbf{R}$ with the expected value of 0 (i.e., $E(\mathbf{R}) = 0$), the proposed method uses $\mathbf{R}$ with $E(\mathbf{R}) > 0$. We use *Kendall*'s τ_b correlation to compute vector similarities in the resulting non-Gaussian spaces. Most importantly, since $E(\mathbf{R}) > 0$, weighting methods such as positive pointwise mutual information (PPMI) can be applied to PoP-constructed spaces after their construction for efficiently transferring PoP embeddings onto spaces that are discriminative for semantic similarity assessments. Our PoP-constructed models, combined with PPMI, achieve an average score of 0.75 in the *MEN relatedness test*, which is comparable to results obtained by state-of-the-art algorithms.

1 Introduction

The development of data-driven methods of natural language processing starts with an educated guess, a distributional hypothesis: We assume that some properties of linguistic entities can be modelled by 'some statistical' observations in language data. In the second step, this statistical information (which is determined by the hypothesis) is collected and represented in a mathematical framework. In the third step, tools provided by the chosen mathematical framework are used to implement a similarity-based logic to identify linguistic structures, and/or to verify the proposed hypothesis. Harris's distributional hypothesis (Harris, 1954) is a well-known example of step one that states that meanings of words correlate with the environment in which the words appear. Vector space models and η-normed-based similarity measures are notable examples of steps two and three, respectively (i.e., word space models or word embeddings).

However, as pointed out for instance by Baroni et al. (2014), the *count-based models* resulting from the steps two and three are not discriminative enough to achieve satisfactory results; instead, *predictive models* are required. To this end, an additional transformation step is often added. Turney and Pantel (2010) describe this extra step as a combination of *weighting* and *dimensionality reduction*.[1] This transformation from count-based to predictive models can be implemented simply via a collection of rules of thumb (such as frequency threshold to filter out highly frequent and/or rare context elements), and/or it can involve more sophisticated mathematical transformations, such as converting raw counts to probabilities and using matrix factorization techniques. Likewise, by exploiting the large amounts of computational power available nowadays, this transformation can be achieved via neural word embedding techniques (Mikolov et al., 2013; Levy and Goldberg, 2014).

To a large extent, the need for such transformations arises from the *heavy-tailed* distributions that we often find in statistical natural language models (such as the Zipfian distribution of words in contexts when building word spaces). Consequently, count-based models are sparse and high-dimensional and therefore both computationally expensive to manipulate (due of the high dimensionality of models) and nondiscriminatory (due to the combination of the high-dimensionality of the

---

[1] Similar to topics of feature weighting, selection, and engineering in statistical machine learning.

*Proceedings of the Fifth Joint Conference on Lexical and Computational Semantics (*SEM 2016), pages 189–198,*
Berlin, Germany, August 11-12, 2016.

models and the sparseness of observations—see Minsky and Papert (1969, chap. 12)).[2]

On the one hand, although neural networks are often the top performers for addressing this problem, their usage is costly: they need to be trained, which is often very time-consuming,[3] and their performance can vary from one task to another depending on their *objective function*.[4] On the other hand, although methods based on random projections efficiently address the problem of reducing the dimensionality of vectors—such as random indexing (RI) (Kanerva et al., 2000), reflective random indexing (RRI), (Cohen et al., 2010), ISA (Baroni et al., 2007) and random Manhattan indexing (RMI) (Zadeh and Handschuh, 2014)—in effect they retain distances between entities in the original space.[5] Moreover, since these methods use asymptotic Gaussian or Cauchy random projection matrices $\mathbf{R}$ with $\mathrm{E}(\mathbf{R}) = 0$, their resulting vectors cannot be adjusted and transformed using weighting techniques such as PPMI. Consequently, these methods often do not outperform neural embeddings and combinations of PPMI weighting of count-based models followed by matrix factorization—such as the truncation of weighted vectors using singular value decomposition (SVD).

To overcome these problems, we propose a new method called *positive-only projection (PoP)*. PoP is an incremental semantic space construction method which employs random projections. Hence, building models using PoP does not require training but simply generating random vectors. However, in contrast to RI (and previous methods), the PoP-constructed spaces can undergo weighting transformations such as PPMI, after their construction and at a reduced dimensionality. This is due to the fact that PoP uses random vectors that contain only positive integer values. Because the PoP method employs random projections, models can be built incrementally and efficiently. Since the vectors in PoP-constructed models are small (i.e., with a dimensionality of a few hundred), applying weighting methods such

as PPMI to these models is incredibly faster than applying them to classical count-based models. Combined with a suitable weighting method such as PPMI, the PoP algorithm yields competitive results concerning accuracy in semantic similarity assessments, compared for instance to neural net-based approaches and combinations of count-based models with weighting and matrix factorization. These results, however, are achieved without the need for heavy computations. Thus, instead of hours, models can be built in a matter of a few seconds or minutes. Note that even without weighting transformation, PoP-constructed models display a better performance than RI on tasks of semantic similarity assessments.

We describe the PoP method in § 2. In order to evaluate our models, in § 3, we report the performance of PoP in the MEN relatedness test. Finally, § 4 concludes with a discussion.

2   Method

2.1   Construction of PoP Models

A transformation of a count-based model to a predictive one can be expressed using a matrix notation such as:

$$\mathbf{C}_{p \times n} \times \mathbf{T}_{n \times m} = \mathbf{P}_{p \times m}. \tag{1}$$

In Equation 1, $\mathbf{C}$ denotes the count-based model consisting of p vectors and n context elements (i.e., n dimensions). $\mathbf{T}$ is the transformation matrix that maps the p n-dimensional vectors in $\mathbf{C}$ to an m-dimensional space (often, but not necessarily, $m \neq n$ and $m \ll n$). Finally, $\mathbf{P}$ is the resulting m-dimensional predictive model. Note that $\mathbf{T}$ can be a composition of several transformations, e.g., a weighting transformation $\mathbf{W}$ followed by a projection onto a space of lower dimensionality $\mathbf{R}$, i.e., $\mathbf{T}_{n \times m} = \mathbf{W}_{n \times n} \times \mathbf{R}_{n \times m}$.

In the proposed PoP technique, the transformation $\mathbf{T}_{n \times m}$ (for $m \ll n$, e.g., $100 \leq m \leq 7000$) is simply a randomly generated matrix. The elements t_{ij} of $\mathbf{T}_{n \times m}$ have the following distribution:

$$t_{ij} = \begin{cases} 0 & \text{with probability } 1 - s \\ \lfloor \frac{1}{U^\alpha} \rfloor & \text{with probability } s \end{cases}, \tag{2}$$

in which U is an independent uniform random variable in $(0, 1]$, and s is an extremely small number (e.g., $s = 0.01$) such that each row vector of $\mathbf{T}$ has at least one element that is not 0 (i.e.,

---

[2]That is, the well known *curse of dimensionality* problem.

[3]Baroni et al. (2014) state that it took *Ronan Collobert* two months to train a set of embeddings from a Wikipedia dump. Even using GPU-accelerated computing, the required computation and training time for inducing neural word embeddings is high.

[4]Ibid, see results reported in supplemental materials.

[5]For η-normed space that they are designed for, i.e., $\eta = 2$ for RI, RRI, and ISA and $\eta = 1$ for RMI.

$\sum_{i=1}^{m} t_{ji} \neq 0$ for each row vector $t_j \in \mathbf{T}$). For α, we choose $\alpha = 0.5$. Given Equations 1 and 2 and using the distributive property of multiplication over addition in matrices,[6] the desired semantic space (i.e., $\mathbf{P}$ in Equation 1) can be constructed using the two-step procedure of incremental word space construction (such as used in RI, RRI, and RMI):

Step 1. Each context element is mapped to one m-dimensional *index vector* $\vec{r}$. $\vec{r}$ is randomly generated such that most elements in $\vec{r}$ are 0 and only a few are positive integers (i.e., the elements of $\vec{r}$ have the distribution given in Equation 2).

Step 2. Each target entity that is being analysed in the model is represented by a *context vector* $\vec{v}$ in which all the elements are initially set to 0. For each encountered occurrence of this target entity together with a context element (e.g., through a sequential scan of a corpus), we update $\vec{v}$ by adding the index vector $\vec{r}$ of the context element to it.

This process results in a model built directly at the reduced dimensionality m (i.e., $\mathbf{P}$ in Equation 1). The first step corresponds to the construction of the randomly generated transformation matrix $\mathbf{T}$: Each index vector is a row of the transformation matrix $\mathbf{T}$. The second step is an implementation of the matrix multiplication in Equation 1 which is distributed over addition: Each context vector is a row of $\mathbf{P}$, which is computed in an iterative process.

2.2 Measuring Similarity

Once $\mathbf{P}$ is constructed, if desirable, similarities between entities can be computed by their *Kendall's* τ_b ($-1 \leq \tau_b \leq 1$) correlation (Kendall, 1938). To compute τ_b, we adopt an implementation of the algorithm proposed by Knight (1966), which has a computational complexity of $O(n \log n)$.[7]

In order to compute τ_b, we need to define a number of values. Given vectors $\vec{x}$ and $\vec{y}$ of the same dimension, we call a pair of observations (x_j, y_j) and (x_{j+1}, y_{j+1}) in $\vec{x}$ and $\vec{y}$ *concordant* if $(x_j < x_{j+1} \wedge y_j < y_{j+1}) \vee (x_j > x_{j+1} \wedge y_j > y_{j+1})$. The pair is called *discordant* if $(x_j < x_{j+1} \wedge y_j > y_{j+1}) \vee (x_j > x_{j+1} \wedge y_j < y_{j+1})$. Finally, the pair is called *tied* if $x_j = x_{j+1} \vee y_j = y_{j+1}$. Note that a tied pair is neither concordant nor discordant. We define n_1 and n_2 as the number of pairs

with tied values in $\vec{x}$ and $\vec{y}$, respectively. We use n_c and n_d to denote the number of concordant and discordant pairs, respectively. If m is the dimension of the two vectors, then n_0 is defined as the total number of observation pairs: $n_0 = \frac{m(m-1)}{2}$. Given these definitions, Kendall's τ_b is given by

$$\tau_b = \frac{n_c - n_d}{\sqrt{(n_0 - n_1)(n_0 - n_2)}}.$$

The choice of τ_b can be motivated by generalising the role that cosine plays for computing similarities between vectors that are derived from a standard Gaussian random projection. In random projections with $\mathbf{R}$ of (asymptotic) $\mathcal{N}(0, 1)$ distribution, despite the common interpretation of the cosine similarity as the angle between two vectors, cosine can be seen as a measure of the product-moment correlation coefficient between the two vectors. Since $\mathbf{R}$ and thus the obtained projected spaces have zero expectation, Pearson's correlation and the cosine measure have the same definition in these spaces (see also Jones and Furnas (1987) for a similar claim and on the relationships between correlation and the inner product and cosine). Subsequently, one can propose that in Gaussian random projections, Pearson's correlation is used to compute similarities between vectors.

However, the use of projections proposed in this paper (i.e., $\mathbf{T}$ with a distribution set in Equation 2) will result in vectors that have a non-Gaussian distribution. In this case, τ_b becomes a reasonable candidate for measuring similarities (i.e., correlations between vectors) since it is a nonparametric correlation coefficient measure that does not assume a Gaussian distribution (see Chen and Popovich (2002)) of projected spaces. However, we do not exclude the use of other similarity measures and may employ them in future work. In particular, we envisage additional transformations of PoP-constructed spaces to induce vectors with Gaussian distributions (see for instance the log-based PPMI transformation used in the next section). If a transformation to a Gaussian-like distribution is performed, then it is expected that the use of Pearson's correlation, which works under the assumption of Gaussian distribution, yields better results than Kendall's correlation (as confirmed by our experiments).

2.3 Some Delineation of the PoP Method

The PoP method is a *randomized algorithm*. In this class of algorithms, at the expense of a tolera-

---

[6]That is $(\mathbf{A} + \mathbf{B}) \times \mathbf{C} = \mathbf{A} \times \mathbf{C} + \mathbf{B} \times \mathbf{C}$.

[7]In our evaluation, we use the implementation of Knight's algorithm in the *Apache Commons Mathematics Library*.

ble loss in accuracy of the outcome of the computations (of course, with a certain acceptable amount of probability) and by the help of *random decisions*, the computational complexity of algorithms for solving a problem is reduced (see, e.g., Karp (1991), for an introduction to randomized algorithms).[8] For instance, using Gaussian-based sparse random projections in RI, the computation of eigenvectors (often of the complexity of $O(n^2 \log m)$) is replaced by a much simpler process of random matrix construction (of an estimated complexity of $O(n)$)—see Bingham and Mannila (2001). In return, randomized algorithms such as the PoP and RI methods give different results even for the same input.

Assume the difference between the optimum result and the result from a randomized algorithm is given by δ (i.e., the error caused by replacing deterministic decisions with random ones). Much research in theoretical computer science and applied statistics focuses on specifying bounds for δ, which is often expressed as a function of the probability ϵ of encountered errors. For instance, δ and ϵ in Gaussian random projections are often derived from the lemma proposed by Johnson and Lindenstrauss (1984) and its variations. Similar studies for random projections in ℓ_1-normed spaces and deep neural networks are Indyk (2000) and Arora et al. (2014), respectively.

At this moment, unfortunately, we are not able to provide a detailed mathematical account for specifying δ and ϵ for the results obtained by the PoP method (nor are we able to pinpoint a theoretical discussion about PoP's underlying random projection). Instead, we rely on the outcome of our simulations and the performance of the method in an NLP task. Note that this is not an unusual situation. For instance, Kanerva et al. (2000) proposed RI with no mathematical justification. In fact, it was only a few years later that Li et al. (2006) proposed mathematical lemmas for justifying very sparse Gaussian random projections such as RI (QasemiZadeh, 2015). At any rate, projections onto manifolds is a vibrant research both in theoretical computer science and in mathematical statistics. Our research will benefit from this in the near future. If δ refers to the amount of distortion in pairwise ℓ_2 norm correlation measures in a PoP space,[9] it can be shown that δ and its variance σ_δ^2

are functions of the dimension m of the projected space, that is: $\sigma_\delta^2 \approx \frac{1}{m}$, based on similar mathematical principles proposed by Kaski (1998) (and of Hecht-Nielsen (1994)) for the *random mapping*.

Our empirical research and observations on language data show that projections using the PoP method exhibit similar behavioural patterns as other sparse random projections in α-normed spaces. The dimension m of random index vectors can be seen as the capacity of the method to memorize and distinguish entities. For m up to a certain number ($100 \leq m \leq 6000$) in our experiments, as was expected, a PoP-constructed model for a large m shows a better performance and smaller δ than a model for a small m. Since observations in semantic spaces have a *very*-long-tailed distribution, choosing different values of non-zero elements for index vectors does not effect the performance (as mentioned, in most cases 1, 2 or 3 non-zero elements are sufficient). Furthermore, changes in the adopted distribution of t_{ij} only slightly affect the performance of the method.

In the next section, using empirical investigations we show the advantages of the PoP model and support the claims from this section.

3   Evaluation & Empirical Investigations

3.1   Comparing PoP and RI

For evaluation purposes, we use the MEN relatedness test set (Bruni et al., 2014) and the UKWaC corpus (Baroni et al., 2009). The dataset consists of 3000 pairs of words (from 751 distinct tagged lemmas). Similar to other 'relatedness tests', Spearman's rank correlation ρ score from the comparison of human-based ranking and system-induced rankings is the figure of merit. We use these resources for evaluation since they are in public domain, both the dataset and corpus are large, and they have been used for evaluating several word space models—for example, see Levy et al. (2015), Tsvetkov et al. (2015), Baroni et al. (2014), Kiela and Clark (2014). In this section, unless otherwise stated, we use cosine for similarity measurements.

Figure 1 shows the performance of the simple count-based word space model for lemmatized-context-windows that extend symmetrically around lemmas from MEN.[10] As expected, up to

---

[8]Such as many classic search algorithms that are proposed for solving NP-complete problems in artificial intelligence.

[9]As opposed to pairwise correlations in the original high-

dimensional space.

[10]We use the tokenized preprocessed UKWaC. However, except for using part-of-speech tags for locating lemmas

a certain context-window size, the performance using count-based methods increases with an extension of the window.[11] For context-windows larger than 25+25 the performance gradually declines. More importantly, in all cases, we have $\rho < 0.50$.

We performed the same experiments using the RI technique. For each context window size, we performed 10 runs of the RI model construction. Figure 1 reports for each context-window size the average of the observed performances for the 10 RI models. In this experiment, we used index vectors of dimensionality 1000 containing 4 non-zero elements. As shown in Figure 1, the average performance of the RI is almost identical to the performance of the count-based model. This is an expected result since RI's objective is to retain Euclidean distances between vectors (thus cosine) but in spaces of lowered dimensionality. In this sense, RI is successful and achieves its goal of lowering the dimensionality while keeping Euclidean distances between vectors. However, using RI+cosine does not yield any improvements in the similarity assessment task.

We then performed similar experiments using PoP-constructed models, with the same context window sizes and the same dimensions as in the RI experiments, averaging again over 10 runs for each context window size. The performance is also reported in Figure 1. For the PoP method, however, instead of using the cosine measure we use Kendall's τ_b for measuring similarities. The PoP-constructed models converge faster than RI and count-based methods and for smaller context-windows they outperform the count-based and RI methods with a large margin. However, as the sizes of the windows grow, performances of these methods become more similar (but PoP still outperforms the others). In any case, the performance of PoP remains above 0.50 (i.e., $\rho > 0.50$). Note that in RI-constructed models, using Kendall's τ_b also yield better performance than using cosine.

3.2 PPMI Transformation of PoP Vectors

Although PoP outperforms RI and count-based models, compared to the state-of-the-art methods,

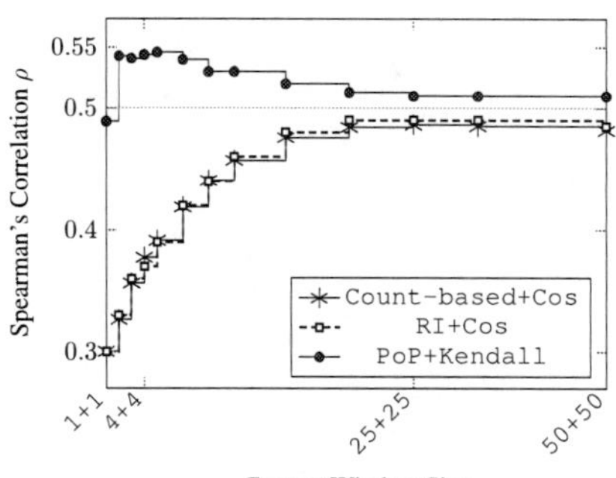

Figure 1: Performance of the classic count-based a-word-per-dimension model vs. RI vs. Pop in the MEN relatedness test. Note that count-based and RI models show almost an identical performance in this task.

its performance is still not satisfying. Transformations based on association measures such as PPMI have been proposed to improve the discriminatory power of context vectors and thus the performance of models in semantic similarity assessment tasks (see Church and Hanks (1990), Turney (2001), Turney (2008), and Levy et al. (2015)). For a given set of vectors, pointwise mutual information (PMI) is interpreted as a measure of information overlap between vectors. As put by Bouma (2009), PMI is a mathematical tool for measuring how much the actual probability of a particular co-occurrence (e.g., two words in a word space) deviate from the expected probability of their individual occurrences (e.g., the probability of occurrences of each word in a words space) under the assumption of independence (i.e., the occurrence of one word does not affect the occurrences of other words).

In Figure 2, we show the performance of PMI-transformed spaces. Count-based PMI+Cosine models outperform other techniques including the introduced PoP method. The performance of PMI models can be further enhanced by their normalization, often discarding negative values[12] and using PPMI. Also, SVD truncation of PPMI-weighted spaces can improve the performance slightly (see the above mentioned references) requiring, however, expensive computations of eigenvectors.[13] For a $p \times n$ matrix with elements v_{xy}, $1 \leq x \leq p$ and $1 \leq y \leq n$, we compute the

---

listed in MEN, we do not use any additional information or processes (i.e., no frequency cut-off for context selection, no syntactic information, etc.).

[11]After all, in models for relatedness tests, relationships of topical nature play a more important role than other relationships such as synonymy.

[12]See Bouma (2009) for a mathematical delineation. Jurafsky and Martin (2015) also provide an intuitive description.

[13]In our experiments, applying SVD truncation to models results in negligible improvements between 0.01 and 0.001.

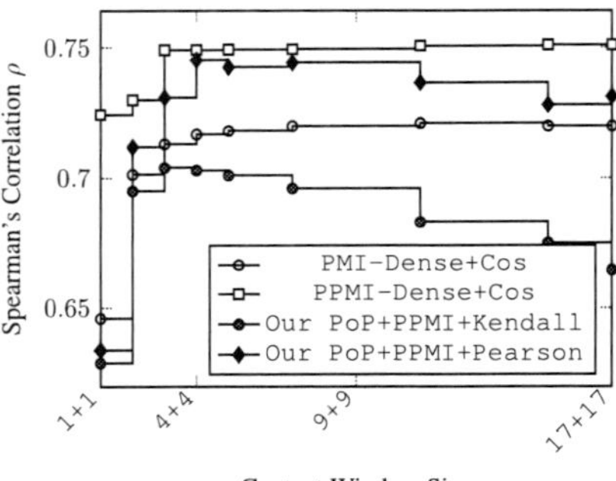

Figure 2: Performances of (P)PMI-transformed models for various sizes of context-windows. From context size 4+4, the performance remains almost intact (0.72 for PMI and 0.75 for PPMI). We also report the average performance for PoP-constructed models constructed at the dimensionality $m = 1000$ and $s = 0.002$. PoP+PPMI+Pearson exhibits a performance similar as dense PPMI-weighted models, however, much faster and using far less amount of computational resources. Note that reported PoP+PMI performances can be enhanced by using $m > 1000$.

PPMI weight for a component v_{xy} as follows:

$$ppmi(v_{xy}) = \max(0, \log \frac{v_{xy} \times \sum_{i=1}^{p} \sum_{j=1}^{n} v_{ij}}{\sum_{i=1}^{p} v_{iy} \times \sum_{j=1}^{n} v_{xj}}). \quad (3)$$

The most important benefit of the PoP method is that PoP-constructed models, in contrast to previously suggested random projection-based models, can be still weighted using PPMI (or any other weighting techniques applicable to the original count-based models). In an RI-constructed model, the sum of values of row and column vectors of the model are always 0 (i.e., $\sum_{i=1}^{p} v_{iy}$ and $\sum_{j=1}^{n} v_{xj}$ in Equation 3 are always 0). As mentioned earlier, this is due to the fact that a random projection matrix in RI has an asymptotic standard Gaussian distribution (i.e., transformation matrix $\mathbf{R}$ has $E(\mathbf{R}) = 0$). As a result, PPMI weights for the RI-induced vector elements are undefined. In contrast to RI, the sum of values of vector elements in the PoP-constructed models is always greater than 0 (because the transformation is carried out by a projection matrix $\mathbf{R}$ of $E(\mathbf{R}) > 0$). Also, depending on the structure of data in the underlying count-based model, by choosing a suitably large value of s, it can be guaranteed that the sum of column vectors is always a non-zero value. Hence, vectors in PoP models can undergo the PPMI transformation defined in Equation 3. Moreover, the PPMI trans-

formation in PoP models is much faster, compared to the one performed on count-based models, due to the low dimensionality of vectors in the PoP-constructed model. Therefore, the PoP method makes it possible to benefit both from the high efficiency of randomized techniques as well as from the high accuracy of PPMI transformation in semantic similarity tasks.

If we put aside the information-theoretic interpretation of PPMI weighting (i.e., distilling statistical information that matters), the logarithmic transformation of probabilities in the PPMI definition plays the role of a *power transformation* process for converting long-tailed distributions in the original high-dimensional count-based models to Gaussian-like distributions in the transformed models. From a statistical perspective, any variation of PMI transformation can be seen as an attempt to stabilize the variance of vector coordinates and therefore to make the observations more similar/fit to Gaussian distribution (a practice with a long history in research, particularly in the biological and psychological sciences).

To exemplify this phenomenon, in Figure 3, we show histograms of the distributions of the assigned weights to the vector that represents the lemmatized form of the verb 'abandon' in various models. As shown, the raw collected frequencies in the original high-dimensional count-based model have a long tail distribution (see Figure 3a). Applying the log transformation to this vector yields a vector of weights with a Gaussian distribution (Figure 3b). Weights in the RI-constructed vector (Figure 3c) have a perfect Gaussian distribution but with an expected value of 0 (i.e., $\mathcal{N}(0, 1)$). The PoP method, however, largely preserves the long tail distribution of coordinates from the original space (Figure 3d), which in turn can be weighted using PPMI and thereby transformed into a Gaussian-like distribution.

Given that models after the PPMI transformation have bell-shaped Gaussian distributions, we expect that a correlation measure such as Pearson's r, which takes advantage of the prior knowledge about the distribution of data, outperforms the non-parametric Kendall's τ_b for computing similarities in PPMI-transformed spaces.[14] This is indeed the case (see Figure 2).

---

[14]Note that using correlation measures such as Pearson's r and Kendall's τ_b in count-based model may excel measures such as cosine. However, their application is limited due to the high-dimensionality of count-based methods.

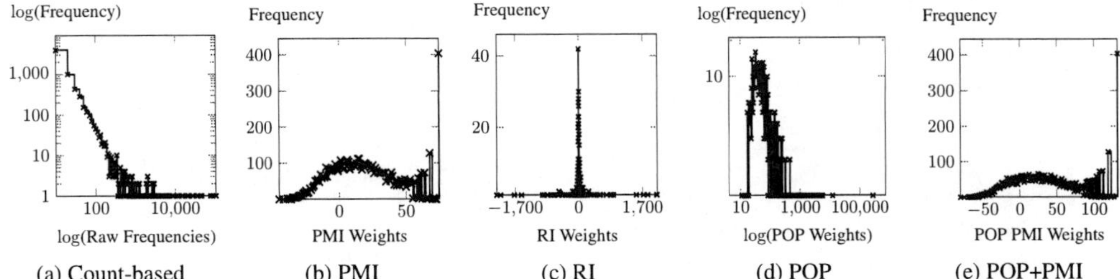

(a) Count-based   (b) PMI   (c) RI   (d) POP   (e) POP+PMI

Figure 3: A histogram of the distribution of frequencies of weights (i.e., the value of the coordinates) in various models built from 1+1 context-windows for the lemmatized form of the verb 'abandon' in the UKWaC corpus.

3.3 PoP's Parameters, its Random Behavior and Performance

As discussed in § 2.3, PoP is a randomized algorithm and its performance is influenced by a number of parameters. In this section, we study the PoP method's behavior by reporting its performance in the MEN relatedness test under different parameter settings. To keep evaluations and reports to a manageable size, we focus on models built using context-windows of size 4+4.

Figure 4 shows the method's performance when the dimension m of the projected index vectors increases. In these experiments, index vectors are built using 4 non-zero elements; thus, as m increases, s in Equation 2 decreases. For each m, $100 \leq m \leq 5000$, the models are built 10 times and the average as well as the maximum and the minimum observed performances in these experiments are reported. For PPMI transformed PoP spaces, with increasing dimensions, the performance boosts and, furthermore, the variance in performance (i.e., the shaded areas)[15] gets smaller.

However, for the count-based PoP method without PPMI transformation (shown by the dash-dotted lines) and with the number of non-zero elements fixed to 4, increasing m over 2000 decreases the performance. This is unexpected since an increase in dimensionality is usually assumed to entail an increase in performance. This behavior, however, can be the result of using a very small s; simply put, the number of non-zero elements are not sufficient to build projected spaces with adequate distribution. To investigate this matter, we study the performance of the method with the dimension m fixed to 3000 but with index vec-

---

[15]Evidently, the probability of worst and best performances can be inferred from the reported average results.

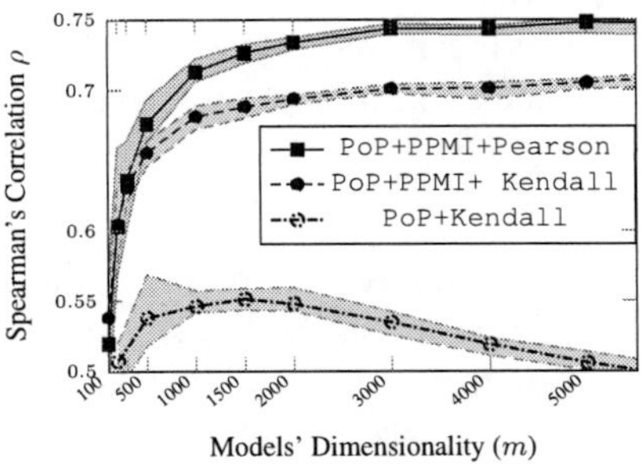

Figure 4: Changes in PoP's performance when the dimensionality of models increases. The average performance in each set-up is shown by the marked lines. The margins around these lines show the minimum and maximum performance observed in 10 independent executions.

tors built using different numbers of non-zero elements, i.e., different values of s.

Figure 5 shows the observed performances. For PPMI-weighted spaces, increasing the number of non-zero elements clearly deteriorates the performance. For unweighted PoP models, an increase in s up to the limit that does not result in non-orthogonal index vectors enhances performances. As shown in Figure 6, when the dimensionality of the index vectors is fixed and s increases, the chances of having non-orthogonal vectors in index vectors are boosted. Hence, the chance of distortions in similarities increases. These distortions can enhance the result if they are controlled (e.g., using a training procedure such as the one used in neural net embedding). However, when left to chance, they can often lower the performance. Evidently, this is an oversimplified justification: in fact, s plays the role of a switch that controls the resemblance between the distribution of data in

195

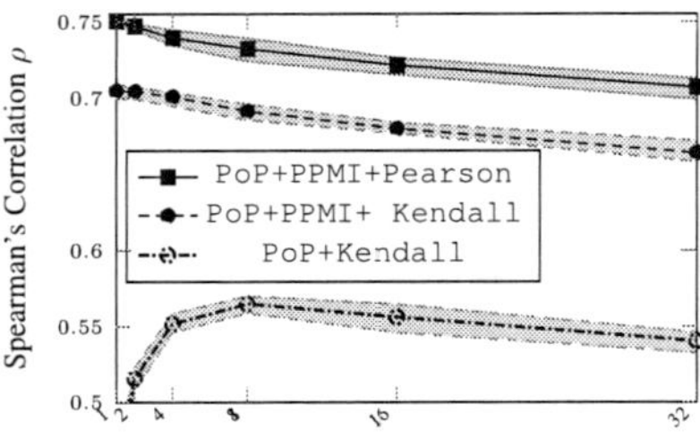

Figure 5: Changes in PoP's performances when the dimensionality of models are fixed to $m = 3000$ and the number of non-zero elements in index vectors (i.e., s) increases. The average performances in each set-up are shown by marked lines. The margins around these lines show the minimum and maximum performance observed in 10 independent executions.

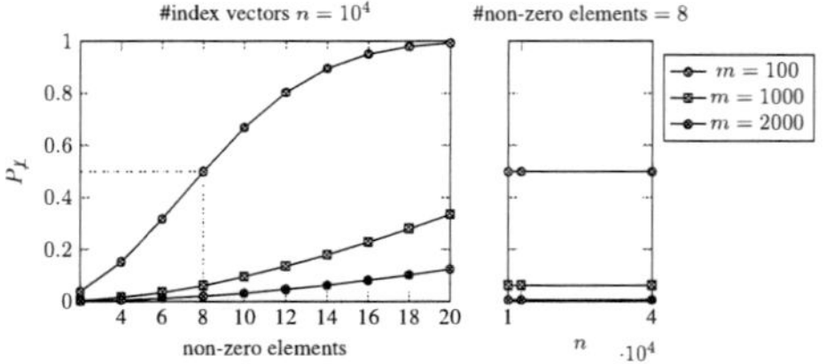

Figure 6: The proportion of non-orthogonal pairs of index vectors ($P_{\not\perp}$) obtained in a simulation for various dimensionality and number of non-zero elements. The left figure shows the changes of $P_{\not\perp}$ for a fixed number of index vectors $n = 10^4$ when the number of non-zero elements increases. The right figure shows $P_{\not\perp}$ when the number of non-zero elements is fixed to 8 but the number of index vectors n increases. As shown, $P_{\not\perp}$ is determined by the number of non-zero elements and the dimensionality of index vectors and independently of n.

the original space and the projected/transformed spaces. It seems that the sparsity of vectors in the original matrix plays a role in finding the optimal value for s. If PoP-constructed models are used directly (together with τ_b) for computing similarities, then we propose $0.002 < s$. If PoP-constructed models are subject to an additional weighting process for stabilizing vector distributions into Gaussian-like distributions such as PPMI, we propose using only 1 or 2 non-zero elements.

Last but not least, we confirm that by carefully selecting context elements (i.e., removing stop words and using lower and upper bound frequency cut-offs for context selection) and fine tuning PoP+PPMI+Pearson (i.e., increasing the dimension of models and scaling PMI weights as in Levy et al. (2015)) we achieve an even higher score in the MEN test (i.e., an average of 0.78 with the max of 0.787). Moreover, although improvements from applying SVD truncation are negligible, we can employ it for reducing the dimensionality of PoP vectors (e.g., from 6000 to 200).

4 Conclusion

We introduced a new technique called PoP for the incremental construction of semantic spaces. PoP can be seen as a dimensionality reduction method, which is based on a newly devised random projection matrix that contains only positive integer values. The major benefit of PoP is that it transfers vectors onto spaces of lower dimensionality without changing their distribution to a Gaussian

shape with zero expectation. The obtained transformed spaces using PoP can, therefore, be manipulated similarly to the original high-dimensional spaces, only much faster and consequently requiring a considerably lower amount of computational resources.

PPMI weighting can be easily applied to PoP-constructed models. In our experiments, we observe that PoP+PPMI+Pearson can be used to build models that achieve a high performance in semantic relatedness tests. More concretely, for index vector dimensions $m \geq 3000$, PoP+PPMI+Pearson achieves an average score of 0.75 in the MEN relatedness test, which is comparable to many neural embedding techniques (e.g., see scores reported in Chen and de Melo (2015) and Tsvetkov et al. (2015)). However, in contrast to these approaches, PoP+PPMI+Pearson achieves this competitive performance without the need for time-consuming training of neural nets. Moreover, the processes involved are all done on vectors of low dimensionality. Hence, the PoP method can dramatically enhance the performance in tasks involving distributional analysis of natural language.

Acknowledgments

The work described in this paper is funded by the Deutsche Forschungsgemeinschaft (DFG) through the 'Collaborative Research Centre 991 (CRC 991): The Structure of Representations in Language, Cognition, and Science".

References

Sanjeev Arora, Aditya Bhaskara, Rong Ge, and Tengyu Ma. 2014. Provable bounds for learning some deep representations. In *Proceedings of the 31st International Conference on Machine Learning, ICML 2014, Beijing, China, 21-26 June 2014*, pages 584–592.

Marco Baroni, Alessandro Lenci, and Luca Onnis. 2007. ISA meets Lara: An incremental word space model for cognitively plausible simulations of semantic learning. In *Proceedings of the Workshop on Cognitive Aspects of Computational Language Acquisition*, pages 49–56, Prague, Czech Republic, June. Association for Computational Linguistics.

Marco Baroni, Silvia Bernardini, Adriano Ferraresi, and Eros Zanchetta. 2009. The wacky wide web: a collection of very large linguistically processed web-crawled corpora. *Language Resources and Evaluation*, 43(3):209–226.

Marco Baroni, Georgiana Dinu, and Germán Kruszewski. 2014. Don't count, predict! a systematic comparison of context-counting vs. context-predicting semantic vectors. In *Proceedings of the 52nd Annual Meeting of the Association for Computational Linguistics (Volume 1: Long Papers)*, pages 238–247, Baltimore, Maryland, June. Association for Computational Linguistics.

Ella Bingham and Heikki Mannila. 2001. Random projection in dimensionality reduction: applications to image and text data. In *Proceedings of the Seventh ACM SIGKDD International Conference on Knowledge discovery and data mining*, KDD '01, pages 245–250, New York, NY, USA. ACM.

Gerlof Bouma. 2009. Normalized (pointwise) mutual information in collocation extraction. In *Proceedings of the Biennial GSCL Conference*.

Elia Bruni, Nam Khanh Tran, and Marco Baroni. 2014. Multimodal distributional semantics. *J. Artif. Int. Res.*, 49(1):1–47, January.

Jiaqiang Chen and Gerard de Melo. 2015. Semantic information extraction for improved word embeddings. In *Proceedings of the 1st Workshop on Vector Space Modeling for Natural Language Processing*, pages 168–175, Denver, Colorado, June. Association for Computational Linguistics.

Peter Y. Chen and Paula M. Popovich. 2002. *Correlation: Parametric and Nonparametric Measures*. Quantitative Applications in the Social Sciences. Sage Publications.

Kenneth Ward Church and Patrick Hanks. 1990. Word association norms, mutual information, and lexicography. *Comput. Linguist.*, 16(1):22–29, March.

Trevor Cohen, Roger Schvaneveldt, and Dominic Widdows. 2010. Reflective random indexing and indirect inference: A scalable method for discovery of implicit connections. *Journal of Biomedical Informatics*, 43(2):240 – 256.

Zellig Harris. 1954. Distributional structure. *Word*, 10(2-3):146–162.

Robert Hecht-Nielsen. 1994. Context vectors: general purpose approximate meaning representations self-organized from raw data. *Computational Intelligence: Imitating Life*, pages 43–56.

Piotr Indyk. 2000. Stable distributions, pseudorandom generators, embeddings and data stream computation. In *41st Annual Symposium on Foundations of Computer Science*, pages 189–197.

William Johnson and Joram Lindenstrauss. 1984. Extensions of Lipschitz mappings into a Hilbert space. In *Conference in modern analysis and probability (New Haven, Conn., 1982)*, volume 26 of *Contemporary Mathematics*, pages 189–206. American Mathematical Society.

William P. Jones and George W. Furnas. 1987. Pictures of relevance: A geometric analysis of similarity measures. *Journal of the American Society for Information Science*, 38(6):420–442.

Daniel Jurafsky and James H. Martin, 2015. *Speech and Language Processing*, chapter Chapter 19: Vector Semantics. Prentice Hall, 3rd edition. Draft of August 24, 2015.

Pentti Kanerva, Jan Kristoferson, and Anders Holst. 2000. Random indexing of text samples for latent semantic analysis. In *Proceedings of the 22nd Annual Conference of the Cognitive Science Society*, pages 103–6. Erlbaum.

Richard M. Karp. 1991. An introduction to randomized algorithms. *Discrete Applied Mathematics*, 34(13):165 – 201.

Samuel Kaski. 1998. Dimensionality reduction by random mapping: fast similarity computation for clustering. In *The 1998 IEEE International Joint Conference on Neural Networks*, volume 1, pages 413–418.

Maurice G. Kendall. 1938. A new measure of rank correlation. *Biometrika*, 30(1-2):81–93.

Douwe Kiela and Stephen Clark. 2014. A systematic study of semantic vector space model parameters. In *Proceedings of the 2nd Workshop on Continuous Vector Space Models and their Compositionality (CVSC)*, pages 21–30, Gothenburg, Sweden, April. Association for Computational Linguistics.

William R. Knight. 1966. A computer method for calculating kendall's tau with ungrouped data. *Journal of the American Statistical Association*, 61(314):436–439.

Omer Levy and Yoav Goldberg. 2014. Neural word embedding as implicit matrix factorization. In Z. Ghahramani, M. Welling, C. Cortes, N. D. Lawrence, and K. Q. Weinberger, editors, *Advances in Neural Information Processing Systems 27*, pages 2177–2185. Curran Associates, Inc.

Omer Levy, Yoav Goldberg, and Ido Dagan. 2015. Improving distributional similarity with lessons learned from word embeddings. *Transactions of the Association for Computational Linguistics*, 3:211–225.

Ping Li, Trevor J. Hastie, and Kenneth W. Church. 2006. Very sparse random projections. In *Proceedings of the 12th ACM SIGKDD International Conference on Knowledge Discovery and Data Mining*, KDD '06, pages 287–296, New York, NY, USA. ACM.

Tomas Mikolov, Ilya Sutskever, Kai Chen, Greg S Corrado, and Jeff Dean. 2013. Distributed representations of words and phrases and their compositionality. In C. J. C. Burges, L. Bottou, M. Welling, Z. Ghahramani, and K. Q. Weinberger, editors, *Advances in Neural Information Processing Systems 26*, pages 3111–3119. Curran Associates, Inc.

Marvin Lee Minsky and Seymour Papert. 1969. *Perceptrons: An Introduction to Computational Geometry*. MIT Press.

Behrang QasemiZadeh. 2015. Random indexing revisited. In *20th International Conference on Applications of Natural Language to Information Systems, NLDB*, pages 437–442. Springer.

The Apache Commons Mathematics Library [Computer Software]. 2016. KendallsCorrelation Class. Retrieved from https://commons.apache.org/proper/commons-math/javadocs/api-3.6.1/index.html.

Yulia Tsvetkov, Manaal Faruqui, Wang Ling, Guillaume Lample, and Chris Dyer. 2015. Evaluation of word vector representations by subspace alignment. In *Proceedings of the 2015 Conference on Empirical Methods in Natural Language Processing*, pages 2049–2054, Lisbon, Portugal, September. Association for Computational Linguistics.

Peter D. Turney and Patrick Pantel. 2010. From frequency to meaning: Vector space models of semantics. *J. Artif. Int. Res.*, 37(1):141–188, January.

Peter D. Turney. 2001. Mining the web for synonyms: PMI-IR versus LSA on TOEFL. In *Proceedings of the 12th European Conference on Machine Learning*, EMCL '01, pages 491–502, London, UK, UK. Springer-Verlag.

Peter D. Turney. 2008. The latent relation mapping engine: Algorithm and experiments. *J. Artif. Int. Res.*, 33(1):615–655, December.

Behrang Q. Zadeh and Siegfried Handschuh. 2014. Random Manhattan integer indexing: Incremental L1 normed vector space construction. In *Proceedings of the 2014 Conference on Empirical Methods in Natural Language Processing, EMNLP 2014, October 25-29, 2014, Doha, Qatar, A meeting of SIGDAT, a Special Interest Group of the ACL*, pages 1713–1723.

A   Supplemental Material

Codes and resulting embeddings from experiments are available from `https://user.phil-fak.uni-duesseldorf.de/~zadeh/material/pop-vectors`.

A Compositional-Distributional Semantic Model for Searching Complex Entity Categories

Juliano Efson Sales[1], André Freitas[1], Brian Davis[2], Siegfried Handschuh[1]
[1]Department of Computer Science and Mathematics - University of Passau
Innstrasse 43, ITZ-110, 94032 Passau, Germany
{juliano-sales,andre.freitas,siegfried.handschuh}@uni-passau.de
[2]Insight Centre for Data Analytics - National University of Ireland Galway
IDA Business Park, Lower Dangan, Galway, Ireland
brian.davis@insight-centre.org

Abstract

Users combine attributes and types to describe and classify entities into categories. These categories are fundamental for organising knowledge in a decentralised way acting as tags and predicates. When searching for entities, categories frequently describes the search query. Considering that users do not know in which terms the categories are expressed, they might query the same concept by a paraphrase. While some categories are composed of simple expressions (e.g. *Presidents of Ireland*), others have more complex compositional patterns (e.g. *French Senators Of The Second Empire*). This work proposes a hybrid semantic model based on syntactic analysis, distributional semantics and named entity recognition to recognise *paraphrases of entity categories*. Our results show that the proposed model outperformed the comparative baseline, in terms of recall and mean reciprocal rank, thus being suitable for addressing the vocabulary gap between user queries and entity categories.

1 Introduction

A significant part of search queries on the web target entities (e.g. people, places or events) (Pound et al., 2010). In this context, users frequently use the characteristics of the target entity to describe the search query. For example, to find *Barack Obama*, it is reasonable that a user types the query *Current President of United States*.

The combination of attributes and types of an entity in a grammatically correct fashion defines an *entity category*, which groups a set of entities that share common characteristics. Examples of entity categories are *French Female Artistic Gymnasts*, *Presidents of Ireland* and *French Senators Of The Second Empire*. Considering that users do not know in which terms the categories are expressed, they might query the same concept by a paraphrase, i.e. using synonyms and different syntactic structures.

The following text excerpt from Wikipedia shows an example where *Embraer S.A* is defined as *Brazilian aerospace conglomerate*:

> *"Embraer S.A. is a **Brazilian aerospace conglomerate** that produces commercial, military, executive and agricultural aircraft and provides aeronautical services. It is headquartered in São José dos Campos, São Paulo State."*[1]

The flexibility and richness of natural language allow describing **Brazilian aerospace conglomerate** both as *Brazilian Planemaker*[2] or as *Aircraft manufacturers of Brazil*[3].

In addition to their occurrence in texts, entity categories are also available in the form of structured data. The Yago project (Suchanek et al., 2007) shares unary properties associating hundreds of thousands of descriptive categories manually created by the Wikipedia community to DBpedia entities (Auer et al., 2007). Thus, a mechanism to recognise paraphrases can make a shortcut between a natural language expression and a set of entities. Table 1 shows a list of entity categories and associated paraphrases.

This paper focuses on the recognition of *paraphrases of entity categories*, which is designed as an information retrieval task. To

---

[1]Extracted from https://en.wikipedia.org/wiki/Embraer

[2]In *Brazilian Planemaker Unveils Its Biggest Military Jet Yet* published by Business Insider.

[3]The Wikipedia category *Aircraft manufacturers of Brazil*.

*Proceedings of the Fifth Joint Conference on Lexical and Computational Semantics (*SEM 2016)*, pages 199–208,
Berlin, Germany, August 11-12, 2016.

Original	*Paraphrased*
Prehistoric Canines	Ancestral Wolves
Soviet Pop Music Groups	Popular Musical Bands in the USSR
American Architectural Styles	Fashions of American Building Design
Defunct Companies of Finland	Bankrupt Finnish Businesses

Table 1: Examples of paraphrases.

deal with this problem, we propose an approach which combines syntactic analysis, distributional semantics and named entity recognition. To support reproducibility and comparability, we provide the test collection and the source code related to this work at `http://bit.ly/cat-test-collection` and `http://bit.ly/linse-code`.

2 Understanding the Structure of an Entity Category

An entity category names and classifies a set of entities. It is composed of a central concept, called *core*, and its *specialisations*. For example, the entity category *2008 Film Festivals* embraces *festivals*, which defines the category's core. More specifically, this category covers those *festivals* that are related to *films* and occurred in *2008*. In its turn, *Populated Coastal Places in South Africa* embraces *places* (the core) that are *populated*, in the coast (*coastal*) and within *South Africa*. While *festivals* and *places* act as cores, all other terms work as *specialisations*, defining characteristics such as *temporality* (specialisations of time), *localization* (specialisations of place) and other general characteristics. These three types of terms are respectively classified as *temporal named entity*, *spatial named entity*, and *general specialisation*.

By analysing a large set of entity categories generated in a decentralised setting, Freitas et al. (2014) described them according to a group of recurring features: *contains verbs, contains temporal references, contains named entities, contains conjunctions, contains disjunctions* and *contains operators*. These features suggest a syntactic pattern that can be described as a combination of simple relations based on the lexical categories of their constituent terms (Freitas et al., 2014). In this manner, we apply a list of parsing rules to determine the graph structure/hierarchy according to Table 2, which defines *the core-oriented segmentation model*.

During the parsing process, categories are ana-

POS Pattern	Core-side
[VB, IN]	left
[NN, VBG]	left
[IN]	left
[","]	left
[POS]	right
[CC]	left

Table 2: Rules to construct the graph of an entity category.

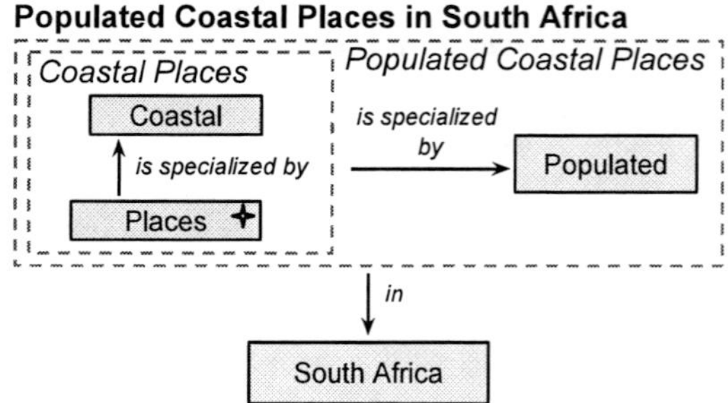

Figure 1: Graph of *Populated Coastal Places in South Africa*.

lysed from left to right. Once a pattern is identified, the *core-side* attribute specifies the side where the core is located. Both parts are then recursively analysed, where the opposite part is treated as specialisation(s). The order of the rules determines their precedence. To simplify the rule list, some tags are normalised, e.g. POS-tag *TO* is converted to *IN* and *NNPS* is converted to *NNP*. When no pattern is identified, the last term in the resulting chunk is admitted as the *core* and all others as *specialisations*, if any.

Figure 1 shows the graph generated by the core-oriented segmentation method for the entity category *Populated Coastal Places in South Africa*. The graph root (*places*) represents the core.

3 Semantic Approximation & Compositionality

From a finite set of words, it is possible to express unlimited utterances and ideas. This property is credited to the principle of *semantic compositionality* (Baroni et al., 2014a).

Distributional semantics is based on the hypothesis that words co-occurring in similar contexts tend to have similar meaning (Harris, 1954; Turney and Pantel, 2010). Distributional semantics supports the automatic construction of semantic models from large-scale unstructured corpora, using vector space models to represent the meaning of a word. The process to construct distributional models ranges from statistical methods to models based on machine learning (Dumais et al., 1988; Mikolov et al., 2013; Jeffrey Pennington, 2014).

Distributional semantics allows measuring the semantic compositionality by combining an appropriate *word representation* and a suitable method to *semantically compose* them. Its meaning representation supports the construction of more comprehensive semantic models which have semantic approximation at its centre. We compute the semantic similarity and relatedness between two terms using vector operations in the vector space.

4 Compositional-Distributional Model

This work proposes *a hybrid model that combines the core-oriented segmentation model with semantic approximation based on distributional semantics to provide a semantic search approach for entity categories*. This approach segments the entity categories and stores their constituent parts according to their type in a graph-based data model.

The graph data model has a signature $\Sigma = (C, Z, R, S, E)$, where C, Z, R and S represent the sets of *cores*, *general specialisations*, *temporal specialisations* and *spatial specialisations* respectively. E contains sets of edges, where each set represents a graph. The elements in C and Z are natural language terms indexed in distributional semantics spaces. The elements in R are closed integer intervals representing the temporal expressions in years. The elements in S are sets of equivalent terms referring to a geographic place and its demonyms. The proposed graph data model is inspired by the τ-*Space* (Freitas et al., 2011), which represents graph knowledge in a distributional space.

Distributional semantics spaces represent terms by distributional vectors. The distributional vectors are generated from a large external corpus to capture the semantic relation in a broader scenario. It allows that even when dealing with a small dataset, the semantic representation is not limited to that context. The distributional space allows searching by measuring the geometric distances or vector angles between the query term and the indexed terms.

Temporal and spatial specialisations do not use the same representation strategy. In the case of spatial named entities, our tests have shown poor performance when using general-purpose distributional semantics models to compare them. The problem resides in the fact that places and demonyms have a high relatedness with common nouns. For example, in one distributional model[4], *American* has a higher relatedness with *war* than with *Texas*. To avoid this kind of misinterpretation, spatial expressions are compared using their names, acronyms, and demonyms.

Because of the numerical and ordered nature of temporal references, temporal specialisations are represented as year intervals. By this representation, two expressions of time are compared by computing the interval intersection. We consider them as semantically related if the intersection is not empty.

4.1 Constructing the Knowledge Representation Model

The first step is to build the data model based on the target set of entity categories. For each entity category in the set, the segmentation model presented in Section 2 generates a graph representation $G = (V, E)$. The set of vertices (V) is the union of the core term $\vec{c}$, the set of general specialisations (Z'), the set of temporal specialisations (R') and the set of spatial specialisations (S'), i.e. $V = \{c'\} \cup Z' \cup R' \cup S'$. Any of these three sets of specialisations can eventually be empty. The process of building the data space from a target set of entity categories T is described in Algorithm 1. In line 6, the category t is decomposed by the core-oriented segmentation model. Each term is indexed in their respective index according to their type: the core ($\vec{c}$) in the core space (C) and the specialisations in the general specialisation space (Z),

---

[4]Distributional models used in the context of this work are presented in Section 5.

temporal space (R) and spatial space (S).

Spatial specialisations are identified by the longest string matching method comparing against a dictionary which contains the name, acronym and demonym of places. Temporal expressions are converted to an interval of years. Terms that are considered neither spatial nor temporal specialisations fall into the general specialisation case.

Algorithm 1 Construction

1: **input** : T : target set of entity categories.
2: **output** : Σ : a filled graph data model.
3:
4: $C \leftarrow \emptyset, Z \leftarrow \emptyset, R \leftarrow \emptyset, S \leftarrow \emptyset, E \leftarrow \emptyset$
5: **for** t $\in$ T **do**
6: $\quad \vec{c}, Z', R', S', E' \leftarrow graphOf(\text{t})$
7: $\quad C \leftarrow \bigcup \{\vec{c}\}$
8: $\quad Z \leftarrow \bigcup Z'$
9: $\quad R \leftarrow \bigcup R'$
10: $\quad S \leftarrow \bigcup S'$
11: $\quad E \leftarrow \bigcup \{flat(E')\}$
12: **return** Σ

To illustrate visually, Figure 2 depicts a diagram where the entity categories *2000s Film Festivals* and *Populated Coastal Places in South Africa* are represented within the model. The cores *festivals* and *places* are stored in the core distributional space (C: geometric representation). The first category has two specialisations: the time interval 2000-2009, indexed in the temporal space (R: interval representation); and *film*, indexed in the general specialisation space (Z: also geometric representation). Next, the second category has three specialisations: the spatial named entity *South Africa*, indexed in the spatial index (S: expanded index); and the general specialisations *coastal* and *populated*, indexed in (Z). Dashed lines connecting the cores to their specialisations represent the flattened edges of the graphs, i.e. all specialisations are connected directly to their respective core.

4.2 Searching as Semantic Interpretation

Algorithm 2 describes the interpretation process that receives the query and the graph data model Σ as inputs. Queries are paraphrases that follow the same syntactic pattern of entity categories. The process starts by generating the graph of the input query (line 4). Considering the graph structure, each vertex becomes a sub-query to be submitted to their respective specific index (representation space).

The core defines the first sub-query. It needs to be semantically aligned to relevant cores in Σ. In line 5, $distSearch(\vec{c}, C)$ searches for cores semantically related to the query core $\vec{c}$. In addition to the simple searching of terms and synonyms, the vector cosine defines how related $\vec{c}$ is to the cores present in C. Given a threshold η, distributional search returns $K = \{(\vec{k}, h)|\vec{k} \in C, h = cosine(\vec{k}, \vec{c}), h > \eta\}$. The semantic relatedness threshold η determines the minimum distance or angle between the query core and the target cores that makes them semantically relevant. In the context of this work, η is defined dynamically according to the result set. Let X be the descending-order set of returned cosine scores, $(\eta = x_n | x_n \in X, x_{n+1} \in X, x_n/2 > x_{n+1})$. The distributional search returns a set of pairs $(\vec{k}, h)$ where $\vec{k}$ is a core term and h is the normalised $cosine(\vec{k}, \vec{c})$. Entity categories containing relevant cores are select for the next search step (lines 6, 7).

The next step deals with the specialisations. Spatial and temporal named entities found in the query are searched in their respective subsets, identifying equivalent spatial representations (lines 11-13) and comparing the time intervals (lines 14-20). Temporal expressions out-of-range are penalised by a negative score (line 20). The pairing of general specialisations (lines 22-24) follows the same principle of the core search. When there are two or more general specialisations, the method $maximiseMatching$ aims to avoid that two terms from one side match to the same term on the other side, selecting the pairs that maximise the final score.

The final score is determined by the composition of all scores proportionally to the number of terms in the categories according to the expressions in the lines 26-29.

In the example of Figure 2, *2008 Movie Celebrations* is the query which is segmented in *celebration* (core), *movie* (general specialisation) and *2008* (temporal interval). The core term *celebrations* feeds a sub-query in the distributional core space. The alignment is defined by computing a distributional semantic relatedness function between *celebrations* and all cores in the core space and by filtering out all the elements which are below the semantic relatedness threshold η.

Navigating over the graph structure, the query

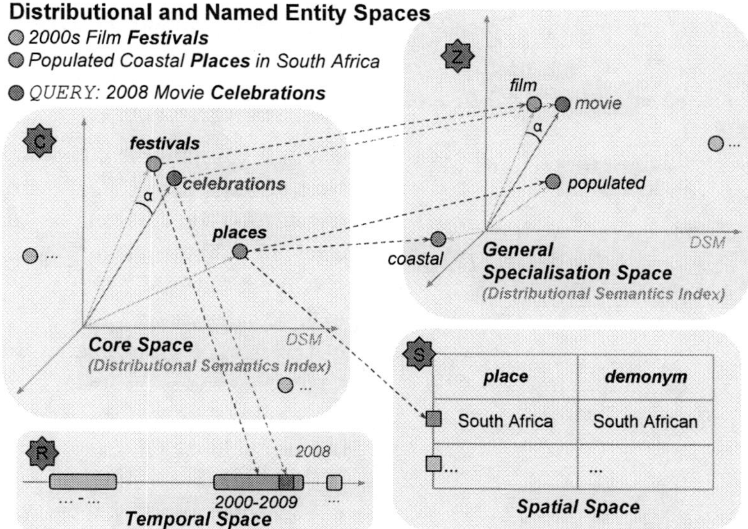

Figure 2: Depiction of the structured distributional vector space model.

terms representing specialisations are searched in the subspaces according to their type. In the given query example, *movie* is semantically aligned in the general specialisation space applying the same approach described in the core space. In its turn, the intersection is calculated for the temporal specialisation *2008* in the temporal space.

5 Evaluation

The evaluation focuses on comparing the compositional-distributional model to baseline approaches and assessing the performance of different distributional semantic models in combination with our representation model. The evaluation scenarios are designed to measure the individual contribution of each component.

5.1 Setup

The evaluation has three comparative baselines:

Bag-of-words search: Target entity categories are indexed in a state-of-the-art information retrieval system treating each category as a separate document. Additionally, the document is enriched by synonyms obtained from WorNet (Miller, 1995). Lucene[5] 4.10.1 is the information retrieval system used in the experiment.

Pure core-oriented segmentation: The core-oriented segmentation model incorporated by this work is applied in an isolated fashion, i.e. without the distributional component but making use of simple string matching, WordNet expansion and temporal and spatial named entity indices.

Sum-algebraic-based method: Entity categories are compared by an algebraic operation that sums up component vectors using the resulting vectors to calculate the cosine similarity. This method results in many scenarios, one for each distributional model.

Five different models are analysed in this work: **Latent Semantic Analysis** (Dumais et al., 1988): LSA is a distributional semantic space that extracts statistical relations between words in narrow context windows. It is characterised for executing a costly operation to reduce the space dimensionality.

Random Indexing (RI) (Sahlgren, 2005): Random Indexing was proposed to avoid the dimensional reduction. It dynamically accumulates *context vectors based on the occurrence of words in contexts* to generate the semantic space.

Explicit Semantic Analysis (Gabrilovich and Markovitch, 2007): ESA uses entire documents as contexts. It was created under the assumption of *concept hypothesis*[6] which states that a portion of information such as an article or document is associated with a particular concept, and the space model could take advantage of this information.

Continuous Skip-gram Model (W2V) (Mikolov et al., 2013): Skip-gram is a vector space model created by deep learning techniques focused on lo-

---

[6] Studies contest the existence of this hypothesis (Gottron et al., 2011).

Algorithm 2 Semantic Interpretation Process
____

1: **input** : `query` and $\Sigma = (C, Z, R, S, E)$
2: **output** : `Z` : related categories and their score.
3:
4: $\vec{c}, Z^q, R^q, S^q, E^q \leftarrow graphOf(\texttt{query})$
5: $U \leftarrow distSearch(\vec{c}, C)$
6: **for** $(\vec{k}, h) \in K$ **do**
7: $\quad D \leftarrow selectGraphsByCore(\vec{k}, E)$
8: $\quad$ **for all** $D' \in D$ **do**
9: $\quad\quad \vec{k}, Z^c, R^c, S^c, E^c \leftarrow D'$
10: $\quad\quad a \leftarrow 0$
11: $\quad\quad$ **for** $s^c \in S^c$ **do**
12: $\quad\quad\quad$ **if** $\exists s \in S^q \mid s^c \equiv s$ **then**
13: $\quad\quad\quad\quad a \leftarrow a + 1$
14: $\quad\quad b \leftarrow 0$
15: $\quad\quad$ **for** $r^c \in R^c$ **do**
16: $\quad\quad\quad$ **if** $\exists r \in R^q \mid r^c \equiv r$ **then**
17: $\quad\quad\quad\quad b \leftarrow b + 1$
18: $\quad\quad\quad$ **else**
19: $\quad\quad\quad\quad$ **if** $R^q \neq \emptyset$ **then**
20: $\quad\quad\quad\quad\quad b \leftarrow b - 0.5$
21: $\quad\quad X \leftarrow \emptyset$
22: $\quad\quad$ **for** $\vec{o^c} \in O^c$ **do**
23: $\quad\quad\quad J \leftarrow distSearch(\vec{o^c}, O^q)$
24: $\quad\quad\quad X.append(J)$
25: $\quad\quad Y \leftarrow maximiseMatching(X)$
26: $\quad\quad n^q \leftarrow \mid E^q \mid$
27: $\quad\quad n^c \leftarrow \mid E^c \mid + 1$
28: $\quad\quad u \leftarrow h + a + b + (\sum_{x=1}^{n} y_x \mid y_x \in Y)$
29: $\quad\quad u \leftarrow u * (n^q / n^c)$
30: $\quad\quad U.append(D', u)$
31: **return** $sort(U)$
____

cal context windows.

Global Vectors (GloVe) (Jeffrey Pennington, 2014): GloVe aims to conciliate the statistical co-occurrence knowledge present in the whole corpus with the local pattern analysis (proposed by the skip-gram model) applying a hybrid approach of conditional probability and machine learning techniques.

DINFRA (Barzegar et al., 2015), a SaaS distributional infrastructure, provided the distributional vectors. We generated all five ditributional models using the English Wikipedia 2014 dump as a reference corpus, stemming by the Porter algorithm (Porter, 1997) and removing stopwords. For LSA, RI and ESA, we used the SSpace Package (Jurgens and Stevens, 2010), while W2V and GloVe were generated by the code shared by the respec-

tive authors. All models used the default parameters defined in each implementation.

5.2 Test Collection

The test collection is composed of a knowledge base of more than 350,000 entity categories obtained from the complete set of Wikipedia 2014 categories, but removing those containing non-ASCII characters. Each category has between one to three paraphrases.

The creation of the queries was guided by seed target categories. The use of seed entity categories was deliberately decided to ensure the presence of one paraphrase equivalence for each query.

Queries were generated by asking a group of English-speaking volunteers to paraphrase the subset of 105 categories. They were instructed to describe the same meaning using different words and, if possible, different syntactic structures. After that, we applied a curation process conducted by two researchers to validate the paraphrase's equivalence intuitively. In the end, we admitted a set of 233 paraphrased pairs.

To create various degrees of difficulty in the topics, we balanced the test collection with categories varying in size (two to ten terms), in the occurrence of places and demonyms references, in the presence of temporal expressions and, in the occurrence of noun phrase components (verbs, adjectives, adverbs).

Test collection files are available at `http://bit.ly/cat-test-collection`.

5.3 Results and Discussion

We evaluate our approach in three scenarios. The first considers the TOP-10 list of each execution. The second considers the TOP-20 list and the third the TOP-50.

For each query in the test collection, we calculate the recall and mean reciprocal ranking, together with their aggregate measures (Table 3). Figure 3 provides a visual representation of the recall scores. In the experiment, we assumed that only one category corresponded to the correct answer. This assumption makes *precision* a redundant indicator since it can be derived from *recall* ($precision = recall/range \mid range \in \{10, 20, 50\}$).

The evaluation shows that distributional semantic models address part of the semantic matching tasks since distributional approaches outperform simple stemming string search and WordNet-

Approaches	Recall			MRR		
	Top 10	*Top 20*	*Top 50*	*Top 10*	*Top 20*	*Top 50*
Lucene	0.0904	0.1040	0.1357	0.0410	0.0420	0.0429
Core-Oriented Segmentation	0.0985	0.1126	0.1361	0.0613	0.0623	0.0630
Sum-algebraic-based method	-	-	-	-	-	-
with LSA	0.1126	0.1621	0.2117	0.0595	0.0631	0.0645
with RI	0.0630	0.0945	0.1216	0.0348	0.0371	0.0379
with ESA	0.0540	0.0900	0.1486	0.0271	0.0296	0.0312
with W2V	0.2657	0.3333	0.3963	0.1356	0.1403	0.1422
with GloVe	0.2702	0.3558	0.4324	0.1417	0.1476	0.1501
Our proposed method	-	-	-	-	-	-
with LSA	0.3545	0.4000	0.4590	0.1981	0.2013	0.2033
with RI	0.3073	0.3743	0.4078	0.1768	0.1813	0.1823
with ESA	0.2818	0.3182	0.4000	0.1822	0.1846	0.1872
with W2V	**0.3727**	**0.4364**	**0.4909**	**0.2448**	**0.2491**	**0.2510**
with GloVe	**0.3727**	0.4090	0.4500	0.2274	0.2300	0.2314

Table 3: Results for recall and mean reciprocal rank (MRR).

based query expansion. By applying either *sum-algebraic-based method* and *our proposed method*, most of the distributional models present significant performance improvement in comparison to non-distributional methods. It is also important to stress that Word2Vec and GloVe consistently deliver better results for the test collection. Apart the controversies about predictive-based and count-based distributional models (Baroni et al., 2014b; Lebret and Collobert, 2015; Levy and Goldberg, 2014), in the context of this work, these results suggest that predictive-based distributional models outperform count-based methods (despite the proximity of LSA results).

Regarding the compositional method, the results of the *core-oriented strategy* combined with the named entity recognition exceeded all results delivered by the *sum-algebraic-based method* when comparing the same distributional model. The performance increases not only in the recall, which represents more entity categories retrieved but also in the mean reciprocal rank, reflecting that the target categories are better positioned in the list. Our proposed method succeed in almost 50% of the test collection when considered the Top-50 scenario.

Sales et al. (2015) shows a prototype demonstration of this work.

5.4 Analysing Unsuccessful Cases

The most significant limitation is the restriction of comparing words one-by-one, assuming that each word in a paraphrase is semantically equivalent to only one word in the target categories and vice-versa. For example, the pair (*Swedish Metallurgists, Metal Workers from Sweden*) is ranked at #1173 when using W2V. It occurs because *metallurgists* and *workers* have low relatedness (0.0031). Comparing the relatedness of *metallurgists* to *metal workers* would have a higher score.

Concerning named entities, we observed three relevant issues. Our approach uses a simple longest string matching method to identify places. Categories containing terms such as *Turkey* are always considered a spatial named entity. In the pair (*American Turkey Breeds* and *Chicken Breeds Originating in the US*) the terms *turkey* and *chicken* would not be semantically compared, since *Turkey* is always considered a spatial named entity. Secondly, when searching for *Water Parks in the USA*, all parks at *Texas, Tennessee* or *Pennsylvania* are also relevant for the user. Our model does not contain this hierarchical information to provide a geographic match. Finally, expressions such as *WWI* and *USSR* should be identified as the paraphrasing of *Wold War I* and *the Soviet Union* or even other variations, what is not available in our model.

6 Related Work

Balog and Neumayer (2012) propose the *hierarchical target type identification problem* which aims to identify the most specific type grounded in a given ontology that covers all entities sought

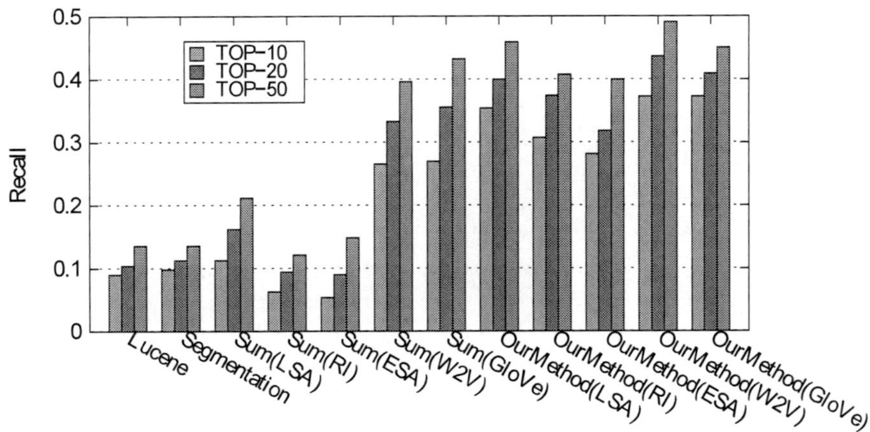

Figure 3: Chart of recall values grouped by different approaches.

by a query. Yao et al. (2013) propose an *entity type prediction* considering the *universal schema*. In this work, a predictor is expected to label a given entity with types. This schema is composed of all types from diverse available ontologies. To identify types from texts, they compose named entity recognition with dependency parsing. These works focus on identifying the ontological types that are sought by the query.

Regarding *entity similarity*, Moreau et al. (2008) propose a method to calculate entity similarity based on Soft-TFIDF. Liu and Birnbaum (2007) propose a method based on the Open Directory Project (ODP) to capture category names in all pages where the named entity appears to generate a vector space. Liu et al. (2008) describe a method that uses the set of URLs in which entities are present to measure similarity. The difference to these works is that they focus on comparing named entities, not based on their description, but based on non-linguistic attributes.

Other related topics are *paraphrasing* and *text entailment*. Androutsopoulos and Malakasiotis (2010) present an extension overview of datasets and approaches applied in these fields. Papers in this context deal with the paraphrasing of complete sentences (formed of subject and predicate) which cannot benefit from the core-oriented segmentation model. The different format of their target datasets inhibits a direct comparison, while their lack of association with entities does not create the required bridge between unstructured and structured data.

This work distinguishes mainly from existing approaches by proposing a novel compositional method grounded in syntactic analysis to combine distributional vectors and by using distributional semantics models generated from external resources. The target knowledge base (the dataset of categories) is not part of the data used to produce the distributional models. This isolation supports a more comprehensive semantic matching.

7 Conclusion

This work proposes a compositional-distributional model to recognise paraphrases of entity categories. Distributional semantics in combination with the proposed compositional model supports a search strategy with robust semantic approximation capabilities, largely outperforming string and WordNet-based approaches in recall and mean reciprocal rank. The proposed compositional strategy also outperforms the tradional *vector-sum method*.

This work also provides additional evidence to reinforce *(i)* the suitability of distributional models to cross the semantic gap (Freitas et al., 2012; Aletras and Stevenson, 2015; Agirre et al., 2009; Freitas et al., 2015) and *(ii)* suggest that prediction methods generate better semantic vectors when compared to count-based approaches. Considering the controversies about the comparisons between predictive-based and count-based distributional models (Baroni et al., 2014b; Lebret and Collobert, 2015; Levy and Goldberg, 2014), this evidence is restricted to the distributional models involved in the experiment and cannot be generalised. In the context of our work, we conjecture that the better performance is credited to the fact that our problem comprises much more *paradig-*

matic than *syntagmatic* relations.

Additionally, the use of distributional semantic models provides a better base for transporting the solution to multi-lingual scenarios, since it does not depend on manually constructed resources.

Future work will focus on the investigation of specialised named entity distributional methods in the context of the semantic search problem.

Acknowledgments

This publication has emanated from research supported by the National Council for Scientific and Technological Development, Brazil (CNPq) and by a research grant from Science Foundation Ireland (SFI) under Grant Number SFI/12/RC/2289. The authors also would like to thank Douglas N. Oliveira (Florida Institute of Technology) and the anonymous reviewers for the valuable critical comments.

References

Eneko Agirre, Enrique Alfonseca, Keith Hall, Jana Kravalova, Marius Paşca, and Aitor Soroa. 2009. A study on similarity and relatedness using distributional and WordNet-based approaches. In *Proceedings of Human Language Technologies: The 2009 Annual Conference of the North American Chapter of the Association for Computational Linguistics*, NAACL '09.

Nikolaos Aletras and Mark Stevenson. 2015. A hybrid distributional and knowledge-based model of lexical semantics. In *Proceedings of the Fourth Joint Conference on Lexical and Computational Semantics*, June.

Ion Androutsopoulos and Prodromos Malakasiotis. 2010. A survey of paraphrasing and textual entailment methods. *J. Artif. Int. Res.*, 38(1):135–187, May.

Sören Auer, Christian Bizer, Georgi Kobilarov, Jens Lehmann, Richard Cyganiak, and Zachary Ives. 2007. DBpedia: A nucleus for a web of open data. In *Proceedings of the 6th International The Semantic Web and 2Nd Asian Conference on Asian Semantic Web Conference*, ISWC'07/ASWC'07, pages 722–735, Berlin, Heidelberg. Springer-Verlag.

Krisztian Balog and Robert Neumayer. 2012. Hierarchical target type identification for entity-oriented queries. In *Proceedings of the 21st ACM International Conference on Information and Knowledge Management*, CIKM'12.

Marco Baroni, Raffaella Bernardi, and Roberto Zamparelli. 2014a. Frege in space: A program for compositional distributional semantics. *Linguistic Issues in Language Technology*, 9.

Marco Baroni, Georgiana Dinu, and Germán Kruszewski. 2014b. Don't count, predict! a systematic comparison of context-counting vs. context-predicting semantic vectors. In *Proceedings of the 52nd Annual Meeting of the Association for Computational Linguistics*, June.

Siamak Barzegar, Juliano Efson Sales, Andre Freitas, Siegfried Handschuh, and Brian Davis. 2015. DINFRA: A one stop shop for computing multilingual semantic relatedness. In *Proceedings of the 38th International ACM SIGIR Conference on Research and Development in Information Retrieval*, SIGIR '15.

S. T. Dumais, G. W. Furnas, T. K. Landauer, S. Deerwester, and R. Harshman. 1988. Using latent semantic analysis to improve access to textual information. In *Proceedings of the Conference on Human Factors in Computing Systems*.

André Freitas, Edward Curry, João Gabriel Oliveira, and Seán O'riain. 2011. A distributional structure semantic space for querying RDF graph data. *International Journal of Semantic Computing*, 05(04):433–462.

André Freitas, Edward Curry, and Seán O'Riain. 2012. A distributional approach for terminological semantic search on the linked data web. In *Proceedings of the 27th Annual ACM Symposium on Applied Computing*, SAC '12.

André Freitas, Rafael Vieira, Edward Curry, Danilo Carvalho, and João Carlos Pereira da Silva. 2014. On the semantic representation and extraction of complex category descriptors. In *Natural Language Processing and Information Systems*, volume 8455 of *Lecture Notes in Computer Science*.

Andre Freitas, Juliano Efson Sales, Siegfried Handschuh, and Edward Curry. 2015. How hard is this query? measuring the semantic complexity of schema-agnostic queries. In *Proceedings of the 11th International Conference on Computational Semantics*, pages 294–304, London, UK, April. Association for Computational Linguistics.

Evgeniy Gabrilovich and Shaul Markovitch. 2007. Computing semantic relatedness using Wikipedia-based explicit semantic analysis. In *Proceedings of the 20th International Joint Conference on Artifical Intelligence*, IJCAI'07.

Thomas Gottron, Maik Anderka, and Benno Stein. 2011. Insights into explicit semantic analysis. In *Proceedings of the 20th ACM International Conference on Information and Knowledge Management*, CIKM'11.

Zellig Harris. 1954. Distributional structure. *Word*, 10(23).

Christopher Manning Jeffrey Pennington, Richard Socher. 2014. Glove: Global vectors for word representation. In *Proceedings of the

2014 Conference on Empirical Methods in Natural Language Processing (EMNLP), October.

David Jurgens and Keith Stevens. 2010. The S-Space Package: An open source package for word space models. In *Proceedings of the ACL 2010 System Demonstrations*, ACLDemos '10, pages 30–35, Stroudsburg, PA, USA. Association for Computational Linguistics.

Rémi Lebret and Ronan Collobert, 2015. *Rehabilitation of Count-Based Models for Word Vector Representations*, pages 417–429. Springer International Publishing, Cham.

Omer Levy and Yoav Goldberg. 2014. Linguistic regularities in sparse and explicit word representations. In *Proceedings of the Eighteenth Conference on Computational Natural Language Learning*, pages 171–180, Ann Arbor, Michigan, June. Association for Computational Linguistics.

Jiahui Liu and L. Birnbaum. 2007. Measuring semantic similarity between named entities by searching the web directory. In *Web Intelligence, IEEE/WIC/ACM International Conference on*, Nov.

Hui Liu, Jinglei Zhao, and Ruzhan Lu. 2008. Mining the URLs: An approach to measure the similarities between named-entities. In *Innovative Computing Information and Control, 2008. ICICIC '08. 3rd International Conference on*, June.

Tomas Mikolov, Kai Chen, Greg Corrado, and Jeffrey Dean. 2013. Efficient estimation of word representations in vector space. In *ICLR Workshop Papers*.

George A. Miller. 1995. WordNet: A lexical database for english. *Commun. ACM*, 38(11), November.

Erwan Moreau, François Yvon, and Olivier Cappé. 2008. Robust similarity measures for named entities matching. In *Proceedings of the 22nd International Conference on Computational Linguistics (Coling 2008)*, August.

Martin F. Porter. 1997. Readings in information retrieval. chapter An Algorithm for Suffix Stripping, pages 313–316. Morgan Kaufmann Publishers Inc., San Francisco, CA, USA.

Jeffrey Pound, Peter Mika, and Hugo Zaragoza. 2010. Ad-hoc object retrieval in the web of data. In *Proceedings of the 19th International Conference on World Wide Web*, WWW '10, pages 771–780, New York, NY, USA. ACM.

Magnus Sahlgren. 2005. An introduction to random indexing. In *In Methods and Applications of Semantic Indexing Workshop at the 7th International Conference on Terminology and Knowledge Engineering, TKE 2005*.

Juliano Efson Sales, André Freitas, Siegfried Handschuh, and Brian Davis. 2015. Linse: A distributional semantics entity search engine. In *Proceedings of the 38th International ACM SIGIR Conference on Research and Development in Information Retrieval*, SIGIR '15, pages 1045–1046, New York, NY, USA. ACM.

Fabian M. Suchanek, Gjergji Kasneci, and Gerhard Weikum. 2007. Yago: A core of semantic knowledge. In *Proceedings of the 16th International Conference on World Wide Web*, WWW '07, pages 697–706, New York, NY, USA. ACM.

Peter D. Turney and Patrick Pantel. 2010. From frequency to meaning: Vector space models of semantics. *J. Artif. Int. Res.*, 37(1):141–188, January.

Limin Yao, Sebastian Riedel, and Andrew McCallum. 2013. Universal schema for entity type prediction. In *Proceedings of the Workshop on Automated Knowledge Base Construction*.

Approximating Givenness in Content Assessment through Distributional Semantics

Ramon Ziai   **Kordula De Kuthy**   **Detmar Meurers**
Collaborative Research Center 833
University of Tübingen
{rziai,kdk,dm}@sfs.uni-tuebingen.de

Abstract

Givenness (Schwarzschild, 1999) is one of the central notions in the formal pragmatic literature discussing the organization of discourse. In this paper, we explore where distributional semantics can help address the gap between the linguistic insights into the formal pragmatic notion of Givenness and its implementation in computational linguistics.

As experimental testbed, we focus on short answer assessment, in which the goal is to assess whether a student response correctly answers the provided reading comprehension question or not. Current approaches only implement a very basic, surface-based perspective on Givenness: A word of the answer that appears as such in the question counts as GIVEN.

We show that an approach approximating Givenness using distributional semantics to check whether a word in a sentence is similar enough to a word in the context to count as GIVEN is more successful quantitatively and supports interesting qualitative insights into the data and the limitations of a basic distributional semantic approach identifying Givenness at the lexical level.

1   Introduction

Givenness is one of the central notions in the formal pragmatic literature discussing the organization of discourse. The distinction between *given* and *new* material in an utterance dates back at least to Halliday (1967) where *given* is defined as "anaphorically recoverable" and the notion is used to predict patterns of prosodic prominence. Schwarzschild (1999) proposes to define Givenness in terms of the entailment of the existential f-closure between previously mentioned material and the GIVEN expression, hereby also capturing the occurrence of synonyms and hyponyms as given.

On the theoretical linguistic side, a foundational question is whether an approach to Information Structure should be grounded in terms of a Given-New or a Focus-Background dichotomy, or whether the two are best seen as complementing each other. Computational linguistic research on short answer assessment points in the direction of both perspectives providing performance gains (Ziai and Meurers, 2014). On the empirical side, the characteristic problem of obtaining high inter-annotator agreement in focus annotation (Ritz et al., 2008; Calhoun et al., 2010) can be overcome through an incremental annotation process making reference to questions as part of an explicit task context (Ziai and Meurers, 2014; De Kuthy et al., 2016).

In short answer assessment approaches determining whether a student response correctly answers a provided reading comprehension question, the practical value of excluding material that is mentioned in the question from evaluating the content of the answer has been clearly established (Meurers et al., 2011; Mohler et al., 2011). Yet these computational linguistic approaches only implement a very basic, completely surface-based perspective on Givenness: A word of the answer that appears as such in the question counts as GIVEN.

Such a surface-based approach to Givenness fails to capture that the semantic notion of Givenness

i) may be transported by *semantically similar* words,

ii) *entailment* rather than identity is at stake, and

iii) so-called *bridging* cases seem to involve *semantically related* rather than *semantically similar* words.

209

*Proceedings of the Fifth Joint Conference on Lexical and Computational Semantics (*SEM 2016)*, pages 209–218,
Berlin, Germany, August 11-12, 2016.

Computational linguistic approaches to classifying Givenness (Hempelmann et al., 2005; Nissim, 2006; Rahman and Ng, 2011; Cahill and Riester, 2012) have concentrated on the information status of noun phrases, without taking into account other syntactic elements. Furthermore, they do not explicitly make use of similarity and relatedness between lexical units as we propose in this paper. Our approach thus explores a new avenue in computationally determining Givenness.

Theoretical linguistic proposals spelling out Givenness are based on formal semantic formalisms and notions such as logical entailment, type shifting, and existential f-closure, which do not readily lend themselves to extending the computational linguistic approaches. As already alluded to by the choice of words "semantically similar" and "semantically related" above, in this paper we want to explore whether distributional semantics can help address the gap between the linguistic insights into Givenness and the computational linguistic realizations. In place of surface-based Givenness checks, as a first step in this direction we developed an approach integrating distributional semantics to check whether a word in a sentence is similar enough to a word in the context to count as GIVEN.

In section 2, we provide the background on Schwarzschild's notion of Givenness and conceptually explore what a distributional semantic perspective may offer. Section 3 then introduces the application domain of content assessment as our experimental sandbox and the CoMiC system (Meurers et al., 2011) we extended. The distributional model for German used in extending the baseline system is built in section 4. In section 5 we then turn to the experiments we conducted using the system extended with the distributional Givenness component and provide quantitative results. Section 6 then presents the qualitative perspective, discussing examples to probe into the connection between the theoretical linguistic notion of Givenness and its distributional semantic approximation, and where it fails. Finally, section 7 concludes with a summary of the approach and its contribution.

2   Linking Givenness and the distributional semantic perspective

Before turning to the computational realization and a quantitative and qualitative evaluation of the idea, let us consider which classes of data are handled by the theoretical linguistic approach to Givenness and where an approximation of Givenness using distributional semantics can contribute.

Let us first define Givenness according to Schwarzschild (1999, p. 151): an utterance U counts as GIVEN iff it has a salient antecedent A and either i) A and U co-refer or ii) A entails the Existential F-Closure of U. In turn, the Existential F-Closure of U is defined as "the result of replacing F-marked phrases in U with variables and existentially closing the result, modulo existential type shifting" (Schwarzschild, 1999, p. 150).

Schwarzschild uses Givenness to predict where in an utterance the prosodic prominence falls. Consider the question-answer pair in (1), example (12) of Schwarzschild (1999).

(1) John drove Mary's red convertible. What did he drive before that?

A: He drove her BLUE convertible.

Here the prominence does not fall on *convertible* as the rightmost expression answering the question, as generally is the case in English, but instead on the adjective *blue* because the *convertible* is GIVEN and thus is de-accented according to Schwarzschild. With respect to our goal of automatically identifying Givenness, such cases involving **identical lexical material** that is repeated (here: *convertible*) are trivial for a surface-based or distributional semantic approach.

A more interesting case of Givenness involves **semantically similar** words such as synonyms and hypernyms, as exemplified by *violin* and *string instrument* in (2), mentioned as example (7) by Büring (2007).

(2) (I'd like to learn the violin,) because I LIKE string instruments.

The existence of a violin entails the existence of a string instrument, so *string instrument* is GIVEN and deaccented under Schwarzschild's approach. Such examples are beyond a simple surface-based approach to the identification of Givenness and motivate the perspective pursued in this paper: investigating whether a distributional semantic approach to semantic similarity can be used to capture them.

Before tackling these core cases, let us complete the empirical overview of the landscape of cases that the Givenness notion is expected to handle. A relevant phenomenon in this context is **bridging**. It can be exemplified using (3), which is example (29) of Schwarzschild (1999).

(3) a. John got the job.

    b. I KNOW. They WANTed a New Yorker.

The part of the formal definitions that is intended to capture the deaccenting of *New Yorker* in a context where *John* is known to be from that city simply refers to salience (Schwarzschild, 1999: "An utterance U counts as GIVEN iff it has a salient antecedent A ..."), which Schwarzschild readily admits is not actually modeled: "Exactly which propositions count as in the background for these purposes remains to be worked out". While beyond the scope of our experiments, approaches computing semantic similarity in more local contexts, such as Dinu and Lapata (2010), may be able to provide an avenue for handling such narrowly contextualized notions of common ground in the evolving, dynamic discourse.

A more straightforward case arises when such bridging examples involve semantic relatedness between expressions that are richly represented in corpora. For example, the fact that Giuliani was the mayor of New York and thus can be identified as semantically related to New Yorker in (4) is within reach of a distributional semantic approach.

(4) a. Giuliani got the job.

    b. I KNOW. They WANTed a New Yorker.

When exactly such bridging based on semantically related material results in GIVEN material and its deaccenting, as far as we are aware, has not been systematically researched and would be relevant to explore in the future.

An interesting case related to bridging that adds a further challenge for any Givenness approach is exemplified by (5), originating as example (4) in Büring (2007). The challenge arises from the fact that it does not seem to involve an apparent semantic relation such as entailment – yet the accent falling on *strangle* can only be explained if *butcher* is GIVEN, i.e., entailed by the context.

(5) a. Did you see Dr. Cremer to get your root canal?

    b. (Don't remind me.) I'd like to STRANgle the butcher.

The linguistic approaches to Givenness do not formally tackle this since the lexical semantic specification and contextual disambiguation of *butcher* as a particular (undesirable type of) *dentist* is beyond their scope. The fact that *butcher* counts as GIVEN is not readily captured by a general distributional semantic approach either since it is dependent on the specific context and the top-down selection of the meaning of *butcher* as referring to people who brutally go about their job. Distributional semantic approaches distinguishing specific word senses (Iacobacci et al., 2015) could be applicable for extending the core approach worked out in this paper to cover such cases.

Overall, at the conceptual level, a realization of Givenness in terms of distributional semantics can be seen as nicely complementing the theoretical linguistic approach in terms of the division of labor of formal and distributional factors.

3 Content Assessment: Baseline System and Gold Standard Data

To be able to test the idea we conceptually motivated above, we chose short answer assessment as our experimental testbed. The content assessment of reading comprehension exercises is an authentic task including a rich, language-based context. This makes it an interesting real-life challenge for research into the applicability of formal pragmatic concepts such as Givenness. Provided a text and a question, the content assessment task is to determine whether a particular response actually answers the question or not.

In such a setting, the question typically introduces some linguistic material about which additional information is required. The material introduced is usually not the information required in a felicitous answer. For example, in a question such as 'Where was Mozart born?', we are looking for a location. Consequently, in an answer such as 'Mozart was born in Salzburg', we can disregard the words 'Mozart', 'was' and 'born' on account of their previous mention, leaving only the relevant information 'in Salzburg'.

Short answer assessment is thus a natural testbed since the practical value of excluding material that is mentioned in the question from evaluating the content of the answer has been clearly established (Meurers et al., 2011; Mohler et al., 2011) – yet these approaches only integrated a basic surface-based perspective on Givenness. The CoMiC system (Meurers et al., 2011) is freely available, so we used it as baseline approach and proceeded to replaced its surface-based Givenness filter with our distributional semantic approach to Givenness.

3.1 Baseline system

CoMiC is an alignment-based Content Assessment system which assesses student answers by analyzing the quantity and quality of alignment links it finds between the student and the target answer. For content assessment, it extracts several numeric features based on the number and kind of alignments found between non-GIVEN answer parts. The only change we made to the baseline setup is to replace the TiMBL (Daelemans et al., 2007) implementation of k-nearest-neighbors with the WEKA package (Hall et al., 2009), setting k to 5 following the positive results of Rudzewitz (2016).

The CoMiC system we use as baseline for our research employs a surface-based Givenness filter, only aligning tokens not found in the question. The surface-based Givenness filter thus ensures that parts of the answer already occurring in the question are not counted (or could be fed into separate features so that the machine learner making the final assessment can take their discourse status into account).

3.2 Gold-standard content assessment corpus

The data we used for training and testing our extension of the CoMiC system are taken from the CREG corpus (Ott et al., 2012), a task-based corpus consisting of answers to reading comprehension questions written by American learners of German at the university level. It was collected at Kansas University (KU) and The Ohio State University (OSU). The overall corpus includes 164 reading texts, 1,517 reading comprehension questions, 2,057 target answers provided by the teachers, and 36,335 learner answers.

The CREG-5K subset used for the present experiments is an extended version of CREG-1032 (Meurers et al., 2011), selected using the same criteria after the overall, four year corpus collection effort was completed. The criteria include balancedness (same number of correct and incorrect answers), a minimum answer length of four tokens, and a language course level at the intermediate level or above.

4 Creating a distributional model

To model Givenness as distributional similarity, we need an appropriate word vector model. As there is no such model readily available for German, we trained one ourselves.

As empirical basis, we used the DeWAC corpus (Baroni et al., 2009) since it is a large corpus that is freely available and it is already lemmatized, both of which have been argued to be desirable for word vector models. Further preprocessing consisted of excluding numbers and other undesired words such as foreign language material and words the POS tagger had labelled as non-words. The whole corpus was converted to lowercase to get rid of unwanted distinctions between multiple possible capitalizations.

To select an implementation for our purpose, we compared two of the major word vector toolkits currently available, word2vec (Mikolov et al., 2013) and GloVe (Pennington et al., 2014). While word2vec is a prediction-based approach that optimizes the probability of a word occurring in a certain context, GloVe is a counting approach based on co-occurrences of words.

We compared the two on the lexical substitution task designed for GermEval 2015 (Miller et al., 2015). The task can be seen as related to recognizing Givenness: deciding what a good substitute for a word in context is requires similar mechanisms to deciding whether the meaning of a word is already present in previous utterances. For GloVe, we used the models trained by Dima (2015), which were also trained on a large German web corpus and were shown to perform well. However, results on the lexical substitution task put both of word2vec's training approaches, continuous bag-of-words (CBOW) and skip-gram, ahead of GloVe using the models previously mentioned, so we continued with word2vec.

Finally, to select the optimal training algorithm for word2vec for our purpose, we again used the GermEval task as a benchmark. We explored both CBOW and skip-gram with negative sampling and hierarchical softmax, yielding four combinations. Among these, CBOW with hierarchical softmax significantly outperformed all other combinations, so we chose it as our training algorithm.

The German model we obtained has a vocabulary of 1,825,306 words and uses 400 dimensions for each, the latter being inspired by Iacobacci et al. (2015).

5 Experiment and Quantitative Results

Now that we have a baseline content assessment system (section 3) and a distributional model for German (section 4) in place, we have all the components to quantitatively and qualitatively evaluate the idea to model Givenness through semantic similarity measures. To do so, we simply replaced the surface-based Givenness filter of the baseline CoMiC system with a distributional-semantics based Givenness filter based on the model described in the previous section. For this we must make concrete, how exactly distributional-semantic distances are used to determine the words in an answer counting as GIVEN.

The parameters to be estimated relate to two different ways one can determine semantic relatedness using word vectors for two words w_1 and w_2:

I. Calculate cosine similarity of w_1 and w_2 and require it to be at least equal to a threshold t.

II. Calculate n nearest words to w_1 and check whether w_2 is among them.

For the first method, one needs to estimate the threshold t, while for the second method one needs to determine how many neighbors to calculate (n). We explored both methods. For the threshold parameter t, we experimented with values from 0.1 to 0.9 in increments of 0.1. For the number of nearest neighbors n, we used a space from 2 to 20 with increments of 2.

To cleanly separate our test data from the data used for training and parameter estimation, we randomly sampled approximately 20% of the CREG-5K data set and set it aside as the final test set. The remaining 80% was used as training set. All parameter estimation was done before running the final system on the test set and using only the training data.

Table 1 shows the results in terms of classification accuracy for 10-fold cross-validation on the training data. The table includes the performance of the system without a Givenness filter as well as with the basic surface-based approach. Training and testing was done separately for the two

	KU	OSU
# answers	1466	2670
Without Givenness	75.4%	76.7%
Surface Givenness	82.4%	83.0%
Best threshold t	0.3	0.5
Accuracy using t	82.7%	**83.6%**
Best n nearest-words	20	10
Accuracy using n	**83.2%**	**83.6%**

Table 1: Content Assessment results on training set

sub-corpora of CREG-5K corresponding to the universities where they were collected, KU and OSU.

First, the results confirm that an alignment-based content assessment system such as CoMiC greatly benefits from a Givenness filter, as demonstrated by the big gap in performance between the no-Givenness and surface-Givenness conditions. Second, both the threshold method and the nearest-words method outperform the surface baseline, if only by a small margin.

Turning to the actual testing, we wanted to find out whether the improvements found for the distributional-semantic Givenness filters carry over to the untouched test set. We trained the classifier on the full training set and used the best parameters from the training set. The results thus obtained are summarized in Table 2.

	KU	OSU
# answers	348	654
No Givenness	74.7%	74.2%
Surface Givenness	80.7%	81.2%
Accuracy using t	81.0%	**81.8%**
Accuracy using n	**81.9%**	81.0%

Table 2: Content Assessment results on test set

We can see that results on the test set are generally lower, but the general picture for the test set is the same as what we found for the 10-fold CV on the training data: Surface-based-Givenness easily outperforms the system not employing a Givenness filter, and at least one of the systems employing a distributional semantic Givenness filter (marginally) outperforms the surface-based method.

Interestingly, the two data sets seem to differ in terms of which relatedness method works best for recognizing Givenness: while the threshold method works better for OSU, the n-nearest-words method is the optimal choice for the KU data set. This may be due to the fact that the OSU data set is generally more diverse in terms of lexical variation and thus presents more opportunities for false positives, i.e., words that are somewhat related but should not be counted as given. Such cases are better filtered out using a global threshold. The KU data set, on the other hand, contains less variation and hence profits from the more local n-nearest-words method, which always returns a list of candidates for any known word in the vocabulary, no matter whether the candidates are globally very similar or not.

6 Qualitative Discussion

While the quantitative results provide a useful ball-park measure of how well a Givenness filter based on distributional semantics performs and that it can improve the content assessment of reading comprehension questions, the relatively small and heterogeneous nature of the data set for a complex task such as the content assessment of reading comprehension means that such quantitative results by themselves are best interpreted cautiously. For the conceptual side of our proposal, it is more interesting to see whether semantic similarity can adequately capture the different types of Givenness that we discussed in section 2.

6.1 Successfully identifying Givenness through distributional semantics

To illustrate how exactly the Givenness filter in the CoMiC system ensures that only the material that is not already present in the question is aligned for assessing the similarity of a student and a target answer, let us start by taking a look at a simple example from CREG where the answers repeat lexical material from the question, as shown Figure 1.

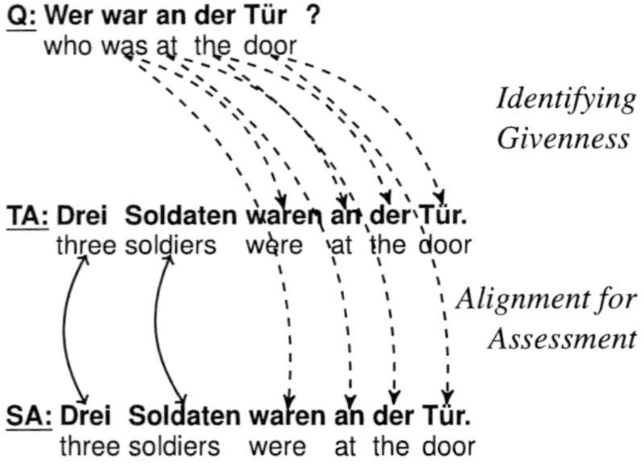

Figure 1: Simple Givenness alignment

The dotted arrows show which words in the question trigger Givenness marking of which items in the target and the student answer. The solid arrows illustrate the actual alignments between words in the target and the student answer used in the content assessment.

The Givenness filter ensures that the words *waren* (*was*), *an* (*at*), *der* (*the*), and *Tür* (*door*) of the student (SA) and the target (TA) answers are marked as GIVEN with respect to the question and are thus not aligned in order to calculate the similarity of the two answers.

A type of Givenness that a surface-based Givenness filter cannot handle, but that is captured by our distributional similarity approach, occurs in examples where parts of the question are picked up by semantically similar words in the target and student answer. This is illustrated by Figure 2.

The verbs *glaubte* (*believed*) and *meinte* (*thought*) are semantically close enough to the verb *verstand* (*understood*) in the question for them to be identified as GIVEN. They consequently can be excluded from the content assessment of the student answer (SA) in relation to the target answer (TA).

The core idea to use semantic similarity as identified by distributional semantics to identify the words which are GIVEN in a context thus nicely captures real cases in authentic data.

6.2 Overidentifying Givenness

At the same time, there are two aspects of distributional semantics that can also lead to overidentification of Givenness.

Entailment is not symmetric, but semantic similarity and relatedness are The first difficulty arises from the fact that semantic similarity and semantic relatedness are symmetric, whereas the entailment relation used to define Givenness is not. As a result, our distributional semantic model wrongly identifies a word as GIVEN that is more specific than, i.e., a hyponym of the word in the context as illustrated in Figure 3.

The entire NP *praktische Erfahrung im Controlling eines Finanzservice-Unternehmens* (*practical experience in controlling of a financial service company*) consists of new material in both the target answer and the student answer and should thus be aligned for the content assessment of the student answer. But since *Finanzservice-Unternehmen* (*financial service company*) is semantically similar to the noun *Firma* (*company*) occurring in the question, it is marked as GIVEN under the current setting of our distributional similarity approach and incorrectly excluded from the content assessment.

Under the notion of Givenness as defined by Schwarzschild, *Finanzservice-Unternehmen* (*financial service company*) would not count as GIVEN, since the mentioning of *company* in the prior discourse does not entail the existence of a *financial service company*.

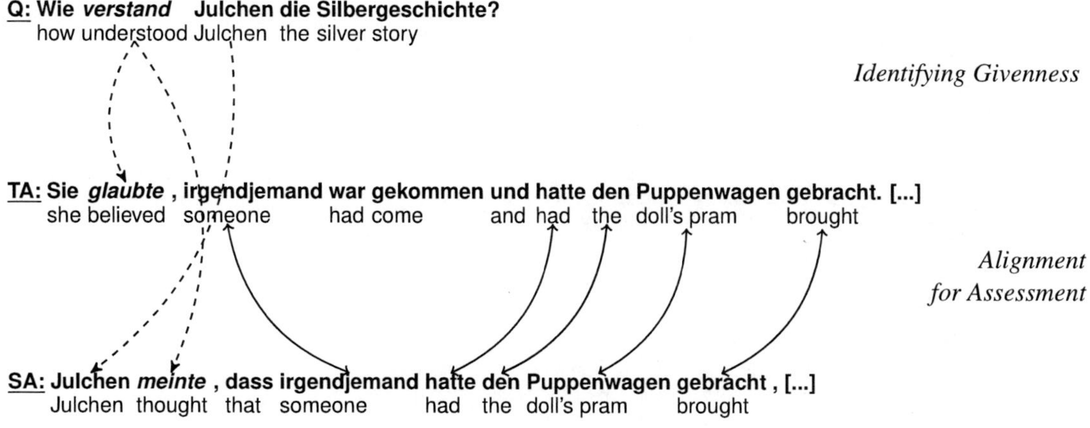

Figure 2: CREG example illustrating Semantic similarity

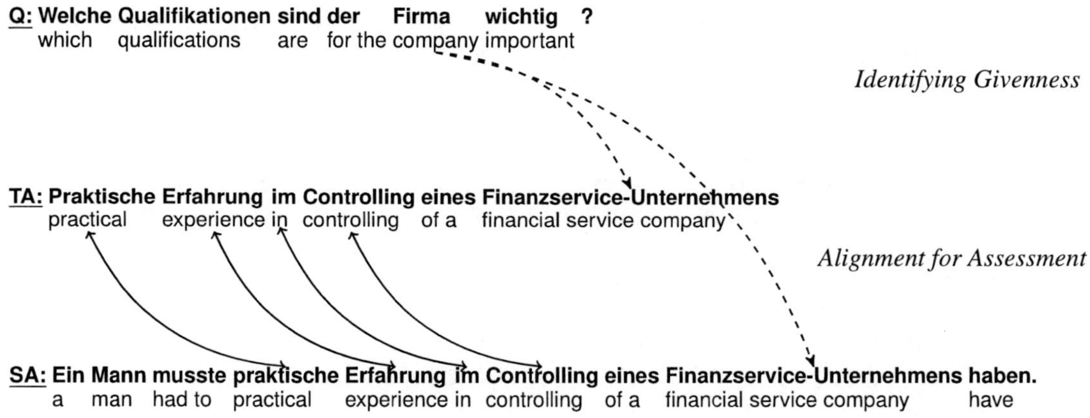

Figure 3: CREG example illustrating entailment in wrong direction

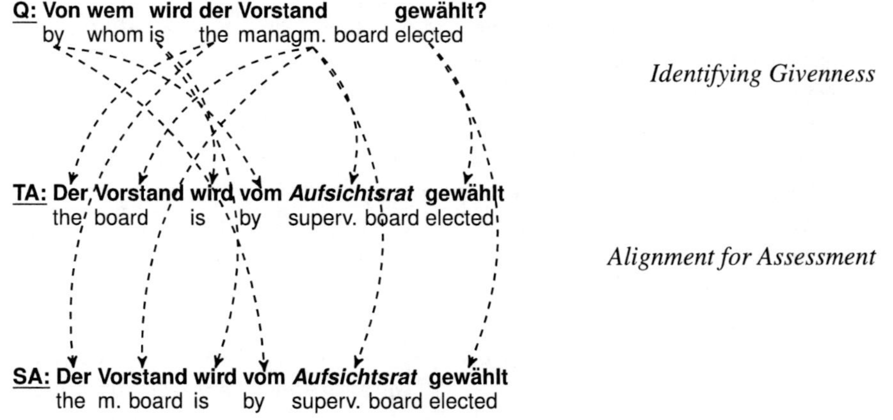

Figure 4: CREG example illustrating Semantic Relatedness

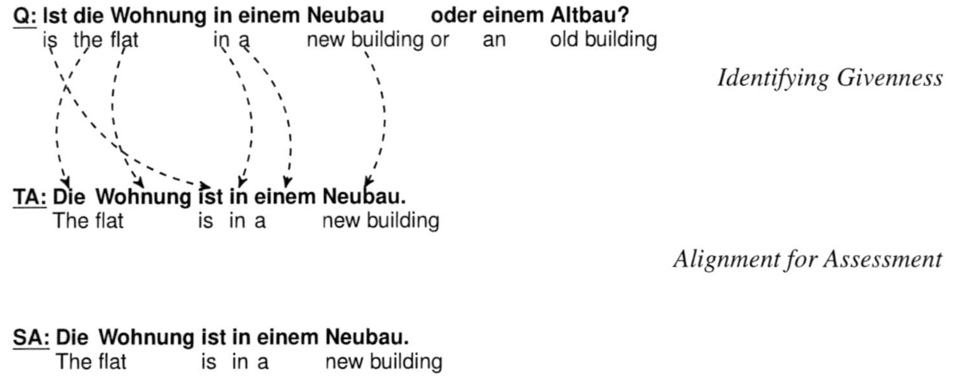

Figure 5: CREG example illustrating overidentification by Givenness filter

Semantic relatedness is not semantic similarity Second, it is difficult for distributional semantic approaches to distinguish semantic similarity from semantic relatedness (cf., e.g., Kolb, 2009). In the discussion of bridging in section 2 we saw that cases such as (4) could arguably benefit from the use of semantic relatedness to identify Givenness. Yet, allowing all semantic related material to count as GIVEN clearly overestimates what counts as GIVEN and can therefore be deaccented. As a result, our approach wrongly identifies some semantic relatedness cases as Givenness. Consider the semantically related words *Vorstand* (*management board*) and *Aufsichtsrat* (*supervisory board*) in the example shown in Figure 4.

The Givenness filter ensures that the lexical material *der* (*the*), *Vorstand* (*management board*), *wird* (*is*), *gewählt* (*elected*) that is repeated in the answers is marked as GIVEN and thus excluded from the content assessment. But under the current setting of our distributional similarity approach, the noun *Aufsichtsrat* (*supervisory board*) that is semantically related to the noun *Vorstand* (*advisory board*) is also marked as GIVEN and thus excluded from the content assessment. As a consequence all material in the answers is excluded from the alignment and the CoMiC system fails to classify the student answer as a correct answer. A general solution to this kind of misidentification seems to be beyond the scope of an analysis based on the word level – an issue which also turns out to be a problem in another, systematic set of cases, which we turn to next.

Comparing lexical units not enough The Givenness filter under both approaches, surface-based Givenness as well as distributional similarity,

sometimes also overidentifies Givenness because the analysis is based on lexical units rather than entailment between sentence meanings. Recall that the way this filter works is to exclude tokens from alignment which are GIVEN in the question. But what if the lexical material required by the question is actually explicitly spelled out as an option by the question itself? This actually happens systematically for alternative questions, where one has to pick one out of an explicitly given set of alternatives. Consider the example in Figure 5, where target and student answer happen to be identical (and for visual transparency only the arcs between question and target answer are shown, not also the identical arcs that link the question and the student answer).

The question asks whether the apartment is in a new or in an old building. Both alternatives are GIVEN in the question, however only one is correct, namely that the apartment is in a new building. The student correctly picked that alternative, but the Givenness filter excludes all material from alignment for content assessment. Hence, classification fails to mark this as a correct answer. As a simple fix, one could integrate an automatic identification of question types and switch off the Givenness filter for alternative questions. More interesting would be an approach that explores when material provided by the question constitutes alternatives in the sense of focus alternatives (Krifka, 2007), from which a selection in the answer should be counted as informative. This essentially would replace the Givenness filter with an approach zooming in to the material in Focus in the answer in the context of the question. At the same time, realizing this idea would require development of an approach automatically identifying Focus, an alternative avenue to pursue in future research.

7 Conclusion

The paper investigated how the formal pragmatic notion of Givenness can be approximated using current computational linguistic methods, and whether this can capture a number of distinct conceptual subcases. We tested the idea in a real-life computational linguistic task with an established external evaluation criterion, content assessment of learner answers to reading comprehension questions.

In place of a surface-based Givenness filter as employed in previous content assessment work, we developed an approach based on distributional semantics to check whether a word in an answer is similar enough to a word in the question to count as GIVEN. The quantitative evaluation confirms the importance of a Givenness filter for content assessment and improved content assessment accuracy for the distributional approach. We experimented with absolute cosine similarity thresholds and with calculating the nearest n words for a candidate word and found that which of the two works better potentially depends on data set characteristics such as lexical diversity.

In the qualitative evaluation, we confirmed that the approximation of Givenness through semantic similarity does indeed capture a number of conceptual cases that a pure surface-based Givenness approach cannot handle, such as bridging-cases involving semantically related words – though this can also lead to over-identification. In future research, integrating more context-sensitive notions of semantic similarity, such as proposed by Dinu and Lapata (2010), may provide a handle on a more narrowly contextualized notion of Givenness in the common ground of discourse participants.

Acknowledgments

We would like to thank Mohamed Balabel for his work on training and selecting the distributional model. Furthermore, we are grateful to the anonymous reviewers of JerSem and *Sem for their comments, which were very helpful in revising the paper.

References

Marco Baroni, Silvia Bernardini, Adriano Ferraresi, and Eros Zanchetta. 2009. The wacky wide web: A collection of very large linguistically processed web-crawled corpora. *Journal of Language Resources and Evaluation*, 3(43):209–226.

Daniel Büring. 2007. Intonation, semantics and information structure. In Gillian Ramchand and Charles Reiss, editors, *The Oxford Handbook of Linguistic Interfaces*. Oxford University Press.

Aoife Cahill and Arndt Riester. 2012. Automatically acquiring fine-grained information status distinctions in german. In *Proceedings of the 13th Annual Meeting of the Special Interest Group on Discourse and Dialogue*, pages 232–236. Association for Computational Linguistics.

Sasha Calhoun, Jean Carletta, Jason Brenier, Neil Mayo, Dan Jurafsky, Mark Steedman, and David Beaver. 2010. The NXT-format switchboard corpus: A rich resource for investigating the syntax, semantics, pragmatics and prosody of dialogue. *Language Resources and Evaluation*, 44:387–419.

Walter Daelemans, Jakub Zavrel, Ko van der Sloot, and Antal van den Bosch, 2007. *TiMBL: Tilburg Memory-Based Learner Reference Guide, ILK Technical Report ILK 07-03*. Induction of Linguistic Knowledge Research Group Department of Communication and Information Sciences, Tilburg University, Tilburg, The Netherlands, July 11. Version 6.0.

Kordula De Kuthy, Ramon Ziai, and Detmar Meurers. 2016. Focus annotation of task-based data: a comparison of expert and crowd-sourced annotation in a reading comprehension corpus. In *Proceedings of the 10th Edition of the Language Resources and Evaluation Conference (LREC)*.

Corina Dima. 2015. Reverse-engineering language: A study on the semantic compositionality of german compounds. In *Proceedings of the 2015 Conference on Empirical Methods in Natural Language Processing*, pages 1637–1642, Lisbon, Portugal, September. Association for Computational Linguistics.

Georgiana Dinu and Mirella Lapata. 2010. Measuring distributional similarity in context. In *Proceedings of the 2010 Conference on Empirical Methods in Natural Language Processing*, pages 1162–1172, Cambridge, MA, October. Association for Computational Linguistics.

Mark Hall, Eibe Frank, Geoffrey Holmes, Bernhard Pfahringer, Peter Reutemann, and Ian H. Witten. 2009. The weka data mining software: An update. In *The SIGKDD Explorations*, volume 11, pages 10–18.

Michael Halliday. 1967. Notes on transitivity and theme in english. part 1 and 2. *Journal of Linguistics*, 3:37–81, 199–244.

Christian F. Hempelmann, David Dufty, Philip M. McCarthy, Arthur C. Graesser, Zhiqiang Cai, and Danielle S. McNamara. 2005. Using LSA to automatically identify Givenness and Newness of noun phrases in written discourse. In B. G. Bara, L. Barsalou, and M. Bucciarelli, editors, *Proceedings of the 27th Annual Meeting of the Cognitive Science Society*, pages 941–949, Stresa, Italy. Erlbaum.

Ignacio Iacobacci, Mohammad Taher Pilehvar, and Roberto Navigli. 2015. Sensembed: learning sense embeddings for word and relational similarity. In *Proceedings of ACL*, pages 95–105.

Peter Kolb. 2009. Experiments on the difference between semantic similarity and relatedness. In Kristiina Jokinen and Eckhard Bick, editors, *Proceedings of the 17th Nordic Conference on Computational Linguistics (NODALIDA)*, pages 81–88.

Manfred Krifka. 2007. Basic notions of information structure. In Caroline Fery, Gisbert Fanselow, and Manfred Krifka, editors, *The notions of information structure*, volume 6 of *Interdisciplinary Studies on Information Structure (ISIS)*, pages 13–55. Universitätsverlag Potsdam, Potsdam.

Detmar Meurers, Ramon Ziai, Niels Ott, and Janina Kopp. 2011. Evaluating answers to reading comprehension questions in context: Results for German and the role of information structure. In *Proceedings of the TextInfer 2011 Workshop on Textual Entailment*, pages 1–9, Edinburgh, July. ACL.

Tomas Mikolov, Ilya Sutskever, Kai Chen, Greg S Corrado, and Jeff Dean. 2013. Distributed representations of words and phrases and their compositionality. In *Advances in neural information processing systems*, pages 3111–3119.

Tristan Miller, Darina Benikova, and Sallam Abualhaija. 2015. GermEval 2015: LexSub – A shared task for German-language lexical substitution. In *Proceedings of GermEval 2015: LexSub*, pages 1–9, sep.

Michael Mohler, Razvan Bunescu, and Rada Mihalcea. 2011. Learning to grade short answer questions using semantic similarity measures and dependency graph alignments. In *Proceedings of the 49th Annual Meeting of the Association for Computational Linguistics: Human Language Technologies*, pages 752–762, Portland, Oregon, USA, June. Association for Computational Linguistics.

Malvina Nissim. 2006. Learning information status of discourse entities. In *Proceedings of the 2006 Conference on Emprical Methods in Natural Language Processing*, Sydney, Australia.

Niels Ott, Ramon Ziai, and Detmar Meurers. 2012. Creation and analysis of a reading comprehension exercise corpus: Towards evaluating meaning in context. In Thomas Schmidt and Kai Wörner, editors, *Multilingual Corpora and Multilingual Corpus Analysis*, Hamburg Studies in Multilingualism (HSM), pages 47–69. Benjamins, Amsterdam.

Jeffrey Pennington, Richard Socher, and Christopher Manning. 2014. Glove: Global vectors for word representation. In *Proceedings of the 2014 Conference on Empirical Methods in Natural Language Processing (EMNLP)*, pages 1532–1543. Association for Computational Linguistics.

Altaf Rahman and Vincent Ng. 2011. Learning the information status of noun phrases in spoken dialogues. In *Proceedings of the 2011 Conference on Empirical Methods in Natural Language Processing*, pages 1069–1080, Edinburgh, Scotland, UK., July. Association for Computational Linguistics.

Julia Ritz, Stefanie Dipper, and Michael Götze. 2008. Annotation of information structure: An evaluation across different types of texts. In *Proceedings of the 6th International Conference on Language Resources and Evaluation*, pages 2137–2142, Marrakech, Morocco.

Björn Rudzewitz. 2016. Exploring the intersection of short answer assessment, authorship attribution, and plagiarism detection. In *Proceedings of the 11th Workshop on Innovative Use of NLP for Building Educational Applications*, San Diego, CA.

Roger Schwarzschild. 1999. GIVENness, AvoidF and other constraints on the placement of accent. *Natural Language Semantics*, 7(2):141–177.

Ramon Ziai and Detmar Meurers. 2014. Focus annotation in reading comprehension data. In *Proceedings of the 8th Linguistic Annotation Workshop (LAW VIII, 2014)*, pages 159–168, Dublin, Ireland. COLING, Association for Computational Linguistics.

Learning Embeddings to lexicalise RDF Properties

Laura Perez-Beltrachini and **Claire Gardent**
CNRS, LORIA, UMR 7503
Vandoeuvre-lès-Nancy
F-54500, France
{laura.perez, claire.gardent}@loria.fr

Abstract

A difficult task when generating text from knowledge bases (KB) consists in finding appropriate lexicalisations for KB symbols. We present an approach for lexicalising knowledge base relations and apply it to DBPedia data. Our model learns low-dimensional embeddings of words and RDF resources and uses these representations to score RDF properties against candidate lexicalisations. Training our model using (i) pairs of RDF triples and automatically generated verbalisations of these triples and (ii) pairs of paraphrases extracted from various resources, yields competitive results on DBPedia data.

1 Introduction

In recent years, work on the Semantic Web has led to the publication of large scale datasets in the so-called Linked Data framework such as for instance DBPedia or Yago. However, as shown in (Rector et al., 2004), the basic standards (e.g., RDF, OWL) established by the Semantic Web community for representing data and ontologies are difficult for human beings to use and understand. With the development of the semantic web and the rapid increase of Linked Data, there is consequently a growing need in the semantic web community for technologies that give humans easy access to the machine-oriented Web of data.

Because it maps data to text, Natural Language Generation (NLG) provides a natural means for presenting this data in an organized, coherent and accessible way. It can be used to display the content of linked data or of knowledge bases to lay users; to generate explanations, descriptions and summaries from DBPedia or from knowledge bases; to guide the user in formulating knowledge

base queries; and to provide ways for cultural heritage institutions such as museums and libraries to present information about their holdings in multiple textual forms.

In this paper, we focus on an important subtask of generation from RDF data namely lexicalisation of RDF properties. Given a property, our goal is to map this property to a set of possible lexicalisations. For instance, given the property HASWONPRIZE, our goal is to automatically infer lexicalisations such as *was honored with* and *received*.

Our approach is based on learning low-dimensional vector embeddings of words and of KB triples so that representations of triples and their corresponding lexicalisations end up being similar in the embedding space. Using these embeddings, we can then assess the similarity between a property and a set of candidate lexicalisations by simply applying the dot product to their vector embeddings.

One difficulty when lexicalising RDF properties is that, while in some cases, there is a direct and simple relation between the name of a property and its verbalisation (e.g., BIRTHDATE / "was born on"), in other cases, the relation is either indirect (e.g., ROUTEEND / "finishes at") or opaque (e.g., CREW1UP / "is the commander of").

To account for these two possibilities, we therefore explore two main ways of creating candidate lexicalisations based on either *lexical-* or on *extensional-relatedness*. Given some input property p, lexically-related candidate lexicalisations for p are phrases containing synonyms or derivationally related words of the tokens making up the name of the input property. In contrast, extensionally-related candidate lexicalisations are phrases containing named entities which are in its extension. For instance, given the property CREW1UP, if the pair of entities (STS-

*Proceedings of the Fifth Joint Conference on Lexical and Computational Semantics (*SEM 2016)*, pages 219–228,
Berlin, Germany, August 11-12, 2016.

130, GEORGE_D._ZAMK) is in its extension (i.e., there exists an RDF triple of the form ⟨ STS-130, CREW1UP, GEORGE_D._ZAMK ⟩), all sentences mentioning STS-130, GEORGE_D._ZAMK or both will be retrieved and exploited to build the set of candidate lexicalisations for CREW1UP. Figure 1 shows some example L- and E-candidate lexicalisations phrases.

In summary, the key contribution made in this paper is a novel method for lexicalising RDF properties which differs from previous work in two ways. First, while lexical and extensional relatedness have been used before for lexicalising RDF properties (Walter et al., 2013), ours is the first lexicalisation approach which jointly considers both sources of information. Second, while previous approaches have used discrete representations and similarity metrics based on Wordnet, our method exploits continuous representations of both words and KB symbols that are learned and optimised for the lexicalisation task.

2 Related Work

We situate our work with respect to previous work on ontology lexicons but also to research on relation extraction (extracting verbalisations of knowledge base relations) and to embeddings-based approaches.

Ontology Lexicons (Trevisan, 2010) proposes a simple lexicalisation approach which exploits the tokens included in a property name to build candidate lexicalisations. In brief, this approach consists in tokenizing and part-of-speech tagging relation names with a customized tokenizer and part-of-speech (PoS) tagger. A set of hand-defined mappings is then used to map PoS sequences to lexicalisations. For instance, given the property name HASADRESS, this approach will produce the candidate lexicalisation "the address of S is O" where S and O are place-holders for the lexicalisations of the subject and object entity in the input RDF triple.

(Walter et al., 2013; Walter et al., 2014a; Walter et al., 2014b) describes an approach for inducing a lexicon mapping DBPedia properties to possible lexicalisations. The approach combines a label-based and a pattern-based method. The label-based method extracts lexicalisations from property names using additional information (e.g., synonyms) from external resources. The pattern-based method extract lexicalisations from a text corpus by retrieving sentences containing entities that are related by a DBPedia property and generalising over the dependency paths that connect them using hand-written patterns and frequency counts.

While these approaches can be effective, (Trevisan, 2010)'s approach fails to account for "opaque" property names (i.e., property such as CREW1UP whose lexicalisation is not directly deducible from the tokens making up that property name) and the pattern-based approach of (Walter et al., 2013), because it relies on frequency counts rather than lexical relatedness, allows for lexicalisations that may be semantically unrelated to the input property. In contrast, we learn continuous representations of both KB properties and words and exploit these to rank candidate lexicalisations which are either lexically- or extensionally-related to the properties to be lexicalised. In this way, we consider both types of property names while systematically checking for semantic relatedness.

Relation Extraction Earlier Information Extraction (IE) systems learned an extractor for each target relation from labelled training examples (Riloff, 1996; Soderland, 1999). For instance, (Riloff, 1996) first extract relation mention patterns from the corpus then rank these based on the number of time a relation pattern occurs in a text labelled with the target relation.

More recent work on Open IE has focused on building large scale knowledge bases such as Reverb by extracting arbitrary relations from text (Wu and Weld, 2010; Fader et al., 2011; Mohamed et al., 2011; Nakashole et al., 2012).

While relation extraction can be viewed as the mirror task of relation lexicalisation, there are important differences. Our lexicalisation task differs from domain specific IE in that it is unsupervised (we do not have access to annotated data). It also differs from open IE in that the set of properties to be lexicalised is predefined whereas, by definition, in open IE, the set of relations to be extracted is unrestricted. That is, while we aim to find the possible lexicalisations of a given set of relations (here DBPedia properties), open IE seeks to extract an unrestricted set of relations from text. Nevertheless, (Nakashole et al., 2012) includes a clustering phase which permits grouping relation clusters with a predefined set of properties such as, in particular, DBPedia properties. In Section 6, we therefore compare our results with the lexical-

Property	CROSSES
L-Candidate lexicalisation	"Old Blenheim Bridge spans Schoharie Creek"

Property	CREW1UP
RDF Triple	⟨ STS-130, CREW1UP, GEORGE_D._ZAMKA ⟩
E-Candidate lexicalisation	"Zamka served as the commander of mission STS-130"

Figure 1: Example L- and E-candidate lexicalisation phrases.

isations output by (Nakashole et al., 2012)'s approach.

Embedding-based Approaches The model we propose is inspired by (Bordes et al., 2014). In (Bordes et al., 2014), low dimensional embedding of words and KB symbols are learned so that representations of questions and their corresponding answers end up being similar in the embedding space. The embeddings are learned using automatically generated questions from KB triples and a dataset of questions marked as paraphrases (WikiAnswers, (Fader et al., 2011)). We adapt this model to the lexicalisation task by generating noisy lexicalisations of KB triples using a simple generation approach and by exploiting different paraphrase resources (c.f. Section3). Our approach further differs from (Bordes et al., 2014) in that we combine this embedding based framework with a pre-selection of candidate lexicalisations which reflects knowledge about the property extension and the property name. As mentioned in Section 1, E-related candidate lexicalisation phrases are sentences mentioning subject and/or object of the property being considered for lexicalisation while L-related candidate lexicalisation phrases are phrases containing synonyms or derivationally related words of the token making up the name of that property. In this way, we provide a joint modelling of the impact of lexical and extensional similarity on lexicalisation.

3 Approach

Given a KB property p, our task is to find a set of possible lexicalisations L_p for p. For instance, given the property HASWONPRIZE, our goal is to automatically infer lexicalisations such as *was honoured with* and *received*.

3.1 Lexicalisation Algorithm

Our lexicalisation algorithm is composed of the following steps:

Embeddings Using distant supervision, we learn embeddings of words and KB symbols such that the representations of KB triples, of sentences artificially generated from these triples and of their paraphrases are similar in the embedding space.

Candidate Lexicalisations Using WordNet and the extension of RDF properties (i.e., the set of pairs of entities related by that property), we build sets of candidate lexicalisation phrases. "Subject Relation Object" phrases are extracted from the set of candidate sentences using Reverb (Etzioni et al., 2011). Reverb is a tool for Open IE which extracts relation mentions from text based on frequency counts and regular expression filters.

Ranking Using the dot product on embedding based representations of triples and candidate lexicalisation phrases, we rank candidate lexicalisations of properties.

Extractions We apply some normalisation rules on the relation mention of the ranked lexicalisations to eliminate "duplicates". These rules consist in a small set of basic patterns to detect and remove adverbs, adjectives, determiners, etc. For instance, given the following relation mentions *always led by*, *is also led by* and *is currently led by* only one version will be extracted that is *led by*. From the top ranked lexicalisation phrases according to some threshold (e.g. top 10), we extract the lexicalisation set L_p for property p. Lexicalisations in L_p are relation mentions from the ranked lexicalisation phrases.

3.2 Learning Words and KB symbols Embeddings

Similar to the work of (Bordes et al., 2014), we use distant supervision and multitask training to learn embeddings of words and KB symbols.

Training Set Generation We train on two datasets, one aligning KB triples with automatically generated verbalisations of these triples and the other, aligning paraphrases. The first dataset ($\mathcal{T}$) is used to learn a similarity function between KB symbols and words, the second ($\mathcal{P}$) to account for the many ways in which a given property may be verbalised.

Triples and Sentences ($\mathcal{T}$) We build a training corpus of KB triples and Natural Language sentences by combining the pattern based lexicalisation approach of (Trevisan, 2010) (c.f. Section 2) with a simple grammar based generation step. We apply this approach to map KB property names to syntactic constructions and then use a simple grammar to generate sentences from KB triples. For instance, the triple in (1a) will yield the sentences in (1b-g):

(1) a. $\langle$ DUMBARTON_BRIDGE, LOCATEDINAREA,
        MENLO_PARK_CALIFORNIA $\rangle$
     b. "The Dumbarton Bridge should be located in menlo park california."
     c. "It should be located in menlo park california."
     d. "Dumbarton Bridge located in menlo park california."
     e. "Dumbarton Bridge which should be located in menlo park california."
     f. "Menlo Park California in which dumbarton bridge is located."
     g. "The Dumbarton Bridge should be located in menlo park california."

On average, each property is associated with 5.9 sentences. Given a training pair (t, s) such that $t = (s_k, p_k, o_k)$, we generate negative examples by corrupting the triple i.e., by producing pairs of the form (t', s) such that $t' = (s_k, p'_k, o_k)$ and $(s_k, o_k) \notin p'_k$.

Paraphrases ($\mathcal{P}$). To learn embeddings and a similarity function that takes into account the various ways in which a property can be lexicalised, we supplement our training data with pairs of paraphrases contained in the PPDB paraphrase database, in the WikiAnswers dataset and in DBPedia (DBPP). Positive examples (p_i, p_j) are taken from these datasets and negative examples are produced by creating corrupted pairs (p_i, p_l) such that p_i is not in the paraphrase dataset of p_l and vice versa.

The PPDB database was extracted from bilingual parallel corpora following (Bannard

and Callison-Burch, 2005)'s bilingual pivoting method[1]. PPDB comes pre-packaged in 6 sizes: S to XXXL. The smaller packages contain only better-scoring, high-precision paraphrases, while the larger ones aim for high coverage. Additionally PPDB is broken down into lexical paraphrases (i.e. one word to one word), phrasal paraphrases (i.e. multi-word phrases), as well as syntactic paraphrases which contain non-terminals. We use PPDB version 2.0 M size lexical and phrasal sets which contain overall 3525057 paraphrase pairs. We choose to use medium size sets to incorporate some variability while still favouring higher quality paraphrases. As for the type of paraphrases, we took only the lexical and phrasal ones given that our goal is geared to acquiring alternative lexicalisations in terms of wording rather than syntactic variation.

Wikianswers is a corpus of 18M question-paraphrase pairs collected by (Fader et al., 2013), with 2.4M distinct questions in the corpus. Because these pairs have been labelled collaboratively, the data is highly noisy ((Fader et al., 2013) estimated that only 55% of the pairs were actual paraphrases).

Finally, the BDPP dataset consists of (entity, class) pairs extracted from the DBPedia ontology. They provide a bridge between the entity names appearing in the DBPedia triples and the more generic common nouns which may be used in text.

Using the resources and tools just described, we create a triple/sentence corpus $\mathcal{T}$ consisting of 317853 triple/sentence pairs obtained from 53384 KB triples of 149 relations. The paraphrase corpus $\mathcal{P}$ contains 3525057 (PPDB), 220998 (WikiAnswers) and 54489 (DBPP) paraphrase pairs. Figure 2 shows some positive and negative training examples drawn from the $\mathcal{T}$ and $\mathcal{P}$ datasets.

Training Using a training corpus created as described in the previous section, we learn a similarity function S between triples and candidate lexicalisations which is defined as:

$$S_{t/s}(t, s) = f(t)^{\top} . g(s) \tag{1}$$

with

$$f(t) = K^{\top} . \phi(t) \tag{2}$$

and

$$g(s) = W^{\top} . \psi(s) \tag{3}$$

---

[1]Briefly, the intuition underlying the bilingual pivoting method is that expressions sharing the same translation into a target language are paraphrases.

T

| (t, s) | $(\langle$ ARISTOTLE, INFLUENCED, CHRISTIAN_PHILOSOPHY $\rangle$, "Christian philosophy who is influenced by Aristotle.") |
| (t', s) | $(\langle$ ARISTOTLE, COMPUTINGMEDIA, CHRISTIAN_PHILOSOPHY $\rangle$, "Christian philosophy who is influenced by Aristotle.") |

$\mathcal{P}$ (PPDB)

(p_i, p_j)	("collaborate", "cooperate")
(p_i, p_l)	("collaborate", "improving")
(p_i, p_j)	("is important to emphasize that", "is notable that")
(p_i, p_l)	("is important to emphasize that", "are using")

$\mathcal{P}$ (Wikianswers)

| (p_i, p_j) | ("much coca cola be buy per year", "much do a consumer pay for coca cola") |
| (p_i, p_l) | ("much coca cola be buy per year", "information on neem plant") |

$\mathcal{P}$ (DBPP)

| (p_i, p_j) | ("Amsterdam", "Place") |
| (p_i, p_l) | ("Amsterdam", "Novels first published in serial form") |

Figure 2: Examples of positive examples present in the $\mathcal{T}$ and $\mathcal{P}$ training datasets with their corresponding corrupted negative counterpart.

$K \in \mathbb{R}^{n_k \times d}$ and $W \in \mathbb{R}^{n_w \times d}$ are the embedding matrices for KB symbols and for words respectively with n_k, the number of distinct symbols in the knowledge base and n_w, the number of distinct word forms in the text corpus. Furthermore, $\phi(t)$ and $\psi(s)$ are binary vectors indicating whether a KB symbol/word is present or absent in t/s. Thus, $f(t)$ and $g(s)$ are the embeddings of t and s and $S_{t/s}$ scores their similarity by taking their dot product.

To learn word embeddings which capture the similarity between a triple and a set of paraphrases (rather than just the similarity between a triple and artificially synthesised sentences), we multi-task the training of our model with the task of paraphrase detection. That is, the weights of the W matrix for words are learnt with the training of the triple/sentence similarity function $S_{t/s}$ and the training of a similarity function S_p for paraphrases which uses the same embedding matrix W for words and is trained on $\mathcal{P}$, the paraphrase corpus. The phrase similarity function S_p between two natural language phrases p_i and p_j is defined as follows:

$$S_p(p_i, p_j) = f(p_i)^\top . f(p_j) \qquad (4)$$

Similarly to (Bordes et al., 2014), we train our model using a margin-based ranking loss function so that scores of positive examples should be larger than those of negative examples by a margin of 1. That is, for $S_{t/s}$, we minimize:

$$\forall i, j, \forall [1 - S_{s/t}(t_i, s_i) + S_{s/t}(t_j, s_i)] \qquad (5)$$

where (t_i, s_i) is a positive triple/sentence example and (t_j, s_i) a negative one. Similarly, when training on paraphrase data, the ranking loss function to minimise is:

$$\forall i, j, l, \forall [1 - S_p(p_i, p_j) + S_p(p_i, p_l)] \qquad (6)$$

where (p_i, p_j) is a positive example from the paraphrase corpus $\mathcal{P}$ and (p_i, p_l) a negative one.

4 Implementation

The model is implemented in Python using the Keras(Chollet, 2015) library with Theano backend.

We initialise the W matrix with pre-trained vectors which already provide a rich representation for words. We use the publicly available GloVe (Pennington et al., 2014) vectors[2] of length 100. These vectors were trained on 6 billions words from Wikipedia and the English Gigaword. We set the dimension d of the K and W matrices to 100. For K we use uniform initialisation.

The size of the vocabulary for the W matrix, the n_w dimension, is 130970 words. This is considering all words appearing in the $\mathcal{T}$ and $\mathcal{P}$ sets. The size of the K matrix, the n_k dimension, is 43797 counting both KB entities and relations.

The training for both similarity functions $S_{t/s}$ and S_p is performed with Stochastic Gradient Descent. The learning rate is set to 0.1 and the number of epochs to 5. Training run approximately 15 hours[3].

---

[2] http://nlp.stanford.edu/projects/glove/

[3] A first phase run on a machine with 1 CPU Intel Xeon

223

5 Experiments

DBPedia[4] is a crowd-sourced knowledge based extracted from Wikipedia and available on the Web in RDF format. Available as Linked Dataon the web, the DBPedia knowledge base defines Linked Data URIs for millions of concepts. It has become a de facto central hub of the web of data and is heavily used by systems that employ structured data for applications such as web-based information retrieval or search engines.

Like many other large knowledge bases (e.g., Freebase or Yago) available on the web, DBPedia lacks lexical information stating how DBPedia properties should be lexicalised. We apply our lexicalisation model to DBPedia object properties. We construct candidate lexicalisation sets in the following way.

Candidate Lexicalisations As mentioned in Section 1, we consider two main ways of building sets of candidate lexicalisations for a given property p.

E-LEX$_p$: Let WKP$_p$ be the set of sentences extracted from Wikipedia which contain at least one mention of two entities that are related in DB-Pedia by the property p. WKP$_p$ was built using the pre-processing tools[5] of the MATOLL framework (Walter et al., 2013; Walter et al., 2014b). Then E-LEX$_p$ is the corpus of candidate lexicalisations extracted from WKP$_p$ using Reverb.

L-LEX$_p$: Given WKP the corpus of Wikipedia sentences, L-LEX$_p$ is the corpus of relation mentions extracted from WKP using Reverb and filtered to contain only mentions which include words that are lexically related to the tokens making up the property name. Lexically related words include all synonyms and all derivationally related words listed in Wordnet for a given token.

6 Evaluation and Results

We compare the output of our lexicalisation method with the following resources and approaches.

TEAM, COUNTRY, ORDER, DEATHPLACE, OCCUPATION, KINGDOM, NATIONALITY, BATTLE, HOMETOWN, AWARD, PREDECESSOR, PUBLISHER, DISTRIBUTOR, OWNER, RECORDEDIN, ALBUM, PRODUCT, PARENT, AFFILIATION, EDUCATION, ROUTEEND, ORIGIN, NEARESTCITY, ARCHITECT, COMPOSER, MOUNTAINRANGE, FOUNDEDBY, INFLUENCED, GARRISON, LEADER, PROGRAMMINGLANGUAGE

Table 1: Set of DBPedia object properties used in the evaluation.

DBlexipedia$_e$: a lexicon[6] automatically inferred from Wikipedia using the method described in (Walter et al., 2013; Walter et al., 2014a; Walter et al., 2014b) (c.f. section 2). Lexical entries are inferred using either the extension of the properties (by retrieving sentences containing entities that are related by a DBPedia property and generalising over the dependency paths that connect them.) or synonyms of the words contained in the property name.

PATTY: a lexicon automatically inferred from web data using relation extraction and clustering (c.f. (Nakashole et al., 2012)).

QUELO: a lexicon automatically derived using the method described in (Trevisan, 2010) (c.f. section 2). Lexical entries are derived by first, tokenizing and pos tagging property names and second, mapping the resulting pos-tagged sequences to pre-defined mention patterns.

For the quantitative evaluation, we use the lexicon developed manually for DBPedia properties by (McCrae et al., 2011) as a gold standard[7]. We test on a held-out set of 30 properties[8] chosen from DBPedia and which were present in the gold standard lexicon, in the other systems we compare with and in the available E-Lex$_p$ corpus. Table 1 lists the set of properties.

We compute precision (Correct/Found), recall

X3440, 4 cores/CPU, 16GB RAM and a second phase on a machine with 2 CPUs Intel Xeon L5420, 4 cores/CPU, 16GB RAM.

[4] http://wiki.dbpedia.org/

[5] https://github.com/ag-sc/matoll

[6] For this evaluation we use the version available for download at http://dblexipedia.org/download and we use only the English lexical entries.

[7] This lexicon is available at https://github.com/ag-sc/lemon.dbpedia

[8] The selection of these properties was based, on one hand, on the frequency with a third of the selected properties appearing more than 80000 times in DBPedia, a third appearing less than 20000 times and a third appearing between 20000 and 80000 times (min. is 5936 for PROGRAMMINGLANGUAGE and max. is 1825970 for TEAM). On the other hand, we include properties with different name/label patterns imposing differences in verbalisation difficulty, e.g. compound nouns as ROUTEEND or PROGRAMMINGLANGUAGE.

(Correct/GOLD) and F1 measure of each of the above resources. Recall is the proportion of (property, lexicalisation) pairs present in GOLD which are present in the resource being evaluated, precision the proportion in a resource which is also present in GOLD and F1 is the harmonic mean of precision and recall[9].

In our setup though, precision (and therefore F1) values are artificially decreased because the reference lexicon is small (2.4 lexicalisations in average per property) and often fails to include all possible lexicalisations. The number of correct lexicalisations can therefore be under-estimated while the number of found lexicalisations is usually larger than the number of gold lexicalisations and therefore much larger than the number of correct (= GOLD ∩ Found) lexicalisations.

We report results using different sets of lexicalisation candidates (L-LEX, E-LEX, their union and their intersection) and different thresholds or methods for selecting the final set of lexicalisations. These include: retrieving the n-best lexicalisations (k=10) *versus* using an adaptive threshold which varies depending on the size of the set of candidate lexicalisations and on the distributions of its ranking scores. We tried taking all lexicalisations over the median (median), over the mid-range ((min+max)/2) or in the third quartile (Q3). We also tested an alternative ranking technique where the score of each lexicalisation is the product of its similarity score (dot product of the embedding vectors representing the property and the lexicalisation) with the frequency of this particular lexicalisation in the set of candidate lexicalisations[10]. We rerank the lexicalisations using these new scores and consider only the lexicalisations in the third quartile of the distribution (FreqQ3). Further if this results in having either less than 7 or more than 25 lexicalisations, we ignore the Q3 constraint and take the 7 and 25 best respectively (FreqQ3Limit(7,25)).

Table 3 summarises the results.

---

[9]To determine whether a given property lexicalisation is correct, i.e. present in the GOLD, we use "soft" comparison rather than strict string matching. This consists in checking whether the stemmed gold lexicalisation is contained in a given candidate lexicalisation. For instance, the candidate "main occupation of" and gold "occupation of" are considered as a match.

[10]In the set of candidate lexicalisations, the same lexicalisation may occur with minor variations. We compute the frequency of a given lexicalisation by removing adjectives and adverbs and counting the number of repeated occurrences after removing these.

Recall In terms of recall, our results generally outperform QUELO, PATTY and DBlexipedia$_e$.

The low recall score of QUELO shows that simply using patterns based on the property name does not suffice to find appropriate property lexicalisations. This is true in particular of properties such as ROUTEEND where the correct lexicalisation is difficult to guess from the property name.

DBlexipedia$_e$ at k=10 scores lower (0.29) than the corresponding version of our approach union(k=10), R:0.38). Interestingly, for our approach, better recall values are consistently obtained using L-LEX suggesting that many of the verbalisations found in GOLD can be extracted from text that is unrelated to the extension of DBPedia properties. This is a nice feature as this permits avoiding the data sparsity issue which arises when a DBPedia property has either a restricted extension or a small set WKP_p of candidate lexicalisations. Indeed, we found that out of a set of 149 DBPedia properties, the MATOLL corpus did not provide any sentences for 19 of them. In such cases, an approach based only on extensionally related sentences of the property would have zero recall. This is in line with the results of (Walter et al., 2013; Walter et al., 2014a) who observe that such an approach yields a recall of 0.35 whilst combining it with a lexically based approach (using synonyms of the tokens occurring in the property name) permits increasing recall to 0.5.

Finally, although PATTY has a comparatively high recall value (0.59), its precision is very low (0.0015) and versions of our approach with comparable precision (e.g., E-LEX(All)) have a much higher recall (R: 0.80).

Precision As shown in Table 3, the retrieval approach which gives the best results in terms of both precision and F1 is in fact to take the 10-best. Together with the much lower precision achieved by the random baselines (Random*k=10), this result suggests that the similarity function learned by our model appropriately captures the similarity between DBPedia properties and their lexicalisations.

Unsurprisingly, QUELO has the highest precision as it only guesses lexicalisation based on the tokens making up the property name. For instance, for noun property names like OWNER it produces the following two lexicalisations: "owner" and "owner of"; for verb based property names like RECORDEDIN it produces the lexicalisation

225

System/goldLemonDBPPatterns	Avg.NB	Recall	Precision	F1
L-LEX(k=10)	9.9	0.3611	0.0875	**0.1409**
L-LEX(median)	343	**0.7500**	0.0052	0.0104
L-LEX((min+max)/2)	216	0.6250	0.0069	0.0137
L-LEX(Q3)	104	0.5000	0.0115	0.0225
L-LEX(FreqQ3)	104	0.5139	0.0118	0.0231
L-LEX(FreqQ3Limit(7,25))	218	0.4583	**0.0505**	0.0909
L-LEX(All)	687.4	**0.8194**	0.0029	0.0057
E-LEX(k=10)	10	0.3333	0.0800	**0.1290**
E-LEX(median)	778.2	**0.7222**	0.0022	0.0044
E-LEX((min+max)/2)	301.8	0.6806	0.0054	0.0107
E-LEX(Q3)	251	0.6250	0.0059	0.0118
E-LEX(FreqQ3)	251	0.6250	0.0059	0.0118
E-LEX(FreqQ3Limit(7,25))	23.3	0.5000	0.0514	0.0933
E-LEX(All)	1557	**0.8056**	0.0012	0.0025
union(k=10)	10	0.3889	0.0933	0.1505
union(median)	543	**0.8194**	0.0036	0.0072
union((min+max)/2)	47.7	0.6389	0.0320	0.0610
union(Q3)	86.7	0.5972	0.0165	0.0320
union(FreqQ3)	85.8	0.6667	0.0185	0.0361
union(FreqQ3Limit(7,25))	10.8	0.4861	**0.1080**	**0.1768**
union(All)	2162.5	0.9444	0.0010	0.0021
intersec(k=10)	0.4	0.0556	0.3636	0.0964
intersec(median)	35.27	**0.4444**	0.0305	0.0571
intersec((min+max)/2)	14.8	0.3333	0.0547	0.0939
intersec(Q3)	8.6	0.2639	0.0748	0.1166
intersec(FreqQ3)	12.3	0.2917	0.0575	0.0961
intersec(FreqQ3Limit(7,25))	2.2	0.2500	**0.2813**	**0.2647**
intersec(All)	81.9	0.5417	0.0159	0.0309
L-LEXRandom(k=10)	9.9	0.2083	0.0505	0.0813
E-LEXRandom(k=10)	10	0.0833	0.0200	0.0323
QUELO	2.13	0.2917	0.3281	0.3088
DBlexipedia$_e$(k=10)	5.4	0.2500	0.1104	0.1532
PATTY	936	0.5694	0.0015	0.0029

Figure 3: Micro-averaged Precision, Recall and F1 with respect to GOLD. The column Avg.NB indicates the averaged number of candidate lexicalisations for each system.

PROGRAMMINGLANGUAGE	*written in*, **uses**, include, **based on**, supports, is a part of, **programming language for** (4/1)
AFFILIATION	member of, associated with, *affiliated with*, **affiliated to**, **affiliate of**, **accredited by**, tied to, founded in, president of, associate member of (4/1)
COUNTRY	village in, **part of**, one of, *located in*, commune in, town in, born in, refer to, county in, country in, city in (2/1)
MOUNTAINRANGE	**mountain in**, **located in**, **include**, range from, **mountain of**, **mountain range in**, *part of*, **lies in**, reach, peak in, **find in**, highest mountain in (8/1)
DISTRIBUTOR	sell, appear in, allocate to, air on, **release**, **make**, star in, appear on (2/2)
LEADER	lead to, **leader of**, **led by**, **is a leader in**, visit, become, **lead**, lead producer of, *president of*, **elected leader of**, left (6/3)

Figure 4: Example Lexicalisations output by our System (Union.FreqQ3Limit7-25). Gold items are in italics. Items in bold indicates a correct lexicalisation absent from the gold. The number N/G in bracket indicates the number N of lexicalisations produced by our system that are not in the gold standard and the number G of items in the gold standard.

"recorded in". On these two properties, QUELO perfectly coincides with the entries defined in GOLD. This explains the high F1 obtained by QUELO. However, as argued in the previous section, QUELO's approach fails to account for cases where the relation name is indirect or opaque. Moreover, it does not support the generation of alternative lexicalisations. For the property EDUCATION, the gold standard defines the the lexical entries "attend", "go to" and "study at" which QUELO fails to produce.

DBlexipedia$_e$ has a precision score (0.11) comparable to the corresponding version of our approach (union(k=10), P:0.09) and PATTY has a very low precision (P:0.0015). A manual examination of the data shows that the relation extraction approach fails to find a sufficiently large number of distinct property lexicalisations. The lexicalisations found often contain many near repetitions (e.g., "has graduated from, graduated from, graduates") but few distinct paraphrases (e.g., "graduate from, study at").

To better assess, the precision of our system we therefore manually examined the results of our system and annotated all outputs lexicalisations which were correct but not in the gold. Based on this updated gold, precision for union.FreqQ3Limit7-25 is in fact, 0.289.

Example Output Table 4 shows some example output of our system (for union.FreqQ3Limit7-25)[11]. These examples show that our system correctly predicts additional lexicalisations that are absent from GOLD.

They also show that our approach can produce both L- and E-related lexicalisations. Thus for instance, for the property PROGRAMMINGLANGUAGE, our model produces the lexicalisation "programming language for" which is clearly an L-lexicalisation that can be directly derived from the property name. However, it also derives more context-sensitive E-lexicalisations such as "written in", "uses" and "based on" which are not lexically related to the property name but can be found by considering E-related candidate lexicalisations i.e., sentences such as "FastTacker Digit was written in Pascal" which contain entities that are arguments of the PROGRAMMINGLANGUAGE property.

---

[11]The complete set of extractions is available at `http://www.loria.fr/~perezlla/content/sw_resources/union.FreqQ3Limit.txt`.

Similarly, the COUNTRY property whose gold lexicalisation is "located in" (the RDF triple ⟨ Sakhalin_Oblast, country, Russia ⟩ can be verbalised as " Sakhalin Oblast is located in Russia"), is correctly assigned the lexicalisations "located in" and "part of". Interestingly, our approach also yield more specific lexicalisations such as "is a village/commune/town/county in" which may also be correct lexicalisations given the appropriate subject. For instance, "is a town in" is a correct lexicalisation of the COUNTRY property given the triple ⟨ Paris, country, France ⟩.

7 Conclusion

We use an embeddings based framework for identifying plausible lexicalisations of KB properties. While embeddings have been much used in domains such as question answering, semantic parsing and relation extraction, they have not been used so far for the lexicalisation task. Conversely, existing approaches to lexicalisation which exploits the similarity between property name and candidate lexicalisations do so on the basis of discrete representations such as WordNet Synsets. In contrast, we learn embeddings of words and KB symbols using distant supervision. We show that, when applied to DBPedia object properties, our approach yields competitive results with these discrete approaches.

As future work, we plan to conduct a larger scale evaluation. This will include the application of the approach to datatype properties and test on a larger set of properties.

The scoring function used by our approach is based on a bag-of-words representation of natural language phrases. We have observed that tuples and candidate lexicalisation phrases like ⟨ AMERICAN_FILM_INSTITUTE, LOCATION, CALIFORNIA ⟩ and "A new city was built on a nearby location" are scored high as they share some highly related words. We plan to explore whether a more complex representation of natural language phrases could remedy this shortcoming.

Acknowledgements

We thank the French National Research Agency for funding the research presented in this paper in the context of the WebNLG project. We would also like to thank Sebastian Walter for kindly providing us with the MATOLL corpus.

References

Colin Bannard and Chris Callison-Burch. 2005. Paraphrasing with bilingual parallel corpora. In *Proceedings of the 43rd Annual Meeting on Association for Computational Linguistics*, pages 597–604. Association for Computational Linguistics.

Antoine Bordes, Jason Weston, and Nicolas Usunier. 2014. Open question answering with weakly supervised embedding models. *CoRR*, abs/1404.4326.

Fran¸cois Chollet. 2015. Keras. `https://github.com/fchollet/keras`.

Oren Etzioni, Anthony Fader, Janara Christensen, Stephen Soderland, and Mausam Mausam. 2011. Open information extraction: The second generation. In *IJCAI*, volume 11, pages 3–10.

Anthony Fader, Stephen Soderland, and Oren Etzioni. 2011. Identifying relations for open information extraction. In *Proceedings of the Conference on Empirical Methods in Natural Language Processing*, pages 1535–1545. Association for Computational Linguistics.

Anthony Fader, Luke S Zettlemoyer, and Oren Etzioni. 2013. Paraphrase-driven learning for open question answering. In *ACL (1)*, pages 1608–1618. Citeseer.

John McCrae, Dennis Spohr, and Philipp Cimiano. 2011. Linking lexical resources and ontologies on the semantic web with lemon. In *The semantic web: research and applications*, pages 245–259. Springer.

Thahir P Mohamed, Estevam R Hruschka Jr, and Tom M Mitchell. 2011. Discovering relations between noun categories. In *Proceedings of the Conference on Empirical Methods in Natural Language Processing*, pages 1447–1455. Association for Computational Linguistics.

Ndapandula Nakashole, Gerhard Weikum, and Fabian Suchanek. 2012. Discovering and exploring relations on the web. *Proceedings of the VLDB Endowment*, 5(12):1982–1985.

Jeffrey Pennington, Richard Socher, and Christopher D. Manning. 2014. Glove: Global vectors for word representation. In *Empirical Methods in Natural Language Processing (EMNLP)*, pages 1532–1543.

A. Rector, N. Drummond, M. Horridge, J. Rogers, H. Knublauch, R. Stevens, H. Wang, and C. Wroe. 2004. Owl pizzas: Practical experience of teaching owl-dl: Common errors & common patterns. *Engineering Knowledge in the Age of the Semantic Web*, pages 63–81.

Ellen Riloff. 1996. Automatically generating extraction patterns from untagged text. In *Proceedings of the national conference on artificial intelligence*, pages 1044–1049.

Stephen Soderland. 1999. Learning information extraction rules for semi-structured and free text. *Machine learning*, 34(1-3):233–272.

Marco Trevisan. 2010. A portable menuguided natural language interface to knowledge bases for querytool. Master's thesis, Free University of Bozen-Bolzano (Italy) and University of Groningen (Netherlands).

Sebastian Walter, Christina Unger, and Philipp Cimiano. 2013. A corpus-based approach for the induction of ontology lexica. In *Natural Language Processing and Information Systems*, pages 102–113. Springer.

Sebastian Walter, Christina Unger, and Philipp Cimiano. 2014a. Atolla framework for the automatic induction of ontology lexica. *Data & Knowledge Engineering*, 94:148–162.

Sebastian Walter, Christina Unger, and Philipp Cimiano. 2014b. M-atoll: a framework for the lexicalization of ontologies in multiple languages. In *The Semantic Web–ISWC 2014*, pages 472–486. Springer.

Fei Wu and Daniel S Weld. 2010. Open information extraction using wikipedia. In *Proceedings of the 48th Annual Meeting of the Association for Computational Linguistics*, pages 118–127. Association for Computational Linguistics.

Author Index